A MILITARY
OF PERTHSHIRE
1899–1902

EDITED BY

THE MARCHIONESS OF TULLIBARDINE

WITH A ROLL
OF THE PERTHSHIRE MEN OF THE PRESENT
DAY WHO HAVE SEEN ACTIVE SERVICE
UNDER THE BRITISH FLAG

COMPILED BY

THE EDITOR & JANE C. C. MACDONALD

WITH PORTRAITS, ILLUSTRATIONS, AND MAPS

PERTH
R. A. & J. HAY
GLASGOW | EDINBURGH
J. MACLEHOSE & SONS | WILLIAM BROWN
1908

Printed by BALLANTYNE, HANSON & Co.
At the Ballantyne Press, Edinburgh

TO

PERTHSHIRE SOLDIERS AND SAILORS

PAST AND PRESENT

AS A SMALL TRIBUTE TO THE SERVICES THEY HAVE
RENDERED TO THEIR COUNTRY

PREFACE

THIS volume is intended in the first instance as an appreciation of the services rendered by Perthshire men who served in South Africa during the late war, and indirectly, as a tribute to British soldiers and sailors in general. The names (and in most cases the portraits) of the Forfarshire men who took part in the earlier stages of the South African War were recorded in "The Muster-Roll of Angus," published in 1900, and Miss Jane C. C. Macdonald, who had been one of the promoters of the Angus book, undertook, at the suggestion of some friends in Perthshire, to compile a similar record for this county. The work was begun during the course of the war, but in the absence of the many officers and men who were then serving abroad, considerable difficulty was experienced in obtaining the necessary information.

In the winter of 1902–1903, some months after my return from South Africa, I was invited by Miss Macdonald to complete the record which she had inaugurated, and after some months of preliminary work I finally accepted the responsibility of the editorship. Though only too conscious that on the grounds of literary experience I had no qualification whatever for the work of an editor, I felt that, as the wife and sister of Perthshire men who had served in South Africa, I could not but do what in me lay to further the compilation of such a record, and that my connection with the Army might afford me facilities for procuring information. Generous help in the way of amassing material had already been given by the parish ministers and others resident in the county ; the kindness of the officers commanding the depôts of the various Scots regiments now procured me additional lists ; and the information obtained from local sources was, wherever possible, verified and supplemented from regimental records. The result has been the collection of brief records of some 170 officers and 1370 non-commissioned officers and men, with portraits of the great majority of the officers and men in question.

Under the original scheme the book was to record only the services of men who had served in the South African War, but at an early stage I felt that it would gain in interest, and would not be enlarged to any considerable extent, if it included the names of the Perthshire men who had served in the Soudan Expedition of 1898 and the various campaigns on the Indian Frontier during the ten years previous to 1903—the year in which I took up the work. So far, therefore, as I have been able to trace them, a brief outline is here presented of the services of all the Perthshire men, living or dead, who saw active service under the British flag from 1893 to 1903, and of such survivors of earlier campaigns as were living in the latter year. But no one is more aware than I that, with the best will in the world, such a record must necessarily be incomplete, and I would fain ask forgiveness beforehand of those officers and men whose names may have been inadvertently omitted from these pages.

It should be added that space has been found in the Roll for a mention of the men of the Yeomanry and Scottish Horse, who, enlisting for active service towards the end of the South African War, arrived in South Africa to find that peace had been concluded.

As the term " Perthshire man " is open to different interpretations, I may here explain that, following the lines on which the book had already been begun, I have included not only natives of the county, but men who, though not born in Perthshire, have resided therein in a civilian capacity for a period of not less than five years. The definition may perhaps be regarded as too comprehensive, but in a record such as this I would rather be accused of including too many than too few. It will, however, be readily understood that so wide a category has considerably added to the difficulties of compilation.

From the first Miss Macdonald had intended that the records of the Perthshire men of the present day should be accompanied by letterpress, including some essays illustrative of the military achievements of the county in the past. The last four years have seen so wide a development of the historical portion of this scheme, besides a large increase in the number of records amassed, that it has been found impossible to publish all the material within the limits of one volume, and it has further been felt desirable that the work, instead of appearing, as originally proposed, under the name of " The Muster-Roll of Perthshire," should bear the more distinctive title of a " Military History " of the county from 1660 onwards. The present volume, therefore, besides the records and portraits of officers and men of the present day, and appreciations of three distinguished men connected with the county who lost their lives in the late South African War, includes only articles dealing with that war. All historical matter prior to 1899 will be found in " A Military History of Perthshire, 1660-1902," which is published uniformly with this volume.

The extension of the historical portion of the book is chiefly responsible for the fact that the publication has been delayed so long beyond the date originally contemplated ; but few perhaps will realise what incessant correspondence and laborious work have been involved in the arrangement, amplification, and verification of the records of service, or how long it was before I was able to seriously devote my attention to more purely literary matters. Indeed it was not until many months after I had set to work that some of the regimental depôts to which I had applied were able to furnish me with all the necessary information.

In a work the material for which has been gathered from so many different sources, editor and compiler alike are indebted to many for assistance. In the first instance thanks are due to the respective contributors of the articles on the Black Watch in South Africa, the account of the principal engagements in which the Scottish Horse took part, and the three appreciations already referred to ; also to Captain Lord George Stewart Murray and Captain the Hon. Maurice Drummond, adjutants respectively of the 1st and 2nd Battalions of the Black Watch, for help in compiling the table showing the services of the officers of their regiment in South Africa. The illustrations to the articles on the Black Watch are the work of the respective authors of those articles ; while the compilers are indebted to Miss Jane B. Constable for her admirable sketch of a Scottish Horse trooper ; to Lord Tullibardine for the map showing the engagement at Moedwil ; and to Mr. Colin B. Phillip, A.R.W.S., for permission to reproduce a picture which he generously gave to be disposed of for the benefit of a fund for providing copies of this book for the non-commissioned officers and men whose services are recorded herein.

In the initial stages of the work Miss Macdonald derived much assistance from the late Mr. David Farquharson, A.R.A., Mr. John Hassall, R.I., Mr. W. G. Burn-Murdoch, the late Dr. Hugh Macmillan, and the late Mr. Ness of Braco. And from first to last, long is the list of those who have assisted in the collection of the soldiers' records and portraits. Ministers of the Established and other Churches (especially the Rev. James Meikle, at Alyth) have rendered invaluable help ; and among others to whom the compilers owe a debt of gratitude on this score are Miss H. M. O. Wedderburn, Miss Jean Hope, the late Miss Buchanan of Leny, Miss E. J. Bairnsfather, Miss Murray MacGregor, Captain R. M. Christie, late 4th Volunteer Battalion The Black Watch, Lieutenants T. Buchanan and C. Willison and Sergeant-Instructor G. Strathearn, all of the 5th Volunteer Battalion, Sergeant T. Robertson, late 5th Volunteer Battalion, Dr. John Irvine, Mr. A. Stuart Erskine, Mr. R. Doig, Scone, and Mr. J. Roberts, Dunkeld. But above all they are indebted to Miss Mary Masterson, Honorary Treasurer and Secretary of the Perthshire Branch of the Soldiers' and Sailors' Families Association, for her untiring zeal in procuring information with regard to the many men belonging to Perth, whose names are to be found in this book.

I must also record my thanks to the officers commanding the various regimental and departmental depôts to which I applied, also to their respective staffs, and to the Permanent Staff of the two Volunteer battalions in the county, for their kindness in furnishing me with the requisite information. The labour involved in preparing the lists of the men of the Black Watch must have been particularly heavy, and I am most grateful to Colonel E. G. Grogan, C.B., late commanding the 42nd Regimental District, for his never-failing courtesy in replying to my queries, and to Quartermaster-Sergeant Alexander Kelman, and Private Angus McPhee, who, under his direction, compiled voluminous tables for my benefit.

I should like to take this opportunity of thanking the many contributors to the Soldiers' Copies Fund already referred to, and Captain R. M. Christie and the members of the Dundee and Celtic Football Clubs, who most kindly gave the proceeds of a football match to help towards the considerable expenditure involved in the production of the book. I wish to thank also the many soldiers' and sailors' relatives who entrusted the compilers with photographs for reproduction.

Mrs. William J. Watson (Miss E. C. Carmichael), editor of *The Celtic Review*, has very kindly read through the proofs of this volume, and I have received from her much helpful advice on various points. I am also indebted to Miss C. G. Barclay and Captain Arthur Ramsay for help in correcting the proofs of the records of service, and to my husband and Lieutenant-Colonel Angel Scott, 3rd (Militia) Battalion The Black Watch, for information on various technical points.

Though full explanations of the scheme of arrangement are given in the text, it may perhaps be mentioned here that the officers' records are arranged alphabetically, grouped in two parts, according to the connection of each individual with Perthshire. The records of the non-commissioned officers and men, on the other hand, are arranged according to regiments, the different units being given in the correct order of precedence, and the records of each regiment being in alphabetical order. The portraits of officers have been grouped wherever possible according to family or clan; those of non-commissioned officers and men under their respective regiments, though such pictorial effect as was possible has been preferred to an alphabetical arrangement. As will readily be believed, the expense of reproducing so many photographs has been considerable, and the portraits of non-commissioned officers and men being especially numerous, it was found impossible to include them except in a very small size. In many cases the photographs of non-commissioned officers and men sent could not be reproduced without another process. This was skilfully accomplished by Messrs. D. Milne and Son, photographers, Blairgowrie. It should be added, in fairness to Messrs. Carl Hentschel, Limited, who are responsible for the reproduction of the illustrations, that many of the photographs sent to them were of an extremely faulty nature, and that under the circumstances they have produced surprisingly good results.

A reference to each portrait included will be found in the corresponding record, and as the scale on which the portraits of non-commissioned officers and men have been reproduced precludes the possibility of printing the names below them, each photo has been numbered, and a Portrait Index has been included, to which the numbers on the photos are the key. Finally, the extremely careful Indexes which have been compiled by Mr. Andrew Ross, Ross Herald, and his son, Mr. Alastair Ross, make it a simple matter to refer to any person or regiment mentioned in the book. A list of the abbreviations used in the records and the Indexes will be found on page 64.

Indian place-names mentioned in the text of records of officers and men I have, as far as possible, spelt as in Wilson's *Gazetteer*. The names of the various clasps on medals, however, have been reproduced as on the clasps themselves. Names of regiments, past or present, I have given as in contemporary *Army Lists*, and the records of all officers of the Imperial forces have been verified—indeed, mainly compiled—from the same source.

It is the earnest hope of the compilers that this tribute to the Perthshire soldiers and sailors of the present day may serve to stimulate the patriotism of their descendants, and that in the future, as in the past, Perthshire men, by their readiness to share in the toils, the privations, and the dangers incident to war, will show that even that terrible scourge of humanity, when entered upon in vindication of just rights or principles, may call out the noblest qualities alike in the individual and the nation.

In conclusion I should like to record my thanks to the subscribers, who, with so much kindly patience and forbearance, have awaited the publication of this volume.

K. M. TULLIBARDINE.

BLAIR CASTLE,
1907.

CONTENTS

THE BLACK WATCH IN SOUTH AFRICA
1899–1902

PAGE

I. The First Battalion, 1901–1902. By An Officer 1

II. The Second Battalion, 1899–1902. By A Company Officer . . 4

Appendix I. Table showing Services, Promotions, Casualties, &c., of
officers of The Black Watch in South Africa, 1899–1902 :—

    A. Officers of the 1st and 2nd Battalions 22

    B. Officers attached to the 2nd Battalion from the Reserve of
    Officers 27

    C. Officers of the 3rd (Militia) Battalion 27

    D. Officers of the Volunteer Battalions 27

    E. Officers attached to the 2nd Battalion from other units . 28

    F. Civilian attached as Officer to the 2nd Battalion . . . 28

Appendix II. N.C.O.s and Men of the 2nd Battalion The Black Watch
who received rewards for services in South Africa 28

Appendix III. N.C.O.s and Men of the 2nd Battalion The Black Watch
who were mentioned in despatches for services in South Africa . 29

THE SCOTTISH HORSE

The Raising and Organisation of the Regiment. By the Editor . . 30

The Scottish Horse in Action. By A Squadron Officer—
Bakenlaagte (October 30th, 1901) 38

    The War in the West—
    Moedwil (September 30th, 1901) 49

    Rooiwal (April 11th, 1902) 55

PAGE

Appendix I. Officers and Men of the Scottish Horse who received rewards for services performed while with the Regiment . . . 60

Appendix II. Officers and Men of the Scottish Horse who were mentioned in despatches for services performed while with the Regiment . . 61

List of Abbreviations used in Records of Officers, Warrant Officers, Non-commissioned Officers, and Men; in the Table showing the Services of Officers of The Black Watch, pp. 22–28; and in the Indexes to Portraits, to Persons, and to Military Units and Departments 64

ROLL OF PERTHSHIRE OFFICERS WHO HAVE SEEN ACTIVE SERVICE

Part I. 67

Part II. 90

David William Stanley Ogilvy, eighth Earl of Airlie, 1856–1900. By A. Francis Steuart 97

Lieutenant-Colonel the Hon. Andrew David Murray, 1863–1901. By Lieutenant-Colonel Lord Lovat, C.B., C.V.O., D.S.O. . . . 99

Lieutenant-Colonel William Henry Dick-Cunyngham, V.C., 1851–1900. By the Hon. Mrs. Forbes of Brux 101

ROLL OF PERTHSHIRE WARRANT-OFFICERS, NON-COMMISSIONED OFFICERS, AND MEN, WHO HAVE SEEN ACTIVE SERVICE

Royal Navy 147

     Australian Naval Brigade— New South Wales Section 147

The Army— The Cavalry— 2nd Life Guards 147

       Royal Horse Guards (The Blues) 147

       2nd Dragoon Guards (Queen's Bays) 147

Contents XV

The Cavalry (*continued*)—
PAGE

4th (Royal Irish) Dragoon Guards 148
6th Dragoon Guards (Carabiniers) 148
2nd Dragoons (Royal Scots Greys) 148
6th (Inniskilling) Dragoons 150
7th (The Queen's Own) Hussars 150
9th (The Queen's Royal) Lancers 150
10th (The Prince of Wales's Own Royal) Hussars . . . 151
12th (The Prince of Wales's Royal) Lancers 151
13th Hussars 151
14th (The King's) Hussars 151
17th (The Duke of Cambridge's Own) Lancers 152
18th Hussars 152
19th (Alexandra, Princess of Wales's Own) Hussars . . . 152
20th Hussars 153

Royal Regiment of Artillery—
Royal Horse Artillery 153
Royal Field Artillery 153
Royal Garrison Artillery—
Mountain Division 154
Garrison Companies 154

Corps of Royal Engineers 155

The Foot Guards—
Scots Guards 156

Infantry of the Line, Militia, and Volunteers—
The Royal Scots (Lothian Regiment) 159
The Queen's (Royal West Surrey Regiment) 160
The Buffs (East Kent Regiment) 160
The Royal Scots Fusiliers 161
The South Wales Borderers 162
The King's Own Scottish Borderers 162
The Cameronians (Scottish Rifles) 163
The Worcestershire Regiment 164
The Border Regiment 164
The Hampshire Regiment 164

Infantry of the Line, Militia, and Volunteers (*continued*)—   PAGE
The Welsh Regiment 165
The Black Watch (Royal Highlanders) 165
The King's Royal Rifle Corps 188
The Duke of Edinburgh's (Wiltshire Regiment) . . . 188
The Highland Light Infantry 188
Seaforth Highlanders (Ross-shire Buffs, The Duke of Albany's) 192
The Gordon Highlanders 197
The Queen's Own Cameron Highlanders 201
The Royal Irish Rifles 204
Argyll and Sutherland Highlanders (Princess Louise's) . . 204
The Royal Dublin Fusiliers 208
Scottish Cycle Corps 208

Army Service Corps 208
Royal Army Medical Corps 209
Army Ordnance Department 209
Army Pay Department 209
Army Post Office Corps 209
Remount Department 210

Imperial Yeomanry—
4th Battalion—
7th (Leicestershire) Company 210
28th Company (Compton's Horse) 210
5th Battalion—
16th (Worcestershire) Company 210
6th Battalion—
18th (Lanarkshire) Company 210
20th (Fife and Forfarshire Light Horse) Company . . 210
107th (Lanarkshire) Company 212
108th (Queen's Own Royal Glasgow) Company . . . 212
11th Battalion—
34th (Middlesex) Company 212
15th Battalion—
57th (Buckinghamshire) Company 212

Contents xvii

Imperial Yeomanry (*continued*)—
17th Battalion—

PAGE

   50th (Hampshire) Company 212

18th Battalion—

   70th (Sharpshooters) Company 213
   72nd (Rough Riders) Company 213

21st Battalion—

   81st (Sharpshooters) Company 213

22nd Battalion—

   78th (Rough Riders) Company 213

24th Battalion (Metropolitan Mounted Rifles) 213
26th Battalion (Younghusband's Horse)—

   121st Company 214

31st Battalion (Fincastle's Horse) 214
37th Battalion (Highland Horse) 214
Duke of Cambridge's Own Imperial Yeomanry . . 215

Corps partly Imperial Yeomanry and partly Irregular—
Lovat's Scouts 215
The Scottish Horse 216

Indian and Colonial Volunteer and Irregular Corps—
Ashburner's Light Horse 225
Bethune's Mounted Infantry 225
Canadian Mounted Rifles 225
Cape Garrison Artillery 225
Cape Pioneer Regiment 225
Cape Railway Sharpshooters 225
Cape Town Highlanders 225
Ceylon Mounted Infantry 226
Colonial Scouts 226
Commander-in-Chief's Bodyguard 226
Diamond Fields Horse 226
Duke of Edinburgh's Own Volunteer Rifles . . . 226
Durban Light Infantry 226
Eastern Province Horse 226
Imperial Light Horse 226

Indian and Colonial Volunteer and Irregular Corps (*continued*)—   PAGE

    Imperial Light Infantry 227
    Indian Ambulance Corps. 227
    Johannesburg Mounted Rifles 227
    Kimberley Mounted Corps 227
    Kimberley Rifles 227
    Kitchener's Fighting Scouts 228
    Kitchener's Horse 228
    Lumsden's Horse 228
    Marshall's Horse 228
    Mennie's Scouts 228
    Natal Carbineers 229
    Natal Volunteer Artillery 229
    New England Mounted Rifles 229
    New South Wales Mounted Rifles 229
    New Zealand Mounted Infantry 229
    New Zealand Rough Riders 229
    Prince Alfred's Volunteer Guard 230
    Prince of Wales's Light Horse 230
    Roberts' Horse 230
    Scott's Railway Guards 230
    South African Light Horse 230
    Steinaecker's Horse 230
    Strathcona's Horse 231
    Thorneycroft's Mounted Infantry 231
    Volunteer Ambulance Corps 231
    Western Province Mounted Rifles 231

Town Guards—

    Kimberley Town Guard 231
    Port Elizabeth Town Guard 232

Constabulary and Police—

    British South Africa Police 232
    Cape Police 232
    South African Constabulary 232

Index to Portraits of Warrant Officers, Non-commissioned Officers, and Men   269

Contents

Addenda—   PAGE
    Roll of Officers, Part I. 286

    Roll of Non-commissioned Officers and Men—
        The Highland Light Infantry 287
        Seaforth Highlanders (Ross-shire Buffs, The Duke of Albany's) 287

    Imperial Yeomanry (6th Battalion)—
        18th (Lanarkshire) Company 287

    South African Constabulary 287

Subscribers' Index 288

Index to Persons 293

Index to Military Units and Departments 312

ILLUSTRATIONS

Schiehallion from the Head of Loch Tummel . . . *Frontispiece*
(From a Water-colour Painting by Colin B. Phillip, A.R.W.S. *Original presented by the Artist for the benefit of the Soldiers' Copies Fund*)

Trek Companies of the Black Watch fording the Wilge River, near Tafelkop, O.R.C. . . . . *To face page* 3

Block-house held by Detachment of the 1st Battalion The Black Watch on Reitz Hill, near Harrismith, O.R.C. . ,, 3

A Trooper of the Scottish Horse . . . . . . ,, 30
(From a Water-colour Drawing by Jane B. Constable)

Gun-carriage of the 84th Battery, R.F.A. . . . . ., 30
(Presented by the War Office in recognition of the gallantry of the Scottish Horse at Bakenlaagte, 30th October 1901)

Portraits of Officers . . . . *Page* 105

Portraits of Non-commissioned Officers and Men . . . . ,, 239

MAPS AND PLANS

PAGE

Sketch Map of Magersfontein, 11th December 1899 7

Sketch Map of Paardeberg, 18th February 1900 11

Sketch showing Highland Brigade Marches from 21st July to 9th August 1900 16

Hand Sketch showing Disposition of Troops at Retief's Nek, 23rd and 24th July 1900 17

Sketch Plan of the Action at Bakenlaagte, 30th October 1901, showing roughly the lie of the ground where Colonel Benson made his last stand 42

Sketch Map of the Action at Moedwil, 30th September 1901 . . 51

THE BLACK WATCH IN SOUTH AFRICA
1899–1902

I.—THE FIRST BATTALION
1901–1902

TOWARDS the end of 1901 it was rumoured that certain regiments from India, including the 1st Battalion The Black Watch (which was then quartered at Kampti, in the Central Provinces), were about to take the place of some of the war-worn battalions in South Africa. After a few weeks of suspense, these rumours were happily confirmed by the receipt, on the 13th of November, of orders for the Black Watch to proceed at once on active service. A large number of time-expired men availed themselves of the bounty then offered, and extended their service in order to accompany the regiment to the front.

On the 6th of December, 22 officers,[1] 2 warrant officers, and 953 non-commissioned officers and men, under the command of Lieutenant-Colonel E. G. Grogan, embarked on board the transport *Armenian* at Bombay, and after a calm but very hot voyage, lasting sixteen days, reached Durban on the 22nd of the same month.

On the afternoon of the 24th the battalion started up-country in two trains, its destination being Standerton, in the Transvaal. The first train, under Major Wolrige-Gordon, arrived there early on Christmas morning, just about the hour at which the Boers were rushing the Yeomanry camp at Tweefontein.

Consequent on this disaster, the second train was stopped by a telegram twenty miles south of Standerton, and the whole regiment was ordered to turn and join Lieutenant-General Sir Leslie Rundle's diminished force in the Orange River Colony as quickly as possible.

On the morning of the 27th of December, headquarters and four companies reached Harrismith. One company was left there, and the remainder immediately set out on an eighteen-mile march to Elands River Bridge, where they were joined, twenty-four hours later, by the rest of the battalion, with the exception of the company left in Harrismith. Considering that it was the hot weather,

---

[1] Seven officers joined the battalion in South Africa. For the names of the officers who served with the 1st and 2nd Battalions respectively, see Appendix I. of this section.

II.   A

and that the men had been seventeen days on board ship and three consecutive days in the train, they covered the distance very well, and a flattering letter was received from the General to that effect.

Somewhat over a week was spent at Elands River Bridge, during which time the regiment was employed in throwing up a fort, and in covering the construction of a line of block-houses to Elands River Drift. It then joined General Rundle's headquarters near Tweefontein, and during the next two or three weeks helped to construct block-houses between Harrismith and Bethlehem.

On the afternoon of the 8th of January 1902, the force made a short march of about four miles to Tyger's Spruit. Unaware of this, a party of Boers, returning to De Wet's commando from the direction of Witzies Hoek, stumbled right upon the camp in the dark. They were met by a heavy fire from the picquets, and—according to information supplied several weeks afterwards by two separate batches of Boer prisoners—sustained some seventeen or eighteen casualties from the fusillade.

The next five or six nights were cold, and heavy rain fell, accompanied by the violent thunder and lightning peculiar to South Africa. During these unpleasant hours of darkness the " clip-clop " of the Boer Mauser was no unfamiliar sound, and at a place called Hattingsdal, where the force bivouacked on the 13th of January, one of our sentries was killed by a Boer sniper, a few paces in front of his picquet.

Before the end of January block-houses had been run up as far as Bethlehem, and headquarters and four companies had been withdrawn to Harrismith to form part of the garrison. The defences of the town were placed in charge of Colonel Grogan ; and by the middle of February the whole of the battalion, (except C and G Companies), had joined headquarters at Harrismith.

Later in the month the battalion formed the greater portion of what might be called the " bag " of a huge net, into which our mobile columns drove about 1000 Boers, thus forcing them to surrender to us.

Immediately after this " drive," A and H Companies, under Major Burton and Captain Lloyd, and F and E Companies, under Captains Grant-Duff and Walker, joined Colonel Rimington's and Colonel S. D. Gordon's columns respectively, in relief of four companies of the 2nd Battalion, which had had several months of hard trekking.

The greater part of G and C Companies meantime had taken over from the East Yorks a line of twenty block-houses extending from Elands River to Tradouw. In the course of one of the " drives " which followed, we lost a most promising young N.C.O. (Lance-Corporal W. Scott), who was in charge of a new block-house, specially put up for a big " drive " organised by Major-General Locke Elliot. Scott was killed at a range of over a mile on the night of the 27th of March, during an unsuccessful attempt made by the Boers to break through our line.

With Rimington's column, Major Burton's and Captain Lloyd's companies marched through the Orange River Colony, Eastern Transvaal, and Natal,

TREK COMPANIES OF THE BLACK WATCH FORDING THE WILGE RIVER,
NEAR TAFELKOP, O. R. C.

BLOCK-HOUSE HELD BY DETACHMENT OF THE 1ST BATTALION THE BLACK WATCH
ON REITZ HILL, NEAR HARRISMITH, O. R. C.

between the 1st of March and 31st of May, chiefly in pursuit of De Wet. Captain Grant-Duff's and Captain Walker's men joined Colonel Gordon's column (forming part of Colonel Garratt's force) at Elands River on the 3rd of March, and participated in much the same " drives " as A and H. The four companies marched over a thousand miles before the conclusion of hostilities on the 31st of May, and the combined efforts of the several columns engaged in these " drives " resulted in the capture of a considerable number of prisoners and cattle.

The following " Force Order " was published by Colonel Rimington on the break-up of his column after peace had been declared. " The O.C. Column desires to thank the officers, N.C.O.s, and men of the 1st Black Watch for the excellent work they have done with this column, and to place on record his high opinion of their soldier-like qualities, good discipline, and magnificent marching powers, and further to thank them for the cheerful way in which they have helped the transport at difficult drifts, &c."

Colonel Gordon also wrote to Colonel Grogan as follows :—

" MY DEAR COLONEL GROGAN,—Your two companies under Captain Grant-Duff have left my column this morning to join your headquarters, and I wish to place on record with you my high appreciation of their discipline and behaviour whilst under my command. We have not fought any battles during this period, but there has been plenty of hard work ; long weary marches, especially for them, and much trying night picquet duty. During these marches I have always felt my baggage to be safe in their charge, and at night I knew my most exposed flank was safe in their hands. I never heard of any grumbling or slackness, and anything I asked them to do was done as I wished it. I cannot give them higher praise than this, and what I say of the men of course applies in even a greater degree to the officers. I shall always be proud to have had them under my command, and can only hope I shall be equally lucky on some future occasion."

· The close of the war found the whole of the regiment at Harrismith, the two battalions meeting for the first time in their history.

About the middle of September the 2nd Battalion received orders to be ready to proceed to India, and 238 N.C.O.s and men were accordingly transferred from the 1st Battalion, 170 N.C.O.s and men not qualified to serve in India being received in return. On the 24th of September the 1st Battalion left Harrismith for Durban on its way home, with a strength of 22 officers, 2 warrant officers, and 635 non-commissioned officers and men.

The casualties of the 1st Battalion in South Africa were :—3 N.C.O.s and men killed and died of wounds ; 2 men died of injuries or disease, and 3 men wounded.

II.—THE SECOND BATTALION
1899–1902

BY A COMPANY OFFICER

BEFORE beginning his meagre record the narrator feels he owes a humble apology to the honoured memory of his brave comrades for being so little able to do one tithe of the justice due to the gallant soul of the regiment. The company officer's view is so restricted that he can only describe what happens on a mile or two of ground, and therefore all his impressions are those of a man looking at a picture while standing a few inches from the canvas.

1899. The mobilisation order for the 1st Army Corps, of which the 2nd Battalion The Black Watch was a part, reached Aldershot on the 7th of October 1899. On the 11th came news of the ultimatum. Then our reservists, every one of whom reported himself, arrived from Perth:—27 officers, 954 rank and file (of whom 430 were reservists) embarked in the *Orient* (Captain Symons) at Tilbury, on Sunday the 22nd of October, and 59 more came by a second ship shortly afterwards. The *Daily Chronicle* of the 23rd of October said of the regiment at Tilbury, " A more splendid body of men has never been seen on any parade ground since the substitution of short for long service in the Army."

After a most comfortable voyage we dropped anchor in Table Bay on the evening of the 13th of November, and came alongside on the following afternoon.

We at once loaded up two trains, and were away up the line early on the 15th across the dreary Karroo, arriving at De Aar on the 17th, where we found the General, Andrew Wauchope, our old Colonel, with his staff.

A few days afterwards we left by rail for Naauwpoort Junction, where a culvert over which we had just passed was blown up. On the 23rd Captain Cumming-Bruce's company (C), when acting as part of an escort to General French's reconstruction train, came under the fire of a few Boers near Arundel. Three of the mounted infantry escort and five Boers were wounded.

At Naauwpoort we left our claymores and sporrans. To replace the sporran an apron of khaki drill was worn. All ranks carried the rifle.

On the 1st of December came news of Modder River fight and sudden orders to entrain, one half-battalion being railed through to Modder River, the other marching from Orange River (fifty-five miles). On the 7th the Boers made an attempt to cut the railway behind us at Enslin, and on the same day we heard of Captain H. Scott Turner's death while bravely leading a successful sortie from Kimberley on the 28th of November. In him the regiment lost a most gallant, capable, and popular officer.

At Modder River we came under Lord Methuen's command, and the Highland Brigade was collected together—the 1st Highland Light Infantry, the 2nd Seaforth Highlanders, the 1st Argyll and Sutherland Highlanders, and ourselves. The total force under Lord Methuen must have been some 14,000 men of all arms.

At 2.30 P.M. on Sunday the 10th of December, in pouring rain, the Highland Brigade paraded for the attack on the Magersfontein kopjes. At the same time the 9th Lancers and four batteries of artillery moved off, the Lancers protecting our right flank. In the brigade every one carried a blanket (an unwieldy piece of furniture), a rifle, and 150 rounds of ammunition in pouches. Every man had his mess tin, and every other man a one-pound tin of beef.

A and B Companies of the regiment were the advanced-guard. We proceeded some three miles in a north-easterly direction and then lay down while all our artillery—field-guns, howitzers, and 4.7 naval guns—poured a tremendous hail along the upper ridges of Magersfontein Hill. From Dr. Ramsbotham, then head of the Free State Ambulance, the narrator heard long afterwards that not a single Boer was killed, and only two or three slightly wounded, by this storm of projectiles.

The rain stopped during the afternoon, but a heavy thunderstorm broke in the evening. At dark the brigade fell back, and bivouacked under the shelter of some rising ground in mass of quarter columns—*i.e.* each company behind the other, at a distance of eight paces.

During the evening Colonel Coode explained to all his officers General Wauchope's instructions :—that we should advance at 12.30 A.M. in brigade mass of quarter column ; that Major G. E. Benson, R.A., would lead us a little to the east of the most northerly point of the hill before us ; that at the foot of the hill the brigade would deploy (*i.e.* form line for attack) to the left ; that the H.L.I. (the rear battalion) would form the "second line" ; that each of the other three battalions would at first have two companies in the firing line, two in support, four in reserve ; that the crest of the hill was held by the enemy, and had to be taken by this partial turning movement ; and that the General would be with the H.L.I.

At 12.30 A.M. on Monday the 11th of December we moved off, the Black Watch leading. While charging magazines two rifles were accidentally discharged in the brigade, but the storm must have prevented the report being heard at any distance. The left guide of each company held a rope knotted every ten yards. It was a pitch-black night, and ever and again the glare of the Kimberley search-light would flash on us and intensify the surrounding darkness. At about 2 A.M. the thunderstorm was at its height. The only human noise was caused by men stumbling and falling as we moved over the rocky ground. On the right there was occasionally confusion owing to men from other companies and other regiments losing touch in the darkness, and some men of the Seaforth got as far forward as our second company. The General marched on the left at the head of the column behind Major Benson, who was assisted by Captain Cumming-Bruce. There were constant halts to check the direction, but we veered about a good deal, as the lightning affected the magnetic compasses. The Boers had a lamp showing on the hill at one time during the night, but it was probably not for signalling purposes. At about 2.30 A.M. the rain ceased. Shortly after 3 A.M. we came on a thick line of bushes, through which the two leading companies moved in "fours." The brigade again formed up on the other side of these, our right close to a barbed-wire farm fence. The dawn was beginning to show behind the hill to our right front, so that we seemed to be considerably to the west of the line we were intended to take. The General then sent back to order the three leading battalions to deploy to the right instead of to the left, and, under Colonel Coode's orders, A, the leading company, went forward, extended to five paces interval, while B Company, with each half-company in single rank, followed as support.

A had advanced a hundred and fifty yards, with B seventy yards behind, when the foot of the hill in front of them burst into a sheet of fire. A Company received orders direct from the General, who, with Colonel Coode, had moved forward with it, to lie down and fire, evidently whilst waiting for the brigade to deploy. B then doubled up in line, fixing bayonets as it did so. The fire was going high, but a good many men were hit. Captain Cumming-Bruce was mortally wounded just behind A Company, and close by fell the Colonel. General Wauchope must have been killed almost at once, as he never spoke, although his galloper was asking for him near the spot where he was afterwards found dead. Part of C Company under Lieutenant Edmonds ran forward into the ranks of A and B, so that the men were almost shoulder to shoulder. Part of F under 2nd Lieutenant Maurice Drummond (who was almost at once hit in the thigh), also came into the ranks of A at a place where 2nd Lieutenant Nunneley and a few men were in a small trench. Lieutenant F. G. Tait also brought some men of F into the ranks of B, but the bulk of this company, under Major (now Lieutenant-Colonel) Mowbray Berkeley, deployed with the rest of the battalion to the right. The confusion was due to the new orders for deployment having scarcely reached every one when the enemy's fire first began.

In the position in which the leading companies found themselves they were enfiladed by a slight fire from both flanks, and were some three hundred yards from the Boer trenches. Two rushes were made to enable the men to spread out a little, and then they settled down to good deliberate firing. A sharpish fire was also coming from the rear, where another regiment, which did not know of our companies in front, had lain down and was replying to the Boer fire—the heaviest we ever experienced during the war, not excepting Paardeberg. As daylight broke this advanced party, of whom a large number had been hit, found itself isolated by a spur jutting out on its right which the Boers had occupied, but by collecting ammunition from dead and wounded and by firing only when a Boer exposed himself, fire was kept up until after 10 A.M. At about 5 A.M. our guns began and kept the Boer fire down, and although a shell would occationally burst back (two of our men being hit thus), the benefit done by keeping the enemy quiet could not be over-estimated. This body—originally some 200

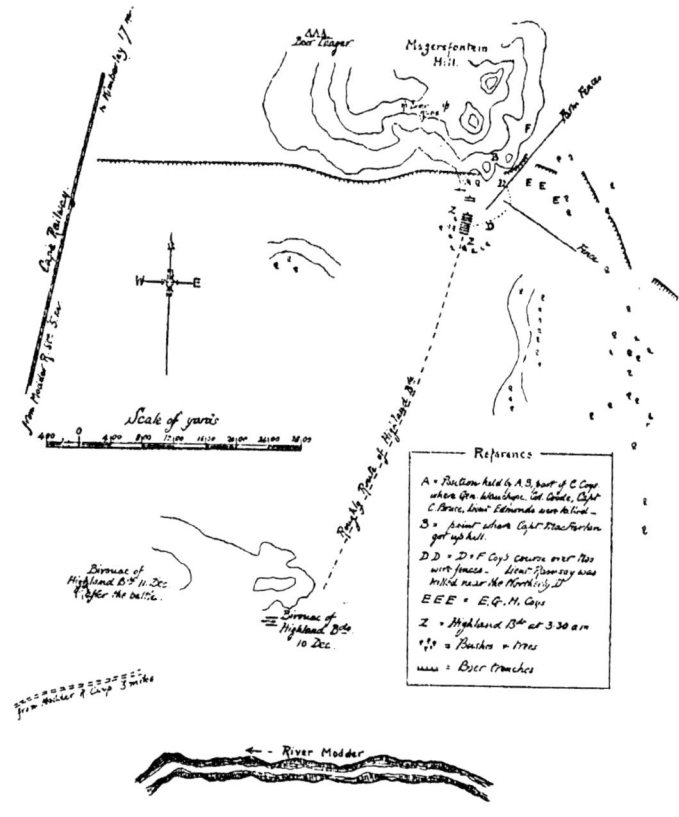

SKETCH MAP OF MAGERSFONTEIN, 11TH DECEMBER 1899

strong—waited all day for a reinforcement, and, weakened as it was by heavy casualties, could not charge the trenches alone. At daylight, from the spot where Lieutenant Tait, hit in the leg, lay under a small thorn tree, to where some hundred and twenty yards away the General's galloper, Lieutenant Arthur Wauchope, was lying, wounded in both legs, there were not fifteen men untouched.

It was here that our casualties were heaviest; our General some forty yards to the left of Lieutenant Wauchope, Colonel Coode just between A and B Companies, Lieutenant Edmonds some yards to the Colonel's left, and Captain Cumming-Bruce, were all killed. A Company had 23 killed, 28 wounded; B 15 killed, 40 wounded; and C about the same.   The summer sun and the innumerable flies were maddening to the wounded men.

Receiving no order to retire, this small force hung on until dark, and then those who could walk fell back, led by two of the company officers who were unhit—about twenty-five men in all, at whom, as they withdrew, the Boers most chivalrously forbore to fire.   They reached the bivouac of the brigade at about 9 P.M. and got food—their previous meal having been at mid-day on Sunday.

To return to the greater portion of the battalion.   When the fire commenced they moved to the right at the double, and each company turned to its front as soon as it got clear.   Owing to the brigade having closed up, the rear company, after turning " fours right," had to incline a little to the right, and so in some way interfered with the front companies of the Seaforth.   D, E, and F Companies went through two wire farm fences, and shortly after going through the second wire fence, Lieutenant Nigel Ramsay, who was leading the left half of D Company, was killed—not more than two hundred yards from the Boer trench. Owing to the small spur shown on the map west of B, all these men lost touch with the men of A, B, and C Companies on the left of the spur.   A certain number of men with Captain MacFarlan, the Adjutant (who had been hit in the wrist in the first fire), went up the hill at the point marked B on the sketch. They were stopped by a sudden fire in front, whereupon they lay down and returned the fire, but were eventually driven down by our own artillery, and fell back somewhere near F (see map).   Captain MacFarlan walked back along the line doing most noble work, and was killed close to where he started up the hill.

Lieutenants Cox and Wilson of the Seaforth also led a mixed company of our men and theirs round by the point marked F—to which place Sergeant Fraser of the Black Watch managed to bring some more of our men—so that the Boers were almost taken in rear.   This party, however, was enfiladed by the enemy, and was driven down by our own artillery fire, five men being taken prisoner. It was our own shrapnel too that made the companies at the north point D fall back at about 7 A.M. to the line EE, under a severe enfilading fire from the Boer trenches on the right.   This line EE they held—ammunition being passed along from some unknown supply on the left—until 10 A.M., when the casualties were so heavy that this could no longer be done, and the ammunition gave out.   The line then fell back a short way facing still more to the right, *i.e.* east-north-east, on to a supporting line of the Seaforth.

Our right flank was now in touch with the Guards Brigade, which was in the bushes shown in the sketch running south to the Modder River, and at about 1 P.M. Colonel Hughes-Hallett gave an order to the centre to retire.   This retirement gave the Boers a chance they were quick to seize of pouring in a tremendous fire, which caused many casualties.   A second position was taken up further back, but there was little fighting in this part of the field after 4 P.M.   The brigade was finally brought back to a spot just west of the bivouac occupied on the previous night.

The bitter cold after the heat of the daytime was very trying to the wounded, most of whom lay all night where they had fallen. The Boers gave them water, but they had no medical attendance until next day. Our medical officer, Lieutenant H. E. M. Douglas, was severely wounded after doing magnificent work under fire, for which he subsequently received the Victoria Cross; but there is no space to tell of the countless individual acts of heroism performed that day. Our roll of dead and wounded should speak for itself :—7 officers, 88 N.C.O.s and men were killed, and 11 officers, 207 N.C.O.s and men wounded, of the 25 officers, 918 rank and file who went into action ; 42 men, some of whom were wounded, were captured on the hill when they fell back at the commencement of our artillery fire.

The following morning we stood to arms at 3.30 A.M., and the order to march back to Modder River came as a very bitter blow to the regiment, as we had scarcely realised that we were not to have one more chance of trying to take the hill.

Lord Methuen then sent out parties of men to bring in our wounded and bury the dead. General Wauchope's body was brought to Modder River, and the regiment he had once commanded, that loved him as he loved it, paid him the last honours at his grave. Captain Elton, Lieutenant Ramsay, and twenty-five rank and file were also laid to rest at Modder River that day. The others were buried where they fell on the field of Magersfontein.

Some comment was afterwards caused at home by the fact that no return was sent in of men of the Black Watch who had distinguished themselves in this engagement. The Commanding Officer decided that where all had done their share it would be unjust to select names.

The next few weeks were full of hard work for the shrunken battalion.

1900. On New Year's Day the Caledonian Society of Capetown sent up every man in the brigade a pint of beer and a generous gift of tobacco, and during this time presents arrived from numerous kind friends at home.

On the 23rd of January Major-General Hector MacDonald, C.B., arrived and took command of the brigade. Colonel Carthew-Yorstoun came from the 1st Battalion to command us ; Lieutenant Grieve, adjutant of the Royal Scots of Sydney, was attached to the regiment, and all the officers and men who had not been severely wounded rejoined during these weeks. Sixty-five of our 3rd Battalion also arrived.

On the 3rd of February a force under General MacDonald, consisting of the Highland Brigade, two squadrons 9th Lancers, the 62nd Battery R.F.A., and a detachment R.E., with pontoons, started for Koedoesberg, some twenty-four miles west down the left bank of the Riet River. We had a long halt on the 3rd, and arrived after a hot march on the 4th, whereupon the Boers fell back from Koedoesberg Drift (which they had occupied on hearing of the movement of our force), on to a hill behind. In the next two days the brigade crossed and occupied the southern crest of the " berg." On the 7th the brigade cleared the hill, but we lost two most valuable officers—one mortally wounded, the other killed outright—Captain Eykyn and Lieutenant Tait.

The Boers rode away in a north-easterly direction, a cavalry brigade arriving too late to intercept them. The casualties in the regiment were 2 officers and 2 men killed, 7 N.C.O.s and men wounded.

We heard afterwards that this feint of a move to the relief of Kimberley had puzzled the Boers most successfully.

The whole force arrived back at Modder River on the 9th, and found that Lord Roberts had come up. He made a most complimentary speech to the brigade on the following day.

On the 12th of February the brigade, which now formed part of the 9th Division under General Colvile, moved by rail to Enslin (eighteen miles south), and starting on the 13th at 6 A.M., crossed the frontier of the Orange Free State.

During the next few days we made long marches, but saw no fighting until we reached the Modder River at Paardeberg Drift, which we did shortly before midnight on the 17th of February. There, owing to the capture of a large convoy by the Boers at Waterval Drift on the 15th, we were only served with half-rations of biscuit and tea, but we had a full ration of meat.

We bivouacked on the morning of the 18th close to Paardeberg Drift, and, just before " breakfasts " were " up " at 5.30 A.M., we heard shots fired at some mounted infantry from the opposite (the right or northerly) bank of the river, and the brigade fell in.

We marched a quarter of a mile to the east in single file, and then turned to our left and faced the river, from the banks of which, as also from a ridge on our right, broke a sharp fire. These banks were precipitous, and about ten or twelve feet high, covered with bush and stunted thorn. On the right bank several Boers had climbed into the trees, but little damage was done by the enemy's fire. Cronje's main laager was to the brigade's right front. General MacDonald was on the extreme left of the brigade (at a point where some bushes are shown on the left of the sketch), and behind us was " Kitchener's Kop," where stood Lord Kitchener, who was in command of all three divisions. By 7 A.M. some of the companies on the left of the brigade—A and B Companies of the Black Watch and a company of the Seaforth under 2nd Lieutenant McClure—were at the river bank. The river was in spate and said to be unfordable. However, one of our officers and a piper, Donald Cameron (Doune), tested it, and the officer, thinking that if he could cross he could clear the bush on the right bank of snipers, proceeded to call up his widely-extended company to the spot where a crossing was possible. Each lot of ten as they came up linked arms, hung their ammunition pouches round their necks, and plunged in. A bugler, Purdie, was nearly swept away, but was seized by Sergeant Millar (Alyth) and saved. The water was up to the men's waists. Piper Cameron was the first across, and helped the officer out ; he received the Distinguished Conduct Medal for his gallantry on this occasion. Two more companies of the Black Watch and the company of the Seaforth followed across, and extended at right angles to the river, with their right moving along the river bank ; but owing to the formation of the ground the three companies on the left got rather widely separated from the directing company. As the four companies moved forward they were met by a sharpish fire from a deep donga, and to their left front sixty mounted Boers rode away at a gallop. After advancing some six hundred yards along the bank,

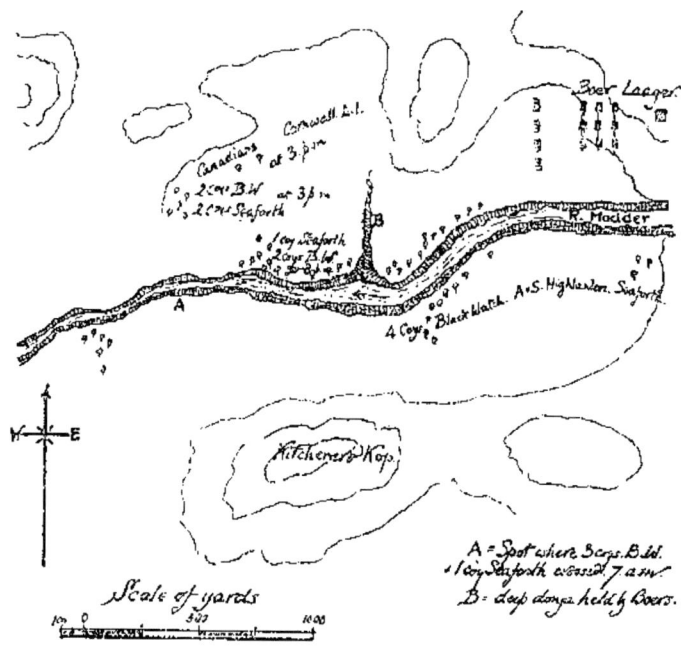

SKETCH MAP OF PAARDEBERG, 18TH FEBRUARY 1900

and being then three hundred and fifty yards from the donga, the officer in charge received orders from the left bank to halt, and hold on to the ground gained, as these companies were now masking the fire of the rest of the brigade on the opposite side of the river.

A fourth company of the Black Watch and some more men of the Seaforth now reinforced the left companies of this detachment, while the right company on the river bank was reinforced by some of the Shropshire Light Infantry. The pioneers of the regiment, under Sergeant Howden (who also has received the Distinguished Conduct Medal for this engagement) brought over large supplies of ammunition. At about 3 P.M. the 19th Brigade (our sister brigade) made a charge over the open in which all the companies of our brigade on the right bank of the river took part—except our extreme right company, which was too far in advance to form part of the charging line. This charge failed to get home, though it cleared the donga and drove the Boers into the laager.

Meantime on the right, across the river, the remainder of the battalion was firing into the double tier of small trenches near the laager on the right bank and into another row of trenches on the left bank, at about seven hundred yards. The right bank being higher than the left, the Boers had practically three tiers of fire, but in spite of this E Company fought its way to the left bank of the river. It was here that Colonel Carthew-Yorstoun, Major Maxwell, and Major Berkeley were wounded. The battalion was for twelve hours fiercely engaged until nightfall, when the whole force withdrew, with the exception of the company on the right of the river, which, with a company of the Shropshires, entrenched itself, as if it had fallen back the snipers could have again occupied the bushes near the donga. Other men who received the Distinguished Conduct Medal for this day were Sergeant Millar, Lance-Corporal Forrett, Private J. Smith, and Pioneer Hastie.

We lost a most excellent officer killed, who was attached to one of the companies north of the river—Lieutenant J. G. Grieve, of the New South Wales Permanent Forces. Our total casualties were 1 officer, 18 N.C.O.s and men killed, 5 officers, 74 N.C.O.s and men wounded, out of 15 officers, 640 N.C.O.s and men who went into action.

The following day the battalion, which had now only eight officers (one other being down with enteric), was employed on reconnaissance with the Argylls, while the company across the river, which had found four dead Boers and several horses in the deserted donga, was relieved at about 10 A.M. by some of the 19th Brigade. This company was rationed at mid-day, after having been thirty-six hours without a meal. The rumour of Cronje's surrender on Monday the 19th raised every one's spirits to the highest pitch, so that, when it proved false, the next few days of constant bombardment fell rather flat.

On the night of the 26th of February two companies, A and B, were sent over to General Smith-Dorrien, and formed part of the picquet line surrounding the laager, with orders to prevent any Boer stragglers breaking away. During the night the 6-inch howitzers spoke from time to time. At 2 A.M. on the 27th (Amajuba Day), the Canadians, who had sapped to within forty yards of the laager, and the Shropshire Light Infantry, at a much longer range, began pouring in a heavy fire towards the laager, from which we were five thousand yards distant. It was very dark, so the fire must have been unaimed. The Boers replied to it, but the Canadians were the only sufferers. The moon rose at 2.20, and at 3.30 the firing ceased. As soon as it was light the laager, which had been knocked to pieces by our shells, was seen to be displaying white flags everywhere, and news of Cronje's surrender with 3700 Boers reached us at 7 A.M.

Three Krupp guns, one quick-firing gun, quantities of ammunition, and plenty of food were found in the laager. The ground was littered with clothing, tins, letters, books, and carcases of horses and oxen. The smells were appalling. The trenches, which extended for a mile and a half on both banks, were each about six feet long, five feet deep, and thirty inches wide, beautifully constructed, and well concealed. A small building in the laager was used as a hospital, with a German doctor in charge.

Several officers and men joined us during this week from various hospitals and from home.

On the 4th of March we started again, trekking towards Bloemfontein. We had had a very damp week of it at Paardeberg, and the drinking water had been very yellow and smelly, so we were glad to get on the move. Our clothes and shoes also were much in need of repair, but the Queen's telegram of congratulation on the Paardeberg capture was a very pleasing incentive to spur us all on.

We were now moving on the right bank of the Modder River.

On the 7th of March we left Makouw's Drift at 5.15 a.m., the brigade being in front of the 9th Division, in échelon from the right. At about 7 a.m. one of the enemy's guns opened fire on us from a steep kopje on the other (south) side of the river at a range of five thousand yards. Our three naval 12-pounders replied. The Argylls were on the bank of the river, we next them, and beyond us the Seaforth. General Colvile ordered B, C, and A Companies of the regiment to push on along the river with the Argylls, but the brigade was considerably delayed by the fact that we were ahead of all the cavalry on the left bank, owing to their having to make a long détour. As we advanced the enemy ran like rabbits, after firing a few shots at fourteen hundred yards, and one or two of our picked shots made very pretty shooting at this range. We found meat cooking in the hastily-dug trenches the enemy had deserted, and three or four miles further east could see their waggons trekking as hard as possible towards Bloemfontein. They left tents, blankets, and ammunition behind them.

From where we were we saw our whole army spread out—the 6th Division on our left, then the mounted infantry and 19th Brigade, while on our right were the cavalry and the 7th Division. There were eight casualties in the 9th Division, none in the regiment. The 6th Division captured two guns. At 4.30 p.m. we reached the farm-house at Poplar Grove just quitted by Steyn and Kruger. On the 8th we recrossed the Modder River to the left bank.

On the 10th of March the 6th Division was hotly engaged at Driefontein, but we were not under fire—although as no clasp was given for Poplar Grove, we received the "Driefontein" clasp. A company was detailed as a burying party and buried 110 of the enemy's dead.

We proceeded on our march, averaging sixteen miles daily, through a pleasant enough country, and on the 13th of March arrived at Ferreira Spruit, five miles south of Bloemfontein. We moved to Bloemfontein town commonage on the 15th of March, and proceeded to try to refit in the shops. This town, of some 10,000 inhabitants, is now well known—a well-kept, clean little place. Our camp, owing to the incessant rains, soon became a veritable quagmire, but nevertheless the brigade suffered less from sickness than any other part of the force which was lying there.

In about a week the railway was opened, and after that all the reservists of Section D (many of whom had joined on hearing the news of Magersfontein), the Militia Reserve of our 3rd Battalion, the 1st Volunteer Company under Captain R. Millar, old officers who had volunteered for the " Reserve of Officers," all came pouring in and swelled the regiment to 31 officers and nearly 900 rank and file.

On the 31st of March the battalion formed part of the force which, under General Colvile, marched to Sanna's Post, to try to recover the seven guns of U and Q Batteries, R.H.A.; but we reached Waterval Drift (twenty-four miles) too late. We were never under heavy fire that day, and had no casualties, the only ones in the brigade being two men of the Argylls, wounded. We arrived back in Bloemfontein on the 3rd of April.

On the 24th of April General Colvile's command, consisting of the Highland Brigade, two naval 4.7-inch guns, one battery R.F.A., and fifty mounted men, moved east very lightly equipped, leaving tents and all surplus baggage at Bloemfontein.

We started marching north on the 2nd of May with the town of Winburg as our objective. The battalion as advanced-guard carried on the 4th of May a big hill named Baviansberg, with a loss of 3 men wounded—a fight of which Lord Roberts wrote in his daily report—" The Black Watch distinguished themselves and were very well led." We arrived on the 6th at Winburg, which had sur-rendered to General Ian Hamilton the previous day. E Company left us here, and joined Lord Roberts' main army as escort to the naval guns of the 11th Division. This company took part in the actions of Johannesburg, Diamond Hill, and Belfast, and rejoined the battalion in November 1900.

We left Winburg at 9 P.M. on the 17th and reached Ventersburg (thirty-four miles) at 3 P.M. next day. On the 23rd we again moved on, having been reinforced by 5 officers and 100 men. We made an eighteen-mile march on the Queen's birthday. On the 25th and 26th we were opposed when going into Lindley by a force of some 1000 Boers under Prinsloo. The battalion lost 1 killed and 9 wounded; but owing to the way in which the brigade was handled it had altogether only a few casualties and hardly met with a check, although our small mounted force, which had suffered greatly, had shrunk to thirty-five men. That evening we were sniped in our camping-ground outside the town.

At Lindley we had expected a reinforcement of Imperial Yeomanry under Colonel Spragge, but as General Colvile had to be in Heilbron by the 30th of May we pushed on next day without them. The regiment was the rearguard, and was sniped at all day during the seventeen-mile march by some fifty Boers, who hung about two thousand yards behind us. On the 28th the Seaforth and Argylls bore the brunt of the fighting on the right flank and in rear. The Boers, whose total force must have numbered fully 2800 men, under the two De Wets and Prinsloo, opened fire with two guns from a kopje three thousand yards to our left front, but our naval guns quickly persuaded them to move. We know that the enemy suffered severely, as we afterwards found many of their wounded in Heilbron.

The following day they avoided coming within any reasonable range, and tried to check our advance by fire from three guns placed on a hill named Spitz Kop, outside Heilbron (these guns were always on this hill to greet us on every subsequent occasion on which we marched by this road). After a long march we arrived in Heilbron on the night of the 29th—a hundred and twenty-six miles in eight days. All our advanced, rear, and flank guards had been performed by infantry, so many men must have covered an average of well over twenty miles a day. There was no falling out or straggling, and in brigade orders General MacDonald said of his force—"Their coolness and discipline through the long and trying march was most marked, and only for their cheerful determination to overcome all obstacles and gain their destination on the date appointed by Lord Roberts, I feel certain the distance could not have been completed in face of the opposition met with."

We had for some time been on half-rations of everything but meat, and on the 4th of June a convoy of 160 details, bringing provisions from the railway, eighteen miles distant, failed to reach us. However there was plenty of flour in the town, and we were never really short of provisions, and could have reached the railway at any time if it had been necessary. The Boers, said to number 4000, sniped the picquets daily, but did no damage.

On the 2nd of June our force was increased by a most useful body of men—100 Lovat's Scouts—another 100 of whom joined the brigade later.

On the 7th of June Lord Methuen came in from Lindley with three infantry regiments, fourteen guns, and 1500 yeomanry. The battalion and 50 Lovat's Scouts, all under Colonel Carthew-Yorstoun, went out with them on the 9th to bring back a convoy.

On the 10th we were going south, and were west of the railway line, when we heard several explosions on it, and at about 1 P.M. the regiment found itself in face of three small kopjes, which were strongly held. The enemy, however, did not wait, and we could see 600 to 1000 Boers riding south over the veld. We had one man wounded (at two thousand yards), took nine prisoners, and found three dead Boers.

We came straight on the ransacked camp of the unfortunate Derbyshire Militia—a pitiful sight, with the graves close by.

On the 19th of June we met with some opposition when returning to Heilbron.

We were out from the 27th to the 29th on the Kroonstad road, but failed to get in touch with the enemy—some 1000 Boers with three guns—who trekked south.

The branch railway to Heilbron had now been open a few days, and on the 1st of July three battalions of the Highland Brigade, together with a large mounted force, moved off with fourteen days' supplies to join General Hunter at Frankfort, thirty miles east of Heilbron. The Argylls remained as a temporary garrison to Heilbron. We averaged fourteen miles a day, and early on the 9th of July reached Bethlehem, which General Clements had occupied on the 7th.

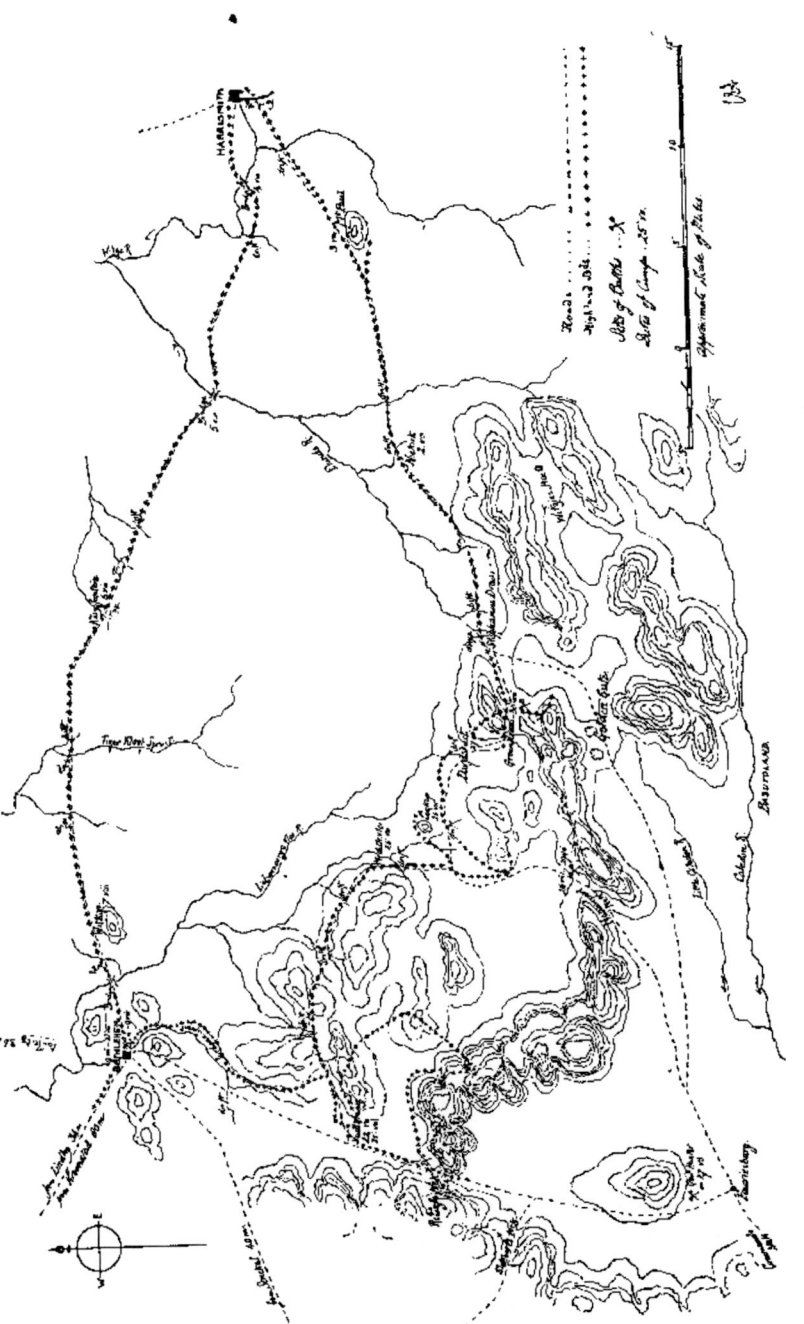

SKETCH SHOWING HIGHLAND BRIGADE MARCHES FROM 21ST JULY TO 9TH AUGUST 1900

The town lies 5300 feet above the sea, and is some seventy-five miles south of Frankfort. Owing to the altitude the nights were bitterly cold.

On the 22nd of July the brigade moved out of Bethlehem to Vaal Krantz Farm, five miles north of Retief's Nek. The sketch below represents the general appearance of the hills from a kopje just south of the farm.

The situation roughly was as follows :—Inside a semicircle of high precipitous hills, resembling the giant parapet of a redoubt, lies the little town of Fouriesburg. This natural redoubt is fifteen miles from north to south, forty miles from east to west, and its gorge is closed by the Caledon River—the Basutoland march. Inside the mountain parapet is a rich and more level country. The whole is known as the Brandwater Basin, and the hills are the Wittebergen. There are only five entrances into the basin—Commando Nek in the south-west

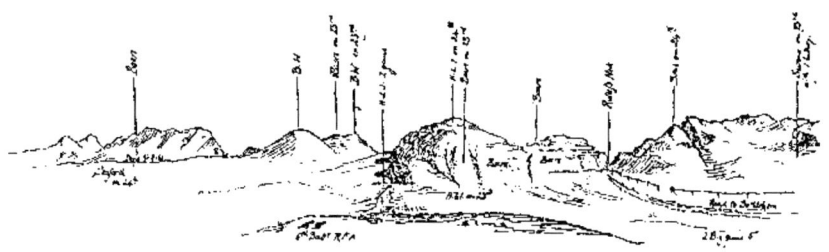

HAND SKETCH SHOWING DISPOSITION OF TROOPS AT RETIEF'S NEK,
23RD AND 24TH JULY 1900

corner, Slabbert Nek on the western side, Retief's Nek in the north-west corner, Naauwpoort Nek on the north, and the Golden Gate on the east.

Inside the basin were, when we arrived at Bethlehem, 8000 Free Staters under Steyn, Christian De Wet, and Prinsloo. Steyn and De Wet, with 2000 men, seeing the net being drawn round them, on the night of the 15th of July managed to pass out of Slabbert Nek within a mile of a British column, without being detected. On the 22nd, when supplies reached us, a general advance was made on all the western entrances.

The night of the 22nd was bitterly cold, and the snow was lying three inches deep on the ground. General Hunter was with the brigade, and had besides Lovat's Scouts, Rimington's Guides, one battery artillery, and two 5-inch guns, while the Sussex Regiment and an additional battery R.F.A. co-operated with the brigade on the extreme right. Lovat's Scouts having thoroughly reconnoitred the two north-eastern neks, the Black Watch was sent at 4.30 A.M. on the 23rd to the round hill (marked B.W. on the sketch), with a view to gaining the saddle-backed hill behind. The two 5-inch guns, from a small kopje on the plain below, rained their shells into the nek, and the noise of Paget's guns away to the west firing into Slabbert Nek sounded as if the British were clamouring at the fortress gates for admittance. The H.L.I. in the centre were firing

II.   B at the big hill to the left of Retief's Nek. The Sussex, who had had a very long march, appeared at mid-day, and in most gallantly advancing towards the right of the nek, which was impregnable, lost more than fifty men. However, the Black Watch on the left managed to press forward, and at 6 P.M. rushed fourteen hundred yards of bare valley under cover of the fire of two companies left on the round kopje, topped the saddle-back, and opened a heavy fire on the flying Boers at two hundred yards range. This saddle-backed kopje commanded the whole of the back of the big hill on the left of the nek, and our possession of it rendered the nek untenable by the enemy. Here we bivouacked. At day-break the Boers, who had not disclosed a gun on the 23rd, fired a few shells at us from two guns, but by 8 A.M. were on the move south. The Seaforth moved up on our left and fired at them as they fled down a deep donga running east-south-east.

On the 24th Slabbert Nek was also evacuated by the enemy.

On the 23rd at Retief's Nek we suffered a very heavy loss in the death of Major Ernest Willshire, who was mortally wounded. Our other casualties were 1 man killed, 1 officer and 15 men wounded. The Boers lost a good many killed. On the night of the 24th we bivouacked inside Retief's Nek.

The next day General Hunter went on to Fouriesburg, while the brigade, under General MacDonald, joined General Bruce Hamilton's force, and marched outside the mountain wall to Naauwpoort Nek, the battalion on the 26th carrying a position held by the Harrismith Commando at Davels Rust with a loss of six wounded. Meantime the Camerons and Lovat's Scouts, assisted by the 5-inch guns, captured Naauwpoort Nek.

On the 29th General Hunter heliographed the welcome news of Prinsloo's surrender with 5000 Boers inside the basin—the biggest capture made during the war.

Our portion of the force went on to Harrismith, which we entered on the 4th of August. The hoisting of the Union Jack was greeted enthusiastically by the inhabitants, of whom a large number were Scots.

From Harrismith we returned *viâ* Bethlehem and Lindley to Heilbron, which we reached after an engagement in which the H.L.I. on our right flank had fifty casualties, mostly caused by shell-fire from Spitz Kop.

From the 14th to the 26th of August we rested after our daily marching, and managed to get in some sadly-needed stores of clothing and shoes.   From Heilbron we went to Kroonstad and then back to Winburg, marching daily some fifteen miles and scouring the country as we went; but it was not until the 13th of September that we ran into a convoy of 700 Boers under Haasbroek at Karree-fontein, twenty-five miles south of Winburg. The Boers broke at once, pursued by Lovat's Scouts. Eight prisoners and thirty waggons of stores were captured, also 80,000 rounds of rifle and 75 rounds of big-gun ammunition, and dynamite besides. We continued our marching through this country, and on the 17th of September formed part of a combined movement on the Doornberg, a long hill north of Winburg, where General Rundle captured four guns and thirty waggons.

After trekking north we were ordered into Kroonstad, and sent down by rail to Bloemfontein, whence we marched out to Ladybrand.

Up to the 13th of October 1900 the battalion had covered by road (not including any deviations for fighting and flanking movements) well over twelve hundred miles.

1900–01. From the 13th of October 1900 to the 25th of September 1901 we formed the garrison of the Ladybrand district. Our picquets, which enclosed over a hundred square miles of country, formed part of a chain of posts running from Bloemfontein to the Basutoland border. The Boers never tried to break through our part of the line, though occasionally our outer posts were fired at and our various mounted infantry posts were constantly in touch with the enemy. Until the 22nd of August 1901 we were invariably successful, but on that date a force of fifty mounted infantry which had been detached to surprise a farm named Evening Star, found itself surrounded at dawn on an isolated kopje. In order to guard the horses the party was split up round the base of the hill, and after fourteen hours' fighting, the ammunition being exhausted, each small section of the force was successively overpowered, 1 man being killed and 1 officer and 4 men wounded. This was the only capture of any of our men during the war, with the exception of the forty-two men on the hill at Magersfontein, and two men, one of whom lost his way, and the other of whom was engaged on telegraph work at Heilbron.

In September 1901 the battalion was railed to Natal to help to meet Louis Botha's threatened attack, and a detachment was sent on to Zululand.

1901–02. From November 1901 to February 1902 four companies were with Colonel Rimington's column and took part in the great " drives " in the Orange River Colony. One N.C.O. was killed on the 23rd of February. Two other companies which also took part in these " drives " were with Colonel Byng, and three were with General Spens. The 1st Battalion relieved these companies in March 1902.

A mounted infantry company from the 2nd Battalion served with Colonel Western's column in the " drives " in the Western Transvaal which were carried out by General Walter Kitchener in March, and by Sir Ian Hamilton in May 1902. This company also took part in the successful surprise of Schweizer Reneke by Colonel Rochfort in April. In March it covered a hundred and fifty miles in less than three days without losing a man or horse.

A smaller detachment of fifty was in all the " drives " in the Northern Transvaal, and one officer, twenty-five N.C.O.s and men, formed the garrison of No. 9 Armoured Train from July 1901 onwards.

From March 1902 until the end of the war (31st May 1902) the battalion formed part of the garrison of Harrismith, which (as related elsewhere) also included our 1st Battalion. The two battalions therefore, for the first time on record, had the pleasure of serving together.

After having been two years and seven months on active service the 2nd Battalion sailed for India in October 1902.

Throughout the campaign 77 officers, 2437 N.C.O.s and men passed through the ranks of the battalion; 11 officers (including Lieutenant Grieve, attached), 119 N.C.O.s and men were killed or died of wounds while serving with it; 71 men died of disease; 17 officers and some 340 N.C.O.s and men were wounded.

In addition, both of our medical officers were wounded—Lieutenant H. E. M. Douglas (who subsequently received the V.C. and D.S.O.) at Magersfontein, and Captain G. H. Goddard at Paardeberg.

Scattered on the lonely veld are the graves of those who fell in South Africa. Over many the wail of " Lochaber no more " never sounded, but the gaps in the ranks are filled, and still the red hackle and dark tartan are guarding the marches of the Empire.

APPENDICES

APPENDIX I

Table showing Services, Promotions, Casualties, &c., of Officers of The Black Watch in South Africa, 1899–1902.

N.B.— In the following table the words "1st Batt." and "2nd Batt.," when the name of the regiment is not given, refer to The Black Watch. For list of abbreviations see p. 64.

A.—OFFICERS OF THE 1st AND 2nd BATTALIONS.

NAME.	RANK ON PROCEEDING TO S. AFRICA.	UNITS AND PERIODS OF SERVICE IN S. AFRICA.	PROMOTIONS DURING WAR.	HONOURS.	CASUALTIES. WOUNDS.	CASUALTIES. DEATHS.
Allan, W. D.	Lce.-Cpl. (in Vols.)	1st Vol. Service Coy. Seaforth Highlanders (as Lce.-Cpl.), 1900-1. 1st Batt. Black Watch (as 2nd Lieut. in Army), 1902.	...	...	...	...
Berkeley, T. M. Mowbray	Major	2nd Batt., 1899-1902	Lieut. (in Impl. Yeo.). 2nd Lieut. (in Army), 8. 2. 02.	Brev. Lt.-Col., 29. 11. 00. Despatches, 10. 9. 01.	Magersfontein, 11. 12. 99. Paardeberg, 18. 2. 00.	...
Berthon, H. C. W.	Lieut.	2nd Batt., 1899	...	...	Magersfontein, 11. 12. 99.	Dd. of wounds, Wynberg, 15. 12. 99.
Blair, J. M.	2nd Lieut.	2nd Batt., 1901 and (Mtd. Infy. Coy.), 1901-2.	...	...	...	...
Bruce, Honble. J. F. T. Cumming-	Captain	2nd Batt., 1899	...	...	...	Kd. Magersfontein 11. 12. 99.
Bulloch, R. A.	2nd Lieut.	2nd Batt., 1899-1902	Lieut., 13. 11. 00.	...	Magersfontein, 11. 12. 99.	...
Burton, St. G. E. W.	Major	1st Batt. 1901-2.	...	Brev. Major, 29. 11. 00. Despatches, 10. 9. 01.	...	...
Cameron, A. M.	Captain	2nd Batt., 1899-1902. (Adjt., 1900-2)	...	...	Magersfontein, 11. 12. 99.	...
Campbell, D.	Lieut. (in Mil.)	Attd. 2nd Batt. (from Mil.), 1900-1. 1st Batt. (as 2nd Lieut. in Army), 1901-2.	2nd Lieut. (in Army), 27. 10. 00. Lieut., 24. 5. 02.	...	...	...
Campbell, K. J.	2nd Lieut.	1st Batt., 1901 2.	...	...	...	...
Campbell, W. MacL.	Captain	Attd. 2nd Scottish Horse, 1902.	...	...	...	...

Name	Rank	Service		Despatches		
Collins, J. G.	Captain	1st Batt., 1901-2. 2nd Batt., 1902.				
Comyn, D. C. E. ff.	2nd Lieut.	2nd Batt., 1900-1. Mtd. Infy., 1902.	Lieut., 20.5.01.			Kd. Magersfontein, 11.12.99.
Coode, J. H. C.	Lieut.-Col.	Lieut.-Col. Comdg. 2nd Batt., 1899.		Despatches, 10.9.01.		
Cunyngham, Sir W. Stewart-Dick, Bt.	Lieut.	Special Service, 1900. Scottish Horse, as Adjt. 1st Regt. 1900-1; as Regtl.-Adjt., 1901; as Second-in-Comd. 1st Regt., 1901-2.	Capt., 13.11.00. Local Major, 1901-2.			
Cuthbertson, N. W.	Major	2nd Batt., 1899-1900 (comdg., Feb. to March 1900). Staff, 1900-1.		Despatches, 8.2.01.	Magersfontein, 11.12.99.	
Dalglish, C. A., de G.	2nd Lieut.	1st Batt., 1901-2.				
Davidson, W. B. F.	Hon. Lieut. and Qrmr.	1st Batt., 1901-2.				
Dawes, E. S.	Captain	2nd Batt., 1902.	Major, 12.12.99.		Magersfontein, 11.12.99.	
Deane, J.	Captain	Adjt. 4th Batt. Argyll and Suth. Highlanders, 1899-1900. Staff of Governor of Cape Colony, 1901-2.				
Drummond, Honble. M. C. A.	2nd Lieut.	2nd Batt., 1899 and 1901. No. 9 Armrd. Train, 1901-2.	Lieut., 5.9.00.	Despatches, 29.7.02.	Magersfontein, 11.12.99.	
Duff, A. Grant-	Captain	1st Batt., 1902.				
Duff, A. Gordon	Major	2nd Batt., 1899-1900. 1st Batt., 1901-2. Press Censor, 1902.	Lieut.-Col., 24.5.02.		Magersfontein, 11.12.99.	
Duff, P. A.	2nd Lieut.	2nd Batt., 1901. 2nd Mtd. Infy., 1901-2. 2nd Batt. Black Watch, 1902.				
Eden, S. H.	Lieut.	1st Batt., 1901-2.				Kd. Magersfontein, 11.12.99.
Edmonds, N. G.	Lieut.	2nd Batt., 1899.				Kd. Magersfontein, 11.12.99.
Elton, E. G.	Captain	2nd Batt., 1899.				
Evans, L. P.	2nd Lieut.	2nd Batt., 1900-2.	Lieut., 1.5.01.			Dd. of wounds, 8.2.00.
Eykyn, C.	Captain	2nd Batt., 1899-1900.			Koedoesberg, 7.2.00.	
Farquharson, D. L. Wilson-	Captain	2nd Batt., 1900-2.	Major, 24.5.02.			
Forrester, R. E.	Private (in Impl. Yeo.)	6th Batt. Impl. Yeo. (as Pte. and Lce.-Cpl.), 1900-1. 2nd Batt. Black Watch (as 2nd Lieut.), 1901. Mtd. Infy., 1901-2.	Lce.-Cpl., 1900. 2nd Lieut., 26.6.01. Lieut., 16.2.01.	Despatches, 10.9.01. 29.7.02. D.S.O. D.C.M.		
Gordon, C. W. E.	2nd Lieut.	2nd Batt., 1899-1900, 1900-1, and (Mtd. Infy. Coy.), 1902.		Despatches, 10.9.01.		
Gordon, W. G. Wolrige-	Major	1st Batt., 1901-2.				
Grant, A. S.	2nd Lieut.	2nd Batt., 1899-1900. No. 3 Armrd. Train, 1900-2.	Lieut., 26.7.00. Local Capt. while comdg. Armrd Train.	Despatches, 18.7.02. D.S.O.		

APPENDIX I.—*continued.*

NAME.	RANK ON PROCEEDING TO S. AFRICA.	UNITS AND PERIODS OF SERVICE IN S. AFRICA.	PROMOTIONS DURING WAR.	HONOURS.	CASUALTIES. WOUNDS.	CASUALTIES. DEATHS.
Grant, C. J. P. MacA.	Lieut. (in Mil.)	4th Batt. Argyll and Suth. Highlanders (as Lieut. in Mil.), 1899–1900.	2nd Lieut. (in Army), 4. 4. 00. Lieut., 12. 11. 01.	...	...	...
Green, W.	Lieut.	1st Batt., 1901–2.	Colonel, 24. 5. 02.	Despatches, 29. 7. 02. C.B.	...	...
Grogan, E. G.	Lieut.-Col.	Lieut.-Col. Comdg. 1st Batt., 1901–2 .				
Hadow, R. W.	2nd Lieut.	1st Batt., 1901–2.	Capt., 12. 12. 99.	D.S.O.	Paardeberg, 18. 2. 00.	...
Hamilton, J. G. H.	Lieut.	2nd Batt., 1899–1902 (Act. Adjt. Dec. 1899–Feb. 1900; Mtd. Infy. Coy., 1901–2).		Despatches, 8. 2. 01. and 10. 9. 01.		
Hamilton, N. A. B. Baillie-	2nd Lieut.	2nd Batt., 1900. 22nd Mtd. Infy., 1901–2	Lieut., 11. 5. 01.	...	...	...
Harvey, J.	Lieut.	2nd Batt., 1899–1900 (Act. Adjt. Feb. to March 1900).	Capt., 16. 7. 00.	...	Magersfontein. 11. 12. 99.	...
Harvey, W. J. St. J.	Lieut.	2nd Batt., 1899–1900. Adjt. 1st Batt., 1901–2.	Capt., 13. 11. 00.	Despatches, 29. 7. 02.	Magersfontein. 11. 12. 99.	...
Henderson, C. R. B.	2nd Lieut.	2nd Batt., 1901–2.	...	...	...	...
Henderson, N. G. B.	2nd Lieut.	2nd Batt., 1902.				...
Innes, S. A.	2nd Lieut.	2nd Batt., 1899 and 1900	Lieut., 9. 2. 00.	...	...	...
Kedie, W. T.	2nd Lieut.	1st Batt., 1901–2.	2nd Lieut. (in Army) 19. 10. 01	...	...	...
Krook, A. D. C.	Lieut. (in Mil.)	6th Batt. Lancashire Fusiliers (as Lieut. in Mil.), 1900–1. 1st Batt. Black Watch (as 2nd Lieut. in Army), 1901–2	Lieut., 11. 5. 01.			
Lamb, C. C.	2nd Lieut.	2nd Batt., 1900–2 .		...	...	...
Laverton, H. C.	Lieut.	2nd Batt., 1900–1 and 1902.	...	Despatches, 10. 9. 01. Brev. Lt.-Col. 22. 8. 02.	...	...
Livingston, P. J. C.	Major.	2nd Batt., 1900. Staff, 1900–2				...
Lloyd, T. O.	Captain	1st Batt., 1901–2.	...	...	...	Kd. Magersfontein. 11. 12. 99.
MacFarlan, W.	Captain	Adjt. 2nd Batt., 1899				
McLean, C.	Lieut.	2nd Batt., 1900. 1st Batt. 1901–2 .	Capt., 30. 11. 00.	...	...	...

24

Name	Rank	Service	Rank attained	Despatches / Honours	Medal	Killed
MacRae, C. W.	Captain	2nd Batt., 1900-2.	...	...	...	...
Marindin, A. H.	Lieut.	Special Service, 1899-1900. 1st Batt., 1902				
Maxwell, J. G.	Colonel, D.S.O.	Infy. Bgde., 1900; Mily. Gov., Pretoria, 1900-2; Comdg. Western District, Transvaal, 1902.	Capt., 21.10.00. Local Major-Gen., 10.4.00	Despatches, 10.9.01. Despatches, 16.4.01. and 29.7.02. K.C.B. C.M.G. D.S.O. Despatches, 10.9.01.	...	...
Maxwell, Honble. H. E.	Major	2nd Batt., 1899-1902 (comdg. Dec. 1899-Jan. 1900).	...	...	Paardeberg, 18.2.00.	...
Morris, J. B. Pollok-	Lieut.	2nd Batt., 1900-1. Adjt. 6th Batt. Impl. Yeo., 1901-2.	Capt., 19.4.00.	...	...	...
Murray, F. D.	Lieut.	Staff, 1899-1900. Staff of Governor of Natal, 1900-1. Attd. 2nd Scottish Horse as Officer Comdg. (local Major) 1901.	Capt., 13.11.00. Local Major while comdg. 2nd Scottish Horse.	Despatches, 19.6.00. and 9.11.00. Brev. Major, 17.2.01.	...	Kd. Bakenlaagte, 30.10.01.
Murray, Lord G. Stewart	Lieut.	Attd. 2nd Batt. Gordon Highlanders, 1899-1900. Attd. 2nd Batt. Black Watch, 1900. Staff, 1900. Adjt. 1st Scottish Horse, 1901-2.	Capt., 11.5.01.	Despatches, 29.7.02.	...	...
Murray, H. F. F.	2nd Lieut.	S. Africa, 1901. 2nd Batt. 1902	Lieut., 12.11.01.	...	...	...
Murray, J. T. C.	Captain	2nd Batt. 1901-2.	...	...	...	...
Nunneley, W. P.	2nd Lieut.	2nd Batt., 1899-1900. Staff, 1900. 2nd Batt., 1900-1.	Lieut., 12.12.99.			
Parker, A. E.	2nd Lieut. (in Mil.)	Attd. 2nd Batt. (from Mil.), 1900-1; 2nd Batt. (as 2nd Lieut. in Army), 1901-2 (with Mtd. Infy. Coy., 1902).	2nd Lieut. (in Army), 5.1.01.	...	...	...
Ramsay, N. N.	Lieut.	2nd Batt., 1899	...	...	...	...
Rennie, J. G.	Captain	Staff, 1899. 2nd Batt., 1899-1902	...	D.S.O. Despatches, 16.4.01.	...	Kd. Magersfontein, 11.12.99.
Richmond, G. M.	2nd Lieut.	1st Batt., 1902.	...	...	...	...
Robertson, F. M. B.	Lieut.	S. African Constabulary, 1901-2.	...			
Robrtson, R. M.	2nd Lieut.	2nd Batt., 1901-2.	...			
Rose, H.	Major	1st Batt., 1901-2.	...			
Ruthven, Honble. C. M.	2nd Lieut.	2nd Batt., 1899-1900. 12th Mtd. Infy., 1900-2.	Lieut., 21.10.00.	Despatches, 16.3.00. 10.9.01. 29.7.02. D.S.O.	...	...
Steuart, B. C. A.	Trooper (in Irreg. Corps)	Lumsden's Horse (as Trooper), 1900. 1st Batt. Black Watch (as 2nd Lieut.), 1901-2.	2nd Lieut., 17.10.00. Lieut., 17.4.02.	...	...	...

APPENDIX I.—continued.

Name.	Rank on proceeding to S. Africa.	Units and Periods of Service in S. Africa.	Promotions during War.	Honours.	Casualties. Wounds.	Casualties. Deaths.
Steward, O. H. D'A.	Lieut.	1st Batt., 1901-2.	...	...	...	...
Stewart, C. E.	Captain	2nd Batt., 1899-1900. Staff, 1900-2	...	Despatches, 10. 9. 01.	...	...
Stewart, W.	Lieut.	1st Batt., 1901-2.	...	...	...	...
Strahan, C. E.	2nd Lieut.	1st Batt., 1902.	...	...	...	...
Studley, H.	Hon. Lieut. and Qrmr.	2nd Batt., 1899-1902	...	Despatches, 10. 9. 01. 29. 7. 02.	...	...
Suttie, G. D. Grant-	Lieut.	1st Batt., 1901-2.	...	...	Magersfontein, 11. 12. 99.	Kd. Koedoesberg, 7. 2. 00.
Tait, F. G.	Lieut.	2nd Batt., 1899-1900	...	...	Kimberley, 25. 11. 99.	Kd. Kimberley, 28. 11. 99.
Turner, H. Scott-	Capt. and Brev. Major	Staff (comdg. mtd. troops, Kimberley), 1899.	Local Lieut.-Col. Capt., 17. 4. 02.	Despatches, 4. 5. 00.	...	...
Urquhart, E. F. M.	Lieut.	1st Batt., 1901-2.	Capt., 25. 10. 01.	...	...	...
Walker, J. D. G.	Lieut.	Attd. 2nd Batt. Gordon Highlanders, 1899. Staff, 1899-1900. 1st Batt. 1901-2.	...	Despatches, 8. 2. 01. D.S.O.	...	...
Wauchope, Andrew G.	Major-Gen., C.B., C.M.G.	Staff (comdg. Highland Bgde.), 1899	...	...	...	Kd. Magersfontein, 11. 12. 99.
Wauchope, Arthur G.	Lieut.	2nd Batt., 1899. Staff of Governor of Cape Colony, 1901-2.	Capt., 30. 10. 01.	Despatches, 16. 4. 01. D.S.O.	Magersfontein, 11. 12. 99.	...
Wavell, A. G.	Local Major-Gen.	Staff (comdg. 15th Infy. Bgde.), 1900.	...	Despatches, 8. 2. 01. C.B.	...	...
Wavell, A. P.	2nd Lieut.	2nd Batt., 1901-2.	...	Despatches, 8. 2. 01.	...	...
West, C. C.	2nd Lieut.	2nd Batt., 1899-1902 (Mtd. Infy. Coy., 1901-2).	Lieut., 30. 11. 00.	...	...	...
Willshire, E. M.	Major	2nd Batt., 1900 (comdg., March to April, 1900).	...	C.B. Despatches, 8. 2. 01.	Retief's Nek, 23. 7. 00. Paardeberg, 18. 2. 00.	Dd. of wounds, 25. 7. 00.
Yorstoun, A. M. Carthew-	Lieut.-Col.	Lt.-Col. Comdg. 2nd Batt., 1900-2.	...	Despatches, 8. 2. 01.	...	...

B.—OFFICERS ATTACHED TO THE 2ND BATTALION FROM THE RESERVE OF OFFICERS.

			Despatches, 17. 6. 02. D.S.O. Prom. Major, Res. of Officers.	
Bald, A. C.	Captain	2nd Batt., 1900-1. Staff, 1901-2	...	...
Davie, F. A. Ferguson-	Lieut.	2nd Batt., 1900-2.	...	...
Moubray, W. H. H. C.	Captain	2nd Batt., 1900-2	Prom. Major, Res. of Officers.	...
Scott, W. A.	Major and Hon. Lt.-Col.(in Mil.)	2nd Batt., 1900. Press Censor, 1900-1	Prom. Major, Res. of Officers.	...

C.—OFFICERS OF THE 3RD (MILITIA) BATTALION.

Moubray, P. L.	2nd Lieut. (in Mil.)	Attd. and Batt., 1900-1. Remount Dept., 1901-2.	...	...
Richardson, Sir E. A. Stewart-, Bt.	Capt. (in Mil.)	2nd Queens'and Mtd. Infy., 1900. Attd. 2nd Batt. Black Watch, 1900-1.	...	...
Robertson, S.	Capt. (in Mil.)	Remount Dept., and attd. 14th Hussars, 1900.	...	Dd. Kroonstad, 6. 6. 00.

D.—OFFICERS OF THE VOLUNTEER BATTALIONS.

Byers, J.	Capt. (in Vols.)	(2nd Vol. Batt.) Attd. 2nd Batt., 1900-2.	...	...
Christie, R. M.	Capt. (in Vols.)	4th Vol. Batt.) Attd. and Batt., 1901-2.	...	...
Corrie, A. B.	Lieut. (in Vols.)	(1st Vol. Batt.) Attd. 2nd Batt., 1901-2.	...	...
Ferguson, T.	Lieut. (in Vols.)	(5th Vol. Batt.) Attd. 2nd Batt., 1902.	...	...
Millar, R. H.	Capt. (in Vols.)	(2nd Vol. Butt.) Attd. 2nd Batt., 1900-1	...	...
Smith, H. K.	Lieut.(in Vols.)	(3rd Vol. Batt.) Attd. 2nd Batt., 1900-1	Hon. Capt. (in Army), 17. 6. 01. Hon. Lieut. (in Army), 17. 6. 01.	Retief's Nek, 23. 7. 00.
Stirling, R.	Surg.-Maj. (in Vols.), M.D., F.R.C.S.	(4th Vol. Batt.) Attd. Scottish National Red Cross Hospital, 1900. Attd. 18th Bgde., 1900.	Despatches, 29. 11. 00.	...
Tosh, E.	Lieut.(in Vols.)	(1st Vol. Batt.) Attd. 2nd Batt. and Staff, 1900-1.	Hon. Lieut. (in Army), 17. 6. 01.	Capt. (in Vols.), 21. 5. 02.
Valentine, A.	Lieut. (in Vols.)	(1st Vol. Batt.) Attd. 2nd Batt., 1900-1.	...	...
Walker, C. E. C.	Lieut.(in Vols.)	(1st Vol. Batt.) Attd. 2nd Batt., 1902.	...	...
White, F. H. Buchanan-	Lieut.(in Vols.)	(5th Vol. Batt.) Attd. 2nd Batt., 1901-2.	...	...

NAME.	RANK ON PROCEEDING TO S. AFRICA.	UNITS AND PERIODS OF SERVICE IN S. AFRICA.	PROMOTIONS DURING WAR.	HONOURS.	CASUALTIES. WOUNDS.	CASUALTIES. DEATHS.
E.—OFFICERS ATTACHED TO THE 2ND BATTALION FROM OTHER UNITS.						
Douglas, H. E. M.	Lieut.	(Royal Army Med. Corps) Attd. 2nd Batt. Black Watch, 1899.	...	Despatches, 16. 3. 00. V.C., D.S.O.	Magersfontein, 11. 12. 99.	...
Fraser, L.	Scripture Reader.	2nd Batt., 1900.	...			...
Goddard, G. H.	Lieut., M.R.C.S., L.R.C.P.	(Royal Army Med. Corps) Attd. 2nd Batt. Black Watch, 1900-1.	Capt., 28. 1. 02.	...	Paardeberg, 18. 2. 00.	...
Grieve, J. G.	Lieut.	(New South Wales Perm. Forces) Attd. 2nd Batt. Black Watch, 1900.	...	...	...	Kd. Paardeberg, 18. 2. 00.
F.—CIVILIAN ATTACHED AS OFFICER TO THE 2ND BATTALION.						
Mackay, J. A.	Hon. Lieut.	Attd. 2nd Batt., 1900-1 and 1902	...	...	Evening Star, 22. 8. 01.	...

APPENDIX II

N.C.O.s and Men of the 2nd Battalion The Black Watch who received rewards for services in South Africa.

Sergeant-Major J. Anderson
Colour-Sergeant A. Millar
Pioneer-Sergeant T. Howden
Sergeants J. Baxter, H. Harrison, and A. Wilson
Lance-Sergeant G. Gaynor } Distinguished Conduct Medal.
Lance-Corporal W. Forrett
Piper D. Cameron
Pioneer J. Hastie
Privates R. McGregor, R. Ormonde, and J. Smith

APPENDIX III

N.C.O.s and Men of the 2nd Battalion The Black Watch who were mentioned in despatches for services in South Africa.

Sergeants-Major J. Anderson (twice), W. Fowler, and E. Parker.
Colour-Sergeant A. Millar (twice).
Pioneer-Sergeant T. Howden (twice).
Signalling-Sergeant G. L. Weir.
Sergeants J. Baxter, D. Grant, H. Harrison, C. Leicester, J. Niven, and
    A. Wilson (twice).
Lance-Sergeant G. Gaynor (twice).
Corporals A. Hamilton and D. Miller.
Lance-Corporals W. Forrett (three times), J. McIntosh, and J. Noble.
Pipers G. Burns and D. Cameron (twice).
Pioneer J. Hastie (twice).
Privates G. Foote, R. McGregor (twice), A. Murdoch, R. Ormonde, and
    J. Smith.

THE SCOTTISH HORSE

THE RAISING AND ORGANISATION OF THE REGIMENT

BY THE EDITOR

WHEN in November 1900 Lord Kitchener took over the command of the forces in South Africa, preparations were immediately begun for a vigorous campaign which was to be mainly conducted by mounted troops. For this more mounted men were urgently required, and the formation of various new regiments of mounted infantry was accordingly sanctioned without delay. Among other offers of help came a suggestion from the Caledonian Society of Johannesburg that a corps should be raised under the name of "The Scottish Horse," to be recruited from Scotsmen in South Africa. As the Society could guarantee a number of men, and as the name of the corps seemed one calculated to attract the numerous South Africans of Scots descent, the Commander-in-Chief readily agreed to the proposal. No well-known Scotsman, however, was immediately forthcoming as commanding officer, and recruiting for the new corps hung fire for a week or two, until Lord Kitchener offered the command to Captain the Marquess of Tullibardine, D.S.O. (Royal Horse Guards), who was then at Newcastle in Natal—wiring to him to "send out the fiery cross." The raising of the new corps then commenced in earnest. Lord Tullibardine appointed Captain A. Blair, D.S.O. (King's Own Scottish Borderers) and Captain Sir William Dick-Cunyngham (the Black Watch), second-in-command and adjutant respectively, and started at once for Johannesburg, sending Captain Blair to recruit in Cape Town, and Sir William Dick-Cunyngham to enlist the help of the Caledonian Societies of Durban and Maritzburg, and of the leading Scotsmen in Natal. The Scottish Horse was gazetted on December the 15th, 1900,[1] and within a week Lord Tullibardine had established a recruiting office and regimental depôt at Johannesburg, and had raised there his first troop. He then returned to Maritzburg, where for the next five weeks he was busy recruiting, organising, equipping, and training his men. Recruiting was not easy, as so many new corps were being raised, but Lord Tullibardine and his officers worked hard ; Caledonian Societies and Scotsmen generally gave what help they could ; and, though the Commanding Officer was very particular as to the class of men he enlisted, by the beginning of February 1901 the Scottish Horse

---

[1] Lord Tullibardine was given local rank of major and shortly afterwards local rank of lieutenant-colonel while commanding the Scottish Horse. Captain Blair was given local rank of major.

30

A TROOPER OF THE SCOTTISH HORSE

(From a Water-colour Drawing by Jane B. Constable)

GUN-CARRIAGE OF THE 84TH BATTERY R.F.A., PRESENTED BY THE WAR OFFICE IN
RECOGNITION OF THE GALLANTRY OF THE SCOTTISH HORSE AT
BAKENLAAGTE, 30TH OCTOBER 1901

was a regiment four squadrons strong,[1] with full complement of officers, and included besides, fifty special scouts and fifty picked cyclists.

The men were recruited mainly from Natal, though about a squadron came from the Cape ; more than half were Scots or of Scots descent. The enlistment was for six months only, and the pay (as in all the South African Irregular Corps) was 5s. a day for a trooper, other ranks being paid in proportion. Lord Tullibardine was fortunate in securing from the first the aid of several capable and experienced officers, who rendered valuable service. One of the first to join was Captain "Pete" Rattray, a Perthshire man, who was shortly followed by his three brothers.

Early in February 1901 the Scottish Horse left Maritzburg for Johannesburg, and from thence was sent to join a column commanded by Colonel Flint, then operating in the Western Transvaal. Under Colonel Flint, and later under Colonel Shekleton, the regiment was for some weeks busily engaged in helping to clear the Losberg and Gatsrand Mountains and the basin of the Vaal— a fertile region which up to that time had been De Wet's base of supplies. The column did its work so thoroughly that De Wet was never afterwards able to get supplies from that district. Towards the end of March Brigadier-General Cunningham assumed command of the column, and operations were then begun in the Magaliesberg Mountains and the surrounding country—ground which the men of the Scottish Horse were to know well before the end of the war.

In the meantime Lord Tullibardine, wishing to command a more representative Scots corps, had obtained Lord Kitchener's leave to apply for Scotsmen from Home and from Australia. He accordingly wired early in January 1901 to ask the Highland Society of London and the Caledonian Society of Melbourne to get him recruits. A ready response came from Australia that 250 Victorians were ready to join him. They sailed shortly afterwards, and landed in Cape Town on March the 8th—a fine body of men, well educated, of sturdy, independent character, and first-rate horsemen. Several officers were appointed from their number. As the regiment which had already been raised in South Africa was up to the requisite strength, the Australians became the nucleus of a second regiment of Scottish Horse, and the organisation of this new unit proceeded apace.

The Highland Society of London was as ready to help as the Victorian Government, but the military authorities at Home were at first afraid that if recruiting for the Scottish Horse were sanctioned it might interfere with the extensive recruiting which was then going on for the Yeomanry. With the help of the Duke of Atholl, however, Sir Fitzroy Maclean and a deputation from the Highland Society finally arranged the matter with the Secretary of State, and in February, March, and April, 4 officers and 397 men, of whom 309 were Scotsmen, were sent out in successive drafts to the Scottish Horse. They were classed as Imperial Yeomanry, but from the day of their arrival in

---

[1] Squadrons A, B, C, and D.

South Africa they were directly under Lord Tullibardine—not the Yeomanry authorities. They were enlisted for a year, or until the end of the war. Most of these men were sent to join the Australians, and completed the establishment of the 2nd Regiment.

It was decreed however, to the great disappointment of the Commanding Officer, that the two regiments were not to be kept together in the field, and it thus henceforward became impossible for him to be permanently with either. In view of this and of the constant recruiting necessitated by the short period for which the South Africans and Australians were enlisted, Lord Kitchener judged it best for Lord Tullibardine to establish his headquarters at Johannesburg—from thence to pay visits in turn to both regiments, to keep them constantly supplied with fresh drafts of men and horses, and, while controlling both, to leave the actual command of the regiments in the field to commanding officers who could be permanently there. The wisdom of this step was fully justified by events; the Scottish Horse increased steadily in numbers—not by recruiting in South Africa (where it soon became almost impossible, owing to competition, to get a good class of men), but by further drafts from Home and from Australia ; the regimental organisation was immensely improved, and the officers and men in the field were kept supplied with horses, transport, clothing, food-stuffs, &c., in a way which would have been impossible had there been no central regimental staff at Johannesburg.

In March 1901 Lord Tullibardine appointed Major F. D. Murray (the Black Watch) and Captain Michael Lindsay (Seaforth Highlanders)—both most gallant and capable officers—commanding officer and adjutant respectively of the 2nd Scottish Horse. About a fortnight was spent at Middleburg in organisation, equipment, and training, and by the middle of April the new regiment took the field—a fine corps, four squadrons strong,[1] composed equally of Australians and Scotsmen from Home.[2] These men had the good fortune to be placed in a column commanded by that most able officer, Colonel G. E. Benson, R.A. (who had as intelligence officer Lieutenant-Colonel Wools Sampson), and for many months they trekked continuously, and with great success—sometimes north of the railway line to Delagoa Bay, sometimes south of it—but always in the Eastern Transvaal. Colonel Benson wrote of the 2nd Scottish Horse that " both men and horses were excellent," that " their organisation was one to be copied," and that he " defied any troops to scout better." A system devised by Lord Tullibardine, under which native scouts, commanded by one of their own chiefs, were attached to each regiment, was also much praised by Colonel Benson. The chief undertook to have a certain number of men always with the regiment, and as he was made responsible for their behaviour and could enforce obedience, the work done by these scouts was admirable.

From April to October 1901 the 2nd Regiment took part in several gallant fights and many forced marches (frequently by night), resulting in large captures

[1] Squadrons E, F, G, and H.
[2] In May a fifth squadron (L), composed of men from Home, joined the 2nd Regiment.

of Boers with their horses, cattle, and ammunition. A fight at Elandskloof on the 3rd of July deserves special mention ; there Major Murray and some twenty-six officers and men withstood the attack of sixty Boers for three-quarters of an hour. The firing was at close quarters and very hot, but the Scottish Horse held its own until reinforcements came, when the Boers withdrew. Several officers and men were recommended for gallantry on this occasion, and Lieutenant W. J. English was awarded the V.C. Colonel Benson and his column were known and feared throughout the Eastern Transvaal ; the enemy fled ever at their approach; and it was only when Botha had concentrated a large body of men for his attempted invasion of Natal that the Boers dared to attack them, determined if possible by their superior numbers to wipe out this small force which had done them so much harm. The engagement which followed is described later ; it suffices here to say that on October the 30th, near Baken-laagte, the Boers overwhelmed the rearguard of Colonel Benson's column, killing Colonel Benson himself, Major Murray, Captain Lindsay, and three other officers and twenty-eight men of the Scottish Horse. The regiment also had four officers and thirty-six men wounded, most of whom were hit in several places. No words can describe the loss the Scottish Horse suffered that day ; but that heroic stand on the ridge by the guns was not in vain ; it saved the camp and the rest of the column from total destruction, and it remains for all time an instance of that self-sacrifice and devotion to duty in the face of overwhelming odds, for which the British soldier has ever been famous.

But to return to the 1st Scottish Horse. In April, after an engagement at Slipstein Kopjes in which the cyclist corps suffered some loss, the command of the column was given to Brigadier-General Dixon. Shortly afterwards Major C. E. Duff (8th Hussars) was appointed to command the regiment, with Major Blair as second-in-command ; and as Sir William Dick-Cunyngham at the same time took up the duties of regimental adjutant at the headquarters in Johannesburg, Captain H. A. F. Watson (Lancashire Fusiliers) became adjutant 1st Scottish Horse. Early in May Lord Tullibardine obtained leave to recruit men from the 1st Volunteer Service Companies of Scots regiments. These companies were about to return Home, but about a hundred men joined the Scottish Horse and formed a very fine squadron—J—which was sent to the 1st Regiment, and which subsequently gained for itself a reputation extending far beyond the column with which it trekked. Another squadron — K — consisting of a contingent from Home which arrived about this time, was also sent to the 1st Regiment. Some of the 1st Scottish Horse were present during the latter part of the engagement at Vlakfontein in May 1901 ; they arrived on the scene at a critical moment of the fight and rendered very good service. In June a good many of the South-African-enlisted men left the 1st Regiment, owing to the expiry of their engagement, but Lord Tullibardine, anticipating this, had already cabled to the Duke of Atholl to raise him two more squadrons. The Duke immediately arranged with the War Office to open recruiting stations for the Scottish Horse at Inverness, Aberdeen, Perth, Stirling, and Edinburgh.

He himself was put in charge of the recruiting, and the result was the despatch in June of a fine body of Scotsmen, 224 strong, with four officers. These men arrived in July, and after training at Elandsfontein, were sent out to the 1st Regiment as squadrons C and D, to replace two of those originally raised. In August the 1st Scottish Horse once more changed its column commander— but for the last time ; henceforth it was under Colonel Kekewich (the defender of Kimberley), and led by him, with Major Duff as its Commanding Officer, the regiment made many successful treks and large captures of Boers and stock.

But, like the 2nd Regiment, the 1st was also to have its hour of trial. Early on the morning of September the 30th, Delarey and Kemp, seizing an occasion when Colonel Kekewich's force was temporarily isolated and reduced in numbers, made a fierce attack on his camp at Moedwil. An account of this fight is given elsewhere, but it may be mentioned here that Colonel Kekewich's column made a most gallant stand, and that the attack was repulsed, though with terrible loss. The Scottish Horse had three officers (including its very capable adjutant, Captain Watson) and seventeen men killed, besides twelve officers and forty-one men wounded. The losses occurred chiefly among the men of the two new squadrons, who stood their ground nobly, though receiving their baptism of fire. Major Blair was severely wounded, and Sir William Dick-Cunyngham became second-in-command of the 1st Scottish Horse. On October the 30th the regiment, though reduced in numbers and sadly short of officers, captured seventy-five Boers at Beestekraal, on the Crocodile River, after a long night march.

To replace the casualties at Moedwil Lord Tullibardine obtained permission to apply for two more squadrons from Home, and the Duke of Atholl accordingly once more began recruiting. After the further losses at Bakenlaagte, a month later, the raising of yet another two squadrons was sanctioned ; but no difficulty whatever was found in getting men—and men of the right sort. They were keen, brave, well-disciplined, and good shots, and though they could not ride when they left home, a month's training under a good riding-master at Johannesburg made them fit for trek.

More Australians too were to come. Most of the first contingent had returned to Australia in September—their time being up—but another draft of two hundred took their place, and many of the original contingent returned when they heard of the casualties among their comrades at Bakenlaagte. What had been Colonel Benson's column was given after his death to Lieutenant-Colonel C. J. Mackenzie (Seaforth Highlanders) ; Major A. Jennings-Bramly (19th Hussars) was appointed to command the 2nd Scottish Horse, and Captain G. A. Thomas, an Australian officer, became adjutant. Major Bramly was killed, however, near Lake Banagher on the 20th of December 1901—a great loss to the regiment. His place was filled by Major L. C. Jones (Indian Staff Corps), who commanded the 2nd Regiment until the end of the war, during which period Colonel Mackenzie's column, ever on the move, took part in the "drives" organised by General Bruce Hamilton in the Eastern Transvaal.

Changes had also taken place in the 1st Regiment, for in November 1901 Captain Lord George Stewart Murray (the Black Watch) was appointed adjutant, and in December Major H. P. Leader (6th Dragoon Guards) became commanding officer *vice* Major Duff, who left to take up the command of the 8th Hussars. Till the end of the war the 1st Scottish Horse was trekking continuously in the Western Transvaal, and ably led by Major Leader, the regiment helped to score many successes for Colonel Kekewich's column. One notable engagement was at Gruisfontein on February the 5th, 1902, where the Scottish Horse, after a night march in which the mounted troops of Colonel Hickie's column also joined, surrounded Commandant Sarel Alberts' laager just before dawn, and though met by a hot fire, captured his entire force, 139 strong.[1]

Another very successful, though minor, affair was a raid made by Lord Tullibardine and sixty Australian recruits on a Boer remount farm some miles out from the Standerton-Ermelo line of block-houses. Though pursued by a force of more than double its number and engaged in a heavy rearguard action for about eighteen miles, this small party succeeded in bringing back to the block-house line over 150 horses, most of which were utilised as remounts.

In March 1902 the 2nd Scottish Horse was divided into two wings, one of which, composed of Scotsmen, was given to Major Blair, who had by now recovered from his wounds. The other, consisting entirely of Australians, remained under the command of Major Jones. The Right (or Scots) Wing was transferred to Colonel Kekewich's column, so that henceforth all the men who came from Home—and they now formed the majority of the 1st Regiment—were together. This immensely increased the *esprit de corps* which from the beginning had been a marked characteristic of the Scottish Horse. Together the 1st Regiment and Right Wing of the 2nd Regiment withstood the Boer attack at Rooiwal[2] on the 11th of April, and greatly distinguished themselves there, though two of the squadrons of the Right Wing were under fire for the first time that day.

One more " drive " from Klerksdorp right across to Mafeking and back was to end the treks of the 1st Scottish Horse and Right Wing, while General Bruce Hamilton's operations in the South-Eastern Transvaal, in which the Australians of the Left Wing had for six months borne a continuous and arduous part, were also brought to a close by the signing of peace on the 31st of May.

Another squadron—M—making the tenth sent from Home, had been raised by the Duke of Atholl in April. The men were recruited in only nine days, but they could not be embarked before May the 17th; they consequently landed at Cape Town—to their great disappointment—too late for hostilities.

After despatching at extremely short notice a contingent of officers and men to represent the Scottish Horse at the Coronation, both regiments were brought into camp near Johannesburg for disbandment, and for a month all who wished

---

[1] Major Leader, who was in command of the troops, received a brevet of lieutenant-colonel for this capture.

[2] An account of this engagement is given later.

to remain in South Africa were busily engaged in finding situations. Lord Tulli-bardine had been beforehand in obtaining offers of employment for his men, and partly owing to his exertions, and partly to the men's own good character and to the fact that most of them were trained to some trade, about seven hundred were settled in the country. A hundred officers and men joined the Natal Mounted Police on the understanding that they should be kept together as a squadron, and that they should be allowed to retain the black-cocks' tails in their hats, and other distinctive badges of the Scottish Horse.

Two hundred and fifty Australians returned to their homes, and the remainder of the corps—about seven hundred men—came back to Scotland, and were dis-banded in Edinburgh on September the 3rd, after having been entertained at luncheon by the Corporation—a great honour, and one much appreciated both by officers and men.

The main feature to be noted in connection with the Scottish Horse was its truly Imperial character—the men being drawn, as has been seen, not only from Scotland, but in large numbers also from South Africa and Australia. The corps included besides New Zealanders and Canadians, and it is probable that had the war not ended when it did, negotiations in which Lord Tullibardine was then engaged would have resulted in a large draft being sent from the Dominion.

From first to last, some 3500 men passed through the ranks, but owing to the short period for which the Colonials enlisted, the numbers were continually fluctuating, and this necessitated constant recruiting and reorganisation. 1843 officers and men in the field (exclusive of those on the high seas or at Home) was the highest number reached at any one time—a considerable increase this on the total of 500, which was originally to have been the strength of the Scottish Horse. Mere numbers, however, would have been nothing without the *esprit de corps* for which Scotsmen all over the world are famous, or without the splendid services rendered by the officers, both Regular and Irregular, whose help Lord Tullibardine was fortunate enough to secure. The Regular officers were more numerous than in most Colonial corps, and to this fact, and more especially to the work done by such officers as Lieutenant-Colonel Duff, Lieutenant-Colonel Leader, Major Blair, Major Murray, Major Jones, and others too numerous to mention, the success of the regiment was in great measure due. The Irregular officers too, of whom the greater number were Australians and South Africans, did extremely well, and there were many fine squadron-leaders among them. The men were for the most part of such a high class that it was possible to replace by promotion from the ranks the majority of the losses in officers caused by the fights at Moedwil and Bakenlaagte. Forty-six officers in all were appointed in this way.

From the first Lord Kitchener gave the Commanding Officer a very free hand in the management of the Scottish Horse, with the result that the corps was run on its own lines—a system which completely succeeded. Some special features have already been noticed, but another one may be mentioned, *i.e.* the establishment of an advanced depôt for each regiment at a point on the railway line near the district in which the regiment happened to be trekking. These advanced depôts became also remount depôts, and by this means the Scottish Horse was more easily and quickly supplied with fresh horses than most other corps.

Another special feature was the establishment, in January 1902, of a convalescent camp, to which every man on leaving hospital was sent before returning to duty. This ensured that the men did not get lost by being drafted down country to distant convalescent camps, which was often otherwise the case.

With the Commanding Officer lay the appointment and promotion of every officer, Regular or Irregular, though the appointments had to be ratified by the Commander-in-Chief. What an immense responsibility this was will be seen, when it is realised that altogether 157 officers served with the corps, and that the permanent establishment at the end of the war was 91.

In all, 1250 officers and men went from Home to join the Scottish Horse, and for the raising of 831 of these the Duke of Atholl was personally responsible. He also rendered valuable service in connection with the drafts sent out in the spring of 1901.

It should be mentioned that, before leaving Johannesburg, Lord Tullibardine helped to organise two regiments of Scots Volunteers—one a mounted, the other an infantry, corps—which, entitled respectively " The Transvaal Scottish " and " The Scottish Horse," carry on the tradition of his regiment in South Africa. He is their honorary colonel ; the infantry therefore have kilts of Atholl tartan, and both regiments wear the characteristic black-cocks' tails in their hats.[1]

Early in 1903 Lord Tullibardine was appointed to raise and command a regiment of Imperial Yeomanry, to be recruited from Argyllshire, Perthshire, Aberdeenshire, Banffshire, and Morayshire, a part of Scotland which, generally speaking, has hitherto produced but few mounted troops. This corps has now reached its establishment of some 950 officers and men, and is divided into two regiments, the first of which has been raised entirely in Perthshire. It perpetuates the name of the Scottish Horse in this country, and it may be confidently anticipated that the reputation gained by the old regiment in South Africa will be honourably upheld by the new one.

The foregoing pages, as has been seen, deal chiefly with the *personnel* and organisation of the Scottish Horse. How officers and men bore themselves in action will be told in the following accounts of the three principal engagements in which they took part.

[1] 1907. Since this article went to press, the Scottish Horse has been disbanded by the new Transvaal Government.

THE SCOTTISH HORSE IN ACTION[1]

BY A SQUADRON OFFICER

BAKENLAAGTE—MOEDWIL—ROOIWAL

BAKENLAAGTE, MOEDWIL, and ROOIWAL are the three especial " honours " of the Scottish Horse. A corps composed of men of all classes, upbringings, professions, and occupations—farmers, soldiers, lawyers, business men, Highlanders, Lowlanders, Australians, South Africans, moulded together and united partly by a semi-feudal idea, partly by a semi-clannish instinct, partly by an excellent organisation, primarily by a stolid sense of duty to their country—the Scottish Horse came into the field at a time when service was more irksome than during the earlier stages of the war.

At Bakenlaagte, Moedwil, and Rooiwal they were tried and passed their test, emerging from the war with a record for phlegmatic gallantry which was beyond question, and which in the eyes of the world placed them in the front rank of fighting corps, Regular or Irregular.

Yet what they chanced to do on those particular three days, they would have done whenever asked on any other occasion, and their conduct, " abounding in a spirit of courage and zeal, should neither be disfigured nor forgotten."

BAKENLAAGTE [2] (*October* 30*th*, 1901)

" Stranger, go tell the Lacedæmonians that we died in obedience to their laws."
—*Epitaph of the Spartans at Thermopylæ.*

The column under Colonel G. E. Benson, R.A., acting upon information received by its intelligence officer, Lieutenant-Colonel Wools Sampson, had been operating in the Bethel District, Eastern Transvaal, and on the evening of the 29th of October was encamped at Quaggaslaagte, about forty miles south of Brug Spruit. Few of the enemy had been seen on the preceding days, but Boers had been reported to be concentrating in force on the high ground to the north-west, and the column commander had judged it advisable to fall back upon the line of block-houses until the situation could be met by a force of greater strength.

[1] It should be borne in mind that this article has been written chiefly with a view to showing the part taken by the Scottish Horse in the engagements described. Comparatively little mention therefore has been made of other regiments which distinguished themselves on the same occasions.—[ED.]

[2] The paper on Bakenlaagte has already in substance appeared in vol. v. of *The Times History of the War*, this article and the preceding one—as the only material available with regard to the Scottish Horse—having been lent in response to a request for information about the regiment.

In case the use of the terms "front" and "rear" in this paper should not be clearly understood, it must be explained that these terms are used in their relation to the column as a whole, and not to any position taken up by the rearguard. Thus the ground between the rearguard and the rest of a column is termed the "front," even when the rearguard is faced about and in action.—[ED.]

The column marched from camp at 4.30 A.M. (daylight) on the 30th of October. The rearguard, consisting of three companies [1] of the 3rd Mounted Infantry (180 rifles), one company of infantry (80 rifles), and a pom-pom ("CC" Section), was under the command of Major F. G. Anley (Essex Regiment). The 2nd Scottish Horse at this time formed part of the main body, and marched on the right of the transport in company with the remainder of the infantry and guns.

The *terrain* is a slightly undulating country. Viewed from a distance, the veld hereabouts rolls gently like an Atlantic sea on a calm day. The rise and fall are so gradual that the traveller finds it hard to say at what moment he is upon the highest point of the undulation. Hence dominating ground is not easily distinguishable.

The day was cold with a thick mist; rain was imminent, and the ground being heavy and holding, the going could hardly have been worse for transport.

As soon as the force moved off parties of Boers began to press upon the rearguard, and soon the front and flanks of the column were also engaged. Though firing was at extreme ranges, one man of the rearguard was killed as early as 4.45 A.M. A little later, the convoy and main body were slowly crossing a drift, while the mounted men of the rear party were clinging to the high ground some 4000 yards behind. A little band of Boers stole round the mounted screen and captured seven stragglers of the infantry; shortly afterwards these men were returned to the main body stripped of all but their shirts. At 9 A.M. the company of infantry, being somewhat exhausted, was ordered forward to join the waggons, and the officer commanding the company was told to take up defensive positions covering the mounted troops, whenever the convoy should halt. The rearguard now consisted only of two companies of the mounted infantry and the pom-pom. Flanking parties of the third company—the Dublin Fusiliers—were kept out very wide, as the rearguard commander feared that the enemy might work round between him and the main body.

Till nine o'clock the day was only threatening, but at about that hour a cold rain began to fall, driving such dense sheets into the faces of the men of the rearguard that they could see no further than a hundred paces behind them, and making it impossible to tell where the full force of the Boer attack would fall. The march of the column, however, continued unchecked, and the convoy still laboured slowly forward; but waggons kept sticking fast in the clammy ground, and by one o'clock two of these had sunk so deep into the mud that they had dropped a considerable way behind the rest. The rearguard therefore halted upon some higher ground close to a reedy marsh, while the rest of the column proceeded on its march, and never halted again until it came into laager at Bakenlaagte farm. A second pom-pom (" R_2 ") was shortly afterwards sent back to reinforce the rearguard.

The rain and mist now came on more heavily than ever, and the main body

[1] *i.e.* one company each of the Yorkshire Light Infantry, the North Lancashire Regiment, and the Dublin Fusiliers.

had no sooner moved off than a hot fire was opened on the rear screen from almost every quarter of the compass (as it seemed) but chiefly from the rear—the increased severity of the attack being due to the arrival of Botha with a force of some 1000 men, and to the fact that the Boers on the front and flanks of the column, disliking the rain in their faces, had worked round to the rear in order to fight with the rain behind them. A message was therefore despatched to Colonel Benson informing him of the situation.

Still the Boers continued to press on their attack, and Major Anley, finding the position by the marshes an unfavourable one, decided at length to abandon the waggons and to fall back upon a second rise some 800 yards nearer the column. This retirement was safely carried out—the rear screen being hotly engaged all the while—and in a few moments Colonel Benson himself arrived, bringing with him two weak squadrons [1] of the Scottish Horse (73 in all), under Major F. D. Murray.[2] It was these men, together with a company of the 3rd Mounted Infantry, a section of the 84th Battery and its escort of some twenty men each of the Scottish Horse and 25th Mounted Infantry [3] (60th Rifles), who were destined to be the heroes of Bakenlaagte. The flank and advanced-guards of the column, though engaged throughout the day, were never very seriously pressed; the glorious story therefore of Bakenlaagte is the story of the rearguard.

Many minutes had not passed before Colonel Benson had realised that the second position taken up could not be held, and he accordingly ordered a retirement on to a third rise, about 1500 yards nearer camp, which he believed to be held by some 200 infantry and two guns of the 84th Battery. The artillery and two companies of infantry had, as a matter of fact, been sent back to this rise by Colonel Wools Sampson, who, as soon as the heavy rain came on, knowing the Boers' habits, foresaw that their attack on flanks and front would diminish, and that the danger to the rearguard would be correspondingly increased. Together with the guns and their escort, two companies of infantry were to hold the ridge, while the infantry company which had originally been with the rearguard, and which had not yet reached camp, was expected to cover the retirement of the mounted troops.

Each leaving a covering section, and preceded by "CC" pom-pom, which had done good service all the morning and had now been ordered to gallop straight into camp,[4] the Scottish Horse and 3rd Mounted Infantry retired simultaneously from their second position, and as they did so, were followed up

[1] *i.e.* Squadrons H and L.—[ED.]
[2] Captain and brevet-major the Black Watch; commanding 2nd Scottish Horse. He had served for some time on the staff of the Governor of Natal, and in the early days of the war had been signalling officer to Lord Dundonald. Major Murray was twenty-nine years of age, and had joined the Black Watch in 1891.
[3] This section of the 25th Mounted Infantry did not form part of the gun-escort at the beginning of the day, but was sent to reinforce it at about 11 A.M.—[ED.]
[4] "R₂" had jammed about five minutes previously, and had already been sent on to camp. The two pom-poms had fired about 2000 rounds during the day.—[ED.]

at a gallop by some 1000 Boers about 1200 yards away. The ridge was reached in safety—the retirement being aided by a well-sustained fire from Lieutenant Kelly and the Scottish Horse of the gun-escort, who had been pushed out to the left rear [1] of the hill. The guns with the remainder of the escort were found in position on the hill marked A in sketch; but no companies of infantry were to be seen, and it was discovered afterwards that the men who should have been on the ridge were sheltering from the heavy rain in a dip beyond it, while the other company had by that time reached a hollow in rear of hill A, from which it could give little or no assistance. Also in the hollow, but nearer the ridge, was a smaller body of infantry which had been told off as additional escort to the guns.

Major Murray and Captain Lindsay [2] dismounted by the guns at the head of the Scottish Horse, commanding and beseeching all who heard them "to stop and hold the ridge or else they'd lose the guns," in the forlorn hope of checking the Boers until the guns could be taken away by reinforcements. Their appeal was nobly answered by all the mounted troops. The Scottish Horse and Yorkshire Company of the mounted infantry dismounted and formed a straggling line to right and left of the guns—mostly to the right—while the Lancashire Mounted Infantry Company under Major Anley took up a position on a rise some 1500 yards away to the left (see hill marked B in sketch). The Scottish Horse of the gun-escort were called up by Major Murray, and their ammunition being scarce, they were told off as horse-holders. Most of the horses of the regiment were now sent on to camp—about twenty remaining in charge of six men of the escort.[3]

In the meantime, as the covering troop of Scottish Horse under Lieutenant E. O. Straker abandoned the second position, the leading Boers were only 100 yards in rear of them, and nothing now checked the onslaught of the whole Boer force.[4]

Pouring from around a farm to the south-east at which they had been seen massing, they galloped round to the south-west end of the first rise, surmounted the second, and without a check charged like a regiment of cavalry in open order. Firing from their horses as they came, and, to use the words of a spectator, "yelling like savages," they galloped straight into the infantry in rear of hill A. The men of the smaller party made a gallant resistance, losing nineteen killed and wounded out of thirty. The others were knocked down and ridden over or were clubbed by the Boer rifles, and the remainder in a few

---

[1] *i.e.* right front as they faced the enemy.

[2] Captain, Seaforth Highlanders and adjutant, 2nd Scottish Horse; son of Mr. Walter Lindsay (Windsor Herald). Captain Lindsay had been wounded with the Seaforth Highlanders at Magersfontein (where he was noticed for conspicuous gallantry), and again with the 2nd Scottish Horse at Roodekranz on April the 30th, 1901.

[3] Of these twenty horses only one could finally be brought into camp, and it was hit in three places.

[4] The Boers, who, it is believed, were upwards of 2000 strong, were led by Grobelaar of Ermelo, Erasmus of Carolina, and by Britz and Steyn with the Swaziland Police. Louis Botha (who is said to have ridden sixty miles to join Grobelaar) was in chief command.

moments held up their hands in sign of surrender. Lieutenant Straker, with the Boers "on top of him" (as he describes it), had been forced to gallop as fast as his horses could move to reach Colonel Benson and the rearguard on the third rise, and as he was surmounting the latter, his horse stumbled and fell. He picked himself up shaken and half stunned, and realised that a Boer had shot at him from a few yards off and missed him. The next instant another Boer clubbed his rifle and struck him on the head from behind, and he lost consciousness until some hours afterwards, when he awoke to find himself without coat or boots lying on the ground.[1] The men of his covering party—thirteen in number—were also overtaken before they could reach the rise, and were made prisoners.

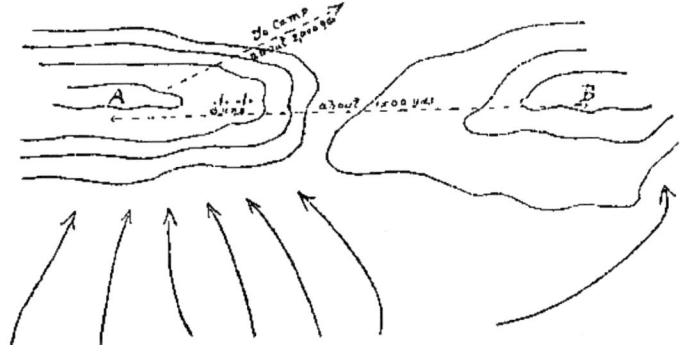

Sketch Plan of the Action at Bakenlaagte, 30th October 1901, showing roughly the lie of the ground where Colonel Benson made his last stand.
The arrows denote the direction of the Boer attack.

Dropping a few of their number to disarm the infantry, the Boers galloped on in extended order, and wheeling to their left as they approached, took advantage of some dead ground below the rise marked A to dismount. They then advanced on foot as near as they could to the guns and brought an overwhelm-

[1] As Straker opened his eyes he saw a commandant upbraiding a crowd of Boer laggards and telling them that he would beat them if they didn't return to the fight, "for if only they came now they would capture the guns." The laggards then went forward, and four Boers were left behind to escort the prisoners back to a farm named Kruisemefontein where the laager was. The prisoners numbered about one hundred, and included (besides the fourteen Scottish Horse mentioned in the text), one man of the R.A. and six "M.I." They were all wet and cold, without coats or boots. The main body of Boers arrived in laager about seven o'clock. They were jubilant, and brought in the guns. "O Khakis," they said, "we'll give you lots of whisky to-night. We're going to take your convoy now." But in the morning all they said was that the columns were coming and that they must retire, and at about 8 A.M. Commandant Brets formed up the prisoners and said "It had been a very good fight, and the English had had over 200 casualties, including Major Murray, and the prisoners would be released at three o'clock." At about four o'clock, accordingly, the prisoners were released and walked over to Bakenlaagte camp, five miles off.

ing rifle fire to bear on this part of the ridge. The attack made on the rise marked B was less fierce, the approach to it being very exposed; the enemy, however, demonstrated in such force from all points that it was impossible for Major Anley to reinforce those on hill A. Hill B was held until dark, when the Lancashire Mounted Infantry fell back on the camp, to assist in its defence.

The doomed guns were in position at about thirty yards interval from one another. The rise on which they stood was a gentle wave of veld—there was no definite summit—and between them and the nearest Boers was a strip of open space about twenty yards broad, dotted with ant-heaps.

The mêlée which followed—in which the casualties now became so terrific —of which the survivors are so few—is not easy to describe.

Major Murray crouched down in the open and under a terrific volume of fire from the Boers began to use his pistol; the men too settled down to their rifles and brought a good fire to bear. Right and left of the guns lay seventy-nine men of the Scottish Horse, and to the left of these the Yorkshire Mounted Infantry Company, but both right and left of guns and escort were completely "in the air," inasmuch as on the right the higher continuation of the ridge, being unoccupied, was at once seized by the Boers, while to the left of the guns was ground which it had been intended should have been held by the infantry. The latter, however, had surrendered just below it, and the Boers had also possessed themselves of this part of the ridge. Ground therefore both to the immediate left and to the immediate right of the guns was in the enemy's hands, and an intolerable fire was at once directed upon the gun-escort from right, left, and front, at ranges never greater than 300 yards, for the most part not greater than twenty yards—from three quarters of the compass—by an enemy who outnumbered it by nearly seven to one.[1]

The position of the mounted troops and the doomed guns began therefore to be desperate in the extreme, but for some time the Boers did not advance closer. They brought the same fire to bear from the front, but from the flanks their fire intensified. They had quickly seen that they could not at present advance nearer, and had determined to shoot the entire gun-escort from commanding ground to right and left before seizing the guns.

I continue the story in the words of a non-commissioned officer of the Scottish Horse who at this moment was lying beside an ant-heap near the guns. Ten yards to his left Colonel Benson himself lay behind another smaller ant-heap; some five yards from him Major Murray was crouching behind another, and a little to his right lay Captain Lindsay.

" The guns now fired three shots, of which the last two were case and at a range of about fifty yards. They then ceased fire and could never fire again, for all the gunners were killed or wounded in the first three minutes whilst they served the guns.

" There were a great many ant-heaps near the guns, but no shelter what-

[1] This is estimating the number of Boers attacking the ridge at 1500. The British troops, so far as can be ascertained, were about 220 or 230.—[Ed.]

ever for the gunners. I had been looking for Major Murray, as my place was by him, and he was at once conspicuous to me, for he wore a double felt hat and was half on his knees firing his pistol. The Boers were only about twenty yards off, and looked to me like two rows of infantry in extended order, covering an enveloping front of about 1200 yards. I heard Major Guinness [1] call out to his sergeant-major to fetch up the gun teams which were just behind the ridge. There were no gunners left to handle up the limbers, and sending for the teams of horses when no man dared even show his head above an ant-heap was a most desperate attempt. As soon as the teams came up the Boers concentrated such a fire upon them that I saw all the horses fall in an instant like corn cut with a scythe, and the artillery sergeant-major who was leading the first team was shot through the head and all the drivers wounded or killed."

According to this N.C.O. it was immediately after this that Major Murray and Captain Lindsay were killed—the latter being hit three times. Sergeant Skinner (Scottish Horse), who was lying about six yards to Major Murray's right, relates that Captain Inglis of the regiment was killed a few minutes later, and about the same time Lieutenant Woodman, an Australian officer of the Scottish Horse, was mortally wounded.

" Soon after this," (to quote the same authority,) " I happened to look at Colonel Benson, who was lying behind a very small ant-heap about ten yards from me on my left. He seemed to have been hit in the knee, for it was tied up, and I saw that he had turned round with his back to the Boers and was watching the column which was laagered up on the low ground, some 2000 yards behind us."

Even as Colonel Benson looked, his assistant staff officer, Captain Eyre Lloyd [2] (Coldstream Guards), appeared and dismounted on the farther edge of the rise, about a hundred yards away, throwing the reins of his horse to a trooper. In almost the same second, as it seemed, man and horse fell dead. Captain Lloyd saw this happen, but he walked on towards Colonel Benson with a characteristic smile, and in a manner which can only be described as leisurely. He was not even carrying a revolver, and his right hand was casually slipped into his breast [3] as he sauntered defiantly and quite upright across the open space, shot at by half a thousand rifles at not more than thirty or forty yards' range. All who saw him wondered at his glorious bravado—a precious example to every soldier, and one for which he paid the price—for he was severely wounded while only a few paces from his chief, and never succeeded in reaching him. [4]

[1] 84th Battery R.F.A.

[2] Captain Lloyd had been sent on by Colonel Benson earlier in the day to lay out the camp, but when he heard of the severe fighting and of the column commander being wounded, he felt his place was by Colonel Benson's side, and he accordingly galloped back to the ridge.—[ED.]

[3] This must have been in order to hide a wound in the right wrist which he had received a few minutes before.—[ED.]

[4] Captain Lloyd was mortally wounded a few minutes later, while being attended by Lieutenant J. M. Sloan, R.A.M.C. (attached Scottish Horse), and died next morning.—[ED.]

The Scottish Horse at Bakenlaagte 45

Of Captain Lloyd the above-mentioned N.C.O. said, " He was the bravest young officer I ever saw."

Following up their attack on the ridge, the Boers had opened a heavy fire on the camp and had by now almost surrounded it.[1] The survivors of the gun-escort could therefore look for no help from this quarter,[2] and the two companies of infantry, after making ineffectual attempts to reach the rise, were about this time withdrawn for the protection of the camp.

But there was no dribbling back of stragglers from the ridge ; where the Scottish Horse and Yorkshire Light Infantry had dismounted they had lain down. Murray's voice was now silent for ever, but his appeal was still in their ears, and where they lay they died.

Close behind the rise, upon the side nearer camp and among the led horses, stood two ammunition carts. Squadron-Quartermaster-Sergeant Warnock's [3] proper place was in camp with the waggons, but he had seen that his comrades were in a desperate plight and had put himself in charge of these ammunition carts. This man and Trooper A. Cunningham (Scottish Horse) now crawled up to within some twenty yards of the firing line, dragging a box of ammunition. Cunningham was immediately shot dead through the heart. Warnock lay down for a moment, and then undaunted crawled forward again alone, foot by foot, until he came into the firing line. The man nearest to him happened to be Sergeant W. Johnstone (Scottish Horse), who had been severely wounded in three places and was lying disabled. Warnock threw his ammunition right and left to those whom it could reach, and then seizing Johnstone's rifle, knelt and fired again and again right in the open and in full view of the Boers. To the others near by it seemed certain death under the terrific volume of fire from such close quarters, yet for some minutes Warnock bore a charmed life, and went crawling from ant-heap to ant-heap, plying his rifle undismayed, until he emerged right beyond the firing line and was all but in among the Boers, when he was badly wounded in three places. An audacity like this, displayed at such a moment, when three-fourths of the gun-escort had been killed or wounded and resistance was flickering out, will live for ever in the minds of all who saw it.[4] Close behind Warnock came Corporal J. J. M'Carthy [5] (Scottish Horse), and another man, with a second box of ammunition. They too contrived to crawl into the firing line,

[1] A hill commanding the camp was held from noon onwards by three sections of the 25th Mounted Infantry under Captain F. M. Crum, in face of a heavy and continuous fire which caused many casualties. At dark this party fell back on the camp, and the Boers immediately seized the hill.—[ED.]

[2] Reinforcements had been sent out earlier from camp, but had been unable to reach the ridge, though Lieutenant G. Dalby and twenty-five men of the 25th Mounted Infantry managed to get within a hundred yards of the guns.—[ED.]

[3] A Dumfries-shire man who had been for twenty-one years in the King's Own Scottish Borderers ; attached Scottish Horse.

[4] After the fight the Boers were robbing the dead and wounded, and came to Warnock to take his watch. He said to the first of them, "You don't want to take a poor old soldier's watch, do you?" and they, in admiration of his gallantry and respect for his age, abstained.

[5] Subsequently promoted lieutenant.—[ED.]

and Corporal M'Carthy, though three times wounded, threw his ammunition to the men on either side of him.

Meanwhile the Boers were wriggling up closer to the guns, yard by yard. Once they stood up as if to charge, but there still were some five-and-twenty unwounded men upon the ridge ; a straggling volley was fired, the Boer line sank to earth again, and for another fifteen minutes they kept up their fire without advancing.

Then a man leading a grey pony with his rifle in his left hand stood up from among them, and some half-dozen others rose with him.   They seemed to think the fight was over, and came walking towards the guns as if they could now take possession of them. At this moment there were merely six or seven rifles available in the gun-escort, but these poured what fire they could into the group of Boers. The man with the grey horse span round and fell, and the others behind him sank to the ground.

It was perhaps three or four minutes after this that the whole Boer line four or five deep stood upright as one man. The nearest of them were then about twelve yards from the guns, and they all seemed to be dressed in British soldiers' cloaks. One and all were firing furiously so as to stamp out the last embers of resistance from the survivors of the gun-escort.

They were cheering wildly—not as Northern people cheer, but as Kaffirs scream when exultant. Their scream was caught up all along their line, which now closed up and advanced right into the guns, shooting indiscriminately at everything that moved.

It was about this moment that Colonel Benson called out for a volunteer to go back to camp. Trooper N. H. Grierson [1] of the Scottish Horse shouted from behind his ant-heap that he would go, and a message was given to him to the effect that the ambulances were not to be sent out for the wounded, because, as the ridge was now virtually captured, the Boers would use the ambulance mules to drag the guns away. As Grierson rose and stood in front of Colonel Benson to take the message he was hit in the foot, and the self-same bullet glancing on its way pierced Colonel Benson above the left hip, passing right through his body.

The line of Boers surged slowly up and the guns were now lost.

All the officers and all but seven of the men of the Scottish Horse lay dead or wounded ; all four officers of the Yorkshire Light Infantry had been laid low, and seventeen out of twenty Riflemen, while the gun section had lost twenty-nine men out of thirty-two engaged, both its officers being killed.

Lance-Corporal J. Bell [2] (Scottish Horse) was the only unwounded man by the guns as the Boer line advanced. Three men came up to him and called " hands up."   He refused, shot one of them, and was immediately killed by the other two.

As the Boers were stripping the dead and wounded Colonel Benson con-

[1] Now 2nd lieutenant, West India Regiment.—[ED.]
[2] Son of Sir James Bell, ex-Lord Provost of Glasgow.—[ED.]

trived to send off one of his men into camp with an order to Colonel Wools Sampson to open fire at once on the ridge and clear it, in order to prevent the Boers from taking away the guns. Colonel Benson himself was lying grievously wounded by the guns and could not move, and fire from camp would be more likely to wound him again than to hurt any Boer. This order truly displayed a self-sacrificing devotion.

His messenger arrived in camp about half-an-hour later, in his shirt, without coat or boots, and fire was opened on the ridge.

Just at this moment Corporal J. L. Meates [1] (Scottish Horse) rode up to the rise on which the guns stood, with a message for Colonel Benson. The Boers were now among the guns, firing heavily into the mob of led horses, which stood for a moment below the rise and then with one accord stampeded. All the horse-holders of the Scottish Horse were hit, except Corporal H. Haxton.[2] Trooper B. Campbell (Scottish Horse) was badly wounded by this fire and fell off his horse close to Meates. The latter dragged him behind an ant-heap and there they lay together.

All the time the long line of Boers surged slowly over the rise step by step, shooting at dead and dying. And—as if this inferno were not enough—the guns and pom-poms now opened fire upon the ridge from camp, and the few unfortunate survivors of the gun-escort found themselves with "death in front and destruction in the rear"—in a tornado of rifle fire from the Boers—in a storm of shrapnel from their own people.

The line of Boers still came over and down the rise. Meates was accosted by a field cornet, who nodded kindly, saying, "Get behind us here," and the Boer line passed over him and left him alive.

As the shell-fire from camp, however, now intensified, Meates was at a loss where to seek shelter, and was standing up in despair, when a middle-aged Boer touched him on the shoulder, and speaking perfect English said, "Lie down here, my lad, and then you won't be hit," and led him to cover behind an ant-heap.

As the shell-fire continued most of the Boers retired, leaving the guns, but many remained, contemptuous of the fire, stripping dead and wounded men and horses. After about half-an-hour most of these too retired, but several still crawled about on their hands and knees—human jackals—rifling dead and dying.

At 5.30 all the Boers had fallen back under the shell-fire, and Meates stood up again and waved his arm to any who might be alive to see him. He was joined by three other men of the Scottish Horse, and these survivors of Bakenlaagte walked into camp, leaving seventy-three dead and wounded of their regiment on the ground.

Soon after this the ambulance waggons started out to bring in the wounded, and fire from camp ceased.

---

[1] Subsequently promoted lieutenant.—[ED.]
[2] Afterwards promoted sergeant.—[ED.]

Under the cover of the ambulances the Boers took the guns away with oxen. The dead were left where they lay.

The night came very dark, but there was no alarm, and as morning dawned men learnt the truth of the Biblical metaphor " as snow on Salmon," for the rise on which the guns had stood was white with the naked bodies of our dead.

At about 6 A.M. on October the 31st Colonel Benson died, after giving directions for the defence of the camp, and was buried at 12.30 P.M.

On the 1st of November a burial party went out to the rise on which the guns had stood. Of all the dead, only Lieutenant Kelly, Scottish Horse, had not been stripped. His coat—riddled by over thirty bullets—was torn to shreds and not worth the taking.

But this paper ends with the close of a fight, which, for the percentage of wounds and death endured by the defenders of the guns, stands unsurpassed in civilised war, and which for the devotion displayed by them should find a perpetual place in the history of British arms.

For the officers and men who suffered at Bakenlaagte unconsciously bequeathed to those who should live after them the priceless legacy of a glorious example.

CASUALTIES OF COLONEL BENSON'S COLUMN AT BAKENLAAGTE
(Compiled from the official returns)

	Officers.	N.C.O.s and Men.	Total.
Killed and died of wounds .	15	74	89
Wounded	11	138	149

Total, 26   Total, 212   Grand total, 238

(N.B.—These figures include, besides the casualties of the rearguard, those of the whole column on the 30th of October 1901.—ED.)

CASUALTIES OF THE 2ND SCOTTISH HORSE AT BAKENLAAGTE

Officers.	N.C.O.s and Men.	Total.
Killed and died of wounds—		
Major F. D. Murray, Commanding.		
Captains M. W. Lindsay (Adjutant)		
and S. W. Inglis.	28	33
Lieutenants J. B. Kelly and		
C. Woodman.		
Wounded—		
Captain C. Murray.		
Lieutenants W. Campbell, T. Firns,	36	40
and A. T. Wardrop.		

Total, 9   Total, 64   Grand total, 73

out of 79 officers and men engaged on the ridge by the guns.

THE WAR IN THE WEST

"Nemo me impune lacessit"

MOEDWIL (*September 30th*, 1901)

THE war in the west was well waged by the two rival commanders, Kekewich and Delarey. Both Boer and British generals were born leaders. Both tempered daring with caution, both knew when to risk much and when to risk nothing. Colonel Kekewich commanded the unshaken confidence, the respectful affection, and the loyal devotion of all ranks of his force, not only because they saw him for what he was—the best type of English gentleman—but because they well knew that the greater the emergency, the greater would prove the resources of their leader's generalship. Delarey was an enemy worthy of Kekewich : the Stonewall Jackson of the Boers—Puritan—born strategist—a chivalrous but uncompromising enemy—he inspired the respect of the British almost as much as the enthusiasm of the Dutch, and emerged from two and a half years of incessant warfare with the finest reputation of any of his countrymen.

The column commanded by Colonel R. G. Kekewich, composed of five companies of the Derbyshire Regiment under Lieutenant-Colonel Wylly (approximately 400 men), three guns of the 28th Battery Royal Artillery, one pom-pom of " G_2," and eight squadrons of mounted men (about 560 in all), had been operating in the Magaliesberg district throughout the month of September 1901.[1] The mounted troops were composed of six squadrons of the 1st Scottish Horse under Major Duff (8th Hussars), and two squadrons of the 7th Imperial Yeomanry. Major Blair (King's Own Scottish Borderers) was second-in-command of the 1st Scottish Horse, and the squadrons of that regiment were commanded as follows :—

A Squadron, Captain H. G. Field.
B Squadron, Captain J. P. Lambert.
C Squadron, Captain R. H. Dick-Cunyngham (21st Lancers).
D Squadron, Captain P. M. Rattray.
J Squadron, Captain P. N. Field.
K Squadron, Captain I. R. Mackenzie.

---

[1] There had also been some 400 men of the King's Own Scottish Borderers, but these left the column on the 22nd of September.

Of these six Scottish Horse Squadrons, two (C and D, under Dick-Cunyngham and Rattray respectively), although they had landed at Durban in July, had practically never yet been under fire, inasmuch as throughout September Kekewich's column had taken part in those "combined operations" and "closing-in movements" which for the most part characterised the 1901 period of the war. Stragglers from various commandos had been captured, but the column had for several weeks continuously trekked through the Magaliesberg country without any serious engagement.

On the 28th of September Kekewich was at Waterval, but left that spot at 5 A.M. on the 29th, arriving at noon on that day at the point where the road from Rustenberg to Zeerust crosses the drifts over the Selons River and joins the road from Waterval. The veld at this place is marked on the maps "Moedwil (639)," and the camp was pitched at mid-day at a point some 400 yards to the east of the drift over the river, and on slightly rising ground. The camp at Moedwil was set in an open space, roughly speaking, about 1400 or 1500 yards square, completely surrounded by bush of varying degrees of thickness, and beyond the bush bounded on north and west by the Selons River, which had here cut itself deep into the soft soil (see sketch). The camp faced west and its left rested on the Rustenburg-Zeerust main road. The mounted troops were on the right (the Yeomanry being on the extreme right), the guns were in the centre, and the Derbys on the left. Of the outposts the Derbys were responsible for the south-western, southern, and south-eastern aspects, while the mounted men took up a semicircular line covering western, north, and north-eastern sides, and joined hands with the infantry both at the drift over the river and on the road to Magato's Pass. The posts held by the mounted men were formed by one squadron of Yeomanry and C Squadron Scottish Horse, the latter being thrown out about six hundred yards to the right rear of the camp as a detached post (see map).

The ground behind the camp was fairly level, but it fell gently away in front towards the Selons River, rising again beyond it, and the alternative of placing his outposts on the near or far side of the river-bed offered itself to the commander. Outposts placed beyond it would see more, but would have to be pushed far out, and would thus be much more exposed than if posted on the camp side; and again outposts on the right bank of the river would in places be somewhat too near the main body to give timely warning of attack. The latter alternative was the one chosen by Colonel Kekewich, but he gave orders that each picquet was to send out a patrol an hour before daylight, and that two special patrols, each a troop strong, were to move out in north-westerly and south-westerly directions respectively, at 4 A.M. One Derby picquet was to hold the main drift over the Selons River, and another was posted on the further bank.

At 7 P.M. on the 29th the supply column with refugees and prisoners, under an escort of one company of the Derbys, J Squadron Scottish Horse,[1] and a half

---

[1] Less Captain P. N. Field, who took over command of A squadron.

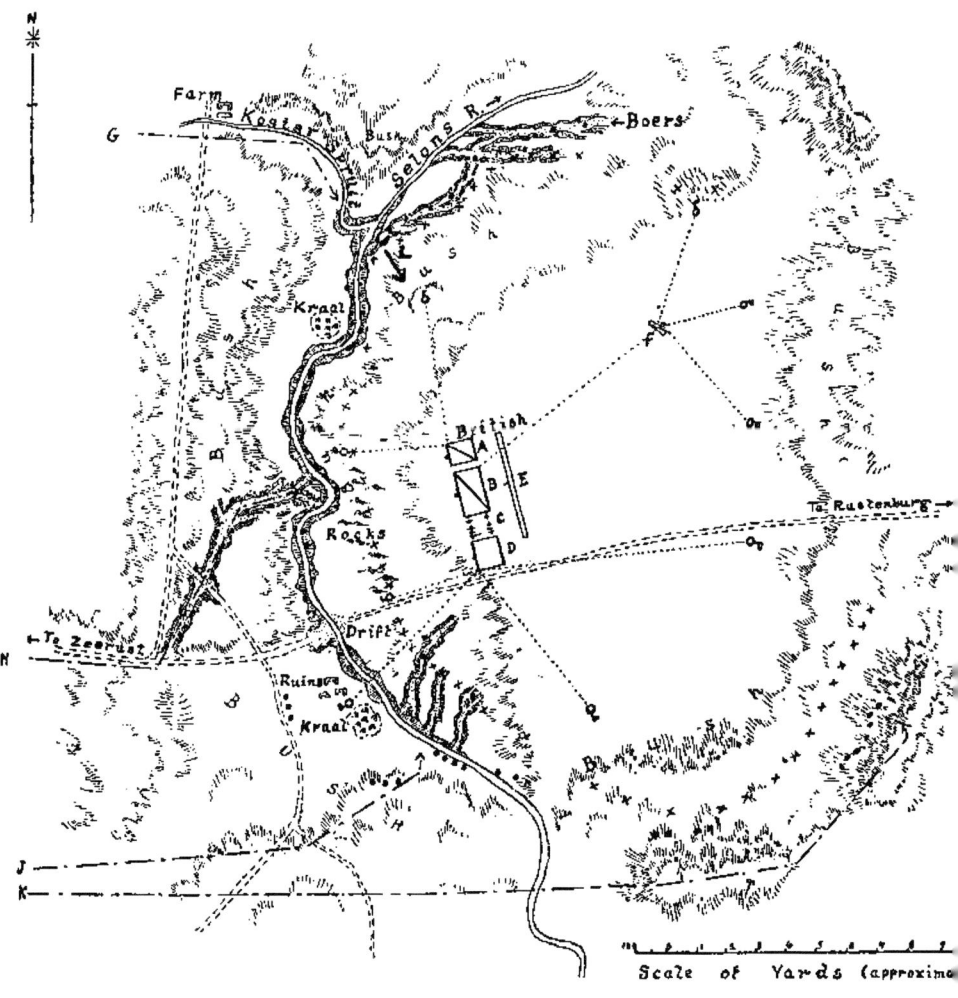

SKETCH MAP OF THE ACTION AT MOEDWIL, 30TH SEPTEMBER 1901.

A = Imperial Yeomanry.
B = Scottish Horse.
C = Artillery and Pom-pom.
D = Derbyshire Regiment.
E = Transport.
F = C Squadron, Scottish Horse.
G = Line of advance of Steinkamp and Osthinzen.

H = Line of advance of Van Tonder, Plessis, and Boshoff.
J = Line of advance of Fowrie and Coetzie.
K = Line of advance of Van Heerden and Kemp.
L = Direction of first Boer attack.
δ = British picquets.
× = Positions the Boers intended to take up.
● = Those they actually took up.

squadron of Yeomanry left the column for Naaupoort to "fill up," and the force in camp that evening resolved itself into four companies of the Derbys and one maxim, six and a half squadrons of mounted men, three guns of the 28th Battery and one pom-pom ; in all, about 900 men and 800 rifles.

The night passed quietly, and at 4.15 A.M., while still quite dark, a patrol moved out from the Devon Yeomanry picquet, on the extreme left of the line held by the mounted troops. Suddenly at about 4.30 some rifle shots were heard coming from the north-west ; the patrol had sighted Boers in the river-bed, had immediately opened fire in order to arouse the camp, and had then retired on the picquet, one man being taken prisoner. The first shots were followed by a loud outburst of fire from the same direction, a general alarm was given, and Colonel Kekewich turned out immediately. His orders were immediate and simple, and from first to last, according to the testimony of many who saw him, he was blessed with a complete coolness and decision which were in themselves the ingredients of victory. The situation which he now had to face was actually as follows :—

Delarey, foremost and astutest of the leaders of the Dutch, had effected a sudden concentration of the western commandos, amounting to about 1100 men. A force under Kemp and Van Heerden, working south, was to occupy higher ground some 5000 yards to the east of the camp, and there to join hands with Steinkamp and Osthuisen pushing round by the north, while the main body under Delarey himself, with Fourie, Coetzc, Van Tonder, Plessis, and Boshoff, was to drive home an attack through the river-bed on to the front of the camp, and force the British to retire into the arms of Kemp. Delarey purposed to repeat the tactics of Kornspruit, and the deep scrubby valley which like a python enveloped two sides of the slope on which Kekewich's camp stood, lent itself to his plan. Collecting some 900 men in the river-bed, he pushed them up into the scrub which everywhere fringed the right bank, and only waited for daylight to come to open a murderous fire.

The first brunt of the attack now fell on the unfortunate picquets, and especially on those of the mounted men who were responsible for the north-western and western sides of the camp ; these men at once found themselves enfiladed and all but engulfed in the firing line of the Boers. Point-blank fire was brought to bear on them from both flanks, and two of the Yeomanry picquets were in a few minutes all but annihilated. The enemy also pushed up the river and overwhelmed the Derby picquet at the main drift—every man but one being either killed or wounded.

The alarm having been given, the officers hastily collected their men and led them forward to the nearest spot, clear of the horse lines and tents, from which a field of fire could be obtained. By 4.45 A.M., and before darkness had fully given place to twilight, every unit had turned out of camp, with the exception of a small party of the Derbys, left behind to guard the ammunition.

The camp, however, which stood on the skyline of the rising ground, came under a heavy fire from west and north-west as the light increased, and many horses and men were hit. The fire was so hot that in a few minutes one of the field-guns was out of action—the detachment being all shot down—and the pom-pom is said to have jammed. Colonel Kekewich gave an order for some of the horses to be saddled up in order to be able to pursue the enemy later, but, to quote the words of one who took part in this attempt—"It was almost hopeless. All the men who were worth their salt were already in the firing line ; moreover the horses were dropping like shelled peas. . . . In one troop-line there stood thirteen horses " (of the Scottish Horse). " Of these, twelve were hit (eight, if I remember right, being killed), and the thirteenth was so panic-stricken that it was found impossible, even after the fight, to saddle him." It was in several fruitless attempts to carry out this order that most of the casualties occurred among the officers and men of the Scottish Horse. Colonel Kekewich himself was hit twice (in the right shoulder and left side) but never discontinued directing operations.

The volume of fire directed on the tents and horses at this period of the fight far exceeded that which was turned upon the men in the firing line, for these were now lying down on the slope and were hardly visible ; hence for the most part the Boer fire passed over their heads until broad daylight came, when the attacking force could better see where the defenders of the camp lay. On the other hand, when the full light of day came, our men could get a better view of the enemy, and so did more execution.

At about 5.15 a report was sent in to Colonel Kekewich to the effect that a large body of the enemy was working round from the north to the east or rear of the camp, and a strong body of the Derbyshire Regiment under Major C. N. Watts moved out eastwards to be ready for eventualities. Major Watts, however, found that this report was incorrect—the Boers apparently not being able to carry out this part of their original plan—and being joined by Captain Mackenzie with a few of the Scottish Horse, and by Major R. A. Browne of the Border Regiment (who with much foresight had collected all the servants, cooks, and orderlies in the camp), Major Watts followed the unbreakable rule of every successful soldier and " marched to the sound of the firing." Although he did not then recognise the fact, he thus eventually decided the day. Swinging his men round towards the north. he advanced with fixed bayonets against the enemy's left, through the ground held by C Squadron, Scottish Horse. This squadron had repulsed two determined attacks of the enemy, but had not been strong enough to drive him back unaided ; now, reinforced in this manner, it joined in an advance which was taken up all along the British line to north and north-west, and which at once became a most effective turning movement. The enemy's left, thus threatened, gave way, and this was the beginning of the end, for at 6 A.M. a general retirement of the Boers from the river-bed began. Picking up their horses, they galloped away towards the north and north-west, and only for a short distance did they come under the fire of our guns.

The last shot was fired at 6.15. The fight had been a costly one, some 25 per cent. of Kekewich's column being killed or wounded—a fact which proves the intensity of the Boer rifle fire and the determination of the attack.

It is evident, however, that the patrols sent out before daylight precipitated matters and upset Delarey's plan. He had intended to delay his attack until Kemp and Steinkamp had worked round to the rear of the camp, and until day should be dawning, when—the camp being on the top of a slope against the skyline—few officers or men would ever have got out of it unhit. As it was, the attack took place before the Boer flanking parties had reached their destination; most of the British troops were in the firing line before dawn; and though, as has been seen, the casualties in camp became very heavy as the light increased, they were far less than would have been the case had the attack been launched twenty minutes later.

It is said that the quality most requisite to successful generalship consists in the faculty of acting normally in abnormal times of emergency. A quick decision and a prompt execution of the only possible course achieved at Moedwil an unqualified success for the defence, when the least vacillation or want of control would have caused an unmitigated disaster.

All the Scottish Horse did well that day, but a brief mention should be made of three Perthshire men who rendered especially good service :—Major Duff, who by his able dispositions materially contributed to the victory; Captain "Pete" Rattray, who gallantly led out his untried squadron to where the fire was hottest; and Surgeon-Captain Kidd, who, though severely wounded early in the day, continued to attend to the wounded until 10 A.M., when he was obliged to give in through loss of blood. Two others should also be noted :— Lieutenant W. Jardine, who, in spite of having received two wounds, remained in command of his men, and Farrier-Sergeant Kirkpatrick, who pursued and killed Boshoff, the leader of the Boer scouts, who had got right into camp. Among those killed was an excellent non-commissioned officer, Scout-Sergeant William McGregor, from Weem.

The following tables show as nearly as can be ascertained the total casualties of the column, and the losses of the Scottish Horse in particular. It may also be mentioned that 327 horses and 185 mules were killed, and that 117 rounds of shrapnel, 800 rounds of maxim, and about 67,000 rounds of small-arm ammunition were expended.

CASUALTIES OF COLONEL KEKEWICH'S COLUMN AT MOEDWIL
(*Compiled from the official returns*)

	Officers.	N.C.O.s and Men.	Total.
Killed and died of wounds . .	5	56	61
Wounded	21	110	131
	Total, 26	Total, 166	Grand total, 192

CASUALTIES OF THE 1ST SCOTTISH HORSE AT MOEDWIL

Officers.	N.C.O.s and Men.	Total.
Killed and died of wounds—		
Captain H. A. F. Watson (Adjutant).		
Lieutenants T. J. Irvine and	17	20
H. N. C. Erskine-Flower.		
Wounded—		
Major C. E. Duff.		
Major A. Blair, D.S.O.		
Captains P. M. Rattray and		
P. N. Field.	41	53
Surgeon-Captain W. S. Kidd.		
Lieutenants J. Stuart-Wortley, D. Rattray,		
W. N. Edwards, M. Prior, D.S.O., W. Loring,		
N. C. G. Cameron, and W. Jardine.		

Total, 15   Total, 58   Grand total, 73

ROOIWAL (*April* 11th, 1902)

ON the night of the 10th of April, in accordance with instructions from General Ian Hamilton (who was in supreme command of all the columns operating in the Western Transvaal), Colonel Kekewich's force, composed of Lieutenant-Colonel Grenfell's and Lieutenant-Colonel Von Donop's columns, which for some months past had been operating in the Klerksdorp district, occupied a line running west and east along the valley of the Brakspruit and facing south. Kekewich's force covered ground from near the farms called Rooiwal and Doornbult to Oshoek (some three miles away to the east), where it joined hands with the Imperial Light Horse, who were on the right of Sir Henry Rawlinson's force. The only information available indicated generally that the majority of the enemy were some distance to the south. General Hamilton's orders to Kekewich for the 11th of April were to move at an early hour to the junction of the Harts River and the Brakspruit, and thence to make a reconnaissance in a west-north-west direction, while Rawlinson's and Walter Kitchener's forces reconnoitred towards the south-west.

The "general idea" on which these dispositions were conceived was that of feeling for the enemy while maintaining close touch between the three forces, so that the cordon should be preserved and the enemy enclosed in the area between the columns and the block-houses.

Some few days prior to this date, General Delarey had passed through Colonel Kekewich's lines on his way to discuss terms of peace with Lord Kitchener at Klerksdorp, but there was no amnesty between the two armies. Kemp appears to have been in command of all the western commandos during

Delarey's absence, and to have caused a large concentration of his men in the neighbourhood of Wolmaranstad on the 10th of April. He had under him some 2000 of various commandos, the toughest veterans of the Boer forces—men who had been continuously in the field since October 1899, and whose pugnacious spirit had been fortified by an intimate experience of British tactics, by their own protracted resistance, and, in an especial sense, by their recent striking victories. Kemp's purpose on the 10th of April was to concentrate every available man in close proximity to Kekewich, and then in repetition of the tactics which had recently been so successful, to envelop the British force and rush into close quarters.

Entirely unaware of any impending conflict, at 6 A.M. on the 11th of April Grenfell's and Von Donop's columns closed on their right and moved west—Von Donop's column leading—towards the junction of the Harts River and the Brakspruit. The country through which the column marched was not only stamped with a natural desolation, but scarred and disfigured with the débris, the putrefying bones and offal, of the recent wayfaring and fighting. At Doornbult [1] lay hundreds of animals ten days dead, and on almost every hillock and hollow were tokens of warfare, bodies and bones of animals, broken boxes, newly-covered graves—back-wash left by the storm. Only the white farmhouse of Rooiwal with its smoking chimney (comfortably nestling by some water in a sheltered hollow, between an orchard and an orange grove) at once struck the traveller's eye as the sole kindly and human feature in a fierce and inhospitable landscape.

At 7.30 A.M. the two columns had almost closed up, the head of Von Donop's column having reached the farm of Rooiwal, and his scouts being about a mile and a half ahead. It is said that a short time before this a little girl of about fourteen years of age had run out from the farmhouse up the hillside to the south and had waved her apron high above her head. It was afterwards conjectured that this had been a signal to call her countrymen to battle, for before the column reached Rooiwal the officer commanding the advanced-guard reported that a large force was approaching from the left and asked if it was Rawlinson. Colonel Von Donop thereupon rode forward to reconnoitre.

At this moment the Scottish Horse,[2] under Lieutenant-Colonel Leader (6th Dragoon Guards), were marching at the head of Grenfell's column and had reached a point about a mile east of Rooiwal farm. They were passing through the low ground along the river-bed, which is here flanked by a large bushy hill on its northern and by a smaller eminence on its southern side—forming a defile from which the view to the front is uninterrupted, but to either flank is limited by the kopjes. I continue the story from the point of view of those who were with the leading files of the Scottish Horse.

As Von Donop's column reached Rooiwal a few irregular shots were heard from the left front, followed immediately by three or four loud regular volleys,

---

[1] Doornbult was the scene of Colonel Cookson's fight, which had taken place a few days before.

[2] *i.e.* 1st Scottish Horse and Right Wing, 2nd Scottish Horse.

and almost simultaneously it was noticed that the fan-shaped regularity of the screen was broken and that there was some unaccountable galloping in front. A general tendency of this galloping in the direction of the north (that is to say, from the left front away towards the right), was also clearly perceived.

A few moments later—out of the distant uproar and across the bare stretch of plain and the deserted left front—galloped *ventre à terre* a hatless horseman straight for Colonel Grenfell. The Scottish Horse watched him growing clearer and wondered who he was. A few seconds later and he was hailed by Colonel Grenfell, and recognised as Percival of the 5th Fusiliers, Colonel Von Donop's aide-de-camp. "Those men in front are all Boers," he calmly but emphatically shouted, "Boers—nothing but Boers. I have galloped right through them myself."

Grenfell looked in the direction indicated and saw against the sky to his left front a thick black line, perhaps a mile away. It might have been anything —cattle or sheep or men—all one could say was that a black line a mile or more in length stretched thick and unbroken all along the skyline, across the front, left front, and left flank. Grenfell threw a glance at the screen—saw that it was not—and realised in a second that he must achieve his own salvation. A second glance at the long black line showed it blacker and longer, and dissipated doubts ; it was men—it was Boers—they were many—and Percival's information (at first so surprising as almost to be incredible), was swallowed and digested. Grenfell had some 1100 rifles, with two guns and a pom-pom, and acting under instructions from Colonel Kekewich, he now gave the following orders :— the guns and pom-pom immediately to come into action facing west ; the 1st and 2nd Scottish Horse (460 rifles) to wheel to their left, dismount and advance towards the Boers, seizing some mealie-covered ground which rose slightly towards the enemy—thus covering the south-west ; the South African Constabulary (290 rifles) to protect the guns ; and the Yeomanry (420 rifles) to come up on the left of the Scottish Horse and face south. Otherwise expressed, Colonel Grenfell's intention was to dispose his column in a crescent-shaped line of dismounted men facing west, south-west, and south, on the best ground available in the few seconds which could be spared. The guns at once began firing at about 1100 yards range, and the Scottish Horse under Leader, being at the head of the column, were the first to get dismounted under a very heavy but inaccurate fire, under which horses were freely hit and some stampeded. Leader and the first troops climbed the slightly rising ground and took up the best position they could find, some fifty yards away from the horses, facing west and south-west. The men then extended and opened fire at about 600 yards, and the rest of the Scottish Horse formed up to right and left of these troops, extending the firing line until something very like what Grenfell purposed was realised.

Just as the remaining troops of the Scottish Horse followed Colonel Leader and the first troops into the firing line, so the other units formed on the Scottish Horse ; and eventually Von Donop's column rallied and formed on Grenfell.

Thus it is literally true that Colonel Leader with the first few troops of the Scottish Horse formed the nucleus of the entire resistance, and in a sense the fortunes of the whole force depended on Leader at once getting every available rifle into occupation of the right ground ; for had the Boers galloped into Grenfell before he had had time to possess himself of the higher ground on his left, they would have been in occupation of a position from which the entire valley would have been at their mercy.

The Boers had advanced slowly so as to give their wings time to swing up and envelop the British force, and this cost them the day. For now the crisis was passed ; the Scottish Horse were lying along the higher ground with a good field of fire before them, and stolid north-countrymen are not easily dismayed by the moral effect of an advancing enemy.

The range rapidly diminished to five, four, and three hundred yards, but still the Boer line in close order, knee to knee, and two and more deep, moved slowly onward at the " trippling " pace of African ponies.

Seldom in the history of small-bore warfare have riflemen or gunners had a surer target than that thick crowded line of horsemen. There was no chance of a man mistaking his range ; each fired point blank as fast as he could fill his magazine, and the guns were using " case." Still, through this terrific fire-zone, on horses, on mules, on foot—the horsemen firing as they rode—the foot-men stopping anon to fire out of the " mealies "—the Boer line surged forward to the charge.

Those who had been at Omdurman had seen a similar imposing spectacle ; none of the rest of a veteran column had ever beheld so Homeric a sight as the confident onslaught of 2000 mounted men, knee to knee, two, three, and four deep.

Some of the leading Boers came to within 100 yards of the Scottish Horse and even closer to the Constabulary, and then the tornado of lead in which they found themselves was too much even for their determination. and they broke and galloped away, the last shot being fired at about 8.10 A.M.

Men now had leisure in which to realise that the day was won. Away on the right a few parties of the enemy were still trying to get round that flank through the scrub jungle on the hillside. To the left and to the front, near and far, were galloping horsemen and clouds of dust, while immediately before the recumbent British line were over 100 dead and wounded Dutchmen. Close to the Scottish Horse Maxim (which had done excellent service) lay Commandant Potgieter, a big man in a blue suit and jack boots ; and near by a lad of fourteen, himself badly wounded, was holding a blanket over a dying old man to shield him from the sun.

At about 9 o'clock, when the horses had been collected, a movement towards the south in échelon of columns to the right rear began. An unbroken line of scouts stretched from the valley of the river for six miles in a southerly direction, and for some three hours a ceaseless cantering pursuit was maintained through mealie fields and over the endless veld. " Only over the next rise "—but beyond that was another and again another, and beyond again the dust clouds of the fugitives, which never seemed the nearer.

Here and there among the mealies lay wounded Boers; here and there limped a wounded horse with sweat marks on his back, dripping blood, into the corn cobs. One might swear the rider was not far to seek; but the pursuit of the dust clouds did not admit of drawing rein. At last in a hollow the Scottish Horse came upon their prize—two beat teams of mules harnessed to the last of the lost field-guns,[1] one pom-pom, a small band of prisoners who held up their hands, and beyond, some waggons. Beyond again, four or five miles to the west, the broken commandos trailed up the hill track for Schweizer Reneke; but the horses were now so exhausted that further pursuit was impossible. The men gave their animals a drink of liquid mud, burnt the waggons (expressing a courteous if not quite sincere regret to the female occupants), and turned their heads towards camp at Rooiwal.

A red-letter day—a day of a thousand days—was done, and a real success, pregnant with results as yet but dimly guessed by those who had achieved it, had been most cheaply won in a country of disasters.

The actual result of the fight, some say, was the end of the war in the west. Be this as it may, Kekewich's column had been privileged to witness a wondrous change in the character of their enemy;—the changing of the leopard's spots— the transmigration of the soul of the Dervish into the heart of the Dutchman.

And the Scottish Horse had seen an even greater thing than that, for they had furnished in themselves an undeniable demonstration of the rule of war that stolid riflemen well led need fear no charge of horsemen, even though the latter be fortified by the prestige of former success.

CASUALTIES OF LIEUTENANT-COLONEL GRENFELL'S COLUMN AT ROOIWAL

1 officer and 4 men killed.
4 officers and 37 men wounded.
200 horses killed.

AMMUNITION EXPENDED BY LIEUTENANT-COLONEL GRENFELL'S COLUMN AT ROOIWAL

Small-arm ammunition, 42,000.
Shell and case, 73.
Pom-pom ammunition, 410.

SCOTTISH HORSE CASUALTIES

1 N.C.O. died of wounds.
8 men wounded.
1 prisoner.

---

[1] The guns lost at De Klip Drift on the 7th of March, 1902.

APPENDIX I

Officers and Men of the Scottish Horse who received rewards for services performed while with the Regiment.[1]

FIRST REGIMENT.

DISTINGUISHED SERVICE ORDER.

Captain I. R. Mackenzie (South African).[2]
Captain P. M. Rattray (South African).

BREVET OF LIEUTENANT-COLONEL.

Major H. P. Leader, Commanding (Canadian ; attached from 6th Dragoon Guards) —for capture of Sarel Alberts' laager at Gruisfontein, 5th February 1902.

DISTINGUISHED CONDUCT MEDAL.

Qrmr. and Hon. Lieut. E. A. Legge[3] (English ; attached from Sq.-Qrmr.-Sergt. 18th Hussars).

SECOND REGIMENT.

VICTORIA CROSS.

Lieutenant W. J. English (Scots)—for gallantry at Elandskloof, 3rd July 1901.

DISTINGUISHED SERVICE ORDER.

Captain O. W. Kelly (Australian).

DISTINGUISHED CONDUCT MEDAL.

Regimental Sergeant-Major J. Sharp (Scots ; attached from Royal Horse Guards).
Regimental Sergeant-Major H. E. Varley (English ; attached from 6th Dgn. Guards).

---

[1] This list does not include the numerous promotions made for merit. As the Scottish Horse had only a temporary existence, and as its numbers and *personnel* were continually fluctuating, very few promotions were made by seniority.

[2] In the case of officers and men attached from the Regular Army, the words " South African," " Canadian," and so on, refer, so far is as known, to the countries to which such officers and men respectively belonged. In other cases they indicate the countries in which officers and men were respectively domiciled at the commencement of the war.

[3] This officer served as quartermaster and honorary lieutenant throughout the period of his service with the Scottish Horse, but at the conclusion of the war was required to revert to his former rank in the 18th Hussars—a strange reward for his services in South Africa.

APPENDIX II

Officers and Men of the Scottish Horse who were mentioned in despatches for services performed while with the Regiment.

Lieut.-Col. the Marquess of Tullibardine, D.S.O., Commanding Scottish Horse (Scots ; seconded from Royal Horse Guards).
Lieut. W. F. Fison (Australian), Regimental Adjutant.

FIRST REGIMENT

Major (afterwards Lieut.-Col.) H. P. Leader, Commanding (Canadian)—for capture of Sarel Alberts' laager at Gruisfontein, 5th Feb. 1902.
Captain R. H. Dick-Cunyngham (Scots ; attached from 21st Lancers)—for services at Moedwil, 30th Sept. 1901.
Captain P. N. Field (South African)—for services in Magaliesberg Mountains, Sept. 1901.
Captain I. R. Mackenzie (South African)—for services in Magaliesberg Mountains, Sept. 1901.
Captain C. E. Rice (Scots)—(1) for services at Beestekraal, 30th Oct. 1901, and (2) for services in action with Delarey, 24th March 1902.
Surg.-Capt. W. S. Kidd (Scots)—for services at Moedwil (wounded), 30th Sept. 1901.
Lieutenant N. C. G. Cameron (Scots)—for services at Moedwil (wounded), 30th Sept. 1901.
Lieutenant W. Jardine (South African)—for services in Magaliesberg Mountains, Sept. 1901, and at Moedwil (wounded), 30th Sept. 1901.
Lieutenant W. A. King (South African)—for services at Beestekraal, 30th Oct. 1901.
Lieutenant (afterwards Captain) W. Lawless (Canadian)—for services at Gruisfontein, 5th Feb. 1902.
Lieutenant S. H. Lewis (South African).
Lieutenant W. Loring (English)—for services at Moedwil (wounded), 30th Sept. 1901.
Lieutenant (afterwards Captain) A. Rattray (South African)—for services at Moedwil, 30th Sept. 1901.
Lieutenant H. T. Selby (Australian)—for services at Gruisfontein, 5th Feb. 1902.
Lieutenant J. H. Symonds (South African)—for services at Moedwil, 30th Sept. 1901.
Lieutenant J. C. Wallace (South African)—for services at Gruisfontein, 5th Feb. 1902.
Lieutenant J. Stuart-Wortley (English)—for services at Moedwil (wounded), 30th Sept. 1901.
Qrmr. and Hon. Lieut. E. A. Legge (English ; attached from 18th Hussars).
Farr.-Major W. Fraser (Scots ; attached from Royal Horse Guards).
Sq. Sergt.-Major G. H. Manley (English ; attached from 13th Hussars).
Sq. Sergt.-Major F. Neale (Scots)—for services at Gruisfontein, 5th Feb. 1902.

Farr.-Sergt. Scout R. H. Tellam (South African).

Farr.-Sergt. T. Kirkpatrick (Scots)—for services at Moedwil, 30th Sept. 1901.

Sergeant (afterwards Sq. Sergt.-Major) G. Gunning (South African)—for services at Gruisfontein, 5th Feb. 1902.

Sergeant C. E. I'Anson (English)—for services at Moedwil (wounded), 30th Sept. 1901.

Sergeant D. McIlwraith (Scots)—(1) for services at Slipstein Kopjes, 4th April 1901, and (2) in despatches of 23rd June 1902.

Corporal Scout W. Ruddy (South African)—for scouting.

Scout T. Gibbons (South African)—for scouting.

Scout M. A. K. Shadwell (South African)—for scouting.

Scout L. N. Smith (South African)—for scouting.

Scout T. Tooms (South African)—for scouting.

Trooper [1] C. Barclay (Scots)—for services at Gruisfontein, 5th Feb. 1902.

Trooper [1] C. H. M. McCallum (Scots)—for services at Gruisfontein, 5th Feb. 1902.

Trooper [1] J. S. Robb (Scots).

Trooper [1] G. Webster (Scots)—for services at Moedwil, 30th Sept. 1901.

SECOND REGIMENT

Major A. Blair, D.S.O., Commanding Right Wing (Scots ; attached from King's Own Scottish Borderers)—for services at Rooiwal, 11th April 1902.

Captain O. W. Kelly (Australian)—for services at Laatste Drift (wounded), 15th July 1901.

Lieutenant J. M. Baker (Scots).

Lieutenant J. L. Jack (Scots ; 2nd Vol. Batt. Argyll and Sutherland Highlanders).

Lieutenant (afterwards Captain) D. Robertson (Scots)—for services at Bakenlaagte, 30th Oct. 1901.

Qrmr. and Hon. Lieut. J. Murray [2] (Scots ; attached from Sq. Qrmr.-Sergt., 3rd Dgn. Guards).

Regimental Sergt.-Major W. G. Austin (Right Wing) (English ; attached from 19th Hussars).

Regimental Sergt.-Major J. Sharp (Scots ; attached from Royal Horse Guards)—for services (1) at the Mauchberg, 14th June 1902, and at Elandskloof, 3rd July 1902 ; (2) at Bakenlaagte, 30th Oct. 1901 ; and (3) (with 1st Regiment) at Gruisfontein, 5th Feb. 1902.

Regimental Sergt.-Major H. E. Varley (English ; attached from 6th Dgn. Guards).

Sq. Sergt.-Major E. Luther (Australian).

Sergeant (afterwards Lieutenant) T. Firns (Australian)—for services at Elandskloof, 3rd July 1901.

Sergeant (afterwards Sq. Qrmr.-Sergt.) R. B. F. Fraser (Scots)—for services at Elandskloof (wounded), 3rd July 1901.

Sergeant J. C. Gange (Australian)—for services at Houtboschloop, 13th June 1901.

Sergeant A. Martin [3] (Right Wing) (Scots)—for services at Rooiwal, 11th April 1902.

Sergeant W. L. Whiteman (Australian)—for services at Elandskloof (wounded), 3rd July 1901.

---

[1] Promoted corporal for gallantry in the field.
[2] This officer was treated at the close of the war in a similar manner to Lieutenant E. A. Legge (see note, p. 60).   [3] Formerly in the 1st Regiment.

Corporal F. H. Helmkemp (Australian).

Corporal (afterwards Sergeant) F. T. Kererouse (Australian)—for services at Laatste Drift, 15th July 1901.

Corporal W. Parker (South African)—for services at Rooiwal (with Right Wing), 11th April 1902. Died of exhaustion the same day.

Lance-Corporal [1] A. Redpath (Scots)—for services at Elandskloof, 3rd July 1901.

Trooper [1] T. Fraser (Australian)—for services at Elandskloof, 3rd July 1901.

Trooper [1] N. H. Grierson (Scots)—for services at Bakenlaagte (wounded), 30th Oct. 1901.

Trooper [1] F. W. Wilkinson (Tasmanian)—for services at Laatste Drift, 15th July 1901.

Though the foregoing articles do not claim to record events beyond 1902, it may be added that down to the present year (1907) the following officers and men of the Scottish Horse have obtained commissions in the Regular Army :—

FIRST REGIMENT

Rank	Name	Commission in
Lieutenant	N. C. G. Cameron	The Northumberland Fusiliers.
Lieutenant	C. A. L. Irvine	The King's Own Scottish Borderers.
Lieutenant	L. A. Jones	The Royal Warwickshire Regiment (for Indian Army).
Lieutenant	J. H. Symonds	12th Lancers.

SECOND REGIMENT

Rank	Name	Commission in
Lieutenant	W. Campbell	The Highland Light Infantry.
Lieutenant	W. J. English	Army Service Corps.
Lieutenant	W. E. Stuart	The King's Own Scottish Borderers.
Corporal	N. H. Grierson	The West India Regiment.
Trooper	C. H. M. McCallum [2]	The Highland Light Infantry.

[1] Promoted corporal for gallantry in the field.

[2] Son of Colonel Sir Henry McCallum, G.C.M.G., A.D.C., Governor of Ceylon.

List of Abbreviations used in Records of Officers, Warrant Officers, Non-Commissioned Officers, and Men; in the Table showing the Services of Officers of The Black Watch, pp. 22–28; and in the Indexes to Portraits, to Persons, and to Military Units and Departments.

A. . . . . = Army
A.A.G. . . = Assistant Adjutant-General
A. and S. H. = Argyll and Sutherland Highlanders
A.B. . . . = Able-bodied Seaman
Abdn. . . = Aberdeen
Act. . . . = Acting
A.D.C. . . = Aide-de-camp
Adjt. . . . = Adjutant
Ammun. . = Ammunition
A.O. . . . = Army Ordnance
Apptd. . . = Appointed
Arm. . . . = Armourer
Armrd. . . = Armoured
Arty. . . . = Artillery
A.S. C. . . = Army Service Corps
Attd. . . . = Attached
Bart. . . } = Baronet
Bt. . . . }
Batt. . . . = Battalion
B.Ch. . . . = Bachelor of Surgery
Bdsman. . . = Bandsman
Bgde. . . . = Brigade
Blk. Watch } = Black Watch
B.W. . . }
Bomb. . . = Bombardier
Brev. . . . = Brevet
Brig. . . . = Brigadier
B. S. A. . . = British South Africa
Cam. . . . = Cameron
Capt. . . . = Captain
Carb. . . . = Carbineers
Cav. . . . = Cavalry
C.B. . . . = Companion of the Bath
C.B. (with number) = Coast Brigade
C.I.E. . . = Companion of the Indian Empire
C. in C. . . = Commander-in-Chief
C.I.V. . . = City Imperial Volunteers
Civ. . . . = Civil
Civiln. . . = Civilian
Cl. . . . . = Class
C.M. . . . = Master of Surgery
C.M.G. . . = Companion of St. Michael and St. George
Col. . . . = Colonel
Colds. . . = Coldstream
Col.-Sergt. . = Colour-Sergeant
Comdg. . . = Commanding
Comdr. . . = Commander
Comdt. . . = Commandant
Condr. . . = Conductor
Corpl. } = Corporal
Cpl. }
Coy. . . . = Company
C.R.E. . . = Commanding Royal Engineers
D.C.M. . . = Distinguished Conduct Medal
Dd. . . . = Died
Dept. . . . = Department
Dgns. . . . = Dragoons
Divn. . . . = Division

Dr. . . . = Driver
Drum. . . = Drummer
D.S.O. . . = Distinguished Service Order
Edin. . . . = Edinburgh
Farr. . . . = Farrier
Fight. . . . = Fighting
F.M. . . . = Field Marshal
F.R.C.S. . . = Fellow of the Royal College of Surgeons
F.R.G.S. . . = Fellow of the Royal Geographical Society
Fus. . . . { = Fusilier, Fusiliers
G.A. . . . = Garrison Artillery
G.C.B. . . = Knight Grand Cross of the Bath
Gds. . . . = Guards
Gen. . . . = General
G.O.C. . . = General Officer Commanding
Gord. . . . = Gordon
Gov. . . . = Governor
Gr. . . . = Gunner
Gren. . . . = Grenadier
H. . . . } = Highlanders
Highdrs. }
H.L.I. . . = Highland Light Infantry
Hon. . . . = Honorary
Honble. . . = Honourable
Hse. . . . = Horse
Huss. . . . = Hussars
Imp. . . . = Imperial
Impl. Yeo. } = Imperial Yeomanry
I.Y. . }
Ind. . . . = Indian
Indt. . . . = Independent
Infy. . . . = Infantry
Instr. . . . = Instructor
Irreg. . . . = Irregular
Johan. . . = Johannesburg
K.C.B. . . = Knight Commander of the Bath
Kd. . . . = Killed
Kitch. . . . = Kitchener
K.O.S.B. . . = King's Own Scottish Borderers
K.T. . . . = Knight of the Thistle
L. . . . = Light
Lan. . . . = Lancers
Lce. . . . = Lance
Lieut. } = Lieutenant
Lt. . . }
Lov. . . . = Lovat's
L.R.C.P. . . = Licentiate of the Royal College of Physicians
M.A. . . . = Master of Arts
Maj. . . . = Major
M.B. . . . = Bachelor of Medicine
M.Ch. . . . = Master of Surgery
M.D. . . . = Doctor of Medicine
Mech. . . = Mechanist
Med. . . . = Medical

Mil. . . . = Militia
Mily. . . . = Military
M.R.C.S. . . = Member of the Royal College of Surgeons
M.R.C.V.S. = Member of the Royal College of Veterinary Surgeons
Mtd. . . . = Mounted
M.V.O. . . = Member of the Royal Victorian Order
N.S.W. . . = New South Wales
N.Z. . . . = New Zealand
Off. . . . { = Officer, Officers
Ordly. Rm. . = Orderly Room
Perm. . . . = Permanent
P.O. . . . = Post Office
Pol. . . . = Police
Prom. . . . = Promoted
Pte. . . . = Private
Qrmr. . . . = Quartermaster
R. . . } = Royal
Rl. . . }
R.A. . . . = Royal Artillery
R.A.M.C. . . = Royal Army Medical Corps
Rdrs. . . . = Riders
R.E. . . . = Royal Engineers
Regt. . . . = Regiment
Res. . . . = Reserve
R.F.A. . . = Royal Field Artillery
R.G.A. . . = Royal Garrison Artillery
Rgh. . . . = Rough
R.H.A. . . = Royal Horse Artillery
Rif. . . . = Rifle, Rifles
R.N. . . . = Royal Navy
S.A. . . . = South African
S.A.C. . . = S. African Constabulary
Sadd. . . . = Saddler
Sapr. . . . = Sapper
Sc. . . } = Scout, Scouts
Scot. . . . = Scottish
Sea. . . . = Seaforth
Secy. . . . = Secretary
Sergt. } = Sergeant
Sgt. . }
Sh. Smith . = Shoeing Smith
Sq. . } = Squadron
Squad. }
Supy. . . . = Supernumerary
Surg. . . . = Surgeon
Temp. . . . = Temporary
Thorn. . . . = Thorneycroft's
Tpr. . . . = Trooper
Tr. . } = Troop
Trp. . }
Tramp. . . = Trumpeter
V.C. . . . = Victoria Cross
Vet. . . . = Veterinary
Vol. . . . = Volunteer
Vols. . . . = Volunteers
Yeo. . . . = Yeomanry
Yr. . . . = Younger

ROLL OF PERTHSHIRE OFFICERS OF THE PRESENT DAY WHO HAVE SEEN ACTIVE SERVICE UNDER THE BRITISH FLAG

NOTE

THE connection of each officer with Perthshire is stated in his record, but it may bo mentioned that Part I. includes men who own property in the county, and their sons ; some grandsons, great-grandsons, and great-great-grandsons (on the paternal side), of landed proprietors of recognised Perthshire families ; sons and grandsons of men who, though not owners of property, are or were long resident in Perthshire, and came of families established in the county ; and men who were born and brought up in Perthshire.

In all cases of ownership of property in Perthshire the preposition " of " is used ; in cases of tenantry only, this preposition is omitted.

A reference at the end of a record denotes the page on which the officer's photo will be found.

This Roll includes officers living in 1903, and of such as were not living in that year, those who had seen active service during the previous ten years. The information in the records is not carried beyond December the 31st, 1903.

ROLL OF OFFICERS

PART I

Airlie, Licut.-Col. David William Stanley, 8th Earl of.[1] Born, 1856. Educated at Eton College and Royal Military College, Sandhurst. Gazetted Unattached Sub-Licut., 1874. Appointed to Scots Fusilier Guards, 1875. Transferred to 10th (The Prince of Wales's Own) Royal Regt. of Hussars, 1876. Promoted Lieut., 1877 (antedated to 1875). Served with 10th Hussars in Afghan War, 1878–1879, being present in attack and capture of Ali Musjid, and in engagement at Futtehabad (medal with clasp). Served with Soudan Expedition, 1884, as Adjt. 10th Hussars, and was present in engagement at Tamai (medal with clasp, 4th class of Medjidie, and Khedive's star). Promoted Capt., 1884. Served as Bgde. Maj. with Nile Expedition, 1884–1885, under Sir Herbert Stewart, and was present in action at Abu Klea (slightly wounded), in engagement at Abu Klea Wells, 16 and 17 Feb. 1885, and in reconnaissance to Metemmeh—slightly wounded (twice mentioned in despatches; brevet of Major; two clasps). Promoted Major, 1892; 2nd in command into 2nd Dragoon Guards (Queen's Bays), 1896; Lieut.-Col. Comdg. into 12th (Prince of Wales's Royal) Lancers, 1897; Hon. Col. 3rd Vol. Batt. Royal Highlanders. Served in South African War, 1899–1900, as Lieut.-Col. Comdg. 12th Lancers, and took part in advance on Kimberley, 1899–1900, including action at Magersfontein, relief of Kimberley, and operations in Orange Free State, Feb. to May 1900, including operations at Paardeberg and action at Driefontein. Wounded at Isabellafontein, May 4, 1900. Took part in operations in Transvaal, June 1900. Killed in action at Diamond Hill, June 11, 1900 (frequently mentioned in despatches; Queen's medal, with four clasps). [p. 109.]

Anderson, Lieut. John, M.B., C.M. Edin. (of Newholme, Pitlochry). Educated at Royal High School, Edinburgh, and Edinburgh University. Served in South African War, 1900–1901, as Civil Surgeon attached to Royal Army Medical Corps (20th Bgde. Bearer Coy.), with temporary rank of Surg. Capt. Took part in operations in Cape Colony and Orange River Colony, 1900, including action at Wittebergen, and in operations in Transvaal. Invalided home and resigned appointment, 1901. (Queen's medal, with four clasps.) Formerly Surg. Lieut. 5th Vol. Batt. The Black Watch. Gazetted Lieut. Scottish Horse (Imperial Yeomanry), 1903. Still serving. [p. 129.]

Anderson, Chief Officer Walter Beveridge (eldest son of the late D. W. Anderson, formerly of Lambhill, Dollar). Educated at Dollar Academy. Enlisted in Kitchener's Horse, 1900. Served in South African War with Kitchener's Horse, 1900–1902, and took part in operations in Cape Colony, Orange Free State, and Transvaal, including action near Diamond Hill. Slightly wounded at Hunt Nek, May 6, 1900. Promoted Sq. Sergt.-Maj., 1901. Discharged on disbandment, 1902 (Queen's medal, with three clasps; King's medal, with two clasps). Served as Chief Officer in H.M. Hospital Ship, *Dunera*, 1902 (Transport medal, with clasp). Relinquished appointment, 1902. [p. 133.]

Barnett, Lieut. Thomas Wilkie (Wester Ballindean, Inchture; eldest son of the late Alexander Barnett, Blindwells, St. Martin's). Educated at Guildtown Public School. For five years in 5th Vol. Batt. The Black Watch. Enlisted in Lovat's Scouts, 1900. Served in South African War, (1) with Lovat's Scouts, 1900–1902; and (2) as Lieut. with 2nd Scottish Horse, 1902. Promoted Corpl. Lovat's Scouts, 1900; Sergt., 1901. Took part in operations in Orange River Colony, 1900, including action at Wittebergen, and in operations in Cape Colony, 1901–1902. Transferred to Scottish Horse and promoted Lieut., 1902. Took part in operations in Western Transvaal, 1902, with Col. Kekewich's' mobile column, including action at Rooiwal (mentioned in despatches; Queen's medal, with three clasps; King's medal, with two clasps). Relinquished appointment at end of war. [p. 127.]

Bissett, Qrmr. and Hon. Major William (3rd son of the late Andrew Bissett, Wester

[1] For short biographical notice of Lord Airlie, see pp. 97, 98.

67

Clow, Dunning). Enlisted in 71st (Highland Light Infantry) Regt., 1867. Promoted Qrmr. and Hon. Lieut., 1882 ; Hon. Capt., 1892. Transferred to 3rd (Militia) Batt. The Highland Light Infantry, 1895. Served in South African War, 1902, with 3rd Batt. H.L.I., and took part in operations in Cape Colony (Queen's medal, with two clasps). Promoted Hon. Major, 1903. Still serving. [p. 131.]

Boyd, Civil Surg. John B., M.B., C.M. Edin. (3rd son of the late W. W. Boyd, of Sylverton House, Scone). Served in South African War, 1902, as Civil Surgeon attached to Royal Army Medical Corps, and was on duty in Orange River Colony (Queen's medal, with two clasps). Relinquished appointment at end of war. [p. 135.]

Bulloch, Lieut. Richard Archibald (youngest son of the late George Bulloch of Kinloch). Educated at Cheam and Harrow Schools, and at Royal Military College, Sandhurst. Gazetted 2nd Lieut. The Black Watch (Royal Highlanders), 1899. Promoted Lieut., 1900. Served in South African War, 1899–1902, with 2nd Batt. The Black Watch, and took part in advance on Kimberley, 1899–1900, including action at Magersfontein—severely wounded ; operations in Orange Free State, Feb. to May 1900, including operations at Paardeberg and action at Vet River ; operations in Orange River Colony, May 1900 to Sept. 1901, including actions at Rhenoster River, Wittebergen, and Witpoort ; operations on Zululand Frontier of Natal, Oct. 1901 ; and operations in Transvaal and Orange River Colony, Nov. 1901 to May 1902 (Queen's medal, with four clasps ; King's medal, with two clasps). Still serving. [p. 131.]

Cameron, Civil Surg. Angus (6th son of the late Angus Cameron, Killichonan, Rannoch). Served in South African War, 1901, as Civil Surgeon attached to 2nd Batt. The Norfolk Regt. with temporary rank of Surg. Capt., and took part in operations in Transvaal (Queen's medal, with two clasps). Invalided home, 1901, in consequence of accident. Died of his injuries at Rannoch, Dec. 31, 1902. [p. 135.]

Campbell, Lieut. Hector (only son of the late Maj.-Gen. R. B. P. P. Campbell, C.B.; greatgrandson and direct representative of John Campbell of Kinloch). Educated on the Continent and at Royal Military College, Sand-

hurst. Gazetted 2nd Lieut. Unattached List, 1897. Served in campaign on North-West Frontier of India under Sir William Lockhart, 1897–1898, with Tirah Expeditionary Force, attached to 1st Batt. The Gordon Highlanders, and took part in actions of Chagru Kotal and Dargai, and capture of the Sampagha and Arhanga Passes. Took part also in operations in the Waran Valley and action of Nov. 16, 1897 ; and in operations in the Bara Valley (medal, with two clasps). Gazetted to Indian Staff Corps (now Indian Army) and appointed Officiating Wing Officer, Corps of Guides (Infantry), 1898. Promoted Lieut., 1899. Served with Allied Forces in China during Boxer Rising, 1900, with 1st Sikh Infantry (medal). Still serving with Corps of Guides. [p. 123.]

Campbell, Capt. the Honble. Ivan (2nd son of John, 6th Earl of Breadalbane). Gazetted 2nd Lieut. 79th (Queen's Own Cameron Highlanders), 1879. Promoted Lieut., 1880. Served with The Cameron Highlanders in Egyptian Campaign, 1882, and was present at battle of Tel-el-Kebir (medal with clasp, and Khedive's star). Retired, 1884. Gazetted Lieut. 3rd (Militia) Batt. The Royal Scots (Lothian Regt.), and promoted Capt., 1900. Served in South African War, 1900–1901, (1) with 3rd Batt. The Royal Scots ; (2) as Comdt. of Provisional Batt. at Kroonstadt ; and (3) as Assistant Press Censor in Cape Colony. Took part in operations in Orange Free State, 1900 (Queen's medal, with three clasps). Retired, and apptd. to Honourable Corps of Gentlemen-at-Arms, 1901. [p. 123.]

Campbell, Lieut. James Colin (eldest son of Col. Alexander Campbell,[1] yr. of Aberuchill and Kilbryde). Born, 1875. Joined Natal Mounted Police, 1898. Appointed Instructor of Maxim Guns to Capt. Hore's Coy. of Volunteers, 1899. Gazetted 2nd Lieut. Cape Garrison Artillery, 1900. Served in South African War, 1900–1902, in command of Armoured Train, in Cape Colony, Orange River Colony, and Transvaal. Promoted Lieut. Killed in accident to No. 15 Armoured Train at Daspoort, near Pretoria, May 5, 1902 (Queen's medal, with clasps ; King's medal, with two clasps). [p. 123.]

Campbell, Col. John Colin Livington (of Achalader). Gazetted Lieut. Corps of Royal Engineers, 1872. Served with Jowaki-Afridi Expedition, 1877–1878 (medal). Served in

[1] Now Sir Alexander Campbell, Bart., of Aberuchill and Kilbryde.

Afghan War, 1878–1880, as Adjutant Royal Engineers, Khaibar Line Force, being present at attack and capture of Ali Musjid (medal, with clasp). Served in Egyptian Campaign, 1882, with 24th Coy. R.E., being present in action at Kassassin, Sept. 9, and in battle of Tel-el-Kebir (medal with clasp, and Khedive's star). Promoted Capt., 1884. Served with Bechuanaland Expedition under Sir Charles Warren, 1884–1885. Promoted Major, 1891; Lieut.-Col., 1898. Comdg. Royal Engineers, Alexandria, 1898–1903; C.R.E. Egypt, Cairo (temp.), 1900–1903. Re-employed on half-pay, 1903.

Campbell, Col. John Hasluck (of Inverardoch). Educated at Trinity College, Glenalmond. Gazetted 2nd Lieut. 93rd (Sutherland Highlanders) (now 2nd Batt. Princess Louise's Argyll and Sutherland Highlanders), 1876. Promoted Lieut., 1877; Capt., 1884; Major, 1893. Served in campaign on North-West Frontier of India under Sir William Lockhart, 1897–1898, with 2nd Batt. A. and S. H., and took part in operations of Tochi Field Force (medal, with clasp). Promoted Lieut.-Col. Comdg. 2nd Batt. A. and S. H., 1899; Colonel, 1903. Half-pay, 1903. [p. 123.]

Chalmers, Major Peter (of Gowanlea, Blairgowrie). Educated in Blairgowrie. Enlisted in Scots Fusilier Guards (now Scots Guards), 1842. Served in Crimea, 1854, during Russian War, as Pay-Sergt. with 1st Batt. Scots Fusilier Guards, and was present in battle of the Alma —severely wounded (medal, with clasp, and Turkish medal). Invalided home and discharged on account of wounds. Appointed Sergt.-Major Royal Perthshire Rifles (Militia), 1855. Gazetted Capt. and Adjt. 1st Clackmannan Rifle Volunteers, 1867; Capt. and Adjt. 1st Stirlingshire Rifle Volunteers, 1873. Retired with hon. rank of Major, 1881. [p. 131.]

Christie, Capt. Robert Main (of Westlands, Dunblane). 4th Vol. Batt. The Black Watch. Served in South African War, 1901–1902, in command of 2nd Vol. Service Coy. attached to 2nd Batt. The Black Watch (Royal Highlanders). Took part in operations in Orange River Colony and Transvaal (Queen's medal, with five clasps). Still serving in 4th Vol. Batt. The Black Watch. [p. 131.]

Clark, Lieut. Francis Maurice Augustus Atkinson (yr. of Port-an-eilean). Educated at Eton College. Gazetted 2nd Lieut. Scots Guards, 1897. Promoted Lieut., 1899. Served in South African War, (1) with 1st Batt. Scots Guards, Nov. 1899 to July 1901 ; and (2) as Adjt. of Rest Camp at Bloemfontein, Aug. 1901 to April 1902. Took part in advance on Kimberley, 1899–1900, including actions at Belmont, Enslin, Modder River, and Magersfontein; operations in Orange Free State, Feb. to May 1900, including operations at Paardeberg and action at Driefontein ; operations in Transvaal, May and June 1900, including actions near Johannesburg and Diamond Hill. Took part also in operations in Orange River Colony, May to Nov. 1900, and in operations in Transvaal, July 1900 to July 1901, including action at Belfast. Died at Bloemfontein, April 21, 1902 (mentioned in despatches ; Queen's medal, with seven clasps ; King's medal, with two clasps). [p. 111.]

Clark, Col. William (of Princeland, Coupar-Angus). Educated at Trinity College, Glenalmond, and Royal Military College, Sandhurst. Gazetted Ensign 43rd (Monmouthshire) Regt. of Foot (Light Infantry) (now 1st Batt. The Oxfordshire Light Infantry), 1862. Promoted Lieut., 1864. Served in New Zealand War, 1863–1866, and took part in action of Gate Pa (severely wounded), and in expeditions into Province of Taranaki (mentioned in despatches ; medal). Appointed Adjt., 1870 ; promoted Capt., 1871 ; Major, 1881. Served in Burmese Expedition, 1886–1887, as Staff-Officer to Shan Column, and with Mtd. Infy. of 3rd Brigade (mentioned in despatches ; brevet of Lieut.-Col. ; medal, with clasp). Also served in Burma, 1887–1889 (clasp) ; with Wuntho and Manipur Expeditions, 1889 (mentioned in despatches ; clasp) ; and in Burma, 1889–1892 (clasp). Promoted Lieut.-Col. Comdg. 2nd Batt. The Oxfordshire Light Infantry, 1891; Colonel, 1895. Commanded 51st and 65th Regimental Districts, 1897–1900. Retired, 1900. [p. 119.]

Clayhills, Lieut. George, D.S.O. (4th son of Thos. Clayhills, and grandson of the late G. D. Clayhills-Henderson of Invergowrie and Hallyards). Educated at Cheltenham College and Trinity Hall, Cambridge. Gazetted 2nd Lieut. The East Lancashire Regt., 1899. Promoted Lieut., 1900. Served in South African War, 1900–1902, with 8th Batt. Mounted Infantry, and took part in operations in Orange Free State, Feb. to May 1900, including operations at Paardeberg and actions at Poplar Grove,

Driefontein, Karree Siding, Vet River, and Zand River; and in operations in Transvaal, May and June 1900, including actions near Johannesburg and Pretoria. Took part also in subsequent operations in Orange River Colony and Eastern and Western Transvaal (twice mentioned in despatches; D.S.O.; Queen's medal, with four clasps; King's medal, with two clasps). Resumed regimental duty, 1902. Still serving. [p. 115.]

Colquhoun, Lieut. John Locke Campbell (4th son of Lieut.-Col. Wm. Campbell Colquhoun of Clathick). Gazetted 2nd Lieut. 3rd (Militia) Batt. The Highland Light Infantry, 1902. Served in South African War, 1902, with 3rd Batt. H.L.I., and took part in operations in Cape Colony (Queen's medal, with two clasps). Promoted Lieut., 1903. Still serving.

Colquhoun, Capt. Julian Campbell (2nd son of Lieut.-Col. Wm. Campbell Colquhoun of Clathick). Gazetted 2nd Lieut. The Prince of Wales's Leinster Regt. (Royal Canadians), 1891. Promoted Lieut., 1893; Capt., 1898. Served in South African War, 1902, with 2nd Batt. The Leinster Regt., and took part in operations in Orange River Colony and Transvaal (Queen's medal, with four clasps). Adjt. 2nd Batt., 1903. Still serving.

Cunyngham, Major Sir William Stewart Dick-, Bart., of Prestonfield (and Killiecrankie Cottage). Gazetted 2nd Lieut. The Black Watch (Royal Highlanders), 1892. Promoted Lieut., 1896. A.D.C. to G.O.C. Scottish District, 1898-1899. Promoted Capt., 1900. Served in South African War, (1) on Special Service in Natal, 1900 (mentioned in despatches); (2) as Adjt. 1st Scottish Horse, 1900-1901; (3) as Regtl. Adjt. Scottish Horse, 1901; and (4) as Second-in-Command 1st Scottish Horse (with local rank of Major), 1901-1902. Took part in operations in Western Transvaal, 1901-1902, with mobile column commanded first by Col. Flint and later by Col. Kekewich, and was present in action at Rooiwal (mentioned in despatches; Queen's medal, with three clasps; King's medal, with two clasps). Resumed regtl. duty, 1902. Retired, 1903. Gazetted Major Scottish Horse (Imperial Yeomanry), 1903. Still serving. [p. 127.]

Drummond, Lieut.-Col. the Honble. Charles

Rowley Hay-[1] (4th son of Thomas, 10th Earl of Kinnoull). Educated at Royal Military College, Sandhurst. Gazetted Ensign and Lieut. Scots Fusilier Guards (now Scots Guards), 1854. Served with Scots Fusilier Guards in Crimea, 1855, during Russian War, including siege and fall of Sevastopol (medal with clasp, and Turkish medal). Promoted Lieut. and Capt., 1856; Capt. and Lieut.-Col., 1862. Retired, 1865. [p. 111.]

Drummond, Lieut.-Col. Francis Henry Rutherford, C.I.E. (oldest surviving son of the late Maj.-Gen. Henry Drummond, and grandson of Col. John Drummond of Stragoath). Educated at Wellington College. Gazetted Sub-Lieut. and promoted Lieut. 109th (Bombay Infy.) Regt., 1875. Served in Afghan War, 1878-1880, being present in engagement at Jagdalak; in subsequent advance to Sherpur under Brig.-Gen. Charles Gough; and in operations round Kabul, Dec. 1879 (twice mentioned in despatches; medal, with clasp. Appointed Lieut. Bengal Staff Corps (now Indian Army), and Officiating Sq. Officer 10th Bengal Cavalry, 1879; Sq. Officer 11th Bengal Cavalry, 1880. Served with Afghan Boundary Delimitation Commission on Russo-Afghan frontier, 1884-1886. Promoted Capt., 1886; Brevet-Maj., 1887; Sq. Comdr. 10th Bengal Cavalry, 1888; Major, 1895. Was in charge of a party of Indian cavalry officers at Queen Victoria's Diamond Jubilee, 1897 (C.I.E.). Appointed Comdt. 1st Regt. Central India Horse (now 38th Central India Horse), with rank of Lieut.-Col., 1900. Promoted Lieut.-Col., 1901. Still serving. [p. 111.]

Drummond, Major Laurence George (only son of the late Admiral the Honble. Sir James Drummond, G.C.B., and grandson of James, 8th Viscount Strathallan). Educated at Eton College and Royal Military College, Sandhurst. Page of Honour to Queen Victoria, 1874-1877. Gazetted 2nd Lieut. Scots Guards, 1879. Promoted Lieut., 1881. Served with Bechuanaland Expedition under Sir Chas. Warren, 1884-1885, with Methuen's Horse. Adjt. 1st Batt. Scots Guards, 1886-1890. (Jubilee medal, 1887.) Promoted Capt., 1888. Appointed Regtl. Adjt., 1892. A.D.C. to G.O.C. Home District, 1892-1897. Served with Ashanti Expedition under Sir Francis Scott, 1895-1896, in command of Guards

1 Assumed surname and arms of Drummond, 1900, on succeeding his brother, Capt. the Honble. Arthur Hay-Drummond, in estates of Cromlix and Innerpeffray.

Company "Special Service Corps" (star). (Clasp to Jubilee medal, 1897.) Promoted Major, 1898. Served in Soudan Campaign under Sir Herbert Kitchener, 1898, on Headquarters Staff, and was present at battle of Khartoum (mentioned in despatches; British medal; and Khedive's medal with clasp). Was Military Secretary to Governor-General of Canada, 1898-1900, and accompanied 1st Canadian Contingent to South Africa, 1899. Served in South African War, (1) on Staff of 1st Divn., 1899 to Feb. 1900 in command of Kimberley mtd. infy., Feb. to April 1900. Took part in advance on Kimberley, 1899-1900, including action at Magersfontein; relief of Kimberley and subsequent operations (mentioned in despatches; Queen's medal, with two clasps). Resumed regtl. duty and appointed Second in Command 3rd Batt. Scots Guards, 1900. Specially mentioned in Coronation Gazette, 1902, to receive rank of full Col. when promoted Lieut.-Col. Still serving. [p. 111.]

Drummond, Capt. Malcolm (of Megginch). Educated at Eton College. Gazetted Lieut. Grenadier Guards, 1876. Appointed A.D.C. and Private Secretary to Governor of Newfoundland, 1881. Promoted Capt., 1885. Served in Soudan Expedition, 1885, with 3rd Batt. Grenadier Guards and 1st Batt. Mtd. Infy., being present in engagement at Hasheen, attack on convoy, engagement at Tamai, and successful attack on Takool under Sir Gerald Graham (medal with clasp, and Khedive's star). (Jubilee medal 1887.) Groom of Privy Chamber to Queen Victoria, 1890-1893; Groom in Waiting in Ordinary, 1893-1901. Clasp to Jubilee medal, 1897. Commander, 1st Class Friedrich Order. Retired, 1890.

Drummond, Lieut. the Honble. Maurice Charles Andrew (3rd son of James, 10th Viscount Strathallan). Educated at Eton College. Page of Honour to Queen Victoria. (Jubilee medal, 1887.) Gazetted 2nd Lieut. 3rd (Militia) Batt. The Black Watch (Royal Highlanders), 1897. Gazetted 2nd Lieut. 2nd Batt. The Black Watch, 1899. Served in South African War, (1) with 2nd Batt. The Black Watch, 1899 and 1901; and (2) in command of No. 9 Armoured Train, 1901-1902. Took part in advance on Kimberley, 1899, including action at Magersfontein (severely wounded). Invalided home, 1900. Promoted Lieut., 1900. Took part in operations in Orange River Colony, Nov. 1900 to Sept. 1901; operations on Zululand Frontier of Natal, Oct. 1901; and operations in Transvaal and Orange River Colony, Nov. 1901 to May 1902 (mentioned in despatches; Queen's medal, with three clasps; King's medal, with two clasps). Resumed regtl. duty, 1902. Still serving. [p. 107.]

Duff, Lieut.-Col. Charles Edward, C.B. (son of the late George Smittan Duff, and grandson of John Duff, Dunkeld). Educated at Uppingham and Cheltenham College. Gazetted 2nd Lieut. 8th (The King's Royal Irish) Hussars, 1878. Served in Afghan War, 1879-1880, with 8th Hussars, being present in action at Messina (medal). Promoted Lieut., 1881; Capt., 1885; Major, 1893. Served in South African War, (1) as Major with 8th Hussars, Feb. 1900 to March 1901; (2) as local Lieut.-Col. Comdg. 1st Scottish Horse, April to Dec. 1901; and (3) as Lieut.-Col. Comdg. 8th Hussars, Dec. 1901 to May 1902. Took part in operations in Orange Free State, Feb. to May 1900; operations in Transvaal, May to Nov. 1900, including actions near Johannesburg and Diamond Hill, and action at Belfast; operations in Eastern Transvaal, Jan. to March 1901. Took part in operations in Western Transvaal, April to Dec. 1901, as local Lieut.-Col. Comdg. 1st Scottish Horse, with mobile column commanded successively by Brig.-Gen. Dixon and Col. Kekewich, and was present in action at Moedwil—slightly wounded. Promoted Lieut.-Col. Comdg. 8th Hussars, Oct. 1901, and took part in operations in Eastern Transvaal, Dec. 1901 to May 1902, successively with mobile columns commanded by Colonels Wing, Parke, Plumer, and Maj.-Gen. Bruce Hamilton (mentioned in despatches; C.B.; Queen's medal, with five clasps; King's medal, with two clasps). Still serving. [p. 109.]

Dundas, Comdr. Colin Mackenzie (of Ochtertyre). Educated at Edinburgh Academy. Gazetted Naval Cadet, Royal Navy, 1855. Served in Russian War, 1855, as Naval Cadet in H.M.S. *Russell* in the Baltic (medal). Promoted Sub-Lieut., 1861; Lieut., 1862. Served as Senior Lieut. in H.M.S. *Dart* in operations for protection of Ada Territory (Gold Coast) from attack by hostile tribes on left bank of River Volta, 1865. Promoted Comdr., 1877. Retired, 1882. [p. 125.]

Dundas, Lieut. David George Minden (eldest son of G. W. M. Dundas, and grandson of the late Sir David Dundas of Dunira, Bart.). Gazetted 2nd Lieut. 6th (Militia) Batt. The Lancashire Fusiliers, 1898. Promoted Lieut., 1899. Gazetted 2nd Lieut. 2nd Batt. The Lancashire Fusiliers, 1901. Served in South African War, 1900-1902, (1) with 6th Batt. The Lancashire Fusiliers, 1900; and (2) with Army Transport. Took part in operations in Cape Colony, Orange River Colony, and Transvaal; severely wounded at Ventersdorp, Oct. 29, 1901 (Queen's medal, with three clasps; King's medal, with two clasps). Attached to North Staffordshire Regt. at Bombay, 1902. Transferred to Indian Army and promoted Lieut., 1903. Still serving.

Erskine, Major James Francis (yr. of Cardross). Educated at Charterhouse. Gazetted Lieut. Scots Guards, 1882. Served in Soudan Expedition, 1885, with 2nd Batt. Scots Guards, and was present in engagements at Hasheen and Tamai (medal with clasp, and Khedive's star). Appointed Adjt. 2nd Batt., 1886; A.D.C. to G.O.C. South-Eastern District, 1891-1892; Regtl. Adjt. Scots Guards 1892-1896. Promoted Capt., 1896. (Jubilee medal, 1897.) Promoted Major, 1899. Was Acting Bgde.-Maj., Bgde. of Guards,1900-1901. Served in South African War, 1901-1902, with 2nd Batt. Scots Guards, and took part in operations in Cape Colony and Orange River Colony (Queen's medal, with four clasps). Still serving.

Erskine, Capt. Seymour Elphinstone (2nd son of H. D. Erskine of Cardross). Gazetted Naval Cadet, Royal Navy, 1876. Promoted Sub-Lieut., 1882. Served with Nile Expedition, 1884-1885. Promoted Lieut., 1885. Took part in bombardment and capture of Sultan of Zanzibar's Palace, 1896 (mentioned in despatches). Served with Benin Expedition, 1897, in command of Scouts (mentioned in despatches; promoted Comdr.; medal with clasp). Served with Allied Forces in China during Boxer Rising, 1900 (medal). Promoted Capt., 1902. Appointed to H.M.S. *Warrior*, 1903. Still serving.

Ewing, Robert Leckie (son of the late Wm. Leckie Ewing of Arngomery). Educated at Edinburgh Academy and in Switzerland. Served in Indian Mutiny, 1858, attached to 84th (York and Lancaster) Regt. of Foot as guest of the officers, and took part in operations of Azamgarh Field Force under Maj.-Gen. Lugard

(medal, and letter of thanks from Government of India). [p. 131.]

Ewing, Lieut. Walter Charles Leckie (youngest son of R. Leckie Ewing, and grandson of the late Wm. Leckie Ewing of Arngomery). Gazetted 2nd Lieut. The Highland Light Infantry, 1900; promoted Lieut., 1901. Served in South African War, 1902, and took part in operations in Cape Colony (Queen's medal, with two clasps). Received Royal Humane Society's bronze medal and diploma, 1903, for attempting to save life, Orange River. Still serving. [p. 131.]

Fenton, Civil Surg. James, M.B., C.M. (of Croft Park, Craigie, Perth). Served in South African War, 1901-1902, as Civil Surg. attached to Royal Army Medical Corps, and was on duty in Natal and Transvaal (Queen's medal, with three clasps). Relinquished appointment at end of war. [p. 135.]

Ferguson, Lieut. Thomas (eldest son of Lieut.-Col. W. S. Ferguson of Friarton, Perth). Gazetted Lieut. 5th Vol. Batt. The Black Watch, 1900. Served in South African War, 1902, with 3rd Vol. Service Coy., attached to 2nd Batt. The Black Watch (Royal Highlanders). Took part in operations in Orange River Colony (Queen's medal, with three clasps). Still serving in 5th Vol. Batt. The Black Watch. [p. 131.]

Fitzmaurice, Capt. Lord Charles George Francis (2nd son of Henry, 5th Marquess of Lansdowne (Baron Nairne)). Gazetted Lieut. 3rd (Militia) Batt. The Royal Scots (Lothian Regt.), 1893. Gazetted 2nd Lieut. 1st (Royal) Dragoons,1895; promoted Lieut., 1898. Served in South African War, (1) with Royal Dragoons, 1899-1900; and (2) on Headquarters Staff, 1900. Took part in relief of Ladysmith, including action at Colenso; operations of Jan. 17-24, 1900, and action at Spion Kop; operations of Feb. 5-7, 1900, and action at Vaalkranz; operations on Tugela Heights, Feb. 14-27, 1900, and action at Pieter's Hill. Took part also in operations in Natal, March 1900, and in Orange Free State, May 1900. Invalided home, 1900 (Queen's medal, with four clasps). Appointed A.D.C. to F.-M. Earl Roberts, and promoted Capt., 1901. Still serving. [p. 109.]

Fleming, Lieut. Hamilton (2nd son of the late Rev. Archibald Fleming of Inchyra). Enlisted in South African Light Horse, 1900. Promoted successively Sergt., 2nd Lieut., and

Lieut., 1900. Served in South African War, 1900–1902, with South African Light Horse, and took part in relief of Ladysmith, including operations of Jan. 17–24, 1900, and action at Spion Kop; operations of Feb. 5–7, 1900, and action at Vaalkranz; operations on Tugela Heights, Feb. 14–27, 1900, and action at Pieter's Hill. Took part also in subsequent operations in Natal, 1900, including action near Laing's Nek; operations in Transvaal, 1900, including action at Belfast; and subsequent operations in Orange River Colony and Cape Colony. Severely wounded at Murraysburg, Jan. 1901 (Queen's medal, with six clasps; King's medal, with two clasps). Relinquished appointment at end of war. Formerly an officer in Queen's Rifle Vol. Bgde. [p. 133.]

Gloag, Lieut. Matthew William (son of Matthew Gloag of St. Albans, Perth). Educated at U.S. College, Westward Ho! and St. Peter's College, Westminster. Gazetted Lieut. 31st Batt. I.Y. (Fincastle's Horse), 1902, and appointed Regtl. Signalling Officer. Served in South African War, 1902, with 31st Batt. I.Y., and took part in operations in Cape Colony (medal, with two clasps). Retired, 1902. Now Lieut. 4th Vol. Batt. The Black Watch. [p. 133.]

Græme, Capt. David Henry (2nd son of Lieut.-Col. L. A. M. Græme, and great-grandson of Col. George Græme of Inchbrakie). Educated at Fettes College. Gazetted 2nd Lieut. 4th (Militia) Batt. The Sherwood Foresters (Derbyshire Regt.), 1893. Gazetted 2nd Lieut. Seaforth Highlanders (Ross-shire Buffs, The Duke of Albany's), 1895. Served in occupation of Crete, 1897. Promoted Lieut., 1898. Served in Soudan Campaign under Sir Herbert Kitchener, 1898, with 1st Batt. Seaforth Highlanders, and was present at battle of Khartoum (British medal, and Khedive's medal with clasp). Promoted Capt., 1901. Served in South African War, 1901–1902, with 18th Batt. Mtd. Infy., and took part in operations in Eastern Transvaal, successively with Col. Parke's, Col. Benson's, and Maj.-Gen. Bruce Hamilton's mobile columns (Queen's medal, with five clasps). Resumed regtl. duty, 1902. Still serving. [p. 113.]

Græme, Hon. Lieut.-Col. Lawrence Anthony Murray (son of the late Major L. Græme, Lieut.-Governor of Tobago, and grandson of Col. George Græme, of Inchbrakie). Educated at Royal Military College, Addiscombe. Gazetted

Ensign Royal Madras Fusiliers (now The Royal Dublin Fusiliers), 1853. Took part in suppression of insurrection in lower part of Bassein River, 1854 (medal, with clasp for Pegu). Promoted Lieut., 1856. Served in Indian Mutiny, 1857–1858, including actions of Mungarwar and the Alambagh under Maj.-Gen. Havelock; defence of the Alambagh, Sept. to Nov. 1857; relief of Lucknow by Sir Colin Campbell; subsequent defence of the Alambagh under Sir James Outram; capture of Lucknow by Sir Colin Campbell; and campaign of 1858 in Oudh (medal with two clasps, and a year's service for Lucknow). Promoted Capt., 1862. Served in Abyssinian Expedition, 1868, in command of Division of Transport Train (mentioned in despatches; brevet of Major, and medal). Promoted Major and Hon. Lieut.-Col., 1875. Retired, 1875. [p. 113.]

Græme, Capt. Laurence Oliphant (eldest son of Lieut.-Col. L. A. M. Græme, and great-grandson of Col. George Græme of Inchbrakie). Educated at Charterhouse and Royal Military College, Sandhurst. Gazetted 2nd Lieut. The Queen's Own Cameron Highlanders, 1892. Promoted Lieut., 1894; Capt., 1898. Adjt. 2nd Batt. Cameron Highlanders, 1897–1901. Served in South African War, (1) with 15th Batt. Mtd. Infy., June to Sept. 1901; and (2) as Adjt. 12th Batt. Mtd. Infy., Sept. 1901 to May 1902. Took part in operations in Orange River Colony and Transvaal, successively with Maj.-Gen. Sir H. Rawlinson's and Col. Dawkins' mobile columns (Queen's medal, with four clasps). Resumed regtl. duty, 1902. Gazetted Adjt. 1st Scottish Horse (I.Y.), 1903. Still serving. [p. 113.]

Græme, Col. Robert Charles (eldest surviving son of the late Henry S. Græme; great-grandson and direct representative of David Græme of Orchill). Educated at Wimbledon. Gazetted Ensign 51st (2nd Yorkshire, West Riding, The King's Own Light Infy.) Regt. (now 1st Batt. The King's Own Yorkshire Light Infy.), 1862. Served with 51st Light Infy. in campaign on North-West Frontier of India (Ambela), 1863. Promoted Lieut., 1867; Capt., 1871. Served with Jowaki-Afridi expedition, 1877 (medal, with clasp). Served also in Afghan War, 1878–1879, with 51st Light Infy., being present at attack and capture of Ali Musjid (mentioned in despatches; medal, with clasp). Promoted Major, 1881; Lt.-Col. Comdg. 2nd Batt. Yorkshire Light Infy., 1887. Half-pay, 1891. Promoted Col., 1893. Comdg. Ashton

Regtl. District, 1893–1898. Col. half-pay Regtl. District, 1898. Retired, 1900. [p. 113.]

Graham, Lient. James, Marquess of (eldest son of Ronald, 5th Duke of Montrose). Educated at Eton College. Served in South African War, (1) as Assistant Press Censor at Capetown, 1899–1900; (2) attached with temporary rank of Lieut. to 27th Coy. Army Service Corps, 1900; and (3) attached with temporary rank of Lieut. to Naval Bgde. landed from H.M.S. *Doris*, 1900. Took part in operations in Orange Free State and Transvaal under Lieut.-Gen. Sir A. Hunter, 1900 (Queen's medal, with three clasps). Formerly Lieut. 5th Vol. Batt. The Black Watch. Gazetted Lieut. Comdg. Clyde Divn. Royal Naval Vol. Reserve, 1903. Still serving. [p. 113.]

Grant, Capt. John Patrick (of Kilgraston). Gazetted 2nd Lieut. Seaforth Highlanders (Ross-shire Buffs, The Duke of Albany's), 1892. Promoted Lieut., 1895. Served with Chitral Relief Force, under Sir Robert Low, 1895, with 2nd Batt. Seaforth Highlanders, and was present in engagement at Mamugai (medal, with clasp). Promoted Capt., 1899. Served in South African War, 1899–1902, with 2nd Batt. Seaforth Highlanders, and took part in advance on Kimberley, 1899–1900, including action at Magersfontein, and in operations in Orange Free State, Feb. to May 1900, including operations at Paardeberg (severely wounded). Took part in operations in Orange River Colony, May 1900 to Jan. 1901, and Jan. to March 1902; and in operations in Cape Colony and Transvaal, Feb. 1901 to May 1902 (twice mentioned in despatches; Queen's medal, with three clasps; King's medal, with two clasps). Still serving. [p. 123.]

Hamilton, Lieut. Arthur Buchanan Baillie-(3rd son of J. B. and Mrs. Buchanan Baillie-Hamilton of Arnprior and Cambusmore). Educated at Winchester College. Formerly in Mtd. Infy. Coy. Queen's Rifle Vol. Bgde. Enlisted in City Imperial Volunteers, 1900. Served in South African War with C.I.V., 1900. Took part in operations in Cape Colony and Orange Free State, 1900, and in Transvaal, May to Nov. 1900, including actions near Johannesburg and Diamond Hill, and action at Belfast (Queen's medal, with five clasps). Discharged, 1900. Gazetted 2nd Lieut. Seaforth Highlanders (Ross-shire Buffs, The Duke of Albany's), 1901. Seconded 1902 for service as Lieut. with 1st Northern Nigerian Regt. West African

Field Force. Served with Kano and Sokoto Expedition, 1903. Still serving. [p. 107.]

Hamilton, Lieut. Neil Alexander Buchanan Baillie- (5th son of J. B. and Mrs. Buchanan Baillie-Hamilton of Arnprior and Cambusmore). Educated at Trinity College, Glenalmond, and Royal Military College, Sandhurst. Gazetted 2nd Lieut. The Black Watch (Royal Highlanders), 1900. Served in South African War, (1) with 2nd Batt. The Black Watch, 1900, and (2) with 22nd Mtd. Infy., 1901–1902. Took part in operations in Orange Free State, Feb. to May 1900. Invalided home, 1900. Promoted Lieut., 1901. Took part in operations in Cape Colony, May 1901, and in Orange River Colony and Transvaal, 1901–1902 (Queen's medal, with three clasps; King's medal, with two clasps). Still serving. [p. 107.]

Harris, Lieut. Henry Hay Marshall (yr. of Glenalmond). Educated at Marlborough College and Royal Military College, Sandhurst. Gazetted 2nd Lieut. The Highland Light Infy., 1898. Served in occupation of Crete, 1898, with 1st Batt. H.L.I., and was present at affair of Sept. 6. Served in South African War, (1) with 1st Batt. H.L.I., 1899–1901, and (2) as Staff Officer to Comdt. at Jamestown, 1901–1902. Took part in advance on Kimberley, including actions at Modder River and Magersfontein ; and in operations in Orange Free State, Feb. to May 1900 (Queen's medal, with two clasps ; King's medal, with two clasps). Promoted Lieut., 1900. Resumed regtl. duty, 1902. Still serving. [p. 119.]

Harris, Col. Thomas Marshall (of Glenalmond). Educated at Royal Military College, Addiscombe. Gazetted 2nd Lieut. Bombay Artillery (now Royal Artillery), 1847. Promoted Lieut., 1852. Served with Persian Expedition, 1856–1857, including storming and capture of Reshire, surrender of Bushire, and bombardment of Mohamrah (medal, with clasp). Served in Indian Mutiny, 1858, including siege and capture of Kotah and pursuit, second capture of Chundari, action of Kotahkeserai and pursuit, capture of Gwalior (mentioned in despatches), bombardment and capture of Puri, actions of Sindwa and Kurai, and surprise and pursuit of rebels at Kundri—severely wounded (medal, with clasp). Promoted Capt., 1858; Major and Lieut.-Col., 1872. A.A.G. for Artillery, Bombay Command, 1872–1877; brevet of Col., and Col., 1877; Col. on Staff, Comdg. Artillery at Gibraltar, 1879–1882. Retired, 1882. [p. 119.]

Hay, Major and Brevet-Lieut.-Col. James Adam Gordon Richardson Drummond-, D.S.O. (of Aberargie; yr. of Seggieden). Gazetted Lieut. Coldstream Guards, 1884. Served in Soudan Expedition, 1885, with 1st Batt. Coldstream Guards, and was present in engagement at Hasheen, attack on convoy and engagement at Tamai (medal with clasp, and Khedive's star). Promoted Capt., 1895; Major, 1899 (Jubilee medal, 1897). Served in South African War, 1899-1902, with 1st Batt. Coldstream Guards, and took part in advance on Kimberley, 1899–1900, including actions at Belmont, Enslin, Modder River, and Magersfontein; operations in Orange Free State, Feb. to May 1900, including actions at Poplar Grove and Driefontein; and operations in Transvaal, May to Oct. 1900, including actions near Johannesburg and Diamond Hill, and action at Belfast. Took part in subsequent operations in Cape Colony, and commanded 1st Batt. Coldstream Guards, Feb. to April 1901 (brevet of Lieut.-Col.; D.S.O.; Queen's medal, with six clasps; King's medal, with two clasps). Still serving. [p. 111.]

Kerry, Capt. Henry William Edmund, Earl of, D.S.O. (eldest son of Henry, 5th Marquess of Lansdowne (Baron Nairne)). Gazetted 2nd Lieut. Grenadier Guards, 1895. Promoted Lieut., 1898. Served in South African War, (1) with 3rd Batt. Grenadier Guards, Nov. 1899 to Feb. 1900; and (2) as A.D.C. on Headquarters Staff, Feb. to Nov. 1900. Took part in advance on Kimberley, 1899–1900, including actions at Belmont, Enslin, Modder River, and Magersfontein; operations in Orange Free State, Feb. to May 1900, including operations at Paardeberg and actions at Poplar Grove and Driefontein; operations in Transvaal, May to Nov. 1900, including actions near Johannesburg and Diamond Hill, and action near Belfast (mentioned in despatches; D.S.O.; Queen's medal, with seven clasps). Transferred to Irish Guards and promoted Capt., 1900. Still serving. [p. 109.]

Kidd, Capt. William Stewart (of Tighnaleigh, Alyth). Gazetted Surg.-Capt. Scottish Horse, 1901. Served in South African War, 1901–1902, with 1st Scottish Horse. Took part in operations in Western Transvaal, Aug. 1901 to May 1902, with Col. Kekewich's column, and

was present in action at Moedwil (severely wounded) and Rooiwal (mentioned in despatches; Queen's medal, with five clasps). Presented with address by fellow-passengers for gallantry in attending wounded under fire during attack on train at Gauna Bridge, Cape Colony, July 20, 1901. Relinquished commission at end of war. Gazetted Capt. Scottish Horse (I.Y.), 1903. Still serving. [p. 127.]

Kinnoull, Archibald FitzRoy George, 12th Earl of. Gazetted Lieut. 42nd (Royal Highland—The Black Watch) (now 1st Batt. The Black Watch (Royal Highlanders)), 1875. Half-pay, 1882. Appointed to Egyptian Army and Gendarmerie, 1883. Served in Soudan Expedition, 1884, with local rank of Col., as Staff Officer to Baker Pasha, and was present in engagements at El-Teb and Tamai (mentioned in despatches; medal with clasp, and Khedive's star; 3rd Class of Osmanieh). Retired, 1886. [p. 123.]

Macdonald, Lieut.-Gen. Alastair McIan (formerly of Dalchosnie and Dunalastair; eldest son of the late Lieut.-Gen. Sir John Macdonald of Dalchosnie, G.C.B.). Gazetted Ensign 92nd (Highland) Regt. of Foot (now 2nd Batt. The Gordon Highlanders), 1846. Promoted Lieut., 1847. A.D.C. to his father, 1848–1854. Served in Crimea, 1854, during Russian War, as A.D.C. to Gen. Pennefather, and took part in battles of the Alma (severely wounded) and Inkerman (severely wounded), and siege of Sevastopol (medal, with three clasps; brevet of Major; 5th Class of Medjidie and Turkish medal). Invalided home. Promoted Major, 1854. Placed on half-pay, 1855. Appointed to Depôt Batt., 1856. Promoted Lieut.-Col. Comdg. 7th Depôt Batt., 1860; Col., 1865. Appointed A.A.G. at Dover, 1870; A.D.C. to H.R.H. the Duke of Cambridge, 1874. Promoted Maj.-Gen., 1877 (antedated to 1870). G.O.C. Scotland, 1881–1885. Promoted Lieut.-Gen., 1885. Retired, 1890. [p. 123.]

McGillewie, Lieut. Patrick (eldest son of the late Donald McGillewie, Pitlochry). Became a burgher of the Transvaal, 1865, and served under Paul Kruger in Boer Commando to help the Orange Free State in a war against Basutos. Served in Boer Commando under President Burgess in campaign against Sekúkúni, 1874. After annexation of the Transvaal by Great Britain, served with Ferreira's Horse in campaign against Sekúkúni, 1878. Served with

Remounts Dept. in Zulu War, 1878, and again in campaign against Sekükûni, 1878, with Border Light Horse under Major Carrington. Left the Transvaal, 1880. Raised No. 1 Troop Queenstown Vol. Mtd. Infy., 1896, and gazetted Lieut. Resigned on account of ill-health, 1899. Served in South African War, 1899-1902, with Queenstown Town Guard. [p. 133.]

MacGregor, Major Charles Frederick Murray (son of the late Gen. Evan Murray MacGregor, and great-grandson of Col. Alex. MacGregor Murray of Napier Ruskie). Educated at Clifton College and Royal Military College, Sandhurst. Served in Zulu War, 1879, and was present in engagement at Gingunhlovo (medal). Served in Bechuanaland Expedition, 1884-1885, under Sir Chas. Warren (medal). Served also in South African War, 1899-1900, as Major, Cape Police, No. 2 Divn., and took part in defence of Kimberley (Queen's medal with two clasps, and star). [p. 129.]

MacGregor, Lieut. Kenneth Murray (eldest son of Major C. F. Murray MacGregor, and great-great-grandson of Col. Alex. MacGregor Murray of Napier Ruskie). Appointed Lieut. Prince Alfred's Guard. Served in South African War with Prince Alfred's Guard, 1900-1902, and took part in operations in Orange Free State, including defence of Wepener, and in subsequent operations in Northern Transvaal (Queen's medal, with three clasps; King's medal, with two clasps). Relinquished appointment at end of war. [p. 129.]

MacGregor, Civil Surg. Thomas (2nd son of the late Duncan MacGregor, Balquhidder). Served in South African War, 1901-1902, as Civil Surg. attached to Royal Army Medical Corps, and was on duty in Cape Colony, Orange River Colony, and Transvaal (Queen's medal, with five clasps). Resigned appointment, 1902. [p. 135.]

Macpherson, Capt. and Brevet Major George Denis (4th son of the late Allan Macpherson of Blairgowrie). Educated at Winchester College and Royal Military College, Sandhurst. Gazetted Lieut. The Royal Munster Fusiliers, 1882. Promoted Capt., 1892. Served in South African War, 1899-1900, with 1st Batt. Munster Fusiliers, and took part in advance on Kimberley, 1899-1900, including actions at Belmont, Enslin, Modder River, and Magersfontein ; also in subsequent operations in Cape Colony, and Orange River Colony, May to Nov. 1900, including

actions at Lindley and Bethlehem—dangerously wounded (mentioned in despatches ; brevet of Major ; Queen's medal, with three clasps). Still serving. [p. 115.]

McVean, Vet. Surg. Hugh Fraser, M.R.C.V.S. (eldest son of the late John McVean, Tyndrum). Served in South African War, 1900-1901, as Vet. Surg. attached to Army Vet. Dept. with temporary rank of Vet. Lieut. :—(1) Was on duty at Kroonstad Vet. Hospital, 1900 ; (2) took part in operations in Orange River Colony, 1900-1901, with Lieut.-Col. Williams's mobile column ; and (3) was on duty at Vet. Hospital, Germiston, 1901 (Queen's medal, with four clasps). Resigned appointment, 1902. [p. 135.]

Marshall, Capt. Francis James (of Duncrievie). Gazetted 2nd Lieut. Seaforth Highlanders (Ross-shire Buffs, The Duke of Albany's), 1895. Served in occupation of Crete, 1897. Promoted Lieut., 1897. Served in Soudan Campaign under Sir Herbert Kitchener, 1898, with 1st Batt. Seaforth Highlanders, and was present at battles of the Atbara and Khartoum (British medal, and Khedive's medal with two clasps). Promoted Capt., 1901. Served in South African War, (1) as Adjt. 18th Batt. Mtd. Infy., Feb. to Nov. 1901 ; and (2) as Assistant Staff Officer with Col. Mackenzie's mobile column, Nov. 1901 to May 1902. Took part in operations in Cape Colony, Orange River Colony, and Transvaal (Queen's medal, with five clasps). Resumed regtl. duty, 1902. Still serving.

Menzies, Capt. Sir Neil James, Bart. (of Menzies). Educated at Harrow School. Gazetted Ensign and Lieut. Scots Fusilier Guards (now Scots Guards), 1874. Promoted Lieut., 1876. Served in Soudan Expedition, 1885, with 2nd Batt. Scots Guards, and was present in engagements at Hasheen and Tamai (medal with clasp, and Khedive's star). During latter part of expedition commanded company of Guards in Major James's Camel Corps. Promoted Capt., 1887. Retired, 1892. [p. 111.]

Mercer, Major William Lindsay (of Huntingtower). Gazetted 2nd Lieut. The Princess of Wales' Own (Yorkshire Regt.), 1881. Promoted Lieut., 1881. Served in Nile Expedition, 1884-1885, with 1st Batt. Yorks. Regt., on Lines of Communication up the Nile. Served with Soudan Frontier Field Force, 1885-1886, in operations on Upper Nile, in command of a division of machine guns, and was present in engagement at Giniss (medal, and Khedive's star). Promoted Capt., 1891. Retired, 1898. As Capt. in Reserve of Officers commanded details of Yorks. Regt. 1900-1902, during South African War. Promoted Major, 1902. [p. 119.]

Moncreiffe, Lieut. John Alexander (8th son of the late Sir Thos. Moncreiffe of Moncreiffe, 7th Bart.). Educated at Harrow School. Enlisted in 5th (Warwickshire) Coy. I.Y., 1900. Promoted Corpl., Sergt., and Lieut., 1900. Served in South African War, (1) with 5th Coy. I.Y., 1900; and (2) with 26th Batt. I.Y., 1902. Took part in operations in Cape Colony, 1900, including engagement at Kheis Drift—severely wounded (mentioned in despatches; Distinguished Conduct Medal). Invalided home, 1900. Appointed Lieut. 26th Batt. I.Y. (Younghusband's Horse), 1902, and took part in operations in Cape Colony, 1902 (Queen's medal, with two clasps). Relinquished commission at end of war. [p. 125.]

Moncreiffe, Midshipman John Robert Guy (eldest son of the late T. G. H. Moncreiffe, and grandson of Sir Thos. Moncreiffe of Moncreiffe, 7th Bart.). Educated at Cheam School and on H.M.S. *Britannia*. Gazetted Naval Cadet and Midshipman, Royal Navy, 1900. Took part in Blockade of Venezuela, 1902-1903, in H.M.S. *Charybdis* and H.M.S. *Columbine*. Still serving. [p. 125.]

Moncreiffe, Capt. Ronald (5th son of the late Sir Thos. Moncreiffe of Moncreiffe, 7th Bart.). Gazetted 2nd Lieut. Worcestershire Yeo. Cav. (now I.Y.), 1887. Promoted Lieut., 1891; Capt., 1895. Served in Matabele Campaign, 1896, on Col. Plumer's Staff (medal). Served also in South African War, 1899-1900, on Col. Baden-Powell's Staff, and took part in defence of Mafeking. Invalided home, 1900 (Queen's medal, with clasp). Still serving in Worcestershire I.Y. [p. 125.]

Moncrieff, Lieut. Alaric Rimmington (3rd son of Col. Sir Alex. Moncrieff, K.C.B., of Bandirran). Educated at Winchester College and Royal Military College, Sandhurst. Gazetted 2nd Lieut. Seaforth Highlanders (Rossshire Buffs, The Duke of Albany's), 1899. Promoted Lieut. 1900. Served in South African War, 1900-1902, with 2nd Batt. Seaforth Highlanders, and took part in advance on Kimberley; operations in Orange Free State, Feb. to May 1900, including operations at Paardeberg (severely wounded); operations in Orange River Colony, May to Nov. 1900, and subse-

quent operations in Transvaal (Queen's medal, with three clasps; King's medal, with two clasps). Transferred to 2nd Dragoons (Royal Scots Greys), 1902. Still serving. [p. 125.]

Moncrieff, Capt. and Brevet-Major Malcolm Matthew (yr. of Bandirran). Educated at Winchester College, at Oxford Military College, and at Royal Military College, Sandhurst. Gazetted 2nd Lieut. 6th Dragoon Guards (Carabiniers), 1896. Promoted Lieut., 1897. Served in South African War with 6th Dragoon Guards, (1) 1899-1900, and (2) 1901-1902. Took part in operations in Cape Colony, 1899-1900, including actions at Colesberg and relief of Kimberley; operations in Orange Free State, Feb. to May 1900, including actions at Karree Siding and Zand River—severely wounded. Invalided home, 1900. Took part in operations in Transvaal, 1901-1902 (brevet of Major; Queen's medal, with three clasps; King's medal, with two clasps). Still serving. [p. 125.]

Moncrieff, Major William Scott (of Fossoway Lodge). Educated at Edinburgh Academy and Royal Military College, Sandhurst. Gazetted 2nd Lieut. 57th (West Middlesex) Regt. of Foot (now 1st Batt. The Duke of Cambridge's Own (Middlesex Regt.)), 1878. Served in Zulu War, 1879, with 57th Regt., being present in action at Ghingunlovu, the relief of Eshowe, and throughout operations of "Clarke's Column" (medal, with clasp). Promoted Lieut., 1880; Capt., 1885; Major, 1896. Served in South African War, 1899-1900, with 2nd Batt. Middlesex Regt. and took part in relief of Ladysmith, including operations of Jan. 17 to 24, 1900, and action at Spion Kop—severely wounded. Invalided home, 1900 (mentioned in despatches; Queen's medal, with clasp). Appointed 2nd-in-command 1st Batt. Middlesex Regt., 1901. Still serving. [p. 125.]

Montrose, Lieut.-Col. Douglas Beresford Malise Ronald, 5th Duke of, K.T., A.D.C. Gazetted Lieut. 5th (Royal Irish) Regt. of Lancers, 1874. Retired 1877, and appointed A.D.C. to G.O.C. South District. Gazetted Lieut.-Col. Comdg. 3rd (Militia) Batt. Argyll and Sutherland Highlanders, 1881; Hon. Col., 1892; Militia A.D.C. to Queen Victoria, and Col., 1897; A.D.C. to King Edward VII., 1901. Served in South African War, 1902, as Lieut.-Col. Comdg. 3rd Batt. A. and S. H., and took part in operations in Cape Colony (Queen's medal, with two clasps). Retired, 1902. [p. 113.]

Moray, Capt. William Home Drummond (of Abercairny). Educated at Eton College. Gazetted Ensign and Lieut. Scots Fusilier Guards (now Scots Guards), 1871. Served in Soudan Expedition, 1885, with 2nd Batt. Scots Guards, and was present in engagements at Hasheen and Tamai (medal with clasp, and Khedive's star). Promoted Capt., 1885. Retired, 1887. [p. 105.]

Murdoch, Lieut. Catesby Burn- (youngest son of John Burn-Murdoch of Gartincaber). Educated at Loretto College. Gazetted Lieut. Lovat's Scouts, 1901. Served in South African War, 1901-1902, with Lovat's Scouts, and took part in operations in Cape Colony and Orange River Colony (Queen's medal, with four clasps). Relinquished commission at end of war. [p. 121.]

Murdoch, Rev. James McGibbon Burn-, M.A., of Greenyards and New Lodge (4th son of the late John Burn-Murdoch of Gartincaber). Educated at Edinburgh Academy and Downing College, Cambridge. Gazetted Cornet 3rd (The Prince of Wales's) Regt. of Dragoon Guards, 1851. Exchanged to 10th (The Prince of Wales's Own) Royal Regt. of (Light) Dragoons, now 10th (The Prince of Wales's Own Royal) Hussars, 1852. Served in Crimea, 1855, during Russian War, with 10th Dragoons, including siege and fall of Sevastopol (medal with clasp, and Turkish medal). Exchanged to 6th Regt. of Dragoon Guards (Carabiniers), 1855. Retired, 1856. Ordained, 1861. [p. 121.] [1]

Murdoch, Brig.-Gen. and Brevet Col. John Francis Burn-, C.B. (only son of Rev. J. McGibbon Burn-Murdoch, and grandson of the late John Burn-Murdoch of Gartincaber). Educated at Eton College. Gazetted 2nd Lieut. 1st (Royal) Dragoons, 1878. Promoted Lieut., 1881. Served in Nile Expedition, 1884-1885, with Camel Corps. Commanded a Transport company in first march to Gakdul, and was present in actions at Abu Klea and El Gubat (medal with two clasps, and Khedive's star). Promoted Capt., 1st Dgns., 1885. Adjt., 1885-1888. Passed Staff College, 1889; Bgde.-Maj. under Inspector Gen. of Cavalry,Horse Gds.,1890-1891. Promoted Maj.,1892; Bgde,-Maj. Cavalry Bgde., Aldershot, 1891-1894. Commanded Egyptian Cavalry 1894-1896 (4th Class of Osmanieh). Served with Dongola Expedition under Sir Herbert

Kitchener, 1896, in command of Egyptian Cavalry, and was present in engagements at Hafir and Firket (mentioned in despatches ; brevet of Lieut.-Col. ; Khedive's medal, with two clasps). Promoted Lieut.-Col. Comdg. 1st (Royal) Dragoons, 1898. Served in South African War, (1) as Lieut.-Col. Comdg. Royal Dragoons, Nov. 1899 to Jan. 1900 ; (2) as Brig.-Gen. on Staff, in command of 1st Cavalry Bgde.,Natal, Feb. to Nov. 1900 ;and (3) as Brig.-Gen. Comdg. Newcastle Sub-District, Nov. 1900 to May 1902. Took part in relief of Ladysmith, including action at Colenso; operations of Jan. 17 to 24, 1900, and action at Spion Kop ; operations of Feb. 5 to 7, 1900, and action at Vaal Kranz ; operations on Tugela Heights, Feb. 14 to 27, 1900, and action at Pieter's Hill. Took part also in operations in Natal, March to June 1900, and in operations in Eastern Transvaal, Feb. and March 1901 (six times mentioned in despatches ; C.B. and brevet of Col. ; Queen's medal, with five clasps ; King's medal, with two clasps). Still serving, in command of Standerton District, Transvaal. [p. 121.]

Murdoch, Major Paul Robert Burn-, of Neuck (son of the late Rev. J. A. H. Burn - Murdoch, and grandson of John Burn - Murdoch of Gartincaber). Gazetted Lieut. Corps of Royal Engineers, 1878. Promoted Capt., 1888. For five years Experimental Officer at Pembroke Dock, and subsequently Assistant Inspector of Submarine Defences at War Office. Promoted Major, 1896. Served in South African War, 1900-1902, in command of 47th Coy. R.E., and took part in operations round Arundel, Feb. 1900 ; advance to and crossing of Orange River ; march to Bloemfontein under Maj.-Gen. Clements ; operations near Dewetsdorp, and Engineer duty on Lines of Communication (twice mentioned in despatches ; Queen's medal, with three clasps ; King's medal, with two clasps). Still serving. [p. 121.]

Murray,[2] Brevet Lieut.-Col. the Honble. Andrew David (2nd son of the late William, Viscount Stormont, and grandson of William, 4th Earl of Mansfield). Born, 1863. Educated at Wellington College. Gazetted Lieut. The Queen's Own Cameron Highlanders,1884. Served during latter part of Nile Expedition, 1885, with Cameron Highlanders (medal with clasp, and

---

[1] Died March 23, 1904.   [2] See biographical notice, pp. 99, 100.

Khedive's star). Served throughout operations of Soudan Frontier Field Force, 1885-1886, with Cameron Highlanders, being present at Kosheh during its investment, and in engagement at Giniss. Promoted Capt., 1893. Served in Soudan Campaign under Sir Herbert Kitchener, 1898, with 1st Batt. Cameron Highlanders, and was present at battles of the Atbara (mentioned in despatches) and Khartoum (mentioned in despatches); took part also in subsequent operations on the Nile above Khartoum, Sept. and Oct. 1898 (mentioned in despatches; brevet of Major; British medal, and Khedive's medal with two clasps). Served in South African War, 1900-1901, as Officer Comdg. Lovat's Scouts, and took part in operations in Orange Free State, April and May 1900; operations in Transvaal, May and June 1900, including actions near Johannesburg, Pretoria, and Diamond Hill; and operations in Orange River Colony, July to Nov. 1900, including action at Wittebergen, where he was in command of Mounted Forces of Highland Bgde. (brevet of Lieut.-Col.). In command of a mobile column took part in operations in Cape Colony and Orange River Colony, Nov. 1900 to Sept. 1901. Killed in attack on camp at Quaggafontein, Sept. 20, 1901 (Queen's medal, with four clasps). [p. 105.]

Murray, 2nd Lieut. Charles John (3rd son of C. A. Murray, Taymount, Stanley). Gazetted 2nd Lieut. Coldstream Guards, 1901. Served in South African War, May 1902, and took part in operations in Cape Colony (Queen's medal, with two clasps). Still serving. [p. 105.]

Murray, Capt. the Honble. Edward Oliphant (2nd son of Montolieu, 10th Baron Elibank). Born, 1871. Gazetted 2nd Lieut. The Queen's Own Cameron Highlanders, 1892. Promoted Lieut., 1893; Capt., 1898. A.D.C. to G.O.C. Forces in Egypt, 1898-1899; A.D.C. to G.O.C. Infy. Bgde., Gibraltar, 1899-1900. Appointed Adjt. Lovat's Scouts, 1901. Served in South African War, 1901, with Lovat's Scouts, and took part in operations in Cape Colony and Orange River Colony. Killed in attack on camp at Quaggafontein, Sept. 20, 1901 (Queen's medal, with three clasps). [p. 105.]

Murray, Capt. Lord George Stewart (2nd surviving son of John, 7th Duke of Atholl). Educated at Farnborough School and Eton College. Gazetted 2nd Lieut. 3rd (Militia) Batt. The Black Watch (Royal Highlanders),

1891. Promoted Lieut., 1892. Gazetted 2nd Lieut. 1st Batt. The Black Watch, 1894. Promoted Lieut., 1898. Served in South African War, (1) attached to 2nd Batt. The Gordon Highlanders, 1899-1900; (2) with 2nd Batt. Black Watch, 1900; (3) as A.D.C. to Sir Henry Colvile, 1900; and (4) as Adjt. 1st Scottish Horse, 1901-1902. Took part in operations in Natal, 1899, including actions at Elandslaagte and Lombard's Kop; defence of Ladysmith, 1899-1900, including action of Jan. 6, 1900; and operations in Orange Free State, April to June 1900. Took part also in operations in Western Transvaal, 1901-1902, with Col. Kekewich's mobile column, including action at Rooiwal (mentioned in despatches; Queen's medal, with five clasps; King's medal, with two clasps). Promoted Capt. The Black Watch, 1901. Resumed regtl. duty, 1902. Appointed A.D.C. to Sir A. Hunter, G.O.C. Scottish District (now G.O.C. Bombay District), 1903. Still serving. [p. 105.]

Murray, Lieut. Lord James Thomas Stewart (3rd surviving son of John, 7th Duke of Atholl). Educated at Farnborough School and Eton College. Gazetted 2nd Lieut. 3rd (Militia) Batt. The Black Watch (Royal Highlanders), 1897. Promoted Lieut., 1899. Gazetted 2nd Lieut. The Queen's Own Cameron Highlanders, 1900. Served in South African War, (1) with 1st Batt. Cameron Highlanders, 1900-1901, and (2) attached to 2nd Scottish Horse, 1901-1902. Took part in operations in Orange Free State, Feb. to May 1900; in Transvaal, May to June 1900, including actions near Johannesburg, Pretoria, and Diamond Hill; operations in Orange River Colony, May 1900 to Jan. 1901, including actions at Wittebergen and Ladybrand; and operations in Eastern Transvaal, Jan. to April 1901, including action at Lake Chrissie. Took part also in operations in Eastern and Western Transvaal, Nov. 1901 to May 1902, with Col. Mackenzie's and Col. Kekewich's mobile columns respectively, including action at Rooiwal (Queen's medal, with four clasps; King's medal, with two clasps). Promoted Lieut. Cameron Highlanders, 1901. Resumed regtl. duty, 1902. Still serving. [p. 105.]

Nason, Brevet Col. Fortescue John, D.S.O. (St. Jerome's, Dunkeld; grandson of the late Chas. A. Williamson of Balgray and Lawers). Gazetted 2nd Lieut. 26th (The Cameronians) (now 1st Batt. The Cameronians (Scottish

Rifles)), 1880. Promoted Lieut., 1881 ; Capt., 1889. Served in operations in Soudan, 1889, with Mtd. Infy., and was present in engagements at Arguin (wounded), and Toski (medal with clasp ; 4th Class of Medjidie, and Khedive's star). Served with Dongola Expedition under Sir Herbert Kitchener, 1896, as Bgde.-Major 1st Bgde., and took part in operations of June 7 and Sept. 19 (mentioned in despatches ; Khedive's medal, with two clasps). Took part also in operations of 1897 (clasp). Promoted Major, 1897. Served with Egyptian Army in Soudan Campaign, under Sir Herbert Kitchener, 1898, and was present at battles of the Atbara and Khartoum (mentioned in despatches), and defeat of Ahmed Fedil's army (mentioned in despatches ; brevet of Lieut.-Col. ; D.S.O. ; British medal, and three clasps to Khedive's medal). Served with Nile Expedition, 1899, in first advance against the Khalifa (3rd Class of Osmanieh ; clasp to Khedive's medal). Promoted Col., 1900. Appointed Governor of Berber and placed on half-pay, 1901. Now Civil Secretary to Governor-General of Soudan. [p. 121.]

Nason, Major Henry Hyde Williamson, D.S.O. (St. Jerome's, Dunkeld ; grandson of the late Chas. A. Williamson of Balgray and Lawers). Gazetted 2nd Lieut. 44th (The East Essex) (now 1st Batt. The Essex Regt.), 1878. Promoted Lieut., 1880 ; Capt., 1884 ; Major, 1895. Served in South African War with 1st Batt. Essex Regt., 1899-1902, and took part in operations in Cape Colony, 1899-1900, including actions at Colesberg ; relief of Kimberley, and operations in Orange Free State, Feb. to May 1900, including operations at Paardeberg, and actions at Poplar Grove, Driefontein, Vet River and Zand River ; operations in Transvaal, May to Nov. 1900, including actions near Johannesburg, Pretoria, and Diamond Hill, and actions at Belfast. Took part also in operations in Transvaal, April and May 1902 (twice mentioned in despatches; D.S.O.; Queen's medal, with six clasps ; King's medal, with clasp). Still serving. [p. 121.]

Ogilvy, Capt. the Honble. Lyulph Gilchrist, D.S.O. (2nd son of David, 7th Earl of Airlie). Served with American Army in Cuba in Spanish-American War, 1898 (medal). Appointed Lieut. 2nd Regt. Brabant's Horse, 1899. Promoted Capt., 1900. Served in South African War, 1899-1900, with 2nd Regt. Brabant's Horse,

and took part in operations in Cape Colony, 1899-1900; operations in Orange River Colony, 1900, including actions at Wittebergen ; and operations in Transvaal, 1900, including actions at Belfast (D.S.O. ; Queen's medal, with three clasps). Resigned appointment, 1900. [p. 109.]

Oliphant, Major-Gen. Laurence James, C.B., C.V.O. (of Condie). Educated at Harrow School and Christchurch College, Oxford. Gazetted Ensign and Lieut. 1st (or Grenadier) Regt. of Foot Guards (now Grenadier Guards), 1866 ; Lieut. and Capt., 1869. Promoted Capt. and Lieut.-Col., 1876 ; Major, 1882. Served with Soudan Expedition, 1885 (medal with clasp, and Khedive's star). Brevet Col., 1886 ; Lieut.-Col. Comdg. 3rd Batt. Grenadier Gds., 1889; Col. Comdg. Gren. Gds. and Regtl. District, 1894 (Jubilee medal, 1897). Promoted Major-Gen. on Staff and appointed to command of Infy. Bgde., Aldershot, 1900. Served in South African War, 1901-1902, as Major-Gen. on Staff, in command of Germiston District, and in command of a section of Lines of Communication (mentioned in despatches ; C.B. ; Queen's medal, with three clasps). Appointed to command 9th Bgde. (of 5th Divn., 2nd Army Corps), and Home District, 1903. Still serving. [p. 111.]

Pullar, Lieut. Herbert S. (son of the late James Pullar, Perth). Enlisted in 20th (Fife and Forfarshire Light Horse) Company Imperial Yeomanry, 1899. Served in South African War, 1900-1901, with 20th Coy. I.Y., and took part in operations in Cape Colony, under Col. Mahon, including relief of Mafeking ; and in operations in Orange River Colony and Transvaal, with column commanded successively by Lieut.-Gen. Sir A. Hunter, Major-Gen. Clements, Col. Benson, and Col. Pilcher (Queen's medal, with four clasps). Promoted Sergt. and Lieut., 1900. Gazetted Lieut. Fife and Forfarshire Light Horse, 1901. Still serving. [p. 133.]

Raitt, Civil Surg. Oswald (3rd son of the late William Raitt of " Bu-Croft," Blairgowrie). Served in South African War, 1902, as Civil Surgeon attached (1) to Col. Doran's Column, and (2) to 17th Lancers. Took part in operations in Cape Colony (Queen's medal, with two clasps). Relinquished appointment at end of war. [p. 133.]

Ramsay, Capt. George, M.R.C.S., L.R.C.P., (eldest son of the late William Ramsay, and grandson of Sir George Ramsay of Bamff, 9th Bart.). Born, 1868. Educated at Cargilfield and Rugby Schools. Passed first into Army Medical College, 1893, and on leaving, gained gold medal for medicine. Gazetted Surg.-Lieut. Indian Medical Service, and appointed to Bengal Medical Dept., 1894. Served with Chitral Relief Force, under Sir Robert Low, 1895 (medal, with clasp). Appointed to detachment 4th Bengal Infy., 1896. Promoted Surg.-Capt., and appointed Officiating Residency Surgeon (ex officio Assistant Political Resident) at Baghdad, in Turkish Arabia, 1897. Died March 24, 1902, at Baghdad. [p. 119.]

Ramsay, Lieut. Nigel Neis (yr. of Bamff). Born, 1876. Educated at Cargilfield School, Winchester College, and Royal Military College, Sandhurst (where he gained Sword of Honour). Gazetted 2nd Lieut. The Black Watch (Royal Highlanders), 1896. Promoted Lieut., 1898. Served in South African War, 1899, with 2nd Batt. The Black Watch, and took part in advance on Kimberley. Killed in action at Magersfontein, Dec. 11, 1899 (Queen's medal, with clasp). [p. 107.]

Rattray, Capt. Andrew (5th son of the late John Rattray, Broom of Dalreoch, Dunning). Enlisted in Thorneycroft's Mtd. Infy., 1899. Served in South African War, (1) with Thorneycroft's Mtd. Infy., 1899-1900 ; (2) with Commander-in Chief's Bodyguard, 1900-1901 ; and (3) with 1st Scottish Horse, 1901-1902. Took part in relief of Ladysmith, 1899-1900, including action at Colenso (wounded); operations of Jan.17 to 24, 1900, including action at Spion Kop ; operations of Feb. 5 to 7, 1900, and action at Vaal Kranz ; operations on Tugela Heights, Feb. 14 to 27, 1900, and action at Pieter's Hill. Took part in operations in Natal, March to June 1900, including action at Laing's Nek, and in subsequent operations in Transvaal. Promoted Sergt. Thorneycroft's Mtd. Infy., 1900. Discharged, 1900. Enlisted in C.-in-C.'s Bodyguard Oct. 1900. Promoted Sergt.-Major. Discharged, 1901. Enlisted in Scottish Horse and appointed Lieut., 1901. Took part in operations in Western Transvaal, 1901-1902, with mobile column commanded successively by Brig.-Gen. Dixon and Col. Kekewich, and was present in actions at Moedwil and Rooiwal. Promoted Capt. (mentioned in despatches ; Queen's medal, with six clasps ; King's medal, with two clasps). Relinquished appointment at end of war. [p. 127.]

II.

Rattray, Lieut. David (4th son of the late John Rattray, Broom of Dalreoch, Dunning). Enlisted in Scottish Horse, 1900. Served in South African War, 1900-1902, with 1st Scottish Horse, and took part in operations in Western Transvaal, with mobile column commanded successively by Cols. Flint and Shekleton, Brig.-Gens. Cunningham and Dixon, and Col. Kekewich, and was present in actions at Moedwil (wounded) and Rooiwal. Promoted Lieut., 1901 (Queen's medal, with clasp). Relinquished appointment at end of war. [p. 127.]

Rattray, Lieut.-Gen. Sir James Clerk, K.C.B. (of Craighall). Educated at Rugby School. Gazetted Ensign 90th Regt. of Foot (Perthshire Vols.) (Light Infy.), (now 2nd Batt. The Cameronians (Scottish Rifles)), 1851. Promoted Lieut., 1854. Served with 90th Regt. in Crimea, 1854-1855, during Russian War, including siege and fall of Sevastopol ; severely wounded in assault on Redan, Sept. 8, 1855 (medal with clasp, and Turkish medal). Promoted Capt., 1855. Served in Indian Mutiny, 1857-1858, including relief and subsequent defence of Lucknow by Maj.-Gen. Havelock (twice mentioned in despatches); defence of the Alambagh by Sir James Outram, and capture of Lucknow by Sir Colin Campbell (medal with two clasps, and a year's service for Lucknow). Promoted Major, 1862 ; Lieut.-Col. Comdg.,1864; Col., 1869; C.B.,1871. Placed on half-pay, 1872. Promoted Maj.-Gen., 1879 ; Lieut.-Gen., 1881 ; K.C.B., 1897. Gazetted Col. The Cameronians (Scottish Rifles), 1899. [p. 119.]

Rattray, Capt. Peter Millar, D.S.O. (eldest son of the late John Rattray, Broom of Dalreoch, Dunning). Served as Sergt. in Mashonaland Rebellion, 1896-1897 (medal, with clasp). Joined Colonial Scouts 1899, and appointed Capt. Served in South African War, (1) with Colonial Scouts, 1899-1900, and (2) with 1st Scottish Horse, 1900-1902. Took part in relief of Ladysmith, 1900, including operations of Feb. 5 to 7, 1900, and action at Vaal Kranz ; operations on Tugela Heights, Feb. 14 to 27, 1900, and action at Pieter's Hill. Relinquished appointment with Colonial Scouts and appointed Capt. Scottish Horse, 1900. Took part in operations in Western Transvaal, 1901-1902, with mobile column commanded successively by Cols. Flint and Shekleton, Brig.-Gens. Cunningham and Dixon, and Col. Kekewich, and was present in actions at Moedwil

F

(wounded) and Rooiwal (mentioned in despatches; D.S.O.; Queen's medal, with five clasps; King's medal, with two clasps). Relinquished appointment at end of war. [p. 127.]

Richardson, Capt. Sir Edward Austin Stewart-, Bart. (of Pitfour). Educated at Rugby School. Gazetted 2d Lieut. 3rd (Militia) Batt. The Black Watch (Royal Highlanders), 1890. Promoted Lieut., 1892. Appointed A.D.C. to Governor of Queensland, 1899. Promoted Capt., 1900. Served in South African War, 1900–1901, (1) as Capt. 2nd Queensland Mtd. Infy., and (2) as 2nd Lieut. attached 2nd Batt. The Black Watch. Took part in operations in Orange Free State, Feb. to May 1900, including actions at Driefontein and Vet River; operations in Orange River Colony, including actions at Rhenoster River, Wittebergen, and Witpoort; and operations in Transvaal (Queen's medal, with four clasps). Still serving in 3rd (Militia) Batt. The Black Watch. [p. 107.]

Richardson, 2nd Lieut. Neil Graham Stewart- (3rd son of the late Sir Jas. Stewart-Richardson, Bart., of Pitfour). Gazetted 2nd Lieut. Seaforth Highlanders (Ross-shire Buffs, The Duke of Albany's), 1901. Served in South African War, 1901–1902, with 2nd Batt. Seaforth Highlanders, and took part in operations in Cape Colony, Orange River Colony, and Transvaal (Queen's medal, with five clasps). Still serving. [p. 107.]

Robertson, Civil Surg. Alistair (son of John Robertson, The Lowes, Dunkeld). Gazetted Surg.-Capt. Imperial Yeomanry, 1901. Served in South African War, 1901, as Civil Surgeon attached to Imperial Yeomanry, with temporary rank of Surg.-Capt. Was on duty at Base Depôt, Elandsfontein (Queen's medal, with two clasps). Resigned commission, 1901. Died at Kintampo, West Africa, Jan. 5, 1903. [p. 135.]

Robertson, Capt. David (son of John Robertson, The Lowes, Dunkeld). Gazetted Lieut. Scottish Horse, 1901. Served in South African War, 1901–1902, with 2nd Scottish Horse, and took part in operations in Eastern Transvaal with mobile column commanded successively by Cols. Benson and Mackenzie, and was present in action at Bakenlaagte. Promoted Capt., 1901 (mentioned in despatches; Queen's medal, with five clasps). Resigned commission, 1902. [p. 129.]

Robertson, Lieut. Duncan (eldest son of John Robertson, J.P., late factor to Duke of Atholl).

Gazetted Lieut. Scottish Horse, 1901. Served in South African War, 1901–1902, with 1st Scottish Horse, and took part in operations in Western Transvaal with mobile column commanded successively by Brig.-Gen. Dixon and Col. Kekewich. Invalided home, 1902, in consequence of accident (Queen's medal, with five clasps). Relinquished commission at end of war. [p. 127.]

Robertson, 2nd Lieut. the Honble. Hugh (younger son of Lord Robertson of Forteviot). Born, 1879. Educated at Radley and Eton Colleges. Gazetted 2nd Lieut. 3rd (Militia) Batt. The Queen's Own Cameron Highlanders, 1899. Appointed A.D.C. to Gen. Montgomery Moore at Aldershot. Seconded for duty with Army Remounts Dept. and sent out with horses to South Africa, 1900. Gazetted 2nd Lieut. 14th Hussars, 1900. Served in South African War with 14th Hussars, 1900–1901, and took part in operations in Transvaal, including action at Belfast. Died at Johannesburg, Feb. 1, 1901 (Queen's medal, with four clasps). [p. 115.]

Robertson, Col. James Peter, C.B. (of Callander Lodge). Gazetted Ensign 31st (The Huntingdonshire) Regt. of Foot (now 1st Batt. The East Surrey Regt.), 1841. Promoted Lieut., 1842. Served with 31st Regt. throughout First Sikh War, 1845–1846, including battles of Mudki, Firozshah, Budiwal, Aliwal, and Sobraon (medal, with three clasps). Promoted Capt., 1848. Served in Crimea, 1855, during Russian War, including siege and fall of Sevastopol, and assaults on Redan June 18 and Sept. 8 (medal with clasp, and Turkish medal). Transferred to Military Train. Promoted Major, 1857. Commanded Military Train, acting as Cavalry, in Indian Mutiny, 1857–1858, and took part in relief of Lucknow by Sir Colin Campbell (being in command at Dilkusha during enemy's attack, Nov. 22, 1857); served also in defence of the Alambagh by Sir James Outram, and in capture of Lucknow by Sir Colin Campbell; afterwards commanded cavalry of Azamgarh Field Force under Maj.-Gen. Lugard, being present at relief of Azamgarh, and capture of Jugdespur (frequently mentioned in despatches; brevet of Lieut.-Col.; C.B.; medal with two clasps, and a year's service for Lucknow). Promoted Col., 1863. Retired, 1870. [p. 119.]

Robertson, Capt. the Honble. Robert B. Fraser (eldest son of Lord Robertson of Forteviot).

Educated at Winchester College and Christ-church College, Oxford. Gazetted 2nd Lieut. 4th (Militia) Batt. The Sherwood Foresters (Derbyshire Regt.), 1892. Promoted Lieut., 1893; Capt., 1895. Enlisted in 3rd (Gloucester-shire) Coy. Imperial Yeomanry, 1899. Promoted Lieut. and Qrmr., 1900. Served in South African War, 1900-1901, with 3rd Coy. I.Y., and took part in operations in Trans-vaal and Orange River Colony, April 1900 to May 1901, including action at Wittebergen; and in operations in Cape Colony, July 1901. Twice wounded (mentioned in despatches; Queen's medal, with four clasps). Gazetted Capt. 21st Lancers, 1901. Still serving. [p. 115.]

Rollo, Gen. the Honble. Robert, C.B. (3rd son of John, 8th Baron Rollo). Educated at Edin-burgh and Brighton. Gazetted Ensign 42nd (or the Royal Highland) Regt. of Foot (now 1st Batt. The Black Watch (Royal Highlanders)), 1832. Promoted Lieut., 1835; Capt., 1841. Was one of two officers sent from Malta on special mission to Tripoli, 1846, and received thanks of Secretaries for Foreign Affairs and Colonies, conveyed through C.-in-C., for his services on that occasion. Brevet of Major, 1854. Served with 42nd Regt. in Crimea, 1854-1855, during Russian War; was Bgde.-Major from battle of Balaclava onwards, until he took command of his regt.; was present in battles of the Alma and Balaclava; commanded 42nd Regt. upon expedition to Kertch and surrender of Yeni-kali, and afterwards at siege of Sevastopol, including assault on Redan, June 18, 1855 (medal, with three clasps; brevet of Lieut.-Col.; Knight of the Legion of Honour; 5th Class of Medjidie, and Turkish medal). Promoted Major and Lieut.-Col., 1855. A.A.G. in Canada, 1855-1860. Promoted Col., 1858. Mily. Secy. to Lieut.-Gen. Sir Fenwick Williams, C.-in-C., British North America, 1860-1865. Promoted Major-Gen., 1868; Lieut.-Gen., 1877; Gen., 1880. Retired 1881. Appointed Col. 93rd (Suther-land Highlanders), 1880; Col. The Black Watch (Royal Highlanders), 1888.[1] [p. 107.]

Ross, Lieut. Alexander (2nd son of the late

John Ross, New Miln, Findo Gask). Enlisted in Colonial Scouts, 1899. Served in South African War, 1899-1900, (1) as Tpr. with Colonial Scouts, and (2) as Lieut. with Imperial Light Horse. Took part in operations in Natal, 1899-1900, including action at Elands-laagte (Queen's medal, with one clasp). Re-signed appointment, 1900. [p. 133.]

Ruthven, Lieut. the Honble. Alexander Gore Arkwright Hore-, V.C. (2nd son of Walter, Baron Ruthven). Gazetted Lieut. 3rd (Militia) Batt. The Highland Light Infantry, 1893. Promoted Capt., 1896. Served with Egyptian Army in Soudan Campaign under Sir Herbert Kitchener, 1898, and was present at capture of Gedarif (mentioned in despatches); V.C.;[2] 4th Class of Osmanieh; British medal; and Khedive's medal, with clasp). Gazetted 2nd Lieut. The Queen's Own Cameron Highlanders, 1899. Served with Egyptian Army in Nile Expedition, 1899, and took part in operations resulting in final defeat of Khalifa (mentioned in despatches; two clasps to Khedive's medal). Promoted Lieut. Cameron Highlanders, 1900. Took part in operations in Somaliland, 1903. Still serving. [p. 115.]

Ruthven, Lieut. the Honble. Christian Malise Hore-, D.S.O. (3rd son of Walter, Baron Ruth-ven). Gazetted 2nd Lieut. The Black Watch (Royal Highlanders), 1899. Served in South African War, (1) with 2nd Batt. The Black Watch, 1899-1900; (2) with 12th Mtd. Infy., 1900-1902. Took part in advance on Kimberley, 1899-1900, including action at Magersfontein; operations in Orange Free State, Feb. to May 1900, in-cluding action at Vet River; and subsequent operations in Orange River Colony, 1900, in-cluding actions at Wittebergen and Witpoort. Took part in operations in Orange River Colony and Transvaal, Nov. 1900 to May 1902 (three times mentioned in despatches; D.S.O.; Queen's medal, with three clasps; King's medal, with two clasps). Promoted Lieut., 1900. Still serving. [p. 115.]

Ruthven, 2nd Lieut. the Honble. Philip James Leslie Hore- (4th son of Walter, Baron Ruthven).

---

[1] K.C.B., 1905. Died, 25th February, 1907.

[2] Captain Hore-Ruthven was awarded the V.C. for the following service: "On the 22nd September 1898, during the action of Gedarif, Captain Hore-Ruthven, seeing an Egyptian officer lying wounded within fifty yards of the advancing Dervishes, who were firing and charging, picked him up and carried him towards the 16th Egyptian Battalion. He dropped the wounded officer two or three times, and fired upon the Dervishes, who were following, to check their advance. Had the officer been left where he first dropped, he must have been killed."

Gazetted 2nd Lieut. The Highland Light Infantry, 1901. Served in South African War, 1901-1902, with 1st Batt. H.L.I. (Queen's medal, with three clasps). Still serving. [p. 115.]

Ruthven, Capt. the Honble. Walter Patrick Hore-, D.S.O., Master of Ruthven (eldest son of Walter, Baron Ruthven). Gazetted 2nd Lieut. Scots Guards, 1891. Promoted Lieut., 1896. (Diamond Jubilee medal, 1897.) Promoted Capt., 1899. Served in South African War, 1899-1901, (1) with 1st Batt. Scots Guards, and (2) as Transport Officer 2nd Cavalry Brigade. Took part in advance on Kimberley, 1899-1900, including actions at Belmont, Enslin, Modder River, and Magersfontein ; relief of Kimberley ; and operations in Orange Free State, Feb. to May 1900, including operations at Paardeberg, and actions at Poplar Grove, Driefontein, Karee Siding, Houtnek (Thoba Mountain), Vet River, and Zand River. Took part also in operations in Transvaal and Orange River Colony, May to Nov. 1900, including actions near Johannesburg, Pretoria, and Diamond Hill, and action at Elands River; also actions at Bethlehem and Wittebergen (three times mentioned in despatches; D.S.O.; Queen's medal, with nine clasps). Invalided home 1901 and resumed regtl. duty. (Coronation medal, 1902.) Now serving as Regtl. Adjt. [p. 115.]

Sandeman, Lieut.-Col. John Glas, M.V.O. (2nd son of the late George Glas Sandeman of Westfield, Hayling Island, and great-grandson of George Sandeman of Springland, Perth. Descended from the Glases of Pittentian). Educated at King's College, London. Gazetted Cornet 1st (Royal) Regt. of Dragoons, 1853. Served with Royal Dragoons in Crimea, 1854-1855, during Russian War, and was present in battles of Inkerman and Balaclava, attack on outpost, Feb. 19, 1855, battle of Tchernaya, first expedition to Kertch, and siege of Sevastopol (medal with three clasps, and Turkish medal). Promoted Lieut., 1855 ; Capt., 1857. Retired, 1859. Appointed to Honourable Corps of Gentlemen-at-Arms, 1869 ; promoted Sub-Officer, 1874. Gazetted Major, Essex Yeomanry Cavalry, 1870. Promoted Lieut.-Col. Commanding, 1874. Retired, 1877. Appointed Hon. Lieut., Royal Naval Reserve, 1875. M.V.O., 1902.

Sandeman, Major Victor Staunton (eldest son of Lieut.-Col. John Glas Sandeman, and great-great-grandson of George Sandeman of Springland). Gazetted Lieut. 3rd (Militia) Batt.

The Black Watch (Royal Highlanders), 1883. Gazetted Lieut. 17th (The Duke of Cambridge's Own) Lancers, 1886. Promoted Capt. and appointed Adjt., 1896. Served in South African War with 17th Lancers, 1900-1901, and took part in operations in Orange Free State, Feb. to May 1900, including actions at Vet River and Zand River, and in operations in Transvaal and Orange River Colony, May to Nov. 1900, including actions near Johannesburg, Pretoria, Diamond Hill, and actions at Elands River. also actions at Bethlehem, Wittebergen, and Caledon River. Took part in operations in Cape Colony and Orange River Colony, Nov. 1900 to Nov. 1901—severely wounded (mentioned in despatches ; brevet of Major ; Queen's medal, with five clasps). Promoted Major, 1903. Still serving. [p. 109.]

Sharp, Civil Surg. Charles William (born and brought up in Comrie). Served in South African War, (1) with Scottish National Red Cross Hospital, 1900, and (2) as Civil Surg. attached to Royal Army Medical Corps, 1901-1902. Was on duty in Cape Colony and Orange River Colony (Queen's medal, with four clasps). Relinquished appointment at end of war. [p. 135.]

Smythe, Lieut.-Col. David Murray (of Methven). Gazetted Lieut. Royal Perthshire Rifles, 1870 ; Lieut. 79th Regt. (Cameron Highlanders), 1874. Retired, 1878, and appointed Capt. Natal Native Contingent. Served with Natal Native Contingent in Zulu War, 1878-1879 (medal, with clasp). Gazetted Capt. Royal Perthshire Rifles (now 3rd (Militia) Batt. The Black Watch (Royal Highlanders)), 1880. A.D.C. Highland Bgde. Infy. Vols., 1888-1892. Promoted Major, 1890 ; Hon. Lieut.-Col., 1892 ; Lieut.-Col. Comdg. 3rd (Militia) Batt. The Black Watch, 1893. Retired, 1897. [p. 107.]

Spalding, Qrmr. and Hon. Lieut. Charles (5th son of James Spalding, Boat Brae. Born and brought up in Rattray). Enlisted in Army Service Corps, 1879. Served in Soudan Expedition, 1885, with A.S.C. Promoted Qrmr. and Hon. Lieut., 1899. Served in South African War, 1899-1902, and took part in operations in Cape Colony and Orange River Colony (Queen's medal, with two clasps ; King's medal, with two clasps). Still serving. [p. 133.]

Speir, Lieut. Kenneth R. N. (2nd son of R. T. N. Speir of Culdees). Enlisted in 8th (Derbyshire) Company Imperial Yeomanry, 1900.

Promoted Lieut., 1900. Served in South African War, 1900, (1) with 8th Coy. I.Y., and (2) as A.D.C. to Major-Gen. Sir C. Parsons. Took part in operations in Cape Colony, Orange River Colony, and Transvaal (Queen's medal, with three clasps). Resigned commission, 1901. [p. 125.]

Steele, Capt. and Brevet-Major George (2nd surviving son of the late Gen. Sir Thomas Steele of Evelick). Educated at Eton College and Royal Military College, Sandhurst. Gazetted 2nd Lieut. 1st (Royal) Dragoons, 1892. Promoted Lieut., 1893 ; Capt., 1899. Appointed Adjt., 1899. Served in South African War, 1899-1902, as Adjt. Royal Dragoons, Oct. 1899 to Jan. 6, 1900, and from Jan. 28, 1900, onwards. Took part in relief of Ladysmith, including action at Colenso ; operations of Feb. 5 to 7, 1900, and action at Vaal Kranz ; operations on Tugela Heights, Feb. 14 to 27, 1900, and action at Pieter's Hill. Took part in subsequent operations in Natal, March to June 1900 ; operations in Orange River Colony, May to Nov. 1900 ; and operations in Transvaal, Orange River Colony, and Cape Colony, Jan. 1901 to May 1902 (three times mentioned in despatches ; brevet of Major ; Queen's medal, with five clasps ; King's medal, with two clasps ; 3rd Class of Red Eagle). Still serving. [p. 109.]

Steele, Capt. and Brevet-Major Julian McCarty (of Evelick ; eldest surviving son of the late Gen. Sir Thomas Steele of Evelick). Educated at Eton College and Royal Military College, Sandhurst. Gazetted 2nd Lieut. Coldstream Guards, 1890. Promoted Lieut., 1896. Adjt. 2nd Batt. Coldstream Gds. 1896-1900. Served in South African War, 1899-1901, with 2nd Batt. Coldstream Gds., and took part in advance on Kimberley, 1899-1900, including actions at Belmont, Enslin, Modder River, and Magersfontein ; operations in Orange Free State, Feb. to May 1900, including actions at Poplar Grove, Driefontein, Vet River, and Zand River ; and operations in Transvaal, May to Oct. 1900, including actions near Johannesburg, Pretoria, and Diamond Hill, and action at Belfast (twice mentioned in despatches ; brevet of Major ; Queen's medal, with seven clasps). (Coronation medal, 1902.) Appointed to command Guards Depôt, 1903. Still serving. [p. 109.]

Steuart, Lieut. Bernard Charles Albert

(4th son of the late John Steuart of Ballechin). Educated at Fort Augustus Abbey School, Inverness. Enlisted in Lumsden's Horse, 1900. Gazetted 2nd Lieut. The Black Watch (Royal Highlanders), 1900. Served in South African War, (1) with Lumsden's Horse, 1900, and (2) with 1st Batt. The Black Watch, 1901-1902. Took part in operations in Orange Free State and Transvaal, 1900, including action near Johannesburg, and in operations in Orange River Colony, 1901-1902 (Queen's medal, with three clasps ; King's medal, with two clasps). Promoted Lieut., 1902. Retired, 1903. [p. 117.]

Stewart, Lieut. Duncan Hubert (2nd son of Alexander Stewart, and grandson of Col. Alexander Stewart, 6th of Strathgarry). Educated at Mostyn House, Cheshire, and Jesus College, Cambridge. Enlisted in Rhodesian Horse Volunteers, and served in Matabele War, 1896 (medal). Discharged Rhodesian Horse Volunteers. Lieut. 2nd Vol. Batt. King's Own Scottish Borderers, 1899. Resigned, and enlisted in 19th (Lothians and Berwickshire) Company Imperial Yeomanry, 1900. Promoted Sergt. Served in South African War, (1) with 19th Coy. I.Y., 1900 ; (2) as Lieut. with Police, 1900 ; (3) as Inspector of Military Police, 1900-1901 ; and (4) as Lieut. with 1st Scottish Horse, 1901. Transferred to Police and appointed Lieut., July 1900. Appointed Inspector of Military Police Aug. 1900. Joined Scottish Horse as Lieut., 1901. Took part in operations in Western Transvaal with mobile column commanded successively by Cols. Flint and Shekleton and Brig.-Gens. Cunningham and Dixon. Severely wounded at Roodeval, July 6, 1901, and invalided home. Returned to South Africa with draft of Scottish Horse, 1902, but arrived after conclusion of hostilities (Queen's medal, with two clasps). Relinquished appointment at end of war. [p. 127.]

Stewart, Major-Gen. George, C.B. (6th son of the late Major W. M. Stewart, and grandson of Wm. Stewart of Ardvorlich). Educated at St. Andrews and London. Gazetted Ensign East India Company's Service, 1856. Promoted Lieutenant, 1857. Served in Indian Mutiny, 1857-1858, (1) in Volunteer Cavalry, with Major-Gen. Havelock's force, 1857-1858 ; took part in actions of Futtehpur, Aoung, Pandu Nuddi, Cawnpore, Unao, Busserutgung (both actions), Bithur, Mungarwar, and the Alambagh ; also relief and subsequent defence of Lucknow. Was also present at capture of Lucknow by Sir Colin Campbell. Served (2) with 1st Sikh Cavalry, 1858, in actions of Simri, Nawabgunge, Bara Banki, reoccupation of Fyzabad, actions of Poorwa, Morar, and Nihow (mentioned in despatches), taking of fort of Simri, actions of Murputgung and Doondiakiera, taking of forts of Omrea and Futtehpur, and action of Koolie-ka-bund—wounded, and horse wounded (medal, with two clasps, and a year's service for Lucknow). Served with 1st Sikh Cavalry throughout campaign in China, 1860, including actions of Sinho (wounded, and mentioned in despatches), Chankiawan, and Palichau, and surrender of Pekin (medal, with two clasps). Served with 11th Bengal Cavalry in campaign on North-West Frontier of India (Ambela), under Gen. Garvock, 1863 (medal, with clasp). Promoted Capt., Bengal Staff Corps, 1868; Comdt. of Cavalry and Squad. Officer Queen's Own Corps of Guides, 1870; Comdt. of Cavalry and Squad. Comdr., 1877. Served with Corps of Guides in Jowaki-Afridi Expedition, 1877-1878, under Gen. Keyes (mentioned in despatches ; clasp). Took part in operations against the Ranizai village of Skakot, and commanded the cavalry in attack on the Utman Khel villages, March 1878. Served in Afghan War, 1878-1880, in command of Guides Cavalry, being present at capture of Ali Musjid, in operations round Kabul, Dec. 1879, and in second engagement at Charasia (mentioned in despatches; brevet of Lieut.-Col. ; medal, with two clasps). Promoted Col., 1883 ; 2nd-in-command and Squad. Comdr., 1884; Major-Gen. and C.B., 1887. Retired, 1887. [p. 117.]

Stewart, Capt. James Anthony (eldest son of the late Col. Anthony Stewart, and great-grandson of Wm. Stewart of Ardvorlich). Gazetted 2nd Lieut. Royal Artillery, 1887. Served in Burma, 1889-1892, and took part in operations of Tonhon Expedition (medal, with clasp). Promoted Lieut., 1890. Served with Chitral Relief Force under Sir Robert Low, 1895, with Mountain Battery, and was present at capture of Malakand Pass, and in actions in Swat Valley, at Panjkora River, and Mamugai (medal, with clasp). Promoted Capt., 1897. Transferred to Royal Garrison Artillery and appointed Ordnance Officer, 4th Class, 1900. Served in South African War, 1900-1902, and took part in operations in Cape Colony, Dec.

1900, and in Transvaal, Dec. 1900 to May 1902 (Queen's medal, with three clasps ; King's medal, with two clasps). Still serving. [p. 117.]

Stewart, Col. John, C.I.E. (of Ardvorlich). Educated at St. Andrews and Royal Military College, Addiscombe. Gazetted 2nd Lieut. Bengal Artillery (now Royal Artillery), 1851. Promoted 1st Lieut., 1857. Served during Indian Mutiny, 1857-1858, with Ordnance Dept. on Lines of Communication between Allahabad and Cawnpore. Promoted Capt., 1861 ; Major, 1872. Employed chiefly in Ordnance Dept. under Civil Administration of the Army, and was Superintendent of Harness and Saddlery Factory at Cawnpore, 1874-1888. Promoted Lieut.-Col., 1878 ; brevet of Col., 1882. C.I.E., 1887. Retired, 1888. [p. 117.]

Stewart, Lieut. John Lindesay (2nd son of Col. Stewart of Ardvorlich). Born, 1875. Educated at Sherborne School and Royal Military College, Sandhurst. Gazetted 2nd Lieut. Indian Staff Corps (now Indian Army), and appointed Officiating Squad. Officer 11th (Prince of Wales's Own) Bengal Lancers, 1894. Served with Chitral Relief Force under Sir Robert Low, 1895, with 11th Bengal Lancers (medal, with clasp). Promoted Lieut., 1897. Served in campaign on North-West Frontier of India under Sir William Lockhart, 1897-1898, with 11th Bengal Lancers, and took part in operations of Malakand Field Force, including operations in Swat (clasp). Appointed to 15th Bengal (Cureton's Multani) Lancers (now 15th Lancers (Cureton's Multanis)), 1900. Died at Murree, June 2, 1902. [p. 117.]

Stewart, Capt. Robert Joseph Tucker (2nd son of the late Col. Anthony Stewart, and great-grandson of Wm. Stewart of Ardvorlich). Gazetted 2nd Lieut. The Northumberland Fusiliers, 1891. Promoted Lieut., 1894. Transferred to Indian Staff Corps (now Indian Army), and appointed Wing Officer 9th Madras Infy., 1895. Wing Officer 22nd Bengal Infy. (now 22nd Punjabis), 1897. Served in campaign on North-West Frontier of India under Sir William Lockhart, 1897-1898, with 22nd Punjab Infy. (1) Took part in operations of Malakand Field Force, including operations in Swat and Bajour, and night attacks of Nawagai. (2) Took part in operations of Mohmand Field Force, including capture of Badmanai Pass, and operations in Mittai and Suran

Valleys. (3) Served on Lines of Communication with Tirah Expeditionary Force (medal, with two clasps). Served in South African War, 1899–1902, as Special Service Officer. Was afterwards on Staff and on Police duty under Military Governor of Pretoria. Took part in operations in Orange Free State, Feb. to May 1900, including operations at Paardeberg, and operations in Transvaal, Nov. 1900 to May 1902 (Queen's medal, with three clasps; King's medal, with two clasps). Promoted Capt., 1901. Resumed regtl. duty, 1902. Served in Kabul-Khel Waziri Expedition, 1902, with 22nd Punjabis. Still serving. [p. 117.]

Stewart, Major William (yr. of Ardvorlich). Gazetted Sub-Lieut. Royal Perthshire Rifles, 1876. Promoted Lieut., 1878. Gazetted 2nd Lieut. 65th (2nd York. N. Riding) Regt., 1879. Promoted 1st Lieut., 1881. Transferred to Bengal Staff Corps (now Indian Army) and appointed Officiating Squad. Officer 10th (The Duke of Cambridge's Own) Bengal Cavalry (now 10th Duke of Cambridge's Own Lancers (Hodson's Horse)), 1885. Promoted Squad. Officer, 1886 ; Officiating Squad. Comdr., 1887 ; Capt., 1890 ; Squad. Comdr., 1891. Served with 10th Bengal Lancers in campaign on North-West Frontier of India under Sir William Lockhart, 1897–1898, and took part in operations of the Malakand and Buner Field Forces, including operations in Swat (medal, with clasp). Promoted Major and retired, 1899. [p. 117.]

Stewart, Capt. William Murray (only son of the late J. A. Stewart, M.A., and great-grandson of Wm. Stewart of Ardvorlich). Educated at Charterhouse and Royal Military College, Sandhurst (where he gained Sword of Honour). Gazetted 2nd Lieut. The Queen's Own Cameron Highlanders, 1895. Promoted Lieut., 1898. Served in Soudan Campaign, 1898, under Sir Herbert Kitchener, with 1st Batt. Cameron Highlanders, and was present at battle of the Atbara. Invalided home (British medal, and Khedive's medal, with clasp). Promoted Capt., 1900. Served in South African War, 1900–1902, with 1st Batt. Cameron Highlanders, and took part in operations in Orange Free State, Feb. to May 1900, including actions at Vet River and Zand River, and in operations in Transvaal, May and June 1900, including actions near Johannesburg and Pretoria. Took part in operations in Orange River Colony, June 1900 to Jan. 1901, including

actions at Wittebergen (wounded) and Ladybrand ; operations in Eastern Transvaal, Jan. to April 1901, including action at Lake Chrissie (wounded); and operations in Western Transvaal, March to May 1902 (mentioned in despatches ; Queen's medal, with two clasps). Still serving. [p. 117.]

Stirling, Capt. Alexander (late of Holme Hill ; son of John Stirling of Fairburn and Holme Hill). Educated at Harrow School. Gazetted Lieut. The Seaforth Highlanders (Ross-shire Buffs, The Duke of Albany's), 1885. Served in Hazara Expedition, 1888, with 2nd Batt. Seaforth Highlanders (medal, with clasp) ; also in Hazara Expedition, 1891, with 2nd Batt. Seaforth Highlanders, in command of Machine Gun Detachment (clasp). Promoted Capt., 1894. Served in South African War, (1) with 12th Batt. Mtd. Infy., March to Dec. 1901, and (2) with 2nd Batt. Seaforth Highlanders, Dec. 1901 to May 1902. Took part in operations in Cape Colony, Orange River Colony, and Transvaal (Queen's medal, with five clasps). Retired, 1903. [p. 123.]

Stirling, Capt. Archibald (of Keir). Educated at Eton College and Cambridge University. Gazetted 2nd Lieut. Scots Guards, 1889. Promoted Lieut., 1892 ; Capt., 1899. Served with Egyptian Army in Nile Expedition, 1899 (Khedive's medal, with clasp). Served in South African War, 1900–1902, with 2nd Batt. Scots Gds., and took part in operations in Orange River Colony, May to Nov. 1900, including actions at Biddulphsberg and Wittebergen; operations in Transvaal, 1901 ; in Cape Colony, 1901–1902 ; and in Orange River Colony, 1902 (Queen's medal, with three clasps ; King's medal, with two clasps). Retired, 1903. Reserve of Officers.

Stirling, Surg.-Major Robert, M.D., F.R.C.S. Edin. (eldest son of D. H. Stirling, M.D., Perth), 4th Vol. Batt. The Black Watch and Army Medical Reserve. Served in South African War, 1900, (1) with Scottish National Red Cross Hospital, and (2) attached to 18th Bgde. Was on duty in Orange River Colony (mentioned in despatches ; Queen's medal, with two clasps). [p. 135.]

Threipland, Capt. William Murray-, D.S.O. (of Fingask). Educated at Fettes College. Gazetted 2nd Lieut. Grenadier Guards, 1887. Promoted Lieut., 1892 ; Capt., 1898. Served in Soudan Campaign under Sir Herbert Kitchener,

1898, with 1st Batt. Grenadier Gds., and was present at battle of Khartoum (British medal, and Khedive's medal with clasp). Served also in South African War with 2nd Batt. Grenadier Gds., 1900-1902, and took part in operations in Orange Free State, April and May 1900 ; operations in Orange River Colony, May to Nov. 1900, including actions at Wittebergen ; and subsequent operations in Transvaal (Queen's medal, with three clasps; King's medal, with two clasps). Retired, 1902. [p. 111.]

Tullibardine, Lieut.-Col. John George, Marquess of, M.V.O., D.S.O. (eldest surviving son of John, 7th Duke of Atholl). Educated at Farnborough School and Eton College. Gazetted 2nd Lieut. 3rd (Militia) Batt. The Black Watch (Royal Highlanders), 1891. Promoted Lieut., 1892. Gazetted 2nd Lieut. Royal Horse Guards (The Blues), 1892. Promoted Lieut., 1893. Seconded to Egyptian Army with rank of Bimbashi, 1898. Served in Soudan Campaign under Sir Herbert Kitchener, 1898, as Staff Officer to Lieut.-Col. Broadword Comdg. Egyptian Cavalry, and was present at cavalry reconnaissance of April 4 up the Atbara and at battles of the Atbara (mentioned in despatches) and Khartoum (mentioned in despatches ; D.S.O. ; British medal, and Khedive's medal with two clasps). Resumed regtl. duty, 1898. Promoted Capt., 1899. Served in South African War, (1) attached to 1st (Royal) Dragoons, Nov. 1899 to Jan. 1900 ; (2) on Staff of 1st Cavalry Bgde., Natal, Feb. to Nov. 1900 ; and (3) as temporary Lieut.-Col. Comdg. Scottish Horse (two regiments), Dec. 1900 to May 1902. Took part in relief of Ladysmith, including action at Colenso ; operations of Jan. 17 to 24, 1900, and action at Spion Kop ; operations of Feb. 5 to 7, 1900, and action at Vaal Kranz ; operations on Tugela Heights, Feb. 14 to 27, 1900, and action at Pieter's Hill. Took part also in operations in Natal, March to June 1900. Apptd. to raise and command Scottish Horse, with temporary rank of Major, Dec. 1900. Temporary rank of Lieut.-Col., 1901. Took part in operations in Western and Eastern Transvaal, in command of 1st and 2nd Scottish Horse, 1901-1902 (three times mentioned in despatches ; brevet of Major ; Queen's medal, with six clasps ; King's medal, with two clasps). Relinquished appointment at end of war. M.V.O., 1902. Apptd. to raise Scottish

Horse (Imperial Yeomanry) and gazetted Lieut.-Col. Comdg., 1903. Still serving. [p. 105.]

Underwood, Col. Thomas Ormsby (of Heath Park, Birnam). Gazetted Ensign, East India Company's Service, and apptd. to 22nd Native Infantry, 1856. Promoted Lieut., 1859. On duty with Sappers and Miners, 1860-1865. Apptd. Squad. Subaltern 4th Punjab Cavalry, 1865 ; 3rd Squad. Officer, 1868. Promoted Capt., 1868 ; Squad. Officer, 1869. Served in campaign on North-West Frontier of India against Bezotis, and with Miranzai Expedition, 1869. Promoted 2nd Squad. Officer, 1871 ; Officiating 2nd in Command, 1872 ; Major, 1876 ; 2nd in Command and Squad. Comdr., 1878 ; was Officiating Commandant, 1878-1880. Served in Afghan War, 1880, and took part in attack on Jundulah. Served also in Mahsúd Waziri Expedition, 1881. Promoted Lieut.-Col. Madras Staff Corps, 1882 ; brevet of Col., 1886. Was Examiner in Hindustani, and Acting Translator to Govt., of Persian and Hindustani. Retired, 1896. [p. 119.]

White, Capt. Francis Hugh Buchanan (eldest son of the late Francis Buchanan White of Annat Lodge, Perth). Apptd. to 5th Vol. Batt. The Black Watch, 1899. Served in South African War, 1901-1902, as Lieut. with 2nd Vol. Service Coy., attached to 2nd Batt. The Black Watch (Royal Highlanders). Took part in operations in Orange River Colony (Queen's medal, with four clasps). Now Capt., 5th Vol. Batt. The Black Watch. [p. 131.]

Whitson, 2nd Lieut. Eric Cecil Hill- (2nd son of Capt. Chas. Hill-Whitson of Parkhill). Educated at Marlborough College. Gazetted 2nd Lieut. 3rd (Militia) Batt. The Royal Scots (Lothian Regt.), 1900; 2nd Lieut. 1st Batt., 1901. Served in South African War, (1) with 3rd Batt. Royal Scots, 1900-1901 ; and (2) with 1st Batt., 1901-1902. Took part in operations in Cape Colony, 1900 : in Orange River Colony, Aug. 1900 to Aug. 1901 ; and in Transvaal, Aug. 1901 to Jan. 1902. Invalided home, 1902. (Queen's medal, with three clasps ; King's medal, with two clasps.) Still serving. [p. 113.]

Whitson, Capt. Thos. Ernest Lynedoch Hill- (yr. of Parkhill). Educated at Harrow School. Gazetted 2nd Lieut. 3rd (Militia) Batt. The Black Watch (Royal Highlanders), 1894. Promoted Lieut., 1895. Gazetted 2nd Lieut. 14th (The King's) Hussars, 1896. Promoted Lieut., 1897. Served in South African War, 1899-1900, with 14th Hussars, and took part in relief of Ladysmith, including operations of Feb. 5 to 7, 1900, and action at Vaal Kranz; operations on Tugela Heights, Feb. 14 to 27, 1900, and action at Pieter's Hill. Took part also in operations in Orange Free State, April and May 1900, including actions at Houtnek (Thoba Mountain) and Zand River; and in operations in Transvaal, May to Nov. 1900, including actions near Johannesburg, Pretoria, and Diamond Hill, and action at Belfast. Invalided home (twice mentioned in despatches; Queen's medal, with seven clasps). Promoted Capt., 1901. Apptd. Adjt. Stafford Imperial Yeomanry, 1902. Still serving. [p. 113.]

Willoughby, Capt. and Brevet-Major the Honble. Charles Strathaven Heathcote-Drummond (2nd son of Gilbert, 1st Earl of Ancaster). Educated at Eton College and Trinity College, Cambridge. Gazetted 2nd Lieut. Scots Guards, 1890. Promoted Lieut., 1894; Capt., 1899. Served in South African War, 1900–1902, with 2nd Batt. Scots Guards, and took part in operations in Orange Free State, April and May 1900, and in operations in Orange River Colony, May to Nov. 1900, including actions at Biddulphsberg and Wittebergen. Served as Adjt. 2nd Batt. Scots Guards, Sept. 1901 to May 1902 (mentioned in despatches; brevet of Major; Queen's medal, with three clasps; King's medal, with two clasps). Still serving.

Willoughby, Capt. the Honble. Claud Heathcote-Drummond (3rd son of Gilbert, 1st Earl of Ancaster). Educated at Eton College. Gazetted 2nd Lieut. Coldstream Guards, 1891. Promoted Lieut., 1897. Served in South African War, 1899–1902, with 2nd Batt. Coldstream Guards, and took part in advance on Kimberley, 1899–1900, including engagement at Belmont (slightly wounded); operations in Orange Free State, Feb. to May 1900, including actions at Poplar Grove, Driefontein, Vet River, and Zand River; operations in Transvaal, May to Nov. 1900, including actions near Johannesburg, Pretoria, and Diamond Hill, and actions at Belfast and Komati Poort. Took part also in operations in Cape Colony, 1901–1902 (Queen's medal, with five clasps; King's medal, with two clasps). Promoted Capt., 1900. Still serving.

Wilson, Lieut. John (son of Peter Wilson, Sunnybrae, Bankfoot). Enlisted in Scottish Horse, 1901. Promoted Lance-Corpl., Corpl., Sergt., and Lieut., 1901. Served in South African War with 2nd Scottish Horse, 1901–1902. Took part in operations in Eastern Transvaal with mobile column commanded successively by Col. Benson and Col. Mackenzie, and was present in action at Bakenlaagte (Queen's medal, with five clasps). Relinquished appointment at end of war. Now serving as Lieut. (Transvaal) Scottish Horse. [p. 127.]

For Addenda to above Roll, see pp. 286–7.

PART II

NOTE.—Part II. includes some officers now or formerly resident in Perthshire; some who were born (but not brought up) in the county; some grandsons (on the maternal side) of landed proprietors of recognised Perthshire families; and some officers connected in other ways with the county, but less closely than those in Part I.

Annat, Lieut. J. W. (formerly resident at Westown of Errol). Enlisted in 92nd (Gordon Highlanders) Regt. of Foot, 1880. Served with 92nd Regt. in Boer War, 1881, taking part in action at Majuba Hill (severely wounded). Transferred to Princess Louise's (Argyll and Sutherland Highlanders), 1881. Transferred to Staff in North-West Provinces of Canada, 1886. Served in Sitting Bull's rebellion, 1900, including action at Pine Bridge (severely wounded). Transferred as Instructor (1) to Staff in New South Wales and (2) to Staff in Queensland. Apptd. Instructor to 3rd Kennedy Regt. and Kennedy Mtd. Infy. Promoted Lieut., 1895. Apptd. to command of Warwick Coy. of Queensland (Vol.) Rifles, 1899. Served in South African War, 1900, with 3rd Queensland Contingent, and took part in operations in Cape Colony and Transvaal. Killed in action at Elands River, Aug. 5, 1900 (Queen's medal, with two clasps). [p. 121.]

Bald, Major Alfred Campbell, D.S.O. (son of Mrs. Bald, Invermay). Educated at Eton College. Gazetted 2nd Lieut. The Black Watch (Royal Highlanders), 1882. Promoted Lieut., 1882. Served with Soudan Expedition, 1884, and was present in engagement at El Teb as Acting Orderly Officer to Maj.-Gen. Davis, Comdg. the 2nd Infy. Bdge., and in engagement at Tamai (medal with clasp, and Khedive's star). Served with Nile Expedition, 1884-1885, with 1st Batt. The Black Watch (clasp). Promoted Capt., 1888. Retired, 1892. Reserve of Officers, 1900. Served in South African War, (1) attached to 2nd Batt. The Black Watch, 1900-1901, and (2) as Transport Officer with Maj.-Gen. Elliot's column, 1901-1902. Took part in operations in Orange Free State, Feb. to May 1900, including action at Vet River, and in operations in Orange River Colony, 1900-1902, including actions at Rhenoster River,

Wittebergen, and Witpoort (mentioned in despatches; D.S.O.; promoted Major, Reserve of Officers; Queen's medal, with two clasps; King's medal, with two clasps).[1] [p. 141.]

Bald, Capt. Ernest Herbert Campbell (son of Mrs. Bald, Invermay). Educated at Eton College. Gazetted 2nd Lieut. 15th (The King's) Hussars, 1894. Promoted Lieut., 1895; Capt., 1899. Served in South African War, 1901-1902, as Adjt. Pietersburg Light Horse, and took part in operations in Transvaal (Queen's medal, with three clasps). Resumed regtl. duty, 1902. Retired, 1903. [p. 141.]

Ballingall, Lieut. Harry Miller (son of Hugh Ballingall, J.P. for Perthshire). Educated at Dundee and at Edinburgh University. For two years Lieut. 16th Middlesex Rifle Volunteers (London Irish Rifles). Gazetted 2nd Lieut. Royal Garrison Artillery, 1899. Served in South African War, (1) with No. 15 Coy. Southern Divn. Siege Train, 1899-1900, and (2) with 61st Batty. Royal Field Artillery, 1900-1902. Took part in operations in Cape Colony, Dec. 1899; operations in Orange Free State, Feb. to May 1900, including operations at Paardeberg, and actions at Driefontein, Vet River, and Zand River; and operations in Transvaal, May and June 1900, including actions near Johannesburg and Pretoria. Took part also in operations in Transvaal and Orange River Colony, 1901-1902 (mentioned in despatches; Queen's medal, with four clasps; King's medal, with two clasps). Promoted Lieut. R.F.A., 1901. Posted to "B" Batty. Royal Horse Artillery, 1903. Still serving. [p. 137.]

Beech, Major John Robert, C.M.G., D.S.O. (resident at Meggernie Castle). Gazetted Vet. Surg., Veterinary Dept., 1881. Served with Veterinary Dept. in Egyptian Campaign, 1882, being present in both actions at Kassassin and in battle of Tel-el-Kebir (medal), with clasp, and Khedive's star). Served also in Soudan Expedition under Sir Gerald Graham, 1884, being present in engagements at El Teb—slightly wounded—and Tamai (mentioned in despatches; two clasps). Served also with Nile Expedition, 1884–1885, being present in actions at Abu Klea and El Gubat (two clasps). Accompanied Sir Gerald Portal's Mission to Abyssinia, 1888 (C.M.G.). Gazetted 2nd Lieut. 21st Hussars, 1888. Promoted Lieut. and Capt. into 20th Hussars, 1889. Served with Egyptian Cavalry in operations near Suakin, Dec. 1888, being present in engagement at Gemaizah (mentioned in despatches; clasp), and in operations of Aug. 1899, including engagements at Arguin and Toski (mentioned in despatches; clasp). Commanded Egyptian Cavalry at taking of Handoub and Tokar, Feb. 1891, and was present in action at Affafib—slightly wounded (D.S.O. and clasp to Khedive's star; 4th Class of Medjidie; 4th Class of Osmanich). Retired, 1895. Reserve of Officers. Served in South African War, March to Nov. 1900, (1) as Transport Officer, and (2) as Assistant Provost Marshal and Camp. Comdt. on Major.-Gen. French's Staff. Took part in operations in Orange Free State, March to May 1900, including action at Zand River; and in operations in Transvaal, May to Nov. 1900, including actions near Johannesburg and Diamond Hill, and action at Belfast (Queen's medal, with five clasps). Gazetted Major Scottish Horse (Imperial Yeomanry), 1903. Still serving. [p. 121.]

Buist, Capt. Arthur Hunter (3rd son of Maj.-Gen. D. S. Buist, who was born and brought up in Perth). Educated at Edinburgh University. Gazetted 2nd Lieut. The Royal Scots Fusiliers, 1891. Promoted Lieut., 1894. Served in campaign on North-West Frontier of India under Sir William Lockhart, 1897–1898, with 1st Batt. Royal Scots Fusiliers, and took part in operations of Tochi Field Force (medal, with clasp). Transferred to Indian Staff Corps and apptd. Wing Officer, 25th Bengal Infy., 1898. Exchanged to Corps of Guides (Infy.), 1900. Promoted Capt., 1901. Still serving. [p. 137.]

Buist, Major David Simson, F.R.G.S. (eldest son of Maj.-Gen. D. S. Buist). Educated at Edinburgh University. Gazetted Lieut. The Hampshire Regt., 1885. Served in Burmese Expedition, 1885–1889, with 1st Batt. The Hamp-

shire Regt. (medal, with two clasps). Transferred to Bengal Staff Corps (now Indian Army), 1889, and apptd. Officiating Squad. Officer, 2nd Cavalry Haiderabad Contingent (now 29th Lancers (Deccan Horse)). Promoted Squad. Officer, 1891; Capt., 1896; Major, 1903. Still serving. [p. 137.]

Buist, Major Herbert John Martin, D.S.O., M.B., M.Ch. Edin. (2nd son of Maj.-Gen. D. S. Buist). Educated at Edinburgh University. Gazetted Surg. Capt., Royal Army Medical Corps, 1891. Served in campaign on North-West Frontier of India under Sir William Lockhart, 1897–1898, with Malakand Field Force and Tirah Expeditionary Force (mentioned in despatches; medal, with two clasps). Served also in South African War, 1899–1902, and took part in operations in Cape Colony, 1899–1900, including action at Colesberg; relief of Kimberley; and operations in Orange Free State, Feb. to May 1900, including operations at Paardeberg and actions at Poplar Grove, Driefontein, Houtnek (Thoba Mountain), and Zand River. Took part also in operations in Transvaal, May to Nov. 1900, including actions near Johannesburg, Pretoria, and Diamond Hill, and actions at Belfast; and subsequent operations in Cape Colony (mentioned in despatches; D.S.O.; Queen's medal, with six clasps; King's medal, with two clasps). Promoted Major, 1903. Still serving. [p. 137.]

Buist, Capt. James Martin, M.B., B.Ch. (5th son of Maj.-Gen. D. S. Buist). Educated at Edinburgh University. Gazetted Lieut., Royal Army Medical Corps, 1899. Served in South African War, 1899–1902, and took part in operations in Cape Colony, 1899–1900: operations in Orange Free State, Feb. 1900, including operations at Paardeberg; and subsequent operations in Orange River Colony and Cape Colony (Queen's medal, with clasps; King's medal, with two clasps). Promoted Capt., 1902, and seconded to South African Constabulary. Still serving. [p. 137.]

Buist, Capt. Keith Lyon (4th son of Maj.-Gen. D. S. Buist). Educated at Edinburgh University. Gazetted 2nd Lieut. The Highland Light Infantry, 1896. Served in campaign on North-West Frontier of India under Sir William Lockhart, 1897–1898, with 2nd Batt. H.L.I., and took part in operations of Malakand Field Force (medal, with clasp). Promoted Lieut., 1899. Served in South African War with 22nd Batt. Mtd. Infy., 1901; severely wounded (loss of right eye) at Doopcut Drift, Orange River Colony (Queen's medal, with five clasps). Promoted Capt., 1901. Still serving. [p. 137.]

Colquhoun, Lieut.-Col. Roderick W. (tenant of Old Faskally). Gazetted 2nd Lieut. The Highland Borderers Light Infantry (now 3rd (Militia) Batt. Princess Louise's (Argyll and Sutherland Highlanders)), 1880. Promoted Lieut., 1881; Capt., 1883; Major and Hon. Lieut.-Col., 1899; Lieut.-Col., 1900. Served in South African War, 1902, with 3rd Batt. A. and S. H., and took part in operations in Cape Colony (Queen's medal, with two clasps). Retired, 1902. [p. 141.]

Cooper, Lieut. Henry Alexander (son of tenant of Glenturret West Lodge). Gazetted 2nd Lieut. 5th (Royal Irish) Lancers, 1901. Promoted Lieut., 1901. Served in South African War, 1901-1902, with 5th Lancers, and took part in operations in Cape Colony (Queen's medal, with three clasps). Still serving. [p. 137.]

Cunyngham, Lieut.-Col. William Henry Dick-,[1] V.C. (grandson of the late Major James Alston-Stewart of Urrard). Born, 1851. Gazetted Sub-Lieut. 92nd (Gordon Highlanders) Regt. of Foot (now 2nd Batt. The Gordon Highlanders), 1872. Promoted Lieut., 1873. Served in Afghan War, 1878-1880, and was present on Transport duty in advance to Kandahar and Khelat-i-Ghilzai under Sir Donald Stewart; served also with Thull Chotiali Force under Maj.-Gen. Biddulph (mentioned in despatches); and with 92nd Gordon Highlanders served in Kuram Valley Field Force under Sir Frederick Roberts, including engagement at Ali Khel. Took part in operations round Kabul, Dec. 1879 (mentioned in despatches), including attack on Sherpur Pass (V.C.[2]); also in Maidan Expedition, 1880, as Acting Adjt. of a wing of his regt., being present in engagement at Charasia (mentioned in despatches). Accompanied Sir F. Roberts in march to Kandahar and was present at reconnaissance of Aug. 31, and at battle of Kandahar (mentioned in despatches; V.C.; medal with two clasps, and Roberts' star). Served in Boer War, 1881, as Adjt. 92nd Gordon Highlanders. Promoted Capt., 1881. Adjt. 4th Vol. Batt., 1883-

1889. Promoted Major into Argyll and Sutherland Highlanders, 1891. Apptd. Station Staff Officer at Delhi, 1893; D.A.A.G. at Lucknow, 1895. Promoted Lieut.-Col. Comdg. back to 2nd Batt. The Gordon Highlanders, 1897. (Jubilee medal, 1897.) Served in South African War, 1899-1900, as Lieut.-Col. Comdg. 2nd Batt. The Gordon Highlanders, and took part in battle of Elandslaagte (severely wounded) and in defence of Ladysmith (Queen's medal, with two clasps). Mortally wounded in attack on Cæsar's Camp at Ladysmith, Jan. 6, 1900. [p. 139.]

Dodd, 2nd Lieut. Percy Reed (born at Parkfield, Perth). Educated at Windermere College and Royal Military College, Sandhurst. Gazetted 2nd Lieut. The Cameronians (Scottish Rifles), 1901. Served in South African War, 1901-1902, (1) with 25th Batt. Mounted Infy., and (2) with 2nd Batt. Scottish Rifles. Took part in operations in Orange River Colony and Transvaal, including the action at Bakenlaagte (Queen's medal, with four clasps). Still serving.

Dudley, Hon. Major William Humble, 2nd Earl of (grandson of Sir Thos. Moncreiffe of Moncreiffe, 7th Bart.). Gazetted Lieut. Worcestershire Yeo. Cav. (now I.Y.), 1885. Promoted Capt., 1888; Major, 1893. Served in South African War, 1900, as D.A.A.G. for I.Y. on Headquarters Staff, and took part in operations in Orange Free State, Feb. to May 1900, including actions at Poplar Grove, Driefontein, Vet River, and Zand River; and in operations in Transvaal, May to Sept. 1900, including actions near Johannesburg and Diamond Hill, and at Belfast (Queen's medal, with five clasps). Hon. Major in the Army. Viceroy of Ireland, 1902. Still serving in Worcestershire I.Y. [p. 143.]

Fincastle, Capt. Alexander Edward, Viscount, V.C. (only son of Charles, 7th Earl of Dunmore; descended from John, 1st Marquess of Atholl). Educated at Eton College. Gazetted 2nd Lieut. 16th (The Queen's) Lancers, 1891. Promoted Lieut., 1894. Served with Dongola Expedition under Sir Herbert Kitchener, 1896, attached to Egyptian Cavalry (British medal, and Khedive's medal with clasp). Served in campaign on North-West Frontier

---

[1] See biographical notice, pp. 101-2.

[2] Lieut. Dick-Cunyngham was awarded the V.C. "for conspicuous gallantry and coolness displayed by him on the 13th Dec. 1879, at the attack on the Sherpur Pass in Afghanistan, in having exposed himself to the full fire of the enemy, and by his example and encouragement rallied the men, who, having been beaten back, were, at the moment, wavering at the top of the hill."

of India under Sir William Lockhart, 1897-1898, with Malakand Field Force, attached to Guides Cavalry, and was present in engagement at Landakai (V.C.[1]); served also with Buner Field Force as A.D.C. to Sir Bindon Blood (three times mentioned in despatches; V.C.; medal, with two clasps). Promoted Capt., 1899. Served in South African War, 1899-1900, (1) attached to 6th (Inniskilling) Dragoons, 1899 to Feb. 1900; (2) with 16th Lancers, Feb. to May 1900; and (3) on Staff of 11th Division, May to Nov. 1900. Took part in operations in Cape Colony, 1899-1900, including actions at Colesberg and relief of Kimberley; operations in Orange Free State, Feb. to May 1900, including operations at Paardeberg, and actions at Poplar Grove and Karree Siding; operations in Transvaal and Orange River Colony, May to Nov. 1900. Apptd. to command 31st Batt. Imperial Yeomanry (Fincastle's Horse) with temporary rank of Lieut.-Col., 1902. Served in South African War as Lieut.-Col. Comdg. 31st Batt. I.Y., 1902, and took part in operations in Cape Colony (mentioned in despatches; Queen's medal, with four clasps). Resumed duty with 16th Lancers, 1903. Still serving. [p. 105.]

Gardyne, Capt. and Brevet - Major Alan David Greenhill- (grandson of William, 9th Viscount Strathallan). Educated at Inverness College, at Charterhouse, and at Royal Military College, Sandhurst. Gazetted 2nd Lieut. The Gordon Highlanders, 1888. Promoted Lieut., 1891. Served with Chitral Relief Force, 1895, with 1st Batt. The Gordon Highlanders, and was present at storming of Malakand Pass (medal, with clasp). A.D.C. to Viceroy of India. Promoted Capt., 1897. A.D.C. to G.O.C. Scottish District, 1898. Served in South African War, (1) with 1st Batt. The Gordon Highlanders, 1899-1900; (2) as Acting Railway Staff Officer at Bloemfontein, 1900-1901; and (3) as Adjt. Steinaecker's Horse, 1901-1902. Took part in operations in Orange River Colony, May to Nov. 1900; in Transvaal, July to Nov. 1900, including actions at Belfast and Lydenburg;

and in Eastern Transvaal, 1901-1902 (mentioned in despatches; brevet of Major; Queen's medal, with three clasps; King's medal, with two clasps). Resumed regtl. duty, 1903. Still serving with the Gordon Highlanders. [p. 141.]

Gardyne, Lieut. Walter Greenhill- (grandson of William, 9th Viscount Strathallan). Educated at Eton College. Enlisted in 20th (Fife and Forfarshire Light Horse) Company Imperial Yeomanry, 1900. Served in South African War, (1) with 20th Company I.Y., 1900 (promoted Lieut.); and (2) as Railway Staff Officer successively at Machadodorp and Klerksdorp, 1900-1902 (Queen's medal, with two clasps; King's medal, with two clasps). Relinquished commission at end of war. [p. 141.]

Hadow, 2nd Lieut. Ronald Walter (grandson of George, 11th Earl of Kinnoull). Educated at Trinity College, Glenalmond, and Harrow School. Received Royal Humane Society's medal, 1900. Gazetted 2nd Lieut. The Black Watch (Royal Highlanders), 1901. Served in South African War, 1901-1902, with 1st Batt. The Black Watch, and took part in operations in Orange River Colony and Transvaal (Queen's medal, with four clasps). Still serving. [p. 139.]

Henderson, Surg. Capt. Patrick Jobson, M.B., C.M. Abdn. (formerly resident in Blairgowrie). Educated at Dundee, Edinburgh, and Aberdeen. For three years in Dundee Cadet Corps, and for three years a student in Vol. Medical Staff Corps. Joined Cape Medical Staff Corps, 1901, and apptd. Surg. Capt. Served in South African War, Dec. 1901 to May 1902, and took part in operations in Cape Colony, (1) as Medical Officer with Col. Crewe's Hdqrs., and (2) as Medical Officer No. 2 Divn. Cape Police. Was subsequently Medical Officer at Picquetberg, at Vogelvlei Remounts Camp, and at Endekuil; also Recruiting Officer at Capetown (Queen's medal, with three clasps). Relinquished appointment at end of war. [p. 129.]

Lamb, Lieut. Claud Carnegie (son of D. I. Lamb, Beechwood, Dunkeld). Educated at Trinity College, Glenalmond, and Royal Military

---

[1] Lord Fincastle was awarded the V.C. for conspicuous bravery as follows: "During the fighting at Nawa Kili, in Upper Swat, on the 17th August 1897, Lieut.-Col. R. B. Adams proceeded with Lieuts. H. L. S. MacLean and Viscount Fincastle, and five men of the Guides, under a very heavy and close fire, to the rescue of Lieut. R. T. Greaves, Lancashire Fusiliers, who was lying disabled by a bullet wound and surrounded by the enemy's swordsmen. In bringing him under cover he (Lieut. Greaves) was struck by a bullet and killed. Lieut. MacLean was mortally wounded, whilst the horses of Lieut.-Col. Adams and Lieut. Viscount Fincastle were shot, as well as two troop horses."

College, Sandhurst. Gazetted 2nd Lieut. The Black Watch (Royal Highlanders), 1900. Served in South African War, 1900-1902, with 2nd Batt. The Black Watch, and took part in operations in Orange Free State, Feb. to May 1900, including action at Vet River; operations in Orange River Colony, May 1900 to Sept. 1901, including actions at Rhenoster River, Wittebergen, and Witpoort; operations on Zululand Frontier of Natal, Oct. 1901, and operations in Transvaal and Orange River Colony, Nov. 1901 to May 1902 (Queen's medal, with three clasps; King's medal, with two clasps). Promoted Lieut., 1901. Still serving. [p. 139.]

Logan, Lieut. David (formerly resident in Callander). Apptd. Lieut. Scottish Horse, 1900. Served in South African War, 1900-1901, with 1st Scottish Horse, and took part in operations in Western Transvaal, with mobile column commanded successively by Cols. Flint and Shekleton, and Brig.-Gens. Cunningham and Dixon (Queen's medal, with four clasps). Invalided home, 1901. Resigned appointment, 1902. [p. 129.]

Login, Capt. Spencer Henry Metcalfe (grandson of the late John Campbell of Kinloch). Educated at Wellington College. Gazetted Naval Cadet, Royal Navy, 1865. Promoted Sub-Lieut., 1872. Served in Ashanti War, 1874, in command of advance-guard of Naval Bgde. (medal, and promoted Lieut). Served in Soudan Expedition, 1884-1885, (1) as Naval Transport Officer at Suakin, and (2) as Chief Transport Officer (medal, with clasp; Khedive's star, and thanks of Board of Trade). Promoted Comdr., 1888. Comdr. of H.M.S. *Anson*, 1888-1891. Comdr. of H.M.S. *Excellent*, 1892-1894. Promoted Capt., 1894. Flag-Capt. to Vice-Admiral Sir A. Buller in H.M.S. *Centurion*, 1895-1898. Capt. of Royal Naval College, Greenwich, 1898-1900. Capt. of H.M.S. *Repulse*, 1900-1903. Still serving. [p. 143.]

Macdonald, Lieut. Alexander, F.R.G.S. (formerly resident at Elcho Park). Apptd. Lieut. 1st Australian (New South Wales) Bushmen, 1900. Served in South African War with 1st Australian Bushmen, 1900-1902, and formed part of Rhodesian Field Force, 1900. Took part also in operations in Transvaal under Maj.-Gen. Bruce Hamilton, 1901-1902 (Queen's medal, clasps unknown; King's medal, with two clasps (?)). Invalided home and relinquished appointment, 1902. [p. 129.]

McLetchie, Lieut. and Hon. Capt. Thomas (formerly resident at Balcairn, Blairgowrie). Educated at Kinloch Parish School and Blairgowrie Public School. For four years in 5th Vol. Batt. The Black Watch. Apptd. Lieut. Scottish Horse, 1901. Served in South African War, (1) with 2nd Scottish Horse, 1901, and (2) with 1st Scottish Horse, 1902. Took part in operations in Eastern Transvaal with Col. Benson's mobile column, April to July 1901; severely wounded at Wagon Drift, July 15, 1901, and invalided home. Took part in operations in Western Transvaal with Col. Kekewich's mobile column, 1902. Relinquished appointment at end of war. [p. 129.]

Macmaster, Civil Surg. Charles, M.B., C.M. (resident in Perth). Educated in Perth. Served in South African War, 1901-1902, as Civil Surgeon attached to Royal Army Medical Corps, and was on duty in Cape Colony, Orange River Colony, and Transvaal (Queen's medal, with five clasps). Relinquished appointment at end of war. [p. 135.]

Meiklejohn, Major-Gen. Sir William Hope, K.C.B., C.M.G. (grandson of the late John Campbell of Kinloch). Educated at Rugby. Gazetted Ensign Bengal Infantry, General List, 1861. Promoted Lieut. 20th Bengal Infy., 1862. Served in Hazara Campaign, 1868, including operations on Black Mountain (medal, with clasp). Promoted Capt., 1871. Served with Jowaki-Afridi Expedition, 1877-1878, under Gen. Keyes (mentioned in despatches; clasp). Served with 20th Bengal Infy. in Afghan War, 1878-1880, being present at attack and capture of Ali Musjid, and with Zaimusht Expedition (medal, with clasp). Served also with Mahsud-Waziri Expedition, 1881. Brevet-Major and Major, 1881. Served with 20th Bengal Infy. in Egyptian Campaign, 1882, and was present in battle of Tel-el-Kebir (mentioned in despatches; medal, with clasp; 4th class of Osmanieh, and Khedive's star). Promoted Lieut.-Col., 1887. Served with Waziristan Delimitation Escort, 1894, as Lieut.-Col. Comdg. 20th Bengal Infy. (mentioned in despatches), and with Waziristan Field Force, 1894-1895 (mentioned in despatches; C.B., and clasp). Promoted Col., 1893. Commanded Malakand Bgde. in Campaign on North-West Frontier under Sir Wm. Lockhart, 1897, and was present during night attacks on camp, throughout defence of Malakand, and at relief of Chakdara Fort; was in command of relieving column, and was present at engagement at Landakai (mentioned in despatches); also commanded a Bgde. during expedition into Mohmand country (mentioned in despatches), and commanded 1st Bgde. Buner Field Force, being present at capture of Tanga Pass (mentioned in despatches; K.C.B.; and medal, with two clasps). Promoted Major-Gen., 1900. Now Officiating in Command, Oudh. [p. 137.]

Neish, 2nd Lieut. William (grandson of James Pattullo of Ashmore). Gazetted 2nd Lieut. The Gordon Highlanders, 1901. Served in South African War, 1901–1902, with Mtd. Infy. Coy. of Gordon Highdrs., and took part in operations in Transvaal and Orange River Colony (Queen's medal, with five clasps). Still serving. [p. 139.]

Ogilvy, Major Angus Howard Reginald, D.S.O. (grandson of George, 9th Baron Kinnaird). Educated at Eton College. Gazetted 2nd Lieut. 13th Hussars, 1881. Promoted Lieut., 1881. A.D.C. to Governor of Victoria, 1887–1888. Promoted Capt., 1888. Adjt. of East Kent Yeomanry, 1890–1895. Served in South African War with 13th Hussars, 1900–1901 (mentioned in despatches; D.S.O.; Queen's medal, with two clasps.) Promoted Major, 1901. Retired, 1902. Apptd. Cavalry Instructor to Forces of Sultan of Morocco, 1903.[1] [p. 143.]

Ogilvy, Comdr. Frederick Charles Ashley (grandson of George, 9th Baron Kinnaird). Educated on H.M.S. *Britannia*. Gazetted Naval Cadet, Royal Navy, 1880. Promoted Midshipman, 1882; Sub-Lieut., 1886; Lieut., 1888. Apptd. 1st and Torpedo Lieut. in H.M.S. *Polyphemus*, 1893; in H.M.S. *Defiance*, 1897; and in H.M.S. *Terrible*, 1898. Served in South African War, 1899-1900, as Lieut. in command of battery of 12-pounders landed from H.M.S. *Terrible*, and took part in relief of Ladysmith, including action at Colenso; operations of Jan. 17 to 24, and action at Spion Kop; operations of Feb. 5 to 7, and action at Vaal Kranz; operations of Feb. 14 to 27, and action at Pieter's Hill (mentioned in despatches; promoted Comdr.; Queen's medal, with two clasps). Served with Allied Forces in China during Boxer Rising, 1900, as Comdr. of H.M.S. *Terrible* (medal). Apptd. Comdr. of H.M.S. *Vernon*, 1903. Still serving. [p. 143.]

Richmond, 2nd Lieut. George Mitchell (son of Jas. Richmond, Monzie Castle). Gazetted 2nd Lieut. The Black Watch (Royal Highlanders),

1902. Served in South African War, 1902, with 1st Batt. The Black Watch, and took part in operations in Orange River Colony (Queen's medal, with two clasps). Still serving. [p. 139.]

Robertson, Lieut. Frank Mansfield Boileau (son of David Robertson, cadet of Robertson of Struan). Educated at Eton College. Gazetted 2nd Lieut. The Black Watch (Royal Highlanders), 1898. Promoted Lieut., 1899. A.D.C. to Viceroy of India, 1900–1901. Seconded to South African Constabulary, 1901–1903. Served in South African War, 1901–1902, with South African Constabulary, and took part in operations in Transvaal and Orange River Colony (Queen's medal, with four clasps). Resumed regtl. duty, 1903. Still serving. [p. 139.]

Rorison, 2nd Lieut. William Gilbert Don Gurdon (son of Very Rev. V. L. Rorison, D.D., Perth). Gazetted 2nd Lieut. The Highland Light Infantry, 1901. Served in South African War, 1901–1902, with 1st Batt. H.L.I., and took part in operations in Cape Colony and Orange River Colony (Queen's medal, with four clasps). Still serving. [p. 141.]

Ross, Capt. Charles William Laing (resident in Kincardine). 7th Vol. Batt. Argyll and Sutherland Highlanders. Served in South African War, 1901–1902, as Lieut. with 2nd Vol. Service Coy., attached to 1st Batt. A. and S. H., and took part in operations in Cape Colony, Orange River Colony, and Transvaal (Queen's medal, with five clasps). Still serving in 7th Vol. Batt. A. and S. H. [p. 141.]

Urmston, Major and Brevet-Lieut.-Col. Archibald George Brabazon (grandson of the late John Burn-Murdoch of Gartincaber). Gazetted 1st Lieut. Royal Marine Light Infantry, 1880. Promoted Capt., 1890; Major, 1899. Served in South African War, (1) in command of Royal Marines with 1st Divn., 1899–1900, and (2) on Staff of 9th Divn., 1900. Took part in advance on Kimberley, 1899-1900, including action at Magersfontein; and in operations in Orange Free State, Feb. and March 1900, including operations at Paardeberg, and actions at Poplar Grove and Driefontein (mentioned in despatches; brevet of Lieut.-Col.; Queen's medal, with three clasps). Invalided home, 1900, and resumed regtl. duty. Retired, 1903. Reserve of Officers. [p. 139.]

Urmston, Lieut.-Col. Edward Brabazon, C.B. (grandson of the late John Burn-Murdoch of Gartincaber). Gazetted 2nd Lieut. 93rd (Suther-

---

[1] Died July 4, 1906.

land Highlanders) (now 2nd Batt. Princess Louise's (Argyll and Sutherland Highlanders)), 1878. Promoted Lieut.,1880; Capt.,1886; Major, 1896. Passed Staff College. Served in South African War, (1) with 1st Batt. A. and S. H., 1899–1900 ; (2) as Bgde.-Major, Highland Bgde., Feb. to March 1900; (3) in command of 1st Batt. A. and S. H., 1900–1901 ; and (4) in command of a mobile column, 1901–1902. Took part in advance on Kimberley, 1899–1900, including engagement at Koodoesberg ; operations in Orange Free State, Feb. to May 1900, including operations at Paardeberg and actions at Poplar Grove and Driefontein; operations in Orange River Colony, May to July 1900, and operations in Transvaal, July 1900 to Nov. 1901, including action at Zillikats Nek. Took part also in operations in Eastern Transvaal, Nov. 1901 to May 1902 (twice mentioned in despatches ; C.B. ; brevet of Lieut.-Col. ; Queen's medal, with four clasps; King's medal, with two clasps). Promoted Lieut.-Col. Comdg. 1st Batt. A. and S. H., 1903. Still serving. [p. 139.]

Ward, Lieut. the Honble. Gerald Ernest Francis (grandson of Sir Thos. Moncreiffe of Moncrieffe, 7th Bart.). Gazetted 2nd Lt., 1st Life Guards, and promoted Lieut., 1899. Served in S. African War, 1899–1900, with Composite Regt. of Household Cav., and took part in operations in Cape Colony, 1899–1900, including actions at Colesberg and relief of Kimberley ; operations in Orange Free State, Feb. to May 1900, including operations at Paardeberg and actions at Poplar Grove, Driefontein, Houtnek (Thoba Mountain), Vet River, and Zand River. Took part also in operations in Transvaal, May and June 1900, including actions near Johannesburg and Pretoria ; operations in Orange River Colony, July 1900, including actions at Bethlehem and Wittebergen ; and subsequent operations in Transvaal, including actions at Elands River (Queen's medal, with five clasps). A.D.C. to Viceroy of Ireland, 1902. Still serving. [p. 143.]

Ward, 2nd Lieut. the Honble. John Hubert (grandson of Sir Thos. Moncreiffe of Moncrieffe, 7th Bart.). Gazetted 2nd Lt. Worcestershire Yeo. Cav. (now I.Y.), 1900. Served in South African War, 1899–1900, (1) as Orderly Officer

to Maj.-Gen. Brabazon, Comdg. I.Y.; (2) as A.D.C. to Maj.-Gen. Pretyman ; (3) as A.D.C. to Maj.-Gen. Brabazon ; and (4) as Press Censor on Headquarters Staff. Took part in operations in Cape Colony, 1899–1900; operations in Orange Free State, 1900, including action at Driefontein ; and operations in Transvaal, 1900, including action near Diamond Hill and action at Belfast (Queen's medal, with four clasps). Resigned appointment, 1900. Still serving with Worcestershire I.Y. [p. 143.]

Ward, Capt. the Honble. Reginald, D.S.O. (grandson of Sir Thos. Moncreiffe of Moncreiffe, 7th Bart.). Gazetted 2nd Lt. Royal Horse Guards (The Blues) and promoted Lieut., 1895. Served in South African War, (1) with Composite Regt. of Household Cavalry, 1899–1900, and (2) on Sir John French's Staff, 1901–1902. Took part in operations in Cape Colony, 1899–1900, including actions at Colesberg and relief of Kimberley; operations in Orange Free State, Feb. to March 1900, including operations at Paardeberg and actions at Poplar Grove and Driefontein. Invalided home, 1900, and promoted Capt. Took part in operations in Cape Colony, 1901–1902 (twice mentioned in despatches; D.S.O. ; Queen's medal, with three clasps ; King's medal, with two clasps).[1] [p. 143.]

Ward, 2nd Lieut. the Honble. Robert Arthur (grandson of Sir Thos. Moncreiffe of Moncreiffe, 7th Bart.). Served in South African War, 1899–1901, as A.D.C. to G.O.C. a Bgde. (Queen's medal; clasps unknown). Resigned appointment and gazetted 2nd Lieut. Worcestershire Imperial Yeomanry, 1901. Still serving.

Webster, Major Thomas (born in Perth). Gazetted Lieut. The Cameronians (Scottish Rifles), 1883. Apptd. Wing Officer 12th (The Khelat-i-Ghilzai) Bengal Native Infy. (now 12th Pioneers (The Khelat-i-Ghilzai Regt.)), 1886. Served with Burmese Expedition, 1886–1888 (medal, with two clasps). Transferred to Indian Staff Corps (now Indian Army), 1889. Promoted Capt., 1894 ; Officiating Wing Comdr., 1896. Apptd. District Recruiting Officer, Delhi, 1897 ; Double Company Comdr., 1899. Promoted Major, 1901; Second-in-Command, 1902. Still serving.

---

[1] Died March 7, 1904.

DAVID WILLIAM STANLEY OGILVY, EIGHTH EARL OF AIRLIE

1856–1900

BY A. FRANCIS STEUART

ONE of the most notable figures in the South African War was David, Earl of Airlie, whose devotion to his military career was akin to that of a knight in the Crusades. He came of a family long noted for its Cavalier and Jacobite loyalty, and which had suffered severely for its attachment to the Stuart cause. Destined for a civil life, his passion for soldiering proved too strong, and passing through Sandhurst he entered the Scots Fusilier Guards in 1875 and exchanged a year later into the 10th Hussars.

With this regiment he went to India, where he became an expert horseman and a keen polo player. During 1878–1879 he took part in the Afghan Campaign, and in 1884, after returning home, rejoined his regiment, then on active service at Souakim. Though too late for the battle of El Teb he was present at Tamai, and served until the end of the campaign. He became brigade-major to Sir Herbert Stewart in the Nile Expedition, and was wounded by an Arab spear at Abu Klea in 1885.

In 1886 he married Lady Mabel Gore, daughter of the fifth Earl of Arran, but this did not hinder his active work. In 1889 he was adjutant of the Hampshire Yeomanry, but in 1892 returned to his regiment, then in Ireland, and was keenly interested in the welfare of his men. In December 1896 he became second-in-command of the 2nd Dragoon Guards, and in 1897 commanding officer of the 12th Lancers.

In 1899 orders came for South Africa, and Lord Airlie sailed on October the 23rd. His letters from the seat of war are full of life, and a few extracts show best his real nature. " It all," he wrote, " reminds me of '85 most vividly, which taught me to live and love." He was a disciplinarian, zealous in every work, and took little rest. " I sleep pretty well when there is time and not too many loose horses." At Magersfontein he was described as " over there in the hottest of the fire with seven wounded men round him, as happy as a king," and he himself wrote—" I like the Boers and am very proud to be fighting against them . . . I am very happy "; and what he hoped for was " a merciful and stable peace." On February the 17th, 1900, he wrote after a hard day's march, " All dead tired—hardly any food—little water for many from 2 A.M. till 9 P.M."; and later from the bivouac, " God grant us victory; I think the cavalry has done very well and quite carried out the cavalry rôle." On April the 13th he says, "I want to go on to the end 'a fin' (his family motto) and fight to the end for the dear homeland," and the end was not far off. He fell ill in March at Cape Town, but even before he recovered full strength returned to the front. At Isabellafontein on May the 4th he was wounded in the right arm and was again invalided, but eager for the field he returned to his regiment soon. At Diamond Hill, near Pretoria, on the 11th of June 1900 the end came. After a splendid charge in which he saved the guns, he gave his last command, "Files about—gallop," and fell to the ground with a bullet in his heart. He lies buried there as he desired, his last wish on leaving England being expressed in the words, "Remember if I am killed in action, whatever memorial you put up for me, that you say on it, I had died as I wished."

LIEUTENANT-COLONEL THE HON. ANDREW DAVID MURRAY

1863–1901

BY LIEUTENANT-COLONEL LORD LOVAT, C.B., C.V.O., D.S.O.

BREVET-LIEUTENANT-COLONEL the Hon. Andrew David Murray was born in 1863, was educated at Wellington, and joined The Queen's Own Cameron Highlanders as a lieutenant in 1884.

He served in the Nile Expedition of 1885, and in 1885–1886 throughout the operations of the Soudan Frontier Field Force : he took part in the defence of Kosheh and the engagement at Giniss. In the 1898 campaign he was present with his regiment at the battles of the Atbara and Omdurman, and was on both occasions mentioned in despatches. During the Fashoda operations he was in command of the white troops, was again mentioned in despatches, and received a brevet of major.

In December 1899, shortly after the battle of Magersfontein, Major Murray was asked by Lord Lovat to take command of a body of Scouts which was being raised in the Highlands for service in South Africa ; his experience, his popularity, and the reputation he had already gained on active service pointed him out as one eminently fitted for the post, and one whose appointment would ensure success to the new corps.

In February 1900 Major Murray was duly gazetted commandant of Lovat's Scouts, and at once took up his duties with that quickness for objective and grasp of detail which always characterised him. In March 1900, despite official delays and unforeseen difficulties, he got his command out to South Africa, and in May, by sheer dogged determination, forced his way up to the front and joined the main advance at Kroonstad.

Major Murray was present at the actions near Johannesburg, Pretoria, and Diamond Hill. He then marched with General Hunter to the Wittebergen and was given command of the mounted forces of the Highland Brigade. After Prinsloo's surrender in July 1900 he took part in the fighting round Heilbron and Philipolis, and in some of the pursuits of De Wet.

In November 1900 Major Murray was given a brevet and—what he appreciated much more—a column of his own in Cape Colony. This column consisted of two guns, Lovat's Scouts, District Mounted Troops, Imperial Yeomanry, mounted infantry and Police details. Many weary months of hard trekking and occasional fighting ensued.

99

In September 1901 the larger portion of Lieutenant-Colonel Murray's column was detached to relieve the town of Ladygrey in Cape Colony, and with 100 mounted men and one gun he himself was sent to watch a country known to be the base of supplies to some 400 Boers. The mission was a dangerous one and the end was not long in coming. On the second night, on the Witberg, while the remainder of his column was approaching and was almost within reach, some 250 Boers under Kritzinger, one hour after the moon had set, crawled between his outposts and overwhelmed his little force.

All that mortal man could do Colonel Murray did that night. Taken wholly by surprise, he broke through the Boer fire to get to his men : at once realising the position, he got the Maxim to work, rallied the men who had escaped out of the lines, and at the last—fell—facing his foes, a bullet through his heart, and " no surrender " his last words.

No truer man ever died for his country, nor have many equalled his rugged personality, his power of inspiring affection, or his military genius. As a soldier Andrew Murray was quick, determined, and resourceful ; an absolute competitor for the main object and without a trace of egotism for himself or his command.

Brave as few men are brave, he was nevertheless the most careful of commanders for even the most insignificant unit of his force : he would court death to make certain that a small flank party was secure, and whenever he detached a small force on a more than usually perilous errand it cost him a great mental struggle not to accompany the men to the post of danger. Those who fought with him will always picture him to themselves, perched on the highest anthill on the flank of the firing line with his telescope and map beside him ; a willing target provided he could thereby draw the fire from his men.

Andrew Murray fell in his eighty-sixth engagement, and it may be safely affirmed that, of all the men who have served under him, there is not one whose thoughts do not go out to him in love and admiration.

LIEUTENANT-COLONEL WILLIAM HENRY DICK-CUNYNGHAM, V.C.

1851-1900

BY THE HON. MRS. FORBES OF BRUX

THE youngest son of Sir William Dick-Cunyngham, eighth Baronet of Preston-field and Lambrughton, and descended on his mother's side from the Stewarts of Urrard, Harry, as he was best known to his many friends, was one of those sunny, affectionate, manly dispositions who, incapable of mean actions themselves, never attribute one to another.

Addicted from boyhood to every kind of out-door life, he carried off trophies in all athletic sports. At Sandhurst he hunted the beagles and was considered one of the smartest cadets. Gifted with a fine voice, a singularly good sportsman, and loving manly sports as much as he hated vulgar dissipation, his high standard of conduct made his influence, which was great for so young a man, always for good.

Obtaining a commission in the 92nd Gordon Highlanders, he served throughout the Afghan War of 1878–1880—first on transport duty in the advance to Kandahar and Khelat-i-Ghilzai under Sir Donald Stewart; next with the Thull Chotiali Force under Major-General Biddulph; and afterwards with his regiment, under Sir Frederick (now Lord) Roberts, in the Kuram Valley Expedition, including the engagement at Ali Khel and the operations round Kabul. For his " conspicuous gallantry and coolness " in the attack on the Sherpur Pass he was awarded the Victoria Cross. He acted as adjutant of a wing of the Gordon Highlanders in the Maidan Expedition, including the engagement at Charasia; accompanied Sir Frederick Roberts in the march to Kandahar, and was present at the subsequent battles. He was four times mentioned in despatches, and in the Boer War of 1881 was adjutant of the 92nd.

It was when seen in action that his true character as a born leader of men appeared. Keen of eye, cool and confident in the midst of danger, he knew how to grasp his opportunity—ever eager to show by personal example that his watchword was " Come " not " Go—on."

In 1883 he married Miss Helen Wauchope, and for five years was adjutant of the 4th (Donside) Volunteer Battalion of the Gordon Highlanders, after which he returned to India with his regiment. Entering thoroughly into the serious side of his profession, he read every available military treatise in order to be eligible for staff appointments, and passed the highest standard in Eastern languages. He was appointed station staff officer at Delhi, and was after-wards deputy-assistant-adjutant-general to Sir Robert Low at Lucknow. Pro-moted major into the Argyll and Sutherland Highlanders, he was recalled in 1897 to command his old battalion of the Gordons, and under him the regiment more than maintained its high standard of efficiency.

Serving in the South African War as lieutenant-colonel commanding the 2nd Battalion Gordon Highlanders 1899–1900, he was severely wounded at the battle of Elandslaagte, but in spite of this preferred sharing the dangers and privations of the siege of Ladysmith to seeking safety in the camp at Intombi. When barely recovered he essayed to lead his regiment against the attack on Cæsar's Camp on January the 6th, 1900, but fell mortally wounded—to the over-whelming sorrow of his men, whose universal expression was, " We shall never have another Colonel like him."   He was in deed the hero he looked.

PORTRAITS OF OFFICERS WHOSE SERVICES
ARE RECORDED IN THE FOREGOING ROLL,
AND IN THE ADDENDA, pp. 286–287

Lieut. the Lord JAMES STEWART
MURRAY,
Cameron Highlanders and late
Scottish Horse

Capt. the Lord GEORGE STEWART
MURRAY,
The Black Watch and late
Scottish Horse

Lt.-Col. the Marquess of TULLIBARDINE,
M.V.O., D.S.O.,
Royal Horse Guards and Scottish Horse

Capt. W. H. D. MORAY of Abercairny,
late Scots Guards

2nd Lt. C. J. MURRAY,
Coldstream Guards

(Late) Brevet Lt.-Col. the Hon. A. D. MURRAY,
Cameron Highlanders and Lovat's Scouts

Capt. the Viscount FINCASTLE, V.C.,
Lancers and late Fincastle's Horse

(Late) Capt. the Hon. E. O. MURRAY,
Cameron Highlanders and
Lovat's Scouts

2nd Lt. the Hon. M. C. A. DRUMMOND,
The Black Watch

(Late) Lieut. N. N. RAMSAY,
pr. of Banff,
The Black Watch

Col. D. M. SMYTHE of Methven,
Lt. Col. of, Comdg. 3rd (Mil.) Batt. The
Black Watch

2nd Lt. N. G. STEWART-RICHARDSON,
Seaforth Highlanders

Lt. A. B. BAILLIE-HAMILTON,
Seaforth Highlanders attd. to N.
Nigerian Regt.

(Late) Gen. the Hon. Sir ROBERT ROLLO, K.C.B.,
Colonel, The Black Watch

Capt. Sir EDWARD STEWART-
RICHARDSON of Pitfour, Bart.,
3rd (Mil.) Batt. The Black Watch

Lieut. N. A. B. BAILLIE-HAMILTON,
The Black Watch

Major G. STEELE,
1st (Royal) Dragoons

Capt. the Hon. L. G. OGILVY, D.S.O.,
late Bra'sam's Horse

Capt. Lord HARLEY FITZMAURICE,
1st (Royal) Dragoons

Capt. the Earl of KERRY, D.S.O.,
Irish Guards

(Late) Lt.-Col. the Earl of AIRLIE,
Comg. 12th Lancers

Major J. STEELE of Ewell's,
Coldstream Guards

Major V. S. SANDEMAN,
17th Lancers

Lieut. A. C. E. DRAKE, C.B.
Comg. Artillery

Capt. Sir NEIL MENZIES of Menzies,
Bart.,
late Scots Guards

(Late) Lieut. F. M. A. ATKINSON CLARK,
Scots Guards

Lt.-Col. J. DRUMMOND-HAY, D.S.O.,
x², of Seggieden
Coldstream Guards

Capt. W. MURRAY-THREIPLAND,
D.S.O., of Fingask,
late Grenadier Guards

Major-Gen. L. J. OLIPHANT, C.B., C.V.O.,
Comdg. 5th Brigade and Home District

Lt.-Col. the Hon. C. R. HAY-DRUMMOND,
late Scots Fusilier Guards

Major L. G. DRUMMOND,
Scots Guards

Lt.-Col. F. H. K. DRUMMOND, C.I.E.,
Comdg. 39th Central India Horse

eut, the Marquess of GRAHAM,
sig, Clyde Division, Royal Naval
Volunteer Reserve

Lt.-Col. the Duke of MONTROSE, K.T., A.D.C.,
late Lt.-Col. Comdg. 3rd (Mil.) Batt. Argyll
and Sutherland Highlanders

Capt. T. I. L. HILL-WHITSON,
yr. of Parkhill,
14th Hussars and Stanford Imperial
Yeomanry

Capt. D. H. GRÆME,
Seaforth Highlanders

2nd Lt. E. C. HILL-WHITSON,
Royal Scots

Col. R. C. GRÆME,
Comdg. Ashton Regimental District

Capt. L. O. GRÆME,
Cameron Highlanders and Scottish Horse

Lt.-Col. L. A. M. GRÆME,
late Royal Madras Fusiliers

apt. the Hon. R. B. L. ROBERTSON,
1st Lancers

Lieut. G. A. AYRHILLS, D.S.O.,
East Lancashire Regiment

Capt. the Master of RUTHVEN, D.S.O.,
2nd Dragoons

(Late) 2nd Lt. the Hon. HUGH
ROBERTSON,
14th Hussars

Lieut. the Hon. G. M. HORE-RUTHVEN,
D.S.O.,
The Black Watch

Major G. D. MACPHERSON,
Munster Fusiliers

Lieut. the Hon. A. G. A. HORE-
RUTHVEN, V.C.,
Cameron Highlanders

2nd Lt. the Hon. P. J. L. HORE-
RUTHVEN,
The Highland Light Infantry

Major W. STEWART, yr. of Ardvorlich,
late 10th Bengal Cavalry

C. J. STEWART of Ardvorlich, C.I.E.,
late Royal Artillery

(Later Lieut. J. L. STEWART,
13th Lancers (Cureton's Mooltanis)

Capt. W. M. STEWART,
Cameron Highlanders

Lieut. R. C. A. STUART,
late The Black Watch

Major-Gen. G. STEWART, C.B.,
late Corps of Guides

Capt. R. J. T. STEWART,
22nd Punjabis

Capt. J. A. STEWART,
Royal Garrison Artillery

(Late) Capt. G. RAMSAY
Indian Medical Service

Col. T. M. HARRIS of Grantsmond,
late Royal Artillery

Lieut. H. H. M. HARRIS,
Gordon Highlanders,
late Oxford Light Infantry

Major W. L. MERCER of Huntingtower,
late the Yorkshire Regiment

Col. W. CHALK of Priestland,
late Commdg. 5th and 12th Regimental District

Col. T. O. UNDERWOOD,
late Madras Staff Corps

Col. J. P. ROBERTSON, C.B.,
late Military Train

Lieut.-Gen. Sir JAMES, etc.

Col. L. J. NASON, D.S.O.,
late Cameronians (Scottish Rifles)

Major J. R. BEECH, C.M.G., D.S.O.,
Scottish Horse

Major H. H. W. NASON, D.S.O.,
Essex Regiment

Lieut. C. BURN-MURDOCH,
late Lovat's Scouts

late Rev. J. M. BURN-MURDOCH,
M.A. of Greenyards and New Lodge,
late 6th Dragoon Guards

Brig.-Gen. J. F. BURN-MURDOCH, C.B.,
Comdg. Stockton Brigade

late Lieut. J. W. ANNAL,
Queensland Volunteer Rifles

Major F. BURN-MURDOCH of Nanton,
Royal Engineers

Capt. the Hon. IVAN CAMPBELL,
late 3rd (Militia) Batt. Royal Scots

Earl of KINNOULL,
late Lieut. The Black Watch and late
Col. Egyptian Gendarmerie

Lieut. H. CAMPBELL,
Corps of Guides

Col. J. H. CAMPBELL of Inverarloch,
late Lt.-Col. Comdg. 2nd Batt. Argyll
and Sutherland Highlanders

Capt. J. P. GRANT of Kilgraston,
Seaforth Highlanders

Lieut.-Gen. A. M. MACDONALD

Capt. A. STIRLING,
late Seaforth Highlanders

(Late) Lieut. J. C. CAMPBELL,
Cape Garrison Artillery

Lieut. K. R. N. SPEIR,
late Imperial Yeomanry

Midshipman J. R. G. MONCKEIFFE,
Royal Navy

Lieut. A. K. MONCRIEFF,
2nd Dragoons (Scots Greys)

Capt. R. MONCREIFFE,
Worcestershire Imperial Yeomanry

Major M. M. MONCRIEFF,
7th Dragoon Guards

Major W. SCOTT-MONCRIEFF,
Middlesex Regiment

Comdr. C. DUNDAS of Ochtertyre,
late Royal Navy

Lieut. J. A. MONCRIEFF,
late Argyll and Sutherland Highlanders

Lieut. D. ROBERTSON.
late Scottish Horse

Lieut. J. WILSON,
late Scottish Horse

Major Sir WM. STEWART DICK
CUNYNGHAM of Prestonfield, Bart.,
Scottish Horse

Lieut. D. RATTRAY,
late Scottish Horse

Lieut. T. W. BARNET,
late Scottish Horse

Lieut. D. H. STEWART,
late Scottish Horse

Capt. A. RATTRAY,   Qrmr.-Sgt. A. RATTRAY,
late Scottish Horse   late Steelmecker's Horse

Capt. P. M. RATTRAY, D.S.O.,
late Scottish Horse

Capt. W. S. KIDD,
Scottish Horse

Major C. F. MURRAY MACGREGOR,
Late Cape Police

Lieut. A. MACDONALD,
Late 1st Australian Battalion

Lieut. F. MURRAY MACGREGOR,
Late Cape Police

Surg. Capt. P. J. HENDERSON,
Late Cape Medical Staff Corps

Lieut. D. LOGAN,
Late Scottish Horse

Capt. E. M. ELLIOT,
Late Scottish Horse

Lieut. J. ANDERSON,
Scottish Horse

Lieut. D. LOGAN,
Late Scottish Horse

II.   L.

Qmr. and Hon. Major W. BISSETT,
1/Mil/ Batt, The Highland Light Infantry

Capt. E. H. BUCHANAN WHITE,
5th Vol. Batt. The Black Watch

Major B. CHALMERS,
1st Stirling Rifle Volunteers

Capt. R. M. CHRISTIE,
4th Vol. Batt. The Black Watch

Sergt. J. FERGUSON,
4th Vol. Batt. The Black Watch

Lieut. R. A. BULLOCH,
The Black Watch

R. LECKIE EWING

Lieut. W. LECKIE EWING,
The Highland Light Infantry

Lieut. H. FLEMING,
late South African Light Horse

Lieut. A. ROSS,
late Imperial Light Horse

Lieut. M. W. GEORG,
4th Vol. Batt. The Black Watch

Lieut. F. MITCHELL,
late Queenstown Town Guard

Chief Off. W. B. ANDERSON

Civil Surg. C. W. SHARP

Civil Surg. C. MACMASTER

(Late) Civil Surg. A. CAMERON

(Late) Civil Surg. A. ROBERTSON

Civil Surg. E. MACGREGOR

Surg. Major E. STEELING
4th Vol. Batt. H. B. & K. W. R.

Civil Surg. J. BOYD

Civil Surg. J. LINTON

Vol. Surg. H. MACKAY

Major H. A. M. RossE, D.S.O.,
Royal Army Medical Corps

Major Gen. Sir WILLIAM H. MEIKLEJOHN
K.C.B., M.D.

Major Gen. B. R.

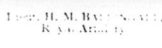

Lieut. H. M. BALL N.
Royal Artillery

Lt.-Col. A. G. B. URMSTON,
Royal Marine Light Infantry

(Late) Lt.-Col. W. H. DICK-CUNYNGHAM, V.C.,
Comg. 2nd Batt. Gordon Highlanders

Lt.-Col. F. B. URMSTON, C.B.,
Comg. 1st Batt. Argyll and Sutherland
Highlanders

Lieut. C. C. LAMB,
The Black Watch

2nd Lieut. W. NEISH,
Gordon Highlanders

2nd Lieut. R. W. HAROW,
The Black Watch

2nd Lieut. G. M. RICHMOND,
The Black Watch

Lieut. M. B. ROBERTSON,
The Black Watch

Major A. D. GREENHILL-GARDYNE,
Gordon Highlanders.

Lieut. The Master of Ruthven,
Argyll and Sutherland Highlanders.

Lieut. W. GREENHILL-GARDYNE,
Lincolnshire Imperial Yeomanry.

Major W. D. C. CAMPBELL-PRESTON,
2nd Battalion, The Black Watch.

Lieut. C. W. J. ROSS,
Argyll and Sutherland Highlanders.

Cmdr. E. C. A. OGILVY,
Royal Navy

Late Major A. H. R. OGILVY, D.S.O.,

Capt. H. M. OGILVY,
Navy

Capt. H. M. H. WARD,
Westmoreland Imp. Yeomanry

Lieut. H. G. L. J. WARD,

Late Capt. Philip
R. WARD, D.S.O.,
Royal Horse Guards

M. de la E. J. WARD,
Westmoreland Imp. Yeomanry

ROLL OF PERTHSHIRE WARRANT OFFICERS,
NON-COMMISSIONED OFFICERS, AND MEN
OF THE PRESENT DAY WHO HAVE SEEN
ACTIVE SERVICE UNDER THE BRITISH FLAG

NOTE

THE following Roll includes natives of Perthshire, residents of not less than five years' standing, and one or two men who were neither born in the county nor reside in it, but who belong to recognised Perthshire families. The records are grouped according to regiments and corps, the records in each unit being arranged alphabetically. The units of the Regular Army are mentioned in order of precedence, followed by the Departments of the Army, the Imperial Yeomanry, the Indian and Colonial forces (the regiments of which are given in alphabetical order), and other similar corps, arranged in like manner.

Except in the case of members of a separate Volunteer unit such as the Scottish Cycle Corps, Militiamen and Volunteers who served in the South African War are shown under the Regular regiments to which their respective corps are affiliated, or under the regiment with which they last proceeded on active service. The records of the Scottish Cycle Corps immediately follow those of the Infantry of the Line.

The record of every man who enlisted in a regiment the title of which has been changed since his enlistment, will be found under the present name of the regiment, the former title being mentioned in his record.

When a man has served in more than one corps his record is given with those of the unit with which he last proceeded on active service.

The name of the place or parish in Perthshire with which each man is connected is given in brackets at the beginning of his record. In cases in which a man is connected with more than one part of the county, the place of birth, when known, has been preferred to the place of residence. The Roll includes men who were born in those districts of Perthshire which were transferred to other counties under the Boundary Commissioners' Order of 1891, or who resided in those districts for not less than five years prior to that date.

The mention of a Volunteer battalion in a record refers, unless otherwise stated, to a Volunteer battalion of the regiment under which the record in question is found.

As mentioned in the Preface, the information contained in the great majority of the records has been verified at the various regimental depôts, but when local sources failed to supply information as to a man's regimental number, such verification became difficult, often impossible. Again, in the case of Colonial regiments disbanded at the end of the South African War, verification of the records was out of the question, and even when an authoritative statement had been procured as to the clasps to which a man was entitled, I was not always definitely informed as to the years in which he had been on active service. Dots . . . have therefore been used to indicate the probability—in some cases, certainty—that certain records are not complete.

As in the case of the Roll of Officers, this Roll includes men living in 1903; while of those not living in that year, only men who had been on active service during the previous ten years have been included. The information contained in the records is not carried beyond December the 31st, 1903.

A number in brackets at the end of a record refers to the man's portrait. Where no such number appears, no portrait has been obtainable. The portraits will be found on pp. 239 to 267, and an Index to the same on p. 271 *et seq.*

The Table of Contents shows the page on which the records of each unit commence, and each individual record is referred to in the Index to Persons.

For abbreviations used see list on p. 64.

ROYAL NAVY

—— 1st Class Petty-Officer Gartland, Alexander K. (Cargill). Enlisted 1891. Served in South African War, 1899-1900 (Queen's medal, with clasps "Belmont" and "Modder River"). Serving on H.M.S. *Argonaut*. [1.]

AUSTRALIAN NAVAL BRIGADE
NEW SOUTH WALES SECTION

133. A.B. Ross, James (Bridge of Earn). Joined Royal Naval Reserve 1897. Volunteered to Australian Naval Brigade (New South Wales Section), 1900. Served with Allied Forces in China during Boxer Rising, 1900 (medal; clasps unknown). Discharged 1901. Re-enrolled in R.N. Reserve 1902. Still serving. [2.]

THE ARMY
THE CAVALRY
2ND LIFE GUARDS

—— **Corpl. of Horse McLaren,** George H. A. P. (Bankfoot). Enlisted in Army Service Corps 1887. Transferred to 2nd Life Guards 1894. Served in South African War with Composite Regiment of Household Cavalry, 1899-1900 (Queen's medal, with clasps "Relief of Kimberley," "Paardeberg," "Driefontein," "Johannesburg," and "Wittebergen"). Still serving. [3.]

ROYAL HORSE GUARDS (The Blues)

—— **Corpl. of Horse Sharp,** James (Perth). Enlisted 1892. Served in South African War, (1) with Composite Regiment of Household Cavalry, 1899-1900; (2) as Regtl. Sergt.-Maj. attd. to 2nd Scot. Horse, 1901-1902; and (3) attd. to 1st Scot. Horse, 1902 (three times mentioned in despatches; Distinguished Conduct Medal; Queen's medal, with clasps "Relief of Kimberley," "Paardeberg," "Driefontein," "Johannesburg," "Diamond Hill," and "Wittebergen"; King's medal, with clasps "South Africa, 1901," and "South Africa, 1902"). Still serving. [4.]

2ND DRAGOON GUARDS (Queen's Bays)

3981. Pte. McArthur, John (Perth). Enlisted in Scots Greys 1890. Transferred to 2nd Dragoon Gds. 1892. Served in South African War as Reservist, 1901-1902 (Queen's medal, with clasps "Cape Colony," "Orange Free State," "Transvaal," "South Africa, 1901," and "South Africa, 1902"). [5.]

4TH (ROYAL IRISH) DRAGOON GUARDS

—— Farr.-Maj. Whiteman, John (Perth). Enlisted 1852. Served in Crimea, 1854-1855, during Russian War (medal, with clasps "Balaclava," "Inkerman," and "Sevastopol"; Turkish medal). Long Service medal. Discharged 1873. [6.]

6TH DRAGOON GUARDS (CARABINIERS)

—— Pte. McInnes, James (Dunkeld). Enlisted in 17th Lancers 1889. Transferred to 2nd Dragoon Gds. 1892. Transferred to Reserve 1896. Served in South African War as Reservist, 1900-1902 (Queen's medal, with clasps "Cape Colony," "Orange Free State," "Johannesburg," and "Diamond Hill"; King's medal, with clasps "South Africa, 1901," and "South Africa, 1902"). Discharged 1902. [7.]

2ND DRAGOONS (ROYAL SCOTS GREYS)

4874. Pte. Anderson, James (Scone). Enlisted 1900. Served in South African War, 1900-1902 (Queen's medal, with clasps "Cape Colony," "Orange Free State," and "Transvaal"; King's medal, with clasps "South Africa, 1901," and "South Africa, 1902"). Still serving. [8.]

4810. Pte. Bullions, William (Kinloch). Enlisted 1899. Served in South African War, 1900 . . . (Queen's medal, with clasps "Cape Colony," "Orange Free State," and "Transvaal"). Still serving.

—— Sergt. Coulter, William (Perth). Enlisted 1886. Served in South African War, . . . 1900-1902 (Queen's medal, with clasps "Relief of Kimberley," "Paardeberg," "Driefontein," "Johannesburg," "Diamond Hill," and "Belfast"; King's medal, with clasps "South Africa, 1901," and "South Africa, 1902"). Still serving. [9.]

—— Pte. Edwards, George A. (St. Martins). Enlisted 1895. Served in South African War, . . . 1900-1902; wounded 1901. (Queen's medal, with clasps "Relief of Kimberley," "Paardeberg," "Driefontein," "Johannesburg," "Diamond Hill," and "Belfast"; King's medal, with clasps "South Africa, 1901," and "South Africa, 1902.") Discharged 1902. [10.]

4911. Pte. Edwards, R. (Perth). Enlisted 1900. Served in South African War, 1900 (Queen's medal, with clasps "Cape Colony," "Orange Free State," and "Transvaal"). Still serving.

—— Pte. Elder, John (Alyth). Enlisted 1893. Served in South African War, . . . 1900-1902 (Queen's medal, with clasps "Relief of Kimberley," "Paardeberg," "Driefontein," "Johannesburg," "Diamond Hill," and "Belfast"; King's medal, with clasps "South Africa, 1901," and "South Africa, 1902"). Transferred to Reserve 1902. [11.]

4410. Pte. Firth, Wilmot (Perth). Enlisted 1897. Served in South African War, . . . 1900-1902 (Queen's medal, with clasps "Relief of Kimberley," "Paardeberg," "Driefontein," "Johannesburg," "Diamond Hill," and "Belfast"; King's medal, with clasps "South Africa, 1901," and "South Africa, 1902"). [12.]

4620. Pte. Gregor, James (Perth). Enlisted 1896. Served in South African War, . . . 1900-1902 (Queen's medal, with clasps "Relief of Kimberley," "Paardeberg," "Driefontein," "Johannesburg," and "Diamond Hill"; King's medal, with clasps "South Africa, 1901," and "South Africa, 1902"). Still serving. [13.]

—— Pte. Jackson, William (Errol). Enlisted in 2nd, or Royal North British Dragoons, 1854. Served in Crimea, 1854-1855, during Russian War. Wounded (in seven places) at Balaclava (medal, with clasps "Balaclava" and "Sevastopol," and Turkish medal). Discharged 1864. [14.]

3448. Corpl. Jenner, Charles (Pitlochry). Enlisted 1890. Served in South African War as Reservist, 1899-1900 (Queen's medal, with clasps "Relief of Kimberley," "Paardeberg," "Driefontein," "Johannesburg," "Diamond Hill," and "Belfast"). Invalided home 1900. [15.]

2971. Pte. Kay, James C. (Alyth). Enlisted 1887. Served in South African War, . . . 1900-1902 (Queen's medal, with clasps "Relief of Kimberley," "Paardeberg," "Driefontein," and

"Belfast"; King's medal, with clasps "South Africa, 1901," and "South Africa, 1902"). Still serving. [31.]

4727. Pte. Lauder, W. (Blairgowrie). Enlisted 1899. Served in South African War. Wounded in the Magaliesberg district, September 1901 (Queen's medal, with clasps "Cape Colony," "Orange Free State," "Transvaal," and "South Africa, 1901"). Still serving.

4443. Corpl. Lindsay, William G. (Dunkeld). Enlisted 1898. Served in South African War, ... 1900–1902. Wounded at Bronkhurst Spruit, December 30, 1901 (mentioned in despatches; Queen's medal, with clasps "Cape Colony," "Paardeberg," "Driefontein," "Johannesburg," "Diamond Hill," and "Belfast"; King's medal, with clasps "South Africa, 1901," and "South Africa, 1902"). Still serving. [16.]

—— **Pte. McGinn, Frank** (Perth). Enlisted 1898. Served in South African War, 1899–1900. Wounded near Kimberley, January 14, 1900 (Queen's medal, with clasps "Relief of Kimberley" and "Paardeberg"). Invalided home 1900. [32.]

3599. Sergt. McIntosh, John (Clunie). Enlisted 1891. Served in South African War, ... 1900–1902 (Queen's medal, with clasps "Relief of Kimberley," "Driefontein," "Johannesburg," "Diamond Hill," and "Belfast"; King's medal, with clasps "South Africa, 1901," and "South Africa, 1902"). Still serving. [17.]

4910. Pte. McMartin, Peter (Aberfeldy). Enlisted 1900. Served in South African War, 1900 (Queen's medal, with clasps "Cape Colony," "Orange Free State," and "Transvaal"). Still serving. [18.]

4308. Pte. McWhammel, George (Perth). Enlisted 1896. Served in South African War, ... 1900–1902 (Queen's medal, with clasps "Relief of Kimberley," "Paardeberg," "Driefontein," and "Belfast"; King's medal, with clasps "South Africa, 1901," and "South Africa, 1902"). Transferred to Reserve 1903. [19.]

4548. Sergt. McWhammel, John (Perth). Enlisted 1899. Promoted Lance-Corpl. and Corpl. 1901, Sergt. 1902. Served in South African War, ... 1900–1902 (Queen's medal, with clasps "Cape Colony," "Orange Free State," and "Transvaal"; King's medal, with clasps "South Africa, 1901," and "South Africa, 1902"). Still serving. [20.]

3657. Pte. Meldrum, George (Perth). En-

listed 1892. Transferred to Reserve 1899. Served in South African War as Reservist, ... 1900–1902 (Queen's medal, with clasps "Relief of Kimberley," "Paardeberg," "Johannesburg," and "Diamond Hill"; King's medal, with clasps "South Africa, 1901," and "South Africa, 1902"). [21.]

5213. Pte. Oliphant, John (Caputh). Enlisted 1901. Served in South African War (Queen's medal, with clasps "Cape Colony," "Orange Free State," and "Transvaal"). Still serving. [22.]

4339. Pte. Petrie, Andrew (Perth). Enlisted 1896. Served in South African War, ... 1900–1902 (Queen's medal, with clasps "Cape Colony," "Orange Free State," and "Transvaal"; King's medal, with clasps "South Africa, 1901," and "South Africa, 1902"). Still serving. [23.]

—— **Sh.-Smith Corpl. Rattray, Harry** (Perth). Enlisted 1896. Served in South African War, ... 1900 ... (Queen's medal, with clasps "Relief of Kimberley," "Paardeberg," "Driefontein," "Johannesburg," and "Diamond Hill"). Still serving. [24.]

4539. Trump. Robertson, Charles R. (Perth). Enlisted 1898. Served in South African War, ... 1900–1902 (Queen's medal, with clasps "Cape Colony," "Orange Free State," and "Transvaal"; King's medal, with clasps "South Africa, 1901," and "South Africa, 1902"). Still serving. [25.]

4409. Pte. Scott, John A. (Perth). Enlisted 1897. Served in South African War, (1) 1899–1900 (invalided home 1900); (2) 1900–1902 (Queen's medal, with clasps "Relief of Kimberley," "Paardeberg," "Driefontein," and "Transvaal"; King's medal, with clasps "South Africa, 1901," and "South Africa, 1902"). Still serving. [26.]

5044. Pte. Sharp, David (Glencarse). Enlisted 1900. Served in South African War, 1901–1902. Wounded at Bronkhurst Spruit, Dec. 30, 1901 (Queen's medal, with clasps "Cape Colony," "Transvaal," "South Africa, 1901," and "South Africa, 1902"). Discharged invalided 1902. [27.]

—— **Sh.-Smith Smeaton, Alexander** (Muthill). Enlisted 1892. Served in South African War, 1899–1900 (Queen's medal, with clasps "Relief of Kimberley," "Paardeberg," and "Driefontein"). Invalided home 1900. Discharged invalided. [28.]

2ND DRAGOONS (ROYAL SCOTS GREYS)—*continued*

3927. Pte. Sturrock, John (Rattray). Enlisted 1894. Served in South African War, 1899–1902 (Queen's medal, with clasps " Relief of Kimberley," "Paardeberg," " Driefontein," " Diamond Hill," and " Belfast"; King's medal, with clasps "South Africa, 1901," and " South Africa, 1902 "). Discharged 1902. [33.]

4724. Pte. Sturrock, Thos. P. (Rattray). Enlisted in 11th Hussars 1898. Transferred to Scots Greys 1899. Served in South African War, 1899–1902 (Queen's medal, with clasps " Relief of Kimberley," "Paardeberg," and " Belfast"; King's medal, with clasps " South Africa, 1901," and "South Africa, 1902 "). Still serving. [34.]

4495. Pte. Taylor, George (Rattray). Enlisted 1898. Served in South African War, . . . 1900–1902 (Queen's medal, with clasps "Relief of Kimberley," " Paardeberg," " Drie-

fontein," and " Transvaal"; King's medal, with clasps "South Africa, 1901," and "South Africa, 1902 "). Still serving.

4223. Lance-Sergt. Telford, George (Perth). Enlisted 1895. Served in South African War, 1899–1902 (Queen's medal, with clasps " Relief of Kimberley," " Orange Free State," and " Johannesburg "; King's medal, with clasps " South Africa, 1901," and South Africa, 1902 "). Still serving. [29.]

4607. Sergt. Telford, James (Perth). Enlisted 1899. Served in South African War, 1900–1902. Wounded at Leeuwkop, February 1902 (Queen's medal, with clasps " Cape Colony," " Orange Free State," and " Transvaal " ; King's medal, with clasps "South Africa, 1901," and " South Africa, 1902 "). Still serving. [30.]

6TH (INNISKILLING) DRAGOONS

—— Corpl. Jenner, Albert F. (Pitlochry). Enlisted in Scots Greys 1888. Transferred to 6th (Inniskilling) Dragoons. Served in South African War, . . . 1900 . . . (Queen's medal, with clasps " Cape Colony," " Orange Free State," and " Belfast "). [35.]

3669. Sq. Sergt.-Maj. McPherson, William (Pitlochry). Enlisted 1897. Promoted Corpl 1899, Sergt. 1900, Sq. Sergt.-Maj. 1903.

Served in South African War, 1899–1902 (Queen's medal, with three clasps ; King's medal, with clasps "South Africa, 1901," and " South Africa, 1902 "). Still serving. [36.]

4305. Pte. Milne, William (Perth). Enlisted 1900. Served in South African War, 1900 . . . (Queen's medal, with three clasps). Still serving. [37.]

7TH (THE QUEEN'S OWN) HUSSARS

—— Pte. Reid, Stuart A. (Perth). Enlisted 1901. Served in South African War, 1901–1902 (Queen's medal, with clasps "Cape Colony,"

"Orange Free State," "Transvaal," "South Africa, 1901," and " South Africa, 1902 "). Still serving. [38.]

9TH (THE QUEEN'S ROYAL) LANCERS

4272. Pte. Gilchrist, William (Coupar Angus). Enlisted in 17th Lancers 1896. Transferred to 9th Lancers 1898. Served in South African War, 1899–1900. Wounded at Magersfontein, December 11, 1899 (Queen's medal, with clasps " Belmont," "Modder River," and " Natal "). Invalided home 1900. Transferred to Reserve 1903. [39.]

4241. Pte. McDonald, William (Aberfeldy). Enlisted in 12th Lancers 1897. Transferred to 9th Lancers 1898. Served in South African War, 1899–1900 (Queen's medal, with clasps " Belmont," " Modder River," " Relief of Kimberley," and " Paardeberg "). Killed at Roodepoort, near Thabanchu, April 24, 1900. [40.]

10TH (THE PRINCE OF WALES'S OWN ROYAL) HUSSARS

4006. Sh.-Smith Barty, James C. (Perth). Enlisted 1898. Served in South African War, ... 1900-1902 (Queen's medal, with clasps "Cape Colony" and "Belfast"; King's medal, with clasps "South Africa, 1901," and "South Africa, 1902"). Transferred to Reserve. [41.]

3755. Pte. Donaldson, George (Perth). Enlisted 1897. Served in South African War, ... 1900 ... (Queen's medal, with clasps "Cape Colony," "Johannesburg," "Diamond Hill," and "Wittebergen"). [42.]

—— **Corpl. Lowe, Andrew M.** (Perth). Enlisted 1898. Served in South African War, ... 1900-1902 (Queen's medal, with clasps "Relief of Kimberley," "Paardeberg," "Driefontein," and "Transvaal"; King's medal, with clasps "South Africa, 1901," and "South Africa, 1902"). Still serving. [43.]

4159. Pte. Muckersie, William (Perth). Enlisted 1899. Served in South African War, ... 1900 (Queen's medal, with clasp "Belfast"). Died at Rustenburg, December 24, 1900. [44.]

4100. Corpl. Mullions, Thomas (Perth). Enlisted 1899. Served in South African War, 1900 (Queen's medal, with clasps "Paardeberg," "Driefontein," and "Belfast"). Killed near Belfast, October 15, 1900. [45.]

12TH (THE PRINCE OF WALES'S ROYAL) LANCERS

5156. Pte. Comrie, W. (Crieff). Enlisted 1900. Served in South African War, 1901-1902 (Queen's medal, with clasps "Cape Colony," "South Africa, 1901," and "South Africa, 1902"). Discharged invalided 1903. [46.]

4913. Pte. Thomson, William (Crieff). Enlisted 1900. Served in South African War, 1900 (Queen's medal, with clasps "Cape Colony," "Orange Free State," and "Transvaal"). Invalided home 1901. Still serving. [47.]

13TH HUSSARS

4624. Pte. Gilchrist, George (Rattray). Enlisted 1900. Served in South African War, 1900-1902 (Queen's medal, with clasps "Natal," "Orange Free State," and "Transvaal"; King's medal, with clasps "South Africa, 1901," and "South Africa, 1902"). Now serving in 4th Hussars. [48.]

3067. Pte. Imrie, Joseph (Perth). Enlisted 1897. Served in South African War, 1899-1902 (Queen's medal, with clasps "Tugela Heights," "Relief of Ladysmith," "Transvaal," and "Orange Free State"; King's medal, with clasps "South Africa, 1901," and "South Africa, 1902"). Still serving. [49.]

3111. Pte. Martin, Richard (Perth). Enlisted 1890. Served in South African War, 1899-1902 (Queen's medal, with clasps "Tugela Heights," "Relief of Ladysmith," "Transvaal," and "Orange Free State"; King's medal, with clasps "South Africa, 1901," and "South Africa, 1902"). Discharged 1902. [50.]

4436. Pte. Watson, James (Scone). Enlisted 1899. Served in South African War, 1901-1902 (Queen's medal, with clasps "Transvaal," "Orange Free State," "South Africa, 1901," and "South Africa, 1902"). Discharged 1903. [51.]

4524. Pte. Wrench, Harry (Abernethy). Enlisted 1898. Served in South African War (as Corpl. in Intelligence Department), ... 1901-1902 (Queen's medal, with clasps "Transvaal," "South Africa, 1901," and "South Africa, 1902"). Discharged invalided 1903. [52.]

14TH (THE KING'S) HUSSARS

4284. Pte. Ferrier, Charles (Perth). Enlisted 1899. Served in South African War, ... 1901 (Queen's medal, with clasps "Cape Colony," "Orange Free State," "Transvaal," and "South Africa, 1901"). Still serving. [55.

14TH (THE KING'S) HUSSARS—*continued*

4306. Pte. Lamb, John O. (Blairgowrie). Enlisted 1899. Served in South African War, 1900–1902 (Queen's medal, with clasps "Cape Colony," "Orange Free State," and "Transvaal"; King's medal, with clasps "South Africa, 1901," and "South Africa, 1902"). Still serving. [56.]

4313. Pte. McIntosh, Hugh (Dunkeld). Enlisted 1899. Served in South African War, 1900–1902 (Queen's medal, with clasps "Cape Colony," "Orange Free State," and "Transvaal"; King's medal, with clasps "South Africa, 1901," and "South Africa, 1902"). Still serving. [53.]

145. Corpl. McQueen, James (Pitlochry). Enlisted 1891. Promoted Lance-Corpl. 1892, Corpl. 1895. Served in Matabele Rebellion, 1896–1897. Transferred to Reserve 1898. Served in South African War as Reservist, 1900; wounded at Doornkop, and at Diamond Hill. Invalided home 1900. Served again in South African War, 1901–1902 (Queen's medal, with clasps "Cape Colony," "Orange Free State," "Johannesburg," and "Diamond Hill"; King's medal, with clasps "South Africa, 1901," and "South Africa, 1902"). Still serving with the colours. [57.]

5036. Sq. Qrmr.-Sergt. Pentland, George (Perth). Enlisted 1890. Served in South African War, (1) with 14th Hussars, 1899–1901; (2) with South African Constabulary, 1901–1902 (Queen's medal, with clasps "Tugela Heights," "Relief of Ladysmith," "Cape Colony," "Orange Free State," "Johannesburg," "Diamond Hill," and "Belfast"; King's medal, with clasps "South Africa, 1901," and "South Africa, 1902"). Still serving. [54.]

4307. Pte. Pillans, Lawrence (Blairgowrie). Enlisted 1899. Served in South African War, 1900–1901 (Queen's medal, with clasps "Cape Colony," "Orange Free State," "Transvaal," and "South Africa, 1901"). Still serving.

17TH (THE DUKE OF CAMBRIDGE'S OWN) LANCERS

—— **Lance-Corpl. Davidson, William L. L.** (Abernethy). Enlisted 1900. Served in South African War, 1901–1902 (Queen's medal, with clasps "Cape Colony," "South Africa, 1901," and "South Africa, 1902"). Still serving. [58.]

18TH HUSSARS

5169. Pte. Dewar, Donald (Killin). Enlisted 1900. Served in South African War, 1900–1902 (Queen's medal, with clasps "Cape Colony," "Orange Free State," "South Africa, 1901," and "South Africa, 1902"). Still serving.

3877. Pte. McBain, John (Blairgowrie). Enlisted 1891. Served in South African War, 1899–1902 (Queen's medal, with clasps "Talana," "Defence of Ladysmith," "Laing's Nek," "Orange Free State," and "Belfast"; King's medal, with clasps "South Africa, 1901," and "South Africa, 1902").

4347. Lance-Corpl. Weir, John (Perth). Enlisted 1894. Served in South African War, 1899 (Queen's medal, with clasps "Talana" and "Defence of Ladysmith"). Died of wounds at Ladysmith, December 9, 1899. [59.]

4084. Corpl. Wilson, James (Bonhard). Enlisted 1893. Served in South African War, 1899–1901. Wounded at Rhenoster Kop, December 8, 1900 (Queen's medal, with clasps "Talana," "Transvaal," and "South Africa, 1901"). Invalided home and discharged invalided 1901. [60.]

19TH (ALEXANDRA, PRINCESS OF WALES'S OWN) HUSSARS

3699. Pte. Curr, David (Perth). Enlisted 1887. Served in South African War as Reservist, 1900. Wounded at Sunday's River (Queen's medal, with clasp "Natal"). Invalided home. [61.]

20TH HUSSARS

4395. Pte. Sutherland, Duncan (Auchterarder). Enlisted 1897. Served in South African War (Queen's medal, with four clasps). Still serving. [62.]

4324. Pte. Watt, James (Perth). Enlisted 1897. Served in South African War (Queen's medal, with four clasps). Still serving. [63.]

4318. Pte. Watt, William G. (Perth). Enlisted 1895. Served in South African War (Queen's medal, with four clasps). Still serving. [64.]

ROYAL REGIMENT OF ARTILLERY

ROYAL HORSE ARTILLERY

—— **Qrmr.-Sergt. Bennett,** James (Abernethy). Enlisted 1852. Served in Crimea 1854-1855 during Russian War (medal, with clasps "Alma," "Balaclava," "Inkerman," and "Sevastopol"; Turkish medal). Long Service medal. Discharged 1874. [67.]

R.A. 50221. Dr. McLeod, William A. (Errol). Enlisted 1885. Served in South African War with T Batty. R.H.A., . . . 1900-1902 (Queen's medal, with clasps "Cape Colony," "Orange Free State," "Johannesburg," and "Belfast"; King's medal, with clasps "South Africa, 1901," and "South Africa, 1902"). Discharged 1902. [65.]

R.A. 30500. Bomb. Storrar, John S. (Perth). O Batty. R.H.A. Enlisted 1898. Served in South African War with O Batty. and R.A. Mtd. Rifles, 1899-1902 (Queen's medal, with clasps "Relief of Kimberley," "Paardeberg," "Driefontein," and "Johannesburg"; King's medal, with clasps "South Africa, 1901," and "South Africa, 1902"). Still serving. [66.]

R.A. 44956. Dr. Taylor, David (Perth). Enlisted 1884. Served in South African War, . . . 1900-1901 (Queen's medal, with clasps "Cape Colony," "Orange Free State," "Johannesburg," "Diamond Hill," and "South Africa, 1901"). Discharged 1902. [68.]

ROYAL FIELD ARTILLERY

15941. Sh.-Smith Anderson, Matthew (Rattray). Enlisted 1901. Served in South African War with R.A. Mounted Rifles, 1901-1902 (Queen's medal, with clasps "Cape Colony," "Orange Free State," "Transvaal," "South Africa, 1901," and "South Africa, 1902"). Discharged 1902.

R.A. 30420. Gr. Bannerman, James (Coupar Angus). Enlisted 1898. Served in South African War (with 1-Pounder Maxims), 1900-1902 (Queen's medal, with clasps "Cape Colony," "Orange Free State," and "Transvaal"; King's medal, with clasps "South Africa, 1901," and "South Africa, 1902"). Now serving with No. 26 Coy. R.G.A.

R.A. 59966. Gr. Cameron, Hugh (Crieff). Enlisted 1887. Transferred to Reserve 1895. Served in South African War as Reservist with 2nd Batty. R.F.A., 1900-1902 (Queen's medal, with clasps "Cape Colony," "Wittebergen," "Transvaal"; King's medal, with clasps "South Africa, 1901," and "South Africa, 1902"). [69.]

R.H. and R.F.A. 12342. Gr. Campbell, Andrew (Kirkmichael). Enlisted 1900. Served in South African War with R.F.A. Details, 1901-1902 (Queen's medal, with clasps "Cape Colony," "Orange Free State," "Transvaal," "South Africa, 1901," and "South Africa, 1902"). Now serving in 2nd Batty. R.F.A. [70.]

R.A. 76190. Sergt. Christie, Samuel (Longforgan). Enlisted 1889. Served in South African War with New Zealand Batty. and 9th Local Ammun. Column, 1900-1902 (Queen's medal, with clasps "Rhodesia," "Cape Colony," "Transvaal," and "Orange Free State"; King's medal, with clasps "South Africa, 1901," "South Africa, 1902"). Discharged 1902. [71.]

R.A. 78085. Dr. Dewar, James (Perth). Enlisted 1890. Served in South African War with 37th Batty. R.F.A., 1899-1902 (Queen's medal, with clasps "Cape Colony" and "Transvaal"; King's medal, with clasps "South Africa, 1901," and "South Africa, 1902"). Discharged 1902. [73.]

ROYAL FIELD ARTILLERY—*continued*

C.B. 2430. Sergt. Hendry, John (Coupar Angus). Coast Brigade. Enlisted 1852. Served in Crimea . . . 1855 during Russian War. Wounded by explosion of a magazine before Sevastopol, November 15, 1855 (medal, with clasp "Sevastopol," and Turkish medal). Served also in Indian Mutiny. Long Service medal. Discharged 1874.

R.F.A. 27568. Corpl. Hynd, David (Perth). Enlisted 1885. Transferred to Reserve 1892. Served in South African War as Reservist with 87th Howitzer Batty. and R.A. Mtd. Rifles, 1900-1902 (Queen's medal, with clasps "Cape Colony," "Orange Free State," and "Transvaal"; King's medal, with clasps "South Africa, 1901," and "South Africa, 1902"). Long Service medal. Still serving with 87th Batty. R.F.A. [74.]

R.A. 66199. Gr. McLean, Duncan (Logiealmond). Enlisted 1888. Transferred to Reserve 1896. Served in South African War as Reservist, 1899-1901 (Queen's medal, with clasps "Cape Colony," "Orange Free State," and "South Africa, 1901"). Discharged 1901. [75.]

R.A. 20625. Gr. Maison, John (Blairgowrie). Enlisted 1897. Served in South African War with 68th Batty. R.F.A., 1900-1902; slightly wounded at Dewetsdorp (Queen's medal, with clasps "Cape Colony" and "Orange Free State"; King's medal, with clasps "South Africa, 1901," and "South Africa, 1902"). Still serving with 68th Batty. R.F.A. [72.]

R.A. 66549. Sh.-Smith Marr, James (Crieff). Enlisted 1888. Served in South African War as Reservist with Excess Numbers and 86th Batty. R.F.A., . . . 1900-1901 (Queen's medal, with clasps "Cape Colony" and "South Africa, 1901"). Discharged 1901.

R.A. 24566. Sadd. - Corpl. Purgavie, Charles (Woodside). Enlisted 1897. Served in South African War with 61st Batty. R.F.A., 1899-1902 (Queen's medal, with clasps "Tugela Heights," "Relief of Ladysmith," "Laing's Nek," "Orange Free State," "Belfast," and "Cape Colony"; King's medal, with clasps "South Africa, 1901," and "South Africa, 1902"). Now serving with 76th Batty. R.F.A. [79.]

R.A. 7923. Dr. Robertson, James (Cargill), 75th Batty. R.F.A. Enlisted 1895. Served in South African War, 1899-1900. Wounded at Modder River, November 28, 1899 (Distinguished Conduct medal; Queen's medal, with clasps "Belmont" and "Modder River"). Transferred to Reserve 1902. [76.]

R.H. and R.F.A. 5846. Gr. Sutherland, David (Coupar Angus). Enlisted 1900. Served in South African War with R.A. Mtd. Rifles, 1902 (Queen's medal, with clasps "Cape Colony," "Orange Free State," and "South Africa, 1902"). Now serving with 28th Batty. R.F.A. [77.]

R.H. and R.F.A. 4518. Sh.-Smith Wilson, James (Port of Monteith). Enlisted 1900. Served in South African War with 82nd Batty. R.F.A., 1900-1902 (Queen's medal, with clasps "Wittebergen," "Cape Colony," and "Transvaal"; King's medal, with clasps "South Africa, 1901," and "South Africa, 1902"). Discharged 1902. [78.]

ROYAL GARRISON ARTILLERY

MOUNTAIN DIVISION

R.A. 85784. Sergt. Miller, William C. (Meigle). Served in South African War with 4th Batty. Mountain Arty. R.G.A., 1899-1900 (Queen's medal, with clasps "Tugela Heights" and "Relief of Ladysmith"). Now serving with No. 63 Coy. R.G.A. [80.]

GARRISON COMPANIES

R.A. 25077. Act. Bomb. Amos, John (Woodside). Enlisted 1897. Served in South African War with Excess Numbers R.G.A., Supy. to No. 7 Coy. Southern Divn. R.G.A. 1899-1901 (Queen's medal, with clasps "Tugela Heights," "Relief of Ladysmith," "Laing's Nek," "Transvaal," "Orange Free State," "Cape Colony," and "South Africa, 1901"). Discharged invalided 1901. [81.]

R.G.A. 4279. Gr. Kean, David F. (Perth). Enlisted 1900. Served in South African War

with No. 98 Coy. R.G.A., 1901 (Queen's medal, with clasps "Cape Colony," "Orange Free State," "Transvaal," and "South Africa, 1901"). Now serving on District Establishment, Halifax, Nova Scotia.

CORPS OF ROYAL ENGINEERS

2188. Corpl. Chalmers, William C. (Perth). 38th Coy. (Field). Enlisted 1898. Served in South African War, 1899–1902. Wounded at Koedoesberg, February 1900 (Queen's medal, with clasps "Belmont," "Modder River," "Paardeberg," "Driefontein," and "Wittebergen"; King's medal, with clasps "South Africa, 1901," and "South Africa, 1902"). Still serving.

1852. Mech. Staff-Sergt. Chalmers, Robertson (Perth). Supy. Staff. Enlisted 1898. Served in South African War, 1902 (Queen's medal, with clasps "Cape Colony," "Orange Free State," "Transvaal," and "South Africa, 1902"). Still serving.

2770. Sapr. Dow, William (Crieff). 5th Coy. (Field). Enlisted 1899. Served in South African War, 1900–1902 (Queen's medal, with clasps "Cape Colony" and "Wittebergen"; King's medal, with clasps "South Africa, 1901," and "South Africa, 1902"). Still serving. [82.]

4788. Sapr. Foote, John (Perth). Telegraph Divn. Enlisted 1901. Served in South African War, 1901–1902 (Queen's medal, with clasps "Cape Colony," "Orange Free State," "Transvaal," "South Africa, 1901," and "South Africa, 1902"). Discharged 1902. [85.]

5226. Sapr. Fraser, William (Perth). 46th Coy. (Field). Enlisted 1900. Served in South African War, 1901–1902 (Queen's medal, with clasps "Cape Colony," "South Africa, 1901," and "South Africa, 1902"). Transferred to Reserve 1903.

23289. Sapr. Halkerston, James (Perth). 58th Coy. (Field). Enlisted 1888. Served in South African War, . . . 1900–1901 (Queen's medal, with clasps "Relief of Kimberley," "Paardeberg," "Driefontein," and "South Africa, 1901"). Discharged 1901. [86.]

24071. Sapr. Irvine, John (Coupar Angus). 29th Coy. (Fortress). Enlisted 1889. Served in South African War, . . . 1900–1902 (Queen's medal, with clasps "Cape Colony," "Orange

Free State," and "Transvaal"; King's medal, with clasps "South Africa, 1901," and "South Africa, 1902"). Died at Woodstock, March 18, 1902. [87.]

29662. Farr.-Corpl. Jack, George (Moulin) 26th Coy. (Field). Enlisted 1896. Served in South African War, 1899–1902 (Queen's medal, with clasps "Cape Colony," "Orange Free State," "Johannesburg"; King's medal, with clasps "South Africa, 1901," and "South Africa, 1902"). Still serving. [88.]

3865. Corpl. Jack, James W. Enlisted 1899. Served in South African War with 45th Coy. R.E. (Steam Road Transport), 1901–1902 (Queen's medal, with clasps "Cape Colony," "Orange Free State," "South Africa, 1901," and "South Africa, 1902"). Transferred to Army Service Corps (Mechanical Transport). Still serving.

24658. Sapr. McFarlane, John (Burrelton). 38th Coy. (Field). Enlisted 1890. Served in South African War as Reservist, 1900–1902 (Queen's medal, with clasps "Paardeberg," "Driefontein"; King's medal, with clasps "South Africa, 1901," and "South Africa, 1902"). Discharged 1902. [89.]

23005. Sapr. McLagan, James (Coupar Angus). Enlisted 1887. Served in South African War as Reservist with 9th Coy. (Field), 1899–1901 (Queen's medal, with clasps "Cape Colony," "Paardeberg," "Driefontein," "Transvaal," and "South Africa, 1901"). Discharged 1902.

3925. Sapr. MacQueen, David (Crieff). Telegraph Divn. Enlisted 1899. Served in South African War, 1901–1902 (Queen's medal, with clasps "Cape Colony," "Orange Free State," "South Africa, 1901," and "South Africa, 1902"). Still serving. [90.]

23219. Corpl. Martin, William (Perth). 2nd Balloon Section. Enlisted 1888. Served in South African War, 1899–1901 (Queen's medal, with clasps "Defence of Ladysmith," "Laing's

CORPS OF ROYAL ENGINEERS—*continued*

Nek," "Orange Free State," "Transvaal," "Cape Colony," and "South Africa, 1901"). Still serving. [83.]

29438. Sapr. Robb, Joseph (Perth). Enlisted 1895. Served in South African War with Bridging Batt. ("A" Troop), . . . 1900–1902. Wounded at Hanover Road (Queen's medal, with clasps "Tugela Heights," "Relief of Ladysmith," "Laing's Nek," "Transvaal," and "Cape Colony"; King's medal, with clasps "South Africa, 1901," and "South Africa, 1902"). Transferred to Reserve. [91.]

1819. Lance-Corpl. Ross, John (Findo Gask). 1st Field Troop. Enlisted 1898. Served in South African War, . . . 1900–1902 (Queen's medal, with clasps "Relief of Kimberley," "Paardeberg," "Driefontein," "Johannesburg," and "Diamond Hill"; King's medal, with clasps "South Africa, 1901," and "South Africa, 1902"). Still serving. [92.]

10766. Sapr. Sturrock, Jas. (Perth). (Formerly in 4th Vol. Batt. The Black Watch) Enlisted in R.E. 1902. Served in South African War, (1) with 1st Vol. Service Coy. The Black Watch, 1900–1901; (2) with Telegraph Divn. R.E., 1902 (Queen's medal, with clasps "Transvaal," "Cape Colony," "Wittebergen," "South Africa, 1901," and "South Africa, 1902"). Discharged 1902. [93.]

25390. Sapr. Traill, James A. (Perth). 38th Coy. (Field). Enlisted 1890. Served in South African War, 1899–1902 (Queen's medal, with clasps "Relief of Kimberley," "Paardeberg," "Driefontein," "Wittebergen," and "Transvaal"; King's medal, with clasps "South Africa, 1901," and "South Africa, 1902"). Transferred to Reserve 1902. [84.]

29254. Sapr. Walker, James (Moulin). 37th Coy. (Field). Enlisted 1895. Served in South African War, 1899–1902 (Queen's medal, with clasps "Tugela Heights," "Relief of Ladysmith," "Laing's Nek," "Orange Free State," and "Transvaal"; King's medal, with clasps "South Africa, 1901," and "South Africa, 1902"). Still serving.

THE FOOT GUARDS

SCOTS GUARDS

1263. Pte. Barnett, John T. (Auchterarder). Enlisted 1897. Served in South African War, 1899–1902 (Queen's medal, with clasps "Belmont," "Modder River," "Driefontein," "Johannesburg," "Diamond Hill," and "Belfast"; King's medal, with clasps "South Africa, 1901," and "South Africa, 1902"). Discharged 1902.

1782. Pte. Benvie, George (Errol). Enlisted 1897. Served in South African War, 1899–1902 (Queen's medal, with clasps "Belmont," "Modder River," "Driefontein," "Johannesburg," and "Belfast"; King's medal, with clasps "South Africa, 1901," and "South Africa, 1902"). Transferred to Reserve. [94.]

9954. Pte. Birrell, James (Perth). Enlisted 1892. Served in South African War, 1900–1902 (Queen's medal, with clasps "Cape Colony," "Orange Free State," "Johannesburg," "Diamond Hill," and "Belfast"; King's medal, with clasps "South Africa, 1901," and "South Africa, 1902"). Transferred to Reserve 1903. [95.]

8167. Pte. Black, James (New Scone). Enlisted 1889. Served in South African War, 1900–1902 (Queen's medal, with clasps "Cape Colony," "Orange Free State," "Johannesburg," "Diamond Hill," and "Belfast"; King's medal, with clasps "South Africa, 1901," and "South Africa, 1902"). Discharged 1902. [96.]

3720. Pte. Blair, R. (Port of Monteith). Enlisted 1901. Served in South African War, 1902 (Queen's medal, with clasps "Cape Colony," "Orange Free State," and "South Africa, 1902"). Still serving. [97.]

2547. Pte. Bullion, George T. (Perth). Enlisted 1899. Served in South African War, 1900–1902 (Queen's medal, with clasps "Cape Colony," "Wittebergen," and "Transvaal"; King's medal, with clasps "South Africa, 1901," and "South Africa, 1902"). Transferred to Reserve.

9415. Corpl. Cameron, Daniel (Stanley). Enlisted 1892. Transferred to Reserve 1899. Served in South African War as Reservist

1899 - 1902 (Queen's medal, with clasps "Belmont," "Modder River," "Driefontein," "Johannesburg," "Diamond Hill," and "Belfast"; King's medal, with clasps "South Africa, 1901," and "South Africa, 1902"). [98.]

9938. Sergt. Cameron, William (Crieff). Enlisted 1892. Served in South African War, 1899–1900 (Queen's medal, with clasps "Belmont," "Modder River," and "Driefontein"). Invalided home and transferred to Reserve.

2997. Lance-Corpl. Chalmers, George M. (Perth). Enlisted 1899. Served in South African War, 1901–1902 (Queen's medal, with clasps "Orange Free State," "South Africa, 1901," and "South Africa, 1902"). Still serving. [99.]

8575. Pte. Davidson, David (Errol). Enlisted 1890. Served in South African War, 1900–1902 (Queen's medal, with clasps "Cape Colony," "Driefontein," "Johannesburg," "Diamond Hill," and "Belfast"; King's medal, with clasps "South Africa, 1901," and "South Africa, 1902"). Discharged 1902. [103.]

3759. Pte. Davidson, Stewart (Comrie). Enlisted 1901. Served in South African War, 1902 (Queen's medal, with clasps "Cape Colony," "Orange Free State," and "South Africa, 1902"). Still serving.

2919. Pte. Dewar, Peter (Fortingall). Enlisted 1899. Served in South African War, 1900–1902 (Queen's medal, with clasps "Cape Colony," "Orange Free State," and "Belfast"; King's medal, with clasps "South Africa, 1901," and "South Africa, 1902"). Still serving. [104.]

3405. Pte. Dickson, George (Perth). Enlisted 1900. Served in South African War with Gds. Mtd. Infy., 1901–1902 (Queen's medal, with clasps "Cape Colony," "South Africa, 1901," and "South Africa, 1902"). Still serving. [100.]

3643. Pte. Geekie, Thos. Elder (Coupar Angus). Enlisted 1900. Served in South African War, 1902 (Queen's medal, with clasps "Cape Colony," "Orange Free State," and "South Africa, 1902"). Still serving. [101.]

3290. Pte. Goodfellow, James (Perth). Enlisted 1900. Served in South African War, 1901–1902 (Queen's medal, with clasps "Orange Free State," "South Africa, 1901," and "South Africa, 1902"). [102.]

5387. Lance-Sergt. Lamond, Peter (Rannagulzion). Enlisted 1881. Served in Egyptian Campaign, 1882 (medal, with clasps "Tel-el-Kebir," and Khedive's star). Promoted Corpl. 1882. Transferred to Reserve as Lance-Sergt. 1888. [105.]

1526. Pte. Livingston, Angus (Logiealmond). Enlisted 1897. Served in South African War, 1900–1902 (Queen's medal, with clasps "Cape Colony," "Orange Free State," "Johannesburg," "Diamond Hill," and "Belfast"; King's medal, with clasps "South Africa, 1901," and "South Africa, 1902"). Discharged 1902.

4217. Sergt. McBeth, Donald (Blair Atholl). Enlisted in Scots Fusilier Guards 1851. Served in Crimea, 1854–1855, during Russian War, as Sgt. of Sharpshooters (Distinguished Conduct medal; medal, with clasps "Alma," "Inkerman," "Balaclava," and "Sevastopol," and Turkish medal). Discharged 1856. [108.]

1877. Pte. McDonald, James (New Rattray). Enlisted 1889. Served in South African War, 1900–1902 (Queen's medal, with clasps "Cape Colony," "Transvaal," and "Wittebergen"; King's medal, with clasps "South Africa, 1901," and "South Africa, 1902"). Still serving.

—— **Pte. Macgregor, Thos. Alison** (Scone). Enlisted in Scots Fusilier Guards 1843. Served in Crimea, 1854–1855, during Russian War (medal, with clasps "Alma," "Balaclava," "Inkerman," and "Sevastopol," and Turkish medal). Discharged 1863.

8175. Pte. McKenzie, John (Stanley). Enlisted in Royal Army Medical Corps 1884. Served in Soudan Expedition, 1884 (medal, with clasps "Suakim, 1884," and Khedive's star). Enlisted in Scots Guards 1889. Transferred to Reserve 1896. Served in South African War as Reservist, 1900–1901 (Queen's medal, with clasps "Cape Colony," "Wittebergen," "Transvaal," and "South Africa, 1901"). Now serving with Royal Garrison Regiment. [106.]

9211. Pte. McLay, John (Dunblane). Enlisted 1891. Served in South African War, 1899 - 1902 (Queen's medal, with clasps "Belmont," "Modder River," "Driefontein," "Johannesburg," "Diamond Hill," and "Belfast"; King's medal, with clasps "South Africa, 1901," and "South Africa, 1902"). Still serving.

SCOTS GUARDS—*continued*

9509. Pte. McLean, John (Aberfeldy). Enlisted 1891. Served in South African War, 1899 – 1900 (Queen's medal, with clasps "Belmont," "Modder River," "Driefontein," and "Diamond Hill"). Discharged invalided 1902. [110.]

1536. Piper McLeish, William (Dunkeld). Enlisted 1897. Served in South African War, 1900-1901 (Queen's medal, with clasps "Wittebergen," "Cape Colony," "Transvaal," and "South Africa, 1901"). Invalided home 1901. Still serving. [111.]

9123. Pte. McMullen, James (Perth). Enlisted 1891. Served in South African War, 1899 – 1902 (Queen's medal, with clasps "Belmont," "Modder River," "Driefontein," "Johannesburg," "Diamond Hill," and "Belfast"; King's medal, with clasps "South Africa, 1901," and "South Africa, 1902"). Still serving.

8746. Pte. McRae, Lorn (Forgandenny). Enlisted 1890. Served in South African War, 1899 – 1902 (Queen's medal, with clasps "Belmont," "Modder River," "Driefontein," "Johannesburg," "Diamond Hill," and "Belfast"; King's medal, with clasps "South Africa, 1901," and "South Africa, 1902"). Discharged 1902.

4165. Pte. Owler, George (Blairgowrie). Enlisted in Scots Fusilier Guards 1850. Served in Crimea, 1854, during Russian War (medal, with clasp "Alma," and Turkish medal). Discharged 1855. [107.]

3295. Pte. Pullar, Daniel (Perth). Enlisted 1900. Served in South African War, 1901-1902 (Queen's medal, with clasps "Orange Free State," "South Africa, 1901," and "South Africa, 1902"). Still serving. [114.]

8605. Pte. Robinson, Fred. (Perth). Enlisted 1890. Served in South African War, 1900-1902 (Queen's medal, with clasps "Cape Colony," "Orange Free State," "Johannesburg," "Belfast," and "Diamond Hill"; King's medal, with clasps "South Africa, 1901," and "South Africa, 1902"). Discharged 1902. [113.]

3436. Pte. Roy, John (Tibbermuir). Enlisted 1900. Served in South African War, 1902 (Queen's medal, with clasps "Cape Colony," "Orange Free State," and "South Africa, 1902"). Still serving.

8901. Pte. Scobie, Andrew (Aberfeldy). Enlisted 1891. Served in South African War, 1899-1900 and 1902 (Queen's medal, with clasps "Belmont," "Modder River," and "South Africa, 1902"). Transferred to Reserve. [112.]

3298. Pte. Scott, William (Muthill). Enlisted 1900. Served in South African War with Gds. Mtd. Infy., 1902 (Queen's medal, with clasps "Cape Colony" and "South Africa, 1902"). Discharged 1903.

9269. Piper Sharp, David (Longforgan). Enlisted 1891. Served in South African War, 1900-1902 (Queen's medal, with clasps "Cape Colony," "Wittebergen," and "Transvaal"; King's medal, with clasps "South Africa, 1901," and "South Africa, 1902"). Still serving.

2366. Pte. Sheriff, Christopher (Pitlochry). Enlisted 1898. Served in South African War, 1900-1901 (Queen's medal, with clasps "Cape Colony," "Wittebergen," "Transvaal," and "South Africa, 1901"). Transferred to Reserve 1902.

298. Pte. Slater, Daniel (Stanley). Enlisted 1894. Served in South African War, 1900-1901 (Queen's medal, with clasps "Cape Colony," "Wittebergen," "Transvaal," and "South Africa, 1901"). Discharged 1902.

1135. Sergt. Stevenson, James W. (Muthill). Enlisted 1896. Promoted Corpl. 1898, Sergt. 1900. Served in South African War, 1900-1902 (Queen's medal, with clasps "Cape Colony," "Orange Free State," and "Transvaal"; King's medal, with clasps "South Africa, 1901," and "South Africa, 1902"). [115.]

2134. Pte. Thornton, William J. (Trinity Gask). Enlisted 1898. Served in South African War, . . . 1900-1902 (Queen's medal, with clasps "Cape Colony," "Orange Free State," "Johannesburg," "Diamond Hill," and "Belfast"; King's medal, with clasps "South Africa, 1901," and "South Africa, 1902"). Still serving. [116.]

5942. Pte. Wood, William (Perth). Enlisted in 72nd (Duke of Albany's Own Highlanders) Regt. 1852. Transferred to Scots Fusilier Guards 1855. Served in Crimea, 1855, during Russian War (medal, with clasp "Sevastopol," and Turkish medal). Discharged 1862. [108.]

INFANTRY OF THE LINE, MILITIA, AND VOLUNTEERS

THE ROYAL SCOTS (Lothian Regiment)

138. Pte. Anderson, Duncan (Dull). Enlisted 1881. Served in South African War, . . . 1900–1902 (Queen's medal, with clasps "Cape Colony," "Orange Free State," and "Transvaal"; King's medal, with clasps "South Africa, 1901," and South Africa, 1902"). Still serving. [117.]

7353. Drum. Baxter, Alexander (Perth). Enlisted 1900. Served in South African War, 1902 (Queen's medal, with clasps "Transvaal" and "South Africa, 1902"). Still serving.

4211. Sergt. Baxter, William (Burrelton). Enlisted 1893. Served in South African War, 1899–1900 (Queen's medal, with clasps "Cape Colony," "Orange Free State," and "Belfast"). Died at Telspruit, Nov. 5, 1900. [118.]

7780. Corpl. Brough, Thomas (Perth). Enlisted 1898. Served in South African War, . . . 1900–1902 (Queen's medal, with clasps "Cape Colony" and "Transvaal"; King's medal, with clasps "South Africa, 1901," and "South Africa, 1902").

4195. Pte. Burnett, William (Perth). Enlisted 1891. Served in South African War, 1902 (Queen's medal, with clasps "Transvaal," and "South Africa, 1902").

8374. Pte. Cameron, James S. (Perth). Enlisted 1900. Served in South African War, 1900–1902 (Queen's medal, with clasps "Cape Colony," "Orange Free State," and "Transvaal"; King's medal, with clasps "South Africa, 1901," and "South Africa, 1902").

6564. Pte. Garvie, Peter (Perth). Enlisted 1898. Served in South African War, . . . 1900–1902 (Queen's medal, with clasps "Cape Colony," "Orange Free State," and "Belfast"; King's medal, with clasps "South Africa, 1901," and "South Africa, 1902"). Still serving.

8357. Pte. Gorrie, Thomas (Auchterarder). 3rd (Militia) Batt. Enlisted 1900. Served in South African War, 1900–1902 (Queen's medal, with clasps "Cape Colony" and "Orange Free State"; King's medal, with clasps "South Africa, 1901," and "South Africa, 1902"). Still serving.

6017. Lance-Corpl. Kirk, James C. (Perth). Enlisted 1897. Served in South African War, 1899–1902. Slightly wounded near Wepener (Queen's medal, with clasps "Cape Colony," "Orange Free State," and "Belfast"; King's medal, with clasps "South Africa, 1901," and "South Africa, 1902"). Still serving. [120.]

8034. Pte. Laird, John (Auchterarder). 3rd (Militia) Batt. Enlisted 1899. Served in South African War, 1900–1902 (Queen's medal, with clasps "Cape Colony," "Orange Free State," and "Transvaal"; King's medal, with clasps "South Africa, 1901," and "South Africa, 1902"). Now serving with the Highland Light Infantry. [121.]

8227. Corpl. Lowson, William (Coupar Angus). Vol. Batt. Served in South African War, (1) with 1st Vol. Service Coy., 1900–1901; (2) with 3rd Vol. Service Coy., 1902 (Queen's medal, with clasps "Belfast," "Orange Free State," and "Cape Colony"; King's medal, with clasps "South Africa, 1901," and "South Africa, 1902").

7083. Pte. McConnell, Gilbert (Perth). Enlisted 1900. Served in South African War, 1901–1902 (Queen's medal, with clasps "Cape Colony," "Orange Free State," "Transvaal," "South Africa, 1901," and "South Africa, 1902"). Still serving. [122.]

6435. Lance-Corpl. McFayden, William (Perth). Enlisted 1884. Served in South African War, . . . 1900–1902 (Queen's medal, with clasps "Cape Colony," "Orange Free State," and "Transvaal"; King's medal, with clasps "South Africa, 1901," and "South Africa, 1902").

2422. Pte. Millar, Robert G. R. (Cargill). Enlisted 1885. Transferred to Reserve 1892. Served in South African War as Reservist, 1900–1902 (Queen's medal, with clasps "Cape Colony," "Orange Free State," and "Belfast"; King's medal, with clasps "South Africa, 1901," and "South Africa, 1902"). Discharged 1902. Now serving with South African Constabulary. [123.]

THE ROYAL SCOTS (LOTHIAN REGIMENT)—*continued*

7677. Pte. Milne, Alexander (Perth). 3rd (Militia) Batt. Enlisted 1898. Served in South African War, 1900-1902 (Queen's medal, with clasps " Cape Colony," " Orange Free State," and " Transvaal " ; King's medal, with clasps "South Africa, 1901," and " South Africa, 1902 "). Still serving.

2507. Corpl. Mitchell, William (Dunblane). Enlisted 1887. Transferred to Reserve 1894. Discharged 1899. Re-enlisted in Army Reserve 1899, in order to proceed to South Africa. Died at sea on way out, March 14, 1900. [124.]

5730. Pte. Myles, James (Scone). Enlisted 1896. Served in South African War, 1900-1902 (Queen's medal, with clasps " Cape Colony," " Orange Free State," and " Transvaal " ; King's medal, with clasps " South Africa, 1901," and " South Africa, 1902 "). Transferred to Reserve 1903.

4859. Sergt.-Drum. Rae, William (Perth). Enlisted 1892. Served in South African War, . . . 1900-1902 (Queen's medal, with clasps " Cape Colony," " Orange Free State," and " Transvaal " ; King's medal, with clasps " South Africa, 1901," and "South Africa, 1902 "). Now serving on Permanent Staff of 3rd (Militia) Batt. [125.]

6086. Pte. Reid, Robert (Perth). Enlisted 1898. Served in South African War, . . . 1900-1902 (Queen's medal, with clasps " Cape Colony," " Orange Free State," and " Transvaal " ; King's medal, with clasps " South Africa, 1901," and South Africa, 1902 "). Still serving. [126.]

7463. Pte. Sinclair, David (Perth). Enlisted 1901. Served in South African War, 1902 (Queen's medal, with clasps " Transvaal " and " South Africa, 1902 "). Still serving.

4298. Pte. Speedie, William (Perth). Enlisted 1892. Served in South African War, . . . 1900-1902 (Queen's medal, with clasps " Cape Colony," Orange Free State," and " Belfast " ; King's medal, with clasps " South Africa, 1901," and " South Africa, 1902 ").

7412. Pte. Stewart, Frank (Callander). . . . Vol. Batt. Served in South African War with 2nd Vol. Service Coy., 1902 (Queen's medal, with clasps " Cape Colony," " Orange Free State," " Transvaal," and " South Africa, 1902 "). [127.]

5982. Pte. Wishart, William (Crieff). Enlisted 1898. Served in South African War, . . . 1900-1902 (Queen's medal, with clasps " Cape Colony," " Orange Free State," and " Belfast " ; King's medal, with clasps " South Africa, 1901," and " South Africa, 1902 "). Still serving. [128.]

THE QUEEN'S (ROYAL WEST SURREY REGIMENT)

3749. Pte. Cameron, William (Perth). Enlisted 1892. Served in South African War, 1902 (Queen's medal, with clasps " South Africa, 1902 " . . .). Transferred to Reserve 1903. [129.]

THE BUFFS (EAST KENT REGIMENT)

6200. Pte. Fisken, Charles (Perth). Enlisted 1900. Served in South African War, 1900-1902 (Queen's medal, with clasps " Cape Colony," " Orange Free State," and "Transvaal " ; King's medal, with clasps " South Africa, 1901," and " South Africa, 1902 "). Still serving.

6273. Lance-Corpl. McEwan, Harry (Perth). Enlisted 1900. Promoted Lance-Corpl. 1900. Served in South African War, 1901-1902 (Queen's medal, with clasps " Cape Colony," " Orange Free State," " Transvaal," " South Africa, 1901," and " South Africa, 1902 "). Still serving. [130.]

6274. Pte. Murphy, Edward (Perth). Enlisted 1900. Served in South African War, 1901 (Queen's medal, with clasps " Cape Colony," " Orange Free State," " Transvaal," and " South Africa, 1901 "). Killed at Bakenlaagte, Oct. 30, 1901. [131.]

THE ROYAL SCOTS FUSILIERS

2765. Lance-Corpl. Cameron, Peter (Perth). Enlisted 1890. Served in South African War as Reservist,1899–1902 (Queen's medal, with clasps "Tugela Heights," "Relief of Ladysmith," "Transvaal," and "Cape Colony"; King's medal, with clasps "South Africa, 1901," and "South Africa, 1902"). Discharged 1902. [132.]

7385. Pte. Chalmers, H. (Methven). . . . Vol. Batt. Served in South African War with 1st Vol. Service Coy., 1900–1901 (Queen's medal, with clasps "Orange Free State," "Transvaal," "Natal," and "South Africa, 1901").

3061. Sergt. Clark, James (Perth). Enlisted in 21st (Royal North British) Fusiliers Regt. 1853. Served in Crimea, 1854–1855, during Russian War (medal, with clasps "Alma," "Balaclava," "Inkerman," and "Sevastopol"; Turkish medal). Long Service medal (relinquished later on obtaining Meritorious Service medal). Transferred to Reserve 1874. Discharged 1878. [133.]

5841. Pte. Fraser, John (Crieff). Enlisted 1898. Served in South African War, 1900–1902 (Queen's medal, with clasps "Cape Colony" and "Transvaal"; King's medal, with clasps "South Africa, 1901," and "South Africa, 1902"). Still serving.

6072. Pte. Fraser, Niven (Perth). Enlisted 1899. Served in South African War, 1900–1902 (Queen's medal, with clasps "Natal" and "Transvaal"; King's medal, with clasps "South Africa, 1901," and "South Africa, 1902"). Still serving.

5744. Sergt. Glass, Robert (Perth). Enlisted 1898. Served in South African War, 1900–1902 (Queen's medal, with clasps "Natal," "Cape Colony," and "Transvaal"; King's medal, with clasps "South Africa, 1901," and "South Africa, 1902"). Still serving. [134.]

4518. Sergt. Grubb, John (Rattray). Enlisted 1894. Served in Campaign on North-West Frontier of India (with Tirah Expeditionary Force), 1897–1898 (medal, with clasps "Punjaub Frontier, 1897–8," and "Tirah, 1897–8"). Still serving. [135.]

4517. Pte. Heron, George (Rattray). Enlisted 1894. Served in Campaign on North-West Frontier of India (with Tirah Expeditionary Force), 1897–1898 (medal, with clasps "Punjaub Frontier, 1897–8," and "Tirah,

1897–8." Served also in South African War, 1902 (Queen's medal, with clasps "Transvaal" and "S. Africa, 1902." Transferred to Reserve. [136.]

6035. Pte. King, Archibald (Muthill). Enlisted 1899. Served in South African War, 1900–1902 (latterly with Mtd. Infy.). Wounded at Krugersdorp (Queen's medal, with clasps "Natal" and "Transvaal"; King's medal, with clasps "South Africa, 1901," and "South Africa, 1902").

6526. Pte. Lindsay, Robert (Perth). Enlisted 1900. Served in South African War, 1901–1902 (partly with Mtd. Infy.). (Queen's medal, with clasps "Cape Colony," "Orange Free State," "South Africa, 1901," and "South Africa, 1902"). Still serving.

6531. Pte. McBain, Alex. (Perth). Enlisted 1900. Served in South African War, 1901–1902 (Queen's medal, with clasps "Cape Colony," "Orange Free State," "Transvaal," "South Africa, 1901," and "South Africa, 1902"). Still serving.

5342. Pte. McDougall, Harry (Perth). Enlisted 1897. Served in South African War, 1899–1902 (Queen's medal, with clasps "Tugela Heights," "Relief of Ladysmith," "Cape Colony," and "Transvaal"; King's medal, with clasps "South Africa, 1901," and "South Africa, 1902"). Still serving. [137.]

1394. Pte. McEwan, John (Blairgowrie). Enlisted 1886. Served in South African War, 1899–1902 (Queen's medal, with clasps "Cape Colony," "Orange Free State," and "Transvaal"; King's medal, with clasps "South Africa, 1901," and "South Africa, 1902"). Discharged 1902.

980. Pte. McHardie, William (Perth). Enlisted 1884. Served in Burmese Expedition, 1885–1887 (medal, with clasp "Burma, 1885–87"); also in South African War, 1899–1901 (Queen's medal, with clasps "Tugela Heights," "Relief of Ladysmith," "Cape Colony," "Orange Free State," "Transvaal," and "South Africa, 1901"). Discharged 1901.

4516. Pte. Phillips, William (Blairgowrie). Enlisted 1894. Served in Campaign on North-West Frontier of India (with Tirah Expeditionary Force), 1897–1898. Wounded at Lozaka Pass, Nov. 29, 1897 (medal, with clasps "Punjaub Frontier, 1897–8," and "Tirah,

II. O

THE ROYAL SCOTS FUSILIERS—*continued*

1897-8"). Served also in South African War, 1899-1902 (Queen's medal, with clasps "Tugela Heights," "Relief of Ladysmith," "Cape Colony," and "Transvaal"; King's medal, with clasps "South Africa, 1901," and "South Africa, 1902").

5747. Pte. Robertson, James (Perth). Enlisted 1898. Served in South African War, 1899-1902 (Queen's medal, with clasps "Natal" and "Transvaal"; King's medal, with clasps "South Africa, 1901," and "South Africa, 1902"). Still serving.

2386. Pte. Sinclair, D. (Perth). Enlisted 1888. Served in South African War, 1899-1901 (Queen's medal, with clasps "Relief of Ladysmith" and "South Africa, 1901"). Discharged 1901.

440. Sergt. Stewart, Donald (Errol). Enlisted 1883. Served in Nile Expedition, 1884-

1885 (medal, with clasps "The Nile, 1884-5," and "Abou Klea"; Khedive's star). Served also in Campaign on North-West Frontier of India (with Tirah Expeditionary Force), 1897-1898 (Distinguished Conduct medal; medal, with clasps "Punjaub Frontier, 1897-8," and "Tirah, 1897-8"). Still serving.

3783. Pte. Stewart, D. (Kilmadock). Enlisted 1892. Served in Campaign on North-West Frontier of India (with Tirah Expeditionary Force), 1897-1898 (medal, with clasps "Samana, 1897," and "Punjaub Frontier, 1897-8"). Still serving.

3508. Pte. Thomson, John (Perth). Enlisted 1891. Served in Campaign on North-West Frontier of India (with Tirah Expeditionary Force), 1897-1898 (medal, with clasps "Punjaub Frontier, 1897-8," and "Tirah, 1897-8"). Transferred to Reserve 1902. [138.]

THE SOUTH WALES BORDERERS.

1568. Pte. Meikle, Robert (Burghmuir). Enlisted 1884. Served in South African War, 1899-1900 (Queen's medal, with clasps "Cape Colony" and "Orange Free State." Discharged 1900. [139.]

THE KING'S OWN SCOTTISH BORDERERS

3979. Pte. Ash, Robert (Perth). Enlisted 1892. Served in South African War, ... 1900 (Queen's medal, with clasps "Cape Colony," "Paardeberg," and "Johannesburg"). Transferred to Reserve 1902.

1963. Pte. Beattie, John (Blairgowrie). Enlisted in 25th (The King's Own Borderers) Regt. 1885. Served with Suakim Field Force, 1888 (medal, with clasps "Gemaizah," and Khedive's star). Served also in South African War as Reservist, 1899-1902 (Queen's medal, with clasps "Cape Colony," "Paardeberg," and "Transvaal"; King's medal, with clasps "South Africa, 1901," and "South Africa, 1902"). [140.]

6650. Pte. Burnett, William (Perth). Enlisted 1899. Served in South African War, ... 1900 (Queen's medal, with clasps "Cape Colony," "Orange Free State," and "Johannesburg"). Still serving.

1823. Pte. Conelly, James (New Scone). Enlisted in 25th (The King's Own Borderers)

Regt. 1885. Served with Suakim Field Force, 1888 (medal, with clasps "Gemaizah," and Khedive's star). Served also in South African War, ... 1900-1902 (Queen's medal, with clasps "Cape Colony," "Paardeberg," and "Johannesburg"; King's medal, with clasps "South Africa, 1901," and "South Africa, 1902"). Discharged 1902. [141.]

1656. Pte. Kennedy, Thomas (Blairgowrie). Enlisted in 25th (The King's Own Borderers) Regt. 1885. Served with Suakim Field Force, 1888 (medal, with clasps "Gemaizah," and Khedive's star). Served also in South African War, 1900 (Queen's medal, with clasps "Cape Colony" and "Paardeberg"). Discharged 1901.

3228. Qrmr.-Sergt. Macfarlane, Daniel (Comrie). Enlisted in 25th (The King's Own Borderers) Regt. 1880. Served with Suakim Field Force, 1888 (medal, with clasps "Gemaizah," and Khedive's star). Served also with Chitral Relief Force, 1895, and in Campaign on North-West Frontier of India with Tirah Expeditionary Force, 1897-1898 (medal, with clasps "Relief of Chitral," "Punjaub Frontier, 1897-8," and "Tirah, 1897-8 "). Long Service medal. Discharged 1901. [142.]

5567. Pte. Robertson, A. (Fortingall). Enlisted 1895. Served in South African War 1900-1902 (Queen's medal, with clasps "Cape Colony," "Paardeberg," "Johannesburg," "Diamond Hill," and "Wittebergen"; King's medal, with clasps "South Africa, 1901," and "South Africa, 1902 "). Transferred to Reserve 1903. [143.]

6496. Pte. Robertson, George (New Rattray). Enlisted 1898. Served in South African War, 1900-1902 (Queen's medal, with clasps "Cape Colony," "Orange Free State," and "Johannesburg"; King's medal, with clasps "South Africa, 1901," and "South Africa, 1902 "). Transferred to Reserve 1902. [144.]

THE CAMERONIANS (Scottish Rifles)

6692. Pte. Bruce, Alexander (Perth). Enlisted 1899. Served in South African War, 1900-1902 (Queen's medal, with clasps "Cape Colony," "Orange Free State," and "Transvaal"; King's medal, with clasps "South Africa, 1901," and "South Africa, 1902 "). Still serving.

1574. Pte. Burry, John A. (Comrie). Enlisted 1885. Served in South African War, . . . 1900-1902 (Queen's medal, with clasps "Natal " and "Transvaal"; King's medal, with clasps "South Africa, 1901," and "South Africa, 1902." [145.]

6677. Pte. Cameron, John (Alyth). Enlisted 1900. Served in South African War, 1900-1902 (Queen's medal, with clasps "Cape Colony," "Orange Free State," and "Transvaal"; King's medal, with clasps "South Africa, 1901," and "South Africa, 1902 "). Still serving. [146.]

5388. Pte. Duff, James (Perth). Enlisted 1895. Served in South African War, 1899-1900 (Queen's medal, with clasps "Tugela Heights," "Relief of Ladysmith," "Laing's Nek," and "Transvaal "). Still serving.

2757. Pte. Ferguson, Duncan (Auchtergaven). Enlisted 1888. Served in South African War, 1899-1901 (Queen's medal, with clasps "Tugela Heights," "Relief of Ladysmith," "Laing's Nek," and "Transvaal "). Discharged 1901.

800. Sergt.-Maj. Graham, James (Perth). Enlisted 1883. Served in South African War, 1899-1902 (mentioned in despatches; Distinguished Conduct medal; Queen's medal, with clasps "Tugela Heights," "Relief of Ladysmith," "Laing's Nek," and "Transvaal "; King's medal, with clasps "South Africa, 1901," and "South Africa, 1902 "). Long Service medal. Still serving. [147.]

2594. Pte. Guild, James (Blairgowrie). Enlisted 1887. Served in South African War as Reservist (Queen's medal, with clasps "Natal " and "Transvaal "). [151.]

4662. Sergt. Imrie, James H. D. (Perth). Enlisted 1893. Served in South African War, 1902 (Queen's medal, with clasps "Transvaal " and "South Africa, 1902 "). Still serving.

7872. Corpl. King, William (Muthill). . . . Vol. Batt. Served in South African War with 1st Vol. Service Coy., 1900-1901. Wounded at Laing's Nek, June 11, 1900 (Queen's medal, with clasps "Laing's Nek," "Transvaal," and "South Africa, 1901 "). [148.]

4002. Pte. Littlejohn, David (Perth). Enlisted 1891. Served in South African War as Reservist, 1899-1901 (Queen's medal, with clasps "Tugela Heights," "Relief of Ladysmith," "Transvaal," and "South Africa, 1901 "). [149.]

1260. Qrmr.-Sergt. McDonald, John (Loaninghead.) 4th (Militia) Batt. Enlisted in 26th (The Cameronian) Regt. 1879. Promoted Lance-Corpl. 1880, Corpl. 1881, Sergt. 1883. Transferred to Permanent Staff of 3rd and 4th (Militia) Batts. the Cameronian (Scottish Rifles) 1885 and promoted Col.-Sergt.; Qrmr.-Sergt. 1893. Served in South African War, 1900-1901 (Queen's medal, with clasps "Cape Colony," "Orange Free State," and "South Africa, 1901 "). Long Service medal. Discharged 1901. [157.]

7959. Pte. Macfarlane, John (Callander). Enlisted 1900. Served in South African War, 1901-1902 (Queen's medal, with clasps "Transvaal," "South Africa, 1901," and "South Africa, 1902 "). Discharged 1902. [150.]

—— **Sergt. McLaren, Peter** (Aberfeldy). Enlisted in 26th (The Cameronian) Regt. 1870. Served in Zulu War, 1878-1879. Present in

THE CAMERONIANS (SCOTTISH RIFLES)—*continued*

actions at Kambula and Ulundi, 1879 (medal, with date clasp). Discharged 1896.

4109. Pte. McLaughlin, James (Blairgowrie). Enlisted 1891. Served in South African War, 1899–1901 (Queen's medal, with clasps "Tugela Heights," "Relief of Ladysmith," "Laing's Nek," "Transvaal," and "South Africa, 1901 "). Discharged invalided 1902. [158.]

2820. Pte. Phillips, George P. (Alyth). Enlisted 1888. Served in South African War, 1899–1900. Severely wounded at Spion Kop, Jan. 24, 1900 (Queen's medal, with clasp "Relief of Ladysmith"). Discharged 1901. [152.]

2909. Pte. Ross, Peter (Blairgowrie). Enlisted 1887. Served in South African War as Reservist, . . . 1900. Wounded at Vaalkrantz, Feb. 5, 1900 (Queen's medal, with clasp "Relief of Ladysmith"). [153.]

5919. Lance-Corpl. Spottiswood, William (Alyth). Enlisted 1897. Served in South African War, 1899–1902 (Queen's medal, with clasps "Relief of Ladysmith," "Transvaal," "Orange Free State," and "Cape Colony"; King's medal, with clasps "South Africa, 1901," and "South Africa, 1902 "). Still serving. [154.]

5331. Pte. Watson, George (Alyth). Enlisted 1895. Served in South African War, 1899–1902 (Queen's medal, with clasps "Tugela Heights," "Relief of Ladysmith," "Laing's Nek," and "Transvaal "; King's medal, with clasps "South Africa, 1901," and "South Africa, 1902 "). Still serving. [155.]

5952. Pte. Watson, Thomas (Alyth). Enlisted 1897. Served in South African War, (1) 1899–1900; invalided home 1900 ; (2) 1901–1902 (Queen's medal, with clasps "Tugela Heights," "Relief of Ladysmith," "Laing's Nek," and "Transvaal "; King's medal, with clasps "South Africa, 1901," and "South Africa, 1902 "). Still serving. [156.]

3023. Corpl. Watt, Alexander (Baledgarno). Enlisted 1889. Served in South African War, 1899–1902 (Queen's medal, with clasps "Tugela Heights," "Relief of Ladysmith," "Laing's Nek," and "Transvaal "; King's medal, with clasps "South Africa, 1901," and "South Africa, 1902 "). Discharged 1902. [159.]

3136. Sergt. Young, Robert C. (Crieff). Enlisted 1889. Promoted Lance-Corpl. 1893, Corpl. 1895, Lance-Sergt. 1896, Sergt. 1899. Served in South African War, 1899–1900 (Queen's medal, with clasps "Tugela Heights," "Relief of Ladysmith," and "Laing's Nek "). Invalided home 1900. Discharged 1902. [160.]

THE WORCESTERSHIRE REGIMENT

—— **Pte. Haynes, John** (Muthill). Enlisted 1886. Served in South African War as Reservist 1900 (Queen's medal, with clasp "Cape Colony"). [161.]

THE BORDER REGIMENT

—— **Pte. Barclay, John** (Perth). Enlisted in 34th (The Cumberland) Regt. (now 1st Batt. The Border Regt.) 1858. Served in Indian Mutiny, 1859 (operations in Nepal). (Medal.) Transferred to the Prince Consort's Own Rifle Brigade 1866. Discharged 1883.

998. Pte. Griffiths, Joseph (Perth). Enlisted 1885. Served in South African War, 1899–1901 (Queen's medal, with clasps "Natal," "Transvaal," "Orange Free State," and "South Africa, 1901 "). [162.]

—— **Pte. Keiller, Murdoch** (Pitcastle). Enlisted 1885. Served with Burmah Expedition, 1890 ; also in South African War, 1900–1902 (Queen's medal, with clasps "Natal," "Orange Free State," and "Transvaal "; King's medal, with clasps "South Africa, 1901," and "South Africa, 1902 "). Discharged 1902. [163.]

THE HAMPSHIRE REGIMENT

1014. Pte. Mackay, John (Caputh). Enlisted in 37th (North Hampshire) Regt. 1862. Served in Afghan War, 1879–1880 (medal, with clasps "Charasia " and "Kabul"). Long Service medal. Discharged 1884.

THE WELSH REGIMENT

—— Pte. Cunningham, Thomas (Kincardine on Forth). Enlisted in 69th (South Lincolnshire) Regt. (now 2nd Batt. The Welsh Regt.). Served in Indian Mutiny, 1857. Discharged invalided 1859, owing to loss of sight.

THE BLACK WATCH (Royal Highlanders)

7582. Lance-Corpl. Adams, Walter (Doune). 4th Vol. Batt. Served in South African War with 1st Vol. Service Coy., 1900-1901 (Queen's medal, with clasps "Cape Colony," "Wittebergen," and "South Africa, 1901"). [169.]

7297. Pte. Alexander, James (Perth). Enlisted 1899. Served in South African War, 1901-1902 (Queen's medal, with clasps "Orange Free State," "Transvaal," "South Africa, 1901," and "South Africa, 1902"). Still serving. [164.]

6511. Pte. Allan, Robert (Blairgowrie). Enlisted 1896. Served in South African War, 1901-1902 (Queen's medal, with clasps "Orange Free State," "Transvaal, 1901," and "South Africa, 1902"). Still serving.

7609. Corpl. Allison, Henry H. D. M. (Blairgowrie). 5th Vol. Batt. Served in South African War with 1st Vol. Service Coy., 1900-1901 (Queen's medal, with clasps "Cape Colony," "Orange Free State," and "South Africa, 1901"). Promoted Corpl. 5th Vol. Batt. [165.]

7210. Pte. Ames, James (Perth). Enlisted 1899. Served in South African War, 1899 (Queen's medal, with clasp "Cape Colony"). Killed at Magersfontein, Dec. 11, 1899. [170.]

3650. Pte. Anderson, James (Crieff). Enlisted 1887. Served in South African War as Reservist, 1899 (Queen's medal, with clasp "Cape Colony"). Killed at Magersfontein, Dec. 11, 1899. [171.]

6802. Pte. Anderson, James (Blairgowrie). Enlisted 1897. Served in South African War, . . . 1900-1902 (Queen's medal, with clasps "Cape Colony," "Paardeberg," "Driefontein," "Wittebergen," and "Transvaal"; King's medal, with clasps "South Africa, 1901," and "South Africa, 1902"). [166.]

7064. Pte. Anderson, James (Perth). Enlisted 1898. Served in South African War, . . . 1900-1902 (Queen's medal, with clasps "Cape Colony" and "Wittebergen"; King's medal, with clasps "South Africa, 1901," and "South Africa, 1902")· Still serving.

5212. Col.-Sergt.-Instr. Anderson, John (Logie). Enlisted 1881. Served with Soudan Expedition, 1884, and with Nile Expedition, 1884-1885. Wounded at Kirbekan, Feb. 10, 1885 (medal, with clasps "El-Teb," "Tamai," "Suakim, 1884," "The Nile, 1884-5," and "Kirbekan, 1885"; Khedive's star). Now serving as Col.-Sergt.-Instr. on Permanent Staff 4th Vol. Batt.

8014. Pte. Anderson, Robert (Perth). Enlisted 1900. Served in South African War, 1902 (Queen's medal, with clasps "Orange Free State" and "South Africa, 1902"). Still serving.

7395. Pte. Arthur, William (Perth). Enlisted 1899. Served in South African War, 1901-1902 (Queen's medal, with clasps "Orange Free State," "Transvaal," "South Africa, 1901," and "South Africa, 1902"). Still serving.

8965. Pte. Baillie, R. (Methven). 4th Vol. Batt. Served in South African War with 2nd Vol. Service Coy., 1901-1902 (Queen's medal, with clasps "Cape Colony," "Orange Free State," "Transvaal," "South Africa, 1901," and "South Africa, 1902").

2370. Col.-Sergt.-Instr. Bain, William (Logie). Enlisted 1881. Served with Egyptian Expedition, 1882, with Soudan Expedition, 1884, and with Nile Expedition, 1884-1885 (medal, with clasps "Tel-el-Kebir," "El-Teb—Tamai," "Suakim, 1884," "The Nile, 1884-5," and "Kirbekan, 1885"; Khedive's star). Appointed Pipe-Major 1st Batt. 1886. Transferred to Permanent Staff 5th Vol. Batt. and appointed Col.-Sergt.-Instr., 1901. Served in South African War with 3rd Vol. Service Coy., 1902 (Queen's medal, with clasps "Cape Colony," "Orange Free State," and "South Africa, 1902"). Still serving. [183.]

5686. Pte. Barr, Archibald (Perth). Enlisted 1894. Served in South African War, 1901-1902 (Queen's medal, with clasps "Orange Free State," "Transvaal," "South Africa, 1901," and "South Africa, 1902"). Still serving.

THE BLACK WATCH (Royal Highlanders)—*continued*

6115. Pte. Black, Alexander (Almondbank). Enlisted 1895. Served in South African War, 1901–1902 (Queen's medal, with clasps "Orange Free State," "Transvaal," "South Africa, 1901," and "South Africa, 1902"). Transferred to Reserve 1902.

3760. Pte. Black, Robert (Methven). Enlisted 1888. Transferred to Reserve 1896. Served in South African War as Reservist, 1899–1900 (Queen's medal, with clasp "Cape Colony"). Invalided home. Discharged 1901. [167.]

9159. Pte. Blair, David (Perth). 4th Vol. Batt. Served in South African War with 3rd Vol. Service Coy., 1902 (Queen's medal, with clasps "Cape Colony," "Orange Free State," "South Africa, 1902"). [172.]

7512. Pte. Blair, William (Perth). Enlisted 1900. Served in South African War (Queen's medal, with clasps "Cape Colony," "Orange Free State," and "Transvaal"). Still serving.

7581. Pte. Brand, William (Perth). 4th Vol. Batt. Served in South African War with 1st Vol. Service Coy., 1900–1901 (Queen's medal, with clasps "Cape Colony," "Wittebergen," and "South Africa, 1901"). [173.]

2765. Pte. Brown, Alexander (Perth). Enlisted 1885. Served in South African War as Reservist (Queen's medal, with clasps "Cape Colony" and "Orange Free State"). Discharged 1902. [207.]

8987. Pte. Brown, Andrew (Alyth). 5th Vol. Batt. Served in South African War with 2nd Vol. Service Coy., 1901–1902 (Queen's medal, with clasps "Cape Colony," "Orange Free State," "Transvaal," "South Africa, 1901," and "South Africa, 1902"). [168.]

8995. Pte. Brown, Duncan (Killin). 5th Vol. Batt. Served in South African War with 2nd Vol. Service Coy., 1901–1902 (Queen's medal, with clasps "Cape Colony," "Orange Free State," "Transvaal," "South Africa, 1901," and "South Africa, 1902"). [174.]

7055. Pte. Brown, George (Perth). Enlisted 1898. Served in South African War, 1900–1902 (Queen's medal, with clasps "Cape Colony," "Paardeberg," "Driefontein," "Wittebergen," and "Transvaal"; King's medal, with clasps "South Africa, 1901," and "South Africa, 1902"). Still serving. [175.]

7719. Lance-Corpl. Brown, Thomas (Dunblane). Enlisted 1899. Served in South African War, 1902 (Queen's medal, with clasps "Cape Colony," "Orange Free State," "Transvaal," and "South Africa, 1902"). Still serving.

7190. Lance-Corpl. Brown, Thomas K. W. (Crieff). Enlisted 1898. Served in South African War, 1899–1900; wounded at Magersfontein, Dec. 11, 1899, and invalided home. Returned to South Africa, and invalided home again (Queen's medal, with clasps, "Cape Colony" and "Orange Free State"). Discharged invalided 1902. [195.]

2366. Sergt. Bruce, Charles (Moulin). Enlisted 1884. Served in South African War, . . . 1900 (Queen's medal, with clasps "Cape Colony" and "Wittebergen"). Discharged 1901.

5780. Pte. Bruce, James (Blairgowrie). Enlisted 1894. Died at sea on way to South Africa, Dec. 17, 1901. [189.]

8966. Lance-Corpl. Bruce, William Brown (Perth). 4th Vol. Batt. Served in South African War with 2nd Vol. Service Coy., 1901–1902 (Queen's medal, with clasps "Cape Colony," "Orange Free State," "Transvaal," "South Africa, 1901," and "South Africa, 1902"). [206.]

9051. Lance-Corpl. Bryson, James F. (Coupar Angus). 1st Vol. Batt. Served in South African War with 2nd Vol. Service Coy., 1901–1902 (Queen's medal, with clasps "Cape Colony," "Orange Free State," "Transvaal," "South Africa, 1901," and "South Africa, 1902"). [201.]

9064. Lance-Corpl. Buchan, Andrew S. (Perth). 4th Vol. Batt. Served in South African War with 2nd Vol. Service Coy., 1901–1902 (Queen's medal, with clasps "Cape Colony," "Orange Free State," "Transvaal," "South Africa, 1901," and "South Africa, 1902"). [184.]

6812. Lance-Corpl. Buchan, David (Cargill). Enlisted 1897. Served in South African War, 1899–1902 (Queen's medal, with clasps "Cape Colony," "Paardeberg," "Driefontein," "Wittebergen," and "Transvaal"; King's medal, with clasps "South Africa, 1901," and "South Africa, 1902"). Still serving. [176.]

8951. Corpl. Buchan, Mungo (Perth). 4th Vol. Batt. Served in South African War with 1st Vol. Service Coy., 1900-1901 (Queen's medal, with clasps "Cape Colony," "Orange Free State," "Transvaal," and "South Africa, 1901"). [185.]

8961. Pte. Buchanan, John (Callander). 4th Vol. Batt. Served in South African War with 2nd Vol. Service Coy., 1901-1902 (Queen's medal, with clasps "Cape Colony," "Orange Free State," "Transvaal," "South Africa, 1901," and "South Africa, 1902"). [177.]

—— **Pte. Burns, Edward (Blairgowrie).** Enlisted in 3rd (Militia) Batt. 1890. Served in South African War (Queen's medal, with clasps . . .). [190.]

3030. Pte. Butchart, James (Rattray). Enlisted 1884. Transferred to Reserve 1892. Re-enlisted 1899. Died at sea on way to South Africa, Feb. 1900. [198.]

4060. Pte. Calderwood, Matthew (Perth). Enlisted in 3rd (Militia) Batt. 1891. Served in South African War, . . . 1900 (Queen's medal, with clasps "Cape Colony," "Paardeberg," and "Driefontein"). Discharged invalided 1901. [186.]

6269. Piper Cameron, Donald (Doune). Enlisted 1895. Served in South African War, 1899-1902 (Distinguished Conduct medal; [1] Queen's medal, with clasps "Cape Colony," "Paardeberg," "Driefontein," and "Wittebergen"; King's medal, with clasps "South Africa, 1901," and "South Africa, 1902"). Discharged 1902.

6962. Pte. Cameron, James (Errol). Enlisted 1898. Served in South African War, . . . 1900-1902 (Queen's medal, with clasps "Cape Colony," "Orange Free State," and "Transvaal"; King's medal, with clasps "South Africa, 1901," and "South Africa, 1902"). Transferred to Reserve 1902.

6575. Pte. Cameron, John (Crieff). Enlisted 1897. Served in South African War, 1899 (Queen's medal, with clasp "Cape Colony"). Killed at Magersfontein, Dec. 11, 1899.

6884. Pte. Cameron, John (Perth). Enlisted 1898. Served in South African War, . . . 1900-1902 (Queen's medal, with clasps "Cape Colony," "Orange Free State," and "Transvaal"; King's medal, with clasps "South Africa, 1901," and "South Africa, 1902"). Died June 1903. [199.]

8360. Pte. Cameron, Robert (Crieff). Enlisted 1901. Served in South African War, 1902 (Queen's medal, with clasps "Orange Free State" and "South Africa, 1902"). Still serving.

7606. Lance-Corpl. Campbell, Duncan S. (Killin). 5th Vol. Batt. Served in South African War with 1st Vol. Service Coy., 1900-1901 (Queen's medal, with clasps "Cape Colony," "Wittebergen," and "South Africa, 1901"). [205.]

6569. Pte. Campbell, John (Dull). Enlisted 1897. Served in South African War, 1901-1902 (Queen's medal, with clasps "Orange Free State," "Transvaal," "South Africa, 1901," and "South Africa, 1902"). Still serving.

6807. Corpl. Campbell, William (Perth). Enlisted 1897. Served in South African War (Queen's medal, with clasps "Cape Colony" and "Orange Free State"). Discharged invalided 1903. [191.]

7579. Pte. Campsie, William (Dunblane and Lecropt). 4th Vol. Batt. Served in South African War with 1st Vol. Service Coy., 1900-1901 (Queen's medal, with clasps "Cape Colony," "Orange Free State," and "South Africa, 1901"). [178.]

7576. Pte. Carmichael, John Napier (Comrie). Joined 4th Vol. Batt. 1897. Served in South African War with 1st Vol. Service Coy., 1900-1901 (Queen's medal, with clasps "Cape Colony," "Wittebergen," and "South Africa, 1901"). [202.]

2519. Pte. Carr, Michael (Alyth). Enlisted 1884. Served with Soudan Expedition, 1884, and with Nile Expedition, 1884-1885 (medal, with clasps "El-Teb—Tamai," "The Nile, 1884-5," and "Kirbekan, 1885"; Khedive's star). Served also in South African War, 1900-1902 (Queen's medal, with clasps "Cape Colony" and "Wittebergen"; King's medal, with clasps "South Africa, 1901," and "South Africa, 1902"). Discharged 1902. [210.]

6088. Pte. Carr, William (Perth). Enlisted 1895. Served in South African War, 1901-1902 (Queen's medal, with clasps "Orange Free State," "Transvaal," "South Africa, 1901," and "South Africa, 1902"). Transferred to Reserve 1902.

8971. Sergt. Chalmers, Robert (Bankfoot). Fifteen years in 5th Vol. Batt. Served in

---

[1] See article on the 2nd Batt. The Black Watch in South Africa, p. 10.

THE BLACK WATCH (Royal Highlanders)—*continued*

South African War with 1st Vol. Service Coy., 1900-1901 (Queen's medal, with clasps "Cape Colony," "Orange Free State," "Transvaal," and "South Africa, 1901"). [181.]

6497. Pte. Chalmers, Williamson (Perth). Enlisted 1896. Served in South African War, 1901-1902 (Queen's medal, with clasps "Orange Free State," "Transvaal," "South Africa, 1901," and "South Africa, 1902"). Still serving. [204.]

6930. Pte. Clark, Robert (Perth). Enlisted 1898. Served in South African War, . . . 1900-1902 (Queen's medal, with clasps "Cape Colony," "Orange Free State," and "Transvaal"; King's medal, with clasps "South Africa, 1901," and "South Africa, 1902"). Still serving. [182.]

3710. Pte. Clark, William (St. Martin's). Enlisted 1888. Served in South African War, 1899-1901. Wounded at Paardeberg, Feb. 18, 1900 (Queen's medal, with clasps "Cape Colony," "Paardeberg," and "South Africa, 1901"). Discharged 1901. [192.]

5470. Pte. Clement, David (Crieff). Enlisted 1894. Served in South African War, . . . 1900-1902 (Queen's medal, with clasps "Cape Colony," "Paardeberg," "Driefontein," and "Wittebergen"; King's medal, with clasps "South Africa, 1901," and "South Africa, 1902"). Still serving. [213.]

6231. Pte. Cochrane, Peter (Scone). Enlisted 1895. Served in South African War, 1901-1902 (Queen's medal, with clasps "Orange Free State," "Transvaal," "South Africa, 1901," and "South Africa, 1902"). Transferred to Reserve 1902.

9065. Pte. Connelly, Patrick (Doune). 4th Vol. Batt. Served in South African War with 2nd Vol. Service Coy., 1901-1902 (Queen's medal, with clasps "Cape Colony," "Transvaal," "Orange Free State," "South Africa, 1901," and "South Africa, 1902").

9066. Lance-Corpl. Cowie, James M. (Perth). 4th Vol. Batt. Served in South African War with 2nd Vol. Service Coy., 1901-1902 (Queen's medal, with clasps "Cape Colony," "Orange Free State," "Transvaal," "South Africa, 1901," and "South Africa, 1902"). [187.]

6973. Pte. Cowper, James (Errol). Enlisted 1898. Served in South African War, 1899-1900. Wounded at Paardeberg, Feb. 18, 1900 (Queen's medal, with clasps "Cape Colony" and "Paardeberg"). Discharged invalided 1901.

2113. Pte. Crawford, Thomas (Muthill). Enlisted 1883. Served with Soudan Expedition, 1884, and with Nile Expedition, 1884-1885 (medal, with clasps "El-Teb—Tamai," and "The Nile, 1884-5"; Khedive's star). Discharged 1891. [188.]

7578. Pte. Crerar, John M'Ewan (Crieff). Joined 4th Vol. Batt. 1896. Served in South African War with 1st Vol. Service Coy., 1900-1901 (Queen's medal, with clasps "Cape Colony," "Wittebergen," and "South Africa, 1901"). Promoted Sergt. in 4th Vol. Batt. 1902. [203.]

7443. Pte. Crichton, Peter (Meigle). Enlisted 1899. Served in South African War, 1902 (Queen's medal, with clasps "Orange Free State," "Transvaal," and "South Africa, 1902"). Still serving. [196.]

4013. Pte. Cruickshanks, Robert (Perth). Enlisted 1890. Served in South African War, . . . 1900-1902 (Queen's medal, with clasps "Cape Colony," "Paardeberg," "Driefontein," and "Wittebergen"; King's medal, with clasps "South Africa, 1901," and "South Africa, 1902"). Re-engaged on Reserve 1902.

6446. Pte. Cunnison, William (Moulin). Enlisted 1896. Served in South African War, 1901-1902 (Queen's medal, with clasps "Orange Free State," "Transvaal," "South Africa, 1901," and "South Africa, 1902"). Still serving.

6852. Pte. Cuthbert, William (Dunkeld). Enlisted 1897. Served in South African War, 1899 (Queen's medal, with clasp "Cape Colony"). Killed at Magersfontein, Dec. 11, 1899. [214.]

7103. Pte. Davidson, John (Crieff). Enlisted 1898. Served in South African War, 1899-1900. Wounded at Magersfontein, Dec. 11, 1899 (Queen's medal, with clasp "Cape Colony"). Discharged invalided 1900. [200.]

9001. Pte. Davidson, William (Killin). 5th Vol. Batt. Served in South African War with 2nd Vol. Service Coy., 1901-1902 (Queen's medal, with clasps "Cape Colony," "Orange Free State," "Transvaal," "South Africa, 1901," and "South Africa, 1902").

5272. Sergt. Dewar, William (Marlee). Enlisted 1893. Served in South African War, 1901–1902 (Queen's medal, with clasps "Orange Free State," "Transvaal," "South Africa, 1901," and "South Africa, 1902"). Transferred to Reserve 1902. [193.]

6566. Pte. Dingwall, James (Perth). Enlisted 1897. Served in South African War, 1901–1902 (Queen's medal, with clasps "Orange Free State," "Transvaal," "South Africa, 1901," and "South Africa, 1902"). Still serving. [197.]

7384. Lance-Corpl. Donaldson, John (Aberfeldy). Enlisted 1899. Served in South African War, ... 1900–1902 (Queen's medal, with clasps "Cape Colony" and "Orange Free State"; King's medal, with clasps "South Africa, 1901," and "South Africa, 1902"). Still serving.

7148. Lance-Corpl. Douglas, John (Dunning). Enlisted 1898. Served in South African War, ... 1900–1902 (Queen's medal, with clasps "Cape Colony" and "Wittebergen"; King's medal, with clasps "South Africa, 1901," and "South Africa, 1902"). Discharged 1902. [215.]

4280. Pte. Douglas, Robert (Perth). Enlisted 1890. Transferred to Reserve 1897. Served in South African War as Reservist, 1899 (Queen's medal, with clasp "Cape Colony"). Killed at Magersfontein, Dec. 11, 1899.

7129. Lance-Corpl. Drummond, James (Crieff). Enlisted 1898. Served in South African War, ... 1900–1902 (Queen's medal, with clasps "Cape Colony" and "Wittebergen"; King's medal, with clasps "South Africa, 1901," and "South Africa, 1902"). Still serving.

8955. Corpl. Duff, David (Perth). 4th Vol. Batt. Served in South African War with 2nd Vol. Service Coy., 1901–1902 (Queen's medal, with clasps "Cape Colony," "Orange Free State," "Transvaal," "South Africa, 1901," and "South Africa, 1902"). [225.]

8102. Drum. Duff, John (Perth). Enlisted 1900. Served in South African War, 1901–1902 (Queen's medal, with clasps "Transvaal," "Orange Free State," "South Africa, 1901," and "South Africa, 1902"). Still serving. [216.]

8999. Sergt. Duff, John (Stanley). Joined 5th Vol. Batt. 1894. Served in South African War with 2nd Vol. Service Coy., 1901–1902

(Queen's medal, with clasps "Cape Colony," "Orange Free State," "Transvaal," "South Africa, 1901," and "South Africa, 1902"). Still in 5th Vol. Batt. [217.]

5846. Pte. Duncan, David (Blairgowrie). Enlisted 1894. Served in South African War, 1901–1902 (Queen's medal, with clasps "Orange Free State," "Transvaal," "South Africa, 1901," and "South Africa, 1902"). Still serving. [194.]

2858. Pte. Duncan, John (Perth). Enlisted 1886. Served in South African War, 1900 (Queen's medal, with clasps "Cape Colony" and "Wittebergen"). [218.]

5191. Corpl. Dunn, Robert (Perth). Enlisted 1892. Served in South African War, ... 1900 (Queen's medal, with clasps "Cape Colony," "Paardeberg," "Driefontein," and "Wittebergen"). Transferred to Reserve 1901.

6445. Pte. Duthie, Crombie (Blair Atholl). Enlisted 1896. Served in South African War, 1901–1902 (Queen's medal, with clasps "Orange Free State," "Transvaal," "South Africa, 1901," and "South Africa, 1902"). Transferred to Reserve 1903. [219.]

8960. Pte. Easson, James T. (Dunblane). 4th Vol. Batt. Served in South African War with 2nd Vol. Service Coy., 1901–1902 (Queen's medal, with clasps "Cape Colony," "Orange Free State," "Transvaal," "South Africa, 1901," and "South Africa, 1902"). [226.]

7468. Pte. Edwards, David (Perth). Enlisted 1899. Served in South African War, ... 1900–1902 (Queen's medal, with clasps "Cape Colony" and "Orange Free State"; King's medal, with clasps "South Africa, 1901," and "South Africa, 1902"). Still serving.

7206. Corpl. Elder, James (Blairgowrie). Enlisted 1899. Served in South African War, 1900–1902 (Queen's medal, with clasps "Cape Colony," and "Orange Free State"; King's medal, with clasps "South Africa, 1901," and "South Africa, 1902"). Still serving. [227.]

7598. Pte. Emslie, Jas. Watson (Kilspindie). Joined 5th Vol. Batt. 1897. Served in South African War with 1st Vol. Service Coy., 1900–1901 (Queen's medal, with clasps "Cape Colony," "Wittebergen," and "South Africa, 1901"). [220.]

7597. Pte. Erskine, Wm. Macdonald (Coupar Angus). 5th Vol. Batt. Served in South African War with 1st Vol. Service Coy., 1900–

THE BLACK WATCH (ROYAL HIGHLANDERS)—*continued*

1901 (Queen's medal, with clasps "Cape Colony," "Wittebergen," and "South Africa, 1901"). [208.]

9157. Pte. Evans, James (Perth). 4th Vol. Batt. Served in South African War with 3rd Vol. Service Coy., 1902 (Queen's medal, with clasps "Cape Colony," "Orange Free State," and "South Africa, 1902"). [221.]

3619. Corpl. Faichney, John (Muthill). Enlisted 1887. Transferred to Reserve 1894. Served in South African War as Reservist, 1899-1900. Promoted Lance-Corpl. Wounded at Paardeberg, Feb. 18, 1900 (Queen's medal, with clasps "Cape Colony" and "Paardeberg"). Invalided home. Discharged invalided. [209.]

8974. Pte. Ferguson, Daniel (Strathtay). 6th Vol. Batt. Served in South African War with 2nd Vol. Service Coy., 1901-1902 (Queen's medal, with clasps "Cape Colony," "Orange Free State," "Transvaal," "South Africa, 1901," and "South Africa, 1902").

7587. Pte. Ferguson, David (Dunblane and Lecropt). 4th Vol. Batt. Served in South African War with 1st Vol. Service Coy., 1900-1901 (Queen's medal, with clasps "Cape Colony," "Wittebergen," and "South Africa, 1901"). [179.]

8968. Corpl. Ferguson, John (St. Fillans). 4th Vol. Batt. Served in South African War with 1st Vol. Service Coy., 1900-1901. Promoted Lance-Corpl. and Corpl., 1900 (Queen's medal, with clasps "Transvaal," "Orange Free State," "Cape Colony," and "South Africa, 1901"). [211.]

6596. Pte. Ferguson, Murdoch (Perth). Enlisted 1897. Served in South African War, 1900-1902 (Queen's medal, with clasps "Cape Colony," "Paardeberg," "Driefontein," and "Transvaal"; King's medal, with clasps "South Africa, 1901," and "South Africa, 1902"). Still serving. [222.]

5271. Pte. Fitzpatrick, Thomas (Bankfoot). Enlisted 1893. Served in South African War, 1900-1902 (Queen's medal, with clasps "Cape Colony," "Orange Free State," and "Transvaal"; King's medal, with clasps "South Africa, 1901," and "South Africa, 1902"). Transferred to Reserve 1902.

6550. Pte. Foote, George (Perth). Enlisted 1897. Served in South African War, 1900-

1902 (mentioned in despatches; Queen's medal, with clasps "Cape Colony," "Paardeberg," "Driefontein," "Johannesburg," "Diamond Hill," and "Belfast"; King's medal, with clasps, "South Africa, 1901," and "South Africa, 1902"). Still serving. [228.]

5376. Pte. Forbes, Alexander (Perth). Enlisted 1893. Served in South African War, 1901-1902 (Queen's medal, with clasps "Orange Free State," "Transvaal," "South Africa, 1901," and "South Africa, 1902"). Still serving.

4138. Pte. Ford, Michael (Perth). Enlisted 1890. Transferred to Reserve 1898. Served in South African War as Reservist, 1899-1902 (Queen's medal, with clasps "Cape Colony" and "Wittebergen"; King's medal, with clasps "South Africa, 1901," and "South Africa, 1902"). Re-engaged on Reserve 1902. [212.]

7209. Pte. Fowler, Robert (Perth). Enlisted 1899. Served in South African War, ... 1900-1902 (Queen's medal, with clasps "Cape Colony," "Paardeberg," "Driefontein," and "Wittebergen"; King's medal, with clasps "South Africa, 1901," and "South Africa, 1902"). Still serving. [223.]

7596. Corpl. Fraser, D. (Scone). Joined 5th Vol. Batt. 1898. Served in South African War with 1st Vol. Service Coy., 1900-1901. Wounded at Retief's Nek, July 23, 1900 (Queen's medal, with clasps "Cape Colony," "Wittebergen," and "South Africa, 1901"). Invalided home. Resigned from 5th Vol. Batt. as Corpl. 1903. [224.]

7480. Pte. Gardiner, Alexander (Perth). Enlisted 1899. Served in South African War, 1900 (Queen's medal, with clasps "Cape Colony," "Orange Free State," and "Transvaal"). Still serving. [231.]

4209. Pte. Gardiner, W. (Perth). Enlisted 1890. Served in South African War, 1899 (Queen's medal, with clasp "Cape Colony"). Killed at Magersfontein, Dec. 11, 1899.

6926. Pte. Garvie, William (Perth). Enlisted 1898. Served in South African War, 1899-1902 (Queen's medal, with clasps "Cape Colony," "Paardeberg," "Driefontein," and "Wittebergen"; King's medal, with clasps "South Africa, 1901," and "South Africa, 1902"). Still serving. [119.]

3825. Pte. Gavin, Philip (Perth). Enlisted

1888. Served in South African War, 1899–1901; wounded at Magersfontein, Dec. 11, 1899 (Queen's medal, with clasps "Cape Colony," "Orange Free State," and "South Africa, 1901"). Discharged 1901.

3894. Pte. Geekie, James (Perth). Enlisted 1889. Served in South African War as Reservist, 1899–1900 (Queen's medal, with clasps "Cape Colony" and "Orange Free State"). Invalided home 1900. Discharged 1902. [252.]

8963. Corpl. Glass, David (Perth). 4th Vol. Batt. Served in South African War with 2nd Vol. Service Coy., 1901–1902 (Queen's medal, with clasps "Cape Colony," "Orange Free State," "Transvaal," "South Africa, 1901," and "South Africa, 1902"). [232.]

5749. Corpl. Godfrey, Daniel (Stormontfield). Enlisted 1894. Served in South African War, 1899–1902 (Queen's medal, with clasps "Cape Colony," "Orange Free State," and "Transvaal"; King's medal, with clasps "South Africa, 1901," and "South Africa, 1902"). Transferred to Reserve 1902. [233.]

7028. Lance - Corpl. Gow, Alexander (Crieff). Enlisted 1898. Served in South African War, 1899–1902 (Queen's medal, with clasps "Cape Colony," "Paardeberg," "Driefontein," "Wittebergen," and "Transvaal"; King's medal, with clasps "South Africa, 1901," and "South Africa, 1902"). Still serving. [234.]

3135. Pte. Gow, Forbes (Perth). Enlisted 1886. Transferred to Reserve 1896. Served in South African War as Reservist, 1900–1902 (Queen's medal, with clasps "Cape Colony," "Orange Free State," and "Johannesburg"; King's medal, with clasps "South Africa, 1901," and "South Africa, 1902"). Discharged 1902. [245.]

3604. Pte. Gowrie, Thos. Fell (Coupar Angus). Enlisted 1887. Served in South African War as Reservist, 1899 (Queen's medal, with clasp "Cape Colony"). Killed at Magersfontein, Dec. 11, 1899. [240.]

3363. Pte. Graham, Alexander (Perth). Enlisted 1887. Transferred to Reserve 1895. Served in South African War as Reservist 1900–1902 (latterly attached to No. 9 Armoured Train) (Queen's medal, with clasps "Cape Colony," "Wittebergen," and "Transvaal"; King's medal, with clasps "South Africa, 1901," and "South Africa, 1902"). Re-transferred to Reserve 1903. [243.]

4081. Pte. Grant, James (Perth). Enlisted 1890. Served in South African War as Reservist, 1899 (Queen's medal, with clasp "Cape Colony"). Killed at Magersfontein, Dec. 11, 1899. [235.]

7071. Pte. Grant, John (Perth). Enlisted 1898. Served in South African War, ... 1900–1902 (Queen's medal, with clasps "Cape Colony" and "Orange Free State"; King's medal, with clasps "South Africa, 1901," and "South Africa, 1902"). Still serving.

8224. Pte. Gray, David (Perth). Enlisted 1901. Served in South African War, 1902 (Queen's medal, with clasps "Cape Colony," "Orange Free State," and "South Africa, 1902"). Still serving.

2748. Pte. Gray, James (Perth). Enlisted 1885. Served in South African War, ... 1900–1902 (Queen's medal, with clasps "Cape Colony," "Orange Free State," and "Transvaal"; King's medal, with clasps "South Africa, 1901," and "South Africa, 1902"). Discharged 1902. [236.]

2845. Pte. Guthrie, William (Blairgowrie). Enlisted 1885. Served in South African War, ... 1900–1902 (Queen's medal, with clasps "Cape Colony" and "Wittebergen"; King's medal, with clasps "South Africa, 1901," and "South Africa, 1902"). Discharged 1902. [237.]

7030. Pte. Halley, David (Perth). Enlisted 1892. Served in South African War, 1901–1902 (Queen's medal, with clasps "Orange Free State," "Transvaal," "South Africa, 1901," and "South Africa, 1902"). Still serving.

7585. Pte. Hampton, John (Perth). 4th Vol. Batt. Served in South African War with 1st Vol. Service Coy., 1900–1901 (Queen's medal, with clasps "Cape Colony," "Wittebergen," and "South Africa, 1901"). [239.]

8989. Pte. Harrier, James (Scone). 5th Vol. Batt. Served in South African War with 2nd Vol. Service Coy., 1901–1902 (Queen's medal, with clasps "Cape Colony," "Orange Free State," "Transvaal," "South Africa, 1901," and "South Africa, 1902").

3746. Sergt. Harrison, Herbert (Perth), Enlisted 1888. Served in South African War, 1899–1902 (Distinguished Conduct medal; Queen's medal, with clasps "Cape Colony," "Paardeberg," "Driefontein," and "Wittebergen"; King's medal, with clasps "South Africa, 1901," and "South Africa, 1902"). Died of wounds at Harrismith, March 6, 1902. [229.]

THE BLACK WATCH (ROYAL HIGHLANDERS)—continued

7112. Pte. Hay, George (Perth). Enlisted 1898. Served in South African War, ... 1900-1902 (Queen's medal, with clasps "Cape Colony," "Paardeberg," and "Driefontein"; King's medal, with clasps "South Africa, 1901," and "South Africa, 1902"). Still serving. [238.]

7039. Piper Henderson, Joseph A. (Perth). Enlisted 1898. Served in South African War, 1899-1900 (Queen's medal, with clasps "Cape Colony," "Paardeberg," and "Driefontein". Died at Bloemfontein, May 14, 1900. [230.]

4693. Pte. Herd, Thomas (Alyth). Enlisted in 3rd (Militia) Batt. 1892. Served in South African War, ... 1900-1902 (Queen's medal, with clasps "Cape Colony," "Paardeberg," "Driefontein," and "Wittebergen"; King's medal, with clasps "South Africa, 1901," and "South Africa, 1902"). Transferred to Militia Reserve. [244.]

7119. Pte. Hilson, Adam (Perth). Enlisted 1898. Served in South African War, ... 1900-1902 (Queen's medal, with clasps "Cape Colony," "Orange Free State," and "Transvaal"; King's medal, with clasps "South Africa, 1901," and "South Africa, 1902"). Still serving.

4287. Pte. Hobson, James (Perth). Enlisted 1890. Transferred to Reserve 1897. Served in South African War, ... 1900 (Queen's medal, with clasps "Cape Colony," "Paardeberg," and "Transvaal"). Re-engaged on Reserve 1902. [241.]

8976. Pte. Hood, David (Alyth). 5th Vol. Batt. Served in South African War with 2nd Vol. Service Coy., 1901-1902 (Queen's medal, with clasps "Cape Colony," "Orange Free State," "Transvaal," "South Africa, 1901," and "South Africa, 1902").

7583. Corpl. Hounan, James (Perth). 4th Vol. Batt. Served in South African War with 1st Vol. Service Coy., 1900-1901 (Queen's medal, with clasps "Cape Colony," "Wittebergen," and "South Africa, 1901"). Formerly in Durham Light Infantry. [250.]

2791. Lance-Corpl. Hume, David (Alyth). Enlisted 1885. Transferred to Reserve 1892. Served in South African War as Reservist, 1900-1902 (Queen's medal, with clasps "Cape Colony" and "Wittebergen"; King's medal, with clasps "South Africa, 1901," and "South Africa, 1902"). Discharged 1902. [242.]

6868. Pte. Hunter, Robert (Dunblane). Enlisted 1898. Served in South African War, ... 1900-1902 (Queen's medal, with clasps "Cape Colony," "Paardeberg," "Driefontein," and "Wittebergen"; King's medal, with clasps "South Africa, 1901," and "South Africa, 1902"). Still serving.

2213. Pte. Hutchison, James (Perth). Enlisted 1884. Transferred to Reserve 1891. Served in South African War as Reservist, 1900-1901 (Queen's medal, with clasps "Cape Colony," "Wittebergen," and "South Africa, 1901"). Discharged 1901. [255.]

7615. Pte. Hutchison, James (Perth). Enlisted 1886. Served in South African War, 1900-1902 (Queen's medal, with clasps "Cape Colony," "Paardeberg," "Driefontein," and "Wittebergen"; King's medal, with clasps "South Africa, 1901," and "South Africa, 1902"). [246.]

6643. Pte. Hynd, Alexander (Perth). Enlisted 1897. Served in South African War, 1899-1900 (Queen's medal, with clasps "Cape Colony" and "Paardeberg"). Still serving.

3412. Pte. Irons, Peter (Stanley). Enlisted 1887. Transferred to Reserve 1894. Discharged from Reserve 1899. Served in South African War (having volunteered), 1899-1900. Wounded at Paardeberg, February 18, 1900 (Queen's medal, with clasps "Cape Colony" and "Paardeberg"). Invalided home and discharged invalided 1900. [249.]

5704. Pte. Johnstone, James (Perth). Enlisted 1894. Served in South African War, ... 1900-1902 (Queen's medal, with clasps "Cape Colony," "Paardeberg," and "Driefontein"; King's medal, with clasps "South Africa, 1901," and "South Africa, 1902"). Transferred to Reserve 1902.

5402. Pte. Jones, William (Perth). Enlisted 1893. Served in South African War, 1901-1902 (Queen's medal, with clasps "Orange Free State," "Transvaal," "South Africa, 1901," and "South Africa, 1902"). Still serving.

6782. Pte. Keir, Alexander (Dunkeld). Enlisted 1897. Served in South African War, 1899-1900 (Queen's medal, with clasps "Cape Colony," "Orange Free State," and "Transvaal"). Invalided home 1900. Still serving. [247.]

The Black Watch

9047. Pte. Kennedy, Frank (Longforgan). 1st Vol. Batt. Served in South African War with 2nd Vol. Service Coy., 1901–1902 (Queen's medal, with clasps "Cape Colony," "Orange Free State," "Transvaal," "South Africa, 1901," and "South Africa, 1902"). Now serving with B. S. A. Police. [248.]

2195. Pte. Kennedy, George D. S. (Logierait). Enlisted 1883. Served with Nile Expedition 1884–1885 (medal, with clasps "The Nile, 1884–5," and "Kirbekan, 1885"; Khedive's star). Discharged 1895. [253.]

6062. Pte. Kennedy, Hugh (Stanley). Enlisted 1895. Served in South African War, 1901–1902 (Queen's medal, with clasps "Orange Free State," "Transvaal," "South Africa, 1901," and "South Africa, 1902"). Transferred to Reserve 1902. [251.]

6576. Pte. Kennedy, James (Aberfeldy). Enlisted 1897. Served in South African War, ... 1900–1902 (Queen's medal, with clasps "Cape Colony," "Paardeberg," "Driefontein," "Wittebergen," and "Transvaal"; King's medal, with clasps "South Africa, 1901," and "South Africa, 1902"). Still serving.

5872. Pte. Kenwell, Arthur (Perth). Enlisted 1894. Served in South African War, 1901–1902 (Queen's medal, with clasps "Orange Free State," "Transvaal," "South Africa, 1901," and "South Africa, 1902"). Transferred to Reserve 1902.

7510. Lance-Corpl. Kerr, Robert (Perth). Enlisted 1900. Served in South African War, 1900–1902 (Queen's medal, with clasps "Cape Colony" and "Orange Free State"; King's medal, with clasps "South Africa, 1901," and "South Africa, 1902"). Still serving. [254.]

4673. Sergt.-Maj. King, John (Strathtay). Enlisted in 42nd (Royal Highland—The Black Watch) Regt. 1880. Served in Egyptian Campaign, 1882 (medal, with clasp "Tel-el-Kebir," and Khedive's star). Promoted Col-Sergt. Now serving as Regtl. Sergt.-Maj. on Permanent Staff 5th Vol. Batt. [256.]

5446. Pte. King, John (Perth). Enlisted 1893. Served in South African War, 1901–1902 (Queen's medal, with clasps "Orange Free State," "Transvaal," "South Africa, 1901," and "South Africa, 1902"). Still serving.

3741. Pte. Kinnear, Thomas (Perth). Enlisted 1888. Served in South African War, ... 1900 (Queen's medal, with clasps "Cape Colony," "Paardeberg," "Driefontein," "Jo-

hannesburg," "Diamond Hill," and "Belfast"). Discharged 1901.

2733. Lance-Corpl. Kirkaldy, Charles (Lethendy). Enlisted 1885. Served in South African War as Reservist (for three months attached to Bloemfontein Police) (Queen's medal, with clasps "Cape Colony" and "Orange Free State"). Discharged 1902. [261.]

6028. Pte. Kirkwood, John (Crieff). Enlisted 1895. Served in South African War, 1899–1902 (latterly with Mtd. Infy.) (Queen's medal, with clasps "Cape Colony," "Paardeberg," "Driefontein," and "Wittebergen"; King's medal, with clasps "South Africa, 1901," and "South Africa, 1902"). Transferred to Reserve 1902. [262.]

6589. Pte. Laing, Charles (Perth). Enlisted 1897. Served in South African War, 1901–1902 (Queen's medal, with clasps "Orange Free State," "Transvaal," "South Africa, 1901," and "South Africa, 1902"). Still serving.

6611. Pte. Lawson, Thomas (Coupar Angus). Enlisted 1897. Served in South African War, 1901–1902 (Queen's medal, with clasps "Orange Free State," "Transvaal," "South Africa, 1901," and "South Africa, 1902"). [265.]

7338. Pte. Leithwaite, Alexander (Perth). Enlisted 1899. Served in South African War, ... 1900–1902 (Queen's medal, with clasps "Cape Colony" and "Orange Free State"; King's medal, with clasps "South Africa, 1901," and "South Africa, 1902"). Still serving.

9035. Pte. Leslie, D. R. (New Scone). 5th Vol. Batt. Served in South African War with 2nd Vol. Service Coy., 1901–1902 (Queen's medal, with clasps "Cape Colony," "Orange Free State," "Transvaal," "South Africa, 1901," and "South Africa, 1902"). [257.]

7135. Pte. Loudfoot, William (Scone). Enlisted 1898. Served in South African War, 1900–1902 (Queen's medal, with clasps "Cape Colony," "Paardeberg," "Driefontein," and "Wittebergen"; King's medal, with clasps "South Africa, 1901," and "South Africa, 1902"). Still serving. [263.]

9036. Pte. Low, Robert (Blairgowrie). 5th Vol. Batt. Served in South African War with 2nd Vol. Service Coy., 1901 (Queen's medal, with clasps "Cape Colony," "Orange Free State," and "South Africa, 1901"). [264.]

5897. Pte. McAinsh, John (Pitlochry). Enlisted 1895. Served in South African War, 1899–1902 (Queen's medal, with clasp "Cape Colony"; King's medal, with clasps "South Africa, 1901," and "South Africa, 1902"). Transferred to Reserve 1902.

7518. Pte. McAndrew, Peter J. (Perth). Enlisted 1900. Served in South African War, 1900–1902 (Queen's medal, with clasps "Cape Colony," "Orange Free State," and "Transvaal"; King's medal, with clasps "South Africa, 1901," and "South Africa, 1902"). Still serving.

7050. Lance-Corpl. MacAra, Jas. Scott (Auchterarder). Enlisted 1898. Served in South African War, 1899–1902 (latterly with Mtd. Infy.) (Queen's medal, with clasps "Cape Colony," "Paardeberg," "Driefontein," "Wittebergen," and "Transvaal"; King's medal, with clasps "South Africa, 1901," and "South Africa, 1902"). Still serving. [266.]

6222. Pte. McCann, Frederick (Perth). Enlisted 1895. Served in South African War, 1901–1902 (Queen's medal, with clasps "Orange Free State," "Transvaal," "South Africa, 1901," and "South Africa, 1902"). Transferred to Reserve 1902.

7608. Pte. McCulloch, Donald (Braes of Rannoch). 5th Vol. Batt. Served in South African War with 1st Vol. Service Coy., 1900–1901 (Queen's medal, with clasps "Cape Colony," "Wittebergen," and "South Africa, 1901").

9037. Pte. MacDiarmid, Peter (Kenmore). 5th Vol. Batt. Served in South African War with 2nd Vol. Service Coy., 1901–1902 (Queen's medal, with clasps "Cape Colony," "Orange Free State," "Transvaal," "South Africa, 1901," and "South Africa, 1902"). Died at Wynburg, April 24, 1902.

6265. Pte. McDonald, Alexander (Aberfeldy). Enlisted 1896. Served in South African War, 1901–1902 (Queen's medal, with clasps "South Africa, 1901," and "South Africa, 1902"). Transferred to Reserve 1902.

5523. Pte. McDonald, John (Perth). Enlisted 1892. Served in South African War, 1901–1902 (Queen's medal, with clasps "Orange Free State," "Transvaal," "South Africa, 1901," and "South Africa, 1902"). Still serving. [267.]

6524. Pte. McDonald, Peter (Perth). Enlisted 1896. Served in South African War, 1901–1902 (Queen's medal, with clasps "Orange Free State," "Transvaal," "South Africa, 1901," and "South Africa, 1902"). Still serving.

4430. Lance-Corpl. McDonald, William (Perth). Enlisted 1890. Served in South African War, . . . 1900–1902 (Queen's medal, with clasps "Cape Colony," "Orange Free State," and "Transvaal"; King's medal, with clasps "South Africa, 1901," and "South Africa, 1902"). Still serving.

6458. Pte. McDonald, William (Aberfeldy). Enlisted 1896. Served in South African War, . . . 1900–1902 (Queen's medal, with clasps "Cape Colony" and "Wittebergen"; King's medal, with clasps "South Africa, 1901," and "South Africa, 1902"). Still serving.

7258. Pipe-Maj. McDougall, John M. (Perth). Enlisted 1899. Served in South African War, . . . 1900–1902 (Queen's medal, with clasps "Cape Colony," "Paardeberg," "Driefontein," and "Wittebergen"; King's medal, with clasps "South Africa, 1901," and "South Africa, 1902"). Still serving. [268.]

6847. Pte. McDougall, P. (Perth). Enlisted 1897. Served in South African War, . . . 1900–1902 (Queen's medal, with clasps "Cape Colony," "Paardeberg," and "Wittebergen"; King's medal, with clasps "South Africa, 1901," and "South Africa, 1902"). Still serving.

8972. Pte. McFarlane, George (Bankfoot). 5th Vol. Batt. Served in South African War with 2nd Vol. Service Coy., 1901–1902 (latterly served with Mtd. Infy.) (Queen's medal, with clasps "Cape Colony," "Orange Free State," "Transvaal," "South Africa, 1901," and "South Africa, 1902"). [269.]

3872. Pte. McFarlane, James (Perth). Enlisted 1888. Served in South African War as Reservist, 1899–1900 (Queen's medal, with clasps "Cape Colony," "Paardeberg," and "Driefontein"). Died at Bloemfontein, April 27, 1900. [271.]

5558. Pte. McFarlane, James (Perth). Enlisted 1894. Served in South African War, 1901–1902 (Queen's medal, with clasps "Orange Free State," "Transvaal," "South Africa, 1901," and "South Africa, 1902"). Transferred to Reserve 1902. [270.]

6290. Pioneer McFarlane, Samuel (Luncarty). Enlisted 1896. Served in South African War, (1) 1899-1900 (invalided home 1900); (2) 1902 (Queen's medal, with clasps "Cape Colony" and "South Africa, 1902"). Again invalided home. Transferred to Reserve 1903. [272.]

3353. Pte. McFarlane, William (Crieff). Enlisted 1887. Served in South African War, . . . 1900-1902 (Queen's medal, with clasps "Cape Colony" and "Orange Free State"; King's medal, with clasps "South Africa, 1901," and "South Africa, 1902"). Transferred to Militia Reserve.

7926. Pte. McFarlane, William (Crieff). Enlisted 1900. Served in South African War, 1901-1902 (Queen's medal, with clasps "Orange Free State," "Transvaal," "South Africa, 1901," and "South Africa, 1902"). Discharged 1902.

7894. Piper McGarry, James (Perth). Enlisted 1900. Served in South African War, 1902 (Queen's medal, with clasps "Orange Free State" and "South Africa, 1902"). Still serving. [273.]

7169. Pte. McGarry, Joseph (Blairgowrie). Enlisted 1898. Served in South African War, 1899-1900 (Queen's medal, with clasp "Cape Colony"). Invalided home and discharged invalided. [298.]

7588. Pte. McGilvary, Robert (Dunblane). 4th Vol. Batt. Served in South African War with 1st Vol. Service Coy., 1900-1901 (Queen's medal, with clasps "Cape Colony," "Orange Free State," and "South Africa, 1901"). [274.]

7924. Pte. McGregor, James (Perth). Enlisted 1900. Served in South African War, 1901-1902 (Queen's medal, with clasps "Orange Free State," "Transvaal," "South Africa, 1901," and "South Africa, 1902"). Still serving.

5657. Pte. McGregor, Robert (Aberfeldy). Enlisted 1894. Served in South African War, 1899-1902. (Distinguished Conduct medal; Queen's medal, with clasps "Cape Colony," "Paardeberg," "Driefontein," and "Wittebergen"; King's medal, with clasps "South Africa, 1901," and "South Africa, 1902"). Discharged 1902.

33. Pte. McGregor, William (Aberfeldy). Enlisted 1881. Served with Soudan Expedition, 1884, and with Nile Expedition, 1884-1885 (medal, with clasps "El Teb—Tamai," "Suakim, 1884," "The Nile, 1884-5," and "Kirbekan, 1885"; Khedive's star). Transferred to Reserve 1889. Enlisted in Royal Scottish Reserve Regt. 1900. Discharged 1901. [299.]

7601. Pte. Macgregor, William J. (Dunkeld). Joined 5th Vol. Batt. 1897. Served in South African War with 1st Vol. Service Coy., 1900-1901 (Queen's medal, with clasps "Cape Colony," "Wittebergen," and "South Africa, 1901"). [275.]

9160. Pte. McInnes, John (Aberfeldy). 5th Vol. Batt. Served in South African War with 3rd Vol. Service Coy., 1902 (Queen's medal, with clasps "Cape Colony," "Orange Free State," and "South Africa, 1902"). [259.]

6202. Pte. McInroy, John W. (Perth). Enlisted 1895. Served in South African War, 1899-1900. Wounded at Magersfontein, Dec. 11, 1899, and invalided home. (Queen's medal, with clasp "Cape Colony.") Discharged invalided 1900.

8959. Pte. McIntosh, Arthur (Logie). 4th Vol. Batt. Served in South African War with 1st Vol. Service Coy., 1900-1901 (Queen's medal, with clasps "Cape Colony," "Orange Free State," "Transvaal," and "South Africa, 1901"). [276.]

8957. Pte. MacIntosh, James (Dunblane). 4th Vol. Batt. Served in South African War with 2nd Vol. Service Coy., 1901-1902 (Queen's medal, with clasps "Cape Colony," "Orange Free State," "Transvaal," "South Africa, 1901," and "South Africa, 1902"). [304.]

7766. Pte. McIntosh, John (Coupar Angus). Enlisted 1900. Served in South African War, 1901-1902 (Queen's medal, with clasps "Orange Free State," "Transvaal," "South Africa, 1901," and "South Africa, 1902"). Transferred to Reserve 1902. [278.]

1273. Pte. McIntyre, Daniel (Coupar Angus). Enlisted 1882. Served with Soudan Expedition, 1884 (medal, with clasps "El Teb" and "Tamai"; Khedive's star). Transferred to Reserve 1889. Discharged 1894.

2272. Pte. McIntyre, James (Perth). Enlisted 1884. Served in South African War, . . . 1900 (Queen's medal, with clasps "Cape Colony" and "Wittebergen"). Discharged 1901.

7038. Pte. McIntyre, John (Perth). Enlisted 1898. Served in South African War, 1899-1902 (Queen's medal, with clasps "Cape Colony" and "Orange Free State"; King's medal, with clasps "South Africa, 1901," and "South Africa, 1902"). Discharged invalided 1903. [279.]

THE BLACK WATCH (Royal Highlanders)—*continued*

8953. Pte. McIntyre, John F. (Logie). 4th Vol. Batt. Served in South African War with 1st Vol. Service Coy., 1900–1901 (Queen's medal, with clasps "Cape Colony," "Orange Free State," "Transvaal," and "South Africa, 1901"). [277.]

6482. Pte. McKay, Alexander (Dunblane). Enlisted 1896. Served in South African War, 1901–1902 (Queen's medal, with clasps "Orange Free State," "Transvaal," "South Africa, 1901," and "South Africa, 1902").

5258. Pte. Mackay, James (Dunning). Enlisted 1893. Served in South African War (as Mtd. Signaller), 1901–1902 (Queen's medal, with clasps "Orange Free State," "Transvaal," "South Africa, 1901," and "South Africa, 1902"). Still serving. [258.]

7594. Ptc. Mackenzie, Duncan H. C. R. (Callander). 5th Vol. Batt. Served in South African War with 1st Vol. Service Coy., 1900–1901 (Queen's medal, with clasps "Cape Colony," "Wittebergen," and "South Africa, 1901"). [260.]

2479. Pte. McKenzie, Francis (Tibbermuir). Enlisted 1884. Transferred to Reserve 1891. Served in South African War as Reservist, 1900–1901 (Queen's medal, with clasps "Cape Colony," "Wittebergen," "Transvaal," and "South Africa, 1901"). Discharged 1901. [305.]

3871. Pte. McKenzie, Henry (Rattray). Enlisted 1889. Served in South African War, 1900–1902 (Queen's medal, with clasps "Cape Colony" and "Wittebergen"; King's medal, with clasps "South Africa, 1901," and "South Africa, 1902"). Discharged 1902. [306.]

9164. Pte. McKenzie, Murdoch (Perth). 5th Vol. Batt. Served in South African War with 3rd Vol. Service Coy., 1902 (Queen's medal, with clasps "Cape Colony," "Orange Free State," and "South Africa, 1902"). [317.]

4180. Pte. McKenzie, Walter (Scone). Served in South African War as Militia Reservist, 1900–1902 (Queen's medal, with clasps "Cape Colony" and "Wittebergen"; King's medal, with clasps "South Africa, 1901," and "South Africa, 1902").

5790. Pte. McKercher, Donald (Perth). Enlisted 1894. Served in South African War, 1901–1902 (Queen's medal, with clasps "Orange Free State," "Transvaal," "South Africa,

1901," and "South Africa, 1902"). Transferred to Reserve 1902.

6100. Pte. McLaren, Donald (Perth). Enlisted 1895. Served in South African War, 1901–1902 (Queen's medal, with clasps "Transvaal," "Orange Free State," "South Africa, 1901," and "South Africa, 1902"). Invalided home and transferred to Reserve 1902. [280.]

7417. Pte. McLaren, James (Collace). Enlisted 1899. Served in South African War, . . . (Queen's medal, with clasps "Cape Colony," "Orange Free State," and "Transvaal"). Discharged 1902. [281.]

7593. Pte. McLaren, John (Callander). 4th Vol. Batt. Served in South African War with 1st Vol. Service Coy., 1900–1901 (Queen's medal, with clasps "Cape Colony," "Wittebergen," and "South Africa, 1901"). Still serving in 4th Vol. Batt. [282.]

8980. Pte. McLaren, Laurence (Pitlochry). 5th Vol. Batt. Served in South African War with 2nd Vol. Service Coy., 1901–1902 (Queen's medal, with clasps "Cape Colony," "Orange Free State," "Transvaal," "South Africa 1901," and "South Africa, 1902").

9069. Pte. McLaren, Peter (Doune). 4th Vol. Batt. Served in South African War with 2nd Vol. Service Coy., 1901–1902 (Queen's medal, with clasps "Cape Colony," "Orange Free State," "Transvaal," "South Africa, 1901," and "South Africa, 1902").

1250. Pte. McLaren, Thomas (Moulin). Enlisted 1882. Served with Soudan Expedition, 1884, and with Nile Expedition, 1884–1885 (medal, with clasps "El Teb" and "The Nile, 1884–5"; Khedive's star). Discharged 1894.

5028. Col.-Sergt. McLaren, William (Perth). Enlisted 1881. Served with Nile Expedition, 1884–1885 (medal, with clasps "The Nile, 1884–5," and "Kirbekan, 1885"; Khedive's star). Now serving on Permanent Staff 6th Vol. Batt. [310.]

5918. Pte. McLaren, William (Auchterarder). Enlisted 1895. Served in South African War, 1901–1902 (Queen's medal, with clasps "Orange Free State," "Transvaal," "South Africa, 1901," and "South Africa, 1902"). Still serving.

6918. Pte. McLauchlan, John (Alyth). Joined 2nd Perthshire Rifle Vols. (now 5th Vol. Batt. the Black Watch), 1879. Enlisted in 3rd (Militia) Batt. the Black Watch, 1885.

Served in South African War as Militia Reservist, 1900 (Queen's medal, with clasps "Cape Colony" and "Wittebergen"). Still in Militia Reserve. [318.]

7346. Pte. McLean, James (Perth). Enlisted 1899. Served in South African War, 1901-1902 (Queen's medal, with clasps "Orange Free State," "Transvaal," "South Africa, 1901," and "South Africa, 1902"). Still serving.

5436. Pte. McLean, Peter (Killin). Enlisted 1893. Served in South African War, 1901-1902 (Queen's medal, with clasps "Orange Free State," "Transvaal," "South Africa, 1901," and "South Africa, 1902"). Still serving.

3798. Pte. McLeish, Andrew (Perth). Enlisted 1888. Served in South African War, . . . 1900 (Queen's medal, with clasps "Cape Colony," "Paardeberg," "Driefontein," and "Wittebergen"). Discharged 1901. [286.]

7184. Corpl. Macmaster, Donald (Kinloch Rannoch). Enlisted 1899. Served in South African War, 1899-1900 (Queen's medal, with clasps "Cape Colony," "Paardeberg," and "Driefontein"). Invalided home 1900. Still serving. [283.]

2718. Col.-Sergt. Macmillan, John (Pitcairngreen). Enlisted 1885. Served in South African War, 1899 (Queen's medal, with clasp "Cape Colony"). Killed at Magersfontein, Dec. 11, 1899. [307.]

9038. Pte. McNab, Peter (Foss). 5th Vol. Batt. Served in South African War with 2nd Vol. Service Coy., 1901-1902 (Queen's medal, with clasps "Cape Colony," "Orange Free State," "Transvaal," "South Africa, 1901," and "South Africa, 1902"). [301.]

9002. Pte. McNaughten, James (Killin). 5th Vol. Batt. Served in South African War with 2nd Vol. Service Coy., 1901-1902 (Queen's medal, with clasps "Cape Colony," "Orange Free State," "Transvaal," "South Africa, 1901," and "South Africa, 1902"). [284.]

4940. Pte. McNie, Malcolm (Balquhidder). Enlisted 1892. Served in South African War, 1901-1902 (Queen's medal, with clasps "Orange Free State," "Transvaal," "South Africa, 1901," and "South Africa, 1902"). Still serving.

2943. Pte. McPherson, Alexander (Coupar Angus). Enlisted in Argyll and Sutherland Highlanders 1885. Transferred to The Black

II.

Watch 1886. Served in South African War, 1900-1902 (Queen's medal, with clasps "Cape Colony" and "Wittebergen"; King's medal, with clasps "South Africa, 1901," and "South Africa, 1902"). Discharged 1902. [287.]

3668. Pte. McPherson, Donald (Perth). Enlisted 1888. Served in South African War, 1899-1900. Wounded at Paardeberg, Feb. 18, 1900 (Queen's medal, with clasps "Cape Colony" and "Paardeberg"). Discharged invalided 1900.

8982. Pte. Macpherson, John (Killiecrankie). 5th Vol. Batt. Served in South African War with 2nd Vol. Service Coy., 1901-1902 (Queen's medal, with clasps "Cape Colony," "Orange Free State," "Transvaal," "South Africa, 1901," and "South Africa, 1902"). [316.]

9166. Sergt. McPherson, John (Kenmore). 5th Vol. Batt. Enlisted in The Black Watch 1895. Discharged 1899. Served in South African War with 3rd Vol. Service Coy., 1902 (Queen's medal, with clasps "Cape Colony," "Orange Free State," and "South Africa, 1902"). [288.]

7438. Pte. McRobbie, George (Longforgan). Enlisted 1899. Served in South African War, . . . 1900-1902 (Queen's medal, with clasps "Cape Colony" and "Orange Free State"; King's medal, with clasps "South Africa, 1901;" and "South Africa, 1902"). Still serving.

625. Col.-Sergt. McVean, John (Ardvorlich). Enlisted in 42nd (Royal Highland—The Black Watch) Regt. 1861. Served in Ashanti War, 1873-1874 (medal, with clasp "Coomassie"). Transferred to Permanent Staff Highland Rifle Militia (now 3rd Batt. Seaforth Highlanders) 1880. Long Service medal. Discharged 1889. [285.]

9158. Pte. McVicar, William (Perth). 4th Vol. Batt. Served in South African War with 3rd Vol. Service Coy., 1902 (Queen's medal, with clasps "Cape Colony," "Orange Free State," and "South Africa, 1902"). [292.]

9018. Pte. McWalter, James (Auchterarder). 3rd Vol. Batt. Served in South African War with 2nd Vol. Service Coy., 1901-1902 (Queen's medal, with clasps "Cape Colony," "Orange Free State," "Transvaal," "South Africa, 1901," and "South Africa, 1902"). [302.]

6808. Lance-Corpl. Maison, Arthur (Blairgowrie). Enlisted 1897. Served in South African War, 1901-1902 (Queen's medal, with clasps "Cape Colony," "Orange Free State,"

P

THE BLACK WATCH (ROYAL HIGHLANDERS)—continued

"Transvaal," "South Africa, 1901," and "South Africa, 1902"). [303.]

7180. Lance-Sergt. Malcolm, William (Perth). Enlisted 1899. Served in South African War, 1900–1902 (Queen's medal, with clasps "Cape Colony" and "Wittebergen"; King's medal, with clasps "South Africa, 1901," and "South Africa, 1902"). Still serving. [322.]

2441. Pte. Mann, Alexander (Blairgowric). Enlisted in 42nd (Royal Highland—The Black Watch) Regt. 1880. Served with Soudan Expedition, 1884, and with Nile Expedition, 1884–1885 (medal, with clasps "El Teb," "Tamai," "The Nile, 1884–5," and "Kirbekan, 1885"; Khedive's star). Transferred to Reserve. Re-enlisted in 11th Hussars 1887. Transferred to Reserve 1895. [320.]

9000. Pte. Martin, Edward (Alyth). 5th Vol. Batt. Served in South African War with 2nd Vol. Service Coy., 1901–1902 (Queen's medal, with clasps "Cape Colony," "Orange Free State," "Transvaal," "South Africa, 1901," and "South Africa, 1902"). [300.]

5787. Pte. Meldrum, Simpson (Perth). Enlisted 1894. Served in South African War, . . . 1900–1902 (Queen's medal, with clasps "Cape Colony," "Paardeberg," "Driefontein," and "Wittebergen"; King's medal, with clasps "South Africa, 1901," and "South Africa, 1902"). Transferred to Reserve 1902. [289.]

7393. Pte. Mellis, Albert (Perth). Enlisted 1899. Served in South African War, 1900–1902 (Queen's medal, with clasps "Cape Colony" and "Orange Free State"; King's medal, with clasps "South Africa, 1901," and "South Africa, 1902"). Discharged 1902.

2299. Pte. Melville, George (Crieff). Enlisted 1884. Served with Nile Expedition, 1884–1885 (medal, with clasp "The Nile, 1884–5," and Khedive's star). Transferred to Reserve 1892. Served in South African War as Reservist, 1900–1901 (Queen's medal, with clasps "Cape Colony," "Wittebergen," and "South Africa, 1901"). Discharged 1901.

9071. Lance-Corpl. Menzies, Daniel (Perth). 4th Vol. Batt. Served in South African War with 2nd Vol. Service Coy., 1901–1902 (Queen's medal, with clasps "Cape Colony," "Orange Free State," "Transvaal," "South Africa, 1901," and "South Africa, 1902"). [293.]

4007. Col.-Sergt. Millar, Alexander (Alyth). Enlisted 1890. Served in South African War, 1899–1902 (with Mtd. Infy. 1900–1902). Wounded at Magersfontein, Dec. 11, 1899, and at Paardeberg, Feb. 18, 1900 (twice mentioned in despatches; Distinguished Conduct medal;[1] Queen's medal, with clasps "Cape Colony," "Paardeberg," "Wittebergen," and "Transvaal"; King's medal, with clasps "South Africa, 1901," and "South Africa, 1902"). Still serving. [308.]

4471. Pte. Miller, Charles (Perth). Enlisted 1891. Served in South African War, . . . 1900 (Queen's medal, with clasps "Cape Colony," "Paardeberg," and "Driefontein"). Re-engaged on Reserve 1903. [294.]

2694. Pte. Milne, James (Perth). Enlisted 1885. Served in South African War, . . . 1900–1902 (Queen's medal, with clasps "Cape Colony," and "Wittebergen"; King's medal, with clasps "South Africa, 1901," and "South Africa, 1902"). Discharged 1902.

4795. Lance-Corpl. Mitchell, Thomas (Meigle). Enlisted 1892. Appointed Piper 1892. Promoted Lance-Corpl.-Piper 1895. Promoted Pipe-Major, and transferred to Permanent Staff, 3rd (Militia) Batt., 1896. Transferred to Reserve 1899. Served in South African War as Reservist, 1899–1902 (Queen's medal, with clasps "Cape Colony," "Driefontein," and "Transvaal"; King's medal, with clasps "South Africa, 1901," and "South Africa, 1902"). Re-transferred to Reserve 1902. [311.]

7363. Pte. Moir, D. H. (Perth). Enlisted 1899. Served in South African War, 1901–1902 (Queen's medal, with clasps "Orange Free State," "Transvaal," "South Africa, 1901," and "South Africa, 1902"). Still serving.

7217. Pte. Money, Andrew (Blairgowrie). Enlisted 1899. Served in South African War, . . . 1900–1902 (Queen's medal, with clasps "Cape Colony," "Paardeberg," and "Transvaal"; King's medal, with clasps "South Africa, 1901," and "South Africa, 1902"). Still serving.

---

[1] See article on the 2nd Batt. The Black Watch in South Africa, pp. 10, 12.

5618. Pte. Morgan, Thomas (Perth). Enlisted 1894. Served in South African War, 1901–1902 (Queen's medal, with clasps "Orange Free State," "Transvaal," "South Africa, 1901," and "South Africa, 1902"). Still serving.

6478. Pte. Morris, A. (Blairgowrie). Enlisted 1896. Served in South African War, 1901–1902 (Queen's medal, with clasps "Orange Free State," "Transvaal," "South Africa, 1901," and "South Africa, 1902"). Transferred to Reserve 1903. [295.]

7810. Pte. Morris, Charles (Cargill). Enlisted 1900. Served in South African War, 1901–1902 (Queen's medal, with clasps "Orange Free State," "Transvaal," "South Africa, 1901," and "South Africa, 1902"). Still serving. [319.]

7080. Pte. Morris, James (Coupar Angus). Enlisted 1898. Served in South African War, 1899 (Queen's medal, with clasp "Cape Colony"). Killed at Magersfontein, Dec. 11, 1899. [290.]

9155. Pte. Morrison, John (Perth). 4th Vol. Batt. Served in South African War with 3rd Vol. Service Coy., 1902 (Queen's medal, with clasps "Cape Colony," "Orange Free State," and "South Africa, 1902"). [296.]

5154. Pte. Moyes, Thomas (Perth). Enlisted 1893. Served in South African War, . . . 1900–1902 (Queen's medal, with clasps "Cape Colony," "Paardeberg," "Wittebergen," and "Transvaal"; King's medal, with clasps "South Africa, 1901," and "South Africa, 1902"). Transferred to Reserve 1902. [291.]

8958. Lance-Corpl. Murray, George (Doune). 4th Vol. Batt. Served in South African War with 2nd Vol. Service Coy., 1901–1902 (Queen's medal, with clasps "Cape Colony," "Orange Free State," "Transvaal," "South Africa, 1901," and "South Africa, 1902").

9070. Pte. Murrie, John (Perth). 4th Vol. Batt. Served in South African War with 2nd Vol. Service Coy., 1901–1902 (Queen's medal, with clasps "Cape Colony," "Orange Free State," "Transvaal," "South Africa, 1901," and "South Africa, 1902"). [297.]

3659. Pte. Murrie, Robert (Crieff). Enlisted 1888. Served in South African War, . . . 1900 (Queen's medal, with clasps "Cape Colony," "Paardeberg," and "Driefontein"). Discharged 1901.

4031. Pte. Myles, David (Coupar Angus).

Enlisted 1890. Served in South African War, 1899–1902 (Queen's medal, with clasps "Cape Colony," "Paardeberg," "Driefontein," and "Wittebergen"; King's medal, with clasps "South Africa, 1901," and "South Africa, 1902"). Discharged 1902. [315.]

4166. Pte. Mylie, John (Perth). Enlisted 1890. Served in South African War as Reservist, 1899–1900. Wounded at Magersfontein, Dec. 11, 1899 (Queen's medal, with clasps "Cape Colony," "Paardeberg," and "Driefontein"). Invalided home 1900. Discharged 1902. [309.]

7205. Pte. Nicoll, John (Perth). Enlisted 1899. Served in South African War, . . . 1900–1902 (Queen's medal, with clasps "Cape Colony," "Wittebergen," and "Transvaal"; King's medal, with clasps "South Africa, 1901," and "South Africa, 1902"). Still serving. [328.]

7485. Pte. Nicolson, D. (Perth). Enlisted 1899. Served in South African War, 1902 (Queen's medal, with clasps "Orange Free State," "Transvaal," and "South Africa, 1902"). Still serving.

2219. Pte. Oswald, James (Perth). Enlisted 1884. Served in South African War, . . . 1900 (Queen's medal, with clasps "Cape Colony" and "Orange Free State"). Discharged 1901.

7672. Pte. Paton, James W. (Errol). Enlisted 1900. Served in South African War, 1900 (Queen's medal, with clasps "Cape Colony," "Orange Free State," and "Transvaal"). Discharged invalided 1902. [323.]

2625. Pte. Paton, Stewart (Errol). Enlisted 1885. Served in South African War, . . . 1900–1902 (Queen's medal, with clasps "Cape Colony" and "Orange Free State"; King's medal, with clasps "South Africa, 1901," and "South Africa, 1902"). Discharged 1902. [324.]

2147. Corpl. Paul, Henry (Huntingtower). Enlisted 1883. Served with Nile Expedition, 1884–1885 (medal, with clasps "The Nile, 1884–5," and "Kirbekan, 1885"); Khedive's star). Served also in South African War as Reservist, 1900–1901 (Queen's medal, with clasps "Cape Colony" and "Wittebergen"). Discharged 1901.

9039. Pte. Petrie, Alexander (Rattray). 5th Vol. Batt. Served in South African War with 2nd Vol. Service Coy., 1901–1902 (Queen's medal, with clasps "Cape Colony," "Orange Free State," "Transvaal," "South Africa,

THE BLACK WATCH (Royal Highlanders)—*continued*

1901," and "South Africa, 1902"). Died at Standerton, Jan. 3, 1902. [329.]

7628. Pte. Philip, David (Airdler). 2nd Vol. Batt. Served in South African War with 1st Vol. Service Coy., 1900–1901 (Queen's medal, with clasps "Cape Colony," "Wittebergen," and "South Africa, 1901"). Died in Netley Hospital, May 24, 1901.

6180. Pte. Porteous, James (Blackford). Enlisted 1895. Served in South African War, 1901–1902 (Queen's medal, with clasps "Orange Free State," "Transvaal," "South Africa, 1901," and "South Africa, 1902"). Transferred to Reserve 1902.

7599. Corpl. Proudfoot, Alex. (Aberfeldy). 5th Vol. Batt. Served in South African War with 1st Vol. Service Coy., 1900–1901 (Queen's medal, with clasps "Cape Colony," "Wittebergen," and "South Africa, 1901"). [330.]

6586. Drum. Purdie, Louis (Perth). Enlisted 1897. Served in South African War, . . . 1900–1902 (Queen's medal, with clasps "Cape Colony," "Paardeberg," "Driefontein," and "Wittebergen"; King's medal, with clasps "South Africa, 1901," and "South Africa, 1902"). Still serving. [331.]

9165. Pte. Rae, John (Killin). 5th Vol. Batt. Served in South African War with 3rd Vol. Service Coy., 1902 (Queen's medal, with clasps "Cape Colony," "Orange Free State," and South Africa, 1902"). [346.]

6724. Lance-Corpl. Ramsay, Hugh (Burrelton). Enlisted 1897. Served in South African War, 1899–1900. Wounded[1] at Magersfontein, Dec. 11, 1899 (Queen's medal, with clasp "Cape Colony"). Discharged invalided 1900. [314.]

5120. Pte. Rankin, Andrew (Perth). Enlisted 1892. Served in South African War, 1901–1902 (Queen's medal, with clasps "Orange Free State," "Transvaal," "South Africa, 1901," and "South Africa, 1902"). Still serving.

5737. Pte. Ray, Robert (Perth). Enlisted 1894. Served in South African War, 1901–1902 (Queen's medal, with clasps "Orange Free State," "Transvaal," "South Africa,

1901," and "South Africa, 1902"). Transferred to Reserve 1902.

3936. Pte. Reid, Alex. M. (Perth). Enlisted 1889. Served in South African War, 1899–1902. Wounded at Magersfontein, Dec. 11, 1899 (Queen's medal, with clasps "Cape Colony," "Paardeberg," "Driefontein," and "Transvaal"; King's medal, with clasps "South Africa, 1901," and "South Africa, 1902"). Invalided home, and discharged invalided, 1902. [312.]

7796. Pte. Reid, James (Dunkeld). Enlisted 1900. Served in South African War, 1901–1902 (Queen's medal, with clasps "Orange Free State," "Transvaal," "South Africa, 1901," and "South Africa, 1902"). Still serving.

4475. Bdsman. Reid, Thos. Baxter (Perth). Enlisted 1891. Transferred to Reserve 1899. Served in South African War as Reservist, 1899–1902 (latterly with Military Mtd. Police) (Queen's medal, with clasps "Cape Colony," "Paardeberg," "Driefontein," and "Wittebergen"; King's medal, with clasps "South Africa, 1901," and "South Africa, 1902"). Still serving with the colours. [334.]

7350. Pte. Reid, William (Perth). Enlisted 1899. Served in South African War, 1901–1902 (Queen's medal, with clasps "Orange Free State," "Transvaal," "South Africa, 1901," and "South Africa, 1902"). Still serving.

2720. Pte. Reilly, James (Perth). Enlisted 1887. Served in South African War, 1899–1902 (Queen's medal, with clasps "Cape Colony," "Paardeberg," "Driefontein," "Wittebergen," and "Transvaal"; King's medal, with clasps "South Africa, 1901," and "South Africa, 1902"). Transferred to Reserve 1902.

2428. Pte. Robertson, Alexander (Alyth). Enlisted 1884. Transferred to Reserve 1891. Served in South African War as Reservist, 1900 (Queen's medal, with clasps "Cape Colony" and "Wittebergen"). [335.]

6553. Pte. Robertson, Charles S. (Blairgowrie). Enlisted 1897. Served in South African War, 1901–1902 (Queen's medal, with clasps "Transvaal," "Orange Free State,"

---

[1] This man had four bullets through the left leg, and two through the right leg; one was embedded in his right elbow, and one grazed the heart. The left leg was also fractured by a shrapnel shell.

"South Africa, 1901," and "South Africa, 1902"). Still serving. [327.]

3739. Pte. Robertson, David (Perth). Enlisted 1889. Served in South African War as Reservist, 1899-1902 (Queen's medal, with clasps "Cape Colony," "Paardeberg," "Driefontein," and "Wittebergen"; King's medal, with clasps "South Africa, 1901," and "South Africa, 1902"). Re-engaged on Reserve 1902. [332.]

5411. Pte. Robertson, David (New Rattray). Enlisted 1893. Served in South African War, 1901-1902 (Queen's medal, with clasps "Orange Free State," "Transvaal," "South Africa, 1901," and "South Africa, 1902"). Still serving. [313.]

7259. Pte. Robertson, George (Scone). Enlisted 1899. Served in South African War, 1901-1902 (Queen's medal, with clasps "Cape Colony," "Orange Free State," "South Africa, 1901," and "South Africa, 1902"). Killed in action, March 14, 1902.

4476. Pte. Robertson, Harry (Perth). Enlisted 1891. Served in South African War, 1899-1902 (Queen's medal, with clasps "Cape Colony," "Paardeberg," and "Wittebergen"; King's medal, with clasps "South Africa, 1901," and "South Africa, 1902"). Re-engaged on Reserve 1903. [326.]

5914. Pte. Robertson, Henry Kidd (Alyth). Enlisted 1895. Served in South African War, 1901-1902 (Queen's medal, with clasps "Orange Free State," "Transvaal," "South Africa, 1901," and "South Africa, 1902"). Still serving. [333.]

3014. Col.-Sergt. Robertson, James (Caputh). Enlisted 1886. Served in South African War, 1899-1900. Promoted Col.-Sergt. (Queen's medal, with clasps "Cape Colony" and "Paardeberg"). Killed at Paardeberg, Feb. 18, 1900. [336.]

3959. Pte. Robertson, James (Perth). Enlisted 1889. Served in South African War, 1899-1902 (Queen's medal, with clasps "Cape Colony," "Paardeberg," "Driefontein" and "Wittebergen"; King's medal, with clasps "South Africa, 1901," and "South Africa, 1902") Discharged 1902. [340.]

7629. Pte. Robertson, James (Ardler). 2nd Vol. Batt. Served in South African War with 1st Vol. Service Coy., 1900-1901 (Queen's medal, with clasps "Cape Colony," "Wittebergen," and "South Africa, 1901"). [325.]

8973. Pte. Robertson, James (Strathtay). 5th Vol. Batt. Served in South African War with 1st Vol. Service Coy., 1900-1901 (Queen's medal, with clasps "Cape Colony," "Orange Free State," "Transvaal," and "South Africa, 1901"). [341.]

7584. Pte. Robertson, Jas. Lindsay (Perth). 4th Vol. Batt. Served in South African War with 1st Vol. Service Coy., 1900-1901 (Queen's medal, with clasps "Cape Colony," "Orange Free State," and "South Africa, 1901"). [350.]

376. Pte. Robertson, John (Perth). Enlisted in 42nd Royal Highland Regt. 1858. Served in Ashanti War, 1873-1874 (medal). Discharged 1879.

1752. Pte. Robertson, John (Perth). Enlisted in 3rd (Militia) Batt. 1885. Served in South African War, 1900-1902 (Queen's medal, with clasps "Cape Colony," "Paardeberg," "Driefontein," "Johannesburg," "Diamond Hill," and "Belfast"; King's medal, with clasps "South Africa, 1901," and "South Africa, 1902"). Still serving. [321.]

3719. Pte. Robertson, John (Muthill). Enlisted 1888. Served in South African War, 1899-1900. Wounded at Magersfontein, Dec. 11, 1899 (Queen's medal, with clasp "Cape Colony"). Invalided home 1900, and discharged invalided. [337.]

6376. Pte. Robertson, John (Luncarty). Enlisted 1896. Served in South African War, 1899-1902 (Queen's medal, with clasps "Cape Colony," "Paardeberg," "Driefontein," "Wittebergen," and "Transvaal"; King's medal, with clasps "South Africa, 1901," and "South Africa, 1902"). Transferred to Reserve 1903. [342.]

7460. Pte. Robertson, John (Stanley). Enlisted 1899. Served in South African War, 1901-1902 (Queen's medal, with clasps "Orange Free State," "Transvaal," "South Africa, 1901," and "South Africa, 1902"). Still serving.

8983. Pte. Robertson, John M. (Blairgowrie). Joined 5th Vol. Batt. 1899. Served in South African War with 1st Vol. Service Coy., 1900-1901 (Queen's medal, with clasps "Cape Colony," "Orange Free State," "Transvaal," and "South Africa, 1901"). [343.]

6568. Pte. Robertson, Peter (Perth). Enlisted 1897. Served in South African War, . . . 1900-1902 (Queen's medal, with clasps "Cape Colony," "Paardeberg," and "Wittebergen";

THE BLACK WATCH (Royal Highlanders)—*continued*

King's medal, with clasps "South Africa, 1901," and "South Africa, 1902"). Still serving.

5492. Pte. Robertson, Thomas (New Rattray). Enlisted 1894. Served in South African War, 1901–1902 (Queen's medal, with clasps "Orange Free State," "Transvaal," "South Africa, 1901," and "South Africa, 1902"). Still serving. [338.]

7605. Sergt. Robertson, Thomas (Dunkeld). Joined 5th Vol. Batt., 1899. Served in South African War with 1st Vol. Service Coy., 1900–1901 (Queen's medal, with clasps "Cape Colony," "Wittebergen," and "South Africa, 1901"). [344.]

8992. Pte. Robertson, Thos. Henry (Alyth). 5th Vol. Batt. Served in South African War with 2nd Vol. Service Coy., 1901–1902. Served with Mtd. Infy. (Queen's medal, with clasps "Cape Colony," "Orange Free State," "Transvaal," "South Africa, 1901," and "South Africa, 1902"). [339.]

5438. Pte. Rodger, Charles (Coupar Angus). Enlisted 1893. Served in South African War, 1901–1902 (Queen's medal, with clasps "Orange Free State," "Transvaal," "South Africa, 1901," and "South Africa, 1902"). Transferred to Reserve 1902.

7163. Pte. Ruddick, James (Crieff). Enlisted 1899. Served in South African War, 1899–1900. Wounded at Magersfontein, Dec. 11, 1899, and invalided home (Queen's medal, with clasp "Cape Colony"). Discharged invalided 1901. [345.]

7927. Pte. Russell, Alexander (Crieff). Enlisted 1900. Served in South African War 1901–1902 (Queen's medal, with clasps "Orange Free State," "Transvaal," "South Africa, 1901," and "South Africa, 1902"). Invalided home 1902. Still serving. [347.]

7386. Pte. Russell, Peter (Crieff). Enlisted 1899. Served in South African War (with Mtd. Infy.), 1901 (Queen's medal, with clasps "Cape Colony," "Orange Free State," "Transvaal," and "South Africa, 1901"). Died at Kimberley, Oct. 19, 1901. [348.]

6867. Pte. Rutherford, Peter (Perth). Enlisted 1898. Served in South African War, 1901–1902 (Queen's medal, with clasps "Orange Free State," "Transvaal," "South Africa, 1901," and "South Africa, 1902"). Still serving.

800. Sergt.-Maj. Sadler, Benjamin (Perth). Enlisted 1881. Served in Egyptian Campaign, 1882; with Soudan Expedition, 1884, and with Nile Expedition, 1884–1885 (medal, with clasps "Tel-el-Kebir," "Sunkim, 1884," "El Teb—Tamai," "The Nile, 1884-5," and "Kirbekan, 1885"; Khedive's star). Long Service medal. Now serving on Permanent Staff 4th Vol. Batt. [349.]

4523. Corpl. Sage, George (Perth). Enlisted 1891. Served in South African War, 1901–1902 (Queen's medal, with clasps "Orange Free State," "Transvaal," "South Africa, 1901," and "South Africa, 1902"). Discharged 1903. [370.]

7577. Lance-Corpl. Scott, John Burns (Perth). 4th Vol. Batt. Served in South African War with 1st Vol. Service Coy., 1900–1901 (Queen's medal, with clasps "Cape Colony," "Orange Free State," "Transvaal," and "South Africa, 1901"). [351.]

9040. Pte. Scott, J. Malcolm (Blairgowrie). 5th Vol. Batt. Served in South African War with 2nd Vol. Service Coy., 1901–1902 (Queen's medal, with clasps "Cape Colony," "Orange Free State," "Transvaal," "South Africa, 1901," and "South Africa, 1902"). [352.]

5244. Pte. Scott, William (Dunkeld). Formerly in 5th Vol. Batt. Enlisted 1893. Served in South African War, 1901–1902 (Queen's medal, with clasps "Orange Free State," "Transvaal," "South Africa, 1901," and "South Africa, 1902"). Transferred to Reserve 1902. [358.]

9161. Pte. Scrimgeour, Donald (Aberfeldy). 5th Vol. Batt. Served in South African War with 3rd Vol. Service Coy., 1902 (Queen's medal, with clasps "Cape Colony," "Orange Free State," and "South Africa, 1902"). [371.]

2644. Pte. Seth, George (Bankfoot). Enlisted 1881. Served in Egyptian Campaign, 1882 (medal, with clasp "Tel-el-Kebir," and Khedive's star). Transferred to Reserve 1897. Discharged 1901.

4689. Pte. Shanahan, John (Glencarse). Enlisted 1892. Served in South African War, 1899–1900. Wounded at Magersfontein, Dec. 11, 1899 (Queen's medal, with clasp "Cape Colony"). Discharged 1900.

7072. Pte. Sharp, David (Perth). Enlisted

1898. Served in South African War, . . . 1900–1902 (Queen's medal, with clasps "Cape Colony," "Paardeberg," "Driefontein," "Johannesburg," "Diamond Hill," and "Belfast"; King's medal, with clasps "South Africa, 1901," and "South Africa, 1902"). Still serving. [372.]

6619. Pte. Shedden, James (Perth). Enlisted 1897. Served in South African War, 1899–1902 (Queen's medal, with clasps "Cape Colony," "Paardeberg," "Driefontein," and "Wittebergen"; King's medal, with clasps "South Africa, 1901," and "South Africa, 1902"). Still serving. [373.]

5779. Pte. Shepherd, Joseph (Perth). Enlisted 1894. Served in South African War, 1901–1902 (Queen's medal, with clasps "Orange Free State," "Transvaal," "South Africa, 1901," and "South Africa, 1902"). Still serving. [359.]

8988. Lance-Corpl. Short, James (Scone). 5th Vol. Batt. Served in South African War with 2nd Vol. Service Coy., 1901–1902 (Queen's medal, with clasps "Cape Colony," "Orange Free State," "Transvaal," "South Africa, 1901," and "South Africa, 1902").

8977. Pte. Sidey, Thos. (Alyth). 5th Vol. Batt. Served in South African War with 2nd Vol. Service Coy., 1901–1902 (Queen's medal, with clasps "Cape Colony," "Orange Free State," "Transvaal," "South Africa, 1901," and "South Africa, 1902"). [353.]

7580. Pte. Simpson, G. (Perth). 4th Vol. Batt. Served in South African War with 1st Vol. Service Coy., 1900–1901 (Queen's medal, with clasps "Cape Colony," "Wittebergen," and "South Africa, 1901").

2601. Lance-Corpl. Simpson, James (Scone). Enlisted 1885. Served in South African War (Queen's medal, with clasps "Cape Colony" and "Orange Free State"). Discharged invalided 1901. [376.]

5194. Pte. Simpson, Joseph (Perth). Enlisted 1893. Served in South African War, 1901–1902 (Queen's medal, with clasps "Orange Free State," "Transvaal," "South Africa, 1901," and "South Africa, 1902"). Still serving. [360.]

5744. Sergt. Simpson, William A. (Scone). Enlisted 1894. Served in South African War, . . . 1900–1902 (Queen's medal, with clasps "Cape Colony," "Paardeberg," "Driefontein," "Johannesburg," "Diamond Hill," and "Belfast" ; King's medal, with clasps "South Africa, 1901," and "South Africa, 1902"). Still serving. [361.]

7679. Pte. Sinclair, James (Crieff). Enlisted 1900. Served in South African War, 1900–1902 (Queen's medal, with clasps "Cape Colony" and "Orange Free State" ; King's medal, with clasps "South Africa, 1901," and "South Africa, 1902"). Still serving. [362.]

5845. Pte. Sinclair, Robert (Inchture). Enlisted 1894. Served in South African War, 1901–1902 (Queen's medal, with clasps "Orange Free State," "Transvaal," "South Africa, 1901," and "South Africa, 1902"). Still serving.

7603. Pte. Small, Robert Menzies (Dull). 5th Vol. Batt. Served in South African War with 1st Vol. Service Coy., 1900 (Queen's medal, with clasps "Cape Colony" and "Orange Free State"). Died at Bloemfontein, April 10, 1900. [363.]

3918. Pte. Smart, Thos. (Perth). Enlisted 1889. Served in South African War, 1899–1900 (Queen's medal, with clasps "Cape Colony" and "Orange Free State"). Discharged 1900.

8975. Pte. Smith, Allan (Coupar Angus). 5th Vol. Batt. Served in South African War with 2nd Vol. Service Coy., 1901–1902 (Queen's medal, with clasps "Cape Colony," "Orange Free State," "Transvaal," "South Africa, 1901," and "South Africa, 1902"). [364.]

3913. Pte. Smith, John (Perth). Enlisted 1889. Served in South African War, . . . 1900 (Queen's medal, with clasps "Cape Colony" and "Paardeberg"). Discharged 1902.

7487. Pte. Smith, Matthew (Callander). Enlisted 1899. Served in South African War, 1900 (Queen's medal, with clasps "Cape Colony" and "Orange Free State"). Discharged invalided 1902. [365.]

8997. Pte. Smith, Thos. (Alyth). 5th Vol. Batt. Served in South African War with 2nd Vol. Service Coy., 1901–1902 (Queen's medal, with clasps "Cape Colony," "Orange Free State," "Transvaal," "South Africa, 1901," and "South Africa, 1902"). [354.]

5205. Pte. Smith, William (Perth). Enlisted 1893. Served in South African War, . . . 1900–1902 (Queen's medal, with clasps "Cape Colony" and "Orange Free State" ; King's medal, with clasps "South Africa, 1901," and "South Africa, 1902"). Transferred to Reserve 1903. [366.]

THE BLACK WATCH (ROYAL HIGHLANDERS)—*continued*

6464. Pte. Smith, William (Perth). Enlisted 1896. Served in South African War, 1901–1902 (Queen's medal, with clasps "Orange Free State," "Transvaal." "South Africa, 1901," and "South Africa, 1902"). Still serving.

7405. Pte. Smitton, David (Perth). Enlisted 1899. Served in South African War, 1902 (Queen's medal, with clasps "Orange Free State," "Transvaal," and "South Africa, 1902"). Still serving.

3114. Pte. Soutar, William (Crieff). Enlisted 1886. Served in South African War, 1900–1902 (Queen's medal, with clasps "Cape Colony," "Wittebergen," and "Transvaal"; King's medal, with clasps "South Africa, 1901," and "South Africa, 1902"). Discharged 1902.

2255. Sergt.-Maj. Stephen, John (Perth). Enlisted in 42nd Royal Highland Regt. 1844. Served in Crimea (1854–1855) during Russian War (medal, with clasps "Alma." "Balaclava," and "Sevastopol"; Turkish medal). Served also in Indian Mutiny, 1857–1858 (medal, with clasp "Lucknow"). Long Service medal. Discharged 1869. Enlisted in Royal Perthshire Rifles (Militia) 1869. Discharged 1874.

6087. Pte. Stewart, Charles (Perth). Enlisted 1895. Served in South African War, 1901–1902 (Queen's medal, with clasps "Orange Free State," "Transvaal," "South Africa, 1901," and "South Africa, 1902"). Still serving.

8990. Pte. Stewart, Charles (Pitlochry). 5th Vol. Batt. Served in South African War with 2nd Vol. Service Coy., 1901–1902 (Queen's medal, with clasps "Cape Colony," "Orange Free State," "Transvaal," "South Africa, 1901," and "South Africa, 1902").

908. Pte. Stewart, Donald (Methven). Enlisted 1881. Served in Egyptian Campaign, 1882; with Soudan Expedition, 1884, and with Nile Expedition 1884–1885 (medal, with clasps "Tel-el-Kebir," "Suakim, 1884," "El Teb—Tamai," "The Nile, 1884–5," and "Kirbekan, 1885"; Khedive's star). Discharged 1898. Served for one year in Royal Scottish Reserve Regt. during South African War.

4177. Pte. Stewart, James (Perth). Enlisted 1890. Served in South African War, . . . 1900–1902 (Queen's medal, with clasps "Cape Colony," "Paardeberg," "Driefontein," "Wittebergen"; King's medal, with clasps "South Africa, 1901," and "South Africa, 1902"). Discharged 1902. [374.]

4407. Pte. Stewart, James (Blairgowrie). Enlisted in 3rd (Militia) Batt. 1891. Served in South African War, . . . 1900–1902 (Queen's medal, with clasps "Cape Colony," "Paardeberg," "Driefontein," and "Wittebergen"; King's medal, with clasps "South Africa, 1901," and "South Africa, 1902"). [377.]

8954. Pte. Stewart, Jas. Cameron (Perth). 4th Vol. Batt. Served in South African War with 2nd Vol. Service Coy., 1901–1902 (Queen's medal, with clasps "Cape Colony," "Orange Free State," "Transvaal," "South Africa, 1901," and "South Africa, 1902"). [367.]

9041. Lance-Corpl. Stewart, John (Aberfeldy). Three years in 5th Vol. Batt. Served in South African War with 2nd Vol. Service Coy., 1901–1902 (Queen's medal, with clasps "Cape Colony," "Orange Free State," "Transvaal," "South Africa, 1901," and "South Africa, 1902"). [375.]

5554. Pte. Stewart, Robert (Moulin). Enlisted 1894. Served in South African War, . . . 1900–1902 (Queen's medal, with clasps "Cape Colony," "Paardeberg," "Driefontein," and "Wittebergen"; King's medal, with clasps "South Africa, 1901," and "South Africa, 1902"). Transferred to Reserve 1902.

2749. Pte. Stewart, Thomas (Perth). Enlisted 1885. Served in South African War, . . . 1900–1902 (Queen's medal, with clasps "Cape Colony" and "Wittebergen"; King's medal, with clasps "South Africa, 1901," and "South Africa, 1902"). Discharged 1902.

2071. Corpl. Strong, Duncan (Logierait). Enlisted in 42nd (Royal Highland, The Black Watch) Regt. 1872. Served in Ashanti War, 1873–1874. Wounded at Amoaful, Jan. 31, 1874, and at Ordashu, Feb. 5, 1874 (medal, with clasp "Coomassie"). [355.]

9168. Pte. Struth, William (Blairgowrie). 5th Vol. Batt. Served in South African War with 3rd Vol. Service Coy., 1902 (Queen's medal, with clasps "Cape Colony," "Orange Free State," and "South Africa, 1902"). [378.]

7244. Pte. Stuart, Charles E. (Perth). Enlisted 1899. Served in South African War,

. . . 1900–1902 (Queen's medal, with clasps "Cape Colony" and "Wittebergen"; King's medal, with clasps "South Africa, 1901," and "South Africa, 1902"). Still serving. [368.]

9154. Pte. Sutherland, Cornelius (Auchterarder). 4th Vol. Batt. Served in South African War with 3rd Vol. Service Coy., 1902 (Queen's medal, with clasps "Cape Colony," "Orange Free State," and "South Africa, 1902"). [382.]

2374. Sergt. Sutherland, John (Perth). Enlisted in 42nd (Royal Highland, The Black Watch) Regt. 1880. Served in Egyptian Campaign, 1882; with Soudan Expedition, 1884, and with Nile Expedition, 1884–1885 (Distinguished Conduct medal; medal, with clasps "Tel-el-Kebir," "El Teb—Tamai," "The Nile, 1884–5," and "Kirbekan, 1885"; Khedive's star). Transferred to Reserve 1886. Discharged 1896. [369.]

7513. Pte. Sutherland, T. (Perth). Enlisted 1900. Served in South African War, 1901–1902 (Queen's medal, with clasps "Cape Colony," "Orange Free State," "Transvaal," "South Africa, 1901," and "South Africa, 1902"). Still serving. [356.]

3157. Pte. Syme, James (Perth). Enlisted 1887. Served in South African War as Reservist (attached to Army Service Corps), 1900–1902 (Queen's medal, with clasps "Cape Colony" and "Wittebergen"; King's medal, with clasps "South Africa, 1901," and "South Africa, 1902"). Discharged 1903. [357.]

2148. Col.-Sergt. Taylor, Alexander (Auchterarder). Enlisted 1883. Served with Nile Expedition, 1884–1885 (medal, with clasp "The Nile, 1884–5," and Khedive's star). Promoted Corpl. 1888, Sergt. 1890, Col.-Sergt. 1898. Served in South African War, 1899–1902 (Queen's medal, with clasps "Cape Colony," "Paardeberg," "Driefontein," and "Wittebergen"; King's medal, with clasps "South Africa, 1901," and "South Africa, 1902"). Now serving as Col.-Sergt. Instructor on Permanent Staff 4th Vol. Batt. [383.]

5889. Lance-Sergt. Taylor, Charles R. (Perth). Enlisted 1895. Served in South African War, 1901–1902 (Queen's medal, with clasps "Orange Free State," "Transvaal," "South Africa, 1901," and "South Africa, 1902"). Transferred to Reserve 1902.

6700. Pte. Taylor, Robert (Perth). Enlisted 1897. Served in South African War,

1899 (Queen's medal, with clasp "Cape Colony"). Killed at Magersfontein, Dec. 11, 1899. [394.]

8969. Pte. Taylor, William (Perth). 4th Vol. Batt. Served in South African War with 2nd Vol. Service Coy., 1901–1902 (Queen's medal, with clasps "Cape Colony," "Orange Free State," "Transvaal," "South Africa, 1901," and "South Africa, 1902").

9156. Pte. Thompson, James (Perth). 4th Vol. Batt. Served in South African War with 3rd Vol. Service Coy., 1902 (Queen's medal, with clasps "Cape Colony," "Orange Free State," and "South Africa, 1902"). Discharged 1902.

7586. Pte. Thomson, Andrew (Logie). 4th Vol. Batt. Served in South African War with 1st Vol. Service Coy., 1900–1901 (Queen's medal, with clasps "Cape Colony," "Wittebergen," and "South Africa, 1901"). [180.]

9129. Corpl. Thomson, D. (Blairgowrie). 3rd Vol. Batt. Served in South African War (1) with 1st Vol. Service Coy., 1900–1901, and (2) with 3rd Vol. Service Coy., 1902 (Queen's medal, with clasps "Cape Colony," "Orange Free State," "Transvaal," "South Africa, 1901," and "South Africa, 1902").

5894. Pte. Thomson, Edward (Blairgowrie). Enlisted 1895. Served in South African War, . . . 1900–1902 (Queen's medal, with clasps "Cape Colony" and "Wittebergen"; King's medal, with clasps "South Africa, 1901," and "South Africa, 1902"). Still serving.

7049. Pte. Thomson, George (Perth). Enlisted 1898. Served in South African War, 1899–1902 (Queen's medal, with clasps "Cape Colony," "Paardeberg," "Driefontein," and "Wittebergen"; King's medal, with clasps "South Africa, 1901," and "South Africa, 1902"). Still serving. [388.]

9042. Pte. Thomson, George (New Scone). 5th Vol. Batt. Served in South African War with 2nd Vol. Service Coy., 1901–1902 (Queen's medal, with clasps "Cape Colony," "Orange Free State," "Transvaal," "South Africa, 1901," and "South Africa, 1902"). [395.]

7589. Corpl. Thomson, James (Perth). Ten years in 4th Vol. Batt. Served in South African War with 1st Vol. Service Coy., 1900–1901 (Queen's medal, with clasps "Cape Colony," "Orange Free State," "Transvaal," and "South Africa, 1901"). [396.]

THE BLACK WATCH (ROYAL HIGHLANDERS)—*continued*

9076. Pte. Thomson, John (Blairgowrie). 5th Vol. Batt. Served in South African War with 2nd Vol. Service Coy., 1901–1902 [1] (Queen's medal, with clasps "Cape Colony," "Orange Free State," "Transvaal," "South Africa, 1901," and "South Africa, 1902").

9162. Pte. Thomson, P. (Perth). 5th Vol. Batt. Served in South African War with 3rd Vol. Service Coy., 1902 (Queen's medal, with clasps "Cape Colony," "Orange Free State," and "South Africa, 1902"). [389.]

9103. Pte. Thomson, Robert (Blairgowrie). 1st Vol. Batt. Served in South African War with 3rd Vol. Service Coy., 1902 (Queen's medal, with clasps "Cape Colony," "Orange Free State," and "South Africa, 1902"). [397.]

6742. Pte. Wallace, David (Perth). Enlisted 1897. Served in South African War, 1901–1902 (Queen's medal, with clasps "Orange Free State," "Transvaal," "South Africa, 1901," and "South Africa, 1902"). Still serving.

6206. Pte. Wallace, William (Perth). Enlisted 1895. Served in South African War, 1901–1902 (Queen's medal, with clasps "Orange Free State," "Transvaal," "South Africa, 1901," and "South Africa, 1902"). Transferred to Reserve 1902.

9133. Pte. Watson, Robert (Blairgowrie). 3rd Vol. Batt. Served in South African War with 3rd Vol. Service Coy., 1902 (Queen's medal, with clasps "Cape Colony," "Orange Free State," and "South Africa, 1902"). [398.]

6205. Pte. Welsh, William F. (Scone). Enlisted 1895. Served in South African War, 1901–1902 (Queen's medal, with clasps "Orange Free State," "Transvaal," "South Africa, 1901," and "South Africa 1902"). Transferred to Reserve 1902. [379.]

6096. Pte. West, Charles (Cargill). Enlisted 1895. Served in South African War, 1901–1902 (Queen's medal, with clasps "Orange Free State," "Transvaal," "South Africa, 1901," and "South Africa, 1902"). Still serving. [381.]

9043. Pte. West, David (Blairgowrie). 5th Vol. Batt. Served in South African War with 2nd Vol. Service Coy., 1901–1902 (Queen's medal, with clasps "Cape Colony," "Orange Free State," "Transvaal," "South Africa, 1901," and "South Africa, 1902"). [390.]

2099. Sergt. West, F. F. (Cargill). Enlisted 1883. Served with Soudan Expedition, 1884 ; wounded at Tamai, March 13, 1884. Served also with Nile Expedition, 1884–1885 (mentioned in despatches ; Distinguished Conduct medal ; medal, with clasps "El Teb—Tamai," "The Nile, 1884–5" and "Kirbekan, 1885" ; Khedive's star). Served also on West Coast of Africa, 1899–1901, as Col.-Sergt. with West African Field Force. Took part in Bida Expedition (mentioned in despatches ; clasp to Distinguished Conduct medal ; and medal with clasp). Still serving.

152. Pte. West, George (Cargill). Enlisted 1881. Served with Soudan Expedition, 1884, and with Nile Expedition, 1884–1885 (medal, with clasps "El Teb—Tamai," "Suakim, 1884," and "The Nile, 1884–5," ; Khedive's star). Discharged 1890. [380.]

1967. Sergt. White, Daniel (Dunblane). Enlisted 1882. Served with Soudan Expedition, 1884, and with Nile Expedition, 1884–1885 (medal, with clasps "El Teb," "Tamai," "The Nile, 1884–5," and "Abou Klea" ; Khedive's star). Served also in South African War, 1901–1902 (Queen's medal, with clasps "Orange Free State," "Transvaal," "South Africa, 1901," and "South Africa, 1902").

2238. Col.-Sergt. White, Hector (Perth). Enlisted in 42nd (Royal Highland, The Black Watch) Regt. 1873. Served in Ashanti War, 1873–1874 (medal). Served also with Soudan Expedition, 1884. Wounded at El Teb, Feb. 29, 1884 (loss of limb) (medal, with clasp "El Teb," and Khedive's star). Discharged invalided 1884. [399.]

7809. Pte. White, John (Perth). Enlisted 1900. Served in South African War, 1900 (Queen's medal, with clasps "Cape Colony" and "Orange Free State"). Still serving. [400.]

9167. Pte. Whittet, Thomas (Scone). 5th Vol. Batt. Served in South African War with 3rd Vol. Service Coy., 1902 (Queen's medal,

---

[1] Volunteered for South Africa at a few hours' notice to take the place of a brother who was taken ill on the eve of departure.

with clasps "Cape Colony," "Orange Free State," and "South Africa, 1902"). [384.]

7406. Pte. **Whyte, Charles** (Alyth). Enlisted 1899. Served in South African War, 1901–1902 (Queen's medal, with clasps "Orange Free State," "Transvaal," "South Africa, 1901," and "South Africa, 1902"). Still serving. [401.]

8979. Pte. **Whyte, Dugald** (Killin). Joined 5th Vol. Batt. 1898. Served in South African War with 2nd Vol. Service Coy., 1901–1902. Served with Mtd. Infy. (Queen's medal, with clasps "Cape Colony," "Orange Free State," "Transvaal," "South Africa, 1901," and "South Africa, 1902"). Still in 5th Vol. Batt. [402.]

6714. Pte. **Whyte, George** (Perth). Enlisted 1897. Served in South African War, 1899–1900 (Queen's medal, with clasp "Cape Colony"). Discharged invalided 1900. [403.]

8998. Pte. **Whyte, William** (Alyth). 5th Vol. Batt. Served in South African War with 2nd Vol. Service Coy., 1901–1902 (Queen's medal, with clasps "Cape Colony," "Orange Free State," "Transvaal," "South Africa, 1901," and "South Africa, 1902"). [391.]

9163. Pte. **Wighton, Fred.** (Balbeggie). 5th Vol. Batt. Served in South African War with 3rd Vol. Service Coy., 1902 (Queen's medal, with clasps "Cape Colony," "Orange Free State," and "South Africa, 1902"). [392.]

3843. Pte. **Williamson, James A.** (Kinfauns). Enlisted 1889. Transferred to Reserve 1896. Served in South African War as Reservist, 1899–1900. Wounded[1] at Magersfontein, Dec. 11, 1899 (Queen's medal, with clasp "Cape Colony"). Discharged invalided 1900.

3509. Sergt. **Wilson, Alex.** (Muckart). Enlisted 1887. Served in South African War, 1899–1902. Wounded at Paardeberg, Feb. 18, 1900. (Twice mentioned in despatches; Distinguished Conduct medal: Queen's medal, with clasps "Cape Colony," "Paardeberg," "Wittebergen," and "Transvaal"; King's medal, with clasps "South Africa, 1901," and "South Africa, 1902"). Still serving. [385.]

4204. Sergt. **Wilson, Alexander** (Alyth). Enlisted 1890. Served in South African War, 1899–1902. Wounded at Paardeberg, Feb. 18,

1900 (Queen's medal, with clasps "Cape Colony," "Paardeberg," and "Wittebergen"; King's medal, with clasps "South Africa, 1901," and "South Africa, 1902"). Re-engaged on Reserve 1902. [386.]

5559. Pte. **Wilson, David** (Glencarse). Enlisted 1894. Served in South African War, 1901–1902 (Queen's medal, with clasps "Orange Free State," "Transvaal," "South Africa, 1901," and "South Africa, 1902"). Still serving.

5002. Pte. **Winsor, William** (Perth). Enlisted 1892. Served in South African War, 1899–1902 (Queen's medal, with clasps "Cape Colony," "Orange Free State," and "Transvaal"; King's medal, with clasps "South Africa, 1901," and "South Africa, 1902"). Transferred to Reserve 1903. [387.]

7610. Pte. **Winton, William** (Pitlochry). 5th Vol. Batt. Enlisted 1900. Served in South African War with 1st Vol. Service Coy., 1900–1901 (Queen's medal, with clasps "Cape Colony," "Wittebergen," and "South Africa, 1901"). [405.]

7272 Pte. **Wishart, Edward J.** (Perth). Enlisted 1899. Served in South African War, 1902 (Queen's medal, with clasps "Orange Free State" and "South Africa, 1902"). Still serving. [404.]

7397. Pte. **Wishart, George** (Crieff). Enlisted 1899. Served in South African War, 1902 (Queen's medal, with clasps "Orange Free State" and "South Africa, 1902"). Still serving. [406.]

7784. Pte. **Wright, Thos.** Cairns (Dunblane). Enlisted 1900. Served in South African War, 1902 (Queen's medal, with clasps "Orange Free State," "Transvaal," and "South Africa, 1902"). Discharged 1902. [407.]

6864. Pte. **Young, David** (Perth). Enlisted 1898. Served in South African War, 1899–1902 (Queen's medal, with clasps "Cape Colony," "Paardeberg," "Driefontein," and "Wittebergen"; King's medal, with clasps "South Africa, 1901," and "South Africa, 1902"). Still serving. [408.]

14. Pte. **Young, William** (Dunkeld). Enlisted 1881. Served with Soudan Expedition, 1884, and with Nile Expedition, 1884–1885

---

[1] This man was wounded in the left foot, left thigh, left arm (humerus fractured), left shoulder, right shoulder, and right leg. He lay on the field of battle for two days and a night.

THE BLACK WATCH (Royal Highlanders)—continued

(medal, with clasps "El Teb—Tamai," "Suakim, 1884," "The Nile, 1884–5,"; and "Kirbekan, 1885"; Khedive's star). Trans-ferred to Reserve 1889. Discharged 1893. Re-enlisted in Royal Scottish Reserve Regt. 1900. Discharged 1901. [393.]

THE KING'S ROYAL RIFLE CORPS

1126. **Rifleman Geddes**, Thomas (Alyth). Enlisted in the 60th (The King's Royal Rifle Corps) 1864. Served in Afghan War, 1878–1880 (medal, with clasps "Ahmed Kiel" and "Kandahar"; Roberts' star). Served also in Boer War, 1880–1881. Discharged 1889. [409.]

699. **Rifleman Robertson**, John (Perth). Enlisted 1898. Served in South African War, 1899–1902 (Queen's medal, with clasps "Tugela Heights," "Relief of Ladysmith," "Laing's Nek," "Transvaal," and "Cape Colony"; King's medal, with clasps "South Africa, 1901," and "South Africa, 1902"). [410.]

THE DUKE OF EDINBURGH'S (Wiltshire Regiment)

4417. **Pte. Kennedy**, James (Perth). Enlisted 1896. Served in South African War, 1899–1902 (Queen's medal, with clasps "Cape Colony," "Orange Free State," and "Transvaal"; King's medal, with clasps "South Africa, 1901," and "South Africa, 1902"). Transferred to Reserve 1903. [411.]

4452. **Bdsman. Smith**, Morgan Jas. (Perth). Enlisted 1896. Served in South African War, . . . 1900–1902 (Queen's medal, with clasps "Cape Colony," "Wittebergen," and "Transvaal"; King's medal, with clasps "South Africa, 1901," and "South Africa, 1902"). Still serving. [412.]

THE HIGHLAND LIGHT INFANTRY

1298. **Lance-Corpl. Cameron**, Alexander (Crieff). 3rd (Militia) Batt. Enlisted 1899. Served in South African War, 1902 (Queen's medal, with clasps "Cape Colony" and "South Africa, 1902"). Still serving.

4274. **Pte. Cameron**, William (Perth). Enlisted 1891. Served in Campaign on North-West Frontier of India, 1897–1898 (operations of Malakand and Buner Field Forces) (medal, with clasp). Served also in South African War, 1899–1900 (Queen's medal, with clasps "Cape Colony," "Paardeberg," and "Wittebergen"). Killed at Dewetsdorp, Nov. 23, 1900.

4600. **Pte. Campbell**, Alexander (Perth). Enlisted 1892. Served in Campaign on North-West Frontier of India, 1897–1898 (operations of Malakand and Buner Field Forces) (medal, with clasp "Punjaub Frontier, 1897–8"). Served also in South African War, 1901–1902 (Queen's medal, with clasps "Cape Colony," "Orange Free State," "Transvaal," "South Africa, 1901," and "South Africa, 1902"). Discharged 1903.

3686. **Pte. Campbell**, Henry (Perth). Enlisted 1890. Served in South African War, 1899–1900 (Queen's medal, with clasps "Cape Colony" and "Orange Free State"). Discharged 1901.

5456. **Pte. Chapman**, Alexander (Pitlochry). Enlisted 1894. Served in South African War, 1901–1902 (Queen's medal, with clasps "Cape Colony," "Orange Free State," "Transvaal," "South Africa, 1901," and "South Africa, 1902").

6659. **Pte. Cross**, David R. (Perth). Enlisted 1898. Served in South African War, 1900–1902 (Queen's medal, with clasps "Cape Colony" and "Wittebergen"; King's medal, with clasps "South Africa, 1901," and "South Africa, 1902"). Still serving. [413.]

6437. **Pte. Devaney**, Frank (Perth). Enlisted 1897. Served in Occupation of Crete, 1898. Discharged invalided 1903.

5122. **Pte. Devaney**, Patrick (Perth). Enlisted 1893. Served in Campaign on North-West Frontier of India, 1897–1898 (operations of Malakand and Buner Field Forces) (medal, with clasp). Served also in South African War, . . . 1901 (Queen's medal, with clasps "Cape

Colony," "Orange Free State," and "South Africa, 1901"). Transferred to Reserve. [414.]

6956. Pte. Dow, Peter S. (Dunblane). Enlisted 1899. Served in South African War, 1900-1902 (Queen's medal, with clasps "Cape Colony," "Orange Free State," and "Transvaal"; King's medal, with clasps "South Africa, 1901," and "South Africa, 1902"). Discharged 1903. [418.]

5693. Corpl. Duff, Robert (Auchterarder). Enlisted 1894. Served in South African War, 1899-1901 (Queen's medal, with clasps "Modder River," "Wittebergen," and "South Africa, 1901"). Discharged 1901. Died Oct. 8, 1902.

6076. Sergt. Ferguson, Alfred (Logierait). Enlisted 1896. Promoted Corpl. 1898, Sergt. 1901. Served in Occupation of Crete, 1898. Served also in South African War (1), 1899-1900; wounded at Spitzkop, Aug. 14, 1900, and invalided home; (2) 1901-1902 (Queen's medal, with clasps "Cape Colony," "Paardeberg," and "Wittebergen"; King's medal, with clasps "South Africa, 1901," and "South Africa, 1902"). Still serving. [420.]

45. Col.-Sergt. Ferguson, Donald (Logierait). Enlisted in 71st (H.L.I.) Regt. 1857. Served in Indian Mutiny, 1858 (medal, with clasp "Central India"); also on North-West Frontier of India, 1863 (medal, with clasp "Umbeyla"). Long Service medal; (relinquished later on obtaining the Meritorious Service medal). Discharged 1880. [419.]

—— Pte. Ferguson, Peter (Coupar Angus). Enlisted in 71st (H.L.I.) Regt. 1852. Served in Crimea 1855 during Russian War (medal, with clasp "Sevastopol," and Turkish medal). Served also in Indian Mutiny (medal, with clasp "Central India"); and on North-West Frontier of India, 1863 (medal, with clasp "Umbeyla"). Discharged 1872.

2885. Pte. Gibbons, John (Perth). Enlisted in 74th (Highlanders) Regt. (now 2nd Batt. The H.L.I.) 1848. Served in Kaffir War, 1851-1853 (attacks on the Amatolas, the Waterkloof, &c.) (Cape medal). Served also in Indian Mutiny, 1857-1859 (capture of Nurgund) (Distinguished Conduct medal). Discharged 1869. Died Dec. 11, 1903 (after sending in record of service). [424.]

3879. Pte. Glen, James (Coupar Angus). Enlisted 1881. Served in Campaign on North-West Frontier of India, 1897-1898 (operations of Malakand and Buner Field Forces)

(medal, with clasp "Punjaub Frontier, 1897-8"). Served also in South African War, 1899-1902 (Queen's medal, with clasps "Modder River" and "Wittebergen"; King's medal, with clasps "South Africa, 1901," and "South Africa, 1902"). [421.]

3277. Pte. Green, John (Perth). Enlisted 1889. Served in South African War as Reservist, 1899-1902 (Queen's medal, with clasps "Modder River" and "Orange Free State"; King's medal, with clasps "South Africa, 1901," and "South Africa, 1902"). Discharged 1902. [430.]

3161. Corpl. Griffin, Dennis (Blairgowrie). Enlisted 1888. Transferred to Reserve 1897. Re-enlisted in 3rd (Militia) Batt. 1901. Served in South African War, 1902 (Queen's medal, with clasps "Cape Colony" and "South Africa, 1902"). [436.]

4982. Col.-Sergt. Hall, Thomas (Perth). Enlisted 1893. Served in Occupation of Crete, 1898; also in South African War, 1899-1902 (Queen's medal, with clasps "Modder River" and "Orange Free State"; King's medal, with clasps "South Africa, 1901," and "South Africa, 1902"). Still serving. [426.]

5783. Pte. Heron, Andrew (Blairgowrie). Enlisted 1895. Served in Occupation of Crete, 1898; also in South African War, 1899-1902 (Queen's medal, with clasps "Cape Colony," "Paardeberg," and "Wittebergen"; King's medal, with clasps "South Africa, 1901," and "South Africa, 1902"). Discharged 1902. [437.]

7161. Pte. Higgins, Patrick (Perth). Enlisted 1900. Served in South African War, 1901-1902 (Queen's medal, with clasps "Cape Colony," "South Africa, 1901," and "South Africa, 1902"). Discharged 1902.

5123. Pte. Holland, Patrick (Perth). Enlisted 1893. Served in Occupation of Crete, 1898; also in South African War, 1899-1902 (Queen's medal, with clasps "Cape Colony," "Paardeberg," and "Wittebergen"; King's medal, with clasps "South Africa, 1901," and "South Africa, 1902"). [422.]

4006. Pte. Hutchison, Peter (Scone). Enlisted in 71st (H.L.I.) Regt. 1855. Served in Crimea 1855 during Russian War (medal, with clasp "Sevastopol," and Turkish medal). Served also in Indian Mutiny, 1858-1859 (medal, with clasp "Central India"); and on North-West Frontier of India, 1863 (medal,

THE HIGHLAND LIGHT INFANTRY—continued

with clasp "Umbeyla"). Discharged 1867. [432.]

2975. Pte. Limmer, David (Perth). Enlisted 1888. Served in Occupation of Crete, 1898. Still serving.

2254. Pte. McDonald, James (Perth). Enlisted 1886. Served in South African War, 1900–1902 (Queen's medal, with clasps "Cape Colony" and "Wittebergen"; King's medal, with clasps "South Africa, 1901," and "South Africa, 1902"). Discharged 1902.

4980. Pte. McFarlane, John (Gourdie). Enlisted 1893. Served in Campaign on North-West Frontier of India, 1897–1898 (operations of Malakand and Buner Field Forces) (medal, with clasp). Transferred to Reserve.

8417. Pte. McFarlane, William (Crieff). 5th Vol. Batt. Served in South African War with 2nd Vol. Service Coy., 1901–1902 (Queen's medal, with clasps "Cape Colony," "Orange Free State," "South Africa, 1901," and "South Africa, 1902").

7391. Pte. McGregor, Charles (Rannagulzion). Enlisted 1900. Served in South African War, 1901–1902 (Queen's medal, with clasps "Cape Colony," "South Africa, 1901," and "South Africa, 1902"). Discharged 1903. [415.]

2945. Pte. McKenzie, James (Perth). Enlisted 1888. Served in South African War, 1899–1901 (Queen's medal, with clasps "Modder River," "Paardeberg," "Wittebergen," and "South Africa, 1901"). Discharged 1901.

7302. Pte. McLaughlin, William (Perth). Enlisted 1900. Served in South African War, 1901–1902 (Queen's medal, with clasps "Cape Colony," "South Africa, 1901," and "South Africa, 1902"). Still serving.

3154. Pte. McPherson, Peter (Glenlyon). Enlisted 1888. Served in South African War, 1899–1901 (Queen's medal, with clasps "Cape Colony," "Paardeberg," "Wittebergen," and "South Africa, 1901"). [427.]

7345. Pte. McRitchie, James (Blairgowrie). Enlisted 1900. Served in South African War, 1901–1902 (Queen's medal, with clasps "Cape Colony," "South Africa, 1901," and "South Africa, 1902"). Still serving.

5030. Pte. Middlemass, James (Crieff). Enlisted 1893. Served in Campaign on North-West Frontier of India, 1897–1898 (operations of Malakand and Buner Field Forces) (medal, with clasp). Still serving.

3809. Pte. Milligan, George (Perth). Enlisted 1890. Served in South African War, 1899–1902 (Queen's medal, with clasps "Modder River," "Paardeberg," and "Wittebergen"; King's medal, with clasps "South Africa, 1901," and "South Africa, 1902"). Discharged 1902.

4574. Pte. Milne, W. (Aberfeldy). Enlisted 1892. Served in Campaign on North-West Frontier of India, 1897–1898 (operations of Malakand and Buner Field Forces) (medal, with clasp). Served also in South African War, 1900–1902 (Queen's medal, with clasps "Cape Colony," "Orange Free State," and "Transvaal"; King's medal, with clasps "South Africa, 1901," and "South Africa, 1902"). [416.]

3512. Pte. Reid, James (Coupar Angus). Enlisted 1890. Served in Campaign on North-West Frontier of India, 1897–1898 (operations of Malakand and Buner Field Forces) (medal, with clasp). Served also in South African War, 1899–1902 (Queen's medal, with clasps "Modder River" and "Wittebergen"; King's medal, with clasps "South Africa, 1901," and "South Africa, 1902"). Discharged 1902.

4882. Pte. Reid, James (Blairgowrie). Enlisted 1893. Served in Occupation of Crete, 1898; also in South African War, 1899–1902 (Queen's medal, with clasps "Modder River" and "Wittebergen"; King's medal, with clasps "South Africa, 1901," and "South Africa, 1902"). [431.]

3946. Pte. Rentoul, E. (Crieff). Enlisted 1889. Served in Campaign on North-West Frontier of India, 1897–1898 (operations of Malakand and Buner Field Forces) (medal, with clasp "Punjaub Frontier, 1897–8"). Served also in South African War as Reservist, 1899–1902 (Queen's medal, with clasps "Cape Colony," "Orange Free State," and "Transvaal"; King's medal, with clasps "South Africa, 1901," and "South Africa, 1902"). Now serving in South African Constabulary.

5374. Pte. Rentoul, William (Crieff). Enlisted 1894. Served in South African War, 1900–1902 (Queen's medal, with clasps "Cape Colony," "Orange Free State," and "Transvaal"; King's medal, with clasps "South

Africa, 1901," and "South Africa, 1902"). Now serving in South African Constabulary.

6743. Pte. Richardson, John (Perth). Enlisted 1898. Served in South African War, . . . 1900–1902 (Queen's medal, with clasps "Wittebergen" and Cape Colony"; King's medal, with clasps "South Africa, 1901," and "South Africa, 1902"). Still serving.

—— **Sergt. Robertson, Donald** (Stanley). Enlisted in 74th (Highlanders) Regt. (now 2nd Batt. H.L.I.) 1865. Served in Egyptian Campaign, 1882 (medal, with clasp "Tel-el-Kebir," and Khedive's star). Discharged 1886. [425.]

5467. Piper Robertson, Thomas (Pitlochry). Enlisted 1894. Served in Occupation of Crete, 1898; also in South African War, . . . 1901 (Queen's medal, with clasps "Cape Colony" and "South Africa, 1901"). Discharged 1901. [438.]

3048. Corpl. Rumgay, Andrew (New Scone). Enlisted 1888. Promoted Lance-Corpl. 1893. Transferred to Reserve 1896. Served in South African War as Reservist, 1899–1901; promoted Corpl. 1901 (Queen's medal, with clasps "Cape Colony," "Paardeberg," "Wittebergen," and "South Africa, 1901"). Discharged 1901. [439.]

3554. Pte. Shaw, John (Blairgowrie). Enlisted 1890. Served in South African War, 1899–1902 (Queen's medal, with clasps "Cape Colony," "Paardeberg," and "Wittebergen"; King's medal, with clasps "South Africa, 1901," and "South Africa, 1902"). Discharged 1902.

4039. Pte. Shaw, John (Perth). Enlisted 1891. Served in Campaign on North-West Frontier of India, 1897–1898 (operations of Malakand and Buner Field Forces) (medal, with clasp). Served also in South African War, 1899–1902 (Queen's medal, with clasps "Modder River" and "Wittebergen"; King's medal, with clasps "South Africa, 1901," and "South Africa, 1902"). Discharged 1903. [433.]

6407. Sergt. Smith, George (Luncarty). Enlisted 1897. Served in Occupation of Crete, 1898; also in South African War, 1902 (Queen's medal, with clasps "Cape Colony" and "South Africa, 1902"). Still serving.

5301. Pte. Stewart, George (Blairgowrie). Enlisted 1894. Served in Campaign on North-West Frontier of India, 1897–1898 (operations of Malakand and Buner Field Forces) (medal, with clasp "Punjaub Frontier, 1897–8").

Served also in South African War, 1900–1902 (Queen's medal, with clasps "Cape Colony" and "Orange Free State"; King's medal, with clasps "South Africa, 1901," and "South Africa, 1902"). Discharged 1902. [440.]

3768. Pte. Stewart, John (Perth). Enlisted 1890. Served in Campaign on North-West Frontier of India, 1897–1898 (operations of Malakand and Buner Field Forces) (medal, with clasp "Punjaub Frontier, 1897–8"). Served also in South African War, 1899–1902 (Queen's medal, with clasps "Modder River," "Paardeberg," and "Wittebergen"; King's medal, with clasps "South Africa, 1901," and "South Africa, 1902"). Discharged 1902. [434.]

3840. Col.-Sergt. Stewart, Peter (Bankfoot). Enlisted 1890. Served in Campaign on North-West Frontier of India, 1897–1898 (operations of Malakand and Buner Field Forces) (medal, with clasp "Punjaub Frontier, 1897–8"). Royal Humane Society's Bronze Medal for saving life. Still serving. [417.]

8423. Pte. Stewart, William (Ballinluig). 5th Vol. Batt. Served in South African War with 2nd Vol. Service Coy., 1901–1902 (Queen's medal, with clasps "Cape Colony," "Orange Free State," "South Africa, 1901," and "South Africa, 1902"). [435.]

3087. Corpl. Taylor, Alexander (Muthill). Enlisted 1888. Transferred to Reserve 1896. Served in South African War as Reservist, 1899–1901 (Queen's medal, with clasps "Modder River," "Paardeberg," "Wittebergen," and "South Africa, 1901"). Discharged 1901. [423.]

8278. Pte. Watson, Ronald (Logie). . . . Vol. Batt. Served in South African War with 1st Vol. Service Coy., 1900–1901 (Queen's medal, with clasps "Cape Colony," "Orange Free State," "Transvaal," and "South Africa, 1901").

3140. Pte. Welsh, William (Auchterarder). Enlisted 1888. Served in Occupation of Crete, 1898; severely wounded. Served also in South African War, 1899–1901 (Queen's medal, with clasps "Modder River," "Paardeberg," "Wittebergen," and "South Africa, 1901"). Discharged 1901. [428.]

7556. Pte. Wisely, Peter (Bridge of Earn). Enlisted 1901. Served in South African War, 1902 (Queen's medal, with clasps "Cape Colony" and "South Africa, 1902"). Still serving. [429.]

THE HIGHLAND LIGHT INFANTRY—continued

5054. Corpl. Young, John (Kincardine on Forth). Enlisted 1893. Served in Campaign on North-West Frontier of India, 1897–1898 (operations of Malakand and Buner Field Forces) (medal, with clasp "Punjaub Frontier, 1897–8"). Discharged 1902.

SEAFORTH HIGHLANDERS (Ross-shire Buffs, The Duke of Albany's)

6618. Pte. Adams, James (Perth). Enlisted 1899. Served in South African War, . . . 1900–1902 (Queen's medal, with clasps "Cape Colony," "Orange Free State," and "Transvaal"; King's medal, with clasps "South Africa, 1901," and "South Africa, 1902"). Still serving. [441.]

6571. Pte. Aird, Alexander (Perth). Enlisted 1899. Served in South African War, . . . 1900–1902 (Queen's medal, with clasps "Cape Colony," "Orange Free State," and "Transvaal"; King's medal, with clasps "South Africa, 1901," and "South Africa, 1902"). Still serving.

6869. Pte. Allan, David (Perth). Enlisted 1899. Served in South African War, 1900–1902 (Queen's medal, with clasps "Cape Colony," "Orange Free State," and "Transvaal"; King's medal, with clasps "South Africa, 1901," and "South Africa, 1902"). Still serving.

2447. Col.-Sergt. Allan, John (Coupar Angus). Enlisted 1887. Served with Hazara Expedition, 1891 (medal, with clasp "Hazara, 1891"); also with Chitral Relief Force, 1895 (medal, with clasp "Relief of Chitral"). Still serving.

5091. Pte. Allison, John (Perth). Enlisted 1894. Served in Soudan Campaign, 1898 (medal, and Khedive's medal, with clasps "The Atbara" and "Khartoum"). Transferred to Reserve.

5067. Pte. Anderson, Allan (Perth). Enlisted 1894. Served in Soudan Campaign, 1898 (medal, and Khedive's medal, with clasps "The Atbara" and "Khartoum"). Served also in South African War, 1901–1902 (Queen's medal, with clasps "Cape Colony," "Orange Free State," "Transvaal," "South Africa, 1901," and "South Africa, 1902"). [461.]

3746. Pte. Anderson, Thomas (Perth). Enlisted 1891. Served with Chitral Relief Force, 1895 (medal, with clasp "Relief of Chitral"); and in Soudan Campaign, 1898 (medal, and Khedive's medal, with clasps "The Atbara" and "Khartoum"). Served also in South African War, . . . 1900–1902 (Queen's medal, with clasps "Cape Colony," "Paardeberg," "Driefontein," and "Transvaal"; King's medal, with clasps "South Africa, 1901," and "South Africa, 1902"). Discharged 1903.

4784. Sergt. Bisset, Daniel (Scone). Enlisted 1894. Served with Chitral Relief Force, 1895 (medal, with clasp "Relief of Chitral"); also in Occupation of Crete, 1897, and in Soudan Campaign, 1898 (medal, and Khedive's medal, with clasp "Khartoum"). Also served on West Coast of Africa with Northern Nigerian Regiment in (1) The Abuja Expedition, 1902, (2) the Kano and Sokoto Expedition, 1903, and (3) the Expedition in the Kafe Country, 1903. Still serving. [467.]

3002. Col.-Sergt. Brownie, Charles E. (Dunning). Enlisted 1889. Served in Hinterland of West Africa, 1898–1899 (medal, with clasp "1898"). Now serving as Col.-Sergt.-Instr. on Permanent Staff Royal Jersey Militia. [442.]

1711. Sergt. Bruce, Peter (Errol). Enlisted 1885. Served in Soudan Campaign, 1898 (medal, and Khedive's medal, with clasps "The Atbara" and "Khartoum"). Still serving.

6712. Pte. Calderwood, James (Perth). Enlisted 1899. Served in South African War, 1900–1902 (Queen's medal, with clasps "Cape Colony," "Orange Free State," and "Transvaal"; King's medal, with clasps "South Africa, 1901," and "South Africa, 1902"). Still serving. [468.]

3047. Pte. Campbell, Henry M. (Kincardine on Forth). Enlisted 1889. Served with Chitral Relief Force, 1895 (medal, with clasp "Relief of Chitral"). Served also in South African War, 1899–1902. Wounded at Magersfontein, Dec. 11, 1899 (Queen's medal, with clasps "Cape Colony," "Transvaal," and "Wittebergen"; King's medal, with clasps "South Africa, 1901," and "South Africa, 1902"). Discharged 1902. [443.]

2397. Pte. Campbell, John (Tenandry). Enlisted 1887. Served with Hazara Expedition,

1891 (medal, with clasp "Hazara, 1891"). Served also in South African War, (1) 1899; wounded at Magersfontein, Dec. 11, 1899, and invalided home. Served (2) in South African War, 1900-1902 (Queen's medal, with clasps "Cape Colony," "Orange Free State," and "Transvaal"; King's medal, with clasps "South Africa, 1901," and "South Africa, 1902"). Discharged 1902.

564. Pte. Cassidy, William (Blairgowrie). Enlisted in 72nd (Duke of Albany's Own Highlanders) Regt. (now 1st Batt. Seaforth Highlanders) 1880. Served in Egyptian Campaign, 1882 (medal, with clasp "Tel-el-Kehir," and Khedive's star). Served with Hazara Expedition, 1888 (medal, with clasp "Hazara, 1888"); and with Chitral Relief Force, 1895 (medal, with clasp "Relief of Chitral"). Served also in Soudan Campaign, 1898 (medal, and Khedive's medal, with clasps "The Atbara" and "Khartoum"). Discharged 1898.

1895. Col.-Sergt. Cook, John (Errol). Enlisted 1886. Served with Hazara Expedition, 1891 (medal, with clasp "Hazara, 1891"); and with Chitral Relief Force, 1895 (medal, with clasp "Relief of Chitral"). Served also in South African War, 1901 (Queen's medal, with clasps "Cape Colony" and "South Africa, 1901"). Still serving.

5155. Pte. Cook, Thomas (St. Madoes). Enlisted 1895. Served in Soudan Campaign, 1898 (medal, and Khedive's medal, with clasps "The Atbara" and "Khartoum"). Served also in South African War, 1901-1902 (Queen's medal, with clasps "Cape Colony," "Orange Free State," "Transvaal," "South Africa, 1901," and "South Africa, 1902"). Transferred to Reserve.

3230. Sergt.-Maj. Crabb, Joseph (Blairgowrie). Enlisted in 71st (H.L.I.) Regt. 1878. Transferred to Seaforth Highlanders. Served with Hazara Expeditions, 1888 and 1891 (medal, with clasps "Hazara, 1888," and "Hazara, 1891"); also with Chitral Relief Force, 1895 (medal, with clasp "Relief of Chitral"). Appointed Sergt.-Instr. to 1st. Vol. Batt. 1897. Promoted Sergt.-Maj. 1902. Died 1903.

3035. Pte. Cree, John (Perth). Enlisted in 72nd (Duke of Albany's Own Highlanders) Regt. (now 1st Batt. Seaforth Highlanders) 1854. Served in Crimea, 1855, during Russian War (medal, with clasp "Sevastopol," and Turkish medal). Discharged 1865.

II.

9866. Pte. Doig, Charles (Alyth). Enlisted 1901. Served in South African War, 1902 (Queen's medal, with clasps "Cape Colony," "Orange Free State," "Transvaal," and "South Africa, 1902"). Still serving. [473.]

3437. Pte. Douglas, Robert (Cargill). Enlisted 1890. Served with Chitral Relief Force, 1895 (medal, with clasp "Relief of Chitral"). Served also in South African War, 1899 (Queen's medal, with clasp "Cape Colony"). Killed at Magersfontein, Dec. 11, 1899.

5279. Pte. Duff, James (Perth). Enlisted 1895. Served in Soudan Campaign, 1898 (medal, and Khedive's medal, with clasps "The Atbara" and "Khartoum"). Served also in South African War, . . . 1900-1901 (Queen's medal, with clasps "Cape Colony," "Paardeberg," "Driefontein," and "South Africa, 1901"). Transferred to Reserve.

1525. Bdsman. Duff, Thomas (Blairgowrie). Enlisted in 72nd (Duke of Albany's Own Highlanders) Regt. (now 1st Batt. Seaforth Highlanders) 1879. Served in Afghan War, 1879-1880 (medal, with four clasps, and Roberts' star). Served also in Egyptian Campaign, 1882 (medal, with clasp "Tel-el-Kebir," and Khedive's star). Long Service medal. Discharged 1890. [444.]

2849. Col.-Sergt. Dunbar, George (Crieff). Enlisted 1888. Served in Soudan Campaign, 1898 (medal, and Khedive's medal, with clasps "The Atbara" and "Khartoum"). Mediterranean Service medal. Still serving. [445.]

3478. Col.-Sergt. Edward, Robert (Perth). Enlisted in 72nd (Duke of Albany's Own Highlanders) Regt. (now 1st Batt. Seaforth Highlanders) 1878. Served in Afghan War, 1879-1880 (medal, with four clasps, and Roberts' star); also in Egyptian Campaign, 1882 (medal, with clasp "Tel-el-Kebir," and Khedive's star). Served also with Hazara Expedition, 1888 (medal, with clasp "Hazara, 1888"). Now serving in Indian Barrack Department.

4834. Pte. Farquharson, John (Blairgowrie). Enlisted 1894. Served in Soudan Campaign, 1898 (medal, and Khedive's medal, with clasps "The Atbara" and "Khartoum"). Served also in South African War, . . . 1900-1902 (Queen's medal, with clasps "Cape Colony," "Paardeberg," "Driefontein," "Wittebergen," and "Transvaal"; King's medal, with clasps "South Africa, 1901," and "South Africa, 1902"). Transferred to Reserve. [469.]

Q

SEAFORTH HIGHLANDERS—continued

8244. Pte. Faulds, John (Perth). Enlisted 1900. Served in South African War, 1902 (Queen's medal, with clasps "Cape Colony," "Orange Free State," "Transvaal," and "South Africa, 1902"). Still serving.

1169. Col.-Sergt. Fenton, Andrew (Kinnoull). Enlisted 1885. Promoted Corpl. 1890, Sergt. 1893, Col.-Sergt. 1897. Served with Hazara Expedition, 1891, and with Waziristan Field Force, 1894 (medal, with clasps "Hazara, 1891," and "Waziristan, 1894-5"). Served also with Chitral Relief Force, 1895 (medal, with clasp "Relief of Chitral"). Now serving as Sergt.-Instr. on Permanent Staff of 2nd Vol. Batt. (1st Sutherland Highland Rifle Volunteers). [446.]

3004. Qrmr.-Sergt. Fenton, John (Kinnoull). Enlisted 1889. Served in Occupation of Crete, 1897 ; also in Soudan Campaign, 1898 (medal, and Khedive's medal, with clasps "The Atbara" and "Khartoum"). Still serving. [447.]

6713. Pte. Firth, Walter (Perth). Enlisted 1899. Served in South African War, . . . 1900-1902 (Queen's medal, with clasps "Cape Colony," "Orange Free State," and "Transvaal"; King's medal, with clasps "South Africa, 1901," and "South Africa, 1902"). Still serving.

6046. Pte. Flynn, Charles M. (Perth). Enlisted 1898. Served in South African War, 1901-1902 (Queen's medal, with clasps "Cape Colony," "Orange Free State," "Transvaal," "South Africa, 1901," and "South Africa, 1902"). Still serving.

6112. Pte. Gordon, David (Perth). Enlisted 1898. Served in South African War, 1899 (Queen's medal, with clasp "Cape Colony"). Killed at Magersfontein, Dec. 11, 1899. [448.]

7132. Pte. Gordon, David (Perth). Enlisted 1900. Served in South African War, 1902 (Queen's medal, with clasps "Cape Colony," "Orange Free State," "Transvaal," and "South Africa, 1902"). Still serving.

1640. Pte. Grant, James (Crieff). Enlisted 1885. Served with Hazara Expeditions, 1888 and 1891 (medal, with clasps "Hazara, 1888," and "Hazara, 1891"). Served also in South African War, . . . 1900-1902 (Queen's medal, with clasps "Cape Colony," "Paardeberg," "Driefontein," "Wittebergen," and "Trans-

vaal" ; King's medal, with clasps "South Africa, 1901," and "South Africa, 1902"). Discharged 1902.

5315. Pte. Halley, John (Crieff). Enlisted 1895. Served in Soudan Campaign, 1898 (medal, and Khedive's medal, with clasps "The Atbara" and "Khartoum"). Served also in South African War, 1901-1902 (Queen's medal, with clasps "Cape Colony," "Orange Free State," "Transvaal," "South Africa, 1901," and "South Africa, 1902"). Still serving. [449.]

2957. Corpl. Heard, John (Perth). Enlisted 1889. Served with Hazara Expedition, 1891 (medal, with clasp "Hazara, 1891"); also with Chitral Relief Force, 1895 (medal, with clasp "Relief of Chitral"). Served also in South African War as Reservist, 1899. Wounded at Magersfontein, Dec. 11, 1899 (Queen's medal, with clasp "Cape Colony"). Discharged invalided 1900. [450.]

9586. Lance-Corpl. Kidd, John (Perth). Enlisted 1901. Served in South African War, 1902 (Queen's medal, with clasps "Cape Colony," "Orange Free State," "Transvaal," and "South Africa, 1902"). Still serving. [451.]

3038. Pte. Laing, William (Perth). Enlisted 1889. Served with Chitral Relief Force, 1895 (medal, with clasp "Relief of Chitral"); also in South African War (Queen's medal, with clasp "Cape Colony"). Discharged 1902.

1788. Corpl. Lamb, George (Perth). Enlisted in 72nd (Duke of Albany's Own Highlanders) Regt. (now 1st Batt. Seaforth Highlanders) 1868. Served in Afghan War, 1879-1880 (medal, with three clasps, and Roberts' star). Discharged 1886.

3264. Pte. McFarlane, Alex. (Perth). Enlisted 1890. Served in South African War, 1899-1902 (Queen's medal, with clasps "Cape Colony," "Paardeberg," "Driefontein," and "Johannesburg"; King's medal, with clasps "South Africa, 1901," and "South Africa, 1902"). [452.]

5815. Pte. MacGregor, George (Perth). Enlisted 1897. Served in South African War, 1899-1902 (Queen's medal, with clasps "Cape Colony," "Paardeberg," "Driefontein," "Wittebergen," and "Transvaal"; King's medal, with clasps "South Africa, 1901," and "South Africa, 1902"). Still serving. [462.]

4559. Pte. McInroy, George (Scone). Enlisted 1893. Served in Soudan Campaign, 1898 (medal, and Khedive's medal, with clasps "The Atbara" and "Khartoum"). Served also in South African War, 1900–1902 (Queen's medal, with clasps "Cape Colony" and "Wittebergen"; King's medal, with clasps "South Africa, 1901," and "South Africa, 1902"). Transferred to Reserve.

5051. Pte. McInroy, Kenneth (Perth). Enlisted 1894. Served in Soudan Campaign, 1898 (medal, and Khedive's medal, with clasps "The Atbara" and "Khartoum"). Served also in South African War, 1901–1902 (Queen's medal, with clasps "Cape Colony," "Orange Free State," "Transvaal," "South Africa, 1901," and "South Africa, 1902"). Transferred to Reserve. [470.]

6557. Pte. McKenzie, David (Clunie). Enlisted 1899. Served in South African War, . . . 1900–1902 (Queen's medal, with clasps "Cape Colony," "Orange Free State," and "Transvaal"; King's medal, with clasps "South Africa, 1901," and "South Africa, 1902"). Still serving.

5604. Pte. McKinlay, Alexander (Strathbraan). Enlisted 1896. Served in Soudan Campaign, 1898 (medal, and Khedive's medal, with clasps "The Atbara" and "Khartoum"). Served also in South African War, 1901–1902 (Queen's medal, with clasps "Cape Colony," "Orange Free State," "Transvaal," "South Africa, 1901," and "South Africa, 1902") Still serving. [453.]

1056. Pte. McLaren, Daniel (Strathyre). Enlisted in 72nd (Duke of Albany's Own Highlanders) Regt. 1878. Served in Afghan War, 1879–1880 (medal, with three clasps, and Roberts' star). Served also in Egyptian Campaign, 1882 (medal, with clasp "Tel-el-Kebir," and Khedive's star). Discharged 1890.

2599. Pte. McOwen, John (Rhynd). Enlisted 1884. Served in Egyptian Campaign (medal, and Khedive's star); also with Hazara Expeditions, 1888 and 1891 (medal, with clasps "Hazara, 1888," and "Hazara, 1891"). Served also in South African War, . . . 1901 (Queen's medal, with clasps "Cape Colony," "Orange Free State," "Transvaal," and "South Africa, 1901"). Discharged 1901. [471.]

6462. Pte. Matthews, John (Perth). Enlisted 1899. Served in South African War, . . . 1900–1902 (Queen's medal, with clasps "Cape Colony," "Orange Free State," and "Transvaal"; King's medal, with clasps "South Africa, 1901," and "South Africa, 1902"). Still serving.

6714. Pte. Mitchell, James (Perth). Enlisted 1899. Served in South African War, 1900–1902 (Queen's medal, with clasps "Orange Free State" and "Cape Colony"; King's medal, with clasps "South Africa, 1901," and "South Africa, 1902"). Still serving. [454.]

1463. Pte. Morrison, Donald (Auchterarder). Enlisted in 72nd (Duke of Albany's Own Highlanders) Regt. (now 1st Batt. Seaforth Highlanders) 1868. Served in Afghan War, 1879–1880 (medal, with clasps "Charisia," "Kabul," and "Kandahar"; Roberts' star). Served also in Egyptian Campaign, 1882 (medal, with clasp "Tel-el-Kebir," and Khedive's star). Discharged 1888. [474.]

6285. Pte. Noble, Fleming (Stanley). Enlisted 1898. Served in South African War, . . . 1900–1902 (Queen's medal, with clasps "Cape Colony," "Orange Free State," and "Transvaal"; King's medal, with clasps "South Africa, 1901," and "South Africa, 1902"). Still serving.

5717. Pte. Paterson, Alexander (Alyth). Enlisted 1896. Served in South African War, . . . 1900–1902 (Queen's medal, with clasps "Cape Colony," "Wittebergen," and "Transvaal"; King's medal, with clasps "South Africa, 1901," and "South Africa, 1902"). Still serving.

6113. Pte. Proudfoot, James (Perth). Enlisted 1898. Served in South African War, . . . 1900–1902 (Queen's medal, with clasps "Cape Colony," "Paardeberg," "Driefontein," "Wittebergen," and "Transvaal"; King's medal, with clasps "South Africa, 1901," and "South Africa, 1902"). Still serving. [455.]

1745. Pte. Robertson, Donald (Ballinluig). Enlisted 1885. Served with Hazara Expedition, 1891 (medal, with clasp "Hazara, 1891"); also in South African War, . . . 1900 (Queen's medal, with clasps "Cape Colony" and "Paardeberg"). Discharged 1902. [463.]

1365. Pte. Robertson, George T. (Perth). Enlisted in 72nd (Duke of Albany's Own Highlanders) Regt. (now 1st Batt. Seaforth Highlanders) 1868. Served in Afghan War, 1879–1880 (medal, with clasps "Charisia,"

SEAFORTH HIGHLANDERS—*continued*

"Kabul," and "Kandahar"; Roberts' star). Served also in Egyptian War, 1882 (medal, with clasp "Tel-el-Kebir," and Khedive's star). Long Service medal. Discharged 1889. [456.]

5762. Drum. **Robertson, John** (Perth). Enlisted 1879. Served in South African War, . . . 1900 (Queen's medal, with clasps "Cape Colony," "Paardeberg," and "Driefontein"). Still serving. [472.]

4988. Pte. **Smith, John** (Blairgowrie). Enlisted 1894. Served in Soudan Campaign, 1898 (medal, and Khedive's medal, with clasps "The Atbara" and "Khartoum"). Transferred to Reserve.

—— Pte. **Smith, Myles** (Blairgowrie). Enlisted in 78th (Highland—Ross-shire Buffs) Regt. (now 2nd Batt. Seaforth Highlanders) 1874. Served with Suakim Field Force, 1888 (medal, with clasp "Gemaizah," and Khedive's star). Discharged 1886. Enlisted in the King's Own Scottish Borderers, 1887. Discharged 1903.

486. Lance-Corpl. **Sorley, James** (Corsiehill). Enlisted in 71st (H.L.I.) Regt. 1868. Discharged 1877. Re-enlisted for active service in 72nd (Duke of Albany's Own Highlanders) Regt. (now 1st Batt. Seaforth Highlanders) 1879. Served in Afghan War, 1880. Wounded at Kandahar, Sept. 1, 1880 (medal, with four clasps, and Roberts' star). Promoted Lance-Corpl. 1889. Long Service medal. Discharged 1892. Now serving as Sergt. Master Tailor with . . . Vol. Batt. The Royal Scots (Queen's Rifle Vol. Bgde.). [464.]

2965. Sergt. **Spiers, William** (Blairgowrie). Enlisted 1889. Served with Chitral Relief Force, 1895 (medal, with clasp "Relief of Chitral"). Still serving.

8245. Pte. **Stewart, Douglas** (Perth). Enlisted 1900. Served in South African War, 1902 (Queen's medal, with clasps "Cape Colony," "Orange Free State," "Transvaal," and "South Africa, 1902"). Still serving.

—— Pte. **Stewart, James** (Perth). Enlisted in 72nd (Duke of Albany's Own Highlanders) Regt. (now 1st Batt. Seaforth Highlanders) 1852. Served in Crimea, 1855, during Russian War. Wounded at Sevastopol (medal, with clasp "Sevastopol," and Turkish medal). Served also in Indian Mutiny, 1857–1859 (medal,

with clasp "Central India"). Transferred to Reserve 1863. Discharged 1883. [465.]

3442. Pte. **Stewart, James** (Perth). Enlisted 1890. Served with Chitral Relief Force 1895 (medal, with clasp "Relief of Chitral"); in Occupation of Crete, 1897; and in Soudan Campaign, 1898 (medal, and Khedive's medal, with clasps "The Atbara" and "Khartoum"). Served also in South African War as Reservist, 1899–1901 (Queen's medal, with clasps "Cape Colony," "Paardeberg," "Driefontein," "Wittebergen," "Transvaal," and "South Africa, 1901"). Discharged 1902. [475.]

5547. Sergt. **Stewart, John** (Blair Atholl). Enlisted 1896. Served in Soudan Campaign, 1898 (medal, and Khedive's medal, with clasps "The Atbara" and "Khartoum"). Served also in South African War (with Mtd. Infy.), 1901–1902 (Queen's medal, with clasps "Cape Colony," "Orange Free State," "Transvaal," "South Africa, 1901," and "South Africa, 1902"). Still serving. [457.]

2974. Pte. **Taylor, Andrew** (Kincardine). Enlisted 1889. Served with Chitral Relief Force, 1895 (medal, with clasp "Relief of Chitral"); also in South African War, . . . 1900–1902 (Queen's medal, with clasps "Cape Colony," "Paardeberg," "Driefontein," "Wittebergen," and "Transvaal"; King's medal, with clasps "South Africa, 1901," and "South Africa, 1902"). Discharged 1902.

4595. Pte. **Taylor, Archibald** (Blair Drummond). Enlisted 1893. Served in Soudan Campaign, 1898 (medal, and Khedive's medal, with clasps "The Atbara" and "Khartoum"). Served also in South African War, . . . 1900–1902 (Queen's medal, with clasps "Cape Colony," "Wittebergen," and "Transvaal"; King's medal, with clasps "South Africa, 1901," and "South Africa, 1902"). Transferred to Reserve.

1763. Pte. **Thomson, George** (Cargill). Enlisted 1885. Served with Hazara Expedition, 1891 (medal, with clasp "Hazara, 1891"); also in South African War, . . . 1900–1902 (Queen's medal, with clasps "Cape Colony," "Paardeberg," "Driefontein," and "Transvaal"; King's medal, with clasps "South Africa, 1901," and "South Africa, 1902"). Discharged 1902. [476.]

5221. Sergt.-Drum. **Thomson, Robert**

(Perth). Enlisted 1884. Served with Chitral Relief Force, 1895 (medal, with clasp "Relief of Chitral"); also in South African War, . . . 1901 (Queen's medal, with clasps "Rhodesia," "Cape Colony," "Orange Free State," "Transvaal," and "South Africa, 1901"). Killed in attack on Armoured Train, Aug. 8, 1901. [458.]

3241. Lance-Corpl. Tyrie, Robert (Errol). Enlisted 1890. Served in South African War, . . . 1900-1902 (Queen's medal, with clasps "Cape Colony," "Paardeberg," "Driefontein," "Wittebergen," and "Transvaal"; King's medal, with clasps "South Africa, 1901," and "South Africa, 1902"). Discharged 1902. [459.]

2619. Pte. Watt, John (Moulin). Enlisted in Cameron Highlanders 1886. Transferred to Seaforth Highlanders 1887. Served with Hazara Expeditions, 1888 and 1891 (medal, with clasps "Hazara, 1888," and "Hazara, 1891"). Served also in South African War, (1) 1899; wounded at Magersfontein, Dec. 11, 1899, and invalided home; (2) 1900-1901; wounded at Ermelo,

Aug. 11, 1901 (whilst attached to Scottish Horse), and invalided home (Queen's medal, with clasps "Cape Colony," "Orange Free State," "Transvaal," and "South Africa, 1901"). Discharged 1902. Enlisted in Scottish Horse (I.Y.) 1903.

355. Pte. Wilson, Andrew (Bankfoot). Enlisted in 72nd (Duke of Albany's Own Highlanders) Regt. (now 1st Batt. Seaforth Highlanders) 1878. Served in Afghan War, 1879-1880 (medal, with clasp "Kandahar," and Roberts' star). Transferred to Reserve 1888. Discharged 1890. Enlisted in Royal Scottish Reserve Regt. 1900. Discharged 1901. [465.]

1105. Pte. Wilson, Charles (Cargill). Enlisted in 72nd (Duke of Albany's Own Highlanders) Regt. (now 1st Batt. Seaforth Highlanders) 1866. Served in Afghan War, 1879-1880 (medal, with three clasps, and Roberts' star). Served also in Egyptian War, 1882 (medal, with clasp "Tel-el-Kebir," and Khedive's star). Discharged 1889. [460.]

THE GORDON HIGHLANDERS

7183. Pte. Aitken, George (Coupar Angus). Enlisted 1900. Served in South African War, 1901-1902 (Queen's medal, with clasps "Cape Colony," "Orange Free State," "Transvaal," "South Africa, 1901," and "South Africa, 1902"). Transferred to Reserve 1903.

4680. Pte. Anderson, James (Auchterarder). Enlisted 1892. Served with Chitral Relief Force, 1895, and in Campaign on North-West Frontier of India (with Tirah Expeditionary Force), 1897-1898 (medal, with clasps "Relief of Chitral," "Punjaub Frontier, 1897-8," and "Tirah, 1897-8"). Served also in South African War, 1899-1901. Wounded at Boemspruit, July 4, 1901, and invalided home (Queen's medal, with clasps "Defence of Ladysmith," "Laing's Nek," "Belfast," and "South Africa, 1901"). Discharged 1902. [485.]

2101. Col.-Sergt. Archer, Jas. Anderson (Alyth). Enlisted in 92nd (Gordon Highlanders) Regt. 1870. Served in Afghan War, 1879-1880 (medal, with clasps "Charasia," "Kabul," and "Kandahar"; Roberts' star). Served also in Boer War, 1881; wounded at Majuba, Feb. 27, 1881. Promoted Corpl. 1882, Lance-Sergt. 1883, Sergt. 1884, Col.-Sergt. 1888. Appointed Sergt.-Instr. to 3rd Vol. Batt. 1901. Discharged 1898. [477.]

6700. Pte. Beharrie, W. (Perth). Enlisted 1899. Served in South African War (Queen's medal, with clasps "Cape Colony," "Paardeberg," "Driefontein," "Transvaal," "South Africa, 1901," and "South Africa, 1902"). Still serving.

2561. Pte. Bennett, Peter (Braco). Enlisted 1887. Served with Chitral Relief Force, 1895, and in Campaign on North-West Frontier of India, 1897-1898 (with Tirah Expeditionary Force) (medal, with clasps "Relief of Chitral," "Punjaub Frontier, 1897-8," and "Tirah, 1897-8"). Served also in South African War, 1899-1902 (Queen's medal, with clasps "Relief of Ladysmith," "Cape Colony," "Orange Free State," and "Transvaal"; King's medal, with clasps "South Africa, 1901," and "South Africa, 1902"). [486.]

4968. Pte. Boyd, Hugh (Bridge of Earn). Enlisted 1893. Served in Campaign on North-West Frontier of India, 1897-1898 (with Tirah Expeditionary Force) (medal, with clasps "Punjaub Frontier, 1897-8," and "Tirah, 1897-8"). Served also in South African War, 1899-1902 (Queen's medal, with clasps "Elandslaagte," "Defence of Ladysmith," and "Transvaal"; King's medal, with clasps "South

THE GORDON HIGHLANDERS—*continued*

Africa, 1901," and "South Africa, 1902").
Discharged 1902.

2240. Sergt. Brown, John Roy (Perth).
Enlisted 1886. · Served with Chitral Relief Force,
1895 ; (wounded at storming of Malakand Pass,
April 3). Served also in Campaign on North-
West Frontier of India, 1897–1898 (with Tirah
Expeditionary Force) (medal, with clasps "Re-
lief of Chitral," " Punjaub Frontier, 1897–8,"
and "Tirah, 1897–8"). Served also in
South African War, 1899–1902 (Queen's medal,
with clasps "Cape Colony," " Paardeberg,"
" Driefontein," " Johannesburg," and " Bel-
fast" ; King's medal, with clasps " South
Africa, 1901," and " South Africa, 1902").
Still serving. [487.]

6282. Lance-Corpl. Calder, David (Dunkeld). Enlisted 1897. Served in South
African War, . . . 1900 (Queen's medal, with
clasps "Cape Colony," " Paardeberg," and
" Driefontein "). Still serving. [479.]

3668. Pte. Charlesworth, W. (Perth). Enlisted 1891. Served in South African War,
1899–1901 (Queen's medal, with clasps " Laing's
Nek," " Belfast," and " South Africa, 1901 ").

3265. Pte. Clark, Archibald (Perth). En-
listed 1889. Served in Campaign on North-
West Frontier of India, 1897–1898 (with Tirah
Expeditionary Force) (medal, with clasps
" Punjaub Frontier, 1897–8," and " Tirah,
1897–8"). Served also in South African
War, 1899–1902 (Queen's medal, with clasps
" Cape Colony," " Paardeberg," " Driefontein,"
and " Johannesburg" ; King's medal, with
clasps " South Africa, 1901," and " South
Africa, 1902"). Discharged 1902. [478.]

5320. Pte. Clark, Archibald (Dowally).
Enlisted 1895. Served in Campaign on North-
West Frontier of India, 1897–1898 (with Tirah
Expeditionary Force) (medal, with clasps
" Punjaub Frontier, 1897–8," and " Tirah,
1897–8 "). Served also in South African War,
1899–1902 (Queen's medal, with clasps " De-
fence of Ladysmith," " Laing's Nek," and
" Belfast " ; King's medal, with clasps " South
Africa, 1901," " South Africa, 1902"). Still
serving. [488.]

5995. Pte. Connor, R. (Perth). Enlisted
1897. Served in South African War, 1899–
1902 (Queen's medal, with clasps " Elandslaagte," " Defence of Ladysmith," and " Trans-

vaal" ; King's medal, with clasps " South Africa,
1901," and "South Africa, 1902"). Still serving.

5861. Pte. Connor, W. (Perth). Enlisted
1896. Served in South African War, 1899–
1900 (Queen's medal, with clasp " Defence
of Ladysmith "). Still serving.

6527. Pte. Dingwall, Arch. Fair (Path of
Condie). Enlisted 1898. Served in South
African War, 1900–1902 (Queen's medal, with
clasps " Laing's Nek " and " Belfast " ; King's
medal, with clasps " South Africa, 1901," and
" South Africa, 1902"). Still serving.

—— Pte. Drysdale, William S. (Kincardine
on Forth). Enlisted 1898. Served in South
African War, 1899–1900. Wounded at Komati
Poort, Sept. 30, 1900 (Queen's medal, with
clasps " Cape Colony," " Paardeberg," "Driefontein," " Johannesburg," and " Belfast ").
Discharged invalided 1901.

3042. Pte. Farquharson, Alexander (Rattray).
Enlisted 1890. Served with Chitral Relief Force,
1895, and in Campaign on North-West Frontier
of India, 1897–1898 (with Tirah Expeditionary
Force) (medal, with clasps " Relief of Chitral,"
" Punjaub Frontier, 1897–8," and " Tirah,
1897–8"). Served also in South African War,
. . . 1900–1902 (Queen's medal, with clasps
" Cape Colony," " Paardeberg," " Driefontein,"
" Johannesburg," and " Belfast" ; King's
medal, with clasps " South Africa, 1901," and
" South Africa, 1902"). Discharged invalided
1903.

5194. Lance-Corpl. Findlay, William (Blairgowrie). Enlisted 1894. Served in Campaign
on North-West Frontier of India, 1897–1898
(with Tirah Expeditionary Force) (medal, with
clasps " Punjaub Frontier, 1897–8," and
" Tirah, 1897–8 "). Served also in South
African War, 1899–1902 (Queen's medal, with
clasps " Elandslaagte," " Defence of Ladysmith," " Laing's Nek," and " Belfast " ; King's
medal, with clasps " South Africa, 1901," and
" South Africa, 1902"). Transferred to Reserve.
[491.]

6504. Pte. Ford, Patrick (Perth). Enlisted
1898. Served in South African War, . . .
1900–1902 (Queen's medal, with clasps " Cape
Colony," " Laing's Nek," and " Belfast";
King's medal, with clasps " South Africa,
1901," and " South Africa, 1902 "). Still serving. [494.]

5619. Pte. Fraser, John Chalmers (Arngask). Enlisted 1896. Served in Campaign on North-West Frontier of India, 1897–1898 (with Tirah Expeditionary Force) (medal, with clasps "Punjaub Frontier, 1897–8," and "Tirah, 1897–8"). Served also in South African War, 1899–1900 (Queen's medal, with clasps "Elandslaagte," "Defence of Ladysmith," "Laing's Nek," and "Transvaal"). Killed at Van Wyk's Vlei, near Belfast, Aug. 21, 1900. [489.]

3264. Pte. Gardiner, Robert (Perth). Enlisted 1889. Served with Chitral Relief Force, 1895, and in Campaign on North-West Frontier of India, 1897–1898 (with Tirah Expeditionary Force) (medal, with clasps "Relief of Chitral," "Punjaub Frontier, 1897–8," and "Tirah, 1897–8"). Served also in South African War, 1899–1901 (Queen's medal, with clasps "Cape Colony," "Paardeberg," "Driefontein," "Johannesburg," and "South Africa, 1901")- [480.]

1122. Pte. Graham, J. (Alyth). Enlisted 1883. Served with Nile Expedition, 1884–1885 (medal, with clasp "The Nile, 1884–5," and Khedive's star); also in South African War, 1899–1901 (Queen's medal, with clasps "Cape Colony," "Orange Free State," "Johannesburg," "Belfast," and "South Africa, 1901").

5930. Pte. Hay, David (Scone). Enlisted 1898. Served in South African War, 1899–1902. Wounded at Lilliefontein, near Belfast, Nov. 2, 1900 (Queen's medal, with clasps "Cape Colony," "Paardeberg," "Driefontein," "Johannesburg," and "Belfast"; King's medal, with clasps "South Africa, 1901," and "South Africa, 1902"). Still serving. [490.]

5156. Pte. Henderson, John (Scone). Enlisted 1895. Served in Campaign on North-West Frontier of India, 1897–1898 (with Tirah Expeditionary Force) (medal, with clasps "Punjaub Frontier, 1897–8," and "Tirah, 1897–8"). Served also in South African War, 1899–1902. Wounded at Elandslaagte, Oct. 21, 1899 (Queen's medal, with clasps "Elandslaagte," "Tugela Heights," "Relief of Ladysmith," "Laing's Nek," and "Belfast"; King's medal, with clasps "South Africa, 1901," and "South Africa, 1902"). Transferred to Reserve 1902. [497.]

4886. Pte. Honeyman, William (Blairgowrie). Enlisted 1893. Served in Campaign on North-West Frontier of India, 1897–1898 (with Tirah Expeditionary Force) (medal, with clasps "Punjaub Frontier, 1897–8," and "Tirah, 1897–8"). Served also in South African War, 1899–1902 (Queen's medal, with clasps "Cape Colony," "Paardeberg," "Driefontein," "Johannesburg," and "Belfast"; King's medal, with clasps "South Africa, 1901," and "South Africa, 1902"). [495.]

3269. Pte. McDonald, John (Perth). Enlisted 1889. Served with Chitral Relief Force, 1895, and in Campaign on North-West Frontier of India, 1897–1898 (with Tirah Expeditionary Force) (medal, with clasps "Relief of Chitral," "Punjaub Frontier, 1897–8," and "Tirah, 1897–8"). Served also in South African War, 1899–1902 (Queen's medal, with clasps "Cape Colony," "Paardeberg," "Driefontein," and "Belfast"; King's medal, with clasps "South Africa, 1901," and "South Africa, 1902"). Discharged 1902. [492.]

7666. Pte. McGregor, Frank (Perth). Enlisted 1901. Served in South African War, 1902 (Queen's medal, with clasps "Cape Colony," "Orange Free State," "Transvaal," and "South Africa, 1902"). Still serving.

4145. Corpl. Macintosh, John J. (Perth). Enlisted 1892. Served with Chitral Relief Force, 1895, and in Campaign on North-West Frontier of India, 1897–1898 (with Tirah Expeditionary Force) (medal, with clasps "Relief of Chitral," "Punjaub Frontier, 1897–8," and "Tirah, 1897–8"). Served also in South African War, 1899–1902 (Queen's medal, with clasps "Elandslaagte," "Defence of Ladysmith," "Laing's Nek," and "Belfast"; King's medal, with clasps "South Africa, 1901," and "South Africa, 1902"). Transferred to Reserve 1902. [481.]

7215. Pte. Mackenzie, Donald (Redgorton). Enlisted 1900. Served in South African War, 1901–1902 (Queen's medal, with clasps "Transvaal," "South Africa, 1901," and "South Africa, 1902"). Still serving. [493.]

402. Pte. Matchett, William (Methven). Enlisted in 92nd (Gordon Highlanders) Regt. 1874. Served in Afghan War, 1879–1880 (medal, with clasps "Charasia," "Kabul," and "Kandahar," Roberts' star). Served also in Egyptian Campaign, 1882 (medal, with clasp "Tel-el-Kebir," and Khedive's star). Discharged 1886.

6699. Pte. Miller, R. (Perth). Enlisted 1899. Served in South African War, 1901–1902

THE GORDON HIGHLANDERS—continued

(Queen's medal, with clasps "Transvaal," "South Africa, 1901," and "South Africa, 1902"). Still serving.

2889. Corporal Mitchell, Archibald (Ardler). Enlisted 1887. Served with Chitral Relief Force, 1895 (medal, with clasp "Relief of Chitral"); also in South African War, . . . 1900. Wounded at Doornkop, May 25, 1900 (Queen's medal, with clasps "Cape Colony," "Paardeberg," "Driefontein," "Johannesburg," and "Belfast"). Discharged 1901. [493.]

6520. Pte. Paterson, E. Donald (Perth). Enlisted 1898. Served in South African War (Queen's medal, with clasps "Cape Colony" and "Orange Free State"). Discharged invalided 1901. [499.]

1021. Corpl. Paton, John (Coupar Angus). Enlisted 1883. Served with Soudan Expedition, 1884. Wounded at Suakim, March 9, 1884 (medal, with clasp "El Teb," and Khedive's star). Discharged 1895.

7036. Pte. Robb, James (Luncarty). Enlisted 1899. Served in South African War, 1900–1902 (Queen's medal, with clasps "Cape Colony," "Orange Free State," and "Transvaal"; King's medal, with clasps "South Africa, 1901," and "South Africa, 1902"). Still serving. [500.]

5933. Pte. Robertson, James (Kinnoull). Enlisted 1897. Served in South African War, . . . 1900–1902 (Queen's medal, with clasps "Relief of Kimberley," "Paardeberg," "Johannesburg," "Diamond Hill," "Wittebergen," and "South Africa, 1901"). Discharged invalided 1901.

3029. Pte. Ross, Alexander (Perth). Enlisted in 92nd (Highland) Regt. 1854. Served in Crimea during Russian War, and in Indian Mutiny. Served also in Afghan War, 1879–1880 (medal, with clasps "Charisia" and "Kabul"). Discharged 1880.

7629. Corpl. Ross, James G. (Perth). Enlisted 1900. Served in South African War, 1902 (Queen's medal, with clasps "Cape Colony," "Orange Free State," "Transvaal," and "South Africa, 1902"). Promoted Corpl. 1903. Still serving.

1462. Pte. Seaton, James (Perth). Enlisted 1884. Served in South African War, 1900–1901 (Queen's medal, with clasps "Cape Colony," "Orange Free State," "Johan-

nesburg," "Belfast," and "South Africa, 1901").

5985. Pte. Sim, Lawrence (Perth). Enlisted 1897. Served in South African War, 1899–1902 (Queen's medal, with clasps "Defence of Ladysmith" and "Transvaal"; King's medal, with clasps "South Africa, 1901," and "South Africa, 1902"). Still serving.

232. Pte. Smith, James (Alyth). Enlisted 1881. Served with Soudan Expedition, 1884, and with Nile Expedition, 1884–1885 (medal, with clasps "El Teb," "Tamai," and "The Nile, 1884–5"; Khedive's star). Transferred to Reserve 1889. Discharged 1893. [496.]

6603. Lance-Corpl. Strang, Thos. (Tulliallan). Enlisted 1898. Served in South African War, 1899–1901 (Queen's medal, with clasps "Cape Colony," "Paardeberg," "Belfast," and "South Africa, 1901"). Still serving.

783. Pte. Strathdee, George (Perth). Enlisted in 92nd (Highland) Regt. 1842. Served in Indian Mutiny, 1858–1859 (medal, with clasp "Central India"). Discharged 1867. [482.]

2995. Pte. Taylor, Charles (Logiealmond). Enlisted 1888. Served with Chitral Relief Force, 1895 (medal, with clasp "Relief of Chitral"); also in South African War, 1899–1901 (Queen's medal, with clasps "Cape Colony," "Paardeberg," "Driefontein," "Johannesburg," "Belfast," and "South Africa, 1901"). Discharged 1901. [483.]

6000. Pte. Thomson, M. (Perth). Enlisted 1897. Served in South African War, 1899–1901 (Queen's medal, with clasps "Defence of Ladysmith," "Laing's Nek," "Belfast," and "South Africa, 1901"). Discharged invalided 1901.

5396. Pte. Welham, W. (Blairgowrie). Enlisted 1895. Served in South African War, 1899–1902 (Queen's medal, with clasps "Defence of Ladysmith" and "Transvaal"; King's medal, with clasps "South Africa, 1901," and "South Africa, 1902"). Transferred to Reserve 1903.

3981. Pte. Wilkie, William (Muthill). Enlisted 1890. Served with Chitral Relief Force, 1895, and in Campaign on North-West Frontier of India, 1897–1898 (with Tirah Expeditionary Force) (medal, with clasps "Relief of Chitral," "Punjaub Frontier, 1897-8," and

"Tirah, 1897-8"). Transferred to Reserve 1899. Served also in South African War as reservist, 1899-1900. Wounded at Paardeberg, Feb. 18, 1900, and invalided home (Queen's medal, with clasps "Cape Colony" and "Paardeberg"). Discharged invalided 1900. [484.]

THE QUEEN'S OWN CAMERON HIGHLANDERS

—— Lance-Sergt. Anderson, James (Perth). Enlisted in 79th (Cameron Highlanders) Regt. 1854. Served in Crimea during Russian War (medal, with clasp "Sevastopol"). Served also in Indian Mutiny (medal). [512.]

3440. Lance-Corpl. Anderson, James (Perth). Enlisted 1892. Served in Soudan Campaign, 1898 (medal, and Khedive's medal, with clasp "Khartoum"). Still serving. [515.]

3700. Pte. Brown, A. (Perth). Enlisted 1895. Served in Soudan Campaign, 1898 (medal, and Khedive's medal, with clasps "The Atbara" and "Khartoum"). Served also in South African War, 1900-1902 (Queen's medal, with clasps "Johannesburg," "Diamond Hill," "Wittebergen," and "Cape Colony"; King's medal, with clasps "South Africa, 1901," and "South Africa, 1902"). Transferred to Reserve. [519.]

876. Pte. Brown, Robert (Scone). Enlisted in 79th (Queen's Own Cameron Highlanders) Regt. 1876. Served with Nile Expedition, 1884-1885 (medal, with clasp "The Nile, 1884-5," and Khedive's star). Discharged 1888.

5091. Lance-Corpl. Cameron, Donald (Blair Atholl). Enlisted 1899. Served in South African War, 1901-1902 (Queen's medal, with clasps "Cape Colony," "Orange Free State," "Transvaal," "South Africa, 1901," and "South Africa, 1902"). Still serving. [521.]

5072. Pte. Cameron, Norman (Blair Atholl). Enlisted 1899. Served in South African War, 1901-1902 (Queen's medal, with clasps "Cape Colony," "Orange Free State," "Transvaal," "South Africa, 1901," and "South Africa, 1902"). Still serving.

239. Pte. Campbell, Duncan (Blair Atholl). Enlisted 1882. Served with Nile Expedition, 1884-1885, and with Soudan Frontier Field Force, 1885-1886 (action at Giniss) (medal, with clasp "The Nile, 1884-5," and Khedive's star). Discharged 1889. Enlisted in Royal Scottish Reserve Regt. 1900. Discharged 1901. [522.]

1538. Corpl. Campbell, John (Blair Atholl).

Enlisted in 1st (The Royal Scots) Regt. 1876. Transferred to Cameron Highlanders 1885. Served with Soudan Frontier Field Force, 1885-1886 (investment of Kosheh and action at Giniss) (medal and Khedive's star). Discharged 1895. [523.]

3911. Pte. Cannon, M. (Kilmadock). Enlisted 1897. Served in South African War, 1901-1902 (Queen's medal, with clasps "Cape Colony," "Orange Free State," "Transvaal," "South Africa, 1901," and "South Africa, 1902"). Discharged invalided 1903.

3960. Pte. Collins, T. (Perth). Enlisted 1897. Served in Soudan Campaign, 1898 (medal, and Khedive's medal, with clasp "Khartoum"). Served also in South African War, 1900-1902 (Queen's medal, with clasps "Cape Colony," "Wittebergen," "Johannesburg," and "Diamond Hill"; King's medal, with clasps "South Africa, 1901," and "South Africa, 1902"). Transferred to Reserve.

—— Pte. Dawson, James (Kincardine). Enlisted in 79th (Cameron Highlanders) Regt. 1855. Served in Indian Mutiny, 1857-1859 (medal, with clasp "Lucknow"). Long Service medal. Discharged 1876.

3699. Pte. Doig, James (Perth). Enlisted 1895. Served in Soudan Campaign, 1898 (medal, and Khedive's medal, with clasps "The Atbara" and "Khartoum"). Served also in South African War (with Mtd. Infy.), 1900 (Queen's medal, with clasps "Cape Colony," "Johannesburg," "Diamond Hill," and "Wittebergen"). Killed at Nooitgedacht, Dec. 13, 1900.

3965. Sergt. Douglas, David (Perth). Enlisted 1897. Served in South African War, 1900-1902 (Queen's medal, with clasps "Cape Colony," "Orange Free State," and "Transvaal"; King's medal, with clasps "South Africa, 1901," and "South Africa, 1902"). Still serving. [501.]

4910. Pte. Forbes, Thomas (Dunblane). Enlisted 1899. Served in South African War, 1901-1902 (Queen's medal, with clasps "Cape Colony," "Orange Free State," "Transvaal,"

THE QUEEN'S OWN CAMERON HIGHLANDERS—*continued*

"South Africa, 1901," and "South Africa, 1902"). Still serving. [502.]

3626. Pte. Grant, William (Blairgowrie). Enlisted 1894. Served in Soudan Campaign, 1898 (medal, and Khedive's medal, with clasps "The Atbara" and "Khartoum"). Served also in South African War as Reservist, 1900–1902 (Queen's medal, with clasps "Cape Colony," "Orange Free State," and "Transvaal"; King's medal, with clasps "South Africa, 1901," and "South Africa, 1902"). Re-enlisted 1902.

368. Pte. Irvine, C. (Blairgowrie). Enlisted in 79th (Queen's Own Cameron Highlanders) Regt. 1875. Served in Egyptian Campaign, 1882 (medal, with clasp "Tel-el-Kebir," and Khedive's star). Transferred to Reserve 1883. Discharged 1888. [503.]

2183. Pte. Keir, John S. (Blairgowrie). Enlisted 1888. Transferred to Reserve. Served in South African War as Reservist, 1900–1901 (Queen's medal, with clasps "Cape Colony," "Johannesburg," "Diamond Hill," "Wittebergen," and "South Africa, 1901"). [504.]

2570. Pte. Knubley, J. (Perth). Enlisted 1891. Served in Soudan Campaign, 1898 (medal, and Khedive's medal, with clasps "The Atbara" and "Khartoum"). Served also in South African War, 1900–1902 (Queen's medal, with clasps "Cape Colony," "Johannesburg," "Diamond Hill," and "Wittebergen"; King's medal, with clasps "South Africa, 1901," and "South Africa, 1902"). Transferred to Reserve.

3788. Pte. McFarlane, J. (Logie). Enlisted 1896. Served in Soudan Campaign, 1898 (medal, and Khedive's medal, with clasps "The Atbara" and "Khartoum"). Died at Cairo, Sept. 30, 1898. [505.]

4182. Pte. McInroy, David (Perth). Enlisted 1897. Served in South African War, 1900–1902 (Queen's medal, with clasps "Cape Colony," "Orange Free State," and "Transvaal"; King's medal, with clasps "South Africa, 1901," and "South Africa, 1902"). Still serving. [506.]

1521. Pte. McIntosh, J. (Pitlochry). Enlisted in 79th (Queen's Own Cameron Highlanders) Regt. 1878. Served in Egyptian Campaign, 1882 (medal, with clasp "Tel-el-Kebir," and Khedive's star). Discharged 1890.

3830. Qrmr.-Sergt. McKenzie, John (Perth). Enlisted in 79th (Cameron Highlanders) Regt. 1854. Served in Crimea, 1855, during Russian War (medal, with clasp "Sevastopol," and Turkish medal); also in Indian Mutiny, 1857–1859 (Distinguished Conduct medal, and medal, with clasp "Lucknow"). Served also in Campaign on North-West Frontier of India 1863 (medal, with clasp "North-West Frontier"). Long Service medal. Transferred to 42nd (Royal Highland—The Black Watch) Regt. 1875. [516.]

1644. Col.-Sergt. Mackenzie, Thomas E. (Perth). Enlisted 1885. Served in Soudan Campaign, 1898 (mentioned in despatches; Distinguished Conduct medal. Medal, and Khedive's medal, with clasps "The Atbara" and "Khartoum"). Served also in South African War, 1900–1902 (Queen's medal, with clasps "Cape Colony," "Johannesburg," "Diamond Hill," and "Wittebergen"; King's medal, with clasps "South Africa, 1901," and "South Africa, 1902"). [509.]

158. Corpl. McKenzie, Thomas (Bridge of Earn). Enlisted in 79th (Cameron Highlanders) Regt. 1860. Served in Campaign on North-West Frontier of India, 1863 (medal, with clasp). Transferred to 42nd (Royal Highland—The Black Watch) Regt. 1873. Served in Ashanti War, 1873–1874. Wounded at Amoaful (medal). Re-transferred to Cameron Highlanders 1874. Discharged invalided 1876. [507.]

2095. Qrmr.-Sergt. McLean, Angus (Perth). Enlisted 1888. Served in Soudan Campaign, 1898 (medal, and Khedive's medal, with clasp "The Atbara"). Served also in South African War, 1900–1902 (Queen's medal, with clasps "Cape Colony," "Johannesburg," "Diamond Hill," and "Wittebergen"; King's medal, with clasps "South Africa, 1901," and "South Africa, 1902"). Still serving. [517.]

5910. Pte. McLellan, John (Logiealmond). Enlisted in the Royal Scots 1899. Transferred to Cameron Highlanders 1901. Served in South African War, 1900–1902 (Queen's medal, with clasps "Cape Colony," "Orange Free State," and "Belfast"; King's medal, with clasps "South Africa, 1901," and "South Africa, 1902"). Died at Elandsfontein, May 5, 1902. [518.]

5362. Pte. MacLennan, Edward (Perth).
Enlisted 1900. Served in South African War,
1902 (Queen's medal, with clasps "Cape
Colony," "Orange Free State," "Transvaal,"
and "South Africa, 1902"). Still serving.

5372. Pte. McManus, Francis (Perth). Enlisted 1900. Served in South African War,
1902 (Queen's medal, with clasps "Cape
Colony," "Orange Free State," "Transvaal,"
and "South Africa, 1902"). Still serving.
[508.]

3597. Pte. Macpherson, Donald (Perth).
Enlisted 1894. Served in Soudan Campaign,
1898 (medal, and Khedive's medal, with clasps
"The Atbara" and "Khartoum"). Served
also in South African War, 1900–1902 (Queen's
medal, with clasps "Cape Colony," "Johannesburg," "Diamond Hill," and "Wittebergen";
King's medal, with clasps "South Africa, 1901,"
and "South Africa, 1902"). Transferred to
Reserve 1902.

1327. Lance-Corpl. Marshall, M. (Methven).
Enlisted 1885. Served in South African War,
1900 (Queen's medal, with clasps "Cape
Colony," "Johannesburg," "Diamond Hill,"
and "Wittebergen"). Killed in action, Aug.
20, 1900.

—— Col. - Sergt. Robertson, Robert
(Pitlochry). Enlisted in 79th (Queen's Own
Cameron Highlanders) Regt. 1877. Served
in Egyptian Campaign, 1882 (medal, with
clasp "Tel-el-Kebir," and Khedive's star).
Long Service medal. Discharged 1898.

631. Sergt. Scott, James (Dull). Enlisted
in 79th (Cameron Highlanders) Regt. 1858.
Served in Campaign on North-West Frontier
of India, 1863 (medal, with clasp "North-West
Frontier") Promoted Corpl. 1874, Sergt. 1878.
Discharged 1880. [510.]

3658. Pte. Smith, J. (Perth). Enlisted 1894.
Served in Soudan Campaign, 1898 (medal, and
Khedive's medal). Served also in South
African War, 1900–1902 (Queen's medal, with
clasps "Cape Colony," "Johannesburg," "Diamond Hill," and "Wittebergen"; King's
medal, with clasps "South Africa, 1901," and
"South Africa, 1902"). Transferred to Reserve.

1644. Pte. Stalker, Wilfred (Kenmore). Enlisted in 79th (Queen's Own Cameron Highlanders)
Regt. 1878. Served with Soudan Frontier
Field Force, 1885–1886 (investment of Kosheh
and action at Giniss) (medal, and Khedive's

star) ; also in Soudan Campaign, 1898 (medal
and Khedive's medal, with clasp "The
Atbara"). Long Service medal. Discharged
1901.

3582. Sergt. Stewart, Daniel (Perth). Enlisted 1892. Served in Soudan Campaign, 1898
(medal, and Khedive's medal, with clasps "The
Atbara" and "Khartoum"). Served also in
South African War, 1900–1902 (Queen's medal,
with clasps "Cape Colony," "Orange Free
State," and "Transvaal"; King's medal, with
clasps "South Africa, 1901," and "South
Africa, 1902"). Transferred to Reserve.

3260. Piper Stewart, J. (Dull). Enlisted
1892. Served in Soudan Campaign, 1898
(medal, and Khedive's medal, with clasp "The
Atbara"). Killed at the Athara, April 8, 1898.

3660. Pte. Stewart, William (Perth). Enlisted 1895. Served in Soudan Campaign,
1898 (medal, and Khedive's medal, with clasps
"The Atbara" and "Khartoum"). Served
also in South African War, 1900–1902 (Queen's
medal, with clasps "Cape Colony," "Johannesburg," "Diamond Hill," and "Wittebergen";
King's medal, with clasps "South Africa,
1901," and "South Africa, 1902"). [511.]

161. Corpl. Stuart, James (Logierait). Enlisted in 79th (Cameron Highlanders) Regt.
1869. Served in Ashanti War. Wounded at
Amoaful, Jan. 31, 1874 (medal, with clasp
"Coomassie"). Served also in Egyptian Campaign, 1882, and with Nile Expedition, 1884–
1885 (medal, with clasps "Tel-el-Kebir" and
"The Nile, 1884–5"; Khedive's star). Discharged 1890.

4997. Pte. Symington, Andrew W. (Alyth).
Enlisted 1899. Served in South African War,
1902 (Queen's medal, with clasps "Cape
Colony," "Orange Free State," "Transvaal,"
and "South Africa, 1902"). Transferred to
Reserve 1902. [513.]

1950. Pte. Thomas, J. (Dunblane). Enlisted 1886. Served in South African War,
1900 (Queen's medal, with clasps "Cape
Colony," "Johannesburg," "Diamond Hill,"
and "Wittebergen").

3675. Pte. Thomson, Robert (Bendochy).
Enlisted in 90th (Perthshire Volunteers—Light
Infantry) Regt. 1852. Transferred to 79th
(Cameron Highlanders) Regt. 1854. Served in
Crimea, 1854–1855, during Russian War (medal,
with clasps "Alma," "Balaclava," and "Sevas-
topol"; Turkish medal). Discharged 1856.

THE QUEEN'S OWN CAMERON HIGHLANDERS—*continued*

571. Pte. Thomson, William (Burrelton). Enlisted 1882. Served with Nile Expedition, 1884–1885, and with Soudan Frontier Field Force, 1885–1886 (medal, with clasp "The Nile, 1884–5," and Khedive's star). Discharged 1888. Now serving with Royal Garrison Regt.

5318. Pte. Wallace, A. (Doune). Enlisted 1900. Served in South African War, 1901 (Queen's medal, with clasps "Cape Colony," "Orange Free State," "Transvaal," and "South Africa, 1902"). Still serving.

2243. Pte. Walls, John (Kincardine on Forth). Enlisted 1889. Served in South African War, 1900–1902 (Queen's medal, with clasps "Cape Colony," "Johannesburg," "Diamond Hill," and "Wittebergen"; King's medal, with clasps "South Africa, 1901," and "South Africa, 1902"). Discharged 1902. [520.]

5482. Pte. Watson, James (Stanley). Enlisted 1900. Served in South African War, 1902 (Queen's medal, with clasps "Cape Colony," "Orange Free State," "Transvaal," and "South Africa, 1902"). Transferred to Reserve 1903. [514.]

THE ROYAL IRISH RIFLES

1163. Pte. Will, Joseph (Perth). Enlisted 1885. Served in South African War, . . . 1901 (Queen's medal, with clasps "Cape Colony,"

"Orange Free State," and "South Africa, 1901"). Still serving. [524.]

ARGYLL AND SUTHERLAND HIGHLANDERS (Princess Louise's)

6997. Pte. Anderson, James (Blairgowrie). Enlisted 1899. Served in South African War, 1900–1902 (Queen's medal, with clasps "Cape Colony," "Orange Free State," and "Transvaal"; King's medal, with clasps "South Africa, 1901," and "South Africa, 1902"). Still serving.

8578. Pte. Andrews, James (Blairlogie). . . . Vol. Batt. Served in South African War, with 2nd Vol. Service Coy., 1901–1902 (Queen's medal, with clasps "Cape Colony," "Orange Free State," "Transvaal," "South Africa, 1901," and "South Africa, 1902"). [539.]

6439. Pte. Blain, Thomas I. (Killin). Enlisted 1898. Served in South African War, 1899–1902 (Queen's medal, with clasps "Modder River," "Orange Free State," and "Transvaal"; King's medal, with clasps "South Africa, 1901," and "South Africa, 1902"). Still serving. [540.]

3891. Corpl. Boyd, John (Perth). 4th Vol. Batt. Served in South African War, with 1st Vol. Service Coy., 1900–1901 (Queen's medal, with clasps "Cape Colony," "Orange Free State," and "South Africa, 1901").

3823. Pte. Brown, Thomas (Perth). Enlisted 1890. Served in Campaign on North-West Frontier of India, 1897–1898 (with Tochi Field Force) (medal, with clasp). Served also in South African War, 1899–1902 (Queen's medal, with clasps "Modder River," "Paardeberg," "Driefontein," and "Transvaal"; King's medal, with clasps "South Africa, 1901," and "South Africa, 1902").

2752. Sergt. Buchanan, William (Doune). Enlisted 1887. Served in South African War as Reservist, 1899–1900 (Queen's medal, with clasps "Modder River," "Paardeberg," "Driefontein," and "Transvaal"). Discharged 1900. [541.]

1745. Lance.-Corpl. Callanan, Thomas (Doune). Enlisted in 91st (Princess Louise's Argyllshire Highlanders) Regt. 1878. Served in Zulu War, 1879 (medal, with clasp "1879"). Discharged 1890.

6829. Pte. Cameron, David (Killin). Enlisted 1899. Served in South African War, 1900–1902 (Queen's medal, with clasps "Cape Colony," "Orange Free State," and "Transvaal"; King's medal, with clasps "South Africa, 1901," and "South Africa, 1902"). Still serving.

5139. Pte. Cameron, Donald (Aberfoyle). 4th Vol. Batt. Served in South African War, (1) with 1st Vol. Service Coy., 1900–1901 ; (2) with 3rd Vol. Service Coy., 1902 (Queen's medal, with clasps "Cape Colony" and "Orange Free State"; King's medal, with clasps "South Africa, 1901," and "South Africa, 1902 ").

3148. Pte. Campbell, James (Auchterarder). Enlisted 1889. Served in South African War, 1899–1902 (Queen's medal, with clasps "Modder River," "Paardeberg," and "Transvaal" ; King's medal, with clasps "South Africa, 1901," and "South Africa, 1902"). Discharged 1902. [545.]

6480. Pte. Campbell, James (Perth). Enlisted 1898. Served in South African War, 1899–1902 (Queen's medal, with clasps "Modder River," "Paardeberg," "Driefontein," and "Transvaal" ; King's medal, with clasps "South Africa, 1901," and "South Africa, 1902"). Still serving. [546.]

624. Col.-Sergt. Campbell, Peter (Dunblane). Enlisted 1882. Served in Campaign on North-West Frontier of India, 1897–1898 (with Tochi Field Force) (medal, with clasp). Now serving on Permanent Staff 5th Vol. Batt. [525.]

6432. Pte. Carmichael, William (Little Dunkeld). Enlisted 1898. Served in South African War, 1899–1900 (Queen's medal, with clasps, "Modder River," "Paardeberg," "Driefontein," and "Transvaal"). Discharged 1903.

7470. Pte. Dingwall, James (Perth). Enlisted 1900. Served in South African War, 1900–1902 (Queen's medal, with clasps "Cape Colony," "Orange Free State," and "Transvaal" ; King's medal, with clasps "South Africa, 1901," and "South Africa, 1902"). Still serving. [526.]

3098. Pte. Docherty, Hugh (Blairgowrie). Enlisted 1889. Served in South African War, 1899–1900 (Queen's medal, with clasps "Modder River," "Paardeberg," "Driefontein," and "Transvaal"). Discharged 1902. [547.]

1814. Sergt. Douglas, Robert (Logicrait). Enlisted in 93rd (Sutherland Highlanders) Regt. (now 2nd Batt. A. and S.H.) 1845. Served in Crimea during Russian War (medal, with clasp, and Turkish medal) ; also in Indian Mutiny, 1857–1859 (medal, with clasps "Relief of Lucknow" and "Lucknow"). Served also in Campaign on North-West Frontier of India, 1863 (medal, with clasp "Umbeyla"). Discharged 1867. Appointed 1st Class Sergt. Instr. to 1st Stirlingshire Rifle Volunteers (now 4th Vol. Batt. A. and S.H.) 1869. Discharged 1884. [527.]

—— **Pte.** Drummond, William (Perth). En-

listed in 93rd (Sutherland Highlanders) Regt. (now 2nd Batt. A. and S.H.) 1853. Served in Crimea, 1854–1855, during Russian War (medal, with clasps "Balaclava" and "Sevastopol" ; Turkish medal). Served also in Indian Mutiny, 1857–1859 (medal, with two clasps) ; also in Campaign on North-West Frontier of India, 1863 (medal, with clasp). Long Service medal.

—— **Sergt.** Duff, John (Perth). Enlisted in 93rd (Sutherland Highlanders) Regt. (now 2nd Batt. A. and S.H.) 1852. Served in Crimea, 1854–1855, during Russian War (medal, with clasps "Alma," "Balaclava," and "Sevastopol" ; Turkish medal). Served also in Indian Mutiny, 1857–1859 (medal, with clasps "Relief of Lucknow" and "Lucknow"). [528.]

4470. Pte. Duncan, John (Dunkeld). Enlisted 1892. Served in South African War, 1899–1902 (Queen's medal, with clasps "Modder River," "Driefontein," and "Transvaal" ; King's medal, with clasps, "South Africa, 1901," and "South Africa, 1902").

5857. Pte. Ellard, Frank (Perth). Enlisted 1896. Served in South African War, 1899–1902 (Queen's medal, with clasps "Modder River," "Paardeberg," and "Transvaal" ; King's medal, with clasps "South Africa, 1901," and "South Africa, 1902"). Still serving.

6706. Lance-Corpl. Ferguson, James (Logierait). Enlisted 1898. Served in South African War, 1899 (Queen's medal, with clasp "Modder River"). Killed at Magersfontein, Dec. 11, 1899. [529.]

7080. Pte. Gow, David (Perth). Enlisted 1899. Served in South African War, 1900–1902 (Queen's medal, with clasps "Cape Colony," "Orange Free State," and "Transvaal" ; King's medal, with clasps "South Africa, 1901," and "South Africa, 1902"). Still serving. [530.]

6079. Sergt. Graham, Thomas (Aberfeldy). Enlisted 1897. Served in South African War, . . . 1900–1902 (Queen's medal, with clasps "Cape Colony," "Paardeberg," "Driefontein," and "Transvaal" ; King's medal, with clasps "South Africa, 1901," and "South Africa, 1902"). Still serving.

3958. Pte. Jenkins, William (Perth). Enlisted 1891. Served in Campaign on North-West Frontier of India, 1897–1898 (with Tochi Field Force) (medal, with clasp "Punjaub Frontier, 1897–8"). Served also in South African War, 1899–1902 (Queen's medal, with

ARGYLL AND SUTHERLAND HIGHLANDERS—*continued*

clasps "Modder River," "Paardeberg," "Drie-fontein," and "Transvaal"; King's medal, with clasps "South Africa, 1901," and "South Africa, 1902").

3088. Pte. Kettles, Andrew (Inchyra). Enlisted 1889. Served with Chitral Relief Force, 1895 (medal, with clasp "Relief of Chitral"); also in South African War, 1899–1902 (Queen's medal, with clasps "Modder River," "Paardeberg," "Driefontein," and "Transvaal"; King's medal, with clasps "South Africa, 1901," and "South Africa, 1902"). Discharged 1902.

2544. Pte. Kidd, Alexander (Perth). Enlisted 1887. Served in South African War, 1900–1902 (Queen's medal, with clasps "Cape Colony," "Orange Free State," and "Transvaal"; King's medal, with clasps "South Africa, 1901," and "South Africa, 1902").

—— **Lance-Corpl. Kininmonth,** Jas. (Perth). Enlisted 1885. Served in South African War (Queen's medal, with clasps "Cape Colony," "Orange Free State," and "Transvaal"). Discharged 1902. [551.]

2588. Lance-Corpl. Kininmonth, Robert (Perth). Enlisted 1887. Served in South African War, . . . 1900–1902 (Queen's medal, with clasps "Cape Colony," "Orange Free State," and "Transvaal"; King's medal, with clasps "South Africa, 1901," and "South Africa, 1902"). [552.]

4504. Pte. Laird, Lindsay (Blairgowrie). Enlisted 1892. Served in South African War, 1899–1900 (Queen's medal, with clasps "Modder River," "Paardeberg," "Driefontein," and "Transvaal"). Transferred to Reserve.

—— **Pte. Lawson,** Angus (Dunkeld). . . . Vol. Batt. Served in South African War with 2nd Vol. Service Coy., 1901–1902 (Queen's medal, with clasps "Cape Colony," "Orange Free State," "Transvaal," "South Africa, 1901," and "South Africa, 1902"). Enlisted in Royal Engineers 1903. Transferred to Cameron Highlanders 1903. Still serving (No. 6769, Cameron Highlanders). [531.]

1910. Sergeant-Major Lindsay, James (Alyth). Enlisted 1878. Served in Zulu War, 1879 (medal, with clasp "1879"). Promoted Warrant Officer. Long Service medal. Silver medal of Victorian Order 1901. Coronation medal 1902. Still serving. [532.]

6551. Pte. Macdonald, John (Crieff). Enlisted 1898. Served in South African War,

1899–1900 (Queen's medal, with clasps "Modder River" and "Paardeberg"). Killed at Paardeberg, Feb. 18, 1900. [533.]

3066. Pte. McDonald, Thos. (Alyth). Enlisted 1889. Served in South African War, 1899–1901 (Queen's medal, with clasps "Modder River," "Paardeberg," "Driefontein," and "South Africa, 1901"). Discharged 1902. [542.]

3043. Pte. McIntosh, James (Perth). Enlisted 1888. Served in South African War, 1899–1900 (Queen's medal, with clasps "Modder River," "Paardeberg," "Driefontein," and "Transvaal"). Discharged 1901. [548.]

7471. Pte. McLaren, James (Kinrossie). Enlisted 1900. Served in South African War, 1900–1902 (Queen's medal, with clasps "Cape Colony," "Orange Free State," and "Transvaal"; King's medal, with clasps "South Africa, 1901," and "South Africa, 1902"). Still serving.

6229. Pte. McLaren, John (Dunblane). Enlisted 1897. Served in South African War, 1899–1902 (Queen's medal, with clasps "Modder River," "Paardeberg," "Driefontein," and "Transvaal"; King's medal, with clasps "South Africa, 1901," and "South Africa, 1902"). Still serving.

3952. Pte. McLean, William (Perth). Enlisted 1891. Served in Campaign on North-West Frontier of India, 1897–1898 (with Tochi Field Force) (medal, with clasp "Punjaub Frontier, 1897–8"). Served also in South African War, 1899–1902 (Queen's medal, with clasps "Modder River," "Paardeberg," "Driefontein," and "Transvaal"; King's medal, with clasps "South Africa, 1901," and "South Africa, 1902"). Discharged 1903. [549.]

7506. Pte. McLeish, R. (Auchterarder). Enlisted 1900. Served in South African War, . . . 1901 (Queen's medal, with clasps "Cape Colony," "Orange Free State," and "South Africa, 1901"). Still serving.

5232. Pte. McNicol, John (Fortingall). Enlisted 1894. Served in Campaign on North-West Frontier of India, 1897–1898 (with Tochi Field Force) (medal, with clasp "Punjaub Frontier, 1897–8"). Served also in South African War, 1902 (Queen's medal, with clasps "Transvaal" and "South Africa, 1902"). Discharged 1902.

—— **Pte. McNie,** James (Kincardine on

Forth). 7th Vol. Batt. Served in South African War, with 2nd Vol. Service Coy., 1901–1902 (Queen's medal, with clasps "Cape Colony," "Orange Free State," "Transvaal," "South Africa, 1901," and "South Africa, 1902"). [534.]

2737. Pte. McPherson, Donald (Blair Atholl). Enlisted 1887. Served in South African War, . . . 1900–1902 (Queen's medal, with clasps "Cape Colony," "Orange Free State," and "Transvaal"; King's medal, with clasps "South Africa, 1901," and "South Africa, 1902").

1549. Pte. Macpherson, Hugh (Blairgowrie). Enlisted 1884. Served in South African War, . . . 1901 (Queen's medal, with clasps "Cape Colony," "Orange Free State," and "South Africa, 1901"). Discharged 1901. [535.]

724. Sergt. McWilliam, Adam (Rattray). Enlisted in 93rd (Sutherland Highlanders) Regt. (now 2nd Batt. A. and S.H.) 1860. Served in Campaign on North-West Frontier of India, 1863 (medal, with clasp "Umbeyla"). Discharged 1871. [553.]

4480. Col.-Sergt. Matthew, Andrew (Auchterarder). Enlisted 1892. Served in South African War, 1899–1902 ; wounded near Heilbron (mentioned in despatches. Queen's medal, with clasps "Modder River," "Paardeberg," "Driefontein," and "Transvaal"; King's medal, with clasps "South Africa, 1901," and "South Africa, 1902").

3053. Lance-Sergt. Matthew, William (Auchterarder). Served in Campaign on North-West Frontier of India, 1897–1898 (with Tochi Field Force) (medal, with clasp "Punjaub Frontier, 1897–8"). Served also in South African War, 1899 (Queen's medal, with clasp "Modder River"). Killed at Magersfontein, Dec. 11, 1899.

6557. Pte. Miller, John (Perth). Enlisted 1898. Served in South African War, 1899–1902 (Queen's medal, with clasps "Modder River," "Paardeberg," "Driefontein," and "Transvaal" ; King's medal, with clasps "South Africa, 1901," and "South Africa, 1902"). Still serving. [536.]

6171. Lance-Corpl. Norrie, Alexander (Greenloaning). Enlisted 1897. Served in South African War, 1899–1902 (Queen's medal, with clasps "Modder River," "Paardeberg," and "Transvaal"; King's medal, with clasps

"South Africa, 1901," and "South Africa, 1902"). Still serving. [537.]

3089. Pte. Paton, James (Perth). Enlisted 1889. Served in South African War, 1899 . . . (Queen's medal, with clasp "Modder River"). Still serving.

3655. Pte. Petrie, James (Perth). Enlisted 1890. Served in South African War, 1899–1902 (Queen's medal, with clasps "Modder River," "Paardeberg," "Driefontein," and "Transvaal"; King's medal, with clasps "South Africa, 1901," and "South Africa, 1902"). Still serving.

5276. Sergt. Reid, James (Moulin). Enlisted 1895. Served in South African War, . . . 1900 (Queen's medal, with clasps "Cape Colony" and "Paardeberg"). Still serving. [538.]

1598. Pte. Sharp, David (Perth). Enlisted 1884. Served in South African War, . . . 1901 (Queen's medal, with clasps "Transvaal," "Cape Colony," "Orange Free State," and "South Africa, 1901"). Discharged 1901. [550.]

3383. Pte. Stewart, Alexander (Crieff). Enlisted 1890. Served in Campaign on North-West Frontier of India, 1897–1898 (with Tochi Field Force) (medal, with clasp "Punjaub Frontier, 1897–8"). Served also in South African War, 1899–1902 (Queen's medal, with clasps "Modder River," "Paardeberg," and "Transvaal"; King's medal, with clasps "South Africa, 1901," and "South Africa, 1902"). Discharged 1902.

3101. Pte. Taylor, John (Logicalmond). Enlisted 1889. Served in South African War (Queen's medal, with clasp "Cape Colony"). Discharged invalided 1900.

929. Pte. Watson, George (Perth). Enlisted 1883. Served in South African War (Queen's medal, with clasps "Cape Colony," "Orange Free State," and "Transvaal"). Discharged 1901.

3116. Qrmr.-Sergt. Weller, W. R. (Scone). Served with Waziristan Field Force, 1894 (medal, with clasp "Waziristan, 1894–5"). Served also in Campaign on North-West Frontier of India, 1897–1898 (with Tochi Field Force) (medal, with clasp "Punjaub Frontier, 1897–8"). Delhi Durbar medal, 1903. [543.]

6904. Pte. Wells, William (Tulliallan). Enlisted 1899. Served in South African War (Queen's medal, with clasps "Cape Colony,"

ARGYLL AND SUTHERLAND HIGHLANDERS—*continued*

"Orange Free State," and "Transvaal"). Invalided home. Still serving.

1448. Col.-Sergt. Wilson, Andrew (Blackford). Enlisted 1884. Served in South African War (Queen's medal, with clasps "Cape Colony" and "Orange Free State"). Still serving. [544.]

6746. Piper Wright, John (Doune). Enlisted 1898. Served in South African War, 1899–1902 (Queen's medal, with clasps "Modder River," "Paardeberg," "Driefontein," and

"Transvaal"; King's medal, with clasps "South Africa, 1901," and "South Africa, 1902"). Still serving.

7044. Pte. Young, William (Perth). Enlisted 1899. Served in South African War, 1900–1902 (Queen's medal, with clasps "Cape Colony," "Orange Free State," and "Transvaal"; King's medal, with clasps "South Africa, 1901," and "South Africa, 1902"). Discharged 1903. [554.]

THE ROYAL DUBLIN FUSILIERS

7028. Pte. Bourke, Thomas (Perth). Enlisted 1900. Served in South African War, 1900–1902 (Queen's medal, with clasps "Cape Colony," "Orange Free State," and "Trans-

vaal"; King's medal, with clasps "South Africa, 1901," and "South Africa, 1902"). Still serving.

SCOTTISH CYCLE CORPS

—— Sergt. Johnston, John G. (Alyth). 6th Vol. Batt. A. and S.H. (Cyclist Coy.). Served in South African War with Scottish Cycle Corps,

1901–1902 (Queen's medal, with clasps "Cape Colony," "Orange Free State," "South Africa, 1901," and "South Africa, 1902"). [555.]

ARMY SERVICE CORPS

I. 13812. Sh.-Smith Coulter, James (Perth). 36th Coy. Enlisted 1898. Served in South African War, 1899–1900 (Queen's medal, with clasps "Relief of Kimberley," "Paardeberg," "Johannesburg," "Diamond Hill," and "Wittebergen"). Died at Aliwal North, Dec. 22, 1900. [557.]

S. 13362. Pte. Gardiner, George D. (Perth). Enlisted 1897. Served in Soudan Campaign, 1898 (medal, and Khedive's medal); also in South African War, 1899–1902 (Queen's medal, with clasp "Natal"; King's medal, with clasps "South Africa, 1901," and "South Africa, 1902"). Transferred to Reserve 1903.

—— 1st Class Warrant Off. Hill, William (Glenalmond). Enlisted in 72nd (Duke of Albany's Own Highlanders) Regt. 1865. Promoted Lance-Corpl. 1866, Corpl. 1867. Transferred to Commissariat and Transport Dept. (now Army Service Corps) as 2nd Corpl. 1876. Promoted Corpl. 1877, Sergt. 1879, 3rd Cl. Staff Sergt. 1881, Conductor of Supplies 1882. Served with Nile Expedition, 1884–1885 (medal,

with clasp "The Nile, 1884–5," and Khedive's star). Discharged 1886. [560.]

1594. Lance-Sergt. Hodge, Andrew (Coupar Angus). Enlisted in Land Transport Corps 1855. Served in Crimea, 1855, during Russian War (medal, with clasp "Sevastopol," and Turkish medal). Discharged 1856. [561.]

285. Corpl. McLaren, Andrew (Perth). Enlisted in 11th Hussars 1855. Transferred to Military Train (now Army Service Corps) 1857. Served in Abyssinian Expedition as Conductor of Transport, 1867–1868 (medal). Discharged 1876. [558.]

—— Qrmr.-Sergt. McLaren, Frederick A. P. (Bankfoot). Enlisted 1890. Served in South African War, 1899–1902 (Queen's medal, with clasps "Cape Colony," "Orange Free State," and "Transvaal"; King's medal, with clasps "South Africa, 1901," and "South Africa, 1902"). Still serving. [562.]

—— Pte. Reoch, Robert (Coupar Angus). Enlisted in the Land Transport Corps (I. Division) 1853. Served in the Crimea, 1855, during Russian War (medal, with clasp "Sevastopol," and Turkish medal). Discharged 1855.

— Pte. Simpson, James (Perth). Enlisted in Land Transport Corps 1854. Served in Crimea, 1855, during Russian War. Slightly wounded at Sevastopol (medal, with clasp "Sevastopol," and Turkish medal). Trans-

ferred to 78th (Highland Ross-shire Buffs) Regt. 1858. Discharged 1861. [559.]

— Pte. Wood, William (Butterstone). Enlisted in Control Department (now Army Service Corps) 1871 (previously in Military Train). Served in Soudan Campaign, 1884–1885 (medal, with clasp "Suakim, 1884," and Khedive's star). Discharged 1888. [556.]

ROYAL ARMY MEDICAL CORPS

11328. Pte. Arnott, William (Auchterarder). Enlisted 1896. Served in South African War, 1900 (Queen's medal, with clasp "Cape Colony"). Died at sea on way home, Feb. 12, 1901. [566.]

13910. Pte. Buchanan, John (Perth). Enlisted 1900. Served in South African War, 1900–1901 (Queen's medal, with clasps "Natal" and "South Africa, 1901"). Transferred to Reserve 1903. [567.]

8061. 2nd Class Staff-Sergt. Maclaren, James (Callander). Enlisted 1888. Served in Northern Nigeria, 1899–1900; also in South African War, 1900 (Queen's medal with clasp . . .). Invalided home 1900. Still serving. [568.]

ARMY ORDNANCE DEPARTMENT

4672. Pte. Bremner, Peter (Dunblane). Enlisted 1900. Served in South African War, 1901–1902 (Queen's medal, with clasps "Cape Colony," "Orange Free State," "Transvaal," "South Africa, 1901," and "South Africa, 1902"). Still serving. [563.]

857. Armr.-Sergt. Jack, Alexander D. (Perth). Enlisted 1898. Served in South African War, 1899–1902; (1) attached to 1st Scots Guards; (2) in charge of Armoury, Port Elizabeth. Wounded at Modder River, Nov. 28, 1899 (Queen's medal, with clasps "Belmont" and "Modder River"; King's medal, with clasps "South Africa, 1901," and "South Africa, 1902"). Still serving (attached to Royal Irish Fusiliers). [564.]

ARMY PAY DEPARTMENT

646. Sergt. Smith, Robert (Perth). Enlisted 1892. Served in South African War, . . . 1900–1902 (Queen's medal, with clasp "Natal"; King's medal, with clasps "South Africa, 1901," and "South Africa, 1902"). Still serving. [565.]

ARMY POST OFFICE CORPS

709. Pte. Jackson, Robert (Birnam). Corpl. in 24th Middlesex (8th Vol. Batt. The Rifle Brigade). Enlisted in Army Post Office Corps 1901. Served in South African War, 1901–1902 (Queen's medal, with clasps "Cape Colony," "Orange Free State," "Transvaal," "South Africa, 1901," and "South Africa, 1902"). Discharged 1902.

— Pte. Muir, William G. (Callander). Eight years in 4th Vol. Batt. Royal Highlanders. Enlisted in Army Post Office Corps 1902. Served in South African War, 1902 (Queen's medal, with clasps "South Africa, 1902" . . .). Discharged 1902. [569.]

II.

R

REMOUNT DEPARTMENT

—— Civiln. Condr. McLaren, Thomas S. (Callander). Served in South African War as Civilian Conductor in Remount Department (Queen's medal, with clasp "Transvaal"). [570.]

IMPERIAL YEOMANRY

4TH BATTALION

7TH (LEICESTERSHIRE) COMPANY

2183. Pte. Kinnison, Kenneth MacKenzie (Butterstone). Enlisted 1900. Served in South African War, 1900-1901 (Queen's medal, with clasps "Cape Colony," "Wittebergen," "Transvaal," and "South Africa, 1901"). Invalided home and discharged invalided 1901. Died Feb. 14, 1902. [597.]

28TH COMPANY (COMPTON'S HORSE)

14976. Pte. Smith, Cuthbert Dinnie (Blairgowrie). Enlisted 1899. Served in South African War, 1900 (Queen's medal, with clasp "Cape Colony"). Discharged invalided 1900. [591.]

5TH BATTALION

16TH (WORCESTERSHIRE) COMPANY

7283. Pte. Keir, James (Blair Atholl). Enlisted 1900. Served in South African War, 1900-1901 (Queen's medal, with clasps "Cape Colony," "Orange Free State," "Transvaal," and "South Africa, 1901"). Discharged 1901. Formerly in 5th Vol. Batt. The Black Watch. [582.]

6TH BATTALION

18TH (LANARKSHIRE) COMPANY

8717. Pte. Mackenzie, Alexander (Glenlyon). Enlisted 1900. Served in South African War, 1900-1901 (Queen's medal, with clasps "Cape Colony," "Wittebergen," "Transvaal," and "South Africa, 1901"). Discharged 1901. [593.]

8715. Farr. McLaren, Alex. (Callander). Enlisted 1900. Served in South African War, 1900-1901 (Queen's medal, with clasps "Cape Colony," "Wittebergen," "Transvaal," and "South Africa, 1901"). Discharged 1901. [583.]

8731. Pte. Robertson, William J. (Braco). Enlisted 1900. Served in South African War, 1900 (Queen's medal, with clasps "Cape Colony," "Orange Free State," and "Transvaal"). Accidentally injured; invalided home and discharged invalided 1901. [594.]

20TH (FIFE AND FORFARSHIRE LIGHT HORSE) COMPANY

29437. Pte. Anderson, George (Alyth). Enlisted 1901. Served in South African War, 1901-1902 (Queen's medal, with clasps "Cape Colony," "Orange Free State," "Transvaal," "South Africa, 1901," and "South Africa, 1902"). Discharged 1902. [571.]

29442. Pte. Boyd, Robert (Scone). Enlisted 1901. Served in South African War,

1901-1902 (Queen's medal, with clasps " Cape Colony," " Orange Free State," " Transvaal," "South Africa, 1901," and " South Africa, 1902 "). Discharged 1902. [856.]

9239. Sh.-Smith Craigon, Peter (Perth). Enlisted 1900. Served in South African War, 1900 (Queen's medal, with clasps " Cape Colony " and "Transvaal "). [572.]

24873. Pte. Davis, Thomas T. A. (Blairgowrie). Served in South African War, 1901-1902 (Queen's medal, with clasps " Cape Colony," " Orange Free State," " Transvaal," "South Africa, 1901," and "South Africa, 1902"). Discharged 1902. [600.]

24874. Pte. Dempster, Hugh (Perth). Enlisted 1901. Served in South African War, 1901 (Queen's medal, with clasps "Cape Colony," " Orange Free State," " Transvaal," and "South Africa, 1901 "). Discharged 1902. [612.]

9236. Sh.-Smith Douglas, Charles (Dunkeld). Formerly in 5th Vol. Batt. The Black Watch. Enlisted in I.Y. 1900. Served in South African War, 1900 (Queen's medal, with clasps " Cape Colony" and " Transvaal"). Transferred on discharge to Imperial Military Railways, 1900. [573.]

24875. Lance - Corpl. Ferrier, Duncan (Alyth). Enlisted 1901. Served in South African War, 1901-1902 (Queen's medal, with clasps "Cape Colony," " Orange Free State," "Transvaal," "South Africa, 1901," and "South Africa, 1902 "). Discharged 1902. [601.]

9161. Pte. Haig, Jas. R. Price (yr. of Blairhill). Enlisted 1900. Served in South African War, 1900-1901. Wounded at Nooitgedacht, Dec. 13, 1900 (Queen's medal, with clasps " Cape Colony," " Orange Free State," "Transvaal," and " South Africa, 1901 "). Discharged 1901. [606.]

9218. Pte. Honeyman, Andrew Lees Muir (Coupar Angus). Enlisted 1900. Served in South African War, 1900-1901 (Queen's medal, with clasps " Cape Colony," " Orange Free State," "Transvaal," and " South Africa, 1901 "). Discharged 1901. [595.]

9213. Trump. Lowe, William (Perth). Enlisted 1900. Served in South African War, 1900-1901 (Queen's medal, with clasps " Cape Colony," "Transvaal," and " South Africa, 1901 "). Discharged 1901. [602.]

24882. Pte. McDonald, Alexander (Straloch). Enlisted 1901. Served in South African War, 1901 (Queen's medal, with clasps "Cape Colony," " Orange Free State," " Transvaal," and " South Africa, 1901 "). Died at Thabanchu, Dec. 28, 1901.

9228. Pte. Minto, Harvey S. (Crieff). Enlisted 1900. Served in South African War, 1900. Wounded near Heckpoort (in Magaliesburg), Sept. 6, 1900 (Queen's medal, with clasps " Cape Colony " and "Transvaal "). [613.]

23400. Pte. Playfair, Charles Gordon (Coupar Angus). Enlisted 1901. Served in South African War, 1901-1902 (Queen's medal, with clasps " Cape Colony," " Orange Free State," "Transvaal," "South Africa, 1901," and "South Africa, 1902 "). Discharged 1902. [609.]

9240. Corpl. Playfair, Harry Lyon (Coupar Angus). Enlisted 1900. Served in South African War, 1900-1901 (Queen's medal, with clasps " Cape Colony," " Orange Free State," "Transvaal," and " South Africa 1901 "). Discharged 1901. [614.]

9136. Pte. Pople, William G. (of Newhouse, Perth). Enlisted 1900. Served in South African War, 1900 (Queen's medal, with clasps "Cape Colony," " Orange Free State," and "Transvaal "). Discharged 1901. [608.]

24886. Pte. Rattray, John (Marlee). Enlisted 1901. Served in South African War, 1901-1902 (Queen's medal, with clasps "Cape Colony," " Orange Free State," "Transvaal," " South Africa, 1901," and "South Africa, 1902 "). Discharged 1902. [615.]

23379. Sergt. Robertson, Geo. Cunningham (Monzievaird). Enlisted 1901. Served in South African War, 1901-1902. Wounded near Bethulie, Oct. 24, 1901 (Queen's medal, with clasps "Cape Colony," " Orange Free State," "Transvaal," "South Africa, 1901," and "South Africa, 1902 "). Discharged 1902. [584.]

25530. Pte. Ross, William (Bridge of Earn). Enlisted 1901. Served in South African War, 1901-1902 (Queen's medal, with clasps "Cape Colony," " Orange Free State," " Transvaal," "South Africa, 1901," and "South Africa, 1902 "). Discharged 1902. [580.]

9158. Pte. Scott, Joseph Garland (Coupar Angus). Enlisted 1900. Served in South African War, 1900-1901 (Queen's medal,

20TH (FIFE AND FORFARSHIRE LIGHT HORSE) COMPANY—*continued*

with clasps "Cape Colony," "Transvaal," and "South Africa, 1901"). Discharged 1901. [599.]

23673. Pte. Thomson, David (Scone). Enlisted 1901. Served in South African War, 1901–1902 (Queen's medal, with clasps "Cape Colony," "Orange Free State," "Transvaal," "South Africa, 1901," and "South Africa, 1902"). Discharged 1902. [607.]

9159. Pte. Wilson, Andrew Taylor (Scone). Enlisted 1900. Served in South African War, 1900 (Queen's medal, with clasps "Cape Colony" and "Transvaal"). Killed at Nooitgedacht, Dec. 13, 1900. [611.]

107TH (LANARKSHIRE) COMPANY

30269. Qrmr.-Sergt. Myers, John Coupar (Pitlochry). Formerly in 6th Vol. Batt. The Black Watch. Enlisted in Scottish Horse 1901. Transferred to I.Y. 1901. Served in South African War, 1901–1902 (Queen's medal, with clasps "Cape Colony," "Orange Free State," "Transvaal," "South Africa, 1901," and "South Africa, 1902"). Discharged 1902. [617.]

108TH (QUEEN'S OWN ROYAL GLASGOW) COMPANY

31006. Pte. Steven, Alexander (Kincardine on Forth). Enlisted 1901. Served in South African War, 1901–1902 (Queen's medal, with clasps "Cape Colony," "Orange Free State," "Transvaal," "South Africa, 1901," and "South Africa, 1902"). Discharged 1902. [604.]

11TH BATTALION

34TH (MIDDLESEX) COMPANY

6346. Sergt. Edmondston, Chas. Biot (Kincardine). Enlisted 1900. Served in South African War, 1900–1901 (Queen's medal, with clasps "Cape Colony," "Wittebergen," "Transvaal," and "South Africa, 1901"). Discharged 1901. [603.]

15TH BATTALION

57TH (BUCKINGHAMSHIRE) COMPANY

34647. Pte. Graham, Christopher (Crieff). Joined 5th West Middlesex Rifle Vols. 1899. Enlisted in I.Y. 1901. Served in South African War, 1901–1902 (Queen's medal, with clasps "Cape Colony," "Orange Free State," "Transvaal," "South Africa, 1901," and "South Africa, 1902"). Discharged 1902. Rejoined Vols. 1902. [581.]

17TH BATTALION

50TH (HAMPSHIRE) COMPANY

—— **Pte. Esplin, George** (Perth). Enlisted 1901. Served in South African War, 1901–1902 (Queen's medal, with clasps "South Africa, 1901," "South Africa, 1902," and . . .). Discharged 1902. [574.]

18TH BATTALION

70TH (SHARPSHOOTERS) COMPANY

12636. Sergt. Deas, Jas. Beatson (Perth). Enlisted 1900. Served in South African War, 1900–1901 (Queen's medal, with clasps "Cape Colony," "Orange Free State," "Rhodesia," and "South Africa, 1901"). Died at Pietermaritzburg, June 27, 1901. Formerly in 4th Vol. Batt. The Black Watch. [610.]

12537. Corpl. Kidd, John (Blairgowrie). Enlisted 1900. Served in South African War, 1900–1901 (Queen's medal, with clasps "Cape Colony," "Orange Free State," "Rhodesia," and "South Africa, 1901"). Discharged 1901. [576].

12550. Corpl. King, John (Muthill). Enlisted 1900. Served in South African War, 1900–1901 (Queen's medal, with clasps "Cape Colony," "Orange Free State," "Rhodesia," and "South Africa, 1901"). Discharged 1901. [577.]

12632. Pte. Macdougall, Duncan A. (Kenmore). Enlisted 1900. Served in South African War, 1900–1901 (Queen's medal, with clasps "Cape Colony," "Orange Free State," "Rhodesia," and "South Africa, 1901"). Discharged 1901.

72ND (ROUGH RIDERS) COMPANY

14572. Lance-Corpl. McLaren, John Hume (Kindallachan). Enlisted 1900. Served in South African War, 1900–1901 (Queen's medal, with clasps "Cape Colony," "Orange Free State," "Transvaal," and "South Africa, 1901"). Discharged 1901. Later joined Corps of Cattlerangers. Died at Pretoria, Aug. 25, 1901. [578.]

21ST BATTALION

81ST (SHARPSHOOTERS) COMPANY

22283. Pte. Selby, Robert E. (Crieff). Enlisted 1901. Served in South African War, 1901–1902 (Queen's medal, with clasps "Cape Colony," "Orange Free State," "Transvaal," "South Africa, 1901," and "South Africa, 1902"). Discharged 1902. [596.]

22ND BATTALION

78TH (ROUGH RIDERS) COMPANY

23419. Sergt. Harris, John Wallace (Alyth). Enlisted 1901. Served in South African War, 1901–1902 (Queen's medal, with clasps "Cape Colony," "Orange Free State," "Transvaal," "South Africa, 1901," and "South Africa, 1902"). Discharged 1902. [588.]

23372. Pte. Nicol, William (Forteviot). Enlisted 1901. Served in South African War, 1901–1902 (Queen's medal, with clasps "Cape Colony," "Orange Free State," "Transvaal," "South Africa, 1901," and "South Africa, 1902"). Discharged 1902. [579.]

24TH BATTALION (METROPOLITAN MOUNTED RIFLES)

——— Lance-Sergt. Gellatly, Wm. Burden (Perth). Enlisted 1901. Promoted Lance-Corpl., Corpl., and Lance-Sergt., 1901. Served in South African War, 1901–1902 (Queen's medal, with clasps "Cape Colony," "Orange Free State," "Transvaal," "South Africa, 1901," and "South Africa, 1902"). Discharged 1902. Formerly in 4th Vol. Batt. The Black Watch and 1st Vol. Batt. The Queen's Royal West Surrey Regt. [575.]

26TH BATTALION (YOUNGHUSBAND'S HORSE)

121ST COMPANY

42052. Pte. McBain, C. (Perth). Enlisted in 20th (Fife and Forfarshire Light Horse) Coy. 1901. Discharged 1902. Enlisted in 121st Coy. 1902. Served in South African War, (1) with 20th Coy. 1901-1902, and (2) with 121st Coy. 1902 (Queen's medal, with clasps "Cape Colony," "Orange Free State," "Transvaal," "South Africa, 1901," and "South Africa, 1902"). Discharged 1902.

31ST BATTALION (FINCASTLE'S HORSE)

—— **Pte. Clark,** David (Scone). Enlisted 1902. Served in South African War, 1902 (Queen's medal, with clasps "Cape Colony" and "South Africa, 1902"). Discharged 1902. [587.]

39851. Pte. Duncan, Adam (Blairgowrie). Enlisted 1902. Served in South African War, 1902 (Queen's medal, with clasps "Cape Colony" and "South Africa, 1902").

37862. Pte. Forbes, James (Doune). Enlisted 1902. Served in South African War, 1902 (Queen's medal, with clasps "Cape Colony" and "South Africa, 1902").

38652. Lance-Corpl. Horne, Thomas (Pitlochry). Enlisted 1902. Served in South African War, 1902 (Queen's medal, with clasps "Cape Colony" and "South Africa, 1902"). Discharged 1902.

38175. Orderly-Room Sergt. Robertson, James W. (Perth). Enlisted 1902. Promoted Sq.-Qrmr.-Sergt. and Orderly-Room Sergt. 1902. Served in South African War, 1902 (Queen's medal, with clasps "Cape Colony" and "South Africa, 1902"). Discharged 1903. [590.]

43794. Lance-Corpl. Robertson, Wm. Peattie (Blairgowrie). Enlisted 1902. Served in South African War, 1902 (Queen's medal, with clasps "Cape Colony" and "South Africa, 1902"). Discharged 1903. [516.]

41099. Pte. Stewart, James (Blairgowrie). Enlisted 1902. Served in South African War, 1902 (Queen's medal, with clasps "Cape Colony" and "South Africa, 1902"). [518.]

38075. Pte. Taylor, John (Perth). Enlisted 1902. Served in South African War, 1902 (Queen's medal, with clasps "Cape Colony" and "South Africa, 1902"). Discharged 1902. [598.]

—— **Sergt. Young,** Alexander (Collace). Enlisted 1902. Served in South African War, 1902 (Queen's medal, with clasps "Cape Colony" and "South Africa, 1902"). Discharged 1903.

37TH BATTALION (HIGHLAND HORSE)

—— **Pte. Gilmour,** William (Crieff). Enlisted 1902 for service in South African War.

—— **Sq.-Qrmr.-Sergt. Keiller,** James M. R. (Perth). Enlisted in Fife and Forfarshire Light Horse 1899. Enlisted 1902 in 37th Batt. I.Y. (Highland Horse) for service in South African War. Discharged 1902. Now serving with Fife and Forfarshire Light Horse. [605.]

42050. Sq.-Qrmr.-Sergt. Lindsay, John (Alyth). 5th Vol. Batt. The Black Watch. Served in South African War as Pte. with 1st Vol. Service Coy., The Black Watch, 1900-1901 (Queen's medal, with clasps "Cape Colony," "Orange Free State," "Transvaal," and "South Africa, 1901"). Enlisted 1902 in 37th Batt. I.Y. (Highland Horse) for service in South African War. Discharged 1903. [589.]

41164. Pte. McLean, A. (Perth). Enlisted 1902 for service in South African War. Died at Aldershot during mobilisation, 1902.

42049. Pte. Mitchell, Peter (Alyth). Enlisted 1902 for service in South African War. Discharged 1903. [585.]

41174. Pte. Mitchell, W. (Blairgowrie). Enlisted 1902 for active service in South African War. Discharged 1903.

42048. **Pte. Thompson, G.** (Alyth). 5th Vol. Batt. The Black Watch. Served in South African War with 1st Vol. Service Coy., The Black Watch, 1900–1901 (Queen's medal, with clasps "Cape Colony," "Wittebergen," and "South Africa, 1901"). Enlisted 1902 in 37th Batt. I.Y. (Highland Horse) for service in South African War. Discharged 1903. [592.]

DUKE OF CAMBRIDGE'S OWN IMPERIAL YEOMANRY

—— **Pte. Robertson, George L.** (Scone). Enlisted 1901. Served in South African War, 1901–1902 (Queen's medal, with clasps "South Africa, 1901," and "South Africa, 1902"). Discharged 1902. [586.]

CORPS PARTLY IMPERIAL YEOMANRY AND PARTLY IRREGULAR

LOVAT'S SCOUTS

37373. **Pte. Cameron, Alexander** (Fortingall). Joined 5th Vol. Batt. The Black Watch 1896. Enlisted in Lovat's Scouts 1901. Served in South African War, (1) with 1st Vol. Service Coy., The Black Watch, 1900–1901 ; (2) with Lovat's Scouts, 1901–1902 (Queen's medal, with clasps "Wittebergen," "Cape Colony," "South Africa, 1901," and "South Africa, 1902"). Discharged 1902. [623.]

8714. **Pte. Crerar, Thomas R.** (Foss). Enlisted 1900. Served in South African War, 1900–1901 (Queen's medal, with clasps "Cape Colony," "Johannesburg," "Diamond Hill," "Wittebergen," and "South Africa, 1901"). Discharged 1901. [619.]

8731. **Pte. Foote, Andrew** (Stanley). Enlisted 1900. Served in South African War, 1900–1901. Wounded at Lindley, July 1900 (Queen's medal, with clasps "Orange Free State" and "South Africa, 1901"). Discharged 1901. [620.]

8754. **Pte. Kennedy, John** (Blairgowrie). Enlisted 1900. Served in South African War, 1900–1901 (Queen's medal, with clasps "Cape Colony," "Wittebergen," and "South Africa, 1901"). Discharged 1901. [625.]

8815. **Pte. McDonald, Alexander** (Blair Atholl). Enlisted 1900. Discharged 1901. Re-enlisted 1901. Served in South African War, (1) 1900–1901, and (2) 1901–1902 (Queen's medal, with clasps "Cape Colony" and "Wittebergen" ; King's medal, with clasps "South Africa, 1901," and "South Africa, 1902"). Discharged 1902. [628.]

8811. **Pte. McFarlane, Duncan** (Pitlochry). Formerly in Scots Greys. Enlisted in Lovat's Scouts 1900. Served in South African War, 1900–1901 (Queen's medal, with clasps "Cape Colony," "Wittebergen," and "South Africa, 1901"). Discharged 1901. [624.]

8835. **Pte. McLauchlan, James** (Logierait). Enlisted 1900. Served in South African War, 1900–1901 (Queen's medal, with clasps "Cape Colony," "Wittebergen," and "South Africa, 1901"). Discharged 1901. [621.]

8776. **Pte. McLean, Robert** (Kenmore). Enlisted 1900. Served in South African War, 1900–1901 (Queen's medal, with clasps "Cape Colony," "Johannesburg," "Diamond Hill," "Wittebergen," and "South Africa, 1901"). Discharged 1901.

36677. **Pte. Simpson, Frederick W.** (Longforgan). Enlisted 1901. Served in South African War, 1901–1902 (Queen's medal, with clasps "Cape Colony," "Orange Free State," "South Africa, 1901," and "South Africa, 1902"). Died at Maraisburg, April 9, 1902.

36779. **Pte. Thomson, James A.** (Dunkeld). Enlisted 1901. Served in South African War, 1901–1902 (Queen's medal, with clasps "Cape Colony," "Orange Free State," "South Africa, 1901," and "South Africa, 1902"). Discharged 1902. [626.]

LOVAT'S SCOUTS—*continued*

36781. Sh. - Smith Turner, Duncan F. (Alyth). Enlisted 1901. Served in South African War, 1901–1902. Wounded at Quaggafontein, Sept. 20, 1901 (Queen's medal, with clasps "Cape Colony," "Orange Free State," "South Africa, 1901," and "South Africa, 1902"). Discharged 1902. [622.]

8911. Pte. Wanliss, George C. (Scone).

Enlisted 1900. Discharged 1901. Re-enlisted 1901. Served in South African War, (1) 1900–1901 and (2) 1901–1902 (Queen's medal, with clasps "Cape Colony," "Orange Free State," and "Johannesburg"; King's medal, with clasps "South Africa, 1901," and "South Africa 1902"). Discharged 1902. [627.]

THE SCOTTISH HORSE

36959. Tpr. Adams, George (Collace). Enlisted 1901. Served in South African War, 1901–1902 (Queen's medal, with clasps "Cape Colony," "Transvaal," "South Africa, 1901," and "South Africa, 1902"). Discharged 1902. [629.]

31366. Lance-Corpl. Alexander, Alexander (Errol). Enlisted 1901. Served in South African War, 1901–1902 (Queen's medal, with clasps "Cape Colony," "Orange Free State," "Transvaal," "South Africa, 1901," and "South Africa, 1902"). Discharged 1902.

37029. Corpl. Alexander, James M. (Alyth). Enlisted 1901. Served in South African War, 1901–1902 (Queen's medal, with clasps "Cape Colony," "Transvaal," "South Africa, 1901," and "South Africa, 1902"). Discharged 1902. [647.]

33376. Tpr. Alexander, John L. (Blairgowrie). Enlisted 1901. Served in South African War, 1901–1902 (Queen's medal, with clasps "Cape Colony," "Orange Free State," "Transvaal," "South Africa, 1901," and "South Africa, 1902"). Coronation medal, 1902. Discharged 1902. [682.]

33382. Tpr. Anderson, Gourlay Steele (Muckart). Enlisted 1901. Served in South African War, 1901–1902 (Queen's medal, with clasps "Cape Colony," "Orange Free State," "Transvaal," "South Africa, 1901," and "South Africa, 1902"). Discharged 1902. [630.]

37670. Tpr. Anderson, William B. (Alyth). Enlisted 1901. Served in South African War, 1902 (Queen's medal, with clasps "Cape Colony," "Orange Free State," "Transvaal," and "South Africa, 1902"). Discharged 1902. [665.]

37137. Tpr. Archer, James (Perth). Enlisted 1901. Served in South African War, 1901–1902 (Queen's medal, with clasps "Transvaal," "South Africa, 1901," and "South Africa, 1902"). Discharged 1902.

36964. Tpr. Band, Henry (Collace). Enlisted 1901. Served in South African War, 1901–1902 (Queen's medal, with clasps "Cape Colony," "Transvaal," "South Africa, 1901," and "South Africa, 1902"). Discharged 1902.

37219. Tpr. Bannerman, George (Coupar Angus). Enlisted 1901. Served in South African War, 1901–1902 (Queen's medal, with clasps "Transvaal," "South Africa, 1901," and "South Africa, 1902"). Discharged 1902.

36961. Tpr. Bannerman, Telford (Coupar Angus). Enlisted 1901. Served in South African War, 1901–1902 (Queen's medal, with clasps "Cape Colony," "Transvaal," "South Africa, 1901," and "South Africa, 1902"). Discharged 1902.

42014. Sergt. Bayne, Thomas M. (Cultoquhey). Formerly in 5th Vol. Batt. The Black Watch. Enlisted in Scottish Horse 1902. Served in South African War, (1) as Corpl. with 2nd Vol. Service Coy., The Black Watch, 1901–1902, (2) as Sergt. with Scottish Horse, 1902 (Queen's medal, with clasps "Cape Colony," "Orange Free State," "Transvaal," "South Africa, 1901," and "South Africa, 1902"). Discharged 1902. [633.]

44016. Sh.-Smith Beattie, Andrew (Coupar Angus). Enlisted 1902. Served in South African War, 1902 (Queen's medal, with clasps "Transvaal" and "South Africa, 1902"). Discharged 1902.

37587. Tpr. Bell, Andrew (Moulin). Enlisted 1902. Served in South African War, 1902

(Queen's medal, with clasps "Transvaal" and "South Africa, 1902"). Transferred 1902 to Scottish Horse Squadron of Natal Mounted Police.

37493. Tpr. Bell, Daniel (Moulin). Enlisted 1902. Served in South African War, 1902 (Queen's medal, with clasps "Transvaal" and "South Africa, 1902"). Transferred 1902 to Scottish Horse Squadron of Natal Mounted Police.

31716. Lance-Corpl. Bell, James (Ardoch). Enlisted 1901. Served in South African War, 1901 (Queen's medal, with clasps "Cape Colony," "Orange Free State," "Transvaal," and "South Africa, 1901"). Killed at Bakenlaagte, Oct. 30, 1901. [694.]

37566. Tpr. Blair, Alexander (Callander). Enlisted 1901. Served in South African War, 1902 (Queen's medal, with clasps "Transvaal" and "South Africa, 1902"). Discharged 1902. [677.]

37246. Tpr. Boyle, John (Madderty). Enlisted 1901. Served in South African War, 1901-1902 (Queen's medal, with clasps "Transvaal" and "South Africa, 1902"). Transferred 1902 to Scottish Horse Squadron of Natal Mounted Police.

31365. Tpr. Brown, Charles (Perth). Enlisted 1901. Served in South African War, 1901-1902 (Queen's medal, with clasps "Cape Colony," "Orange Free State," "Transvaal," "South Africa, 1901," and "South Africa, 1902"). Discharged 1902. [632.]

24302. Sergt. Brown, David (Bankfoot). Formerly in 5th Vol. Batt. The Black Watch. Enlisted in Imperial Yeomanry 1900. Transferred to Scottish Horse 1900. Served in South African War, (1) with 72nd Coy. Imperial Yeomanry, 1900 ; (2) with Scottish Horse, 1900–1901 (Queen's medal, with clasps "Cape Colony," "Orange Free State," "Transvaal," and "South Africa, 1901"). Discharged 1901. [631.]

37067. Tpr. Bruce, David (Alyth). Enlisted 1902. Served in South African War, (1) with 2nd Vol. Service Coy. The Lincolnshire Regiment, 1901-1902 ; (2) with Scottish Horse, 1902 (Queen's medal, with clasps "Cape Colony," "Orange Free State," "Transvaal," "South Africa, 1901," and "South Africa, 1902"). Discharged 1902. [666.]

37119. Sh.-Smith Burnfield, John (Ballathie).

Enlisted 1902. Served in South African War, 1902 (Queen's medal, with clasps "Transvaal" and "South Africa, 1902").

37100. Tpr. Cameron, John (Kintillo). Enlisted 1901. Served in South African War, 1901-1902 (Queen's medal, with clasps "Cape Colony," "Transvaal," "South Africa, 1901," and "South Africa, 1902"). Discharged 1902. [684.]

36954. Tpr. Cameron, William S. (Perth). Enlisted 1901. Served in South African War, 1901-1902 (Queen's medal, with clasps "Cape Colony," "Transvaal," "South Africa, 1901," and "South Africa, 1902"). Discharged 1902.

37194. Tpr. Campbell, Donald (Moulin). Enlisted 1901. Served in South African War, 1901-1902 (Queen's medal, with clasps "Transvaal," "South Africa, 1901," and "South Africa, 1902"). Discharged 1902.

37693. Tpr. Campbell, Duncan (Moulin). Enlisted 1901. Served in South African War, 1902 (Queen's medal, with clasps "Transvaal" and "South Africa, 1902"). Discharged 1902.

37245. Tpr. Campbell, Johnstone (Forgandenny). Enlisted 1901. Served in South African War, 1902 (Queen's medal, with clasps "Transvaal" and "South Africa, 1902"). Discharged 1902. [685.]

44051. Piper Campbell, Stewart (Blairgowrie). Enlisted 1902. Served in South African War, 1902 (Queen's medal, with clasps "Transvaal" and "South Africa, 1902"). Discharged 1902. [667.]

791. Sergt. Chalmers, Alexander (Stanley). Formerly in 5th Vol. Batt. The Black Watch. Enlisted in Scottish Horse 1901. Served in South African War, 1901-1902. Wounded at Beestekraal, Oct. 30, 1901 (Queen's medal, with clasps "Cape Colony," "Orange Free State," "Transvaal," "South Africa, 1901," and "S. Africa, 1902"). Discharged 1902. [635.]

26411. Tpr. Chalmers, James (Gask). Enlisted 1901. Served in South African War, 1901 (Queen's medal, with clasps "Cape Colony," "Orange Free State," "Transvaal," and "South Africa, 1901"). Formerly in 4th Vol. Batt. The Black Watch. Killed at Eland's Drift, Aug. 8, 1901.

30143. Tpr. Christie, David H. (Perth). Enlisted 1901. Served in South African War, 1901-1902 (Queen's medal, with clasps "Cape Colony," "Orange Free State," "Transvaal,"

THE SCOTTISH HORSE—*continued*

"South Africa, 1901," and "South Africa, 1902"). Discharged invalided 1902. [636.]

36970. Tpr. Clarke, Alexander (Dunkeld). Enlisted in Scottish Horse 1901. Served in South African War, 1901–1902 (Queen's medal, with clasps "Cape Colony," "Transvaal," "South Africa, 1901," and "South Africa, 1902"). Discharged 1902. Formerly in Cycle Vol. Corps. [686.]

37589. Tpr. Dair, James (Alyth). Enlisted 1901. Served in South African War, 1902 (Queen's medal, with clasps "Transvaal" and "South Africa, 1902"). Discharged 1902. [668.]

37674. Tpr. Davidson, John (Coupar Angus). Enlisted 1901. Served in South African War, 1902 (Queen's medal, with clasps "Transvaal" and "South Africa, 1902"). Discharged 1902. [669.]

37234. Sadd.-Corpl. Davison, James (Perth). Enlisted 1902. Served in South African War, 1902 (Queen's medal, with clasps "Transvaal" and "South Africa, 1902"). Died at Klerksdorp, March 8, 1902.

37474. Tpr. Dewar, William (Perth). Enlisted 1902. Served in South African War, 1902 (Queen's medal, with clasps "Transvaal" and "South Africa, 1902"). Discharged 1902.

37537. Tpr. Dow, John G. (Perth). Enlisted 1901. Served in South African War, 1902 (Queen's medal, with clasps "Transvaal" and "South Africa, 1902"). Discharged 1902. [637.]

37468. Piper Drummond, James (Muthill). Enlisted 1901. Served in South African War, 1902 (Queen's medal, with clasps "Cape Colony," "Orange Free State," "Transvaal," and "South Africa, 1902"). Coronation medal, 1902. Discharged 1902. [638.]

34482. Sergt. Duff, Peter (Ballinluig). Enlisted in Scots Greys 1887; exchanged into 14th Hussars 1899; enlisted in Scottish Horse 1901. Served in South African War, (1) with 14th Hussars, 1899–1901; (2) with Scottish Horse, 1901–1902 (Queen's medal (with clasps . . .); King's medal, with clasps "South Africa, 1901," and "South Africa, 1902"). Discharged 1902. [671.]

33433. Corpl. Dugan, William (Dunblane). Formerly in Royal Garrison Artillery. En-

listed in Scottish Horse 1901. Served in South African War, 1901–1902 (Queen's medal, with clasps "Cape Colony," "Orange Free State," "Transvaal," "South Africa, 1901," and "South Africa, 1902"). Coronation medal, 1902. Discharged 1902. [634.]

44884. Tpr. Ellis, Thomas (Tullochcurran). Enlisted 1902 for service in South African War. Discharged 1902.

33230. Sh.-Smith Ewan, William (Bankfoot). Formerly in 5th Vol. Batt. The Black Watch. Enlisted in Scottish Horse 1901. Served in South African War, 1901–1902. Wounded at Elandskloof, July 3, 1901 (Queen's medal, with clasps "Cape Colony," "Orange Free State," "Transvaal," "South Africa, 1901," and "South Africa, 1902"). Discharged 1902. [672.]

37185. Piper Ferguson, James (Blairgowrie). Enlisted 1901. Served in South African War, 1901–1902 (Queen's medal, with clasps "Transvaal," "South Africa, 1901," and "South Africa, 1902"). Discharged 1902.

36984. Sergt. Findlay, William (Stanley). Enlisted 1901. Served in South African War, 1901–1902 (Queen's medal, with clasps "Cape Colony," "Transvaal," "South Africa, 1901," and "South Africa, 1902"). Discharged 1902. [643.]

44050. Sh.-Smith Fleming, George (Coupar Angus). Enlisted 1902. Served in South African War, 1902 (Queen's medal, with clasps "Transvaal" and "South Africa, 1902"). Discharged 1902.

36981. Sergt. Flight, John (Burrelton). Enlisted 1901. Served in South African War, 1901–1902 (Queen's medal, with clasps "Cape Colony," "Transvaal," "South Africa, 1901," and "South Africa, 1902"). Discharged 1902. [670.]

37538. Corpl. Foote, Alexander (Stanley). Enlisted 1901. Served in South African War, 1902 (Queen's medal, with clasps "Transvaal" and "South Africa, 1902"). Discharged 1902. [673.]

37586. Tpr. Fraser, John Rutherford (Stanley). Enlisted 1901. Served in South African War, 1902 (Queen's medal, with clasps "Transvaal" and "South Africa, 1902"). Discharged 1902. [639.]

44702. Lance-Corpl. **Fraser, William** (Blair Atholl). 5th Vol. Batt. The Black Watch. Served in South African War with 1st Vol. Service Coy. The Black Watch, 1900–1901. Enlisted in Scottish Horse 1902 for service in South African War (Queen's medal, with clasps "Cape Colony," "Wittebergen," and "South Africa, 1901"). Discharged from Scottish Horse 1902. [640.]

25862. Sh.-Smith **Fulton, Andrew** (Culross). Enlisted 1901. Served in South African War, 1901–1902. Wounded at Bakenlaagte, Oct. 30, 1901 (Queen's medal, with clasps "Cape Colony," "Orange Free State," "Transvaal," "South Africa, 1901," and "South Africa, 1902"). Discharged 1902.

867. Tpr. **Fulton, John** (Doune). Enlisted 1901. Served in South African War, 1901–1902 (Queen's medal, with clasps "Cape Colony," "Orange Free State," "Transvaal," "South Africa, 1901," and "South Africa, 1902"). Discharged 1902.

37460. Tpr. **Gilmour, John** (Crieff). Enlisted 1901. Served in South African War, 1902 (Queen's medal, with clasps "Transvaal" and "South Africa, 1902"). [687.]

37136. Tpr. **Gow, David** (Coupar Angus). Enlisted 1901. Served in South African War, 1901–1902 (Queen's medal, with clasps "Transvaal," "South Africa, 1901," and "South Africa, 1902"). Discharged 1902. [678.]

37491. Tpr. **Grant, Archibald** (Perth). Enlisted 1901. Served in South African War, 1902 (Queen's medal, with clasps "Transvaal" and "South Africa, 1902"). Discharged 1902.

36797. Corpl. **Gray, Bethune J.** (Abernethy). Enlisted 1901. Served in South African War, 1901 (Queen's medal, with clasps "Cape Colony," "Transvaal," and "South Africa, 1901"). Discharged 1901. [690.]

36910. Corpl. **Gray, Harry** (Abernethy). Enlisted 1901. Served in South African War, 1901 (Queen's medal, with clasps "Cape Colony," "Transvaal," and "South Africa, 1901"). Discharged 1901. [691.]

37101. Tpr. **Grieve, John W.** (Abernethy). Enlisted 1901. Served in South African War, 1901–1902 (Queen's medal, with clasps "Transvaal," "South Africa, 1901," and "South Africa, 1902"). Discharged 1902. [641.]

33546. Sergt. **Haxton, Henry** (Forgan-denny). Enlisted 1901. Served in South African War, 1901–1902 (Queen's medal, with clasps "Cape Colony," "Orange Free State," "Transvaal," "South Africa, 1901," and "South Africa, 1902"). Coronation medal 1902. Discharged 1902. Enlisted in Scottish Horse (I.Y.) 1903. [642.]

33411. Farr.-Major **Henderson, Robert** (Perth). Enlisted 1901. Served in South African War, 1901 (Queen's medal, with clasps "Cape Colony," "Orange Free State," "Transvaal," and "South Africa, 1901"). Discharged 1902.

37130. Tpr. **Hood, James** (Blairgowrie). Enlisted 1901. Served in South African War, 1901–1902 (Queen's medal, with clasps "Transvaal," "South Africa, 1901," and "South Africa, 1902"). Discharged 1902.

37666. Corpl. **Hush, John** (Blair Atholl). Enlisted 1901. Served in South African War, 1902 (Queen's medal, with clasps "Transvaal" and "South Africa, 1902"). Discharged 1902. [643.]

44716. Tpr. **Jack, James** (Pitlochry). Enlisted 1902 for service in South African War. Discharged 1902. [649.]

37150. Tpr. **Jack, Thos.** McLaren (Pitlochry). Enlisted 1901. Served in South African War, 1901–1902 (Queen's medal, with clasps "Transvaal," "South Africa, 1901," and "South Africa, 1902"). Discharged 1902. [650.]

37259. Tpr. **Johnstone, Andrew** (Errol). Enlisted 1901. Served in South African War, 1902 (Queen's medal, with clasps "Transvaal" and "South Africa, 1902"). Discharged 1902. [679.]

33267. Sergt.-Major **Johnston, George R.** (Blair Atholl). Enlisted 1901. Served in South African War, 1901–1902 (Queen's medal, with clasps "Cape Colony," "Orange Free State," "Transvaal," "South Africa, 1901," and "South Africa, 1902"). Discharged 1902. [644.]

40923. Sh.-Smith **Johnston, James H.** (Blairgowrie). Enlisted 1902. Served in South African War, 1902 (Queen's medal, with clasps "Transvaal" and "South Africa, 1902"). Discharged 1902. [651.]

33332. Tpr. **Kay, Alexander** (Aberfoyle). Enlisted 1901. Served in South African War, 1901–1902 (Queen's medal, with clasps "Cape Colony," "Orange Free State," "Transvaal,"

THE SCOTTISH HORSE—*continued*

"South Africa, 1901," and "South Africa, 1902"). Discharged 1902. [645.]

31360. Tpr. Kean, William (Perth). Formerly in 4th Vol. Batt. The Black Watch. Enlisted in Scottish Horse 1901. Served in South African War, 1901 (Queen's medal, with clasps "Cape Colony," "Orange Free State," "Transvaal," and "South Africa, 1901"). Died at sea on way home, Jan. 5, 1902. [681.]

820. Tpr. Kerrigan, John (Perth). Enlisted 1901. Served in South African War, 1901. Wounded at Moedwil, Sept. 30, 1901 (Queen's medal, with clasps "Cape Colony," "Orange Free State," "Transvaal," and "South Africa, 1901"). Discharged 1901. [646.]

821. Piper Laidlaw, James (Perth). Enlisted 1901. Served in South African War, 1901–1902 (Queen's medal, with clasps "Cape Colony," "Orange Free State," "Transvaal," "South Africa, 1901," and "South Africa, 1902"). Coronation medal 1902. Discharged 1902. [674.]

37471. Tpr. Laing, David (Ruthvenfield). Enlisted 1901. Served in South African War, 1902 (Queen's medal, with clasps "Transvaal" and "South Africa, 1902"). Discharged 1902. [653.]

37704. Tpr. Laing, George (Ruthvenfield). Enlisted 1901. Served in South African War, 1902 (Queen's medal, with clasps "Transvaal" and "South Africa, 1902"). Discharged 1902.

36992. Tpr. Lamont, James (Stormontfield). Enlisted 1901. Served in South African War, 1901–1902 (Queen's medal, with clasps "Cape Colony," "Transvaal," "South Africa, 1901," and "South Africa, 1902"). Discharged 1902.

37058. Tpr. Leslie, Robert (St. Martins). Enlisted 1901. Served in South African War, 1901–1902 (Queen's medal, with clasps "Cape Colony," "Transvaal," "South Africa, 1901," and "South Africa, 1902"). Discharged 1902. [654.]

37678. Tpr. McCallum, Daniel (Haugh of Aberuthven). Enlisted 1901. Served in South African War, 1902 (Queen's medal, with clasps "Transvaal" and "South Africa, 1902"). Discharged 1902.

37673. Tpr. McCallum, John (Morenish). Enlisted 1901. Served in South African War,

1902 (Queen's medal, with clasps "Transvaal" and "South Africa, 1902"). Discharged 1902.

37247. Tpr. McCulloch, Peter (Madderty). Enlisted 1901. Served in South African War, 1902 (Queen's medal, with clasps "Transvaal" and "South Africa, 1902"). Discharged 1902. [655.]

37490. Tpr. McFarlane, Donald (Stanley). Enlisted 1902. Served in South African War, 1902 (Queen's medal, with clasps "Transvaal" and "South Africa, 1902"). Discharged 1902.

37133. Sh.-Smith McFarlane, Robert (Blair Atholl). Enlisted 1901. Served in South African War, 1901–1902 (Queen's medal, with clasps "Transvaal," "South Africa, 1901," and "South Africa, 1902"). Discharged 1902. [689.]

44667. Tpr. MacGregor, Atholl Murray (Balquhidder). Enlisted 1902 for service in South African War. Discharged 1902. [683.]

37195. Tpr. McGregor, Charles (Perth). Enlisted 1901. Served in South African War, 1901–1902 (Queen's medal, with clasps "Transvaal," "South Africa, 1901," and "South Africa, 1902"). Discharged 1902. [675.]

37570. Tpr. McGregor, Peter (Killin). Enlisted 1902. Served in South African War, 1902 (Queen's medal, with clasps "Transvaal" and "South Africa, 1902"). Discharged 1902.

616. Sc.-Sergt. McGregor, William (Weem). Enlisted in Imperial Light Horse 1899. Discharged 1900. Enlisted in Scottish Horse 1900. Served in South African War, (1) as Hospital Sergt. with Imperial Light Horse, 1899–1900; (2) as Sergt. with Scottish Horse, 1900–1901 (Queen's medal, with clasps "Defence of Ladysmith," "Relief of Mafeking," "Transvaal," and "South Africa, 1901"). Killed at Moedwil, Sept. 30, 1901. [725.]

37387. Pipe-Corpl. McInnes, John (Crieff). Enlisted in The Black Watch 1888 ; in Scottish Horse 1902. Served in South African War, (1) as Reservist with The Black Watch, 1899–1900 (wounded at Paardeberg, Feb. 18, 1900 ; invalided home and discharged 1901) ; (2) as Piper with Scottish Horse, 1902 (Queen's medal, with clasps "Cape Colony," "Paardeberg," "Driefontein," "Transvaal," and "South Africa, 1902"). Coronation medal 1902. Discharged 1902. [731.]

44758. Lance-Corpl. Macintosh, Donald (Weem). Formerly in 5th Vol. Batt. The Black Watch. Served in South African War as Lance-Corpl. with 1st Vol. Service Coy. The Black Watch, 1900-1901. Enlisted in Scottish Horse 1902 for service in South African War (Queen's medal, with clasps "Cape Colony," "Wittebergen," and "South Africa, 1901"). Discharged 1902. [663.]

37492. Corpl. McKay, James W. (Killin). Formerly in 5th Vol. Batt. The Black Watch. Enlisted in Scottish Horse 1901. Served in South African War, (1) as Pte. with 1st Vol. Service Coy. The Black Watch, 1900-1901; (2) as Corpl. with Scottish Horse, 1902 (Queen's medal, with clasps "Cape Colony," "Orange Free State," and "Transvaal ;" King's medal, with clasps "South Africa, 1901," and "South Africa, 1902"). Discharged 1902. [692.]

44751. Tpr. McKay, Patrick (Perth). Enlisted 1902 for service in South African War. Discharged 1902.

37283. Tpr. McKay, Thomas (Dunkeld). Enlisted 1902. Served in South African War, 1902 (Queen's medal, with clasps "Transvaal" and "South Africa, 1902"). Discharged 1902. [656.]

37197. Tpr. McKay, William C. (Burrelton). Enlisted 1901. Served in South African War, 1901-1902 (Queen's medal, with clasps "Transvaal," "South Africa, 1901," and "South Africa, 1902"). Discharged 1902. [737.]

37008. Tpr. McKenzie, James E. (Kinnoull). Served in South African War, 1901-1902. Wounded at Moedwil, Sept. 30, 1901 (Queen's medal, with clasps "Cape Colony," "Transvaal," "South Africa, 1901," and "South Africa, 1902"). Discharged 1902. [688.]

833. Tpr. McKenzie, Robert (Auchterarder), Enlisted 1901. Served in South African War. 1901 (Queen's medal, with clasps "Cape Colony," "Orange Free State," "Transvaal," and "South Africa, 1901"). Died at Rustenburg, Nov. 28, 1901. [664.]

37011. Tpr. McLaren, Alexander (Perth). Enlisted 1901. Served in South African War, 1901-1902. Wounded at Moedwil, Sept. 30, 1901 (Queen's medal, with clasps "Cape Colony," "Transvaal," "South Africa, 1901," and "South Africa, 1902"). Discharged 1902. [736.]

44659. Tpr. McLaren, Thomas (Kindallachan). Enlisted 1902 for service in South African War. Discharged 1902.

37077. Tpr. McLaren, William (Logiealmond). Enlisted 1901. Served in South African War, 1901-1902 (Queen's medal, with clasps "Cape Colony," "Transvaal," "South Africa, 1901," and "South Africa, 1902"). Discharged 1902. [662.]

44742. Tpr. McLauchlan, James (Moulin). Enlisted 1902 for service in South African War. Discharged 1902.

27265. Tpr. McLauchlan, Robert (Perth). Formerly Corpl. in 1st Forfarshire Vol. Artillery. Enlisted in Scottish Horse 1901. Served in South African War, 1901-1902 (Queen's medal, with clasps "Cape Colony," "Orange Free State," "Transvaal," "South Africa, 1901," and "South Africa, 1902"). Discharged 1902. [661.]

37250. Tpr. McLean, Archibald K. (Crieff). Enlisted 1901. Served in South African War, 1902 (Queen's medal, with clasps "Transvaal" and "South Africa, 1902"). Transferred 1902 to Scottish Horse Squadron of Natal Mounted Police. [660.]

44661. Tpr. McLean, James (Dunkeld). Enlisted 1902 for service in South African War. Discharged 1902.

37007. Tpr. McLeish, David (Blackford). Enlisted 1901. Served in South African War, 1901-1902 (Queen's medal, with clasps "Cape Colony," "Transvaal," "South Africa, 1901," and "South Africa, 1902"). Discharged 1902. [659.]

37282. Lance-Corpl. McLeish, Donald K. (Weem). Enlisted 1901. Served in South African War, 1902 (Queen's medal, with clasps "Transvaal" and "South Africa, 1902"). Discharged 1902. [658.]

33287. Tpr. McLeod, James (Blairgowrie). Enlisted 1901. Served in South African War, 1901-1902 (Queen's medal, with clasps "Cape Colony," "Orange Free State," "Transvaal," "South Africa, 1901," and "South Africa, 1902"). Discharged 1902. [693.]

44660. Tpr. McMillan, Alexander (Ballinluig). Enlisted 1902 for service in South African War. Transferred 1902 to Scottish Horse Squadron of Natal Mounted Police. [657.]

36998. Tpr. McPherson, Robert (Pitlochry). Enlisted 1901. Served in South African War, 1901. Wounded at Moedwil, Sept. 30, 1901 (Queen's medal, with clasps "Cape Colony," "Transvaal," and "South Africa, 1901"). Discharged 1902. [680.]

THE SCOTTISH HORSE—continued

37722. Tpr. McPherson, William M. (Alyth). Enlisted 1901. Served in South African War, 1901–1902 (Queen's medal, with clasps "Transvaal," "South Africa, 1901," and "South Africa, 1902"). Discharged 1902. [676.]

44755. Tpr. Malloch, James (Muthill). Enlisted 1902 for service in South African War. Discharged 1902. [735.]

31367. Corpl. Malloy, Joseph (Perth). Enlisted 1901. Served in South African War, 1901–1902 (Queen's medal, with clasps "Cape Colony," "Orange Free State," "Transvaal," "South Africa, 1901," and "South Africa, 1902"). Discharged 1902. [733.]

37385. Sh.-Smith Marshall, George (Crieff). Enlisted 1901. Served in South African War, 1902 (Queen's medal, with clasps "Transvaal" and "South Africa, 1902"). Discharged 1902. [695.]

37001. Pipe-Corpl. Mathewson, John (Balbeggie). Enlisted 1901. Served in South African War, 1901–1902 (Queen's medal, with clasps "Cape Colony," "Transvaal," "South Africa, 1901," and "South Africa, 1902"). Discharged 1902. [728.]

37529. Tpr. Melville, David A. (Alyth). Enlisted 1901. Served in South African War, 1902 (Queen's medal, with clasps "Transvaal" and "South Africa, 1902"). Discharged 1902. [696.]

37703. Tpr. Mersey, Alfred (Blair Atholl). Enlisted 1901. Served in South African War, 1902 (Queen's medal, with clasps "Cape Colony," "Orange Free State," "Transvaal," and "South Africa, 1902"). Discharged 1902. [697.]

37131. Tpr. Michie, John (Forneth). Enlisted 1901. Served in South African War, 1901–1902 (Queen's medal, with clasps "Transvaal," "South Africa, 1901," and "South Africa, 1902"). Discharged 1902.

37010. Tpr. Millar, George (Alyth). Enlisted 1901. Served in South African War, 1901–1902 (Queen's medal, with clasps "Cape Colony," "Transvaal," "South Africa, 1901," and "South Africa, 1902"). Discharged 1902. [698.]

33278. Corpl. Miller, Robert (Perth). Enlisted 1901. Served in South African War, 1901–1902 (Queen's medal, with clasps "Cape Colony," "Orange Free State," "Transvaal," "South Africa, 1901," and "South Africa, 1902"). Discharged 1902.

37115. Tpr. Mitchell, Alexander (Perth). Enlisted 1901. Served in South African War, 1901–1902 (Queen's medal, with clasps "Transvaal," "South Africa, 1901," and "South Africa, 1902"). Discharged 1902. [699.]

36975. Tpr. Mitchell, Robert (Perth). Enlisted 1902. Served in South African War, 1902 (Queen's medal, with clasps "Transvaal" and "South Africa, 1902"). Discharged 1902. [734.]

44662. Tpr. Moffat, Harry F. (Perth). Enlisted 1902 for service in South African War. Discharged 1902. [700.]

44753. Tpr. Moon, James (Port of Monteith). Enlisted 1902 for service in South African War. Discharged 1902. [732.]

25887. Corpl. Murison, John (Alyth). Enlisted 1901. Served in South African War, 1901–1902 (Queen's medal, with clasps "Transvaal," "South Africa, 1901," and "South Africa, 1902"). Discharged 1902. [652.]

37584. Tpr. Neville, Peter (Blackford). Enlisted 1902. Served in South African War, 1902 (Queen's medal, with clasps "Transvaal" and "South Africa, 1902"). Discharged 1902.

37080. Sergt. Paterson, Alex. M. (Abernethy). Enlisted 1901. Served in South African War, 1901–1902 (Queen's medal, with clasps "Cape Colony," "Transvaal," "South Africa, 1901," and "South Africa, 1902"). Discharged 1902.

37135. Tpr. Patton, Alexander (Scone). Enlisted 1901. Served in South African War, 1901–1902 (Queen's medal, with clasps "Transvaal," "South Africa, 1901," and "South Africa, 1902"). Discharged 1902. [706.]

31025. Tpr. Petrie, Robert (Port of Monteith). Enlisted 1901. Served in South African War, 1901–1902 (Queen's medal, with clasps "Cape Colony," "Orange Free State," "Transvaal," "South Africa, 1901," and "South Africa, 1902"). Discharged 1902.

37194. Tpr. Ramsay, David B. (Perth). Enlisted 1901. Served in South African War, 1901–1902 (Queen's medal, with clasps "Transvaal," "South Africa, 1901," and "South Africa, 1902"). Discharged 1902. [701.]

44670. Tpr. Ramsay, John (Perth). Enlisted 1902 for service in South African War. Transferred 1902 to Scottish Horse Squadron of Natal Mounted Police. [702.]

37591. Piper Rattray, Andrew (Pitlochry). Enlisted 1902. Served in South African War, 1902 (Queen's medal, with clasps "Transvaal" and "South Africa, 1902"). Transferred 1902 to Scottish Horse Squadron of Natal Mounted Police. [703.]

37213. Lance-Corpl. Reid, John M. (Coupar Angus). . . . Vol. Batt. The Black Watch. Enlisted in Scottish Horse 1901. Served in South African War, (1) as Lance-Corpl. with 1st Vol. Service Coy. The Black Watch, 1900–1901; (2) with Scottish Horse, 1901–1902 (Queen's medal, with clasps "Cape Colony," "Wittebergen," and "Transvaal"; King's medal, with clasps "South Africa, 1901," and "South Africa, 1902"). Discharged 1902. [739.]

37249. Tpr. Rennet, James (Perth). Enlisted 1901. Served in South African War, 1902 (Queen's medal, with clasps "Transvaal" and "South Africa, 1902"). Discharged 1902.

44699. Tpr. Robertson, Daniel A. (Blair Atholl). Enlisted 1902 for service in South African War. Discharged 1902. [704.]

25890. Tpr. Robertson, David (Alyth). Enlisted 1901. Served in South African War, 1901 (Queen's medal, with clasps "Cape Colony," "Orange Free State," "Transvaal," and "South Africa, 1901"). Discharged 1901. [707.]

31362. Tpr. Robertson, David C. (Blairgowrie). Enlisted 1901. Served in South African War, 1901–1902. Wounded at Bakenlaagte, Oct. 30, 1901 (Queen's medal, with clasps "Cape Colony," "Orange Free State," "Transvaal," "South Africa, 1901," and "South Africa, 1902"). Discharged 1902. Formerly in 4th Vol. Batt. The Black Watch. Now serving in Army Service Corps. [729.]

37012. Tpr. Robertson, Duncan (Cargill). Enlisted 1901. Served in South African War, 1901–1902 (Queen's medal, with clasps "Cape Colony," "Transvaal," "South Africa, 1901," and "South Africa, 1902"). Discharged 1902. [740.]

37284. Tpr. Robertson, George (Alyth). Enlisted 1901. Served in South African War, 1902 (Queen's medal, with clasps "Transvaal" and "South Africa, 1902"). Discharged 1902. [726.]

37572. Lance-Corpl. Robertson, Hugh (Monzievard). Enlisted 1901. Served in South African War, 1902 (Queen's medal, with clasps "Cape Colony," "Orange Free State," "Transvaal," and "South Africa, 1902"). Discharged 1902. [708.]

37588. Sadd.-Corpl. Robertson, James (Alyth). Enlisted 1901. Served in South African War, 1902 (Queen's medal, with clasps "Cape Colony," "Orange Free State," "Transvaal," and "South Africa, 1902"). Discharged 1902. [741.]

37021. Corpl. Robertson, John (Stanley). Enlisted 1901. Served in South African War, 1901–1902 (Queen's medal, with clasps "Cape Colony," "Transvaal," "South Africa, 1901," and "South Africa, 1902"). Transferred 1902 to Scottish Horse Squadron of Natal Mounted Police. [742.]

37271. Lance-Corpl. Robertson, John (Blair Atholl). Enlisted 1901. Served in South African War, 1902 (Queen's medal, with clasps "Transvaal" and "South Africa, 1902"). Transferred 1902 to Scottish Horse Squadron of Natal Mounted Police. [705.]

37587. Sh.-Smith Robertson, Robert (Bankfoot). Enlisted 1902. Served in South African War, 1902 (Queen's medal, with clasps "Transvaal" and "South Africa, 1902"). Discharged 1902.

51. Tpr. Ross, Thomas (Gask). Enlisted 1901. Served in South African War, 1901 (Queen's medal, with clasps "Transvaal" and "South Africa, 1901"). Discharged 1901. [730.]

31029. Tpr. Scott, Alex. M. (Rumbling Bridge). Enlisted 1901. Served in South African War, 1901–1902 (Queen's medal, with clasps "Cape Colony," "Orange Free State," "Transvaal," "South Africa, 1901," and "South Africa, 1902"). Discharged 1902. [719.]

37117. Tpr. Scrimgeour, John (Crieff). Enlisted 1901. Served in South African War, 1901–1902 (Queen's medal, with clasps "Transvaal," "South Africa, 1901," and "South Africa, 1902"). Discharged 1902. [709.]

37116. Tpr. Sim, Peter M. (Pitlochry). Enlisted 1901. Served in South African War, 1901–1902 (Queen's medal, with clasps "Transvaal," "South Africa, 1901," and "South Africa, 1902"). Discharged 1902. [710.]

37173. Piper Stevenson, William (Muthill). Enlisted 1901. Served in South African War, 1901–1902 (Queen's medal, with clasps "Cape Colony," "Orange Free State," "Transvaal,"

THE SCOTTISH HORSE—*continued*

"South Africa, 1901," and "South Africa, 1902"). Coronation medal 1902. Discharged 1902. [727.]

37461. Tpr. **Stewart, Charles** (Blairgowrie). Enlisted 1901. Served in South African War, 1902 (Queen's medal, with clasps "Transvaal" and "South Africa, 1902"). Discharged 1902. [711.]

37022. Tpr. **Stewart, David** (Huntingtower). Enlisted 1901. Served in South African War, 1901–1902 (Queen's medal, with clasps "Cape Colony," "Transvaal," "South Africa, 1901," and "South Africa, 1902"). Discharged 1902. [712.]

44674. Tpr. **Stewart, David H.** (Perth). Enlisted 1902 for service in South African War. Discharged 1902. [713.]

37118. Lance-Corpl. **Stewart, James** (St. Martins). Enlisted 1902. Served in South African War, 1902 (Queen's medal, with clasps "Transvaal" and "South Africa, 1902"). Discharged 1902.

37159. Tpr. **Stewart, James A.** (Ballinluig). Enlisted 1901. Served in South African War, 1902 (Queen's medal, with clasps "Transvaal," "South Africa, 1901," and "South Africa, 1902"). Discharged 1902. Enlisted in Scottish Horse (I.Y.) 1903. [714.]

859. Tpr. **Stewart, Robert D.** (Perth). Enlisted 1901. Served in South African War, 1901–1902 (Queen's medal, with clasps "Cape Colony," "Orange Free State," "Transvaal," "South Africa, 1901," and "South Africa, 1902"). Discharged 1902. [715.]

44706. Tpr. **Strong, Donald** (Thornhill). Joined 4th Vol. Batt. The Black Watch 1901. Enlisted in Scottish Horse 1902 for service in South African War. Transferred to Scottish Horse Squadron of Natal Mounted Police 1902. [716.]

25886. Sergt. **Thomson, Randolph** (Alyth). Enlisted 1901. Served in South African War, 1901–1902. Wounded at Moedwil, Sept. 30, 1901 (Queen's medal, with clasps "Transvaal," "South Africa, 1901," and "South Africa, 1902"). Discharged 1902. [733.]

36933. Tpr. **Wardrope, Robert** (Dunblane). Enlisted 1901. Served in South African War, 1901–1902 (Queen's medal, with clasps "Cape Colony," "Transvaal," "South Africa, 1901," and "South Africa, 1902"). Discharged 1902.

37125. Tpr. **Watt, Duncan** (Perth). Enlisted 1901. Served in South African War, 1901–1902 (Queen's medal, with clasps "Transvaal," "South Africa, 1901," and "South Africa, 1902"). Discharged 1902. [717.]

37024. Tpr. **Whyte, Robert** (Perth). Enlisted 1901. Served in South African War, 1901–1902 (Queen's medal, with clasps "Cape Colony," "Transvaal," "South Africa, 1901," and "South Africa, 1902"). Discharged 1902. [718.]

37152. Lance-Corpl. **Wilson, James** (Glenfarg). Enlisted 1901. Served in South African War, 1902 (Queen's medal, with clasps "Transvaal" and "South Africa, 1902"). Discharged 1902. [720.]

35741. Sergt. **Wilson, Peter** (Bankfoot). Enlisted 1901. Served in South African War, 1901–1902 (Queen's medal, with clasps "Cape Colony," "Orange Free State," "Transvaal," "South Africa, 1901," and "South Africa, 1902"). Died at Middelburg, Jan. 26, 1902. Formerly in 5th Vol. Batt. The Black Watch. [721.]

37025. Tpr. **Wilson, Wm.** (Perth). Enlisted 1901. Served in South African War, 1901 (Queen's medal, with clasps "Cape Colony," "Transvaal," and "South Africa, 1901"). Invalided home 1901. Discharged 1902.

37596. Tpr. **Wishart, Robert** (Crieff). Enlisted 1902. Served in South African War, 1902 (Queen's medal, with clasps "Transvaal" and "South Africa, 1902"). Discharged 1902. [722.]

44663. Tpr. **Yeaman, David** (Perth). Enlisted 1902 for service in South African War. Transferred 1902 to Scottish Horse Squadron of Natal Mounted Police. [723.]

872. Tpr. **Young, Robert** (Bankfoot). Enlisted 1901. Served in South African War, 1901–1902 (Queen's medal, with clasps "Cape Colony," "Orange Free State," "Transvaal," "South Africa, 1901," and "South Africa, 1902"). Discharged 1902. Formerly in 5th Vol. Batt. The Black Watch. [724.]

36880. Tpr. **Young, Robert** (Doune). Enlisted 1901. Served in South African War, 1901–1902 (Queen's medal, with clasps "Transvaal," "South Africa, 1901," and "South Africa, 1902"). Discharged 1902.

INDIAN AND COLONIAL VOLUNTEER AND IRREGULAR CORPS

ASHBURNER'S LIGHT HORSE

—— Tpr. **Robertson,** Duncan (Strathbraan). Formerly in 5th Vol. Batt. The Black Watch. Enlisted in Ashburner's Light Horse 1900. Served in South African War, 1900–1901 (Queen's medal, with clasps "South Africa, 1901"...). Discharged 1901. [779.]

BETHUNE'S MOUNTED INFANTRY

615. Tpr. **MacLeod,** Peter (Crieff). Enlisted 1899. Served in South African War, 1899–1900 (operations in Natal) (Queen's medal; clasps unknown). Discharged 1900. [743.]

—— Qrmr.-Sergt. **Raitt,** Alexander (Blairgowrie). Enlisted 1899. Served in South African War, 1899–1902 (operations in Natal, &c.) (Queen's medal with clasps...; King's medal, with clasps "South Africa, 1901," and "South Africa, 1902"). Discharged 1902. [744.]

CANADIAN MOUNTED RIFLES

276. Corpl. **Robertson,** Alistair Irvine (Blair Atholl). Enlisted 1900. Served in South African War, 1900 (Queen's medal, with clasps "Cape Colony," "Orange Free State," "Johannesburg," and "Diamond Hill"). Discharged 1901. [775.]

CAPE GARRISON ARTILLERY

—— Bomb. **Drury,** James (Perth). Enlisted 1900. Served in South African War, 1900–1902; two years on No. 1 Armoured Train (Queen's medal, with clasps "Cape Colony," "Orange Free State," and "Transvaal"; King's medal, with clasps "South Africa, 1901," and "South Africa, 1902"). [776.]

CAPE PIONEER REGIMENT

—— Sergt. **Anderson,** Alexander (Crieff). Enlisted in Cape Pioneer Regt. 1900. Served in South African War, (1) with Natal Vols., 1899–1900; (2) with Cape Pioneer Regt., 1900–1902 (Queen's medal, with clasps "Relief of Ladysmith" and "Transvaal"; King's medal, with clasps "South Africa, 1901," and "South Africa, 1902"). Discharged 1902.

CAPE RAILWAY SHARPSHOOTERS

1521. Pte. **Whitton,** James (Blairgowrie). Enlisted 1902. Served in South African War, 1902 (Queen's medal, with clasps "Cape Colony" and "South Africa, 1902"). Discharged on disbandment of corps. [777.]

CAPE TOWN HIGHLANDERS

1260. Pte. **Davidson,** William T. (Perth). Enlisted in Cape Town Highlanders 1900. Served in South African War, 1900–1902, latterly with Intelligence Dept. (Queen's medal, with clasps "Cape Colony," "South Africa, 1901," and "South Africa, 1902"). Discharged 1903. Formerly Corpl. in 1st. Vol. Batt. The Cameronians (Scottish Rifles). [778.]

CEYLON MOUNTED INFANTRY

350. Sergt. Hay, Henry M. Drummond (Seggieden). Enlisted 1900. Served in South African War, 1900–1901 (Queen's medal, with clasps "Cape Colony," "Orange Free State," "Johannesburg," "Diamond Hill," and "South Africa, 1901"). Discharged 1901. [780.]

COLONIAL SCOUTS

—— Tpr. Smith, Wm. Ramsay (Caputh). Enlisted 1899. Served in South African War, 1899–1900 (Queen's medal, with clasp "Natal"). Discharged 1900. [745.]

COMMANDER-IN-CHIEF'S BODYGUARD

—— Tpr. Marshall, Andrew M. (Perth). Enlisted in Rhodesian Vols. 1899. Discharged 1900. Enlisted in C.-in-C.'s Bodyguard 1900. Served in South African War, (1) with Rhodesian Vols., 1899–1900; (2) with C.-in-C.'s Bodyguard, 1900–1901 (Queen's medal, with clasps "South Africa, 1901" . . .). Discharged 1901. [746.]

DIAMOND FIELDS HORSE

—— Tpr. Ferguson, Fergus (Coupar Angus). Enlisted 1899. Served in South African War, 1899–1900. Wounded at Kimberley, Nov. 28, 1899, and at Bloemfontein, 1900 (Queen's medal, with clasps "Defence of Kimberley," "Relief of Mafeking," and "Orange Free State"). [747.]

DUKE OF EDINBURGH'S OWN VOLUNTEER RIFLES

—— Sergt. McDiarmid, Donald (Callander). Enlisted 1899. Served in South African War, 1899–1901, (1) as Tpr. in Duke of Edinburgh's Own Vol. Rifles; (2) as Sergt. at depôt of South African Mounted Irregular Forces (Queen's medal, with clasps "Cape Colony" and "South Africa, 1901"). Discharged 1901. [764.]

DURBAN LIGHT INFANTRY

—— Sergt. Rollo, Alexander (Blairgowrie). Enlisted 1899. Served in South African War, 1899–1902. Wounded at Chieveley (Queen's medal with clasps . . . ; King's medal, with clasps "South Africa, 1901," and "South Africa, 1902"). Discharged 1902.

EASTERN PROVINCE HORSE

—— Tpr. Dewar, Charles L. (Kirkmichael). Enlisted 1900. Served in South African War, 1900. Wounded near Heilbron, May 27, 1900 (Queen's medal, with clasp "Cape Colony"). [788.]

IMPERIAL LIGHT HORSE

—— Tpr. Coltart, Charles (Perth). Enlisted in Brabant's Horse 1900. Served in South African War, 1900–1902, (1) with Brabant's Horse, and (2) with Imperial Light Horse (Queen's medal, with clasps . . . ; King's medal, with clasps "South Africa, 1901," and "South Africa, 1902"). Died in South Africa, July 12, 1902. [755.]

—— Tpr. McFarlane, Robert (Crieff). Enlisted 1901. Served in South African War, 1901-1902 (Queen's medal, with clasps " South Africa, 1901," and " South Africa, 1902 "). Discharged 1902.

—— Tpr. Raitt, Robert M. (Blairgowrie). Enlisted 1899. Served in South African War, 1899-1900 (Queen's medal, with clasps "Elands-laagte," " Defence of Ladysmith," and " Relief of Mafeking "). [754.]

1436. Tpr. Whyte, William (Alyth). Enlisted 1902. Served in South African War, 1902 (Queen's medal, with clasps " Orange Free State," " Transvaal," and " South Africa, 1902 "). Discharged 1902. [756.]

IMPERIAL LIGHT INFANTRY

697. Pte. Beat, David (Perth). Enlisted 1899. Served in South African War, 1899-1901 (Queen's medal, with clasps " Tugela Heights," " Relief of Ladysmith," " Laing's Nek," " Transvaal," and " South Africa, 1901 "). Discharged 1901. [791.]

—— Pte. Fleming, William R. (Blacklunans). Enlisted 1899. Served in South African War, 1899-1900 (Queen's medal, with clasps "Tugela Heights," " Relief of Ladysmith," " Laing's Nek," and " Transvaal "). [792.]

—— Pte. Kerrigan, Patrick (Perth). Enlisted 1899. Served in South African War, 1899-1900 (Queen's medal, with clasps " Tugela Heights," " Relief of Ladysmith," and " Laing's Nek "). [793.]

935. Pte. Mackenzie, James B. (Blairgowrie). Enlisted 1899. Served in South African War, 1899-1900 (Queen's medal, with clasps " Tugela Heights " and " Relief of Ladysmith "). [790.]

INDIAN AMBULANCE CORPS

—— Meldrum, Charles G. (Logierait). Served in South African War, 1899-1900, as civilian in charge of portion of Indian Ambulance Corps (Queen's medal, with clasps " Tugela Heights " and " Relief of Ladysmith "). [857.]

JOHANNESBURG MOUNTED RIFLES

—— Sergt. Beaton, Alexander (Killin). Enlisted 1901. Served in South African War, 1901 (Queen's medal, with clasps " South Africa, 1901 " . . .). Transferred to Johannesburg Mounted Police 1901.

729. Tpr. Henderson, John (Blairgowrie). Enlisted 1901. Served in South African War, 1901-1902 (Queen's medal, with clasps " South Africa, 1901," and " South Africa, 1902 "). Discharged 1902. [794.]

KIMBERLEY MOUNTED CORPS

—— Tpr. Scott, Joseph (Auchterarder). Enlisted in Kimberley Light Horse 1899, and in Kimberley Mtd. Corps 1900. Served in South African War, (1) with Kimberley Light Horse, 1899-1900; (2) with Kimberley Mtd. Corps, 1900 (Queen's medal, with clasps " Defence of Kimberley " and " Relief of Mafeking "). Killed at Potchefstroom, July 22, 1900. [757.]

KIMBERLEY RIFLES

—— Pte. Young, David (Tulliallan). Enlisted in Royal Navy 1888. Discharged 1897. Served with Kimberley Rifles in South African War (Queen's medal, with clasps . . .).

KITCHENER'S FIGHTING SCOUTS

—— Sergt. Doig, Robert (Caputh). Formerly in 5th Vol. Batt. The Black Watch. Enlisted in Durban Light Infy. 1899. Transferred to Kitchener's Fighting Scouts 1900. Served in South African War, (1) with Durban Light Infy., 1899–1900, and (2) with Kitchener's Fighting Scouts, 1900–1902 (Queen's medal, with three clasps; King's medal, with clasps "South Africa, 1901," and "South Africa, 1902"). Discharged 1902. [749.]

—— Sergt. Porteous, Peter (Blackford). Enlisted 1900. Served in South African War, 1900–1901 (Queen's medal, with clasps "Cape Colony," "Orange Free State," "Transvaal," and "South Africa, 1901"). Discharged 1901. [750.]

1889. Tpr. Reid, John (Alyth). Enlisted 1902. Served in South African War, 1902 (Queen's medal, with clasp "South Africa, 1902"). Discharged 1902. [751.]

KITCHENER'S HORSE

—— Tpr. Burnfield, William (Kinclaven). Enlisted 1900. Served in South African War, 1900–1901 (Queen's medal, with clasps "South Africa, 1901" . . .). Discharged 1901.

—— Sergt. Douglas, Peter Craigie (Bankfoot). Served in South African War, (1) with the Duke of Edinburgh's Own Volunteer Rifles, 1899–1900; (2) with Kitchener's Horse, 1900–1902 (Queen's medal, with clasps "Cape Colony," "Paardeberg," and "Driefontein"; King's medal, with clasps "South Africa, 1901," and "South Africa, 1902"). Discharged 1902. [781.]

—— Tpr. Neish, George J. (St. Fillans). Enlisted 1900. Served in South African War, 1900 (Queen's medal, with clasps "Cape Colony" and "Transvaal"). Died of wounds at Johannesburg, Dec. 17, 1900. [782.]

LUMSDEN'S HORSE

—— Tpr. Murdoch, James A. H, Burn- (Gartincaber). Enlisted 1900. Served in South African War, 1900. Wounded at Thabanchu (Queen's medal, with clasps "Cape Colony" and "Orange Free State"). Discharged invalided 1901. Formerly in Indian Vol. Cavalry. [748.]

MARSHALL'S HORSE

—— Corpl. Baptie, Robert (Ochtertyre). Enlisted 1899. Served in South African War, 1899–1900 (Queen's medal, with clasps "Relief of Kimberley" and "Paardeberg"). Died at Bloemfontein, June 28, 1900. Formerly in 4th Vol. Batt. The Black Watch, and 3rd Vol. Batt. The Cameronians (Scottish Rifles). [786.]

—— Tpr. Cromb, James (Coupar Angus). Enlisted 1899. Served in South African War, 1899–1900 (Queen's medal, with clasp "Relief of Kimberley" . . .). [785.]

MENNIE'S SCOUTS

1198. Tpr. Littlejohn, Thos. (Perth). Enlisted 1900. Served in South African War, 1900–1902, (1) with Imperial Light Infy.; (2) with Mennie's Scouts (Queen's medal, with clasps . . .; King's medal, with clasps "South Africa, 1901," and "South Africa, 1902"). [752.]

NATAL CARBINEERS

—— Corpl. Comrie, Peter (Dunblane). Enlisted in Richmond Mtd. Rifles 1871. Served in Langalitabelo Expedition. Discharged on disbandment of corps. Subsequently enlisted in Natal Carbineers. Served in Zulu War, 1878–1879 (South African medal, with clasp). Discharged 1879. Re-enlisted 1882, and promoted Lieut. Resigned 1889. Re-enlisted 1899. Served in South African War, 1899–1900 (Queen's medal, with clasp "Defence of Ladysmith"). Killed at Scheeper's Nek, May 20, 1900. [765.]

154. Tpr. Greig, James Elliot (Perth). Enlisted 1896. Served in South African War, 1899–1900. Wounded at Ladysmith (Queen's medal, with clasps "Defence of Ladysmith" "Laing's Nek" . . .). [767.]

—— Tpr. Smythe, David W. (Methven). Enlisted 1896. Served in South African War, 1899–1902 (Queen's medal, with clasps "Defence of Ladysmith," "Laing's Nek," and "Transvaal"; King's medal, with clasps "South Africa, 1901," and "South Africa, 1902"). Still serving. [766.]

NATAL VOLUNTEER ARTILLERY

—— Gr. Kinloch, Archibald D. (Gourdie). Hotchkiss Detachment. Enlisted 1899. Served in South African War, 1899–1900 (Queen's medal, with clasp "Defence of Ladysmith"). Killed on Wagon Hill, January 6, 1900. [753.]

NEW ENGLAND MOUNTED RIFLES

—— Corpl. Proctor, George S. (Blairgowrie). Enlisted 1901. Served in South African War, 1901–1902 (Queen's medal, with clasps "Cape Colony," "South Africa, 1901," and "South Africa, 1902"). Discharged 1902. Died February 4, 1903. [799.]

NEW SOUTH WALES MOUNTED RIFLES

—— Sergt. Keay, William J. (Glenshee). Enlisted 1900. Served in South African War, 1900–1901 (Queen's medal, with clasp "South Africa, 1901"). Discharged 1901. [797.]

—— Sergt. Macdonald, David (Perth). Enlisted in 2nd Contingent N.S.W. Mtd. Rifles 1901. Served in South African War, 1901–1902 (Queen's medal, with clasps "Transvaal," "South Africa, 1901," "South Africa, 1902" . . .). Discharged 1902. [798.]

NEW ZEALAND MOUNTED INFANTRY

—— Tpr. Barty, John H. (Lethendy). Enlisted in 1st Contingent New Zealand Mtd. Infy. 1899. Served in South African War, 1899–1900 (Queen's medal, with clasps "Relief of Kimberley" . . .). Discharged 1900. [760.]

—— Tpr. Henderson, James (Perth). Served in South African War with 3rd Contingent New Zealand Mtd. Infy., 1899–1900 (Queen's medal, with two clasps). [761.]

NEW ZEALAND ROUGH RIDERS

—— Tpr. McDonald, Peter (Strathbraan). Enlisted 1900. Served in South African War, 1900–1901 (Queen's medal, with clasps "South Africa, 1901" . . .). Discharged 1901. [783.]

—— Tpr. Murdoch, Archibald A. U. Burn- (Gartincaber). Enlisted in 3rd Contingent New Zealand Rough Riders 1900. Served in South African War, 1900–1902 (Queen's medal, with clasps "Cape Colony," "Orange Free State," and "Transvaal"; King's medal, with clasps "South Africa, 1901," and "South Africa, 1902"). Discharged 1902. [784.]

PRINCE ALFRED'S VOLUNTEER GUARD

1634. Tpr. Shepherd, Wm. A. (Alyth). Enlisted 1901. Served in South African War, 1901–1902 (Queen's medal, with clasps "Cape Colony," "South Africa, 1901," and "South Africa, 1902"). Discharged 1902. [802.]

PRINCE OF WALES'S LIGHT HORSE

20392. Tpr. Hinshelwood, James (Perth). Enlisted 1900. Served in South African War, 1900–1901 (Queen's medal, with clasps "Cape Colony," "South Africa, 1901" . . .). Discharged 1901. [800.]

20390. Tpr. Hinshelwood, Thomas (Perth). Enlisted 1900. Served in South African War, 1900–1901. Wounded at Hamelsfontein, Feb. 12, 1901 (Queen's medal, with clasps "Cape Colony" and "South Africa, 1901"). Invalided home 1901. [801.]

ROBERTS' HORSE

—— Tpr. Boyd, Alfred (Perth). Served with Transport Dept. in Matabele Rising, 1896–1897 (Matabele medal). Served also in South African War with Roberts' Horse, 1900–1901 (Queen's medal, with clasps "Relief of Kimberley," "Johannesburg," "Diamond Hill," "Wittebergen," and "South Africa, 1901"). Discharged 1901. [787.]

SCOTT'S RAILWAY GUARDS

—— Pte. Skinner, James (Moulin). Served in South African War, (1) with 1st Vol. Service Coy. The Black Watch, 1900–1901; (2) with Scott's Railway Guards (Queen's medal, with clasps "Cape Colony," "Wittebergen," "South Africa, 1901" . . .). Formerly in 5th Vol. Batt. The Black Watch. [758.]

SOUTH AFRICAN LIGHT HORSE

—— Tpr. Thomson, William (Scone). Served in Bechuanaland Campaign, 1897, with Prince Alfred's Vol. Guard; was on survey duty with B. S. A. Police, 1897–1900. Served in South African War, 1901–1902, (1) as Corpl. in Railway Pioneer Regt.; (2) with Scouts of South African Light Horse (Queen's medal, with clasps "South Africa, 1901," "South Africa, 1902" . . .). Now serving in B. S. A. Police. [759.]

STEINAECKER'S HORSE

—— Sq.-Sergt.-Major McGregor, Robert (Blair Drummond). Served in Matabele Risings 1893 and 1896 (Matabele medal, with clasp "Rhodesia, 1896"). Enlisted in Thorneycroft's Mtd. Infy. 1899, and in Steinaecker's Horse 1901. Served in South African War, (1) with Thorneycroft's Mtd. Infy., 1899–1901; and (2) with Steinaecker's Horse, 1901–1902 (Queen's medal, with clasps "Tugela Heights," "Relief of Ladysmith," "Laing's Nek," "Transvaal," "Orange Free State," and "Cape Colony"; King's medal, with clasps "South Africa, 1901," and "South Africa, 1902." Twice mentioned in despatches). Coronation medal 1902. Discharged 1903. [795.]

—— Qrmr.-Sergt. Rattray, Charles (Dunning). Enlisted in C.-in-C.'s Bodyguard 1900, in Scottish Horse 1901, and in Steinaecker's Horse 1902. Served in South African War, (1) with C.-in-C.'s Bodyguard, 1900–1901; (2) with Scottish Horse as Qrmr.-Sergt. 1901–1902; and (3) with Steinaecker's Horse 1902. Wounded 1902 (Queen's medal, with clasps "Cape Colony" and "Transvaal"; King's medal, with clasps "South Africa, 1901," and "South Africa, 1902"). Discharged 1902. [p. 127.]

STRATHCONA'S HORSE

—— Tpr. **Playfair,** William Shaw (Coupar Angus). Enlisted 1900. Served in South African War, 1900–1901. Wounded at Bethulie, Dec. 3, 1900 (Queen's medal, with clasps "Natal," "Orange Free State," "Belfast," and "South Africa, 1901"). Discharged 1901. [768.]

THORNEYCROFT'S MOUNTED INFANTRY

—— Tpr. **Anderson,** Bruce (Muckart). Enlisted 1900. Served in South African War, 1900–1902 (Queen's medal, with clasps "Laing's Nek" . . . ; King's medal, with clasps "South Africa, 1901," and "South Africa, 1902"). Discharged 1902. [772.]

—— Tpr. **Anderson,** James C. L. (Muckart). Enlisted 1899. Served in South African War, 1899–1902. Latterly with Intelligence Dept. (Queen's medal, with clasps "Tugela Heights," "Relief of Ladysmith," "Laing's Nek" . . . ; King's medal, with clasps "South Africa, 1901," and "South Africa, 1902"). Discharged 1902. [771.]

—— Tpr. **Kerrigan,** Hugh (Perth). Enlisted 1899. Served in South African War, 1899–1900 . . . (Queen's medal, with clasps "Tugela Heights," "Relief of Ladysmith," "Laing's Nek," "Transvaal," "Orange Free State" . . .). [773.]

—— Tpr. **MacGregor,** Hamish Sheriff (Trossachs). Enlisted 1899. Served in South African War, 1899–1900 (Queen's medal, with clasp "Tugela Heights"). Killed at Spion Kop, Jan. 24, 1900. [769.]

—— Tpr. **Rattray,** Laurence C. (Blairgowrie). Enlisted 1900. Served in South African War, 1900 (Queen's medal, with clasp "Relief of Ladysmith"). Invalided 1900. [770.]

8914. Sergt. **Stirling,** Benjamin T. (Dunblane). Enlisted 1899. Served in South African War, 1899–1902 (Queen's medal, with clasps "Tugela Heights," "Relief of Ladysmith," "Laing's Nek," "Transvaal," "Orange Free State," and "Cape Colony"; King's medal, with clasps "South Africa, 1901," and "South Africa, 1902"). Discharged 1902. [774.]

VOLUNTEER AMBULANCE CORPS

—— Pte. **Hay,** James (Perth). Enlisted 1899. Served in South African War, 1899–1900 (Queen's medal, with clasps "Cape Colony," "Orange Free State," and "Transvaal"). Discharged 1900. [789.]

WESTERN PROVINCE MOUNTED RIFLES

793. Tpr. **Lowe,** George S. (Alyth). Enlisted 1901. Served in South African War, 1901–1902 (Queen's medal, with clasp "South Africa, 1901," "South Africa, 1902" . , ,). Discharged 1902. [796.]

TOWN GUARDS

KIMBERLEY TOWN GUARD

—— Pte. **McDonald,** Donald (Strathbraan). Enlisted 1899. Served in South African War, 1899–1900 (Queen's medal, with clasp "Defence of Kimberley"; Mayor of Kimberley's siege medal). Formerly in 5th Vol. Batt. The Black Watch. [803.]

—— Staff-Sergt. **Robertson,** James (Strathbraan). Enlisted 1899. Served in South African War, 1899–1900 (Queen's medal, with clasp "Defence of Kimberley"; Mayor of Kimberley's siege medal). [804.]

PORT ELIZABETH TOWN GUARD

—— Pte. Mitchell, James J. (Alyth). Enlisted 1901. Served in South African War, 1901–1902 (Queen's medal, with clasps " Cape Colony," " South Africa, 1901," and " South Africa, 1902 "). Discharged 1902. Died in West Africa, Oct. 1903. [805.]

CONSTABULARY AND POLICE

BRITISH SOUTH AFRICA POLICE

2598. Corpl. Carmichael, Robert (St. Fillans). Enlisted in The Black Watch 1882. Served in Soudan Campaign, 1884, and with Nile Expedition, 1884–1885 (medal, with clasps " El Teb," " The Nile, 1884–5," and " Kirbekan "; Khedive's star). Discharged as Sergt. 1894. Enlisted in Kitchener's Fighting Scouts 1901. Transferred to B. S. A. Police 1901. Served in South African War, (1) with Kitchener's Fighting Scouts, 1901, and (2) with B. S. A. Police 1901–1902 (Queen's medal, with clasps " Cape Colony," " Orange Free State," " Transvaal," " Rhodesia," " South Africa, 1901," and " South Africa, 1902 "). Discharged 1902. [762.]

590. Trp. Sergt.-Major McFarlane, Donald (Amulree). Enlisted 1897. Served in Mashonaland Rebellion 1897 (Matabele medal); also in South African War, 1899–1901 (Queen's medal, with clasps " Relief of Mafeking," " Rhodesia," and " South Africa, 1901 "). Discharged 1903. [763.]

CAPE POLICE

653. Tpr. Johnston, John Buist (Longforgan). Enlisted in Brabant's Horse 1900. Promoted Corpl. Transferred to Western Province Mtd. Rifles (promoted Sergt.), and on disbandment joined Cape Police. Served in South African War, 1900–1902, (1) in Brabant's Horse; (2) in Western Province Mtd. Rifles; (3) in Cape Police (Queen's medal; with clasps . . . ; King's medal, with clasps " South Africa, 1901," and " South Africa, 1902 "). Still serving. [806.]

SOUTH AFRICAN CONSTABULARY

—— Tpr. Aitken, William (Coupar Angus). Enlisted 1901. Served in South African War, 1901–1902 (Queen's medal, with clasps " Cape Colony," " Orange Free State," " South Africa, 1901," and " South Africa, 1902 "). Still serving.

2356. Tpr. Allan, David (Perth). E Divn. S.A.C. Enlisted 1901. Served in South African War, 1901–1902 (Queen's medal, with clasps " Orange Free State," " South Africa, 1901," " South Africa, 1902 " . . .). Still serving. [828.]

—— Tpr. Allan, James (Dunkeld). Enlisted 1901. Served in South African War, 1901 (Queen's medal, with clasps " Transvaal," " South Africa, 1901 " . . .). Invalided home 1901. Formerly in 5th Vol. Batt. The Black Watch. [829.]

—— 1st Cl. Tpr. Anderson, Alexander (Dunkeld). Enlisted 1901. Served in South African War, 1901–1902 (Queen's medal, with clasps " Orange Free State," " South Africa, 1901," " South Africa, 1902 " . . .). Formerly in 5th Vol. Batt. The Black Watch. [807.]

2519. 2nd Cl. Sergt. Anderson, Alex. Menzies (Auchterarder). Hospital Staff, E Divn. S.A.C. Enlisted 1901. Served in South African War, 1901–1902 (Queen's medal, with clasps " Cape Colony," " Orange Free State," " South Africa, 1901," and " South Africa, 1902 "). Still serving. Formerly in 5th Vol. Batt. The Black Watch. [808.]

—— Tpr. Anderson, Thomas (Scone). Enlisted 1901. Served in South African War, 1901–1902 (Queen's medal, with clasps " Cape Colony," " Orange Free State," " Transvaal," " South Africa, 1901 " and " South Africa, 1902 "). Still serving. [809.]

—— Corpl. Balfour, Jas. Haxton (Kinclaven). Enlisted 1901. Served in South African War, 1901–1902 (Queen's medal, with clasps "South Africa, 1901," "South Africa, 1902" . . .). Still serving. [810.]

—— Tpr. Ballingall, William (Blairgowrie). Enlisted in Cape Mtd. Rifles 1897. Discharged 1898. Enlisted in S.A.C. 1900. Served in South African War, 1900 (Queen's medal, with clasps "Orange Free State" . . .). Killed at Staydon's Dam, near Bloemfontein, Nov. 16, 1900. [847.]

—— Tpr. Beaton, Neil (Killin). Enlisted 1901. Served in South African War, 1901–1902 (Queen's medal, with clasps "South Africa, 1901," "South Africa, 1902" . . .). Still serving.

—— Tpr. Boyd, Peter (Scone). Enlisted 1901. Served in South African War, 1901–1902 (Queen's medal, with clasps "Cape Colony," "Orange Free State," "South Africa, 1901," and "South Africa, 1902"). Still serving. [845.]

3054. 3rd Cl. Tpr. Buist, James (Kinnoull). E Divn. S.A.C. Enlisted 1901. Served in South African War, 1901–1902 (Queen's medal, with clasps "Cape Colony," "Orange Free State," "South Africa, 1901," and "South Africa, 1902"). Discharged 1903.

—— Tpr. Cameron, Alexander (Auchterarder). Enlisted 1901. Served in South African War, 1901–1902 (Queen's medal, with clasps "South Africa, 1901," "South Africa, 1902" . . .). Still serving. [811.]

1044. 1st Cl. Tpr. Cameron, Donald (Kinloch Rannoch). C Divn. S.A.C. Enlisted 1901. Served in South African War, 1901–1902 (Queen's medal, with clasps "Cape Colony," "Orange Free State," "Transvaal," "South Africa, 1901," and "South Africa, 1902"). Still serving. [812.]

—— Tpr. Cameron, James (Auchterarder). Enlisted 1901. Served in South African War, 1901–1902 (Queen's medal, with clasps "Transvaal," "South Africa, 1901," "South Africa, 1902" . . .). Discharged 1902. [813.]

3638. 2nd Cl. Tpr. Campbell, John (Kirkmichael). E Divn. S.A.C. Enlisted 1901. Served in South African War, 1901–1902 (Queen's medal, with clasps "Cape Colony," "Orange Free State," "South Africa, 1901," and "South Africa, 1902"). Still serving. [814.]

II.

2750. 3rd Cl. Tpr. Campbell, Robert (Kirkmichael). E Divn. S.A.C. Served in South African War, 1901–1902 (Queen's medal, with clasps "Cape Colony," "Orange Free State," "South Africa, 1901," and "South Africa, 1902"). Still serving. [815.]

—— 1st Cl. Tpr. Comrie, John (Crieff). Served in South African War, 1901–1902 (Queen's medal, with clasps "Transvaal," "South Africa, 1901," "South Africa, 1902" . . .). Still serving. [816.]

1982. Tpr. Cumming, Alexander J. (Perth). Enlisted 1901. Served in South African War, 1901–1902 (Queen's medal, with clasps "Transvaal," "South Africa, 1901," "South Africa, 1902" . . .). Still serving. [846.]

1001. 2nd Cl. Sergt. Davidson, Peter (Perth). B Divn. S.A.C. Enlisted 1901. Served in South African War, 1901–1902 (Queen's medal, with clasps "Cape Colony," "Orange Free State," "Transvaal," "South Africa, 1901," and "South Africa, 1902"). Still serving. Formerly in 1st Forfar Vol. Artillery. [817.]

3102. 1st Cl. Tpr. Doig, David (Alyth). E Divn. S.A.C. Enlisted 1901. Served in South African War, 1901–1902 (Queen's medal, with clasps "Cape Colony," "Orange Free State," "South Africa, 1901," and "South Africa, 1902"). Still serving. Formerly in 1st Vol. Batt. The Black Watch. [830.]

1030. 3rd Cl. Tpr. Douglas, Daniel (Kindallachan). B Divn. S.A.C. Enlisted 1901. Served in South African War, 1901–1902 (Queen's medal, with clasps "Cape Colony," "Orange Free State," "Transvaal," "South Africa, 1901," and "South Africa, 1902"). Still serving.

—— Tpr. Drury, Henry (Perth). Enlisted 1901. Served in South African War, 1901–1902 (Queen's medal, with clasps "Transvaal," "South Africa, 1901," "South Africa, 1902" . . .). Died at Potchefstroom, Feb. 26, 1902. [818.]

923. 3rd Cl. Tpr. Dunn, William (Kenmore). C Divn. S.A.C. Enlisted 1901. Served in South African War, 1901–1902 (Queen's medal, with clasps "Cape Colony," "Orange Free State," "Transvaal," "South Africa, 1901," and "South Africa, 1902"). Discharged 1902. Now in [Transvaal] Scottish Horse [Volunteers].

1644. 3rd Cl. Tpr. Edmondston, Arthur Biot

T

SOUTH AFRICAN CONSTABULARY—*continued*

(Blair Drummond). A Divn. S.A.C. Enlisted 1901. Served in South African War, 1901–1902 (Queen's medal, with clasps "Cape Colony," "Orange Free State," "Transvaal," "South Africa, 1901," and "South Africa, 1902"). Still serving. [852.]

—— Sergt. Ewing, Wm. Leckie (Kippen). Enlisted 1901. Served in South African War, 1901 (Queen's medal, with clasps "Transvaal" "South Africa, 1901" . . .). Discharged invalided 1901. [831.]

1129. Lance-Corpl. Foote, Alfred D. E. (Stanley). B Divn. S.A.C. Enlisted 1901. Served in South African War, 1901–1902 (Queen's medal, with clasps "Cape Colony," "Orange Free State," "Transvaal," "South Africa, 1901," and "South Africa, 1902"). Transferred to S.A.C. Reserve 1902. Discharged 1903. Formerly in Scots Greys. [819.]

—— Tpr. Gardiner, Jas. R. (Perth). Enlisted 1901. Served in South African War, 1901–1902 (Queen's medal, with clasps "Transvaal," "South Africa, 1901," "South Africa, 1902" . . .). Discharged 1902. [848.]

—— Tpr. Gellatly, John (Scone). Enlisted 1901. Served in South African War, 1901–1902 (Queen's medal, with clasps "Orange Free State," "Transvaal," "South Africa, 1901," "South Africa, 1902" . . .) Discharged 1902.

—— Tpr. Glass, Andrew (Scone). Enlisted 1901. Served in South African War, 1901–1902 (Queen's medal, with clasps "Cape Colony," "Orange Free State," "South Africa, 1901," and "South Africa, 1902"). Still serving. [820.]

—— Tpr. Gorrie, James (Crieff). Enlisted 1901. Served in South African War (Queen's medal, with clasp "South Africa, 1902" . . .). Still serving.

309. 1st Cl. Tpr. Hood, James (Alyth). C Divn. S.A.C. Enlisted 1901. Served in South African War, 1901–1902 (Queen's medal, with clasps "Cape Colony," "Orange Free State," "Transvaal," "South Africa, 1901," and "South Africa, 1902"). Discharged 1903. [821.]

—— Corpl. Hutchison, Thomas (Scone). Enlisted 1901. Served in South African War, 1901–1902 (Queen's medal, with clasps "Cape Colony," "Orange Free State," "Transvaal,"

"South Africa, 1901," and "South Africa, 1902"). Still serving. [822.]

1784. 3rd Cl. Tpr. Hynd, Isaac (Perth). E Divn. S.A.C. Enlisted 1901. Served in South African War, 1901–1902 (Queen's medal, with clasps "Cape Colony," "Orange Free State," "South Africa, 1901," and "South Africa, 1902"). Still serving. [833.]

573. 2nd Cl. Tpr. Johnston, Alex. Chalmers (Longforgan). C Divn. S.A.C. Enlisted 1901. Served in South African War, 1901–1902 (Queen's medal, with clasps "Cape Colony," "Orange Free State," "Transvaal," "South Africa, 1901," and "South Africa, 1902"). Still serving. Formerly in 1st Vol. Batt. The Black Watch. [823.]

—— Tpr. Lamond, George (St. Martin's). Enlisted 1901. Served in South African War, 1901–1902 (Queen's medal, with clasps "Cape Colony," "Orange Free State," "Transvaal," "South Africa, 1901," and "South Africa, 1902"). Still serving. [849.]

—— 3rd Cl. Tpr. Laurie, James (Dunblane). Enlisted 1901. Served in South African War, 1901–1902 (Queen's medal, with clasps "South Africa, 1901," "South Africa, 1902" . . .). [851.]

1800. 3rd Cl. Tpr. Lennox, William (Dunblane). E Divn. S.A.C. Enlisted 1901. Served in South African War, 1901 (Queen's medal, with clasps "Cape Colony," "Orange Free State," and "South Africa, 1901"). Killed at Vlakfontein, September 19, 1901. [850.]

—— Tpr. Low, Robt. Kennedy (Alyth). A Divn. S.A.C. Enlisted 1901. Served in South African War, . . . 1902 (Queen's medal, with clasps "South Africa, 1902" . . .). Still serving. [824.]

1281. 3rd Cl. Tpr. McDonald, John (Alyth). C Divn. S.A.C. Served in South African War, 1901–1902 (Queen's medal, with clasps "Cape Colony," "Orange Free State," "Transvaal," "South Africa, 1901," and "South Africa, 1902"). Discharged 1903. [825.]

1064. 3rd Cl. Tpr. McGregor, David Black (Scone). C Divn. S.A.C. Enlisted 1901. Served in South African War, 1901–1902 (Queen's medal, with clasps "Cape Colony," "Orange Free State," "Transvaal," "South Africa,

1901," and " South Africa, 1902 "). Still serving. [853.]

639. 1st Cl. **Tpr. McGregor, William** (Pitlochry). Formerly in 5th Vol. Batt. The Black Watch. Volunteered for active service 1900. Enlisted in C Divn. S.A.C. 1901. Served in South African War, 1901-1902 (Queen's medal, with clasps " Cape Colony," " Orange Free State," " Transvaal," " South Africa, 1901," and " South Africa, 1902 "). Discharged 1902. Enlisted in Scottish Horse (Imperial Yeomanry) 1903. [855.]

—— **Tpr. McIntosh, Thos.** Brew (Alyth). Enlisted 1901. Served in South African War, 1901-1902 (Queen's medal, with clasps " Transvaal," " South Africa, 1901," " South Africa, 1902 " . . .). Still serving. [826.]

—— **Corpl. McKillop, Dugald** (Killin). Formerly in 5th Vol. Batt. The Black Watch. Enlisted in S.A.C. 1901. Served in South African War, (1) with 1st Vol. Service Coy. The Black Watch, 1900–1901 (wounded at Reteif's Nek, July 1900, and invalided home) ; (2) as Corpl. in S.A.C., 1901-1902 (Queen's medal, with clasps " Cape Colony," " Wittebergen," " South Africa, 1901," and " South Africa, 1902 "). Still serving. [827.]

—— **Tpr. McLaggan, David Innes** (Perth). Enlisted 1901. Served in South African War, 1901-1902 (Queen's medal, with clasps " Cape Colony," " Orange Free State," " Transvaal," " South Africa, 1901," and " South Africa, 1902 "). Invalided home and discharged 1902. [835.]

131. Corpl. **McLaggan, James Innes** (Perth). E Divn. S.A.C. Formerly in 4th Vol. Batt. The Black Watch. Served in South African War, (1) with 1st Vol. Service Coy. The Black Watch, 1900 ; (2) with S.A.C., 1900-1901 (Queen's medal, with clasps " Cape Colony," " Wittebergen," and " South Africa, 1901 "). Discharged 1901. [836.]

—— **Tpr. McLaren, Alexander** (Ballinluig). Enlisted 1901. Served in South African War, 1901-1902 (Queen's medal, with clasps " South Africa, 1901," " South Africa, 1902 " . . .). Still serving.

—— **Tpr. McLaren, Archibald** (Ballinluig). Enlisted 1901. Served in South African War, 1901-1902 (Queen's medal, with clasps " South Africa, 1901," " South Africa, 1902 " . . .). Still serving.

—— 3rd Cl. **Tpr. Macmillan, Neil** (Killin).

Enlisted 1901. Served in South African War, 1901-1902 (Queen's medal, with clasps " South Africa, 1901," " South Africa, 1902 " . . .). Discharged 1902. [832.]

—— **Tpr. McTavish, Alexr.** Geo. Anderson (Strathbraan). A Divn. S.A.C. Enlisted 1900. Served in South African War, 1901 (Queen's medal, with clasps " Transvaal " " South Africa, 1901 " . . .). Invalided home and discharged 1902. [837.]

—— **Tpr. McTavish, John** (Strathbraan). A Divn. S.A.C. Enlisted 1901. Served in South African War, 1901–1902 (Queen's medal, with clasps " Transvaal," " South Africa, 1901," " South Africa, 1902 " . . .). Discharged 1903. [838.]

—— 2nd Cl. **Tpr. Marshall, William** (Gilmerton). A Divn. S.A.C. Served in South African War, 1901-1902 (Queen's medal, with clasps " Transvaal," " South Africa, 1901," " South Africa, 1902 " . . .). [834.]

58. Tpr. **Menzies, James** (Struan). B Divn. S.A.C. Enlisted 1901. Served in South African War, 1901-1902 (Queen's medal, with clasps " Cape Colony," " Orange Free State," " Transvaal," " South Africa, 1901," and " South Africa, 1902 "). Still serving. [854.]

1181. 3rd Cl. **Tpr. Pinkerton, James** (Perth). C Divn. S.A.C. Enlisted 1901. Served in South African War, 1901-1902 (Queen's medal, with clasps " Cape Colony," " Orange Free State," " Transvaal," " South Africa, 1901," and " South Africa, 1902 "). Discharged 1903.

1275. 3rd Cl. **Tpr. Ritchie, John** (Perth). E Divn. S.A.C. Enlisted in E Divn. S.A.C. 1901. Served in South African War, 1901-1902 (Queen's medal, with clasps " Cape Colony," " Orange Free State," " South Africa, 1901," and " South Africa, 1902 "). Killed by lightning, Sept. 16, 1902. Formerly in 4th Vol. Batt. The Black Watch ; Royal Scots ; and 10th Hussars. [839.]

667. 3rd Cl. Tpr. **Robertson, Chas.** Stewart (Perth). A Divn. S.A.C. Enlisted 1901. Served in South African War, 1901-1902 (Queen's medal, with clasps " South Africa, 1901," and " South Africa, 1902," and two others). Discharged 1903. [841.]

1935. 3rd Cl. **Tpr. Smith, John** Anderson (Perth). C Divn. S.A.C. Enlisted 1901. Served in South African War, 1901-1902 (Queen's medal, with clasps " Cape Colony," " Orange

SOUTH AFRICAN CONSTABULARY—*continued*

Free State," "Transvaal," "South Africa, 1901,"and "South Africa, 1902 "). Discharged 1902. Formerly in 5th Vol. Batt. The Black Watch. [842.]

1246. 3rd Cl. Tpr. Stewart, David Lamb (Coupar Angus). A Divn. S.A.C. Enlisted 1901. Served in South African War, 1901–1902 (Queen's medal, with clasps "Cape Colony," "Orange Free State," "Transvaal," "South Africa, 1901," and "South Africa, 1902 "). Still serving. [843.]

1931. Tpr. Walker, Robert (Perth). En-listed 1901. Served in South African War, 1901–1902 (Queen's medal, with clasps "Cape Colony," "Orange Free State," "Transvaal," "South Africa, 1901," and "South Africa, 1902 "). Killed by lightning, October 29, 1902. [844.]

—— **Tpr. Whittet,** Andrew (Scone). Enlisted 1901. Served in South African War, 1901–1902 (Queen's medal, with clasps "Cape Colony," "Orange Free State," "Transvaal," "South Africa, 1901," and "South Africa, 1902 "). Still serving. [840.]

PORTRAITS OF WARRANT OFFICERS, NON-COMMISSIONED OFFICERS, AND MEN, WHOSE SERVICES ARE RECORDED IN THE FORE-GOING ROLL AND IN THE ADDENDA, p. 287

NOTE

An Index to the Portraits will be found on p. 269 *et seq.*

121

122

123

124

125

126

127

128

129

131

132

133

13

13

136

13

140

141

142

143

144

145

147

148

149

150

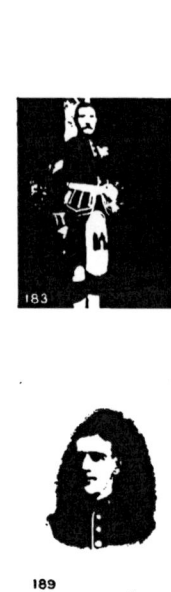

304   305   306   307   308   309

310   311   312   313   314   315

316   318   319   320   321

322   323   324   325   326   327

328   329   330   332

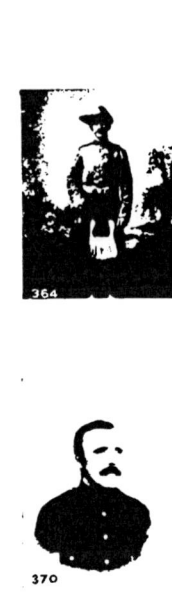
364

368

369

370

371

372

373

374

375

376

377

378

379

380

381

382

383

384

385

386

387

388

389

390

391

392

424 425 426 427 428 429

430 431 432 433 434 435

436 437

442 444 447 448

451 453

545

546

547

548

550

551 552

553

554

555

556

557

558

559

560

561

562

56

564

565

566

567

568

569

570

572

574

605 606 607 608 609 610

611 612 613 614 615 516

617 618 619 620 621 22

623 624 625 626 627 628

62 630 631 632 633

865 666 667 668 669 670

671 672 673 67 675 676

677 678 679 680 681 682

683 684 685 686 687 688

689 690 691 692 694

725 726 727 728 729 730

731 732 733 734 735 736

737 738 739 740 741

743 744 745 746 747 748

749 750 751 752 753 754

785

786

787

788

789

790

791

792

793

794

795

796

797

798

799

802

803

804

805

806

809

812

815

Piper L. Cameron. Bandsman L. Duff. Pte. D. M'Gillivray (Reservist)
Sgt. J. Imrie. Sgt.-Maj. J. Graham. Lce. Cpl. W. Stevenson.

THE PERTHSHIRE MEN OF THE 2ND BATTALION THE CAMERONIANS (SCOTTISH RIFLES), FORMERLY THE 90TH
PERTHSHIRE VOLUNTEERS LIGHT INFANTRY REGIMENT, STANDERTON, TRANSVAAL, 1903.

INDEX TO PORTRAITS OF WARRANT OFFICERS, NON-COMMISSIONED OFFICERS, AND MEN

INDEX TO PORTRAITS OF WARRANT OFFICERS, NON-COMMISSIONED OFFICERS, AND MEN

N.B.—The numbers at the left-hand side of the page refer to the numbers on the portraits of non-commissioned officers and men, pp. 239 to 267.

1.	—	1st Cl. Petty Off.	Gartland, A. K. .	Royal Navy	(Cargill).
2.	133	A. B. . . .	Ross, J. . . .	Australian Naval Brigade .	(Bridge of Earn).
3.	—	Cpl. of Hse. .	McLaren, G.H.A.P.	2nd Life Guards	(Bankfoot).
4.	—	Cpl. of Hse. .	Sharp, J. . . .	Royal Horse Guards . .	(Perth).
5.	3981	Pte.	McArthur, J. . .	2nd Dragoon Guards . .	(Perth).
6.	—	Farr. Maj. .	Whiteman, J. .	4th Dragoon Guards . .	(Perth).
7.	—	Pte.	McInnes, J. . .	6th Dragoon Guards . .	(Dunkeld).
8.	4874	Pte.	Anderson, J. . .	2nd Dragoons (Royal Scots Greys)	(Scone).
9.	—	Sergt. . . .	Coulter, W. . .	,, ,,	(Perth).
10.	—	Pte.	Edwards, G. A. . .	,, ,,	(St. Martin's).
11.	—	Pte.	Elder, J. . . .	,, ,,	(Alyth).
12.	4410	Pte.	Firth, W. . . .	,, ,,	(Perth).
13.	4620	Pte.	Gregor, J. . . .	,, ,,	(Perth).
14.	—	Pte.	Jackson, W. . .	,, ,,	(Errol).
15.	3448	Corpl. . . .	Jenner, C. G. . .	,, ,,	(Pitlochry).
16.	4443	Corpl. . . .	Lindsay, W. G. .	,, ,,	(Dunkeld).
17.	3599	Sergt. . . .	McIntosh, J. . .	,, ,,	(Clunie).
18.	4910	Pte.	McMartin, P. . .	,, ,,	(Aberfeldy).
19.	4308	Pte.	McWhammel, G. .	,, ,,	(Perth).
20.	4548	Sergt. . . .	McWhammel, J. .	,, ,,	(Perth).
21.	3657	Pte.	Meldrum, G. . .	,, ,,	(Perth).
22.	5213	Pte.	Oliphant, J. . .	,, ,,	(Caputh).
23.	4339	Pte.	Petrie, A. . . .	,, ,,	(Perth).
24.	—	Sh. Smith Cpl.	Rattray, H. . .	,, ,,	(Perth).
25.	4539	Trptr. . . .	Robertson, C. R.	,, ,,	(Perth).
26.	4409	Pte.	Scott, J. A. . .	,, ,,	(Perth).
27.	5044	Pte.	Sharp, D. . . .	,, ,,	(Glencarse).
28.	—	Sh. Smith . .	Smeaton, A. . .	,, ,,	(Muthill).
29.	4223	Lce.-Sgt. . .	Telford, G. . .	,, ,,	(Perth).
30.	4607	Sergt. . . .	Telford, J. . .	,, ,,	(Perth).
31.	2971	Pte.	Kay, J. C. . .	,, ,,	(Alyth).
32.	—	Pte.	McGinn, F. . .	,, ,,	(Perth).
33.	3927	Pte.	Sturrock, J. . .	,, ,,	(Rattray).
34.	4724	Pte.	Sturrock, T. P. .	,, ,,	(Rattray).
35.	—	Corpl. . . .	Jenner, A. E. .	6th (Inniskilling) Dragoons	(Pitlochry).
36.	3669	Sq.Sgt.-Maj. .	McPherson, W. .	,, ,,	(Pitlochry).
37.	4305	Pte.	Milne, W. . . .	,, ,,	(Perth).
38.	—	Pte.	Reid, S. A. . .	7th Hussars	(Perth).
39.	4272	Pte.	Gilchrist, W. . .	9th Lancers	(Coupar Angus).
40.	4241	Pte.	McDonald, W. .	,, ...	(Aberfeldy).
41.	4006	Sh. Smith . .	Barty, J. C. . .	10th Hussars	(Perth).
42.	3755	Pte.	Donaldson, G. .	,, ...	(Perth).
43.	—	Corpl. . . .	Lowe, A. M. . .	,, ...	(Perth).

44.	4159	Pte.	Muckersie, W.	10th Hussars	(Perth).
45.	4100	Corpl.	Mullions, T.	,,	(Perth).
46.	5156	Pte.	Comrie, W.	12th Lancers	(Crieff).
47.	4913	Pte.	Thomson, W.	,,	(Crieff).
48.	4624	Pte.	Gilchrist, C.	13th Hussars	(Rattray).
49.	3967	Ptc.	Imrie, J.	,,	(Perth).
50.	3111	Pte.	Martin, R.	,,	(Perth).
51.	4436	Pte.	Watson, J.	,,	(Scone).
52.	4524	Pte.	Wrench, H.	,,	(Abernethy).
53.	4313	Pte.	McIntosh, H.	14th Hussars	(Dunkeld).
54.	5036	Sq. Qrmr.-Sgt.	Pentland, G.	,,	(Perth).
55.	4284	Pte.	Ferrier, C.	,,	(Perth).
56.	4306	Pte.	Lamb, J. C.	,,	(Blairgowrie).
57.	145	Corpl.	McQueen, J.	,,	(Pitlochry).
58.	—	Lce.-Corpl.	Davidson, W.L.L.	17th Lancers	(Abernethy).
59.	4347	Lce.-Corpl.	Weir, J.	18th Hussars	(Perth).
60.	4084	Corpl.	Wilson, J.	,,	(Bonhard).
61.	3699	Ptc.	Curr, D.	19th Hussars	(Perth).
62.	4395	Pte.	Sutherland, D.	20th Hussars	(Auchterarder).
63.	4324	Pte.	Watt, J.	,,	(Perth).
64.	4318	Ptc.	Watt, W. G.	,,	(Perth).
65.	50221	Dr.	McLeod, W. A.	Royal Horse Artillery	(Errol).
66.	30500	Bomb.	Storrar, J. S.	,, ,,	(Perth).
67.	—	Qrmr.-Sgt.	Bennett, J.	,, ,,	(Abernethy).
68.	44956	Dr.	Taylor, D.	,, ,,	(Perth).
69.	59966	Gr.	Cameron, H.	Royal Field Artillery	(Crieff).
70.	12342	Gr.	Campbell, A.	,, ,,	(Kirkmichael.
71.	76190	Sergt.	Christie, S.	,, ,,	(Longforgan).
72.	20625	Gr.	Maison, J.	,, ,,	(Blairgowrie).
73.	78085	Dr.	Dewar, J.	,, ,,	(Perth.)
74.	27568	Corpl.	Hynd, D.	,, ,,	(Perth).
75.	66199	Gr.	McLean, D.	,, ,,	(Logiealmond).
76.	7923	Dr.	Robertson, J.	,, ,,	(Cargill).
77.	5846	Gr.	Sutherland, D.	,, ,,	(Coupar Angus).
78.	4518	Sh. Smith	Wilson, J.	,, ,,	(Port of Monteith).
79.	24566	Sadd. Corpl.	Purgavie, C.	,, ,,	(Woodside).
80.	85784	Sergt.	Miller, W. C.	Royal Garrison Artillery (Mountain Divn.)	(Meigle).
81.	5077	Act. Bomb.	Amos, J.	,, (Garrison Coy.)	(Woodside).
82.	2770	Sapr.	Dow, W.	Royal Engineers	(Crieff).
83.	23219	Corpl.	Martin, W.	,,	(Perth).
84.	25390	Sapr.	Traill, J. A.	,,	(Perth).
85.	4788	Sapr.	Foote, J.	,,	(Perth).
86.	23289	Sapr.	Halkerston, J.	,,	(Perth).
87.	24071	Sapr.	Irvine, J.	,,	(Coupar Angus).
88.	29662	Farr.-Corpl.	Jack, G.	,,	(Moulin).
89.	24658	Sapr.	McFarlane, J.	,,	(Burrelton).
90.	3925	Sapr.	MacQueen, D.	,,	(Crieff).
91.	29438	Sapr.	Robb, J.	,,	(Perth).
92.	1819	Lce.-Corpl.	Ross, J.	,,	(Findo Gask).
93.	10766	Sapr.	Sturrock, J.	,,	(Perth).
94.	1782	Pte.	Benvie, G.	Scots Guards	(Errol).
95.	9954	Pte.	Birrell, J.	,,	(Perth).
96.	8167	Pte.	Black, J.	,,	(New Scone).
97.	3720	Pte.	Blair, R.	,,	(Port of Monteith).
98.	9415	Corpl.	Cameron, D.	,,	(Stanley).
99.	2997	Lce.-Corpl.	Chalmers, G. M.	,,	(Perth).
100.	3405	Pte.	Dickson, G.	,,	(Perth).
101.	3643	Pte.	Geekie, T. E.	,,	(Coupar Angus).
102.	3290	Pte.	Goodfellow, J.	,,	(Perth).
103.	8575	Pte.	Davidson, D.	,,	(Errol).
104.	2919	Pte.	Dewar, P.	,,	(Fortingall).
105.	5387	Lce.-Sgt.	Lamond, P.	,,	(Rannagulzion).

106.	8175	Pte.	McKenzie, J.	Scots Guards	(Stanley).
107.	4165	Pte.	Owler, G.	,,	(Blairgowrie).
108.	5942	Pte.	Wood, W.	,,	(Perth).
109.	4217	Sergt.	McBeth, D.	,,	(Blair Atholl).
110.	9509	Pte.	McLean, J.	,,	(Aberfeldy).
111.	1536	Piper	McLeish, W.	,,	(Dunkeld).
112.	8901	Pte.	Scobie, A.	,,	(Aberfeldy).
113.	8605	Pte.	Robinson, F.	,,	(Perth).
114.	3295	Pte.	Pullar, D.	,,	(Perth).
115.	1135	Sergt.	Stevenson, J. W.	,,	(Muthill).
116.	2134	Pte.	Thornton, W. J.	,,	(Trinity Gask).
117.	138	Pte.	Anderson, D.	The Royal Scots	(Dull).
118.	4211	Sergt.	Baxter, W.	,,	(Burrelton).
119.	6564	Pte.	Garvie, W.	The Black Watch [1]	(Perth).
120.	6017	Lce.-Corpl.	Kirk, J. C.	The Royal Scots	(Perth).
121.	8034	Pte.	Laird, J.	,,	(Auchterarder).
122.	7083	Pte.	McConnell, G.	,,	(Perth).
123.	2422	Pte.	Millar, R. G. R.	,,	(Cargill).
124.	2507	Corpl.	Mitchell, W.	,,	(Dunblane).
125.	4859	Sgt.-Drum.	Rae, W.	,,	(Perth).
126.	6086	Pte.	Reid, R.	,,	(Perth).
127.	7412	Pte.	Stewart, F.	,,	(Callander).
128.	5982	Pte.	Wishart, W.	,,	(Crieff).
129.	3749	Pte.	Cameron, W.	The Queen's (West Surrey Regt.)	(Perth).
130.	6273	Lce.-Corpl.	McEwan, H.	The Buffs (East Kent Rgt.)	(Perth).
131.	6274	Pte.	Murphy, E.	,, ,,	(Perth).
132.	2765	Lce.-Corpl.	Cameron, P.	The Royal Scots Fusiliers	(Perth).
133.	3061	Sergt.	Clark, J.	,, ,,	(Perth).
134.	5744	Sergt.	Glass, R.	,, ,,	(Perth).
135.	4518	Sergt.	Grubb, J.	,, ,,	(Rattray).
136.	4517	Pte.	Heron, G.	,, ,,	(Rattray).
137.	5342	Pte.	McDougall, H.	,, ,,	(Perth).
138.	3508	Pte.	Thomson, J.	,, ,,	(Perth).
139.	1568	Pte.	Meikle, R.	The South Wales Borderers	(Burghmuir).
140.	1963	Pte.	Beattie, J.	The King's Own Scottish Borderers	(Blairgowrie).
141.	1823	Pte.	Conelly, J.	,, ,,	(New Scone).
142.	3228	Qrmr.-Sergt.	Macfarlane, D.	,, ,,	(Comrie).
143.	5567	Pte.	Robertson, A.	,, ,,	(Fortingall).
144.	6496	Pte.	Robertson, G.	,, ,,	(New Rattray).
145.	1574	Pte.	Burry, J. A.	The Cameronians (Scottish Rifles).	(Comrie).
146.	6977	Piper	Cameron, J.	,, ,,	(Alyth).
147.	800	Sergt.-Maj.	Graham, J.	,, ,,	(Perth).
148.	7872	Corpl.	King, W.	,, ,,	(Muthill).
149.	4002	Pte.	Littlejohn, D.	,, ,,	(Perth).
150.	7959	Pte.	Macfarlane, J.	,, ,,	(Callander).
151.	2594	Pte.	Guild, J.	,, ,,	(Blairgowrie).
152.	2820	Pte.	Phillips, G. P.	,, ,,	(Alyth).
153.	2909	Pte.	Ross, P.	,, ,,	(Blairgowrie).
154.	5919	Lce.-Corpl.	Spottiswoode, W.	,, ,,	(Alyth).
155.	5331	Pte.	Watson, G.	,, ,,	(Alyth).
156.	5952	Pte.	Watson, T.	,, ,,	(Alyth).
157.	1260	Qrmr.-Sergt.	McDonald, J.	,, ,,	(Loaninghead).
158.	4109	Pte.	McLaughlin, J.	,, ,,	(Blairgowrie).
159.	3023	Corpl.	Watt, A.	,, ,,	(Baledgarno).
160.	3136	Sergt.	Young, R. C.	,, ,,	(Crieff).
161.	—	Pte.	Haynes, J.	The Worcestershire Regt.	(Muthill).

[1] By mistake photograph No. 119 was sent in bearing the name of Private P. Garvie, the Royal Scots (brother of Private W. Garvie), and it was consequently grouped with the photographs of the other men of the Royal Scots. The mistake was only discovered when it was too late to alter the arrangement.

162.	998	Pte.	Griffiths, J.	The Border Regt.	(Perth).
163.	—	Pte.	Keiller, M.	„	(Pitcastle).
164.	7297	Pte.	Alexander, J.	The Black Watch	(Perth).
165.	7609	Pte.	Allison, H.H.D.M.	„	(Blairgowrie).
166.	6802	Pte.	Anderson, J.	„	(Blairgowrie).
167.	3760	Pte.	Black, R.	„	(Methven).
168.	8987	Pte.	Brown, A.	„	(Alyth).
169.	7582	Lce.-Corpl.	Adams, W.	„	(Doune).
170.	7210	Pte.	Ames, J.	„	(Perth).
171.	3650	Pte.	Anderson, J.	„	(Crieff).
172.	9159	Pte.	Blair, D.	„	(Perth).
173.	7581	Pte.	Brand, W.	„	(Perth).
174.	8995	Pte.	Brown, D.	„	(Killin).
175.	7055	Pte.	Brown, G.	„	(Perth).
176.	6812	Lce.-Corpl.	Buchan, D.	„	(Cargill).
177.	8961	Pte.	Buchanan, J.	„	(Callander).
178.	7579	Pte.	Campsie, W.	„	(Dunblane).
179.	7587	Pte.	Ferguson, D.	„	(Dunblane and Lecropt).
180.	7586	Pte.	Thomson, A.	„	(Logie).
181.	8971	Sergt.	Chalmers, R.	„	(Bankfoot).
182.	6930	Pte.	Clark, R.	„	(Perth).
183.	2370	Col.-Sgt. Instr.	Bain, W.	„	(Logie).
184.	9064	Lce.-Corpl.	Buchan, A. S.	„	(Perth).
185.	8951	Corpl.	Buchan, M.	„	(Perth).
186.	4060	Pte.	Calderwood, M.	„	(Perth).
187.	9066	Lce.-Corpl.	Cowie, J. M.	„	(Perth).
188.	2113	Pte.	Crawford, T.	„	(Muthill).
189.	5780	Pte.	Bruce, J.	„	(Blairgowrie).
190.	—	Pte.	Burns, E.	„	(Blairgowrie).
191.	6807	Corpl.	Campbell, W.	„	(Perth).
192.	3710	Pte.	Clark, W.	„	(St. Martin's).
193.	5272	Sergt.	Dewar, W.	„	(Marloe).
194.	5846	Pte.	Duncan, D.	„	(Blairgowrie).
195.	7190	Lce.-Corpl.	Brown, T. K. W.	„	(Crieff).
196.	7443	Pte.	Crichton, P.	„	(Meigle).
197.	6566	Pte.	Dingwall, J.	„	(Perth).
198.	3030	Pte.	Butchart, J.	„	(Rattray).
199.	6884	Pte.	Cameron, J.	„	(Perth).
200.	7103	Pte.	Davidson, J.	„	(Crieff).
201.	9051	Lce.-Corpl.	Bryson, J. F.	„	(Coupar Angus).
202.	7576	Pte.	Carmichael, J. N.	„	(Comrie).
203.	7578	Pte.	Crerar, J. M.	„	(Crieff).
204.	6497	Pte.	Chalmers, W.	„	(Perth).
205.	7606	Lce.-Corpl.	Campbell, D. S.	„	(Killin).
206.	8966	Lce.-Corpl.	Bruce, W. B.	„	(Perth).
207.	2765	Pte.	Brown, A.	„	(Perth).
208.	7597	Pte.	Erskine, W. M.	„	(Coupar Angus).
209.	3619	Lce.-Corpl.	Faichney, J.	„	(Muthill).
210.	2519	Pte.	Carr, M.	„	(Alyth).
211.	8968	Corpl.	Ferguson, J.	„	(St. Fillans).
212.	4138	Pte.	Ford, M.	„	(Perth).
213.	5470	Pte.	Clement, D.	„	(Crieff).
214.	6852	Pte.	Cuthbert, W.	„	(Dunkeld).
215.	7148	Lce.-Corpl.	Douglas, J.	„	(Dunning).
216.	8102	Drum.	Duff, J.	„	(Perth).
217.	8999	Sergt.	Duff, J.	„	(Stanley).
218.	2858	Pte.	Duncan, J.	„	(Perth).
219.	6445	Pte.	Duthie, C.	„	(Blair Atholl).
220.	7598	Pte.	Emslie, J. W.	„	(Kilspindie).
221.	9157	Pte.	Evans, J.	„	(Perth).
222.	6596	Pte.	Ferguson, M.	„	(Perth).
223.	7209	Pte.	Fowler, R.	„	(Perth).

224.	7596	Corpl.	Fraser, D.	The Black Watch	(Scone).
225.	8955	Corpl.	Duff, D.	,,	(Perth.)
226.	8960	Pte.	Easson, J. T.	,,	(Dunblane).
227.	7206	Corpl.	Elder, J.	,,	(Blairgowrie).
228.	6550	Pte.	Foote, G.	,,	(Perth).
229.	3746	Sergt.	Harrison, H.	,,	(Perth).
230.	7039	Piper	Henderson, J. A.	,,	(Perth).
231.	7480	Pte.	Gardiner, A.	,,	(Perth).
232.	8963	Corpl.	Glass, D.	,,	(Perth).
233.	5749	Corpl.	Godfrey, D.	,,	(Stormontfield).
234.	7028	Lce.-Corpl.	Gow, A.	,,	(Crieff).
235.	4081	Pte.	Grant, J.	,,	(Perth).
236.	2748	Pte.	Gray, J.	,,	(Perth).
237.	2845	Pte.	Guthrie, W.	,,	(Blairgowrie).
238.	7112	Pte.	Hay, G.	,,	(Perth).
239.	7585	Pte.	Hampton, J.	,,	(Perth).
240.	3604	Pte.	Gowrie, T. F.	,,	(Coupar Angus).
241.	4287	Pte.	Hobson, J.	,,	(Perth).
242.	2791	Lce.-Corpl.	Hume, D.	,,	(Alyth).
243.	3363	Pte.	Graham, A.	,,	(Perth).
244.	4693	Pte.	Herd, T.	,,	(Alyth).
245.	3135	Pte.	Gow, F.	,,	(Perth).
246.	7615	Pte.	Hutchison, J.	,,	(Perth).
247.	6782	Pte.	Keir, A.	,,	(Dunkeld).
248.	9047	Pte.	Kennedy, F.	,,	(Longforgan).
249.	3412	Pte.	Irons, P.	,,	(Stanley).
250.	7583	Corpl.	Hounan, J.	,,	(Perth).
251.	6062	Pte.	Kennedy, H.	,,	(Stanley).
252.	3894	Pte.	Geekie, J.	,,	(Perth).
253.	2195	Pte.	Kennedy, G. D. S.	,,	(Logierait).
254.	7510	Lce.-Corpl.	Kerr, R.	,,	(Perth).
255.	2213	Pte.	Hutchison, J.	,,	(Perth).
256.	4673	Sergt.-Major	King, J.	,,	(Strathtay).
257.	9035	Pte.	Leslie, D. R.	,,	(New Scone).
258.	5258	Pte.	Mackay, J.	,,	(Dunning).
259.	9160	Pte.	McInnes, J.	,,	(Aberfeldy).
260.	7594	Pte.	Mackenzie, D.H.C.R.	,,	(Callander).
261.	2733	Lce.-Corpl.	Kirkaldy, C.	,,	(Lethendy).
262.	6028	Pte.	Kirkwood, J.	,,	(Crieff).
263.	7135	Pte.	Loudfoot, W.	,,	(Scone).
264.	9036	Pte.	Low, R.	,,	(Blairgowrie).
265.	6611	Pte.	Lawson, T.	,,	(Coupar Angus).
266.	7050	Lce.-Corpl.	MacAra, J. S.	,,	(Auchterarder).
267.	5523	Pte.	McDonald, J.	,,	(Perth).
268.	7258	Pipe-Major	McDougall, J. M.	,,	(Perth).
269.	8972	Pte.	McFarlane, G.	,,	(Bankfoot).
270.	5558	Pte.	McFarlane, J.	,,	(Perth).
271.	3872	Pte.	McFarlane, J.	,,	(Perth).
272.	6290	Pioneer	McFarlane, S.	,,	(Luncarty).
273.	7894	Piper	McGarry, J.	,,	(Perth).
274.	7588	Pte.	McGilvary, R.	,,	(Dunblane).
275.	7601	Pte.	Macgregor, W. J.	,,	(Dunkeld).
276.	8959	Pte.	McIntosh, A.	,,	(Logie).
277.	8953	Pte.	McIntyre, J. F.	,,	(Logie).
278.	7766	Pte.	McIntosh, J.	,,	(Coupar Angus).
279.	7038	Pte.	McIntyre, J.	,,	(Perth).
280.	6100	Pte.	McLaren, D.	,,	(Perth).
281.	7417	Pte.	McLaren, J.	,,	(Collace).
282.	7593	Pte.	McLaren, J.	,,	(Callander).
283.	7184	Corpl.	Macmaster, D.	,,	(Kinloch Rannoch).
284.	9002	Pte.	McNaughten, J.	,,	(Killin).
285.	625	Col.-Sergt.	McVean, J.	,,	(Ardvorlich).
286.	3798	Pte.	McLeish, A.	,,	(Perth).

287.	2943	Pte.	McPherson, A.	The Black Watch	(Coupar Angus).
288.	9166	Sergt.	McPherson, J.	„	(Kenmore).
289.	5787	Pte.	Meldrum, S.	„	(Perth).
290.	7080	Pte.	Morris, J.	„	(Coupar Angus).
291.	5154	Pte.	Moyes, T.	„	(Perth).
292.	9158	Pte.	McVicar, W.	„	(Perth).
293.	9071	Lce.-Corpl.	Menzies, D.	„	(Perth).
294.	4471	Pte.	Miller, C.	„	(Perth).
295.	6478	Pte.	Morris, A.	„	(Blairgowrie).
296.	9155	Pte.	Morrison, J.	„	(Perth).
297.	9070	Pte.	Murrie, J.	„	(Perth).
298.	7169	Pte.	McGarry, J.	„	(Blairgowrie).
299.	33	Pte.	McGregor, W.	„	(Aberfeldy).
300.	9000	Pte.	Martin, E.	„	(Alyth).
301.	9038	Pte.	McNab, P.	„	(Foss).
302.	9018	Pte.	McWalter, J.	„	(Auchterarder).
303.	6808	Lce.-Corpl.	Maison, A.	„	(Blairgowrie).
304.	8957	Pte.	MacIntosh, J.	„	(Dunblane).
305.	2479	Pte.	McKenzie, F.	„	(Tibbermuir).
306.	3871	Pte.	McKenzie, H.	„	(Rattray).
307.	2718	Col.-Sergt.	Macmillan, J.	„	(Pitcairngreen).
308.	4007	Col.-Sergt.	Millar, A.	„	(Alyth).
309.	4166	Pte.	Mylie, J.	„	(Perth).
310.	5028	Col.-Sergt.	McLaren, W.	„	(Perth).
311.	4795	Lce.-Corpl.	Mitchell, T.	„	(Meigle).
312.	3936	Pte.	Reid, A. M.	„	(Perth).
313.	5411	Pte.	Robertson, D.	„	(New Rattray).
314.	6724	Lce.-Corpl.	Ramsay, H.	„	(Burrelton).
315.	4031	Pte.	Myles, D.	„	(Coupar Angus).
316.	8982	Pte.	Macpherson, J.	„	(Killiecrankie).
317.	9164	Pte.	McKenzie, M.	„	(Perth).
318.	6918	Pte.	McLauchlan, J.	„	(Alyth).
319.	7810	Pte.	Morris, C.	„	(Cargill).
320.	2441	Pte.	Mann, A.	„	(Blairgowrie).
321.	1752	Pte.	Robertson, J.	„	(Perth).
322.	7180	Lce.-Sergt.	Malcolm, W.	„	(Perth).
323.	7672	Pte.	Paton, J. W.	„	(Errol).
324.	2625	Pte.	Paton, S.	„	(Errol).
325.	7629	Pte.	Robertson, J.	„	(Ardler).
326.	4476	Pte.	Robertson, H.	„	(Perth).
327.	6553	Pte.	Robertson, C. S.	„	(Blairgowrie).
328.	7205	Pte.	Nicoll, J.	„	(Perth).
329.	9039	Pte.	Petrie, A.	„	(Rattray).
330.	7599	Corpl.	Proudfoot, A.	„	(Aberfeldy).
331.	6586	Drum.	Purdie, L.	„	(Perth).
332.	3739	Pte.	Robertson, D.	„	(Perth).
333.	5914	Pte.	Robertson, H. K.	„	(Alyth).
334.	4475	Bdsman.	Reid, T. B.	„	(Perth).
335.	2428	Pte.	Robertson, A.	„	(Alyth).
336.	3014	Col.-Sergt.	Robertson, J.	„	(Caputh).
337.	3719	Pte.	Robertson, J.	„	(Muthill).
338.	5492	Pte.	Robertson, T.	„	(New Rattray).
339.	8992	Pte.	Robertson, T. H.	„	(Alyth).
340.	3959	Pte.	Robertson, J.	„	(Perth).
341.	8973	Pte.	Robertson, J.	„	(Strathtay).
342.	6376	Pte.	Robertson, J.	„	(Luncarty).
343.	8983	Pte.	Robertson, J. M.	„	(Blairgowrie).
344.	7605	Sergt.	Robertson, T.	„	(Dunkeld).
345.	7163	Pte.	Ruddick, J.	„	(Crieff).
346.	9165	Pte.	Rae, J.	„	(Killin).
347.	7927	Pte.	Russell, A.	„	(Crieff).
348.	7386	Pte.	Russell, P.	„	(Crieff).
349.	800	Sergt.-Major	Sadler, B.	„	(Perth).

No.	Number	Rank	Name	Regiment	Place
350.	7584	Pte.	Robertson, J. L.	The Black Watch	(Perth).
351.	7577	Lce.-Corpl.	Scott, J. B.	,,	(Perth).
352.	9040	Pte.	Scott, J. M.	,,	(Blairgowrie).
353.	8977	Pte.	Sidey, T.	,,	(Alyth).
354.	8997	Pte.	Smith, T.	,,	(Alyth).
355.	2071	Corpl.	Strong, D.	,,	(Logierait).
356.	7513	Pte.	Sutherland, T.	,,	(Perth).
357.	3157	Pte.	Syme, J.	,,	(Perth).
358.	5244	Pte.	Scott, W.	,,	(Dunkeld).
359.	5779	Ptc.	Shepherd, J.	,,	(Perth).
360.	5194	Pte.	Simpson, J.	,,	(Perth).
361.	5744	Sergt.	Simpson, W. A.	,,	(Scone).
362.	7679	Pte.	Sinclair, J.	,,	(Crieff).
363.	7603	Pte.	Small, R. M.	,,	(Dull).
364.	8975	Pte.	Smith, A.	,,	(Coupar Angus).
365.	7487	Pte.	Smith, M.	,,	(Callander).
366.	5205	Pte.	Smith, W.	,,	(Perth).
367.	8954	Pte.	Stewart, J. C.	,,	(Perth).
368.	7244	Pte.	Stuart, C. E.	,,	(Perth).
369.	2374	Sergt.	Sutherland, J.	,,	(Perth).
370.	4523	Corpl.	Sage, G.	,,	(Perth).
371.	9161	Pte.	Scrimgeour, D.	,,	(Aberfeldy).
372.	7072	Pte.	Sharp, D.	,,	(Perth).
373.	6619	Pte.	Shedden, J.	,,	(Perth).
374.	4177	Pte.	Stewart, J.	,,	(Perth).
375.	9041	Lce.-Corpl.	Stewart, J.	,,	(Aberfeldy).
376.	2601	Lce.-Corpl.	Simpson, J.	,,	(Scone).
377.	4407	Pte.	Stewart, J.	,,	(Blairgowrie).
378.	9168	Pte.	Struth, W.	,,	(Blairgowrie).
379.	6205	Pte.	Welsh, W. F.	,,	(Scone).
380.	152	Pte.	West, G.	,,	(Cargill).
381.	6096	Pte.	West, C.	,,	(Cargill).
382.	9154	Pte.	Sutherland, C.	,,	(Auchterarder).
383.	2148	Col.-Sergt.	Taylor, A.	,,	(Auchterarder).
384.	9167	Pte.	Whittet, T.	,,	(Scone).
385.	3509	Sergt.	Wilson, A.	,,	(Muckart).
386.	4204	Sergt.	Wilson, A.	,,	(Alyth).
387.	5002	Pte.	Winsor, W.	,,	(Perth).
388.	7049	Pte.	Thomson, G.	,,	(Perth).
389.	9162	Pte.	Thomson, P.	,,	(Perth).
390.	9043	Ptc.	West, D.	,,	(Blairgowrie).
391.	8998	Pte.	Whyte, W.	,,	(Alyth).
392.	9163	Pte.	Wighton, F.	,,	(Balbeggie).
393.	14	Ptc.	Young, W.	,,	(Dunkeld).
394.	6700	Pte.	Taylor, R.	,,	(Perth).
395.	9042	Pte.	Thomson, G.	,,	(New Scone).
396.	7589	Corpl.	Thomson, J.	,,	(Perth).
397.	9103	Pte.	Thomson, R.	,,	(Blairgowrie).
398.	9133	Ptc.	Watson, R.	,,	(Blairgowrie).
399.	2238	Col.-Sergt.	White, H.	,,	(Perth).
400.	7809	Pte.	White, J.	,,	(Perth).
401.	7406	Pte.	Whyte, C.	,,	(Alyth).
402.	8979	Pte.	Whyte, D.	,,	(Killin).
403.	6714	Pte.	Whyte, G.	,,	(Perth).
404.	7272	Ptc.	Wishart, E. J.	,,	(Perth).
405.	7610	Pte.	Winton, W.	,,	(Pitlochry).
406.	7397	Pte.	Wishart, G.	,,	(Crieff).
407.	7784	Ptc.	Wright, T. C.	,,	(Dunblane).
408.	6864	Pte.	Young, D.	,,	(Perth).
409.	1126	Rifleman	Geddes, T.	The King's Royal Rifle Corps	(Alyth).
410.	699	Rifleman	Robertson, J.	,,	(Perth).
411.	4417	Pte.	Kennedy, J.	The Wiltshire Regiment	(Perth).
412.	4452	Bdsman.	Smith, M. J.	,, ,,	(Perth).

No.	Reg.	Rank	Name	Regiment		Place
413.	6659	Pte.	Cross, D. R.	The Highland Light Infantry		(Perth).
414.	5122	Pte.	Devaney, P.	,,	,,	(Perth).
415.	7391	Pte.	McGregor, C.	,,	,,	(Rannagulzion).
416.	4574	Pte.	Milne, W.	,,	,,	(Aberfeldy).
417.	3840	Col.-Sergt.	Stewart, P.	,,	,,	(Bankfoot).
418.	6956	Pte.	Dow, P. S.	,,	,,	(Dunblane).
419.	45	Col.-Sergt.	Ferguson, D.	,,	,,	(Logierait).
420.	6076	Sergt.	Ferguson, A.	,,	,,	(Logierait).
421.	3879	Pte.	Glen, J.	,,	,,	(Coupar Angus).
422.	5123	Pte.	Holland, P.	,,	,,	(Perth).
423.	3087	Corpl.	Taylor, A.	,,	,,	(Muthill).
424.	2885	Pte.	Gibbons, J.	,,	,,	(Perth).
425.	—	Sergt.	Robertson, D.	,,	,,	(Stanley).
426.	4982	Col.-Sergt.	Hall, T.	,,	,,	(Perth).
427.	3154	Pte.	McPherson, P.	,,	,,	(Glenlyon).
428.	3140	Pte.	Welsh, W.	,,	,,	(Auchterarder).
429.	7556	Pte.	Wisely, P.	,,	,,	(Bridge of Earn).
430.	3277	Pte.	Green, J.	,,	,,	(Perth).
431.	4882	Pte.	Reid, J.	,,	,,	(Blairgowrie).
432.	4006	Pte.	Hutchison, P.	,,	,,	(Scone).
433.	4039	Pte.	Shaw, J.	,,	,,	(Perth).
434.	3768	Pte.	Stewart, J.	,,	,,	(Perth).
435.	8423	Pte.	Stewart, W.	,,	,,	(Ballinluig).
436.	3161	Corpl.	Griffin, D.	,,	,,	(Blairgowrie).
437.	5783	Pte.	Heron, A.	,,	,,	(Blairgowrie).
438.	5467	Piper	Robertson, T.	,,	,,	(Pitlochry).
439.	3048	Corpl.	Rumgay, A.	,,	,,	(New Scone).
440.	5301	Pte.	Stewart, G.	,,	,,	(Blairgowrie).
441.	6618	Pte.	Adams, J.	Seaforth Highlanders		(Perth).
442.	3002	Col.-Sergt.	Brownie, C. E.	,,	,,	(Dunning).
443.	3047	Pte.	Campbell, H. M.	,,	,,	(Kincardine on Forth).
444.	1525	Bdsman.	Duff, T.	,,	,,	(Blairgowrie).
445.	2849	Col.-Sergt.	Dunbar, G.	,,	,,	(Crieff).
446.	1169	Col.-Sergt.	Fenton, A.	,,	,,	(Kinnoull).
447.	3004	Qrmr.-Sergt.	Fenton, J.	,,	,,	(Kinnoull).
448.	6112	Pte.	Gordon, D.	,,	,,	(Perth).
449.	5315	Pte.	Halley, J.	,,	,,	(Crieff.)
450.	2957	Corpl.	Heard, J.	,,	,,	(Perth).
451.	9586	Lce.-Corpl.	Kidd, J.	,,	,,	(Perth).
452.	3264	Pte.	McFarlane, A.	,,	,,	(Perth).
453.	5604	Pte.	McKinlay, A.	,,	,,	(Strathbraan).
454.	6714	Pte.	Mitchell, J.	,,	,,	(Perth).
455.	6113	Pte.	Proudfoot, J.	,,	,,	(Perth).
456.	1365	Pte.	Robertson, G. T.	,,	,,	(Perth).
457.	5547	Sergt.	Stewart, J.	,,	,,	(Blair Atholl).
458.	5221	Sergt.-Drum.	Thomson, R.	,,	,,	(Perth).
459.	3241	Lce.-Corpl.	Tyrie, R.	,,	,,	(Errol).
460.	1105	Pte.	Wilson, C.	,,	,,	(Cargill).
461.	5067	Pte.	Anderson, A.	,,	,,	(Perth).
462.	5815	Pte.	MacGregor, G.	,,	,,	(Perth).
463.	1745	Pte.	Robertson, D.	,,	,,	(Ballinluig).
464.	486	Lce.-Corpl.	Sorley, J.	,,	,,	(Corsiehill).
465.	—	Pte.	Stewart, J.	,,	,,	(Perth).
466.	355	Pte.	Wilson, A.	,,	,,	(Bankfoot).
467.	4784	Sergt.	Bisset, D.	,,	,,	(Scone).
468.	6712	Pte.	Calderwood, J.	,,	,,	(Perth).
469.	4834	Pte.	Farquharson, J.	,,	,,	(Blairgowrie).
470.	5051	Pte.	McInroy, K.	,,	,,	(Perth).
471.	2599	Pte.	McOwen, J.	,,	,,	(Rhynd).
472.	5762	Drum.	Robertson, J.	,,	,,	(Perth).
473.	9866	Pte.	Doig, C.	,,	,,	(Alyth).
474.	1463	Pte.	Morrison, D.	,,	,,	(Auchterarder).

475.	3442	Pte.	Stewart, J.	Seaforth Highlanders		(Perth).
476.	1763	Pte.	Thomson, G.	,, ,,		(Cargill).
477.	2101	Col.-Sergt.	Archer, J. A.	The Gordon Highlanders		(Alyth).
478.	3265	Pte.	Clark, A.	,,	,,	(Perth).
479.	6282	Lce.-Corpl.	Calder, D.	,,	,,	(Dunkeld).
480.	3264	Pte.	Gardiner, R.	,,	,,	(Perth).
481.	4145	Corpl.	Macintosh, J. J.	,,	,,	(Perth).
482.	783	Pte.	Strathdee, G.	,,	,,	(Perth).
483.	2995	Pte.	Taylor, C.	,,	,,	(Logiealmond).
484.	3981	Pte.	Wilkie, W.	,,	,,	(Muthill).
485.	4680	Pte	Anderson, J.	,,	,,	(Auchterarder).
486.	2561	Pte.	Bennett, P.	,,	,,	(Braco).
487.	2240	Sergt.	Brown, J. R.	,,	,,	(Perth).
488.	5320	Pte.	Clark, A.	,,	,,	(Dowally).
489.	5619	Pte.	Fraser, J. C.	,,	,,	(Arngask).
490.	5930	Pte.	Hay, D.	,,	,,	(Scone).
491.	5194	Lce.-Corpl.	Findlay, W.	,,	,,	(Blairgowrie).
492.	3269	Pte.	McDonald, J.	,,	,,	(Perth).
493.	2889	Corpl.	Mitchell, A.	,,	,,	(Ardler).
494.	6504	Pte.	Ford, P.	,,	,,	(Perth).
495.	4886	Pte.	Honeyman, W.	,,	,,	(Blairgowrie).
496.	232	Pte.	Smith, J.	,,	,,	(Alyth).
497.	5156	Pte.	Henderson, J.	,,	,,	(Scone).
498.	7215	Pte.	Mackenzie, D.	,,	,,	(Redgorton).
499.	6520	Pte.	Paterson, E. D.	,,	,,	(Perth).
500.	7036	Pte.	Robb, J.	,,	,,	(Luncarty).
501.	3965	Sergt.	Douglas, D.	The Cameron Highlanders		(Perth).
502.	4910	Pte.	Forbes, T.	,,	,,	(Dunblane).
503.	368	Pte.	Irvine, C.	,,	,,	(Blairgowrie).
504.	2183	Pte.	Keir, J. S.	,,	,,	(Blairgowrie).
505.	3788	Pte.	McFarlane, J.	,,	,,	(Logie).
506.	4182	Pte.	McInroy, D.	,,	,,	(Perth).
507.	158	Corpl.	McKenzie, T.	,,	,,	(Bridge of Earn).
508.	5372	Pte.	McManus, F.	,,	,,	(Perth).
509.	1644	Col.-Sergt.	MacKenzie, T. E.	,,	,,	(Perth).
510.	631	Sergt.	Scott, J.	,,	,,	(Dull).
511.	3660	Pte.	Stewart, W.	,,	,,	(Perth).
512.	—	Lce.-Sergt.	Anderson, J.	,,	,,	(Perth).
513.	4997	Pte.	Symington, A. W.	,,	,,	(Alyth).
514.	5482	Pte.	Watson, J.	,,	,,	(Stanley).
515.	3440	Lce.-Corpl.	Anderson, J.	,,	,,	(Perth).
516.	3830	Qrmr.-Sergt.	McKenzie, J.	,,	,,	(Perth).
517.	2095	Qtmr.-Sergt.	McLean, A.	,,	,,	(Perth).
518.	5910	Pte.	McLellan, J.	,,	,,	(Logiealmond).
519.	3700	Pte.	Brown, A.	,,	,,	(Perth).
520.	2243	Pte.	Walls, J.	,,	,,	(Kincardine on Forth).
521.	5091	Lce.-Corpl.	Cameron, D.	,,	,,	(Blair Atholl).
522.	239	Pte.	Campbell, D.	,,	,,	(Blair Atholl).
523.	1538	Corpl.	Campbell, J.	,,	,,	(Blair Atholl).
524.	1163	Pte.	Will, J.	The Royal Irish Rifles		(Perth).
525.	624	Col.-Sergt.	Campbell, P.	Argyll and Sutherland Highlanders		(Dunblane).
526.	7470	Pte.	Dingwall, J.	,,	,,	(Perth).
527.	1814	Sergt.	Douglas, R.	,,	,,	(Logierait).
528.	—	Sergt.	Duff, J.	,,	,,	(Perth).
529.	6706	Lce.-Corpl.	Ferguson, J.	,,	,,	(Logierait).
530.	7080	Pte.	Gow, D.	,,	,,	(Perth).
531.	—	Pte.	Lawson, A.	,,	,,	(Dunkeld).
532.	—	Sergt.-Major	Lindsay, J.	,,	,,	(Alyth).
533.	6551	Pte.	MacDonald, J.	,,	,,	(Crieff).
534.	—	Pte.	McNie, J.	,,	,,	(Kincardine on Forth).

535. 1549 Pte. . . . . Macpherson, H. . . Argyll and Sutherland Highlanders . . . (Blairgowrie).
536. 6557 Pte. . . . . Miller, J. . . . " " (Perth).
537. 6171 Lce.-Corpl. . Norrie, A. . . " " (Greenloaning).
538. 5276 Sergt. . . . Reid, J. . . . " " (Moulin).
539. 8578 Pte. . . . . Andrews, J. . . " " (Blairlogie).
540. 6439 Pte. . . . . Blain, T. I. . . " " (Killin).
541. 2752 Sergt. . . . Buchanan, W. . " " (Doune).
542. 3066 Ptc. . . . . McDonald, T. . " " (Alyth).
543. 3116 Qrmr.-Sergt. . Weller, W. R. . " " (Scone).
544. 1448 Col. Sergt. . Wilson, A. . . " " (Blackford).
545. 3148 Pte. . . . . Campbell, J. . . " " (Auchterarder).
546. 6480 Pte. . . . . Campbell, J. . . " " (Perth).
547. 3098 Pte. . . . . Docherty, H. . . " " (Blairgowrie).
548. 3043 Pte. . . . . McIntosh, J. . . " " (Perth).
549. 3952 Pte. . . . . McLean, W. . . " " (Perth).
550. 1598 Pte. . . . . Sharp, D. . . . " " (Perth).
551. — Lce.-Corpl. . Kininmouth, J. . " " (Perth).
552. 2588 Lce.-Corpl. . Kininmouth, R. " " (Perth).
553. 724 Sergt. . . . McWilliam, A. . " " (Rattray).
554. 7044 Pte. . . . . Young, W. . . " " (Perth).
555. — Sergt. . . . Johnston, J. G. . Scottish Cycle Corps . . (Alyth).
556. — Pte. . . . . Wood, W. . . Army Service Corps . . (Butterstone).
557. 113812 Sh. Smith . . Coulter, J. . . " " . . (Perth).
558. 285 Corpl. . . . McLaren, A. . . " " . . (Perth).
559. — Pte. . . . . Simpson, J. . . " " . . (Perth).
560. — 1st Cl.Warr.Off. Hill, W. . . . " " . . (Glenalmond).
561. 1594 Lce.-Sergt. . Hodge, A. . . " " . . (Coupar Angus).
562. — Qrmr.-Sergt. . McLaren, F. A. P. " " . . (Bankfoot).
563. 4672 Pte. . . . . Bremner, P. . . Army Ordnance Department (Dunblane).
564. 857 Armr. Sergt. . Jack, A. D. . . " " (Perth).
565. 646 Sergt. . . . Smith, R. . . . Army Pay Department . (Perth).
566. 11328 Pte. . . . . Arnott, W. . . Royal Army Medical Corps (Auchterarder).
567. 13910 Pte. . . . . Buchanan, J. . " " (Perth).
568. 8061 2nd Cl.Staff Sgt. MacLaren, J. . " " (Callander).
569. — Pte. . . . . Muir, W. . . Army Post Office Corps . (Callander).
570. — Civiln. Condr. McLaren, T. S. . Remounts Department . (Callander).
571. 29437 Pte. . . . . Anderson, G. . . Imperial Yeomanry, 6th Batt. 20th Coy. . . (Alyth).
572. 9239 Sh.-Smith . . Craigon, P. . . " " (Perth).
573. 9236 Sh.-Smith . . Douglas, C. . . " " (Dunkeld).
574. — Pte. . . . . Esplin, G. . . " 17th Batt., 50th Coy. . (Perth).
575. — Lce.-Sergt. . Gellatly, W. B. . " 24th Batt. . . . . (Perth).
576. 12537 Corpl. . . . Kidd, J. . . . " 18th Batt., 70th Coy. . (Blairgowrie).
577. 12550 Corpl. . . . King, J. . . . " " 72nd Coy. . (Muthill).
578. 14572 Lce.-Corpl. . McLaren, J. H. . " " 72nd Coy. . (Kindallachan).
579. 23372 Pte. . . . . Nicol, W. . . . " 22nd Batt., 78th Coy. . (Forteviot).
580. 25530 Pte. . . . . Ross, W. . . . " 6th Batt., 20th Coy. . (Bridge of Earn).
581. 34647 Pte. . . . . Graham, C. . . " 15th Batt., 57th Coy. . (Crieff).
582. 7283 Pte. . . . . Keir, J. . . . " 5th Batt., 16th Coy. . (Blair Atholl.
583. 8715 Farr. . . . McLaren, A. . . " 6th Batt., 18th Coy. . (Callander).
584. 23379 Sergt. . . . Robertson, G. C. . " " 20th Coy. . (Monzievaird).
585. 42049 Pte. . . . . Mitchell, P. . . " 37th Batt. (Highland Horse) . . . . (Alyth).
586. — Pte. . . . . Robertson, G. L. . " Duke of Cambridge's Own . . . . (Scone).
587. — Pte. . . . . Clark, D. . . . " 31st Batt. (Fincastle's Horse) . . . . (Scone).
588. 23419 Sergt. . . . Harris, J. W. . " 22nd Batt., 78th Coy. . (Alyth).
589. 42050 Sq. Qrmr.-Sgt. Lindsay, J. . . " 37th Batt. (Highland Horse) . . . . (Alyth).
590. 38175 Ordly.-Rm. Sgt. Robertson, J. W. . " 31st Batt. (Fincastle's Horse) . . . . . (Perth).

591.	14976	Pte.	Smith, C. D.	Imperial Yeomanry, 4th Batt., 28th Coy. (Blairgowrie).
592.	42048	Pte.	Thompson, G.	,, 37th Batt. (Highland Horse) (Alyth).
593.	8717	Pte.	Mackenzie, A.	,, 6th Batt., 18th Coy. (Glenlyon).
594.	8731	Pte.	Robertson, W. J.	,, ,, ,, (Braco).
595.	9218	Pte.	Honeyman, A.L.M.	,, ,, 20th Coy. (Coupar Angus).
596.	22283	Pte.	Selby, R. E.	,, 21st Batt., 81st Coy. (Crieff).
597.	2183	Pte.	Kinnison, K. M.	,, 4th Batt., 7th Coy. (Butterstone).
598.	38075	Pte.	Taylor, J.	,, 31st Batt. (Fincastle's Horse) (Perth).
599.	9158	Pte.	Scott, J. G.	,, 6th Batt., 20th Coy. (Coupar Angus).
600.	24873	Pte.	Davis, T. T. A.	,, ,, ,, (Blairgowrie).
601.	24875	Lce.-Corpl.	Ferrier, D.	,, ,, ,, (Alyth).
602.	9213	Trump.	Lowe, W.	,, ,, ,, (Perth).
603.	6346	Sergt.	Edmondston, C. B.	,, 11th Batt., 34th Coy. (Kincardine).
604.	31006	Pte.	Steven, A.	,, 6th Batt., 108th Coy. (Kincardine on Forth).
605.	—	Sq. Qrmr.-Sgt.	Keiller, J. M. R.	,, 37th Batt. (Highland Horse) (Perth).
606.	9161	Pte.	Haig, J. R. P.	,, 6th Batt., 20th Coy. (Blairhill).
607.	23673	Pte.	Thomson, D.	,, ,, ,, (Scone).
608.	9136	Pte.	Pople, W. G.	,, ,, ,, (Perth).
609.	23400	Pte.	Playfair, C. G.	,, ,, ,, (Coupar Angus).
610.	12636	Sergt.	Deas, J. B.	,, 18th Batt., 70th Coy. (Perth).
611.	9159	Pte.	Wilson, A. T.	,, 6th Batt., 20th Coy. (Scone).
612.	24874	Pte.	Dempster, H.	,, ,, ,, (Perth).
613.	9228	Pte.	Minto, H. S.	,, ,, ,, (Crieff).
614.	9240	Corpl.	Playfair, H. L.	,, ,, ,, (Coupar Angus).
615.	24886	Pte.	Rattray, J.	,, ,, ,, (Marlee).
616.	43794	Lce.-Corpl.	Robertson, W. P.	,, 31st Batt. (Fincastle's Horse) (Blairgowrie).
617.	30269	Qrmr.-Sergt.	Myers, J. C.	,, 6th Batt., 107th Coy. (Pitlochry).
618.	41099	Pte.	Stewart, J.	,, 31st Batt. (Fincastle's Horse) (Blairgowrie).
619.	8714	Pte.	Crerar, T. R.	,, Lovat's Scouts (Foss).
620.	8731	Pte.	Foote, A.	,, ,, (Stanley).
621.	8835	Pte.	McLauchlan, J.	,, ,, (Logierait).
622.	36781	Sh.-Smith	Turner, D. F.	,, ,, (Alyth).
623.	37373	Pte.	Cameron, A.	,, ,, (Fortingall).
624.	8811	Pte.	McFarlane, D.	,, ,, (Pitlochry).
625.	8754	Pte.	Kennedy, J.	,, ,, (Blairgowrie).
626.	36779	Pte.	Thomson, J. A.	,, ,, (Dunkeld).
627.	8911	Pte.	Wanliss, G. C.	,, ,, (Scone).
628.	8815	Pte.	McDonald, A.	,, ,, (Blair Atholl).
629.	36956	Tpr.	Adams, G.	The Scottish Horse (Collace).
630.	33382	Tpr.	Anderson, G. S.	,, (Muckart).
631.	24302	Sergt.	Brown, D.	,, (Bankfoot).
632.	31365	Tpr.	Brown, C.	,, (Perth).
633.	42014	Sergt.	Bayne, T. M.	,, (Cultoquhey).
634.	33433	Corpl.	Dugan, W.	,, (Dunblane).
635.	791	Sergt.	Chalmers, A.	,, (Stanley).
636.	30143	Tpr.	Christie, D. H.	,, (Perth).
637.	37537	Tpr.	Dow, J. G.	,, (Perth).
638.	37468	Piper	Drummond, J.	,, (Muthill).
639.	37586	Tpr.	Fraser, J. R.	,, (Stanley).
640.	44702	Lce.-Corpl.	Fraser, W.	,, (Blair Atholl).
641.	37101	Tpr.	Grieve, J. W.	,, (Abernethy).
642.	33546	Sergt.	Haxton, H.	,, (Forgandenny).
643.	37666	Corpl.	Hush, J.	,, (Blair Atholl).
644.	33267	Sergt.-Major	Johnston, G. R.	,, (Blair Atholl).
645.	33332	Tpr.	Kay, A.	,, (Aberfoyle).
646.	820	Tpr.	Kerrigan, J.	,, (Perth).

647. 37029 Corpl. . . . Alexander, J. M. The Scottish Horse . . . (Alyth).
648. 36984 Sergt. . . . Findlay, W. . .   "   . . . (Stanley).
649. 44716 Tpr. . . . Jack, J. . . .   "   . . . (Pitlochry).
650. 37150 Tpr. . . . Jack, T. M. . .   "   . . . (Pitlochry).
651. 40923 Sh.-Smith . . Johnston, J. H. .   "   . . . (Blairgowrie).
652. 25887 Corpl. . . . Murison, J. . .   "   . . . (Alyth).
653. 37471 Tpr. . . . Laing, D. . . .   "   . . . (Ruthvenfield).
654. 37058 Tpr. . . . Leslie, R. . . .   "   . . . (St. Martin's).
655. 37247 Tpr. . . . McCulloch, P. . .   "   . . . (Madderty).
656. 37283 Tpr. . . . McKay, T. . . .   "   . . . (Dunkeld).
657. 44660 Tpr. . . . McMillan, A. . .   "   . . . (Ballinluig).
658. 37282 Lce.-Corpl. . McLeish, D. K. .   "   . . . (Weem).
659. 37007 Tpr. . . . McLeish, D. . .   "   . . . (Blackford).
660. 37250 Tpr. . . . McLean, A. K. . .   "   . . . (Crieff).
661. 27265 Tpr. . . . McLauchlan, R. .   "   . . . (Perth).
662. 37077 Tpr. . . . McLaren, W. .   "   . . . (Logiealmond).
663. 44758 Lce.-Corpl. . Macintosh, D. . .   "   . . . (Weem).
664.   833 Tpr. . . . McKenzie, R. .   "   . . . (Auchterarder).
665. 37670 Tpr. . . . Anderson, W. B. .   "   . . . (Alyth).
666. 37067 Tpr. . . . Bruce, D. . . .   "   . . . (Alyth).
667. 44051 Piper . . . Campbell, S. . .   "   . . . (Blairgowrie).
668. 37589 Tpr. . . . Dair, J. . . .   "   . . . (Alyth).
669. 37674 Tpr. . . . Davidson, J. . .   "   . . . (Coupar Angus).
670. 36981 Sergt. . . . Flight, J. . . .   "   . . . (Burrelton).
671. 34482 Sergt. . . . Duff, P. . . .   "   . . . (Ballinluig).
672. 33230 Sh.-Smith . . Ewan, W. . . .   "   . . . (Bankfoot).
673. 37538 Corpl. . . . Foote, A. . . .   "   . . . (Stanley).
674.   821 Piper . . . Laidlaw, J. . .   "   . . . (Perth).
675. 37195 Tpr. . . . McGregor, C. . .   "   . . . (Perth).
676. 37122 Tpr. . . . McPherson, W. M.   "   . . . (Alyth).
677. 37566 Tpr. . . . Blair, A. . . .   "   . . . (Callander).
678. 37136 Tpr. . . . Gow, D. . . .   "   . . . (Coupar Angus).
679. 37259 Tpr. . . . Johnstone, A. .   "   . . . (Errol).
680. 36998 Tpr. . . . McPherson, R. .   "   . . . (Pitlochry).
681. 31360 Tpr. . . . Kean, W. . . .   "   . . . (Perth).
682. 33376 Tpr. . . . Alexander, J. L.   "   . . . (Blairgowrie).
683. 44667 Tpr. . . . MacGregor, A. M.   "   . . . (Balquhidder).
684. 37100 Tpr. . . . Cameron, J. . .   "   . . . (Kintillo).
685. 37245 Tpr. . . . Campbell, J. . .   "   . . . (Forgandenny).
686. 36970 Tpr. . . . Clarke, A. . .   "   . . . (Dunkeld).
687. 37460 Tpr. . . . Gilmour, J. . .   "   . . . (Crieff).
688. 37008 Tpr. . . . McKenzie, J. E.   "   . . . (Kinnoull).
689. 37133 Sh.-Smith . . McFarlane, R. .   "   . . . (Blair Atholl).
690. 36797 Corpl. . . . Gray, B. J. . .   "   . . . (Abernethy).
691. 36910 Corpl. . . . Gray, H. . . .   "   . . . (Abernethy).
692. 37492 Corpl. . . . McKay, J. W. .   "   . . . (Killin).
693. 33287 Tpr. . . . McLeod, J. . .   "   . . . (Blairgowrie).
694. 31716 Lce.-Corpl. . Bell, J. . . .   "   . . . (Ardoch).
695. 37385 Sh.-Smith . . Marshall, G. . .   "   . . . (Crieff).
696. 37529 Tpr. . . . Melville, D. A. .   "   . . . (Alyth).
697. 37703 Tpr. . . . Mersey, A. . .   "   . . . (Blair Atholl).
698. 37010 Tpr. . . . Millar, G. . . .   "   . . . (Alyth).
699. 37115 Tpr. . . . Mitchell, A. . .   "   . . . (Perth).
700. 44662 Tpr. . . . Moffat, H. F. .   "   . . . (Perth).
701. 37194 Tpr. . . . Ramsay, D. B. .   "   . . . (Perth).
702. 44670 Tpr. . . . Ramsay, J. . .   "   . . . (Perth).
703. 37591 Piper . . . Rattray, A. . .   "   . . . (Pitlochry).
704. 44699 Tpr. . . . Robertson, D. A.   "   . . . (Blair Atholl).
705. 37271 Lce.-Corpl. . Robertson, J. .   "   . . . (Blair Atholl).
706. 37135 Tpr. . . . Patton, A. . .   "   . . . (Scone).
707. 25890 Tpr. . . . Robertson, D. .   "   . . . (Alyth).
708. 37572 Lce.-Corpl. . Robertson, H. .   "   . . . (Monzievaird).
709. 37117 Tpr. . . . Scrimgeour, J. .   "   . . . (Crieff).

710.	37116	Tpr.	Sim, P. M.	The Scottish Horse	(Pitlochry).
711.	37461	Tpr.	Stewart, C.	,,	(Blairgowrie).
712.	37022	Tpr.	Stewart, D.	,,	(Huntingtower).
713.	44674	Tpr.	Stewart, D. H.	,,	(Perth).
714.	37159	Tpr.	Stewart, J. A.	,,	(Ballinluig).
715.	859	Tpr.	Stewart, R. D.	,,	(Perth).
716.	44706	Tpr.	Strong, D.	,,	(Thornhill).
717.	37125	Tpr.	Watt, D.	,,	(Perth).
718.	37024	Tpr.	Whyte, R.	,,	(Perth).
719.	31029	Tpr.	Scott, A. M.	,,	(Rumbling Bridge).
720.	37152	Lce.-Corpl.	Wilson, J.	,,	(Glenfarg).
721.	35741	Sergt.	Wilson, P.	,,	(Bankfoot).
722.	37596	Tpr.	Wishart, R.	,,	(Crieff).
723.	44663	Tpr.	Yeaman, D.	,,	(Perth).
724.	872	Tpr.	Young, R.	,,	(Bankfoot).
725.	616	Sc. Sergt.	McGregor, W.	,,	(Weem).
726.	37284	Tpr.	Robertson, G.	,,	(Alyth).
727.	37173	Piper	Stevenson, W.	,,	(Muthill).
728.	37001	Pipe-Corpl.	Mathewson, J.	,,	(Balbeggie).
729.	31362	Tpr.	Robertson, D. C.	,,	(Blairgowrie).
730.	51	Tpr.	Ross, T.	,,	(Gask).
731.	37387	Pipe-Corpl.	McInnes, J.	,,	(Crieff).
732.	44753	Tpr.	Moon, J.	,,	(Port of Monteith).
733.	25886	Sergt.	Thomson, R.	,,	(Alyth).
734.	36975	Tpr.	Mitchell, R.	,,	(Perth).
735.	44755	Tpr.	Malloch, J.	,,	(Muthill).
736.	37011	Tpr.	McLaren, A.	,,	(Perth).
737.	37197	Tpr.	McKay, W. C.	,,	(Burrelton).
738.	31367	Corpl.	Malloy, J.	,,	(Perth).
739.	37213	Lce.-Corpl.	Reid, J. M.	,,	(Coupar Angus).
740.	37012	Tpr.	Robertson, D.	,,	(Cargill).
741.	37588	Sadd.-Corpl.	Robertson, J.	,,	(Alyth).
742.	37021	Corpl.	Robertson, J.	,,	(Stanley).
743.	615	Tpr.	MacLeod, P.	Bethune's Mounted Infantry	(Crieff).
744.	—	Qrmr.-Sergt.	Raitt, A.	,, ,,	(Blairgowrie).
745.	—	Tpr.	Smith, W. R.	Colonial Scouts	(Caputh).
746.	—	Tpr.	Marshall, A. M.	Commander-in-Chief's Bodyguard	(Perth).
747.	—	Tpr.	Ferguson, F.	Diamond Fields Horse	(Coupar Angus).
748.	—	Tpr.	Murdoch, J. A. H. Burn.	Lumsden's Horse	(Gartincaber).
749.	—	Sergt.	Doig, R.	Kitchener's Fighting Scouts	(Caputh).
750.	—	Sergt.	Porteous, P.	,, ,,	(Blackford).
751.	1889	Tpr.	Reid, J.	,, ,,	(Alyth).
752.	1198	Tpr.	Littlejohn, T.	,, ,,	(Perth).
753.	—	Gr.	Kinloch, A. D.	Natal Volunteer Artillery	(Gourdie).
754.	—	Tpr.	Raitt, R. M.	Imperial Light Horse	(Blairgowrie).
755.	—	Tpr.	Coltart, C.	,, ,,	(Perth).
756.	1436	Tpr.	Whyte, W.	,, ,,	(Alyth).
757.	—	Tpr.	Scott, J.	Kimberley Mounted Corps	(Auchterarder).
758.	—	Pte.	Skinner, J.	Scott's Railway Guards	(Moulin).
759.	—	Tpr.	Thomson, W.	South African Light Horse	(Scone).
760.	—	Tpr.	Barty, J. H.	New Zealand Mounted Infantry	(Lethendy).
761.	—	Tpr.	Henderson, J.	,, ,,	(Perth).
762.	2598	Corpl.	Carmichael, R.	British South Africa Police	(St. Fillans).
763.	590	Trp. Sgt.-Major	McFarlane. D.	,,	(Amulree).
764.	—	Sergt.	McDiarmid, D.	Duke of Edinburgh's Own Volunteer Rifles	(Callander).
765.	—	Corpl.	Comrie, P.	Natal Carbineers	(Dunblane).
766.	—	Tpr.	Smythe, D. W.	,,	(Methven).
767.	154	Tpr.	Greig, J. E.	,,	(Perth).

768.	— Tpr.	Playfair, W. S.	Strathcona's Horse	(Coupar Angus).
769.	— Tpr.	MacGregor, H.	Thorneycroft's Mounted Infantry	(Trossachs).
770.	— Tpr.	Rattray, L. C.	,, ,,	(Blairgowrie).
771.	— Tpr.	Anderson, J. C. L.	,, ,,	(Muckart).
772.	— Tpr.	Anderson, B.	,, ,,	(Muckart).
773.	— Tpr.	Kerrigan, H.	,, ,,	(Perth).
774.	8914 Sergt.	Stirling, B. T.	,, ,,	(Dunblane).
775.	276 Corpl.	Robertson, A. I.	Canadian Mounted Rifles	(Blair Atholl).
776.	— Bomb.	Drury, J.	Cape Garrison Artillery	(Perth).
777.	1521 Pte.	Whitton, J.	Cape Railway Sharp-shooters	(Blairgowrie).
778.	1260 Pte.	Davidson, W. T.	Cape Town Highlanders	(Perth).
779.	— Tpr.	Robertson, D.	Ashburner's Light Horse	(Strathbraan).
780.	350 Sergt.	Hay, H. M. D.	Ceylon Mounted Infantry	(Seggieden).
781.	— Sergt.	Douglas, P. C.	Kitchener's Horse	(Bankfoot).
782.	— Tpr.	Neish, G. J.	,, ,,	(St. Fillans).
783.	— Tpr.	McDonald, P.	New Zealand Rough Riders	(Strathbraan).
784.	— Tpr.	Murdoch, A. A. U. Burn.	,, ,,	(Gartincaber).
785.	— Tpr.	Cromb, J.	Marshall's Horse	(Coupar Angus).
786.	— Corpl.	Baptie, R.	,,	(Ochtertyre).
787.	— Tpr.	Boyd, A.	Roberts' Horse	(Perth).
788.	— Tpr.	Dewar, C. L.	Eastern Province Horse	(Kirkmichael).
789.	— Pte.	Hay, J.	Volunteer Ambulance Corps	(Perth).
790.	935 Pte.	MacKenzie, J. B.	Imperial Light Infantry	(Blairgowrie).
791.	697 Pte.	Beat, D.	,, ,,	(Perth).
792.	— Pte.	Fleming, W. R.	,, ,,	(Blacklunans).
793.	— Pte.	Kerrigan, P.	,, ,,	(Perth).
794.	729 Tpr.	Henderson, J.	Johannesburg Mounted Rifles	(Blairgowrie).
795.	— Sq. Sgt.-Maj.	McGregor, R.	Steinaecker's Horse	(Blair Drummond).
796.	793 Tpr.	Lowe, G. S.	Western Province Mounted Rifles	(Alyth).
797.	— Sergt.	Keay, W. J.	New South Wales Mounted Rifles	(Glenshee).
798.	— Sergt.	Macdonald, D.	,, ,,	(Perth).
799.	— Corpl.	Proctor, G. S.	New England Mounted Rifles	(Blairgowrie).
800.	20393 Tpr.	Hinshelwood, J.	Prince of Wales's Light Horse	(Perth).
801.	20390 Tpr.	Hinshelwood, T.	,, ,,	(Perth).
802.	1634 Tpr.	Shepherd, W. A.	Prince Alfred's Volunteer Guard	(Alyth).
803.	— Pte.	McDonald, D.	Kimberley Town Guard	(Strathbraan).
804.	— Staff. Sergt.	Robertson, J.	,, ,,	(Strathbraan).
805.	— Pte.	Mitchell, J. J.	Port Elizabeth Town Guard	(Alyth).
806.	— Tpr.	Johnston, J. B.	Cape Police	(Longforgan).
807.	— 1st Cl. Tpr.	Anderson, A.	South African Constabulary	(Dunkeld).
808.	2519 2nd Cl. Sgt.	Anderson, A. M.	,, ,,	(Auchterarder).
809.	— Tpr.	Anderson, T.	,, ,,	(Scone).
810.	— Corpl.	Balfour, J. H.	,, ,,	(Kinclaven).
811.	— Tpr.	Cameron, A.	,, ,,	(Auchterarder).
812.	1044 1st Cl. Tpr.	Cameron, D.	,, ,,	(Kinloch Rannoch).
813.	— Tpr.	Cameron, J.	,, ,,	(Auchterarder).
814.	3638 2nd Cl. Tpr.	Campbell, J.	,, ,,	(Kirkmichael).
815.	2750 3rd Cl. Tpr.	Campbell, R.	,, ,,	(Kirkmichael).
816.	— 1st Cl. Tpr.	Comrie, J.	,, ,,	(Crieff).
817.	1001 2nd Cl. Sgt.	Davidson, P.	,, ,,	(Perth).
818.	— Tpr.	Drury, H.	,, ,,	(Perth).
819.	1129 Lce.-Corpl.	Foote, A. D. E.	,, ,,	(Stanley).

820.	—	Tpr. . . .	Glass, A. . . .	South African Constabulary		(Scone).
821.	309	1st Cl. Tpr. .	Hood, J. . . .	,,	,,	(Alyth).
822.	—	Corpl. . . .	Hutchison, T. ,	,,	,,	(Scone).
823.	573	Tpr. . . .	Johnston, A. C. .	,,	,,	(Longforgan).
824.	—	Tpr.	Low, R. K. . .	,,	,,	(Alyth).
825.	1281	3rd Cl. Tpr. .	McDonald, J. .	,,	,,	(Alyth).
826.	—	Tpr. . . .	McIntosh, T. B. .	,,	,,	(Alyth).
827.	—	Corpl. . . .	McKillop, D. .	,,	,,	(Killin).
828.	2356	Tpr. . . .	Allan, D. . . .	,,	,,	(Perth).
829.	—	Tpr.	Allan, J. . . .	,,	,,	(Dunkeld).
830.	3102	1st Cl. Tpr. .	Doig, D. . . .	,,	,,	(Alyth).
831.	—	Sergt. . . .	Ewing, W. L. .	,,	,,	(Kippen).
832.	—	3rd Cl. Tpr. .	Macmillan, N. .	,,	,,	(Killin).
833.	1784	3rd Cl. Tpr. .	Hynd, I. . . .	,,	,,	(Perth).
834.	—	2nd Cl. Tpr. .	Marshall, W. . .	,,	,,	(Gilmerton).
835.	—	Tpr. . . .	McLaggan, D. I.	,,	,,	(Perth).
836.	131	Corpl. . . .	McLaggan, J. I. .	,,	,,	(Perth).
837.	—	Tpr. . . .	McTavish, A. G. A.	,,	,,	(Strathbraan).
838.	—	Tpr. . . .	McTavish, J. .	,,	,,	(Strathbraan).
839.	1275	3rd Cl. Tpr. .	Ritchie, J. . .	,,	,,	(Perth).
840.	—	Tpr. . . .	Whittet, A. . .	,,	,,	(Scone).
841.	667	3rd Cl. Tpr. .	Robertson, C. S.	,,	,,	(Perth).
842.	1935	3rd Cl. Tpr. .	Smith, J. A. . .	,,	,,	(Perth).
843.	1246	3rd Cl. Tpr. .	Stewart, D. L. .	,,	,,	(Coupar Angus).
844.	1931	Tpr. . . .	Walker, R. . .	,,	,,	(Perth).
845.	—	Tpr. . . .	Boyd, P. . . .	,,	,,	(Scone).
846.	1982	Tpr. . . .	Cumming, A. J.	,,	,,	(Perth).
847.	—	Tpr. . . .	Ballingall, W. .	,,	,,	(Blairgowrie).
848.	—	Tpr. . . .	Gardiner, J. R. .	,,	,,	(Perth).
849.	—	Tpr. . . .	Lamond, G. . .	,,	,,	(St. Martin's).
850.	1800	3rd Cl. Tpr. .	Lennox, W. . .	,,	,,	(Dunblane).
851.	—	3rd Cl. Tpr. .	Laurie, J. . . .	,,	,,	(Dunblane).
852.	1644	3rd Cl. Tpr. .	Edmondston, A. B.	,,	,,	(Blair Drummond).
853.	1064	3rd Cl. Tpr. .	McGregor, D. B.	,,	,,	(Scone).
854.	58	Tpr. . . .	Menzies, J. . .	,,	,,	(Struan).
855.	639	1st Cl. Tpr. .	McGregor, W. .	,,	,,	(Pitlochry).
856.	29442	Pte.	Boyd, R. . . .	Imperial Yeomanry, 6th Batt., 20th Coy. . . .		(Scone).
857.	—	—	Meldrum, C. G. .	Indian Ambulance Corps .		(Logierait).
858.	4988	Piper . . .	Smith, J. . . .	Seaforth Highlanders . .		(Rattray).
859.	—	Sergt.-Major .	Wilson, J. . . .	Highland Light Infantry .		(Blairgowrie).
860.	1191	Corpl. . . .	Robertson, J. .	South African Constabulary		(Arnprior).
861.	1247	Corpl. . . .	Robertson, W. .	,,	,,	(Arnprior).
862.	21941	Farr. . . .	Campbell, J. . .	Imperial Yeomanry, 6th Batt., 18th Coy. . . .		(Aberfeldy).

ADDENDA

ROLL OF OFFICERS, PART I

Buist, Major-Gen. David Simson (born and brought up in Perth; son of the late Robert Buist, of Perth). Educated at Perth Academy. Gazetted Ensign East India Company's Service and appointed to 27th Bengal Native Infantry (now 27th Punjabis), 1848. Promoted Lieutenant, 1856. Transferred to the Sylet Light Infantry (now 8th Goorkha Rifles), 1857. Served in Indian Mutiny, 1857–1858, with Sylet Light Infantry, (1) in pursuit of the three companies of the 34th Bengal Native Infantry which mutinied at Chittagong on the 18th November 1857; and (2) commanded a detachment of his regiment at the action of Binna Candi in the Cachar district, 12th January 1858 (mentioned in despatches; thanks of Lieut.-Governor of Bengal and Commander-in-Chief in India; and medal). Commanded six companies of the Sylet Light Infantry employed in the Jyntiah Hills in suppressing the Cossiah insurrection in 1860, including skirmishes on the 26th and 28th March, and capture of the stockaded village of Nunjungie (mentioned in despatches). Promoted Captain, 1861. Again served in the Cossiah and Jyntiah Hills during the rebellion of 1862–1863, including the capture of the stockades of Moonsow, Ooksai, Numbraie, Raielyand, and fourth recapture of Moonsow. Served in the Bhutan Expedition of 1865, and was present in the recapture of Dewangiri (mentioned in despatches; promoted 2nd-in-command of Sylet Light Infantry; medal with clasp). Promoted Major, Bengal Staff Corps, and employed on Staff until 1876. Promoted Lieut.-Colonel, 1874; Colonel, and placed on Unemployed Supernumerary List, 1879; Major-General, 1890.

Burleigh, Lieut. the Hon. Robert Bruce, Master of (eldest son of Lord Balfour of Burleigh [1]). Educated at Eton. Gazetted 2nd Lieut. 3rd (Militia) Batt. Princess Louise's Argyll and Sutherland Highlanders, 1898; 2nd Lieut. 1st Butt. A. and S. H., 1900. Served in South African War, (1) with 4th (Militia) Batt. A. and S. H., 1900, and (2) with 1st Batt. A. and S. H., 1900–1902 (Queen's medal, with two clasps; King's medal, with two clasps). Promoted Lieut., 1903. Still serving. [p. 141.]

Campbell, Maj.-Gen. Archibald Edwardes (eldest son of the late Lt.-Gen. John Edwardes Campbell, and grt.-grd.-son of John Campbell of Achalader [2]). Gazetted Ensign 31st Bengal Native Infy. (now 2nd Queen's Own Rajput Light Infy.) 1851. Served in Southal Rebellion, 1855–1856. Promoted Lieut., 1857. Served in Indian Mutiny, 1857–1858, and took part in numerous engagements in the Saugor district of Central India. Severely wounded in the attack on the fortified village of Nurricowli, 18th September 1857 (medal, with clasp). Apptd. Assistant Commissioner in Assam, 1862. Brev.-Capt., 1863; Capt., Bengal Staff Corps, 1866. Deputy Commissioner of the Libsayar district of Upper Assam, 1869–1883. Promoted Major, 1871; Lieut.-Col., 1877; Brev.-Col., 1881. Retired as Senior Deputy Commissioner in Assam, 1888. Placed on Unemployed Supernumerary List, and promoted Major-General, 1892.

---

[1] Lord Balfour of Burleigh owned property in Perthshire until the issue of the Boundary Commissioners' Order of 1891; and in the county *Valuation Roll* he still appears as assessed for the same.

[2] Though the original Achalader was in Argyllshire, John Campbell also owned Ballied, in Perthshire, now known as Achalader.

Murdoch, Lieut.-Col. John Burn- (son of William Burn-Murdoch and grandson of the late John Burn-Murdoch of Gartincaber). Educated at Edinburgh Academy and the Royal Military Academy, Woolwich. Gazetted Lieut. Corps of Royal Engineers, 1872. Served in Afghan War, 1878–1880, and took part in operations of Kuram Valley Field Force under Sir Frederick Roberts, being present in engagement at Charasia, Oct. 6, 1879, and in operations round Kabul, Dec. 1879, including storming of Asmai Heights—wounded (mentioned in despatches; medal with two clasps). Served also in Egyptian Campaign, 1882, with Indian Contingent, being present in battle of Tel-el-Kebir (mentioned in despatches; medal with clasp; 5th class of Medjidie;

Khedive's star). Passed Staff College, 1887–1888. Promoted Capt., 1884; Major, 1891; Lieut.-Col., 1900. Employed for many years on Indian State and Company's Railways. Retired 1900.

Preston, Major Robert William Pigot Clarke Campbell (of Ardchattan and Valleyfield [1]). Educated at Eton and Christ Church, Oxford. Gazetted Lieut. 3rd (Militia) Batt. The Black Watch, 1884. Promoted Capt., 1889. A.D.C. to Governor of New Zealand, 1894–1897. Served in South African War, 1900–1901, attached to 4th (Militia) Batt. Argyll and Sutherland Highlanders, and took part in operations in Cape Colony and Orange River Colony (Queen's medal, with three clasps). Promoted Major 3rd Batt. The Black Watch, 1903. Still serving. [p. 141.]

ROLL OF NON-COMMISSIONED OFFICERS AND MEN

THE HIGHLAND LIGHT INFANTRY

3420. Sgt.-Maj. Wilson, Jas. (Blairgowrie). Enlisted in 71st (Highland) Light Infantry (now The Highland Light Infantry), 1852. Promoted Corpl., 1854; Sergt., 1856. Served in Crimea, 1855–1856, during Russian War, and was present at siege of Sevastopol (medal, with clasp "Sevastopol," and Turkish medal). Served also in Indian Mutiny, 1858–1859; wounded at Gwalior, June 16, 1858 (medal with clasp "Central India"). Good Conduct medal. Apptd. Sergt.-Major 1st Administrative Batt. Perthshire Volunteers (now 5th Vol. Batt. The Black Watch), 1861. Discharged 1892. [859.]

SEAFORTH HIGHLANDERS (ROSS-SHIRE BUFFS, THE DUKE OF ALBANY'S)

4988. Piper Smith, John (Rattray). Enlisted 1894. Served in the Occupation of Crete, 1897, and in Soudan Campaign, 1898 (medal, and Khedive's medal, with clasps "The Atbara" and "Khartoum"). Discharged 1902. [858.]

IMPERIAL YEOMANRY (6TH BATTALION) 18th (Lanarkshire) Company

21941. Farr. Campbell, John (Aberfeldy). Enlisted 1901. Served in South African War, 1901–1902 (Queen's medal, with clasps "Cape Colony," "Orange Free State," "Transvaal," "South Africa, 1901," and "South Africa, 1902"). Discharged 1902. [862.]

SOUTH AFRICAN CONSTABULARY

1191. Corpl. Robertson, James (Amprior). Enlisted 1901. Served in South African War, 1901–1902 (Queen's medal with clasps "Cape Colony," "Orange Free State," "Transvaal," "South Africa, 1901," and "South Africa, 1902"). Promoted Corpl. Still serving. [860.]

1247. Corpl. Robertson, William (Amprior). Enlisted 1901. Served in South African War, 1901–1902 (Queen's medal, with clasps "Cape Colony," "Orange Free State," "South Africa, 1901," and "South Africa, 1902"). Promoted Corpl. Still serving. [861.]

1 Valleyfield was in Perthshire until 1891, when, under the Boundary Commissioners' Order, No. 119, it was transferred to Fife.

SUBSCRIBERS' INDEX

His Majesty the King.

H.R.H. Princess Christian of Schleswig-Holstein.

Adamson, Wm. Shaw, of Careston Castle, Forfarshire.

Allan, George, C.E., 127 Cromwell Road, South Kensington, London.

Allhusen, W. H., Tulliemet, Ballinluig.

Allhusen, Wilton, Pinhay, Lyme Regis, Dorset.

Anderson, Dr. John, Newholme, Pitlochry.

Anderson, J. Chapman, of Aikenhead, Blairgowrie.

Anderson, W. M., Solicitor, Grange Street, Grangemouth.

Ardwall, Lord, 14 Moray Place, Edinburgh.

Armitstead, Lord, 4 Cleveland Square, London.

Asten, Mrs., Laurel Bank, Durham Road, Portobello.

Atholl, Duke of, Blair Castle, Blair Atholl.

Aytoun, Mrs. Rutherford, Easter Bleaton, Bridge of Cally.

Bald, Mrs., 50 Eaton Square, London, S.W.

Balfour, Lady Betty, Fisher's Hill, Woking.

Ballingal, Rev. James, Rhynd Manse, Perth.

Ballingall, Dr. Geo. A., 40 Chapel Park Road, St. Leonards-on-Sea.

Ballingall, Hugh, Ardarroch, Dundee.

Ballingall, Jas. B., LL.B., 6 Abercromby Place, Edinburgh.

Ballingall, Wm., M.A., F.C.S., Ardarroch, Dundee.

Bannerman, Rt. Hon. Sir H. Campbell-, G.C.B., M.P., Belmont Castle, Meigle.

Barbour, Mrs. R. W., Fincastle, Pitlochry.

Barnett, Miss H. M., Wester Ballindean, Inchture.

Beech, Major J. R., Meggernie Castle, Aberfeldy.

Bell, J. Harriott, Rossie, Forgandenny.

Bell, John W., Rossie, Forgandenny.

Bell, Sir James, Bart., Montgreenan, Ayrshire.

Benson, Mrs., Newbrough Hall, Fourstones-on-Tyne.

Bissett, Major W., Woodlands Cottage, Blairgowrie.

Blackett, Mrs., Inverard, Aberfoyle.

Black Watch, The, (Royal Highlanders), 1st Batt., Officers' Mess.

Brand, John, Upland, Kinnoull, Perth.

Brand, Robert, 7 Melville Street, Perth.

Breadalbane, Marquess of, Taymouth Castle, Aberfeldy.

Brickenden, Col. R. H. L., The Albany, Piccadilly, London, W.

Brown, Dr. Wm., Eastfield, Galashiels.

Brown, W., 5 Castle Street, Edinburgh.

Browne, the late Mrs. E. Johnston-, of Kincardine Castle, Auchterarder.

Buchanan, J. Hamilton, of Leny, Callander.

Buist, Major-Gen. D. S., 22 Palmeira Avenue, Hove, Sussex.

Bulloch, Mrs. George, Kinloch, Dunkeld.

Butler, Mrs., Trinity Lodge, Cambridge.

Butter, A., of Faskally, Pitlochry.

Calder, James, of Ardargie, Forgandenny.

Cameron, Miss Catherine, Newburgh, Fife.

Cameronians, The, (Scottish Rifles), 2nd Batt., Officers' Mess.

Campbell, Capt. Hector, Corps of Guides, Junior Naval and Military Club, 96 Piccadilly, W.

Campbell, Lieut.-Col. John H., of Inverardoch, Doune.

Campbell, Major-Gen. A. E., Poltair, Mannamead, Plymouth.

Campbell, Miss Colina, Glan-Llyn, St. Asaph.

Campbell, Miss Margaret, Glan-Llyn, St. Asaph.

Campbell, Miss Mary, Glan-Llyn, St. Asaph.

Campbell, Mrs., Glan-Llyn, St. Asaph.

Campbell, Sir Alexander, Bart., of Aberuchill, Comrie.

Campbell, Sir Duncan, Bart., of Barcaldine, Ridgway Place, Wimbledon.

Campbell, Willison, Acharn, Killin.

Carmichael, James, of Arthurstone, Meigle.

Carnegie, James, of Stronvar, Balquhidder.

Chalmers, Major P., Gowanlea, Blairgowrie.

Chalmers, Mrs. Norman, Mount Linton, Invercargill, New Zealand.

Chambers, C. E. S., of Cardney, Dunkeld.

Chapman, S., 3 King James Place, Perth.

Christie, Capt. R. M., Westlands, Dunblane.

Clark, Capt. J. Hay (late N.S.W. Lancers), 7 Park Place, St. James's, London, S.W.

Clark, Col. W., of Princeland, Coupar Angus.

Clark, G. D. Atkinson, of Belford Hall, Northumberland.

Clark, the late James, F.R.C.V.S., Abbeyhill, Coupar Angus.
Clark, Miss, 7 Park Place, London, S.W.
Cochrane, Mrs., Brookfield, Weston, Bath.
Colquhoun, Col. Campbell, of Clathick, Crieff.
Colquhoun, Lieut.-Col., Old Faskally, Killiecrankie.
Constable, R. R., Cally, Blairgowrie.
Constable, the late Geo., of Balmyle, Blairgowrie.
Cooper, Mrs., 54 Manor Place, Edinburgh.
Cowan, Miss, Lagreach, Pitlochry.
Cox, Albert E., of Dungarthill, Dunkeld.
Cox, Edmund, of Cardean, Meigle.
Cox, Miss, Clement Park, Dundee.
Cox, W. H., of Snaigow, Murthly.
Cumming, W. Skeoch, 29 St. Andrew Square, Edinburgh.
Cunyngham, A. Dick-, 15 Eccleston Square, London, S.W.
Cunyngham, Major Sir Wm. Stewart Dick-, Bart., of Prestonfield, 18 Hobart Place, London.
Cunyngham, Miss Dick-, 7 Ralston Street, Tedworth Square, London, S.W.
Cunyngham, Mrs. W. H. Dick-, 219 Knightsbridge, London, S.W.

Darling, Lord Stormonth, Balvarran, Pitlochry.
Dewar, Sir J., Bart., M.P., Abercairny, Crieff.
Dickson, John, Blair Castle Gardens, Blair Atholl.
Dickson, Mrs. J. F., Newmanswalls, Montrose.
Douglas, Mrs. Pitmuies, Guthrie.
Drummond, A. Hay, of Cromlix, Dunblane.
Drummond, Capt. the Hon. Maurice, The Black Watch.
Drummond, Col. L. G., Scots Guards, 18 Eaton Place, London, S.W.
Drummond, Lady Edith, The Cottage, Kew.
Drummond, Lieut.-Col. F. H. R., Central India House, Pitcairn, Dunning.
Drummond, Lieut.-Col. Home-, of Blair Drummond, Perthshire.
Dudley, Earl of, 7 Carlton Gardens, London, S.W.
Duff, Col. C. E., C.B., Castleton House, Sherborne, Dorset.
Duncan, James, of Jordanstone, Meigle.
Dundas, Comdr., R.N., of Ochtertyre, Stirling.
Dunedin, Lord, of Stenton, 7 Rothesay Terrace, Edinburgh.
Dunmore, Major the Earl of, V.C., 16th Lancers, Aldershot.

Effingham, Earl of, Tusmore Park, Bicester, Oxon.
Elibank, Lord, Darn Hall, Eddleston.
Elibank, Master of, M.P., Juniper Bank, Walkerburn.

Ewing, Henry Leckie, Finglen, Campsie Glen.
Ewing, Robert Leckie, Devon Grove, Dollar.

Fanshawe, Mrs. H. W. R., Lansdowne, Sidmouth, S. Devon.
Ferguson, Rev. R. Menzies, M.A., D.D., Manse of Logie, Bridge of Allan.
Fergusson, J. Grant, of Baledmund, Pitlochry.
Finlayson, Ex-Provost Malcolm, Crieff.
Fleming, George M., of Clayquhat,Blairgowrie.
Fleming, Mrs., of Inchyra, Hamilton House, Perth.
Fleming, Rev. James, M.A., Manse of Kettins, Coupar Angus.
Forbes, Mrs. Drummond, of Millearne, Auchterarder.
Forman, C. M., 6 Drummond Place, Edinburgh.
Fothringham, W. Steuart, of Grandtully and Murthly, Murthly Castle, Murthly.
Fraser, C. C., Blair Castle, Blair Atholl.
Fraser, the late P. Allan, of Blackcraig, Blairgowrie.
Friedlander, J., White Knight's Park, Reading.

Gardyne, Hon. Mrs. Greenhill-, Finavon, Forfar.
Gillespie, James F., Rotmell, Ballinluig.
Gill, Mrs., 60, The Drive, Hove, Sussex.
Gordon, Col., Linnkeith, Blairgowrie.
Gordon, Rev. the Hon. Arthur, M.A., Strathearn Lodge, North Berwick.
Graeme, Col. Laurence, Fonthill, Shaldon, Teignmouth, Devon.
Graeme, Miss, Fonthill, Shaldon, Teignmouth, Devon.
Graham, A. G. Maxtone-, of Cultoquhey and Redgorton, 4 Albion Street, London, W.
Graham, Marquess of, Easton Park, Wickham Market.
Grant, Capt., of Kilgraston, c/o Condie Mackenzie & Co., W.S., Perth.
Grant, Messrs. R., & Son, 107 Princes Street, Edinburgh.
Grimmond, the late Alex. D., of Glencricht, Blairgowrie.
Grimond, Miss, Oak Bank, Blairgowrie.
Guthrie, Sir James, P.R.S.A., 41 Moray Place, Edinburgh.

Halkett, the late Sir Arthur, Bart., of Pitferrane, Dunfermline.
Hamilton, Mrs. Buchanan Baillie, of Cambusmore, Callander.
Harriott, James, Belmont, Dundee.
Harris, Col., Collingwood Tower, Camberley, Surrey.
Hay, Mrs. Drummond-, of Seggieden, Perth.
Hay, R. A., Firwood Villa, Perth.
Henderson, Capt. G. D. Clayhills,- R.N., of Invergowrie, Dundee.
Honey, Rev. John, M.A., The Manse, Inchture.

Honeyman, G., Foxhall, Coupar Angus.
Honeyman, Mrs. Stuart, Greenside, Coupar Angus.
Hood, Dr., Blairgowrie.
Hope, Miss, Donavourd, Crieff.
Hope, Miss Jessie, 6 Canterbury Road, Oxford.
Hutcheson, Andrew, Beechwood, Perth.

ILCHESTER, Dowager Countess of, Abbotsbury Castle, Dorchester.
Inglis, (the late) Mrs. Stephen, 2 East Ascent, St. Leonards-on-Sea.
Irvine, Dr. John, Muthill, Perthshire.

JACK, Mrs., 36 High Street, Crieff.
Jamieson, Mrs., Ardunan, Strathblane.
Japp, William, Broomhall, Alyth.
Johnstone, Ex-Provost, Ashbank, Alyth.
Johnstone, Henry B., The Pass House, Callander.
Johnstone, Laurence, of Sands, Kincardine-on-Forth.

KENNEDY, Rev. H. A. A., Callander.
Kennedy, Rev. W. B., Manse of Eyemouth, Berwickshire.
Kettle, Miss Mackenzie, West Lodge, Callander.
Kidd, Capt. W. S., Scottish Horse, Tighnaleigh, Alyth.
Kincairney, Lord, 6 Heriot Row, Edinburgh.
Kinloch, Charles Y., of Gourdie, Murthly.
Kinloch, Sir John, Bart., of Kinloch, Meigle.
Kinnaird, Lord, Rossie Priory, Inchture.
Kinnoull, Earl of, Dupplin Castle, Perth.

LAMB, D. I., 3 Playfair Terrace, St. Andrews.
Landels, W. Jamieson, c/o Messrs. Redfern, Princes Street, Edinburgh.
Lansdowne, Marquess of, Lansdowne House, Berkeley Square, London, W.
Lindsay, D. C. and Mrs. Rutherford, of Ashintully, Blairgowrie.
Lloyd, Major-Gen., Beechmont, Rathkeale, Co. Limerick.
Login, Miss Edith, Cedars, Aylesford, Kent.
Love, Ex-Lord Provost, Perth.
Low, John L., St. Andrews.

MACALPINE, Alex., Blair Castle, Blair Atholl.
McAra, William, West Lodge, Blair Atholl.
Macdonald, F. F., of Lochlands, Arbroath.
Macdonald, H. L., Wallabadah, N.S.W.
Macdonald, John M. L., of Wallabadah, N.S.W.
Macdonald, Miss J. C. C., Ballintuim House, Blairgowrie.
Macdonald, Miss I. M., M.B., 47 Seymour Street, London, W.
Macdonald, Miss Louisa, M.A., Women's College, The University, Sydney, N.S.W.

Macdonald, Mrs., 95 Harley Street, London, W.
Macdonald, W.K., of Ballintuim, Blairgowrie.
M'Ewen, James, Craigie Bank, Perth.
McFarlane, Wm., Westlands, Guildford, Surrey.
McGillewie, R., Union Bank of Scotland, Dunkeld.
MacGregor, Charlotte, Lady, Hampton Court Palace.
Macgregor, Ex-Provost, Crieff.
MacGregor, John, W.S., 57 Grange Loan, Edinburgh.
MacGregor, Lady Helen, of MacGregor, Edinchip, Balquhidder.
MacGregor, Major Murray, Trelawney, Leckhampton Road, Cheltenham.
MacGregor, Miss, of MacGregor, Edinchip, Balquhidder.
MacGregor, Miss Murray, 7 Barossa Place, Perth.
MacGregor, Mrs. Sheriff, Glengyle, Loch Katrine by Stronachlacher.
MacGregor, Very Rev. Jas., D.D., 3 Eton Terrace, Edinburgh.
McInroy, Wm., of Lude, Blair Atholl.
McKay, Alex., Blair Castle, Blair Atholl.
Mackenzie, Lady Marjory, of Gairloch, 10 Moray Place, Edinburgh.
Mackenzie, Qrmr.-Sgt., 109 Dalkeith Road, Edinburgh.
Mackenzie, Sir Alexander Muir-, Bart., of Delvine, Kennacoil, Dunkeld.
Mackinnon, Major-Gen. Henry, C.V.O., C.B., 13 Ovington Square, London, S.W.
McLagan, C. Gibson, Dunfallandy, Pitlochry.
MacLaren, Surgeon-Lieut.-Col. G. G., M.D., Falcon House, Blairgowrie.
McLauchlan, Miss J., Hill View, Pitlochry.
McLean, John, Blair Castle, Blair Atholl.
MacLeish, Ex-Bailie James, 15 Mill Street, Perth.
McNab, James, Blackcraig, Blairgowrie.
Macnaughton, J., Dunderane, Pitlochry.
Macpherson, Major Denis, Royal Munster Fusiliers, Blairgowrie House, Blairgowrie.
Macpherson, Mrs., of Blairgowrie House, Blairgowrie.
Macpherson, W., Blairgowrie House, Blairgowrie.
Mansfield, Earl of, Scone Palace, Perth.
Marshall, Capt. R., 5th V.B.R.H., Killiecrankie.
Marshall, W. H., of Callander, Perthshire.
Masterson, John, J.P., 28 Mill Street, Perth.
Meikle, Rev. James, The Manse, Alyth.
Meldrum, Rev. A., Logierait, Ballinluig.
Menzies, Miss, of Menzies, 23 Royal Avenue, Chelsea, S.W.
Menzies, Sir Neil, Bart., of Menzies, Farleyer, Aberfeldy.
Menzies, W. Stewart-, of Chesthill, Invervar Lodge, Aberfeldy.

Menzies, W. W. Graham-, of Hallyburton, Coupar Angus.
Middleton, Major W. F., of Baldarroch, Murthly.
Middleton, Miss C. F., Blair Castle, Blair Atholl.
Miller, J. J. W., Ardoch, Braco.
Mitchell, Hugh, Solicitor, Pitlochry.
Molyneux, Miss, Tom-na-Monachan, Pitlochry.
Moncreiffe, Sir Robert, Bart., of Moncreiffe, Bridge of Earn.
Moncrieff, Rev. Robert, Manse of Arngask, Glenfarg.
Moncrieff, the late Sir Alexander, K.C.B., of Bandirran, Perth.
Moray, Capt. Drummond-, of Abercairny, Tealing House, Dundee.
Morison, J. B. Broun-, F.S.A., of Finderlie, Murie House, Errol.
Muir, Lady, Deanston House, Doune.
Murdoch, John Burn-, of Gartincaber, Doune.
Murdoch, Col. J. F. Burn-, C.B., Manor House, Normanton-on-Soar, Loughborough.
Murdoch, the late Rev. Canon, and Mrs. Burn-, The Manor House, Normanton-on Soar, Loughborough.
Murdoch, W. G. Burn-, Arthur Lodge, Dalkeith Road, Edinburgh.
Murray, Capt. Lord George Stewart-, The Black Watch, Blair Castle, Blair Atholl.
Murray, C., Taymount, Stanley.
Murray, Hon. Mrs. Edward, 23 Cadogan Gardens, London, S.W.
Murray, Lady Helen Stewart-, Blair Castle, Blair Atholl.
Murray, Lieut. C. J., Coldstream Guards, Taymount, Stanley.
Murray, Miss, Fintry Lodge, Crieff.
Murray, Mrs. Mackenzie, Woodside House, Coupar Angus.
Murray, Mrs., The Old House, Epsom.
Murray, Rev. H. H., M.A., Manse of Monzie, Crieff.
Murray, Sir Patrick Keith-, Bart., of Ochtertyre, Ardenlea, Crieff.

Ness, the late Patrick, of Braco Castle, Perthshire.

Ogilvy, Capt. the Hon. Lyulph, D.S.O., La Salle, Colorado, U.S.A.
Ogilvy, Mrs. James Wedderburn-, Rannagulzion, Bridge of Cally.
Oliphant, Capt. Blair-, of Ardblair, Blairgowrie.
Osborne, Lady D'Arcy Godolphin, Ladies' Athenæum Club, Dover Street, Piccadilly, W.
Outram, Sir F. B., Bart., Clachnafaire, Pitlochry.

Panton, W. A., of Dalnagairn, Kirkmichael.

Partington, C. Mackenzie-, of Merklands, Blairgowrie.
Paterson, the late D. A., of Dalnaglar, Blairgowrie.
Patullo, the late James, of Ashmore, Blairgowrie.
Patullo, Thomas M., Abertay, Broughty Ferry.
Pearson, Sir Charles, 7 Drumsheugh Gardens, Edinburgh.
Playfair, James, Islabank, Coupar Angus.
Porteous, Sergt. Peter, 903 Great Eastern Road, Glasgow.
Pullar, Edmund, Coneyhill House, Bridge of Allan.
Pullar, Herbert S., Dunbarnie Cottage, Bridge of Earn.
Pullar, the late Mrs. Jas. F., Rosebank, Perth.

Ramsay, Miss, 11 York Buildings, Edinburgh.
Ramsay, Miss I., Bamff, Alyth.
Ramsay, Professor G. G., of Drumore, Blairgowrie.
Ramsay, Sir James, Bart., of Bamff, Alyth.
Rattray, Lieut.-Gen. Sir James Clerk-, K.C.B., of Craighall-Rattray, Blairgowrie.
Rattray, Mrs., Coral Bank, Blairgowrie.
Richardson, Col. E. R. Stewart-, of Ballathie, Stanley.
Richardson, Dowager Lady Stewart-, Westwood Cottage, Balthayock, by Perth.
Richardson, Mrs., Panbride House, Carnoustie.
Richmond, J., Monzie Castle, Crieff.
Rigby, the late Lord Justice, Carlyle House, Chelsea Embankment, London.
Robertson, Capt. F. M. B., The Black Watch, Ruthvenfield, Perth.
Robertson, Edgar W., of Auchleeks, Trinafour.
Robertson, John, The Lowes, Dunkeld.
Robertson, J. Stewart-, of Edradynate, Strathtay.
Robertson, J. W. (late Fincastle's Horse), 13 Kinnoull Causeway, Perth.
Robertson, Lord, 108 Eaton Square, London, S.W.
Robertson, Miss, Dundonnachaidh, Pitlochry.
Robertson, Mrs., Ballandean Farm, Strathtay.
Robertson, Mrs. John, Kindrochet, Pitlochry.
Rodger, Miss J. Kay, Glenpark, Port Glasgow.
Rollo, Col. the Master of, Marshalls Manor, Maresfield, Uckfield.
Rollo, Lord, Duncrub Park, Dunning.
Rollo, the late Gen. the Hon. Sir Robert, K.C.B., Strathearn House, Bournemouth.
Rorison, Rev. Vincent L., D.D., St. John's Rectory, Perth.
Rose, Lauchlan, M.D., Newport, Shropshire.
Rose, Rev. Donald, Dalgety Manse, Aberdour, Fife.

Rose, the late Æneas, West Lodge, Blair Castle, Blair Atholl.

Rube, Mrs., 17 Hill Street, London, W.

Ruthven, Lord, Newland, Gorebridge, Midlothian.

SANDEMAN, George A. C., of Fonab, Pitlochry.

Sandeman, Lieut.-Col. J. Glas, Whin Hurst, Hayling Island.

Scott, John, Allan Street, Blairgowrie.

Selby, Mrs., Mayfield, Crieff.

Sellar, Miss Eleanor, 15 Buckingham Terrace, Edinburgh.

Shaw, William, Rosebank, Alyth.

Sivewright, Sir James, K.C.M.G., Tulliallan Castle, Kincardine-on-Forth.

Small, Mrs., of Dirnanean, Pitlochry.

Smart, Mrs., Ballancleroch, Campsie Glen.

Smith, James, Woodlands, Arbroath.

Smith, Rev. A. Wylie, Manse of Bendochy, Coupar Angus.

Smith, the late Samuel, Orchil, Braco, Perthshire.

Smythe, Col. D. M., of Methven Castle, Perth.

Speid, James, of Forneth, Dunkeld.

Speir, Guy, yr. of Culdees, Muthill.

Speir, R. T. N., of Culdees, Muthill.

Stansfeld, Capt., of Dunninald, Montrose.

Steuart, Capt., of Ballechin, Ballinluig.

Stewart, Aubrey K. Alston-, of Urrard, Killiecrankie.

Stewart, Capt. R. J. T., 22nd Punjabis.

Stewart, Capt. W., 121 Preston Road, Brighton.

Stewart, C. Murray, Kinachoile, Dunblane.

Stewart, Col., C.I.E., of Ardvorlich, Balquhidder.

Stewart, H. D., of Strathgarry, Blair Atholl.

Stewart, Lady, Grantully Castle, Aberfeldy.

Stewart, Lieut. D. H., P.O. Box 141, Barberton, Transvaal.

Stewart, Major Alexander Blair-, of Balnakeilly, Pitlochry.

Stewart, Major-Gen. G., C.B., Baldorran College Road, Upper Norwood.

Stewart, Mrs., Ardvorlich Cottage, Balquhidder.

Stirling, Capt. Archibald, of Keir, Dunblane.

Stirling, Capt. C. H. Graham-, of Strowan, Tomperran, Comrie.

Stirling, J. A., of Kippenross and Kippendavie, Sussex Lodge, Regent's Park, London, N.W.

Stirling, Mrs., Tayview, Birnam.

Strathallan, Viscountess, Machany, Perthshire.

Stroyan, John, of Lanrick Castle, Doune.

THOMAS, John, 25 Barossa Place, Perth.

Thomson, Mr. and Mrs. Inches, Hope Park, Blairgowrie.

Tullibardine, Lt.-Col. the Marquess of, Blair Castle, Blair Atholl.

Turner, Mrs., Grafton House, Buxton.

UNDERWOOD, Col., Heath Park, Birnam.

Urmston, Lieut.-Col. A. G. B., Glenmorven, Drimnin, Argyllshire.

Urmston, Mrs., Glenmorven, Drimnin, Argyllshire.

VAUGHAN, R. Clifton, The Cottage, Knebworth, Herts.

WALKER, Dr. J. H., 122 Harley Street, London, W.

Wauchope, David B., 24 Moray Place, Edinburgh.

Wedderburn, Mrs., Marfield, Blairgowrie.

Wharncliffe, Earl of, Wortley Hall, Sheffield.

Whitelaw, Græme A., Strathallan Castle, Machany.

Whitelaw, J. B., Strowan, Crieff.

White, Major G. Dalrymple, 106 Eaton Square, London, S.W.

Whitson, Capt. Hill-, of Park Hill, Blairgowrie.

Whitson, Lieut. T. E. L., 14th Hussars.

Williams, Mrs. J. G., of Pendley Manor, Tring, Herts.

Williamson, Col. D. R., of Lawers, Comrie.

Willison, Campbell, Acharn, Killin.

Willoughby de Eresby, Lord, 43 Charles Street, Berkeley Square, London, W.

Wilson, John, M.P., of Kippen, Airdrie House, Airdrie.

Wishart, George E., Thessalon, Ontario.

Wood, Mrs., of Freeland, Forgandenny.

Wood, the late C. L., of Freeland, Forgandenny.

Worthington, A. O., Maple Hayes, Lichfield.

Writers to H.M. Signet, Library of Society of.

YOUNGER, W., Ravenswood, Melrose.

INDEX TO PERSONS

(For List of Abbreviations, see p. 64)

ADAMS, George, late Tpr. Scot. Hse., 216, 281
,, James, Ptc. Sea. H., 192, 278
,, R. B., Lt.-Col., 93n
,, Walter, Lce.-Cpl. 4th Vol. Batt. B.W.,
    165, 274
Aird, Alexander, Pte. Sea. H., 192
Airlie, David, 7th Earl of, 80
,, David, 8th Earl of (the late), Lt.-Col.
    Comdt. 12th Lancers, 67, 67n, 97-98
,, Mabel, Countess of Airlie. *See* Gore
Aitken, George, Pte. Gord. H., 197
,, William, Tpr. S.A.C., 232
Albert, Sarel, Boer Comdt., 35, 60, 61
Alexander, Alex., late Lce.-Cpl. Scot. Hse.,
    216
,, James, Pte. B.W., 165, 274
,, James M., late Cpl. Scot. Hse., 216, 282
,, John L., late Tpr. Scot. Hse., 216, 282
Allan, David, Pte. Sea. H., 192
,, David, Tpr. S.A.C., 232, 285
,, James, Tpr. S.A.C., 232, 285
,, John, Col.-Sgt. Sea. H., 192
,, Robert, Pte. B.W., 165
,, W. D., 2nd Lt. B.W., 22
Allison, H. H. D. M., Cpl. 5th Vol. Batt.
    B.W., 165, 274
,, John, Pte. Sea. H., 192
Ames, James (the late), Ptc. B.W., 165, 274
Amos, J., late Act. Bomb. R.G.A., 154-55, 272
Ancaster, Gilbert, 1st Earl of, 89
Anderson, Alex. (Crieff), late Sgt. Cape Picneer
    Regt., 225
,, Alex. (Dunkeld), 1st Cl. Tpr. S.A.C., 232,
    284
,, Alex. M., 2nd Cl.-Sgt. S.A.C., 232, 284
,, Allan, Pte. Sea. H., 192, 278
,, Bruce, late Tpr. Thorn. Mtd. Infy., 231,
    284
,, Duncan, Pte. R. Scots, 159, 273
,, of Lambhill, D. W. (the late), 67
,, George, late Pte. 6th Batt. 20th Coy.
    I.Y., 210, 280
,, G. S., late Tpr. Scot. Hse., 216, 281
,, James, Sgt.-Maj. 2nd Batt. B.W., 28, 29,
    D.C.M.
,, James (Perth), Lce.-Sgt. Cam. H., 201, 279
,, James (Perth), No. 3440, Lce.-Cpl. Cam.
    H. 201, 279
,, James, Pte. 2nd, Dgns., 148, 271
,, James (Crieff, the late), No. 3650, Pte.
    B.W., 165, 274
,, James (Blairgowrie), No. 6802, Pte. B.W.,
    165, 274

Anderson, James (Perth), No. 7064, Pte.
    B.W., 165
,, James, late Pte. Gord. H., 197, 279
,, James, Pte. A. and S.H., 204
,, J. C. L., late Tpr. Thorn. Mtd. Infy., 231,
    284
,, John, M.B., C.M. Edin., Lt. Scot. Hse., 67
,, John, Col.-Sgt.-Instr. 4th Vol. Batt. B.W.,
    165
,, Matthew, Sh.-Smith R.F.A., 153
,, Robert, Pte. B.W., 165
,, Thos. (Scone), Tpr. S.A.C., 232, 284
,, Thos. (Perth), late Pte. Sea. H., 192
,, Walter B., late Chief Off. Hospital Ship, 67
,, Wm. B., late Tpr. Scot. Hse., 216, 282
Andrews, Jas., Pte. A. and S.H., 204, 280
Anley, F. G., Maj. Essex Regt., 39, 40, 41, 43
Annat, J. W. (the late), Lt. Queensland Con-
    tingent, 90
Archer, Jas., late Tpr. Scot. Hse., 216
,, Jas., late Col.-Sgt. Gord. H., 197, 279
Arnott, William (the late), Pte. R.A.M.C.,
    209, 280
Arran, Arthur, 5th Earl of, 97
Arthur, William, Pte. B.W., 165
Ash, Robert, Pte. K.O.S.B., 162
Atholl, John, 1st Marquess of, 92
,, John, 7th Duke of, 31, 33, 34, 35, 37,
    79, 82, 88
Austin, W. G., Regtl. Sgt.-Maj. 2nd Scot.
    Hse., 62

BAILLIE, R., Pte. 4th Vol. Batt. B.W., 165
Bain, Wm., Col.-Sgt.-Instr. B.W., 165, 274
Baker, J. M., Lt. 2nd Scot. Hse., 62
Baker Pasha, 75
Bald, Alfred C., D.S.O. (the late), Major Res.
    of Off., 27, 90
,, Ernest H. C., Capt. 15th Huss., 90
,, Mrs. (Invermay), 90
Balfour of Burleigh, Lord, 6th Baron, 286,
    286n
,, Jas. H., Cpl. S.A.C., 233, 284
Ballingall, Harry M., Lt. R.H.A., 90
,, Hugh, J.P., 90
,, Wm. (the late), Tpr. S.A.C., 233, 285
Band, Henry, late Tpr. Scot. Hse., 216
Bannerman, Geo., late Tpr. Scot. Hse., 216
,, Jas., Gr. R.F.A., 153
,, T., late Tpr. Scot. Hse., 216
Baptie, Rob. (the late), Cpl. Marshall's Hse.,
    228, 284
Barclay, C., Cpl. 1st Scot. Hse., 62

Barclay, John, late Pte. Border Regt., 164
Barnett, Alex. (the late), Blindwells, 67
„ John T., late Pte. Scots Gds., 156
„ T. W., late Lt. Scot. Hse., 67
Barr, Archibald, Pte. B.W., 165
Barty, James C., Sh.-Smith 10th Huss., 151, 276
„ John H., late Tpr., N.Z.Mtd.Infy., 229, 283
Baxter, Alexander, Drum. R. Scots., 159
„ J., D.C.M., Sgt. 2nd Batt. B.W., 28, 29
„ W. (the late), Sgt. R. Scots., 159, 273
Bayne, Thos. M., late Sgt. Scot. Hsc., 216, 281
Beat, David, late Pte. Imp. L. Infy., 227, 284
Beaton, Alex., Sgt. Johan. Mtd. Rif., 227
„ Neil, Tpr, S.A.C., 233
Beattie, Andrew, late Sh.-Smith Scot. Hsc., 216
„ John, Pte. K.O.S.B., 162, 273
Beech, John R., C.M.G., D.S.O., Maj. Scot. Hse. I.Y., 90
Beharrie, W., Pte. Gord. H., 197
Bell, Andrew, late Tpr. Scot. Hsc., 216, 217
„ Daniel, late Tpr. Scot. Hse., 217
„ Sir Jas., ex-Lord Provost of Glasgow, 46n
„ Jas. (the late), Lce.-Cpl. Scot. Hse., 46, 217, 282
Bennett, Jas., late Qrmr.-Sgt. R.H.A., 153, 272
„ Peter, Pte. Gord. H., 197, 279
Benson, G. E. (the late), Col. (formerly Maj. R.A.), 5, 6, 32, 33, 34, 38, 40, 42, 43, 44, 44n, 46, 47, 48, 73, 80, 82, 89, 94
Benvie, George, Pte. Scots Gds., 156, 272
Berkeley, T. M. M., Brev. Lt.-Col. B.W., 6, 12, 22
Berthon, H. C. W. (the late), Lt. B.W., 22
Biddulph, Maj.-Gen., 92, 101
Birrell, Jas., Pte. Scots Gds., 156, 272
Bisset, Daniel, Sgt. Sea. H., 192, 278
Bissett, Andrew (the late), Wester Clow, 67–68
„ W., Qrmr. and Hon. Maj. 3rd (Mil.) Batt. H.L.I., 67, 68
Black, Alexander, Pte. B.W., 166
„ Jas., late Pte. Scots Gds., 156, 272
„ Robert, late Pte. B.W., 166, 274
Blain, Thomas I., Pte. A. and S.H., 204, 280
Blair, A., Maj. 2nd Scot. Hse., 30, 30n, 33, 34–36, 49, 55, 62
„ Alexander, late Tpr. Scot. Hse., 217, 282
„ David, Pte. 4th Vol. Batt. B.W., 166, 274
„ J. M., 2nd Lt. B.W., 22
„ R., Pte. Scots Gds., 156, 272
„ William, Pte. B.W., 166
Blood, Sir Bindon, 93
Boshoff, Boer Leader, 51, 52, 54
Botha, Louis, 19, 33, 40, 41n
Bourke, Thomas, Pte. R. Dub. Fus., 208
Boyd, Alfred, late Tpr. Roberts' Hse., 230, 284
„ Hugh, late Pte. Gord. H., 197
„ John, Cpl. A. and S.H., 204
„ J. B., M.B., C.M. Edin., late Civ. Surg., attd. R.A.M.C., 68
„ Peter, Tpr. S.A.C., 233, 285

Boyd, Robert, late Pte. 6th Batt. 20th Coy. I.Y., 210, 285
„ of Sylverton House, W. W. (the late), 68
Boyle, John, late Tpr. Scot. Hse., 217
Brabazon, Maj.-Gen., 96
Bramly, A. Jennings (the late), Maj. comdg. 2nd Scot. Hse., 34
Brand, Wm., Pte. 4th Vol. Batt. B.W., 166, 274
Breadalbane, John, 6th Earl of, 68
Bremner, Peter, Pte. A.O. Dept., 209, 280
Brets, Commandant, 42n
Britz, Boer Leader, 41n
Broadwood, Lt.-Col., 88
Brough, Thomas, Cpl. R. Scots, 159
Brown, A., Pte. Cam. H., 201, 279
„ Alexander, late Pte. B.W., 166, 274
„ Andrew, Pte. 5th Vol. Batt. B.W., 166, 274
„ Charles, late Tpr. Scot. Hse., 217, 281
„ David, late Sgt. Scot. Hse., 217, 281
„ Duncan, Pte. 5th Vol. Batt. B.W., 166, 274
„ George, Pte. B.W., 166, 274
„ John Roy, Sgt. Gord. H., 198, 279
„ Robert, late Pte. Cam. H., 201
„ Thomas, Lce.-Cpl. B.W., 166
„ Thomas, Pte. A. and S.H., 204
„ Thomas K. W., late Lce.-Cpl. B.W., 166, 274
Browne, R. A., Maj. Bord. Regt., 53
Brownie, Chas. E., Col.-Sgt. Instr. R. Jersey Mil., 192, 278
Bruce, Alexander, Pte. Scot. Rif., 163
„ Charles, late Sgt. B.W., 166
„ David, late Tpr. Scot. Hse., 217, 282
„ James (the late), Pte. B.W., 166, 274
„ Honble. J. F. T. Cumming (the late), Capt. 2nd Batt. B.W., 4, 6, 8, 22
„ Peter, Sgt. Sea. H., 192
„ Wm. B., Lce.-Cpl. 4th Vol. Batt. B.W., 166, 274
Bryson, James F., Lce.-Cpl. 1st Vol. Batt. B.W., 166, 274
Buchan, And. S., Lce.-Cpl., 4th Vol. Batt. B.W., 166, 274
„ David, Lce.-Cpl. B.W., 166, 274
„ Mungo, Cpl. 4th Vol. Batt. B.W., 167, 274
Buchanan, John, Pte. 4th Vol. Batt. B.W., 167, 274
„ John, Pte. R.A.M.C., 209, 280
„ Wm., late Sgt. A. and S.H., 204
Buist, Arthur H., Capt. Corps of Guides, 91
„ D. S., Maj.-Gen., 91, 286
„ David S., F.R.G.S., Maj. 29th Deccan Hse., 91
„ H. J. M., D.S.O., M.B., M.Ch. Edin., Maj. R.A.M.C., 91
„ Jas., late 3rd Cl. Tpr. S.A.C., 233
„ Jas. M., M.B., B.Ch., Capt. R.A.M.C., 91
„ Keith L., Capt. H.L.I., 91–92
„ Robert, of Perth, 286
Buller, Sir A., Vice-Admiral, 94
Bullion, George T., Pte. Scots Gds., 156
Bullions, William, Pte. 2nd Dgns., 148
Bulloch, of Kinloch, George (the late), 68

Bulloch, R. A., Lt. B.W., 22, 68
Burgess, President, 75
Burleigh, Hon. R. B., Master of Burleigh, Lt.
  A. and S.H., 286
Burnett, William, Pte. R. Scots, 159
  „ William, Pte. K.O.S.B., 162
Burnfield, John, Sh.-Smith Scot. Hse., 217
  „ William, late Tpr. Kitch. Hse., 228
Burns, Edward, Pte. 3rd (Mil.) Batt. B.W.,
  167, 274
  „ G., Piper 2nd Batt. B.W., 29
Burry, John A., Pte. Scot. Rif., 163, 273
Burton, St. G. E. W., Maj. B.W., 2, 22
Butchart, James (the late), Pte. B.W., 167,
  274
Buyers, J., Capt. 2nd Vol. Batt. B.W., 27
Byng, Col., 19

Calder, David, Lce.-Cpl. Gord. H., 198, 279
Calderwood, James, Pte. Sea. H., 192, 278
  „ Matthew, late Pte. 3rd (Mil.) Batt. B.W.,
  167, 274
Callanan, Thomas, late Lce.-Cpl. A. and S.H.,
  204
Cambridge, Duke of, 75
Cameron, Alex. (Crieff), Lce.-Cpl. H.L.I., 188
  „ Alex. (Auchterarder), Tpr. S.A.C., 233, 284
  „ Alex. (Fortingal), late Pte. Lov. Sc., 215,
  281
  „ Angus (the late), Killichonan, 68
  „ Angus (the late), Civ. Surg., attd. 2nd
    Batt. Norfolk Regt., 68
  „ A. R., Brev. Maj. B.W., 22
  „ D., D.C.M.,Piper 2nd Batt. B.W.,10, 28, 29
  „ Daniel, Cpl. Scots Gds., 156, 272
  „ David, Pte. A. and S.H., 204
  „ Donald (Blair Atholl), Lce.-Cpl. Cam. H.,
    201, 279
  „ Donald (Doune), Piper 2nd Batt. B.W.,
    10, 167, 167n
  „ Donald (Kinloch Rannoch), 1st Cl. Tpr.
    S.A.C., 233, 284
  „ Donald (Aberfoyle), Pte. 4th Vol. Batt.
    A. and S.H., 204, 205
  „ Hugh, Gr. R.F.A., 153, 272
  „ James, Pte. B.W., 167, 274
  „ James, late Tpr. S.A.C., 233, 284
  „ James S., Pte. R. Scots, 159
  „ John (Crieff) (the late), Pte. B.W., 167
  „ John (Perth) (the late), Pte. B.W., 167
  „ John, Pte. Scot. Rif., 163, 273
  „ John, late Tpr. Scot. Hse., 217, 282
  „ Norman, Pte. Cam. H., 201
  „ N. C. G., Lt. 1st Scot. Hse., 55, 61, 63
  „ Peter,late Lce.-Cpl. R. Scots Fus., 161, 273
  „ Robert, Pte. B.W., 167
  „ William, Sgt. Scots Gds., 157
  „ William, Pte. R. West Surrey Regt., 160,
  273
  „ William (the late), Pte. H.L.I., 188
  „ William S., late Tpr. Scot. Hse., 217
Campbell, of Aberuchill, and Kilbryde, Sir
  Alex., Bart., Col., 68, 68n

Campbell, Alexander, late Pte H.L.I., 188
  „ Andrew, Gr. R.F.A., 153, 272
  „ A. E., Maj.-Gen., 286
  „ B., Tpr. Scot. Hse., 47
  „ Sir Colin, 73, 81, 82, 86
  „ D., 2nd Lt. B.W., 22
  „ Donald, late Tpr. Scot. Hse., 217
  „ Duncan, late Pte. Cam. H., 201, 279
  „ Duncan, late Tpr. Scot. Hse., 217
  „ Duncan S., Lce.-Cpl. 5th Vol. Batt.
    B.W., 167, 274
  „ Hector, Lt. Corps of Guides, 68
  „ Henry, late Pte., H.L.I., 188
  „ Henry M., late Pte. Sea. H., 192, 278
  „ Honble. Ivan, late Capt. 3rd (Mil.) Batt.
    R. Scots, 68
  „ J., Farr. I.Y., 6th Batt. 18th Coy., 285, 287
  „ James (Auchterarder), late Pte. A. and
    S.H., 205, 280
  „ James (Perth), Pte. A. and S.H., 205, 280
  „ James C. (the late), Lt. Cape G.A., 68
  „ of Kinloch, John (the late), 68, 94
  „ John (Dull), Pte. B.W., 167
  „ John (Tenandry), late Pte. Sea. H., 192,
    193
  „ John (Blair Atholl), late Cpl. Cam. H., 201,
    279
  „ John (Kirkmichael), 2nd Cl. Tpr. S.A.C.,
    233, 284
  „ of Achalader, John C. L., Col. R.E., 68-69,
    286, 286n
  „ J. E., Lt.-Gen., 286
  „ of Inverardoch, John H., Lt.-Col. A. and
    S.H., 69
  „ Johnstone, late Tpr. Scot. Hse., 217, 282
  „ K. J., 2nd Lt. B.W., 22
  „ Peter, late Col.-Sgt. A. and S.H., now
    5th Vol. Batt., 205, 279
  „ Robert, 3rd Cl. Tpr. S.A.C., 233, 284
  „ R. B. P. P. (the late), Maj.-Gen., 68
  „ Stewart, late Piper Scot. Hse., 217, 282
  „ W., Lt. 2nd Scot. Hse., 48, 63
  „ William, late Cpl. B.W., 167, 274
  „ W. MacL., Capt. B.W., 22
Campsie, William, Pte. 4th Vol. Batt. B.W.,
  167, 274
Cannon, M., late Pte. Cam. H., 201
Carmichael, J. N., Pte. 4th Vol. Batt. B.W.,
  167, 274
  „ Robert, late Cpl. B.S.A. Police, 232, 283
  „ William, late Pte. A. and S.H., 205
Carr, Michael, late Pte. B.W., 167, 274
  „ William, Pte. B.W., 167
Carrington, Major, 76
Cassidy, William, late Pte. Sea. H., 193
Chalmers, Alex., late Sgt. Scot. Hse., 217, 281
  „ George M., Lce.-Cpl. Scots Gds., 157, 272
  „ H., Pte. Vol. Batt. R. Scots Fus., 161
  „ Jas. (the late), Tpr. Scot. Hse., 217
  „ of Gowanlea, Peter, late Maj. Stirlingshire
    Rif. Vols., 69
  „ Robert, Sgt. 5th Vol. Batt. B.W., 167-68,
    274

Chalmers, Robertson, Mech. Staff-Sgt. R.E., 155
,, William C., Cpl. R.E., 155
,, Williamson, Pte. B.W., 168, 274
Chapman, Alexander, Pte. H.L.I., 188
Charlesworth, W., Pte. Gord. H., 198
Christie, David H., late Tpr. Scot. Hse., 217-18, 281
,, R. M., Capt. 4th Vol. Batt. B.W., 27, 69
,, Samuel, late Sgt. R.F.A., 153, 272
Clark, Archibald (Perth), late Pte. Gord. H., 198, 279
,, Archibald (Dowally), Pte. Gord. H., 198, 279
,, David, late Pte. 31st Batt. I.Y., 214, 280
,, yr. of Port-an-eilan, Francis M. A. (the late), Lt. Scots Gds., 69
,, James, late Sgt. R. Scots Fus., 161, 273
,, Robert, Pte. B.W., 168, 274
,, of Princeland, W., Col. Oxford L.Infy., 69
,, William, late Pte. B.W., 168, 274
Clarke, Alexander, late Tpr. Scot. Hse., 218, 282
Clayhills, Geo., D.S.O., Lt. East Lancashire Regt., 69
,, Thos., son of Invergowrie, 69
Clement, David, Pte. B.W., 168, 274
Clements, Maj.-Gen., 15, 78, 80
Cochrane, Peter, Pte. B.W., 168
Coetze, Boer Leader, 51, 52
Collins, J. G., Capt. B.W., 23
,, T., Pte. Cam. H., 201
Colquhoun, John L. C., Lt. 3rd (Mil.) Batt. H.L.I., 70
,, Julian C., Capt. R. Canadians, 70
,, R. W., late Col. 3rd (Mil.) Batt. A. and S.H., 92
,, of Clathick, Wm. C., Lt.-Col., 70
Coltart, Charles (the late), Tpr. Imp. L. Hse., 226, 283
Colville, Gen., 10, 13, 14, 79
Comrie, John, 1st Cl. Tpr. S.A.C., 233, 284
,, Peter (the late), Cpl. Natal Carb., 229, 283
,, W., late Pte. 12th Lan., 151, 272
Comyn, D. C. E. ff., Lt. B.W., 23
Conelly, James, late Pte. K.O.S.B., 162, 273
Connelly, Pat., Pte. 4th Vol. Batt. B.W., 168
Connor, R., Pte. Gord. H., 198
,, W., Pte. Gord. H., 198
Coode, J. H. C. (the late), Lt.-Col. comdg. 2nd Batt. B.W., 5, 6, 7, 8, 23
Cook, John, Col.-Sgt. Sea. H., 193
,, Thomas, Pte. Sea. H., 193
Cookson, Col., 56n
Cooper, H. A., Lt. 5th Lancers, 92
Corrie, A. B., Lt. 1st Vol. Batt. B.W., 27
Coulter, James (the late), Sh.-Smith A.S.C., 208, 280
,, William, Sgt. 2nd Dgns., 148, 271
Cowie, James M., Lce.-Cpl. 4th Vol. Batt. B.W., 168, 274
Cowper, James, late Pte. B.W., 168
Cox., Lt. 2nd Batt. Sea. H., 8

Crabb, Jos. (the late), Sgt.-Maj. Sea. H., 193
Craigon, Peter, Sh.-Smith 6th Batt. 20th Coy. I.Y., 211, 280
Crawford, Thomas, late Pte. B.W., 168, 274
Cree, John, late Pte. Sea. H., 193
Crerar, John M'E., Pte. 4th Vol. Batt. B.W., 168, 274
,, Thomas R., late Pte. Lov. Sc., 215, 281
Crewe, Col., 93
Crichton, Peter, Pte. B.W., 168, 274
Cromb, James, Tpr. Marshall's Hse., 228, 284
Cronje, Boer Leader, 10, 12
Cross, David R., Pte. H.L.I., 188, 278
Cruickshanks, Robert, Pte. B.W., 168
Crum, F. M., Capt. 25th M.I., 45n
Cumming, Alexander J., Tpr. S.A.C., 233, 285
Cunningham, Brig.-Gen., 31, 81, 85, 94
,, A., Tpr. Scot. Hse., 45
,, Thomas, late Pte. Welsh Regt., 165
Cunnison, William, Pte. B.W., 168
Cunyngham, R. H. Dick-, (21st Lancers) Capt. 1st Scot. Hse., 49, 50, 61
,, Sir William Dick-, 8th Bart., 101
,, William Henry Dick-, V.C., Lt.-Col. 2nd Batt. Gord. H. (Helen his wife, see Wauchope), 92, 92n, 101-2
,, W. S. Dick-, Sir, Bart., Capt. and Local Maj. Scot. Hse., 23, 30, 33, 34, 70
Curr, David, Pte. 19th Huss., 152, 272
Cuthbert, William (the late), Pte. B.W., 168, 274
Cuthbertson, N. W., Maj. B.W., 23

Dair, James, late Tpr. Scot. Hse., 218, 282
Dalby, G., Lt. 25th M.I., 45n
Dalglish, C. A. de G., 2nd Lt. B.W., 23
Davidson, David, Pte. Scots Gds., 157, 272
,, John, late Tpr. Scot. Hse., 218, 282
,, John, late Pte. B.W., 168, 274
,, Peter, 2nd Cl. Sgt. S.A.C., 233, 284
,, Stewart, Pte. Scots Gds., 157
,, William, Pte. 5th Vol. Batt. B.W., 168
,, W. B. F., Hon., Lt. and Qrmr. B.W., 23
,, William L. L., Lce.-Cpl. 17th Lan., 152, 272
,, William T., late Pte. Cape Town H., 225, 284
Davie, F. A. Ferguson-, Lt. B.W., 27
Davis, Maj.-Gen., 90
,, Thomas T. A., late Pte. 6th Batt. 20th Coy. I.Y., 211, 281
Davison, James (the late), Sadd.-Cpl. Scot. Hse., 218
Dawes, E. S., Capt. B.W., 23
Dawkin, Col., 73
Dawson, James, late Pte. Cam. H., 201
Deane, J., Maj. B.W., 23
Deas, Jas. B. (the late), Sgt. 18th Batt. 70th Coy. I.Y., 213, 281
Delarey, Boer Leader, 34, 49, 52, 54, 55, 56, 61
Dempster, Hugh, late Pte. 6th Batt. 20th Coy. I.Y., 211, 281
Devaney, Frank, late Pte. H.L.I., 188

Devaney, Patrick, Pte. H.L.I., 188, 278
Dewar, C. L., Tpr. Eastern Province Hse., 226, 284
,, Donald, Pte. 18th Huss.. 152
,, James, late Dr. R.F.A., 153, 272
,, Peter, Pte. Scots Gds., 157, 272
,, William, late Sgt. B.W., 169, 274
,, William, late Tpr. Scot. Hse., 218
Dickson, George, Pte. Scots Gds., 157, 272
Dingwall, Arch. Fair, Pte. Gord. H., 198
,, James, Pte. B.W., 169, 274
,, James, Pte. A. and S.H., 205, 279
Dixon, Brig.-Gen., 33, 71, 81, 82, 85, 94
Docherty, H., late Pte. A. and S.H., 205, 280
Dodd, P. R., 2nd Lt. Scot. Rif., 92
Doig, Charles, Pte. Sea. H., 193, 278
,, David, 1st Cl. Tpr. S.A.C., 233, 285
,, James (the late), Pte. Cam. H., 201
,, Robert, late Sgt. Kitch. Fight. Sc., 228, 283
Donaldson, George, Pte. 10th Huss., 151, 271
,, John, Lce.-Cpl. B.W., 169
Donop, Von, Lt.-Col., 55-57
Doran, Col., 80
Dorrien, Smith-, Gen., 12
Douglas, Charles, late Sh.-Smith, 6th Batt. 20th Coy. I.Y., 211, 280
,, Daniel, 3rd Cl. Tpr. S.A.C., 233
,, David, Sgt. Cam. H., 201, 279
,, H. E. M., V.C., D.S.O., Lt. B.W., 9, 20, 28
,, John, late Lce.-Cpl. B.W., 169, 274
,, Peter C., late Sgt. Kitch. Hse., 228, 284
,, Robert (the late), Pte. B.W., 169
,, Robert (the late), Pte. Sea. H., 193
,, Robert, late Sgt. A. and S.H., 205, 279
Dow, John G., late Tpr. Scot. Hse., 218, 281
,, Peter S., late Pte. H.L.I., 189, 278
,, William, Sapr. R.E., 155, 272
Drummond, of Cromlix, Hon. Arthur Hay (the late), Capt., 70n
,, Honble. Chas. R. Hay, late Lt.-Col. Scots Gds., 70, 70n
,, Francis H. R., C.S.E., Lt.-Col. Central Ind. Hse., 70
,, Henry (the late), Maj.-Gen., 70
,, James, late Piper Scot. Hse., 218, 281
,, James, Lce.-Cpl. B.W., 169
,, Hon. Sir James R. (the late), Admiral, 70
,, of Strageath, John (the late), Col., 70
,, Laurence G., Maj. Scots Gds., 70
,, of Megginch, Malcolm, late Capt. Gren. Gds., 71
,, Honble. M. C. A., Lt. B.W., 6, 23, 71
,, William, Pte. A. and S.H., 205
Drury, Henry (the late), Tpr. S.A.C., 233, 284
,, James, Bomb. Cape G.A., 225, 284
Drysdale, William S., late Pte. Gord. H., 198
Dudley, William, 2nd Earl of, Maj. Worc. I.Y., 92
Duff, A. Gordon, Lt.-Col. B.W., 23
,, A. Grant, Capt. 1st Batt. B.W., 2, 3, 23
,, Chas. Edward, C.B., 8th Huss., Lt.-Col. comdg. 1st Scot. Hse. and 8th Huss., 33, 34, 35, 36, 49, 54, 55, 71

Duff, David, Cpl. 4th Vol. Batt. B.W., 169, 275
,, George Smittan (the late), 71
,, James, Pte. Scot. Rif., 163
,, James, Pte. Sea. H., 193
,, John (the late), Dunkeld, 71
,, John, Sgt. 5th Vol. Batt. B.W., 169, 274
,, John, Drum. B.W., 169, 274
,, John, Sgt. A. and S.H., 205, 279
,, Peter, late Sgt. Scot. Hse., 218, 282
,, P. A., 2nd Lt. B.W., 23
,, Robert (the late), Cpl. H.L.I., 189
,, Thomas, late Bdsman, Sea. H., 193, 278
Dugan, William, late Cpl. Scot. Hse., 218, 281
Dunbar, George, Col.-Sgt. Sea. H., 193, 278
Duncan, Adam, Pte. 31st Batt. I.Y., 214
,, David, Pte. B.W., 169, 274
,, John, late Pte. B.W., 169, 274
,, John, Pte. A. and S.H., 205
Dundas, of Ochtertyre, Colin M., late Comdr. R.N., 71
,, of Dunira, Sir David, Bart. (the late), 72
,, David G. M., Lt. Ind. Army, 71
,, G. W. M., 71
Dundonald, Lord, 40n
Dunmore, Charles, 7th Earl of, 92
Dunn, Robert, Cpl. B.W., 169
,, William, 3rd Cl. Tpr. S.A.C., 233
Duthie, Crombie, Pte. B.W., 169, 274

Easson, James T., Pte. 4th Vol. Batt. B.W., 169, 275
Eden, S. H., Lt. B.W., 23
Edmonds, N. G. (the late), Lt. B.W., 6, 8, 23
Edmonston, A. B., 3rd Cl. Tpr. S.A.C., 233-34, 285
,, C. B., late Sgt. 11th Batt. 34th Coy. I.Y., 212, 281
Edward, Robert, late Col.-Sgt. Sea. H., now Ind. Barrack Dept., 193
Edwards, David, Pte. B.W., 169
,, George A., late Pte. 2nd Dgns., 148, 271
,, R., Pte. 2nd Dgns., 148
,, W. N., Lt. 1st Scot. Hse., 55
Elder, James, Cpl. B.W., 169, 275
,, John, Pte. 2nd Dgns., 148, 271
Elibank, Montolieu, 10th Baron, 79
Ellard, Frank, Pte. A. and S.H., 205
Elliot, Locke, Maj.-Gen., 2, 90
Ellis, Thomas, late Tpr. Scot. Hse., 218
Elton, E. G. (the late), Capt. B.W., 9, 23
Emslie, Jas., Pte. B.W., 169, 274
English, W. J., V.C., Lt. 2nd Scot. Hse., 33, 60, 63
Erasmus, of Carolina, Boer Leader, 41n
Erskine, of Cardross, H. D., 72
,, yr. of Cardross, J. F., Maj. Scots Gds., 72
,, Wm. M., Pte. 5th Vol. Batt. B.W., 169-70, 274
,, Seymour E., Capt. R.N., 72
Esplin, George, late Pte. 17th Batt. 50th Coy. I.Y., 212, 280

Evans, Jas., Pte. 4th Vol. Batt. B.W., 170, 274
,, L. P., Lt. B.W., 23
Ewan, William, late Sh.-Smith Scot. Hsc., 218, 282
Ewing, Robert L., late attd. York and Lanc. Regt.; 72
,, Walter C. L., Lt. H.L.I., 72
,, William L., late Sgt. S.A.C., 234, 285
,, of Arngomery, Wm. L. (the late), 72
Eykyn, C. (the late), Capt. B.W., 10, 23

FAICHNEY, John, late Cpl. B.W., 170, 274
Farquharson, Alexander, late Pte. Gord. H., 198
,, D. L. Wilson, Maj. B.W., 23
,, John, Pte. Sea. H., 193, 278
Faulds, John, Pte. Sea. H., 194
Fedil, Ahmed, 80
Fenton, Andrew, Col.-Sgt. 1st Sutherland Rifle Vols., 194, 278
,, Jas., M.B., C.M., late Civ. Surg., attd. R.A.M.C., 72
,, John, Qrmr.-Sgt., Sea. H., 194, 278
Ferguson, Alfred, Sgt. H.L.I., 189, 278
,, Daniel, Pte. 5th Vol. Batt. B.W., 170
,, David, Pte. 4th Vol. Batt. B.W., 170, 274
,, Donald, late Col.-Sgt. H.L.I., 189, 278
,, Duncan, late Pte. Scot. Rif., 163
,, F., Tpr. Diamond Fields Hse., 226, 283
,, James, late Piper Scot. Hse., 218
,, James (the late), Lce.-Cpl. A. and S.H., 205, 279
,, John, Cpl. 4th Vol. Batt. B.W., 170, 274
,, Murdoch, Pte. B.W., 170, 274
,, Peter, late Pte. H.L.I., 189
,, Thomas, Lt. 5th Vol. Batt. B.W., 27, 72
,, of Friarton, W. S., Lt.-Col., 72
Ferrier, Charles, Pte. 14th Huss., 151, 272
,, Duncan, late Lce.-Cpl. 6th Batt. 20th Coy. I.Y., 211, 281
Field, H. G., Capt. 1st Scot. Hse., 49
,, P. N., Capt. 1st Scot. Hse., 49, 50n, 55, 61
Fincastle, Alexander, Viscount, V.C., Capt. 16th Lan., 92, 93, 93n
Findlay, William, late Sgt. Scot. Hse., 218, 282
,, William, Lce.-Cpl. Gord. H., 198, 279
Firns, T., Lt. 2nd Scot. Hse., 48, 62
Firth, Walter, Pte. Sea. H., 194
,, Wilmot, Pte. 2nd Dgns., 148, 271
Fisken, Charles, Pte. The Buffs, 160
Fison, W. F., Lt. and Regtl. Adjt. 1st Scot. Hse., 61
Fitzmaurice, Lord Charles George Francis, Capt. 1st Dgns., 72
Fitzpatrick, Thomas, Pte. B.W., 170
Fleming, of Inchyra, Rev. Archibald (the late), 72
,, George, late Sh.-Smith Scot. Hsc., 218
,, Hamilton, late Lt. S.A.L. Hse., 72
,, William R., Pte. Imp. L. Infy., 227, 284
Flight, John, late Sgt. Scot. Hse., 218, 282

Flint, Col., 31, 70, 81, 85, 94
Flower, H. N. C. Erskine, Lt. (the late) 1st Scot. Hse., 55
Flynn, Charles M., Pte. Sea. H., 194
Foote, Alexander, late Cpl. Scot. Hse., 218, 282
,, Alfred D. E., late Lce.-Cpl. S.A.C., 234, 284
,, Andrew, late Pte. Lov. Sc., 215, 281
,, George, Pte. B.W., 29, 170, 275
,, John, late Sapr. R.E., 155, 272
Forbes, Alexander, Pte. B.W., 170
,, James, Pte. 31st Batt. I.Y., 214
,, Thomas, Pte. Cam. H., 201–2, 279
Ford, Michael, Pte. B.W., 170, 274
,, Patrick, Pte. Gord. H., 198, 279
Forrester, R. E., 2nd Lt. B.W., 23
Forrett, W., D.C.M. Lce-Cpl. 2nd Batt. B.W., 12, 28, 29
Fourie, Boer Leader, 51, 52
Fowler, Robert, Pte. B.W., 170, 274
,, W., Sgt.-Maj. 2nd Batt. B.W., 29
Fraser, Sgt. 2nd Batt. B.W., 8
,, D., late Cpl. 5th Vol. Batt. B.W., 170, 275
,, John, Pte. R. Scots Fus., 161
,, John C. (the late), Pte. Gord. H., 198–99, 279
,, John R., late Tpr. Scot. Hse., 218, 281
,, L., Scripture-reader, attd. 2nd Batt. B.W., 28
,, Niven, Pte. R. Scots Fus., 161
,, R. B. F., Sq. Qrmr.-Sgt. 2nd Scot. Hse., 62
,, T., Cpl. 2nd Scot. Hse., 63, 63n
,, W. Farr.-Maj. 1st Scot. Hse., 61
,, William, late Lce.-Cpl. Scot. Hse., 219, 281
,, William, Sapr. R.E., 155
French, Sir John, 4, 96
Fulton, Andrew, late Sh.-Smith, Scot. Hsc., 219
,, John, late Tpr. Scot. Hse., 219

GANGE, J. C., Sgt. 2nd Scot. Hse., 62
Gardiner, Alexander, Pte. B.W., 170, 275
,, George D., Pte. A.S.C. 208
,, Jas. R., late Tpr. S.A.C., 234, 285
,, Robert, Pte. Gord. H., 199, 279
,, W. (the late), Pte. B.W., 170
Gardyne, A. D. Greenhill-, Capt. and Brev.-Maj. Gord. H., 93
,, W. Greenhill-, late Lt. 20th Coy. I.Y., 93
Garratt, Col., 3
Gartland, A. K., 1st Cl. Petty-Off. R.N., 147, 271
Garvie, Peter, Pte. R. Scots, 159, 273n
,, William, Pte. B.W., 170, 273, 273n
Gavin, Philip, late Pte. B.W., 170–71
Gaynor, G., D.C. M Lce.-Sgt. 2nd Batt. B.W., 28, 29
Geddes, Thomas, late Rifleman King's R. Rif., 188, 277
Geekie, James, late Pte. B.W., 171, 275
,, Thomas E., Pte. Scots Gds., 157, 272
Gellatly, John, late Tpr. S.A.C., 234

Gellatly, Wm., late Lce.-Sgt. 24th Batt. I.Y., 213, 280
Gibbons, John (the late), Pte. H.L.I., 189, 278
  ,, T., Scout 1st Scot. Hse., 62
Gilchrist, George, Pte. 4th Huss., 151, 272
  ,, Wm., Pte. 9th Lan., 150, 271
Gilmour, John, Tpr. Scot. Hse., 219, 282
  ,, William, Pte. 37th Batt. I.Y., 214
Glas, of Pittentian, family of, 84
Glass, Andrew, Tpr. S.A.C., 234, 285
  ,, David, Cpl. 4th Vol. Batt. B.W., 171, 275
  ,, Robert, Sgt. R. Scot. Fus., 161, 273
Glen, James, Pte. H.L.I., 189, 278
Gloag, of St. Albans, Matthew, 73
  ,, Matthew Wm., Lt. 4th Vol. Batt. B.W., 73
Goddard, G. H., M.R.C.S., L.R.C.P., Capt. B.W., 20, 28
Godfrey, Daniel, Cpl. B.W., 171, 275
Goodfellow, James, late Pte. Scots Gds., 157, 272
Gordon, C. W. E., Lt. B.W., 23
  ,, David (the late), Pte. Sea. H., 194, 278
  ,, David, Pte. Sea. H., 194
  ,, S. D., Col., 2, 3
  ,, W. G. Wolridge-, Maj. 1st Batt. B.W., 1, 23
Gore, Lady Mabel, Countess of Airlie, 97
Gorrie, James, Tpr. S.A.C., 234
  ,, Thomas, Pte. R. Scots, 159
Gough, Charles, Brig.-Gen., 70
Gow, Alexander, Lce.-Cpl. B.W., 171, 275
  ,, David, Pte. A. and S.H., 205, 279
  ,, David, late Tpr. Scot. Hse., 219, 282
  ,, Forbes, late Pte. B.W., 171, 275
Gowrie, Thos. Fell (the late), Pte. B.W., 171, 275
Græme, of Orchill, David (the late), 73
  ,, David Henry, Capt. Sea. H., 73
  ,, of Inchbrakie, George (the late), Col., 73
  ,, Henry S. (the late), 73
  ,, L. (the late), Major, Lt.-Gov. of Tobago, 73
  ,, L. A. M., late Maj. and Hon. Lt.-Col., 73
  ,, Laur. O., Capt. and Adjt. 1st Scot. Hse., 73
  ,, Robert O., Col. late comdg. Ashton Regtl. Dist., 73
Graham, James, Marquess of, Lt. R.N. Vol. Res., 74
  ,, Alex., late Pte. B.W., 171, 275
  ,, C., late Pte. 15th Batt. 57th Coy. I.Y., 212, 280
  ,, Sir Gerald, 71, 91
  ,, J., Pte. Gord. H., 199
  ,, Jas., Sgt.-Maj. Scot. Rif., 163, 273
  ,, Thomas, Sgt. A. and S.H., 205
Grant, Archibald, late Tpr. Scot. Hse., 219
  ,, A. S., D.S.O., Lt. and local Capt. B.W., 23
  ,, C. J. P. MacA., 2nd Lt. B.W., 24
  ,, D., Sgt. 2nd Batt. B.W., 29
  ,, James (the late), Pte. B.W., 171, 275
  ,, James, late Pte. Sea. H., 194
  ,, John, Pte. B.W., 171
  ,, of Kilgraston, John Patrick, Capt. Sea. H., 74
  ,, William, Pte. Cam. H., 202

Gray, Bethune J., late Cpl. Scot. Hse., 219, 282
  ,, David, Pte. B.W., 171
  ,, Harry, late Cpl. Scot. Hse., 219, 282
  ,, James, late Pte. B.W., 171, 275
Greaves, R. T., Lt., Lancashire Fus., 93n
Green, John, late Pte. H.L.I., 189, 278
  .. W., Lt. B.W., 24
Gregor, James, Pte. 2nd Dgns., 148, 271
Greig, Jas. Elliot, Tpr. Natal Carb., 229, 283
Grenfell, Lt.-Col., 55-59
Grierson, N. H., 2nd Lt. W. Ind. Regt., 46, 46n, 63, 63n
Grieve, J. G., Lt. and Adjt. R. Scots (N.S.W. Perm. Forces), attd. B.W., 9, 12, 20, 28
  ,, John W., late Tpr. Scot. Hse., 219, 281
Griffin, Dennis, Cpl. H.L.I., 189, 278
Griffiths, Jos., Pte. Border Regt., 164, 274
Grobelaar, of Ermelo, Boer Leader, 41n
Grogan, E. G., C.B., Lt.-Col. comdg. 1st Batt. B.W., 1, 2, 3, 24
Grubb, John, Sgt. R. Scot. Fus., 161, 273
Guild, James, Pte. Scot. Rif., 163, 273
Guinness, Maj. 84th Batt. R.F.A., 44
Gunning, Jas., Sq. Sgt.-Maj. 1st Scot. Hse., 62
Guthrie, William, late Pte. B.W., 171, 275

HAASBROEK, Boer Leader, 18
Hadow, Ronald Walter, 2nd Lt. B.W., 24, 93
Haig, yr. of Blairhill, Jas. R. P., late Pte. 6th Batt. 20 Coy. I.Y., 211, 281
Halkerston, James, late Sapr. R.E., 155, 272
Hall, Thomas, Col.-Sgt. H.L.I., 189, 278
Hallett, Hughes-, Col., 8
Halley, David, Pte. B.W., 171
  ,, John, Pte. Sea. H., 194, 278
Hamilton, A., Cpl. 2nd Batt. B.W., 29
  ,, A. B. Baillie-, Lt. Sea. H., 74
  ,, Bruce, Gen., 18, 34, 35, 71, 73, 94
  ,, Sir Ian, Gen., 14, 19, 55
  ,, of Arnprior, J. B. B. Baillie-, 74
  ,, of Arnprior, J. B. B. Baillie-, Mrs., 74
  ,, J. G. H., D.S.O., Capt. B.W., 24
  ,, N. A. B. Baillie-, Lt. B.W., 24, 74
Hampton, John, Pte. B.W., 171, 275
Harrier, James, Pte. B.W., 171
Harris, yr. of Glenalmond, Henry H. M., Lt. H.L.I., 74
  ,, John W., late Sgt. 22nd Batt. 78th Coy. I.Y., 213, 280
  ,, of Glenalmond, Thomas M., Col. R.A., 74
Harrison, Herbert (the late), D.C.M., Sgt. 2nd Batt. B.W., 28, 29, 171, 275
Harvey, J., Capt. B.W., 24
  ,, W. J. St. J., Lt. and Capt. 2nd Batt. B.W., 24
Hastie, J., D.C.M., Pioneer 2nd Batt. B.W., 12, 28, 29
Havelock, Maj.-Gen., 73, 81, 85
Haxton, Henry, late Sgt. Scot. Hse., 47, 47n, 219, 281
Hay, David, Pte. Gord. H., 199, 279
  ,, George, Pte. B.W., 172, 275

Hay, H. M. D., late Sgt. Ceylon Mtd. Infy., 226, 284
,, Jas., late Pte. Vol. Ambulance Corps, 231, 284
,, of Aberargie, James A. G. R. D.-, D.S.O., Maj. and Bt. Lt.-Col. Colds. Gds., 75
Haynes, J., Pte. Worcestershire Regt., 164, 273
Heard, John. late Cpl. Sea. H., 194, 278
Heerden, Van, Boer Leader, 51, 52
Helmkemp, F. H., Cpl. 2nd Scot. Hse., 63
Henderson, C. R. B., 2nd Lt. B.W., 24
,, of Invergowrie, G. D. Clayhills-(the late), 69
,, James, Tpr. N.Z. Mtd. Infy., 229, 283
,, John, Pte. Gord. H., 199, 279
,, John, late Tpr. Johan. Mtd. Rif., 227, 284
,, Joseph A. (the late), Piper B.W., 172, 275
,, N. G. B., 2nd Lt. B.W., 24
,, Patrick Jobson., M.B., C.M. Abdn., late Surg. Cape Med. Staff Corps, 93
,, Robert, late Farr.-Maj. Scot. Hse., 219
Hendry, John, late Sgt. R.F.A., 154
Herd, Thomas, Pte. 3rd (Mil.) Batt. B.W., 172, 275
Heron, Andrew, late Pte. H.L.I., 189, 278
,, George, Pte. R. Scots Fus., 161, 273
Hickie, Col., 35
Higgins, Patrick, late Pte. H.L.I., 189
Hill, William, late 1st Cl. Warrant Off. A.S.C., 208, 280
Hilson, Adam, Pte. B.W., 172
Hinshelwood, James, late Tpr. Prince of Wales's L. Hse., 230, 284
,, Thomas, Tpr. Prince of Wales's L. Hse., 230, 284
Hobson, James, Pte. B.W., 172, 275
Hodge, Andrew, late Lce.-Sgt. A.S.C., 208
Holland, Patrick, Pte. H.L.I., 189, 278
Honeyman, Andrew L. M., late Pte. 6th Batt. 20th Coy. I.Y., 211, 281
,, William, Pte. Gord. H., 199, 279
Hood, David, Pte. 5th Vol. Batt. B.W., 172
,, James, late 1st Cl. Tpr. S.A.C., 234, 285
,, James, late Tpr. Scot. Hse., 219
Hore, Capt., 68
Horne, Thomas, late Lce.-Cpl. 31st Batt. I.Y., 214
Hounan, James, Cpl. 4th Vol. Batt. B.W., 172, 275
Howden, T., D.C.M., Pioneer-Sgt., 2nd Batt. B.W., 11, 28, 29
Hume, David, late Lce.-Cpl. B.W., 172, 275
Hunter, Sir A., Lt.-Gen., 15, 17, 18, 74, 79, 80, 99
,, Robert, Pte. B.W., 172
Hush, John, late Cpl. Scot. Hse., 219
Hutchison, James (Perth) (No. 2213) Pte. B.W., 172, 275
,, Jas. (Perth), No. 7615, Pte. B.W., 172, 275
,, Peter, late Pte. H.L.I., 189-90, 278
,, Thomas, Cpl. S.A.C., 234, 285
Hynd, Alexander, Pte. B.W., 172
,, David, Cpl. R.F.A., 154, 272
,, Isaac, 3rd Cl. Tpr. S.A.C., 234, 285

I'Anson, C. F., Sgt. 1st Scot. Hse., 62
Imrie, James H. D., Sgt. Scot. Rif., 163
,, Joseph, Pte. 13th Huss., 151, 272
Inglis, S. W., Capt. Scot. Hse., 44, 48
Innes, S. A., Lt. B.W., 24
Irons, Peter, late Pte. B.W., 172, 275
Irvine, C., late Pte. Cam. H., 202, 279
,, C. A. L., Lt. 1st Scot. Hse., 63
,, John (the late), Sapr. R.E., 155, 272
,, T. J., Lt. 1st Scot. Hse., 55

Jack, Alex. D., Armr.-Sgt. A.O. Dept., 209, 280
,, George, Farr.-Cpl. R.E., 155, 272
,, James, late Tpr. Scot. Hse., 219, 282
,, James, W., Cpl. R.E., 155
,, J. L., Lt. 2nd Scot. Hse., 62
,, Thos. M'Laren, late Tpr. Scot. Hse., 219, 282
Jackson, Robert, late Pte. Army P.O. Dept., 209
,, Stonewall, 49
,, William, late Pte. 2nd Dgns., 148, 271
James, Major, 76
Jardine, W., Lt. 1st Scot. Hse., 54, 55, 61
Jenkins, William, Pte. A. and S.H., 205-6
Jenner, Albert E., Cpl. 6th Dgns., 150, 271
,, Charles, Cpl. 2nd Dgns., 148, 271
Johnston, Alex. C., 2nd Cl. Tpr. S.A.C., 234, 285
,, George R., late Sgt.-Maj. Scot. Hse., 219, 281
,, James H., late Sh.-Smith Scot. Hse., 219, 282
,, John B., Tpr. Cape Pol., 232, 284
,, John G., Sgt. 6th Vol. Batt. A. and S.H. Scot. Cycle Corps, 208, 280
Johnstone, And., late Tpr. Scot. Hse., 219, 282
,, James, Pte. B.W., 172
,, W., Sgt. Scot. Hse., 45
Jones, L. A., Lt. 1st Scot. Hse., 63
,, L. C., Maj. Ind. Staff Corps, comdg. 2nd Scot. Hse., 34, 35, 36
,, William, Pte. B.W., 172

Kay, Alexander, late Tpr. Scot. Hse., 219-20, 281
,, James C., Pte. 2nd Dgns., 148, 271
Kean, David F., Gr. R.G.A., 155
,, William (the late), Tpr. Scot. Hse., 220, 282
Keay, William J., late Sgt. N.S.W. Mtd. Rif., 229, 284
Kedie, W. T., 2nd Lt. 1st Batt. B.W., 24
Keiller, Jas. M. R., late Sq. Qrmr.-Sgt. 37th Batt. I.Y., 214, 281
,, Murd., late Pte. Border Regt., 164, 274
Keir, Alexander, Pte. B.W., 172, 275
,, James, Pte. 5th Batt. 16th Coy. I.Y., 210, 280
,, John S., Pte. Cam. H., 202, 279
Kekewich, R. G., Col., 34, 35, 49, 50, 52-57, 59, 67, 70, 71, 75, 79, 81, 82, 94
Kelly, J. B., Lt. Scot. Hse., 41, 48

Kelly, O. W., Capt. Scot. Hse., 60, 62
Kemp, Boer Leader, 34, 51, 52, 54–56
Kennedy, Frank, Pte. B.S.A. Pol., 173, 275
„ George D. S., late Pte. B.W., 173, 275
„ Hugh, Pte. B.W., 173, 275
„ James, Pte. B.W., 173
„ James, Pte. Wiltshire Regt., 188, 277
„ John, late Pte. Lov. Sc., 215, 281
„ Thomas, late Pte. K.O.S.B., 162
Kenwell, Arthur, Pte. B.W., 173
Kererouse, F. T., Sgt. 2nd Scot. Hse., 63
Kerr, Robert, Lce.-Cpl. B.W., 173, 275
Kerrigan, H., Tpr. Thorn. Mtd. Infy., 231, 284
„ John, late Tpr. Scot. Hse., 220, 281
„ Patrick, Pte. Imp. L. Infy., 227, 284
Kerry, Henry W. E., Earl of, D.S.O., Capt. Irish Gds., 75
Kettles, Andrew, late Pte. A. and S.H., 206
Keyes, General, 86, 94
Khalifa, The, 80, 83
Kidd, Alexander, Pte. A. and S.H., 206
„ John, late Cpl. 18th Batt. 70th Coy. I.Y., 213, 280
„ John, Lce.-Cpl. Sea. H., 194, 278
„ of Tighnaleigh, W. S., Surg.-Capt. Scot. Hse., 54, 55, 61, 75
King, Archibald, Pte. R. Scots Fus., 161, 173
„ John, Sgt.-Maj. 5th Vol. Batt. B.W., 173, 275
„ John, Pte. B.W., 173
„ John, late Cpl. 18th Batt. 70th Coy. I.Y., 213, 280
„ William, late Cpl. Vol. Batt. Scot. Rif., 163, 273
„ W. A., Lt. 1st Scot. Hse., 61
Kininmonth, Jas., late Lce.-Cpl. A. and S.H., 206, 280
„ Robert, Lce.-Cpl. A. and S.H. 206, 280
Kinloch, Archibald D. (the late), Gr. Natal Vol. Arty., 229, 283
Kinnaird, George, 9th Baron, 95
Kinnear, Thomas, late Pte. B.W., 173
Kinnison, K. MacKenzie (the late), Pte. 4th Batt. 7th Coy. I.Y., 210, 281
Kinnoull, Thomas, 10th Earl of, 70
„ George, 11th Earl of, 93
„ Archibald F., 12th Earl of, local Col. Egypt. Gendarmerie, 75
Kirk, James C., Lce.-Cpl. R. Scots, 159, 273
Kirkaldy, Charles, late Lce.-Cpl. B.W., 173, 275
Kirkpatrick, T., Farr.-Sgt., 1st Scot. Hse., 54, 62
Kitchener, Lord, Sir Herbert, 71, 73, 76, 78–80, 83, 87, 88, 92 ; Lord K., 10, 30–32, 36, 37, 55
„ Walter, Gen., 19, 55
Knubley, J., Pte. Cam. H., 202
Kritzinger, Boer Leader, 100   24
Krook, A. D. C., 2nd Lt. B.W.
Kruger, Paul, 13, 75
II.

Laidlaw, James, late Piper Scot. Hse., 220, 282
Laing, Charles, Pte. B.W., 173
„ David, late Tpr. Scot. Hse., 220, 282
„ George, late Tpr. Scot. Hse., 220
„ William, late Pte. Sea. H., 194
Laird, John, Pte. R. Scots, now H.L.I., 159, 273
„ Lindsay, Pte. A. and S.H., 206
Lamb, C. C., Lt. B.W., 24, 93, 94
„ D. S. Beechwood, Dunkeld, 93
„ George, late Cpl. Sea. H., 194
„ John C., Pte. 14th Huss., 152, 272
Lambert, J. P., Capt. 1st Scot. Hse., 49
Lamoud, George, Tpr. S.A.C., 234, 285
„ Peter, Lce.-Sgt. Scots Gds., 157, 272
Lamont, James, late Tpr. Scot. Hse., 220
Lansdowne, Henry, 5th Marquess of (Baron Nairne), 72, 75
Lauder, W., Pte. 2nd Dgns., 149
Laurie, James, 3rd Cl. Tpr. S.A.C, 234, 285
Laverton, H. C., Lt. B.W., 24
Lawless, W., Capt. 1st Scot. Hse., 61
Lawson, Angus, Pte. Vol. Batt. A. and S.H., now Cam. H., 206, 279
„ Thomas, Pte. B.W., 173, 275
Leader, H. P., 6th Dgn. Gds., Lt.-Col. comdg. 1st Scot. Hse., 35, 33n, 36, 56–58, 60, 61
Legge, E. A., Qrmr. and Hon. Lt. 2nd Scot. Hse., 60, 60n, 61, 62n
Leicester, C., Sgt. 2nd Batt. B.W., 29
Leithwaite, Alexander, Pte. B.W., 173
Lennox, William (the late), 3rd Cl. Tpr. S.A.C., 234, 285
Leslie, D.R., Pte. 5th Vol. Batt. B.W., 173, 572
„ Robert, late Tpr. Scot. Hse., 220, 282
Lewis, S. H., Lt. 1st Scot. Hse., 61
Limmer, David, Pte. H.L.I., 190
Lindsay, James, Sgt.-Major A. and S.H., 206, 279
„ John, late Sq. Qrmr.-Sgt. 37th Batt. I.Y., 214, 280
„ M. W., Capt. and Adjt. 2nd Scot. Hse., 32, 33, 41, 41n, 43, 44, 48
„ Robert, Pte. R. Scots Fus., 161
„ Mr. Walter, Windsor Herald, 41n
„ William G., Cpl. 2nd Dgns., 149, 271
Littlejohn, David, Pte. Scot. Rif., 163, 273
„ Thos., Tpr. Mennie's Sc., 228, 283
Livingston, Angus, late Pte. Scots Gds., 157
„ P. J. C., Brev. Lt.-Col. B.W., 24
Lloyd, Eyre, Capt. Colds. Gds., 44, 44n, 45
„ T. O., Capt. B.W., 2, 24
Lockhart, Sir William, 68, 69, 86, 87, 91, 93, 94
Logan, David, late Lt. 1st Scot. Hse., 94
Login, Spencer H. M., Capt. R.N., 94
Loring, W., Lt. 1st Scot. Hse., 55, 61
Loudfoot, William, Pte. B.W., 173, 275
Lovat, Lord, 99
Low, Sir Robert, 74, 81, 86, 102
„ Robert, Pte. 5th Vol. Batt. B.W., 173, 275

Low, Robert K., Tpr. S.A.C., 234, 285
Lowe, Andrew M., Cpl. 10th Huss., 151, 271
  ,, George S., late Tpr. Western Province
    Mtd. Rif., 231, 284
  ,, William, late Trump. 6th Batt. 20th Coy.
    I.Y., 211, 281
Lowson, William, Cpl. Vol. Batt. R. Scots, 159
Lugard, Maj.-Gen., 72, 82
Lumsden's Horse, 25
Luther, E., Sq. Sgt.-Maj. 2nd Scot. Hse., 62

McAinsh, John, Pte. B.W., 173-74
McAndrew, Peter J., Pte. B.W., 174
Macara, Jas. Scott, Lce.-Cpl. B.W., 174, 275
McArthur, John, Pte. 2nd Dgn. Gds., 147, 271
McBain, Alex., Pte. R. Scots Fus., 161
  ,, C., late Pte. 26th Batt. 121st Coy. I.Y., 214
  ,, John, Pte. 18th Huss., 152
McBeth, Donald, late Sgt. Scots Gds., 157, 273
McCallum, C. H. M., Cpl. 1st Scot. Hse., 62,
    63, 63n
  ,, Sir Henry, G.C.M.G., A.D.C., Gov. of
    Ceylon, 63n
  ,, Daniel, late Tpr. Scot. Hse., 220
  ,, John, late Tpr. Scot. Hse., 220
McCann, Frederick, Pte. B.W., 174
M'Carthy, J. J., Lt. Scot. Hse., 45, 45n, 46
M'Clure, Lt. Sea. H., 10
McConnell, Gilbert, Pte. R. Scots, 159, 273
M'Culloch, Donald, Pte. 5th Vol. Batt.
    B.W., 174
  ,, Peter, late Tpr. Scot. Hse., 220, 282
McDiarmid, Donald, late Sgt. Duke of Edin-
    burgh's own Vol. Rif., 226, 283
  ,, Peter (the late), Pte. 5th Vol. Batt. B.W.,
    174
Macdonald, Alastair McIan, Lt.-Gen., late
    G.O.C. in Scotland, 75
McDonald, Alexander, Pte. B.W., 174
  ,, Alexander (the late), Pte. 6th Batt. 20th
    Coy. I.Y., 211
  ,, Alexander, late Pte. Lov. Sc., 215, 281
Macdonald, Alexander, F.R.G.S., late Lt. 1st
    Aust. Bush, 94
  ,, David, late Sgt. N.S.W. Mtd. Infy., 229,
    284
McDonald, Donald, Pte. Kimberley Town
    Guard, 231, 284
MacDonald, Hector (the late), Maj.-Gen., 9,
    10, 15, 18
  ,, James, late Pte. H.L.I., 190
Macdonald, James, Pte. Scots Gds., 157
  ,, of Dalchosnie, Sir John (the late), G.C.B.,
    Lt.-Gen., 75
  ,, John (the late), Pte. A. and S.H., 206, 279
McDonald, John, late 3rd Cl. Tpr. S.A.C., 234,
    285
  ,, John, Pte. B.W., 174, 275
  ,, John, late Pte. Gord. H., 199, 279
  ,, John, late Qrmr.-Sgt. Scot. Rif., 163, 273
  ,, Peter, Pte. B.W., 174
  ,, Peter, late Tpr. N.Z. Rgh. Rdrs., 229, 284
  ,, Thos., late Pte. A. and S.H., 206, 280

McDonald, William, Lce.-Cpl. B.W., 174
  ,, William, Pte. B.W., 174
  ,, William (the late), Pte. 9th Lan., 150, 271
Macdougall, Duncan A., late Pte. 18th Batt.
    70th Coy. I.Y., 213
McDougall, Harry, Pte. R. Scots Fus., 161, 273
  ,, John M., Pipe-Maj. B.W., 174, 275
  ,, P., Pte. B.W., 174
McEwan, Harry, Lce.-Cpl. the Buffs, 160, 273
  ,, John, late Pte. R. Scots Fus., 161
MacFarlan, W. (the late), Capt. and Adjt.
    2nd Batt. B.W., 8, 24
McFarlane, Alex., Pte. Sea. H., 194, 278
Macfarlane, Daniel, late Qrmr.-Sgt. K.O.S.B.,
    162-63, 273
McFarlane, Donald, late Tpr. Scot. Hse., 220
  ,, Donald, late Trp. Sgt.-Maj. B.S.A. Pol.,
    232, 283
  ,, Duncan, late Pte. Lov. Sc., 215, 281
  ,, George, Pte. 5th Vol. Batt. B.W., 174, 275
  ,, J. (the late), Pte. Cam. H., 202, 279
  ,, James (the late), Pte. B.W., 174, 275
  ,, James, Pte. B.W., 174, 275
  ,, John, Pte. H.L.I., 190
  ,, John, late Sapr. R.E., 155, 272
Macfarlane, John, late Pte. Scot. Rif., 163, 273
McFarlane, Robert, late Sh.-Smith Scot. Hse.,
    220, 282
  ,, Robert, late Tpr. Imp. L. Hse., 227
  ,, Samuel, Pioneer B.W., 175, 275
  ,, William, Pte. Mil. Res. B.W., 175
  ,, William, late Pte. B.W., 175
  ,, William, Pte. 5th Vol. Batt. H.L.I., 190
McFayden, Wm., Lce.-Cpl. R. Scots, 159
McGarry, James, Piper, B.W. 175, 275
  ,, Joseph, late Pte. B.W., 175, 276
McGillewie, Donald (the late), Pitlochry, 75
  ,, Patrick, Lt. Queenst. Town Gd., 75
McGilvary, Robert, Pte. 4th Vol. Batt.
    B.W., 175, 275
McGinn, Frank, Pte. 2nd Dgns., 149, 271
MacGregor, Atholl M., late Tpr. Scot. Hse.,
    220, 282
McGregor, Charles, late Tpr. Scot. Hse., 220,
    282
  ,, Charles, late Pte. H.L.I., 190, 278
MacGregor, Chas. F. M., Maj. Cape Pol., 76
McGregor, David B., 3rd Cl. Tpr. S.A.C.,
    234-35, 285
MacGregor, Duncan (the late), Balquhidder, 76
  ,, Evan M. (the late), Gen., 76
McGregor, Frank, Pte. Gord. H., 199
MacGregor, George, Pte. Sea. H., 194-95, 278
  ,, Hamish Sheriff- (the late), Tpr. Thorn.
    Mtd. Infy., 231, 284
McGregor, James, Pte. B.W., 175
MacGregor, K. M., late Lt. Prince Alfred's
    Gd., 76
McGregor, Peter, late Tpr. Scot. Hse., 220
  ,, R., D.C.M., Pte. 2nd Batt. B.W., 28, 29,
    175
  ,, Robert, late Sq. Sgt.-Maj. Steinaecker's
    Hse., 230, 284

MacGregor, Thomas, late Civ. Surg., attd. R.A.M.C., 76
Macgregor, Thos. Alison, late Pte. Scots Gds., 157
McGregor, William (the late), Sc.-Sgt. Scot. Hse., 54, 220, 283
" William, 1st Cl. Tpr. S.A.C., 235, 285
Macgregor, William, Pte. 5th Vol. Batt. B.W., 175, 276
McGregor, William J., late Pte. B.W., 175, 275
McHardie, William, late Pte. R. Scots Fus., 161
McIlwraith, D., Sgt. 1st Scot. Hse., 62
McInnes, James, late Pte. 6th Dgn. Gds., 148, 271
" John, late Pipe-Cpl. Scot. Hse., 220, 283
" John, Pte. 5th Vol. Batt. B.W., 175, 275
McInroy, David, Pte. Cam. H., 202, 279
" George, Pte. Sea. H., 195
" John W., late Pte. B.W., 175
" Kenneth, Pte. Sea. H., 195, 278
McIntosh, Arthur, Pte. 4th Vol. Batt. B.W., 175, 275
Macintosh, Donald, late Lce.-Cpl. Scot. Hse., 221, 282
McIntosh, Hugh, Pte. 14th Huss., 152, 272
" J., Lce.-Cpl. 2nd Scot. Hse., 29
" J., late Pte. Cam. H., 202
" James, late Pte. A. and S.H., 206, 230
Macintosh, James, Pte. 4th Vol. Batt. B.W., 175, 276
McIntosh, John, Pte. B.W., 175, 275
" John, Sgt. 2nd Dgns., 149, 271
Macintosh, John J., Cpl. Gord. H., 199, 279
McIntosh, Thos. B., Tpr. S.A.C., 235, 285
McIntyre, Daniel, late Pte. B.W., 175
" James, late Pte. B.W., 175
" John, late Pte. B.W., 175, 275
" John F., Pte. 4th Vol. Batt. B.W., 176, 275
McKay, Alexander, Pte. B.W., 176
Mackay, James, Pte. B.W., 176, 275
McKay, Jas. W., late Cpl. Scot. Hse., 221, 282
Mackay, John, late Pte. Hampshire Regt., 164
" J. A., Hon. Lt. B.W., 28
McKay, Patrick, late Tpr. Scot. Hse., 221
" Thomas, late Tpr. Scot. Hse., 221, 282
" William C., late Tpr. Scot. Hse., 221, 283
Mackenzie, Alex., late Pte. 6th Batt. 18th Coy. I.Y., 210, 281
" C. J., Lt.-Col. Sea. H., comdg. column, 34, 76, 79, 82, 89
McKenzie, David, Pte. Sea. H., 195
Mackenzie, Donald, Pte. Gord. H., 199, 279
" Duncan H. C. R., Pte. 5th Vol. Batt. B.W., 176, 275
McKenzie, Francis, late Pte. B.W., 176, 276
" Henry, late Pte. B.W., 176, 276
MacKenzie, I. R., D.S.O., Capt. 1st Scot. Hse., 49, 53, 60, 61
" James, late Pte. H.L.I., 190
MacKenzie, James B., Pte. Imp. L. Infy., 227, 284

McKenzie, James E., late Tpr. Scot. Hse., 221, 282
McKenzie, John, Pte. Scots Gds., now R. Garrison Regt., 157, 273
McKenzie, John, late Qrmr.-Sgt. Cam. H. and B.W., 202, 279
McKenzie, Murdoch, Pte. 5th Vol. Batt. B.W., 176, 276
" Robert (the late), Tpr. Scot. Hse., 221, 282
" Thomas, late Cpl. Cam. H., 202, 279
Mackenzie, Thomas E., Col.-Sgt. Cam. H., 202, 279
McKenzie, Walter, Pte. Mil. Res. B.W., 176
McKercher, Donald, Pte. B.W., 176
McKillop, Dugald, Cpl. S.A.C., 235, 285
McKinlay, Alexander, Pte. Sea. H., 195, 278
McLagan, James, late Sapr. R. E., 155
McLaggan, David I., late Tpr. S.A.C., 235, 285
McLaggan, J. I., Cpl., S.A.C., 235, 285
McLaren, Alex., late Farr. 6th Batt. 18th Coy. I.Y., 210, 280
McLaren, Alexander, late Tpr. Scot. Hse., 221, 283
" Alexander, Tpr. S.A.C., 235
" Andrew, late Cpl. A.S.C., 208, 280
" Archibald, Tpr. S.A.C., 235
" Daniel, late Pte. Sea. H., 195
" Donald, Pte. B.W., 176, 275
" Frederick A. P., Qrmr.-Sgt. A.S.C., 208, 280
" George, H. A. P., Cpl. 2nd Life Gds., 147, 271
Maclaren, James, 2nd Cl. Staff-Sgt. R.A.M.C., 209, 280
McLaren, James, late Pte. B.W., 176, 275
" James, Pte. A. and S.H., 206
" John, Pte. 4th Vol. Batt. B.W., 176, 275
" John, Pte. A. and S.H., 206
" John H. (the late), Lce.-Cpl. 18th Batt. 72nd Coy. I.Y., 213, 280
" Laurence, Pte. 5th Vol. Batt. B.W., 176
" Peter, Pte. 4th Vol. Batt. B.W., 176
" Peter, late Sgt. Scot. Rif., 163–64
" Thomas, late Tpr. Scot. Hse., 221
" Thomas, late Pte. B.W., 176
" Thomas S., civiln. condr. Remount Dept., 210, 280
" William, Col.-Sgt., now 6th Vol. Batt. B.W., 176
" William, Pte. B.W., 176, 276
" William, late Tpr. Scot. Hse., 221, 282
McLauchlan, James, late Tpr. Scot. Hse., 221
" James, late Pte. Lov. Sc., 215, 281
" John, Pte. 3rd (Mil.) Batt. B.W., 176, 276
" Robert, late Tpr. Scot. Hse., 221, 282
McLaughlin, James, late Pte. Scot. Rif., 164, 273
" William, Pte. H.L.I., 190
McLay, John, Pte. Scots Gds., 157
McLean, A. (the late), Pte. 37th Batt. I.Y., 214
" Angus, Qrmr.-Sgt. Cam. H., 202, 279

McLean, Archibald K., Tpr. Scot. Hse., 221, 282

,, C., Capt. B.W., 24

,, Duncan, Gr. R.F.A., 154, 272

Maclean, Sir Fitzroy, 31

,, H. L. S., Lt., 63a

M'Lean, James, Pte. B.W., 177

,, James, late Tpr. Scot. Hse., 221

,, John, late Pte. Scots Gds., 158, 273

,, Peter, Pte. B.W., 177

,, Robert, late Pte. Lov. Sc., 215

,, William, late Pte. A. and S.H., 206, 280

McLeish, Andrew, late Pte. B.W., 177, 275

, David, late Tpr. Scot. Hse., 221, 282

,, Donald K., Lce.-Cpl. Scot. Hse., 221, 282

,, R., Pte. A. and S.H., 206

,, William, Piper Scots Gds., 158, 273

McLellan, John, the late, Pte. Cam. H., 202, 279

Maclennan, Edward, Pte. Cam. H., 203

McLeod, James, late Tpr. Scot. Hse., 221, 282

MacLeod, P., late Tpr. Bethune's Mtd. Infy., 223, 285

M'Leod, William A., late Dr. R.H.A., 153, 272

McLetchie, Thomas, late Lt. and Hon. Capt. 1st Scot. Hse., 64

M'Manus, Francis, Pte. Cam. H., 203, 279

M'Martin, Peter, Pte. 2nd Dgns., 140, 271

Macmaster, Charles, M.B., C.M., late Civ. Surg., attd. R.A.M.C., 94

, Donald, Cpl. B.W., 177, 275

M'Millan, Alexander, Tpr. Scot. Hse., 221, 282

Macmillan, John, the late, Col.-Sgt. B.W., 177, 275

,, Neil, late 3rd C., Tpr. S.A.C., 235, 285

M'Mullen, James, Pte. Scots. Gds., 158

McNab, Peter, Pte. 5th Vol. Batt. B.W., 177, 275

M'Naughten, James, Pte. 5th Vol. Batt. B.W., 177, 275

McNicol, John, late Pte. A. and S.H., 206

McNie, James, late Pte. A. and S.H., 206-7, 280

,, Malcolm, Pte. B.W., 177

McOwen, John, late Pte. Sea. H., 195, 278

M'Pherson, Alexander, late Pte. B.W., 177, 276

Macpherson, of Blairgowrie, Allan, the late, 76

M'Pherson, Donald, late Pte. B.W., 177

Macpherson, Donald, Pte. Cam. H., 203

M'Pherson, Donald, late Pte. A. and S.H., 207

Macpherson, George D., Capt. and Brev. Maj. R. Munster Fus., 76

, Hugh, late Pte. A. and S.H., 207, 280

McPherson, John, Sgt. 5th Vol. Batt. B.W., 177, 276

Macpherson, John, Pte. 5th Vol. Batt. B.W., 177, 276

M'Pherson, Peter, Pte. H.L.I., 190, 278

,, Robert, late Tpr. Scot. Hse., 221, 282

,, Wm. Sq. Sgt.-Maj. 6th Dgns., 150, 271

,, Wm. M., late Tpr. Scot. Hse., 222, 282

MacQueen, David, Sapr. R.E., 155, 272

McQueen, James, Cpl. 14th Huss., 152, 272

MacRae, C. W., Capt. B.W., 25

M'Rae, Lorn, late Pte. Scots Gds., 158

M'Ritchie, James, Pte. H.L.I., 190

M'Robbie, George, Pte. B.W., 177

M'Tavish, Alex. G. A. late Tpr. S.A.C., 235, 285

,, John, late Tpr. S.A.C., 235, 285

McVean, Hugh F., M.R.C.V.S., late Vet. Surg. attd. A. Vet. Dept., 76

,, John, the late, Tyndrum, 76

, John, late Col.-Sgt. B.W., 177, 275

M'Vicar, William, Pte. 4th Vol. Batt. B.W., 177, 276

M'Walter, James, Pte. B.W., 177, 276

M'Whannel, George, Pte. 2nd Dgns., 149, 271

, John, Sgt. 2nd Dgns., 149, 271

M'William, Adam, late Sgt. A. and S.H., 207, 280

Mahon, Col., 80

Maison, Arthur, Lce.-Cpl. B.W., 177-78, 276

, John, Gr. R.F.A., 154, 272

Malcolm, William, Lce.-Sgt. B.W., 178, 276

Malloch, James, late Tpr. Scot. Hse., 222, 283

Malloy, Joseph, late Cpl. Scot. Hse., 222, 283

Manley, G. H., Sgt.-Maj. 1st Scot. Hse., 61

Mann, Alexander, Pte. B.W., 178, 276

Mansfield, William, 4th Earl of, 78

Marindin, A. H., Capt. B.W., 25

Marr, James, late Sh.-Smith R.F.A., 154

Marshall, Andrew M., late Tpr. C.-in-C.'s Body-Gd., 226, 283

, of Duncrievie, F. J., Capt. Sea. H., 76

George, late Sh.-Smith Scot. Hse., 222, 282

, M., the late, Lce.-Cpl. Cam. H., 203

, William, 2nd C., Tpr. S.A.C., 235, 285

Martin, A., Sgt. 2nd Scot. Hse., 62, 62a

,, Edward, Pte. 5th Vol. Batt. B.W., 178, 276

,, Richard, late Pte. 13th Huss., 151, 272

,, William, Cpl. R.E., 155-56, 272

Matchett, William, late Pte. Gord. H., 199

Matthew, Andrew, Col.-Sgt. A. and S.H., 207

,, William, the late, Lce.-Sgt. A. and S.H., 207

Matthews, John, Pte. Sea. H., 195

Mathewson, John, late Pipe Cpl. Scot. Hse., 222, 283

Maxwell, Heutle, H. E., D.S.O., Maj. B.W., 12, 25

Sir J. G., K.C.B., Col. and Local Maj.-Gen., 25

Meates, J. L., Scot. Hse., 47, 47a

Meikle, Robert, late Pte. S. Wales Borderers, 242, 273

Meiklejohn, Sir William Hope, K.C.B., C.M.G., Maj.-Gen. officiating in command Oudh, 94

Meldrum, Chas. G., in Ambulance Corps, 227, 285

, George, Pte. 2nd Dgns., 149, 271

,, Simpson, Pte. B.W., 178, 276

Mellis, Albert, late Pte. B.W., 178

Melville. D. A., late Tpr. Scot. Hse., 222, 282
„ George, late Pte. B.W., 178
Menzies, Daniel, Lce.-Cpl. 4th Vol. Batt.
    B.W., 178, 276
„ James, Tpr. S.A.C., 235, 285
„ of Menzies, Sir Neil James, Bart., late
    Capt. Scots Gds., 76
Mercer, of Huntingtower, William L., Maj.
    Res. of Off., 76
Mersey, Alfred, late Tpr. Scot. Hse., 222, 282
Methuen, Lord, 5, 9, 15
Michie, John, late Trp. Scot. Hse., 222
Middlemass, James, Pte. H.L.I., 190
Millar, Alexander, D.C.M., Col.-Sgt. B.W., 10,
    12, 28, 29, 178, 178n, 276
„ George, late Tpr. Scot. Hse., 222, 282
„ R., Capt. 1st Vol. Serv. Coy. B.W., 14
„ R. G. R., Pte. late R. Scots, now S.A.C.,
    159, 273
„ R. H., Capt. 5th Vol. Batt. B.W., Hon.
    Capt. in Army, 27
Miller, Chas., Pte. B.W., 178, 276
„ D., Cpl. 2nd Batt. B.W., 29
„ John, Pte. A. and S.H., 207, 280
„ R., Pte. Gord. H., 199-200
„ Robert, late Cpl. Scot. Hse., 222
„ William, Sgt. R.G.A., 154, 272
Milligan, George, late Pte. H.L.I., 190
Milne, Alex., 3rd (Mil.) Batt. R. Scots, 160
„ James, late Pte. B.W., 175
„ W., Pte. H.L.I., 190, 277
„ William, Pte. 6th Dgns., 130, 271
Minto, Harvey S., Pte. 6th Batt. 20th Coy.
    I.Y., 211, 251
Mitchell, Alex., late Tpr. Scot. Hse., 222, 282
„ Archibald, late Cpl. Gord. H., 200
„ James, Pte. Sea. H., 195, 275
„ Jas. J. (the late), Pte. Port Elizabeth
    Town Guard, 232, 284
„ Peter, late Pte. 37th Batt. I.Y., 214, 280
„ Robert, late Tpr. Scot. Hse., 222, 282
„ Thomas, Lce.-Cpl. B.W., 178, 276
„ W., late Pte. 37th Batt. I.Y., 214
„ William (the late), Cpl. R. Scots, 160, 273
Moffat, Harry F., late Tpr. Scot. Hse., 222, 282
Moir, D. H., Pte. B.W., 178
Moncreiffe, John, A. late Lt. 26th Batt. I.Y., 77
„ J. R. Guy, Midshipman R.N., 77
„ Ronald, Capt. Worc. I.Y., 77
„ of Moncreiffe, Sir Thomas (the late. 7th
    Bart., 77, 92, 96
„ T. G. H. (the late), 77
Moncrieff, Alaric R., Lt. 2nd Dgns., 77
„ of Bandirran, Col. Sir. Alex., 77
„ yr. of Bandirran, Malcolm M., K.C.B.
    Capt. and Brev. Maj. 6th Dgn. Gds., 77
„ of Fossoway Lodge, Wm. S., Maj.
    Middlesex Regt., 77
Money, Andrew, Pte. B.W., 178
Montrose, Ronald, 5th Duke of, late Lt.-Col.
    comdg. 3rd (Mil.) Batt. A. and S.H., 74, 77
Moon, James, late Tpr. Scot. Hse., 222, 282
Moore, Gen. Montgomery, 82

Moray, of Abercairny, Wm. H. D., late Capt.
    Scots Gds., 78
Morgan, Thomas, Pte. B.W., 179
Morris, A., Pte. B.W., 179, 276
„ Chas., Pte. B.W., 179, 276
„ Jas. (the late), Pte. B.W., 179, 276
„ J. B. Pollok-, Capt. B.W., 25
Morrison, Donald, late Pte. Sea. H., 195, 278
„ John, Pte. 4th Vol. Batt. B.W., 179, 276
Mowbray, P. L., 2nd Lt. 3rd (Mil.) Batt.
    B.W., 27
„ W. H. H. C., Maj. Res. of Off., 27
Moyes, Thomas, late Pte. B.W., 179, 276
Muckersie, William (the late), Pte. 10th
    Huss., 151, 272
Muir, Wm. G., late Pte. A.P.O. Corps, 209, 280
Mullions, Thomas (the late, Cpl. 10th Huss.,
    151, 272
Murdoch, A., Pte. 2nd Batt. B.W., 27
„ Archibald A. C. Burn-, late 1yr. N.Z.
    Rgh. Rifs., 223, 274
„ Catesby Burn-, late Lt. Lov. Sc., 71
„ of Gartincaber J. Burn- 93, 287
    J. Burn-, late L.-Col. R. E., 217
„ the Rev. J. A. H. Burn- (the late, 73
„ J. A. H. Burn-, Tpr. Lanarkn's Hse.,
    222, 213
„ of Greenyards 'the late Rev. J. M'Gibbon
    Burn-, M.A. late Cornet 6th Dgn. Gds.,
    71, 7nn
„ of Gartincaber John Burn the late, 78, 95
„ John F. Burn- C.B. Brig.-Gen. comdg.
    Standerton District, 78
„ of Neuck, P. R. Burn-, Maj. R.E., 71
    'Wm. Burn-, 217
Murison, John, late Cpl. Scot. Hse., 222, 282
Murphy, Edward (the late), Pte. The Buffs,
    167, 273
Murray, Lord George Stewart, Capt. B.W.,
    and Adjt. 1st Scot. Hse. 25, 35, 79
„ Lord James T. Stewart, Lt. Cam. H., 79
„ of Napier Ruskie, Alex. MacGregor the
    late, Col. 75
„ Hon'ble. Andrew D. (the late, Brev. Maj.
    Cam. H. and Brev. Lt.-Col. comdg.
    Lov. Sc., 78, 78n, 79, 99, 100
„ C., Capt. Scot. Hse. 48
„ C. A., Taymount, 79
„ Chas. John, 2nd Lt. Col.-s. Gds., 79
„ Hon'ble. Edward Oliphant (the late. Capt.
    Cam. H. Capt. and Adjt. Lov. Sc. 79
    F. D. (the late), Capt. and Brev. Maj.
    B.W. Local Maj. comdg. 2nd Scot.
    Hse., 25, 32 33, 36 40, 45n 41-45 48
    George Lce.-Col. 4th Vol. Batt. B.W., 179
    H. F. F. Lt. B.W. 25
    J. Qrmr. and Hon. Lt. 2nd Scot. Hse.,
    52, 62n
„ J. T. C., Capt. 2nd Batt. B.W. 25
Murrie, J., Pte. 4th Vol. Batt. B.W. 179, 276
„ Robert, late Pte. B.W., 179
Myers John C., late Qrmr.-Sgt. 6th Batt.
    107th Coy. I.Y., 222, 281

Myles, David, late Pte. B.W., 179, 276
,, James, Pte. R. Scots, 160
Mylie, John, late Pte. B.W., 179, 276

NAIRNE, Baron. *See* Lansdowne
Nason, F. J., D.S.O., Brev. Col., 79–80
,, H. H. W., D.S.O., Maj. Essex Regt., 80
Neale, F., Sq. Sgt.-Maj. 1st Scot. Hse., 61
Neish, G. J. (the late), Tpr. Kitch. Hse., 228, 284
,, William, 2nd Lt. Gord. H., 95
Neville, Peter, late Tpr. Scot. Hse., 222
Nicol, W., late Pte. 22nd Batt. 78th Coy. I.Y., 213, 280
Nicoll, John, Pte. B.W., 179, 276
Nicolson, D., Pte. B.W., 179
Niven, J., Sgt. 2nd Batt. B.W., 29
Noble, Fleming, Pte. Sea. H., 195
,, J., Lce.-Cpl. 2nd Batt. B.W., 29
Norrie, Alex., Lce.-Cpl. A. and S.H., 207, 280
Nunneley, W. P., Lt. B.W., 6, 25

OGILVY, Angus H. R., D.S.O. (the late), Maj. 13th Huss., 95, 95n
,, Fred. C. A., Comdr. R.N., 95
,, Honble. Lyulph G., D.S.O., late Capt. Brabant's Hse., 80
Oliphant, John, Pte. 2nd Dgns., 149, 271
,, of Condie, Laurence J., C.B., C.V.O., Maj.-Gen., 80
Ormonde, R., D.C.M., Pte. 2nd Batt. B.W., 28, 29
Osthuisen, Boer Leader, 51, 52
Oswald, James, late Pte. B.W., 179
Outram, Sir James, 73, 81, 82
Owler, George, late Pte. Scots Gds., 158, 273

PAGET'S guns, 17
Parke, Col. comdg. mobile column, 71, 73
Parker, A. E., 2nd Lt. B.W., 25
,, E., Sgt.-Maj. 2nd Batt. B.W., 29
,, W. (the late), Cpl. 2nd Scot. Hse., 63
Parsons, Sir C., Maj.-Gen., 85
Paterson, Alex., Pte. Sea. H., 195
,, Alex. M., late Sgt. Scot. Hse., 222
,, E. D., late Pte. Gord. H., 200, 279
Paton, Jas., Pte. A. and S.H., 207
,, Jas. W., late Pte. B.W., 179, 276
,, John, late Cpl. Gord. H., 200
,, Stewart, late Pte. B.W., 179, 276
Patton, Alex., late Tpr. Scot. Hse., 222, 282
Pattullo, of Ashmore, James (the late), 95
Paul, Henry, late Cpl. B.W., 179
Pennefather, Gen., 75
Pentland, George, Sq. Qrmr.-Sgt. 14th Huss., 152, 272
Percival, of the 5th Fus., 57
Petrie, Alexander (the late), Pte. 5th Vol. Batt. B.W., 179–80, 276
,, Andrew, Pte. 2nd Dgns., 149, 271
,, James, Pte. A. and S.H., 207
,, Robert, late Tpr. Scot. Hse., 222

Philip, David (the late), Pte. 2nd Vol. Batt. B.W., 180
Phillips, George P., late Pte. Scot. Rif.,164,273
,, William, Pte. R. Scots Fus., 161
Pilcher, Col., 80
Pillans, Lawrence, Pte. 14th Huss., 152
Pinkerton, Jas., 3rd Cl. Tpr. S.A.C., 235
Playfair, Chas. Gordon, late Pte. 6th Batt. 20th Coy. I.Y., 211, 281
,, Harry L., late Cpl. 6th Batt. 20th Coy. I.Y., 211, 281
,, W. S., late Tpr. Strathcona's Hse., 231, 284
Plessis, Boer Leader, 52
Plumer, Col., 71
Pople, William G., late Pte. 6th Batt. 20th Coy. I.Y., 211, 281
Portal, Sir Gerald, 91
Porteous, James, Pte. B.W., 180
,, Peter, late Sgt. Kitch. Fight. Sc., 228, 283
Potgieter, Comdt., 58
Powell, Baden-, Col., 77
Preston, R. W. P. C. C. (of Ardchattan and Valleyfield), Major, 3rd (Militia) Batt. B.W., 287
Pretyman, Maj.-Gen., 96
Prinsloo, Boer Leader, 14, 17, 18, 99
Prior, M., Lt. 1st Scot. Hse., 55
Proctor, George S. (the late), Cpl. New England Mtd. Rif., 229, 284
Proudfoot, Alex., Cpl. 5th Vol. Batt. B.W., 180, 276
,, James, Pte. Sea. H., 195, 278
Pullar, Daniel, Pte. Scots Gds., 158, 273
,, Herbert S., Lt. Fife L. Hse., 80
,, James (the late), 80
Purdie, Bugler 2nd Batt. B.W., 10
,, Louis, Drum. B.W., 180, 276
Purgavie, Chas., Sadd.-Cpl. R.F.A., 154, 272

RAE, John, Pte. 5th Vol. Batt. B.W., 180, 276
,, Wm., Sgt.-Drum., now 3rd (Mil.) Batt. R. Scots., 160, 273
Raitt, Alex., late Qrmr.-Sgt. Beth. Mtd. Infy., 225, 283
,, Oswald, late Civ. Surg., attd. 17th Lan., 80
,, Robert M., Tpr. Imp. L. Hse., 227, 283
,, of Bu-Croft, William (the late), 80
Ramsay, David B., late Tpr. Scot. Hse., 222, 282
,, of Bamff, Sir George (the late), 9th Bart., 81
,, George (the late), M.R.C.S., L.R.C.P., Capt. Ind. Med. Service, 80–81
,, Hugh, late Lce.-Cpl. B.W., 180, 180n, 276
,, John, Tpr. Scot. Hse., 223, 282
,, yr. of Bamff, Nigel N. (the late), Lt. B.W., 8, 9, 25, 81
,, William (the late), 80
Ramsbotham, Dr., Free State Ambulance, 5
Rankin, Andrew, Pte. B.W., 180
Rattray, Andrew, late Capt. Scot. Hse., 50, 61, 81
,, Andrew, Piper Scot. Hse., 223, 282

Rattray, Chas., late Qrmr.-Sgt. Steinaecker's Hse., 230
,, David, late Lt. Scot. Hse., 55, 81
,, Harry, Sh.-Smith Cpl. 2nd Dgns., 149, 271
,, of Craighall, Sir James Clerk, K.C.B., Lt.-Gen., Col. Scot. Rif., 81
,, John, late Pte. 6th Batt. 20th Coy. I.Y., 211, 281
,, John (the late), Broom of Dalreoch, 81
,, L. C., Tpr. Thorn. Mtd. Infy., 231, 284
,, P. M., D.S.O., Capt. 1st Scot. Hse., 31, 49, 54, 55, 60, 81, 82
Rawlinson, Sir Henry, Maj.-Gen., 55, 56, 73
Ray, Robert, Pte. B.W., 180
Redpath, A., Lce.-Cpl. 2nd Scot. Hse., 63, 63n
Reid, Alex. M., late Pte. B.W., 180, 276
,, James, Pte. B.W., 180
,, James, Pte. H.L.I., 190, 278
,, James, late Pte. H.L.I., 190
,, James, Sgt. A. and S.H., 207, 280
,, John, late Tpr. Kitch. Fight. Sc., 228, 283
,, John M., late Lce.-Cpl. Scot. Hse., 223, 283
,, Robert, Pte. R. Scots, 160, 273
,, Stuart A., Pte. 7th Huss., 150, 271
,, Thos. B., Bdsman. B.W., 180, 276
,, William, Pte. B.W., 180
Reilly, James, Pte. B.W., 180
Rennet, James, late Tpr. Scot. Hse., 223
Rennie, J. G., D.S.O., Capt. B.W., 25
Rentoul, E., late Pte. H.L.I., 190
,, Wm., late Pte. H.L.I., 190
Reoch, Robert, late Pte. A.S.C., 208–209
Rice, C. E., Capt. 1st Scot. Hse., 61
Richardson, of Pitfour, Sir Edward A. Stewart-, Bart., Capt. 3rd (Mil.) Batt. B.W., 27, 82
,, of Pitfour, Sir James Stewart, Bart. (the late), 82
,, John, Pte. H.L.I., 191
,, Neil G. Stewart-, 2nd Lt. Sea. H., 82
Richmond, G. M., 2nd Lt. B.W., 25, 93
,, Jas., Monzie Castle, 95
Rimington, Col., 2, 3, 19
Ritchie, John (the late), 3rd Cl. Tpr. S.A.C., 235, 285
Robb, James, Pte. Gord. H., 200, 279
,, Joseph, Sapr. R.E., 156, 272
,, J. S., Tpr. Cpl. 1st Scot. Hse., 62
Roberts, Lord ; (Sir Frederick), 92, 101, 287
,, (Lord R.), 10, 14, 15, 37, 72, 101
Robertson of Forteviot, Lord, 82
Robertson of Struan, family of, 95
,, A., Pte. K.O.S.B., 163, 273
,, Alex., Pte. B.W., 180, 276
,, Alistair (the late), Civ. Surg., attd. I.Y., 82
,, Alistair I., late Cpl. Canadian Mtd. Rif., 225, 284
,, Chas. R., Trump. 2nd Dgns., 149, 271
,, Chas. S., Pte. B.W., 180–81, 276
,, Chas., late 3rd Cl. Tpr. S.A.C., 235, 285
,, D., Capt. 2nd Scot. Hse., 62, 283
,, Daniel A., late Tpr. Scot. Hse., 223, 282
,, David (New Rattray), Pte. B.W., 181, 276

Robertson, David (Perth), Pte. B.W., 181, 276
,, David, Cadet of Robertson of Struan, 95
,, David, late Capt. Scot. Hse., 82
,, David, late Tpr. Scot. Hse., 223, 282
,, David C., late Tpr. Scot. Hse., 223, 283
,, Donald, late Sgt. H.L.I., 191, 278
,, Donald, late Pte. Sea. H., 195, 278
,, Duncan, late Lt. Scot. Hse., 82
,, Duncan, late Tpr. Scot. Hse., 223
,, Duncan, late Tpr. Ashburner's L. Hse., 225, 284
,, Frank, M.B., Lt. B.W., 25, 95
,, George, late Tpr. Scot. Hse., 223, 283
,, George, Pte. K.O.S.B., 163, 273
,, George (the late), Pte. B.W., 181
,, Geo. C., late Sgt. 6th Batt. 20th Coy. I.Y., 211, 280
,, Geo. L., late Pte. I.Y., 215, 280
,, Geo. T., late Pte. Sea. H., 195–96, 278
,, Harry, Pte. B.W., 181, 276
,, Henry K., Pte. B.W., 181, 276
,, Honble. Hugh (the late), 2nd Lt. 14th Huss., 82
,, Hugh, late Lce.-Cpl. Scot. Hse., 223, 282
,, Robertson, J. Cpl. S.A.C., 285, 287
,, James, Staff-Sgt. Kimberley Town Guard, 231, 284
,, James (the late), Col.-Sgt. B.W., 181, 276
,, James, late Sadd.-Cpl. Scot. Hse., 223, 283
,, James, Dr. R.F.A., 154, 272
,, James, Pte. B.W., 181, 276
,, James, Pte. R. Scots Fus., 162
,, James, late Pte. B.W., 181, 276
,, James, Pte. 2nd Vol. Batt. B.W., 181, 276
,, James, Pte. 5th Vol. Batt. B.W., 181, 276
,, James, late Pte. Gord. H., 200
,, Jas. L., Pte. 4th Vol. Batt. B.W., 181, 277
,, James Peter, C.B., late Col. 31st Foot, 82
,, James W., late Orderly-Room Sgt. 31st Batt. I.Y., 214, 280
,, John, The Lowes, 82
,, John (the late), J.P., 82
,, Robertson, John, Blair Atholl, No. 37271, Lce.-Corpl. Scot. Hse., 223, 282
,, John Stanley, No. 37021, Cpl. Scot. Hse., 223, 283
,, John (Perth), No. 376, late Pte. B.W., 181
,, John (Perth), No. 1752, Pte. B.W., 181, 276
,, John (Muthill), late Pte. B.W., 181, 276
,, John (Luncarty), Pte. B.W., 181
,, John (Stanley), Pte. B.W., 181
,, John, Rifleman, King's R. Rif., 188, 277
,, John, Drum. Sea. H., 196, 278
,, John M., Pte. 5th Vol. Batt. B.W., 181, 276
,, Peter, Pte. B.W., 181–82
,, Robert, late Col.-Sgt. Cam. H., 203
,, Robert, late Sh.-Smith Scot. Hse., 223
,, Honble. Robert B. F., Capt. 21st Lan., 82, 83
,, R. M., 2nd Lt. B.W., 25
,, S. (the late), Capt. 3rd (Mil.) Batt. B.W., 27
,, Thomas, Pte. B.W., 182, 276
,, Thomas, Sgt. 5th Vol. Batt. B.W., 182, 276
,, Thos., late Piper H.L.I., 191, 278

Robertson, Thos. H., Pte. 5th Vol. Batt. B.W., 182, 276
„ W., Cpl. S.A.C., 285, 287
„ William J., late Pte. 6th Batt. 18th Coy. I.Y., 210, 281
„ Wm. P., late Lce.-Cpl. 31st Batt. I.Y., 214, 281
Robinson, F., late Pte. Scots Gds., 158, 273
Rochfort, Col., 19
Rodger, Chas., Pte. B.W., 182
Rollo, John, 8th Baron, 83
„ Alex., late Sgt. Durban L. Infy., 226
„ Honble. Sir Robert, K.C.B. (the late), Gen., Col. B.W., 83, 83n
Rorison, Very Rev. V. L., 95
„ William G. D. G., 2nd Lt. H.L.I., 95
Rose, H., Maj. B.W., 25
Ross, Alex., late Lt. Imp. L. Hse., 83
„ Alex., late Pte. Gord. H., 200
„ Chas. Wm. L., Capt. 7th Vol. Batt. A. and S.H., 95
„ James, A.B., R.N. Res., 147, 271
„ James G., Cpl. Gord. H., 200
„ John, Lce.-Cpl. R.E., 156, 272
„ John (the late), New Milne, 83
„ Peter, Pte. Scot. Rif., 164, 273
„ Thomas, late Tpr. Scot. Hse., 223, 283
„ William, late Pte. 6th Batt. 20th Coy. I.Y., 211, 280
Roy, John, Ptc. Scots Gds., 158
Ruddick, James, late Pte. B.W., 182, 276
Ruddy, W., Cpl.-Sc. 1st Scot. Hse., 62
Rumgay, Andrew, late Cpl. H.L.I., 191, 278
Rundle, Sir Leslie, Lt.-Gen., 1, 2, 18
Russell, Alex., Pte. B.W., 182, 276
„ Peter (the late), Pte. B.W., 182, 276
Rutherford, Peter, Pte. B.W., 182
Ruthven, Walter, 6th Baron, 83, 84
„ Honble. Alex. G. A. H.-, V.C., Lt. Cam. H., 83, 83n
„ Honble. Christian M. H.-, D.S.O., Lt. B.W., 25, 83
„ Honble. Philip J. L. H.-, 2nd Lt. H.L.I., 83, 84
„ Honble. Walter P. H.-, D.S.O., Master of Ruthven, Capt. and Regtl. Adjt. Scots Gds., 84

SADLER, B., Sgt.-Maj. 4th Vol. Batt. B.W., 182, 276
Sage, George, late Cpl. B.W., 182, 277
Sampson, Wools, Lt.-Col., 32, 38, 40, 47
Sandeman, of Springland, George (the late), 84
„ of Westfield, Geo. Glas (the late), 84
„ John Glas, M.V.O., late Lt.-Col. Essex Yeo. Cav., 84
„ Victor S., Maj. 17th Lancers, 84
Scobie, Andrew, Pte. Scots Gds., 158
Scott, Alex. M., late Tpr. Scot. Hse., 223, 283
„ Sir Francis, 70
„ Jas., late Sgt. Cam. H., 203, 279
„ J. Malcolm, Pte. 5th Vol. Batt. B.W., 182, 277

Scott, John A., Pte. 2nd Dgns., 149, 271
„ John Burns, Lce.-Cpl. 4th Vol. Batt. B.W., 182, 277
„ Joseph (the late), Kimberley Mtd. Corps, 227, 283
„ Joseph G., late Pte. 6th Batt. 20th Coy. I.Y., 211–12, 281
„ W., Lce.-Cpl. 1st Batt. B.W., 2
„ William, late Pte. Scots Gds., 158
„ William, Pte. B.W., 182, 277
„ W. A., Maj. and Hon. Lt.-Col. in Mil., Maj. Res. of Off., 27
Scrimgeour, Donald, Pte. 5th Vol. Batt. B.W., 182, 277
„ John, late Tpr. Scot. Hse., 223, 282
Seaton, James, Pte. Gord. H., 200
Selby, H. T., Lt. 1st Scot. Hse., 61
„ R. E., late Pte. 21st Batt. 81st Coy. I.Y., 213, 281
Seth, George, late Pte. B.W., 182
Shadwell, M. A. K., Sc. 1st Scot. Hse., 62
Shanahan, John, late Pte. B.W., 182
Sharp, Chas. W., late Civ. Surg., attd. R.A.M.C., 84
„ David, late Pte. 2nd Dgns., 149, 271
„ David, Piper Scots Gds., 158
„ David, Pte. B.W., 182–83, 277
„ David, late Pte. A. and S.H., 207, 280
„ James, Cpl. of Hse. R.H.G. and Regtl. Sgt.-Maj. 2nd Scot. Hse., 60, 62, 147, 271
Shaw, John (Blairgowrie), late Pte. H.L.I., 191
„ John (Perth), late Pte. H.L.I., 191, 278
Shedden, James, Pte. B.W., 183, 277
Shekleton, Col. comdg. column, 31, 81, 85, 94
Shepherd, Joseph, Pte. B.W., 183, 277
„ Wm. A., late Tpr. Prince Alfred's Vol. Gd., 230, 284
Sheriff, Christopher, Pte. Scots Gds., 158
Short, James, Lce.-Cpl. B.W., 183
Sidey, Thos., Pte. B.W., 183, 277
Sim, Lawrence, Pte. Gord. H., 200
„ Peter M., late Tpr. Scot. Hse., 223, 283
Simpson, Frederick W. (the late), Pte. Lov. Sc., 215
„ G., Pte. B.W., 183
„ James, late Lce.-Cpl. B.W., 183, 277
„ James, late Pte. A.S.C., 209, 280
„ Joseph, Pte. B.W., 183, 277
„ William A., Sgt. B.W., 183, 277
Sinclair, D., late Pte. R. Scots Fus., 162
„ David, Pte. R. Scots, 160
„ James, Pte. B.W., 183, 277
„ Robert, Pte. B.W., 183
Sitting Bull, 90
Skinner, Sgt. Scot. Hse., 44
„ Jas., Pte. Scott's Railway Gds., 230, 283
Slater, Daniel, late Pte. Scots Gds., 158
Sloan, J. M., Lt. R.A.M.C., 44n
Small, Robt. M. (the late), Pte. B.W., 183, 277
Smart, Thos., late Pte. B.W., 183
Smeaton, Alex., late Sh.-Smith 2nd Dgns., 149, 271
Smith, Allan, Pte. B.W., 183, 277

Smith, C. D., late Pte. 4th Batt. 28th Coy. I.Y., 210, 281
 ,, George, Sgt. H.L.I., 191
 ,, H. K., Lt. 3rd Vol. Batt. B.W., Hon. Lt. in Army, 27
 ,, J., D.C.M., Pte. 2nd Batt. B.W., 12, 28, 29
 ,, J., Pte. Cam. H., 203
 ,, James, late Pte. Gord. H., 200, 279
 ,, John, late Pte. B.W., 183
 ,, John, Pte. Sea. H., 196
 ,, John, Piper Sea. H., 285, 287
 ,, John A., late 3rd Cl. Tpr. S.A.C., 235-36, 285
 ,, L. N., Sc. 1st Scot. Hse., 62
 ,, Matthew, late Pte. B.W., 183, 277
 ,, Morgan, Jas., Bdsman. Wiltshire Regt., 188, 277
 ,, Myles, late Pte. Sea. H., 196
 ,, Robert, Sgt. Army Pay Dept., 209, 280
 ,, Thos., Pte. 5th Vol. Batt. B.W., 183, 277
 ,, Wm., (Perth) No. 5205, Pte. B.W., 183, 277
 ,, William, (Perth) No. 6464, Pte. B.W., 184
 ,, Wm. R., late Tpr. Colonial Sc., 226, 283
Smitton, David, Pte. B.W., 184
Smythe, of Methven, David M., late Lt.-Col. comdg. 3rd (Mil.) Batt. B.W., 84
 ,, David W., Tpr. Natal Carb., 229, 283
Sorley, Jas., late Lce.-Cpl. Sea. H., 196, 278
Soutar, Wm., late Pte. B.W., 184
Spalding, Chas., Qrmr. and Hon. Lt. A.S.C., 84
 ,, Jas., Boat Brae, 84
Speedie, Wm., Pte. R. Scots, 160
Speir, Kenneth R. N., late Lt. 8th Coy. I.Y., 84
 ,, of Culdees, R. T. N., 84
Speirs, Wm., Sgt. Sea. H., 196
Spens, Gen., 19
Spottiswood, Wm., Lce.-Cpl. Scot. Rif., 164, 273
Spragge, Col. I.Y., 14
Stalker, Wilfred, late Pte. Cam. H., 203
Steele, George, Capt. and Brev. Maj. 1st Dgns., 85
 ,, of Evelick, Julian McCarty, Capt. and Brev. Maj. Colds. Gds., 85
 ,, of Evelick, Gen. Sir Thomas (the late), 85
Steinkamp, Boer Leader, 51, 52, 54
Stephen, John, late Sgt.-Maj. B.W., 184
Stenart, Bernard C. A., late Lt. B.W., 25, 85
 ,, of Ballechin, John (the late), 85
Steven, Alex., late Pte. 6th Batt. 108th Coy. I.Y., 212, 281
Stevenson, Jas. W., Sgt. Scots Gds., 158, 273
 ,, Wm., late Piper Scot. Hse., 223-24, 283
Steward, O. H. D'A., Lt. B.W., 26
Stewarts of Urrard, 101
Stewart, Col. Alex., 5th of Strathgarry (the late), 85
 ,, Alex., son of Strathgarry, 85
 ,, Alex., late Pte. A. and S.H., 207
 ,, Col. Anthony (the late), 86
 ,, Charles, late Tpr. Scot. Hse., 224, 283
 ,, Charles, Pte. B.W., 184

Stewart, Charles, Pte. 5th Vol. Batt. B.W., 184
 ,, C. E., Capt. 2nd Batt. B.W., 26
 ,, D., Pte. R. Scots Fus., 162
 ,, Daniel, Sgt. Cam. H., 203
 ,, David, late Tpr. Scot. Hse., 224, 283
 ,, David H., late Tpr. Scot. Hse., 224, 283
 ,, David L., 3rd Cl. Tpr. S.A.C., 236, 285
 ,, Sir Donald, 92, 101
 ,, Donald, Sgt. R. Scots Fus., 162
 ,, Donald, late Pte. B.W., 184
 ,, Douglas, Pte. Sea. H., 196
 ,, Duncan H., late Lt. 1st Scot. Hse., 85
 ,, Frank, Pte. R. Scots, 160, 273
 ,, George, C.B., Maj.-Gen. late comdg. Guides Cavalry, 85
 ,, George, late Pte. H.L.I., 191, 278
 ,, Sir Herbert, 67, 97
 ,, J. (the late), Piper Cam. H., 203
 ,, James, late Lce.-Cpl. Scot. Hse., 224
 ,, James, Pte. 31st Batt. I.Y., 214, 281
 ,, James (Blairgowrie), Pte. B.W., 184, 277
 ,, James (Perth), late Pte. B.W., 184, 277
 ,, James (Perth), No. 465, late Pte. Sea. H., 196, 278
 ,, James (Perth), No. 3442, late Pte. Sea. H., 196, 279
 ,, J. A., M.A., (the late), 87
 ,, James A., late Tpr. Scot. Hse., 224, 283
 ,, of Urrard, Maj. Jas. Alston-, (the late), 92
 ,, James Anthony, Capt. R.G.A., 86
 ,, Jas. C., Pte. B.W., 184, 277
 ,, of Ardvorlich, C.I.E., John, late Col. R.A., 86
 ,, John, Lce.-Cpl. B.W., 184, 277
 ,, John, late Pte. H.L.I., 191, 278
 ,, John, Sgt. Sea. H., 196, 278
 ,, John L. (the late), Lt. 11th Bengal Lan., 86
 ,, Peter, Col.-Sgt. H.L.I., 191, 278
 ,, Robert, Pte. B.W., 184
 ,, Robert D., late Tpr. Scot. Hse., 224, 283
 ,, Robert J. T., Capt. 22nd Punjabis, 86
 ,, Thomas, late Pte. B.W., 184
 ,, of Ardvorlich, Wm. (the late), 85, 86, 87
 ,, yr. of Ardvorlich, Wm., late Maj. 10th Bengal Lan., 87
 ,, W., Lt. B.W., 26
 ,, Wm., Pte. H.L.I., 191, 278
 ,, Wm., Pte. Cam. H., 203, 279
 ,, Maj. W. M. (the late), 85
 ,, Wm. Murray, Capt. Cam. H., 87
Steyn (President), 13, 17, 41n
Stirling, Alex., late Capt. Sea. H., 87
 ,, of Keir, Archibald, late Capt. Scots Gds., 87
 ,, B. T., late Sgt. Thorn. Mtd. Infy., 231, 284
 ,, D. H., M.D., Perth, 87
 ,, of Fairburn and Holme Hill, John, 87
 ,, Robert, M.D., F.R.C.S. Edin., Surg.-Maj. 4th Vol. Batt. B.W., 27, 87
Stormont, William, Viscount (the late), 78
Storrar, John S., Bomb. R.A., 153, 272
Strahan, C. E., 2nd Lt. B.W., 26
Straker, E. O., Lt. Scot. Hse., 41, 42, 42n
Strang, Thos., Lce.-Cpl. Gord. H., 200

Strathallan, James, 8th Viscount of, 70
„ William, 9th Viscount of, 93
„ James, 10th Viscount of, 71
Strathdee, George, late Pte. Gord. H., 200, 279
Strong, Donald, Tpr. Scot. Hse., 224, 283
„ Duncan, Cpl. B.W., 184, 277
Struth, Wm., Pte. B.W., 184, 277
Stuart, Charles E., Pte. B.W., 184-85, 277
„ James, late Cpl. Cam. H., 203
„ W. E., Lt. 2nd Scot. Hse., 63
Studley, H., Hon. Lt. and Qrmr. 2nd Batt. B.W., 26
Sturrock, Jas., late Sapr. R.E., 156, 272
„ John, late Pte. 2nd Dgns., 150, 271
„ Thos. P., Pte. 2nd Dgns., 150, 271
Sutherland, C., Pte. 4th Vol. Batt. B.W., 185, 277
„ David, Gr. R.F.A., 154, 272
„ Duncan, Pte. 20th Huss., 153, 272
„ John, late Sgt. B.W., 185, 277
„ T., Pte. B.W., 185, 277
Suttie, G, D. Grant-, Lt. B.W., 26
Syme, James, late Pte. B.W., 185, 277
Symington, Andrew W., Pte. Cam. H., 203, 279
Symonds, J. H., Lt. 1st Scot. Hse., 61, 63
Symons, Capt. of the *Orient*, 4

Tait, F. G. (the late), Lt. B.W., 6, 7, 10, 26
Taylor, Alex., Col.-Sgt. 4th Vol. Batt. B.W., 185, 277
„ Alex., late Cpl. H.L.I., 191, 278
„ Andrew, late Pte. Sea. H., 196
„ Archibald, Pte. Sea. H., 196
„ Charles, late Pte. Gord. H., 200, 279
„ Charles R., Lce.-Sgt., B.W., 185
„ David, Dr. R.H.A., 153, 272
„ George, Pte. 2nd Dgns., 150
„ John, late Pte. A. and S.H., 207
„ John, late Pte. 31st Batt. I.Y., 214, 281
„ Robert (the late), Pte. B.W., 185, 277
„ William, Pte. B.W., 185
Telford, George, Lce.-Sgt. 2nd Dgns., 150, 271
„ James, Sgt. 2nd Dgns., 150, 271
Tellam, R. H., Farr.-Sgt. Scout 1st Scot. Hse., 62
Thomas, G. A., Capt. and Adjt. 2nd Scot. Hse., 34
„ J., Pte. Cam. H., 203
Thompson, G., late Pte. 37th Batt. I.Y., 215, 281
Thomson, James, late Pte. B.W., 185
„ Andrew, Pte. B.W., 185, 274
„ D., Cpl. B.W., 185
„ David, late Pte 6th Batt. 20th Coy. I.Y., 212, 281
„ Edward, Pte. B.W., 185
„ George (Perth), Pte. B.W., 185, 277
„ George (New Scone), Pte. B.W., 185, 277
„ George, late Pte. Sea. H., 196, 279
„ James, Cpl. B.W., 185, 277
„ James A., late Pte. Lov. Sc., 215, 281
„ John, Pte. 5th Vol. Batt. B.W., 186, 186n
Thomson, John, Pte. R. Scots Fus., 162, 273

Thomson, M., late Pte. Gord. H., 200
„ P., Pte. 5th Vol. Batt. B.W., 186, 277
„ Randolph, late Sgt. Scot. Hse., 224, 283
„ Robert, Pte. 1st Vol. Batt. B.W., 186, 277
„ Robert (the late), Sgt.-Drmr. Sea. H., 196-97, 278
„ William, Pte. 12th Lan., 151, 272
„ William, Tpr. S.A. Light Hse., 230, 283
„ William, late Pte. Cam. H., 204
Thornton, William J., Pte. Scots Gds., 158, 273
Threipland of Fingask, Wm. Murray, D.S.O., late Capt. Gren. Gds., 87
Tonder, Van, Boer Leader, 51, 52
Tooms, T., Scout 1st Scot. Hse., 62
Tosh, E., Capt. 1st Vol. Batt. B.W., Hon. Lt. in Army, 27
Traill, James A., Sapr. R.E., 156, 272
Tullibardine, John G., Marquess of, M.V.O., D.S.O., Capt. and Brev.-Maj. R. H. Gds., Lt.-Col. comdg. Scot. Hse., 30-37, 61, 88
Turner, Duncan F., late Sh.-Smith Lov. Sc., 216, 281
„ H. Scott (the late), Capt. and Brev.-Maj. B.W., local Lt.-Col., 4, 5, 26.
Tyrie, Robert, late Lce.-Cpl. Sea. H., 197, 278

Underwood, of Heath Park, Thomas O., late Col. Madras Staff Corps, 88
Urmston, Arch. G. B., late Maj. and Brev.-Lt.-Col. R. Marine L. Infy., 95
„ Edward B., Lt.-Col. comdg. 1st Batt. A. and S.H., 95-96
Urquhart, E. F. M., Capt. B.W., 26

Valentine, A., Lt.-Col. 1st Vol. Batt. B.W., 27
Varley, H. E., Regtl. Sgt.-Maj. 2nd Scot. Hse., 60, 62

Walker, C. E. C., Lt. 1st Vol. Batt. B.W., 27
„ James, Sapr. R.E., 156
„ J. D. G., D.S.O., Capt. B.W., 2, 3, 26
„ Robert (the late), Tpr. S.A.C., 236, 285
Wallace, A., Pte. Cam. H., 204
„ David, Pte. B.W., 186
„ J. C., Lt. 1st Scot. Hse., 61
„ William, Pte. B.W., 186
Walls, John, late Pte. Cam. H., 204, 279
Wanliss, Geo. C., late Pte. Lov. Sc., 216, 281
Ward, Honble. Gerald E. F., Lt. 1st Life Gds., 96
„ Honble. John H., 2nd Lt. Worc. I.Y., 96
„ Honble. Reginald D.S.O. (the late), Capt. R.H. Gds., 96, 96n
„ Honble. Robert A., 2nd Lt. Worc. I.Y., 69
Wardrop, A. T., Lt. Scot. Hse., 48
Wardrope, Rob., late Tpr. Scot. Hse., 224
Warnock, Sq. Qrmr.-Sgt. Scot. Hse., 45, 45n
Warren, Sir Charles, 69, 70, 76
Watson, George, Pte. Scot. Hse., 164, 273
„ George, late Pte. A. and S.H., 207
„ H. A. F. (the late), Capt. Lanc. Fus., and Adjt. 1st Scot. Hse., 33, 34, 55
„ James, Pte. Cam. H., 204, 279

Watson, James, late Pte. 13th Huss., 151, 272
,, Robert, Pte. 3rd Vol. Batt. B.W., 186, 277
,, Ronald, Pte. Vol. Batt. H.L.I., 191
,, Thomas, Pte. Scot. Rif., 164, 273
Watt, Alex., late Cpl. Scot. Rif., 164, 273
,, Duncan, late Tpr. Scot. Hse., 224, 283
,, James, Pte. 20th Huss., 153, 272
,, John, late Pte. Sea. H., now Scot. Hse., I.Y., 197
,, William G., Pte. 20th Huss., 153, 272
Watts, C. N., Maj. Derby Regt., 53
Wauchope, Andrew G. (the late), Maj.-Gen., C.B., C.M.G., 4–7, 9, 26
,, Arthur G., D.S.O., Capt. B.W., 7, 26
,, Helen, wife of Lt.-Col. W. H. D.-Cunyngham, V.C., 101
Wavell, A. G., C.B., local Maj.-Gen., 26
,, A. P., 2nd Lt. B.W., 26
Webster, G., Cpl. 1st Scot. Hse., 62
,, Thomas, Maj. Ind. Staff Corps, 96
Weir, G. L., Sig.-Sgt. 2nd Batt. B.W., 29
,, John (the late), Lce.-Cpl. 18th Huss., 152, 272
Welham, W., Pte. Gord. H., 200
Weller, W. R., Qrmr.-Sgt. A. and S.H., 207, 280
Wells, William, Pte. A. and S.H., 207–208
Welsh, William, late Pte. H.L.I., 191, 278
,, William F., Pte. B.W., 186, 277
West, Charles, Pte. B.W., 186, 277
,, C. C., Lt. B.W., 26
,, David, Pte. 5th Vol. Batt. B.W., 186, 277
,, F. F., Sgt. B.W., 186
,, George, late Pte. B.W., 186, 277
Western, Colonel, 19
Wet, De, Boer Leader, 2, 3, 14, 31, 99
,, Christian, 17
White, Daniel, Sgt. B.W., 186
,, of Annat Lodge, F. B. (the late), 88
,, F. H. B., Capt. 5th Vol. Batt. B.W., 27, 88
,, Hector, late Col.-Sgt. B.W., 186, 277
,, John, Pte. B.W., 186, 277
Whiteman, John, late Farr.-Maj. 4th Dgn. Gds., 148, 271
,, W. L., Sgt. 2nd Scot. Hse., 62
Whitson of Parkhill, Capt. Chas. Hill-, 88
,, Eric C. H.-, 2nd Lt. R. Scots, 88
,, yr. of Parkhill, Thos. E. L. H.-, Capt. and Adjt. Stafford I.Y., 88
Whittet, Andrew, Tpr. S.A.C., 236, 285
,, Thomas, Pte. 5th Vol. Batt. B.W., 186–87, 277
Whitton, Jas., late Pte. Cape Railway Sharpshooters, 225, 284
Whyte, Charles, Pte. B.W., 187, 277
,, Dugald, Pte. 5th Vol. Batt. B.W., 187, 277
,, George, late Pte. B.W., 187, 277
,, Robert, late Tpr. Scot. Hse., 224, 283
,, William, late Tpr. Imp. L. Hse., 227, 283
,, William, Pte. B.W., 187, 277
Wighton, Fred., Pte. 5th Vol. Batt. B.W., 187, 277

Wilkie, Wm., late Pte. Gord. H., 200–201, 279
Wilkinson, F. W., Cpl. 2nd Scot. Hse., 63, 63n
Will, Joseph, Pte. Irish Rif., 204, 279
Williams, Lt.-Col. comdg. mobile column, 76
,, Fenwick, Sir, Lt.-Gen., C.-in-C. British North America, 83
Williamson, of Balgray and Lawers, Chas. A., (the late), 79, 80
,, James A., late Pte. B.W., 187, 187n
Willoughby, Honble. Charles S. H. D., Capt. and Brev.-Maj. Scots Gds., 89
,, Honble. Claude H. D., Capt. Colds. Gds., 89
Willshire, Ernest M. (the late). Maj. B.W., 18, 26
Wilson, A. Muckart, No. 3509, D.C.M., Sgt. 2nd Batt. B.W., 28, 29, 187
,, A., Alyth. No. 4204, Sgt. B.W., 187, 277
,, Andrew, late Pte. Sea. H., 197, 278
,, Andrew, Col.-Sgt. A. and S.H., 208, 280
,, Andrew T. (the late), Pte. 6th Batt. 20th Coy. I.Y., 212, 281
,, Charles, late Pte. Sea. H., 197, 278
,, David, late Pte. B.W., 187
,, J., Sgt.-Maj., H.L.I., 285
,, J., Sgt. H.L.I., 287
,, James, late Cpl. 18th Huss., 152, 272
,, James, late Lce.-Cpl. Scot. Hse., 224, 283
,, James, late Sh.-Smith R.F.A., 154, 272
,, John, Lt. Transvaal Scot. Hse., 89
,, Peter, Sunnybrae, 89
,, Peter (the late), Sgt. Scot. Hse., 224, 283
,, R. G., Lt. Sea. H., 8
,, William, late Tpr. Scot. Hse., 224
Wing, Col., 71
Winsor, William, Pte. B.W., 187, 277
Winton, William, Pte. B.W., 187, 277
Wisely, Peter, Pte. H.L.I., 191, 278
Wishart, Edward J., Pte. B.W., 187, 277
,, George, Pte. B.W., 187, 277
,, Robert, late Tpr. Scot. Hse., 224, 283
,, William, Pte. R. Scots, 160, 273
Wood, William, late Pte. Scots Gds., 158, 273
,, William, late Pte. A.S.C., 209, 280
Woodman, C., Lt. Scot. Hse., 44, 48
Wortley, J. Stuart-, Lt. 1st Scot. Hse., 55, 61
Wrench, Harry, late Pte. 13th Huss., 151, 272
Wright, John, Piper A. and S.H., 208
,, Thomas, late Piper B.W., 187, 277
Wylly, Lt.-Col., 49

YEAMAN, D., Tpr. Scot. Hse., 224, 283
Yorstoun, Carthew, C.B., Lt.-Col. comdg. 2nd Batt. B.W., 9, 12, 15, 26
Young, Alex., late Sgt. 31st Batt. I.Y., 214
,, David, Pte. Kimberley Rif., 227
,, David, Pte. B.W., 187, 277
,, John, late Cpl. H.L.I., 192
,, Robert (Bankfoot), late Tpr. Scot. Hse., 224, 283
,, Robert (Doune), late Tpr. Scot. Hse., 224
,, Robert, late Sgt. Scot. Rif., 164, 273
,, William, late Pte. B.W., 187–88, 277
,, William, late Pte. A. and S.H., 208, 280

INDEX TO MILITARY UNITS
AND DEPARTMENTS

(For List of Abbreviations, see p. 64)

ARGYLL and Sutherland Highlanders (Princess Louise's) 1st and 2nd Batts., 5, 12–15, 69, 83, 90, 92, 95, 96, 102, 177, 204–8, 279, 280, 286
„ 3rd (Militia) Batt., 77, 92, 286
„ 4th (Militia) Batt., 286, 287
„ 2nd Vol. Batt. (Sutherland Highland Rif. Vols.), 62, 194
„ 4th Vol. Batt. (1st Stirlingshire Rif. Vol.), 23, 24, 69, 204, 205
„ 5th Vol. Batt., 205
„ 6th Vol. Batt., 208
„ 7th Vol. Batt. (Clackmannan Rif. Vol.), 69, 95, 207
Armoured Train, 68, 71, 171, 197, 225
„ „ No. 3, 23
„ „ No. 9, 23
Army Medical Reserve, 87
Army Ordnance Department, 209, 280
Army Pay Department, 209, 280
Army Post Office Corps, 209, 280
Army Remounts Department, 82
Army Service Corps, 63, 74, 84, 147, 185, 208–9, 223, 280
Army Transport (South Africa), 72
Army Veterinary Department, 76
Ashburner's Light Horse, 225, 284
Australian (New South Wales) Bushmen, 1st, 94
Australian Naval Brigade, New South Wales Section, 147, 271

BENGAL (now Royal) Artillery, 86
Bengal Infantry, 4th, 81
„ „ 12th, 96
„ „ 20th, 94
„ „ 22nd, 86, 88
„ „ 25th, 91
„ „ 27th, 286
„ „ 31st, 286
„ „ 34th, 286
„ Lancers, 10th Duke of Cambridge's Own (Hodson's Horse), 70, 87
„ „ 11th, 70, 86
„ „ 12th, 63
„ „ 15th (Cureton's Multanis), 86
„ Medical Department, 81
Bengal Staff Corps, 70, 85, 86, 87, 91, 286
Bethune's Mounted Infantry, 225, 283

Black Watch, The (Royal Highlanders), 165–88, 202, 215, 216, 220, 221, 232, 271, 274–77
„ 1st Batt., 1–3, 9, 19, 22–27, 30, 70, 71, 75, 79, 83, 85, 90, 93, 95
„ 2nd Batt., 1*n*, 2, 3, 4–20, 22–29, 32, 35, 68, 69, 71, 72, 74, 79, 81, 82, 83, 88, 90, 94, 156
„ 3rd (Militia) Batt., late Royal Perthshire Rifles, 9, 71, 79, 82, 84, 87, 88, 167, 172, 176, 177, 178, 184, 287
„ 3rd (Militia) Batt., Reserve, 14, 181
„ 1st Vol. Batt., 27, 166, 173, 186, 230, 233, 234, 235
„ 2nd Vol. Batt., 27, 180, 181
„ 3rd „ 27, 67, 177, 185, 186
„ 4th Vol. Batt., 27, 69, 71, 73, 87, 156, 165–73, 175–79, 181, 182, 183, 184, 185, 186, 213, 217, 220, 223, 224, 228, 235
„ 5th Vol. Batt., 27, 67, 72, 74, 88, 94, 165–85, 186, 187, 210–12, 214–19, 221, 224–25, 228, 230–32, 235–36, 287
„ 6th Vol. Batt., 176
Bloemfontein Police, 173
Bombay (now Royal) Artillery, 74
Bombay Infantry (late 109th). *See* Royal Inniskilling Fusiliers
Border Light Horse, 76
Border Regiment, The, 53, 164
Brabant's Horse, 2nd Regiment, 80, 226, 232
Brigade, 20th, Bearer Coy., 67
British South Africa Police, 173, 230, 232, 283
Buffs, The (East Kent Regiment), 160, 273

CAMEL Corps, 76
Cameron Highlanders, The Queen's Own, 1st and 2nd Batts., 18, 68, 73, 78, 79, 83, 84, 87, 99, 197, 201–4, 206, 279
„ 3rd (Militia) Batt., 82
Cameronians, The (Scottish Rifles), 1st and 2nd Batts., 79, 81, 92, 96, 163, 164, 203, 273
„ 3rd and 4th (Militia) Batts., 163
„ 1st Vol. Batt., 163, 225
„ 3rd „ 228
Canadian Contingent, 1st, 71
Canadian Mounted Rifles, 225, 284
Cape Garrison Artillery, 68, 225, 284
Cape Medical Staff Corps, 93

Cape Mounted Rifles, 233
Cape Pioneer Regiment, 225
Cape Police, 76, 93, 232, 284
Cape Railway Sharpshooters, 225, 284
Cape Town Highlanders, 225, 284
Central India Horse, 1st Regiment (now 38th C.I.H.), 70
Ceylon Mounted Infantry, 226, 284
City Imperial Volunteers, 74
Clackmannan Rifle Volunteers. *See* 7th Vol. Batt., A. and S.H.
Coldstream Guards, 44, 75, 79, 85, 89
Colonial Scouts, 81, 83, 226, 283
Commander-in-Chief's Bodyguard, 81, 226, 230, 283
Compton's Horse, 210
Control Dept. *See* Army Service Corps
Corps of Cattlerangers, 213
Cumberland Regt. (late 34th). *See* Border Regt.
Cureton's Multanis. *See* 15th Bengal Lancers
Cycle Volunteer Corps, 218

Deccan Horse, 91
Depôt Battalion, 7th, 75
Diamond Fields Horse, 226, 283
District Mounted Troops, 99
Dragoon Guards, 2nd (Queen's Bays), 67, 97, 147, 271
„ 3rd (Prince of Wales's), 62, 78
„ 4th (Royal Irish), 148, 271
„ 6th (Carabiniers), 35, 56, 60, 62, 77, 78, 148, 271
Dragoons, 1st (Royal), 72, 78, 84, 85, 88
„ 2nd (Royal Scots Greys), 77, 147-50, 215, 218, 234, 271
„ 6th (Inniskilling), 93, 150, 271
Duke of Albany's Own (late 72nd). *See* Seaforth Highlanders
Duke of Cambridge's Own. *See* Middlesex Regiment
Duke of Cambridge's Own Imperial Yeomanry, 215, 280
Duke of Edinburgh's Own Volunteer Rifles, 226, 228, 283
Duke of Edinburgh's Own. *See* Wiltshire Regiment
Dundee Cadet Corps, 93
Durban Light Infantry, 226, 228

East Lancashire Regiment, The, 69
East Surrey Regiment, The (late 31st), 82
East Yorkshire Regiment, The, 2
Eastern Province Horse, 226, 284
Essex Regiment, The, 39, 80

Ferreira's Horse, 75
Fife and Forfar Light Horse. *See* Impl. Yeomanry, 6th Batt. 20th Coy.
Forfarshire Volunteer Artillery, 1st Regiment, 221, 233

Gentlemen-at-Arms, The Honourable Corps of, 68, 84

Goorkha Rifles, 8th (late Sylet L. Infy.), 286
Gordon Highlanders, The, 1st and 2nd Batts., 25, 26, 68, 75, 79, 90, 92, 93, 95, 101, 102, 197-201
„ 3rd Vol. Batt., 197
„ 4th (Donside) Vol. Batt., 92, 101
Grenadier Guards, 71, 75, 80, 87, 88
Guards Mounted Infantry, 157, 158
Guides Cavalry, 93
Guides, Queen's Own Corps of, 68, 86, 91

Hampshire Regiment, The (late 37th), 91, 164
Highland Borderers, Light Infantry. *See* A. and S.H., 3rd (Militia) Batt.
Highland Light Infantry, The, 1st and 2nd Batts., 5, 17, 18, 63, 68, 72, 74, 84, 91, 95, 188-93, 196, 278, 285, 287
„ 3rd (Militia) Batt., 68, 70, 83, 188, 189
„ 5th Vol. Batt., 190-91
Highland Rifle Militia. *See* Seaforth Highlanders, 3rd (Militia) Batt.
Hodson's Horse, 87
Hore's Company of Volunteers, Captain, 68
Household Cavalry Composite Regiment, 96, 147
Huntingdonshire Regiment (late 31st). *See* East Surrey Regiment
Hussars, 4th (Queen's Own), 151
„ 7th (Queen's Own), 150, 271
„ 8th (King's Royal Irish), 33, 35, 49, 71
„ 10th (Prince of Wales's Own Royal), 67, 78, 97, 151, 235, 271
„ 11th (Prince Albert's Own), 150, 178, 208
„ 13th, 61, 82, 95, 151, 271
„ 14th (King's), 27, 82, 88, 89, 151-52, 218, 271
„ 15th (The King's), 90
„ 18th, 60, 60n, 61, 152, 271
„ 19th (Alexandra, Princess of Wales's Own), 34, 62, 152, 271
„ 20th, 91, 153, 271
„ 21st, 91

Imperial Light Horse, 55, 83, 220, 226-27, 283
Imperial Light Infantry, 227, 228, 284
Imperial Military Railways (S. Africa), 211
Imperial Yeomanry in Great Britain—
„ 5th Batt., Staffordshire Imperial Yeomanry, 89
„ 19th Batt., Royal East Kent, 95
„ 20th Batt., Hampshire, 97
„ 27th Batt., Duke of Cambridge's Own (Middlesex), 215, 280
„ 31st Batt., Worcestershire, 77, 92, 96
„ 40th Batt., Fife and Forfar Light Horse, 214
„ 49th Batt., Essex, 84
„ 56th Batt., Scottish Horse, 67, 70, 75, 88, 91, 197, 235
Imperial Yeomanry in South Africa, 14, 31, 32, 37, 57, 82, 92, 99, 210-15

Imperial Yeomanry in South Africa—
„ 1st Batt. 3rd Coy. Gloucestershire, 83
„ 2nd Batt. 5th Coy. Warwickshire, 77
„ 4th Batt. 7th Coy. Leicestershire, 210, 281
„ 4th Batt. 8th Coy. Derbyshire, 84, 85
„ 4th Batt. 28th Coy. Bedfordshire, 210, 281
„ 5th Batt. 16th Coy. Worcestershire, 210, 280
„ 6th Batt., 23, 25
„ 6th Batt. 18th Coy. Queen's Own Royal Glasgow and Lower Ward of Lanarkshire, 210, 280, 281, 285, 287
„ 6th Batt. 19th Coy. Lothians and Berwickshire, 85
„ 6th Batt. 20th Coy. Fife and Forfar Light Horse, 80, 93, 210, 211, 212, 214, 280, 281, 285
„ 6th Batt. 107th Coy. Lanarkshire, 212, 281
„ 6th Batt. 108th Coy. Queen's Own Royal Glasgow and Lower Ward of Lanarkshire, 212, 281
„ 7th Batt. 49, 50, 51, 52
„ 7th Batt. 27th Coy. Devon, 52
„ 11th Batt. 34th Coy. Middlesex, 212, 281
„ 15th Batt. 57th Coy. Buckinghamshire, 212
„ 17th Batt. 50th Coy. Hampshire, 212, 280
„ 18th Batt. 70th Coy. Sharpshooters, 213, 281
„ 18th Batt. 72nd Coy. Roughriders, 213, 217, 280
„ 21st Batt. 81st Coy. Sharpshooters, 81, 213
„ 22nd Batt. 78th Coy. Roughriders, 213, 280
„ 24th Batt. Metropolitan Mounted Rifles, 213, 280
„ 26th Batt. Younghusband's Horse, 77, 214
„ 31st Batt. Fincastle's Horse, 73, 93, 214, 280, 281
„ 37th Batt. Highland Horse, 214-15, 280, 281
Indian Ambulance Corps, 227, 285
Indian Barrack Department, 193
Indian Medical Service, 81
Indian Staff Corps, 34, 68, 86, 91, 96
Indian Volunteer Cavalry, 228
Intelligence Department (South Africa), 151, 225, 231

JOHANNESBURG Mounted Police, 227
Johannesburg Mounted Rifles, 227, 284

KENNEDY Mounted Infantry, 90
Kennedy Regiment, 3rd, 90
Kimberley Light Horse, 227
Kimberley Mounted Corps, 227, 283
Kimberley Rifles, 227
Kimberley Town Guard, 231, 284
King's, The. See Shropshire L.I.
„ Own. See Yorks L.I.
„ „ Scottish Borderers, The, 30, 45n, 49, 49n, 62, 63, 162-63, 196, 273
„ „ „ 2nd Vol. Batt., 85

King's Royal Rifle Corps, The (late 60th Rifles), 40, 46, 188, 277
„ „ „ 5th Vol. Batt. (West Middlesex Rif. Vols., 212
Kitchener's Fighting Scouts, 228, 232, 283
Kitchener's Horse, 67, 228, 284

LANCASHIRE Fusiliers, The, 33, 72, 93n
„ 6th (Militia) Batt., 24, 72
„ Mounted Infantry, 41, 43
Lancers, 5th (Royal Irish), 77, 92
„ 9th (Queen's Royal), 5, 9, 150, 271
„ 12th (Prince of Wales's Royal), 63, 67, 97, 150-51, 271
„ 16th (The Queen's), 92, 93
„ 17th (Duke of Cambridge's Own), 80, 84, 148, 150, 152, 271
„ 21st (Empress of India's), 49, 61, 83
„ 29th (Deccan Horse), 91. See Bengal
Land Transport Corps. See Army Service Corps
Leinster Regiment (Royal Canadians), The Prince of Wales's, 70
Life Guards 1st, 96
„ 2nd, 147, 271
Lincolnshire Regiment, The, 2nd Vol. Service Company, 217
Lovat's Scouts, 15, 17, 18, 67, 78, 79, 99-100, 215-16, 281
Loyal North Lancashire Regiment, The, 39n
Lumsden's Horse, 25, 85, 228, 283

MADRAS Infantry, 9th, 86
Madras Staff Corps, 88
Marshall's Horse, 228, 284
Mennie's Scouts, 228, 283
Methuen's Horse, 70
Middlesex Regiment, The, Duke of Cambridge's Own, 1st and 2nd Batts., 77
Military Mounted Police, 180
Military Police, 85
Military Train. See Army Service Corps
Monmouthshire Regiment (late 43rd). See Oxfordshire Light Infantry
Mounted Infantry, 1st Batt., 71
„ 2nd Batt., 23
„ 3rd Batt., 39, 40, 42n
„ 8th Batt., 69
„ 12th Batt., 25, 73, 83, 87
„ 15th Batt., 73
„ 18th Batt., 73, 76
„ 22nd Batt., 23, 24, 74, 91
„ 25th Batt., 40, 40n, 45n, 92
„ in general, 13, 23, 99, 157, 161, 173, 174, 178, 182, 187, 196
„ of 3rd Brigade, 69

NATAL Carbineers, 229, 283
„ Mounted Police, 36, 68
„ „ „ Scottish Horse Squadron, 217, 221, 223, 224
„ Native Contingent, 84

Index to Military Units

Natal Volunteer Artillery, 229
,, Volunteers, 225
Native Infantry. *See* Bengal
Naval Brigade, 74, 94
New England Mounted Rifles, 229, 284
New South Wales. *See* Australian
New South Wales Mounted Rifles, 229, 284
,, ,, ,, Permanent Forces, 12, 28
New Zealand Mounted Infantry, 229, 283
,, ,, Rough Riders, 229, 284
Norfolk Regiment, The, 2nd Batt., 68
North Staffordshire Regiment, The, Prince of Wales's, 72
Northern Nigerian Regiment, 74
Northumberland Fusiliers, The (late 5th), 57, 63, 86

OXFORDSHIRE Light Infantry, The, 1st and 2nd Batts., 69

PERTHSHIRE Rifle Vols. *See* Black Watch, 4th and 5th Vol. Batts.
,, Volunteers (late 90th). *See* Cameronians (Scottish Rifles)
Pietersburg Light Horse, 90
Port Elizabeth Town Guard, 232, 284
Prince of Wales's Light Horse, 230, 284
Prince of Wales's. *See* Leinster Reigment, also North Stafford and West Yorks
Prince Alfred's Volunteer Guard, 76, 230, 284
Princess Louise's. *See* Argyll and Suth. Highs.
Provisional Battalion, Kroonstadt, 68
Punjabis, 22nd, 86, 87
,, 27th, 286
Punjab Cavalry, 4th, 88

QUEEN'S, The. *See* Royal West Surrey
Queen's Own, The. *See* Cameron Highs. and Guides, Corps of
Queen's Rifle Volunteer Brigade, The. *See* Royal Scots, Vol. Batt.
,, Mounted Infantry Company, The, 74
Queensland Contingent, 3rd, 90
Queensland Mounted Infantry, 2nd, 27, 82
Queensland Volunteer Rifles, Warwick Coy., 90
Queenstown Town Guard, 76
,, Volunteer Mounted Infantry, 76

RAILWAY Pioneer Regiment, 230
Remount Department (South Africa), 27, 76, 210, 280
Reserve of Officers, 14, 27, 76, 90, 91
Rhodesian Horse Volunteers, 85, 226
Richmond Mounted Rifles, 229
Rifle Brigade, The (Prince Consort's Own), 164
,, ,, 8th Vol. Batt., 24th Middlesex, 209
,, ,, 16th London Irish Rifles, 90
Rimington's Guides, 17, 19
Roberts' Horse, 230, 284
Ross-shire Buffs (late 78th). *See* Seaforth Highlanders

Royal Army Medical Corps, 28, 44n, 67, 68, 72, 76, 84, 91, 94, 157, 209, 280
Royal Artillery, 5, 32, 38, 40, 42n, 49, 52, 86, 153
,, ,, Mounted Rifles, 154
,, ,, *See* also Bengal and Bombay.
Royal Canadian. *See* Leinster
Royal Dublin Fusiliers, The, 39, 39n, 73, 208
,, Engineers, Corps of, 9, 68, 69, 78, 155–56, 271, 287
,, Field Artillery, 9, 14, 17, 44n, 90, 153–54
,, Garrison Artillery, 86, 90, 154–55, 218, 271
,, ,, ,, Garrison Companies, 154, 155
,, ,, ,, Mountain Division, 154
,, Garrison Regiment, 157, 204
,, Highlanders. *See* Black Watch
,, Horse Artillery, 14, 90, 153, 271
,, ,, Guards (The Blues), 30, 60–62, 88, 96, 147, 271
,, Inniskilling Fusiliers, The, late 109th Bombay Infantry, 70
,, Irish Fusiliers, 209
,, Irish Rifles, The, 204, 279
,, Jersey Militia, 192
,, Madras Fusiliers. *See* Dublin Fusiliers
,, Marine Light Infantry, 95
,, Munster Fusiliers, The, 76
,, Naval Reserve, 84, 147
,, ,, Vol. Reserve, 74
,, Navy, The, 71, 77, 94, 95, 147, 227, 271
,, Perthshire Rifles. *See* Black Watch, 3rd (Mil.) Batt.
,, Scots, The (Lothian Regiment), 88, 159–160, 201, 202, 235, 271
,, ,, 3rd (Militia) Batt., 68, 72, 88, 159, 160
,, ,, Vol. Batt. (Queen's Rifle Vol. Brigade), 196
,, ,, Mounted Infantry Coy., 74
,, Scots of Sydney, 9
,, Scots Fusiliers, The, 91, 161–62, 209, 273
,, ,, ,, Vol. Batt. 161
,, Scots Greys. *See* 2nd Dragoons
,, Scottish Reserve Regiment, 175, 184, 188, 197, 201
,, Sussex Regiment, The, 17, 18
,, Warwickshire Regiment, The, 63
,, West Surrey Regiment (The Queen's), 160
,, ,, ,, 1st Vol. Batt., 213, 273

SAPPERS and Miners, 88
Scots Guards, late Scots Fusilier Guards, 1st, 2nd, and 3rd Batts., 67, 69–72, 76, 78, 84, 87, 89, 97, 156–58, 209, 271–73
Scots Volunteers. *See* Transvaal Scottish and Scottish Horse
Scottish Cycle Corps, 146, 208, 280
Scottish Horse, The, 30–37, 49–55, 63, 70, 82, 85, 88, 89, 94, 197, 212, 216–24, 230, 281–83
,, 1st Regiment, 23, 25, 30–36, 70, 71, 73, 75, 79, 81, 82, 85, 88, 94

Scottish Horse, The, 2nd Regiment, 22, 25, 31–49, 63, 67, 79, 82, 88, 89, 94, 147
,, ,, (Transvaal Vol. Regiment), 37, 89, 224, 233
,, See also Imperial Yeomanry and Natal Mounted Police
,, National Red-Cross Hospital, 27, 84, 87
Scott's Railway Guards, 230, 283
Seaforth Highlanders (Ross-shire Buffs, Duke of Albany's), 1st and 2nd Batts., 5, 6, 8, 10, 11, 13, 14, 18, 32, 34, 41n, 73, 74, 76, 77, 82, 87, 158, 192–97, 208, 209, 278–79, 285, 287
,, 3rd (Militia) Batt., 177
,, 2nd Vol. Batt., 1st Sutherland High. Rifle Vols., 22, 194
Sherwood Foresters, The (Nottinghamshire and Derbyshire Regiment,) 1st Batt., 49, 50, 51, 52, 53
,, 4th (Militia) Batt., 15, 73, 83
Shropshire Light Infantry, The King's, 11, 12
Sikh Cavalry, 1st, 86
,, Infantry, 1st, 68
South African Constabulary, 25, 57, 58, 91, 95, 152, 159, 190, 191, 232–36, 284–287
,, African Light Horse, 72, 73, 230
South Wales Borderers, The, 162, 273
Steinaecker's Horse, 93, 230, 284
Stirlingshire Rifle Vols. See A. and S.H.
Strathcona's Horse, 231, 284

Sutherland Highlanders (late 93rd). See A. and S.H.
Sylet Light Infantry. See Goorkha Rifles

THORNEYCROFT'S Mounted Infantry, 81, 230, 231, 284
Transvaal Scottish, The, 37

VETERINARY Department, 90
,, Hospital, Germiston, 76
,, ,, Kroonstad, 76
Volunteer Ambulance Corps, 231, 284
,, Cavalry (with Havelock, 1857), 85
,, Medical Staff Corps, 93
,, Service Companies of Scots Regiments, 33

WELSH Regiment, The, 2nd Batt. (late South Lincolnshire), 165
West India Regiment, 46n, 63
Western Province Mounted Rifles, 231–32, 284
Wiltshire Regiment, The, Duke of Edinburgh's, 188, 277
Worcestershire Regiment, The, 164, 273

YEOMANRY. See Imperial Yeomanry
York and Lancaster Regiment, The (late 65th and 84th), 72, 87
Yorkshire Light Infantry, The King's Own, 39n, 41, 43, 45, 46, 73
,, Regiment, The Princess of Wales's Own (late 19th), 76, 77

Printed by BALLANTYNE, HANSON & CO.
Edinburgh & London

Lightning Source UK Ltd.
Milton Keynes UK
UKOW051155021111

181354UK00001B/76/P

9 781408 687581